THE
CONFEDERATION
OF
NORTH AMERICA
AND THE
UNITED STATES
OF
MEXICO

# FOR WANT
# OF A NAIL

# FOR WANT OF A NAIL

## IF BURGOYNE HAD WON AT SARATOGA

## Robert Sobel

GREENHILL BOOKS, LONDON
STACKPOLE BOOKS, PENNSYLVANIA

Greenhill Books

This edition of *For Want Of A Nail*
first published 1997 by Greenhill Books,
Lionel Leventhal Limited, Park House, 1 Russell Gardens,
London NW11 9NN
and
Stackpole Books, 5067 Ritter Road, Mechanicsburg, PA 17055, USA

*British Library Cataloguing in Publication Data*
Sobel, Robert, 1931–
For want of a nail: if Burgoyne had won at Saratoga
1. Burgoyne's Invasion, 1777 2. Saratoga Campaign, 1777
3. Imaginary histories
I. Title
355.4'8

ISBN 1-85367-281-5

*Library of Congress Cataloging-in-Publication Data*
1931 Feb. 19–
For want of a nail: if Burgoyne had won at Saratoga/by Robert Sobel.
p. cm.
Originally published: New York: Macmillan, 1973.
Includes bibliographical references and index.
ISBN 1-85367-281-5 (hc)
1. North America—History—Miscellanea. 2. United States—History—
Miscellanea. 3. Imaginary histories.
I. Title.
E46.S63   1997
973—dc21

Publishing History
*For Want Of A Nail* was first published in 1973 (Macmillan, New York), and is
reproduced now exactly as the original edition, complete and unabridged.

Printed and bound in Great Britain by
Creative Print and Design (Wales), Ebbw Vale

*for Jeff Weinper*

# PUBLISHER'S NOTE

The Publisher would like to thank Mr Moshe Feder, on whose recommendation the reprint of this alternate history classic was undertaken.

*For want of a nail the shoe is lost,*
*For want of a shoe the horse is lost,*
*For want of a horse the rider is lost,*
*For want of the rider the battle is lost,*
*For want of the battle the war is lost,*
*For want of the war the nation is lost,*
*All for the want of a horseshoe nail,*

—GEORGE HERBERT (1593–1632)

# CONTENTS

# Contents

# PREFACE

I have always felt a history should stand on its own, and that prefaces are unnecessary. Suffice it to say that this is a book about the interactions and development of two major nations, which are more than neighbors, rather like cousins. They have the same roots, but two centuries ago took different paths. I have tried to describe their journeys, analyze their problems, and indicate why changes took place.

This work is about political and economic history. The reader seeking information and analyses regarding cultural trends will not find such here. Material of this nature was omitted because the author feels the story he has to tell is complicated, and would be made a maze if any threads other than the economic and political were introduced.

I have deliberately neglected to write a concluding chapter to this work. It is my hope that the reader will be able to draw his own conclusions by the time he finishes the journey I have set before him. In its place, I have agreed to have Professor Frank Dana of the University of Mexico City write a *critique*, in which he will indicate objections to my ideas, style, and development. Professor Dana's ideas on the histories of the C.N.A. and the U.S.M. are quite different from my own. I respect his scholarship while retaining the right to reject his conclusions. Knowing Professor Dana, I am certain his comments will be trenchant, to the point, and blunt. I will not see them until the book is published. I would not have it any other way.

A book such as this rests on the work of many men and women. Some of the books I have read or consulted are listed in the *Selected Bibliography*. Portions of the book were read by friends and critics. Professor James Hedge of the University of London was kind enough to read chapters 1–8 and 18. Professor Maude Johnson of Burgoyne University read those chapters dealing with C.N.A. history, while Carlos Olverado, formerly Professor of History at Kinkaid University and now consultant to the Staff at Taiwan University, read those chapters dealing with the U.S.M. My old friend James Duferre, Minister of Home Affairs in the Province of Quebec, read sections on the history of the province and former confederation. Brigadier David

Shaw of the Australian Army gave me the benefit of his ideas regarding the wars of the past two centuries. Special thanks must go to Stanley Tulin, Professor of History at Cortez University and curator of Kramer Associates papers, for permitting me to print a good deal of material he has uncovered in the files, and reading the entire manuscript prior to publication. This book could not have been written without his help, encouragement, and support.

*University of Taiwan*
*February 19, 1972*

# FOR WANT OF A NAIL . . .

# I

# PRELUDE

W HAT many historians call "modern times" began in 1763, when
Great Britain forced the French coalition to accept a humiliating peace at Paris, thus ending the Seven Years' War and initiating
the *Pax Britannica*. Britain was to receive Canada, all Louisiana east of
the Mississippi except New Orleans, and the rich French possessions
in the Indies and India. Last of Europe's major powers to enter the
North American race, Britain was now the victor.

Having won the prize, Britain's leaders set about organizing their
domains. To appreciate the problems and possibilities of this task, one
must first understand the status of British North America in 1763.

There were some two million residents of the thirteen colonies at
that time, although some estimates place the number as low as 1.7
million. Scattered across a broad band that ran from the Maine border
in the north, to Florida in the south, these people had scarcely
scratched the rich surface of the continent. They were, in spite of this,
among the wealthiest and most rapidly developing peoples, not only in
the Empire, but the world. British North America provided excellent
soil and raw materials, and its people were vigorous and ingenious,
though crude and undisciplined. But this would have mattered little
had it not been for the protection and assistance provided the colonists
by Britain, and the benefits accruing to all those who lived under the
imperial umbrella.

Even before 1763, the North American and British economies
were attuned to one another. North America was a leading producer
of raw materials, while British manufactures were the best and cheapest in the world. Thus, American iron, forest products, tobacco, furs,
indigo, and the like were sent to Britain, where they were processed
and used in manufacturing, while the funds earned therefrom were
used to purchase finished goods of domestic origin. While it was true
the Navigation Acts made such trade mandatory and forbade the
Americans from selling and buying their goods outside the Empire,
even without these regulations, the North American trade would have
developed and flourished, since it benefited both sides. Indeed, were it

not for the protection of the Empire, which gave the Americans special privileges in British-controlled ports, the colonies could never have become as prosperous as they did.

By 1763, North America was one of the world's leading iron producers, and its major source of furs. Almost a third of all British ships were constructed in New England, whose oak was unsurpassed in quality and quantity. The region's fishing fleet, which roamed the North Atlantic, operated under the protection of the Royal Navy, and the Navigation Acts permitted the New Englanders to take advantage not only of the lucrative trade with Catholic Europe, but engage most profitably in the African slave trade. Some Virginia planters protested that London factors were taking too large a share of the tobacco trade, but recent studies have shown that the value added by these men was more than their commissions and other charges.[1]

Finally, where the Navigation Acts might have harmed the Americans, they were cheerfully overlooked. The Molasses Act of 1733, the Hat Act of 1732, and the Iron Act of 1750, designed to channel the North American economy along certain lines, were ignored, as New Englanders smuggled molasses and rum, New York made hats, and Pennsylvania produced a variety of iron goods. Nor did the Crown and Parliament attempt to pass strict laws controlling North America. Those that did get through the legislature were usually of minor importance, while the Crown showed little interest in such matters prior to 1763. Indeed, one might have easily concluded that the relations between Britain and North America were as good as those between any mother country and colony in history.

As is so often the case, victory brought many problems, but these were not at first apparent in North America. To southern colonists, the end of the French menace meant an opportunity to expand toward the Mississippi; young Patrick Henry began speculating in western lands at this time, as did Thomas Jefferson, George Washington, and others of the southern upper classes, who hoped in this way to win easy fortunes. Thousands of frontiersmen received the news of the Peace of Paris as a signal to move west, taking Indian lands as they went. To colonists in the New England area, peace meant increased opportunities for trading profits now that the French fleet was out of the way, and the illegal traffic in violation of the Navigation Acts increased sharply.[2] By contrast, the Middle Colonies of New York,

---

1. Herman Hopkins. *The North Atlantic Triangle* (London, 1964), pp. 344–54; Robert Jamieson, "Some Aspects of the Virginia Tobacco Trade in the Late Eighteenth Century," *The Journal of North American History*, LVI (June, 1969), pp. 943–44.

2. George Hinton. *Rebel Rapacity: Land Speculation and Smuggling in North America in the Late Eighteenth Century* (London, 1943), pp. 2–15.

New Jersey, and Pennsylvania were less rapacious, and their leaders, by and large, were fully cognizant of the benefits to be gained by obeying the law and cooperating with London.

It was in London that the first inkling of future problems could be discerned. Britain was in sorry financial condition, caused in large part by the expenses of defending the Empire against the French. The national debt stood at £140 million in 1763, and Prime Minister George Grenville believed the North Americans would have to pay their share of the cost. Furthermore, Grenville was opposed to further wars, since he could see little to be gained in such struggles. Accordingly he urged, and King George accepted, the Proclamation of 1763, under whose provisions three continental provinces were established: Quebec for the St. Lawrence River Valley, and East and West Florida for the former Spanish possessions to the south. The Northwest, the home of the fierce Ottawa and allied tribes, was to be closed to settlers for the time being. Grenville hoped a degree of local autonomy would please the former French and Spanish subjects and dissuade them from possible rebellions. Chief Pontiac of the Ottawa, who had fought on the French side in the Seven Years' War, was still a potent force in 1763, and it was expected that the preservation of his lands and the temporary ban on North American settlement there would prevent a renewal of an Indian war. The southern colonists appeared to understand the problems. To be sure, some homesteaders did transgress the line, but the speculators remained content in the belief that the Northwest would eventually be open to them.

Grenville had more difficulties with his trade policy. He was shocked to learn of the extent of colonial smuggling, and meant to put an end to it while at the same time adding to the national exchequer. In 1764 Parliament passed the Sugar Act, which, while cutting the duties on molasses in half, provided for more stringent collection methods. In addition, the Act raised the duties on sugar, coffee, pimento, indigo, and other West Indies commodities, and prohibited the importation of many products from the non-English colonies.

This last provision struck at the heart of the "triangular trade" between New England, West Africa, and the Indies. In effect, enforcement would mean higher prices for New England rum, a major trading item in the infamous slave trade which was the source of much of New England's prosperity.[3]

Some Boston merchants grumbled when they learned of the provisions of the Sugar Act. To them, it seemed Grenville was sacrificing their interests to please the powerful West Indies lobby in Parliament

---

3. Walter Jennings, Edward Gross, and Edward Fields, *New England and the* *African Slave Trade* (Oxford, 1823), pp. 67–69.

—planters who had long protested the refusal of North Americans to purchase their products. But the Boston merchants did little but talk; they realized enforcement by Britain would be difficult, and that in the future, as in the past, they would find ways to circumvent the law. More important in the long run was the reaction of a young Massachusetts firebrand, Samuel Adams. A malcontent and misfit, Adams was related directly or indirectly to the colony's most prestigious families, and considered by them a black sheep and a crank. Adams charged the Sugar Act with being a case of taxation without representation. He was not silenced when pro-Crown adversaries noted the Act was not a tax but a regulation, and that many British cities were unrepresented in the House of Commons, but nonetheless accepted its laws. For the moment, however, Adams attracted little attention and less support.

A more vocal reaction accompanied passage of the Stamp Act in 1765. Under its provisions, newspapers and some classes of legal documents would be obliged to bear tax stamps, which would provide an additional source of revenue for the mother country. This was not considered an unusual measure in Britain, where a stamp tax was already in operation. Benjamin Franklin, the keenest student of American affairs as well as its most famous resident, opposed the act as unwise, but soon after its passage attempted to win posts for his friends as stamp agents. Richard Henry Lee of Virginia, a well-respected citizen of that colony, hoped to gain a position for himself as stampmaster, and several followed his lead. But others felt differently. In the Virginia House of Burgesses, Patrick Henry, already enraged at his loss of income as a result of the Proclamation of 1763, rose to compare King George with a series of tyrants beginning with Caesar and ending with Charles I. Henry was to Virginia what Sam Adams had become to Massachusetts—a malcontent few listened to or respected. Whatever support he may have had at first was dissipated when he said, "If this be treason, then make the most of it." The House of Burgesses rejected his petition of protest, but it caused great joy in rebel circles in New England. In addition, it provoked the King's Enemies in Parliament to begin an attack on the monarch. Isaac Barré called those Americans who opposed the measure "sons of liberty," but even he did not go so far as to deny Parliament's right to tax the colonies. Passage of the Stamp Act, however, showed that what was later called "a triangle of treason" existed in Charlestown, Boston, and London.[4] This linkage could be seen in the beginnings of rebellious activity in North American ports soon after, much of it ascribed to encouragement from Lon-

---

4. Sir James Wilcox. *The Triangle of Treason* (London, 1962) is the best of the works on the early history of the conspiracy. Also see Robert Grady. *The* London Conspirators (Mexico City, 1966) and Alan Davis. *Patriotism Knows No Boundaries* (Mexico City, 1954).

don. A New England group, known as the Sons of Liberty, acknowledged its debt to the King's Enemies by accepting Barré's words as the name for the organization.[5] Terrorists hounded those favoring the Stamp Act, forcing several to resign. A wave of fear swept the port cities of North America, and this was climaxed by the calling of the Stamp Act Congress in Philadelphia in October of 1765.

Future historians would see in the Stamp Act Congress the seeds of both future difficulties and alignments. There were basically three groups represented at the Congress. The smallest consisted of the future rebels and radicals, men like James Otis of Massachusetts and Thomas Lynch of South Carolina, who demanded an outspoken and blunt statement in opposition to the legislation, but one that would stop short of actual defiance of the monarch. Then there were the "ultras," men who were later accused of being more royalist than King George; Charles Ogden of New Jersey, speaker of that colony's Assembly, was one of these. To him, any attempt to even question the motives and legitimacy of legislative enactments was close to treason.

Finally there were the moderate royalists, led by John Dickinson of Pennsylvania. Dickinson was thirty-three years old at the time, and already a well-known and respected figure in law and politics. The year before he had lost his seat in the Pennsylvania legislature, where he had distinguished himself in debates with Franklin, in which Dickinson had urged more faithful compliance with imperial needs. Although clearly a believer in order and constitutionalism, Dickinson was no ultra. Indeed, he had opposed the Stamp Tax in a brilliant pamphlet entitled, *The Late Regulations Respecting the British Colonies . . . Reconsidered*, and had friends in all camps, who admired not only his mind, but his personal charm and great warmth. It was Dickinson who dominated the Stamp Act Congress, presenting a series of "declarations of the rights and grievances of the colonists in America" which ably put forth the moderate case. Dickinson argued that the colonists were Englishmen by birth and so had certain rights. One of these was representation in Parliament, and since this had been denied them, the Stamp Act was of doubtful validity. Dickinson went on to observe the right of petition was an ancient one, and concluded by saying that the colonists in no way wanted to challenge the rights of the mother country. The proposals were accepted, disappointing both ultras who refused to sign them and radicals who had hoped for more.[6]

5. Sir James Wilcox, *Isaac Barré and the Conspiracy* (London, 1965), pp. 5–10.
6. The literature and history of the Dickinson career is both large and excellent, but the subject's own works are the best introduction to his life and thought. See Sir John Dickinson. *My Life and Work* (Philadelphia, 1804) and *The Late Rebellion*, 3 vols. (Philadelphia, 1784). Also, see Percy Hargrave. *Dickinson of North America*, 6 vols. (London, 1960–1966).

Shortly before the Stamp Act Congress met, but unknown to the members until afterwards, Grenville stepped down as Prime Minister to be replaced by the Marquis of Rockingham, who took command of the government in late July. Rockingham sympathized with the Dickinson position, at one time going so far as to exclaim, "I rejoice that America has resisted." William Pitt, who had always been sympathetic to American radicalism, considered Rockingham his protégé, and the Marquis brought such pro-radicals as General Henry Seymour Conway —who persisted in denying Parliament's right to tax the colonies—into his inner circle.

Rockingham succeeded in repealing the Stamp Act, but at the same time Parliament passed the Declaratory Act, which asserted its right to legislate for the colonies. Then he led a movement to lower the molasses duty, open several West Indies ports to American ships, and increase bounties paid for specified American products. Even his friends now complained Rockingham was sacrificing London for Boston, and his support began to fade. The King was thus able to dismiss him in August, 1766, and replace Rockingham with Pitt, who soon after was given the title of Lord Chatham. Since Chatham was now a member of Lords, others led the government from Commons, and one of them, Charles Townshend, was a man of ambition who sought King George's favor. This was relatively easy to do, since Chatham was old and infirm, unable to cope with the deficit or erase the red ink from the government's ledgers, while Townshend promised to do both.

Townshend introduced his program in January, 1767. At the time, Commons was divided into two factions, the Grenvillites and the Chathamites, with Townshend considered part of the latter group. When Townshend suggested the colonists be made to pay their share of imperial finances, the Grenvillites believed it a trick of some kind, but they changed their minds as Townshend proceeded. He would levy new taxes on tea, paper, paint, and glass, with the money collected used to pay salaries of colonial judges and governors. Since the colonists were divided over the issue of taxation, Townshend thus proposed what seemed on the surface a compromise. The radicals claimed Parliament had no right to tax the North Americans, who were not represented in Commons. But the Townshend program would raise money to be spent in the colonies, and so would not be a tax in the usual sense of the term.[7] In this way, the Townshend program would appear a compromise between the opposite sides, one calculated to heal the breach between

7. Philip Childs. "The Chathamites and the Grenvillites: Factionalism in Parliament on the Eve of the Rebellion," *The* *Journal of North American History*, XLI (January, 1954), pp. 112-23.

North America and Britain. He would raise sufficient revenue to please the Grenvillites while satisfying the constitutional objections of the Chathamites, and in the process make Charles Townshend the next prime minister of Britain.[8] Townshend was attacked on all sides, with Edmund Burke predicting a storm of opposition from North Americans, while Grenville argued the duties would raise insufficient funds and would harm English merchants. But the measures passed Commons by a large margin, and became law in July, 1767.

The Townshend duties (more commonly known at the time as the Revenue Act of 1767) were generally unacceptable to a majority of Americans, and as expected, raised a storm among the radicals. James Otis called for an embargo against British goods, while Sam Adams roused the Sons of Liberty and embarked upon a new wave of terror against those in the Boston area who remained believers in the law. Patrick Henry issued new broadsides from Virginia, and called upon his fellow-representatives to fight the Revenue Act. The most important response, however, came from John Dickinson, who, throughout, was the voice of a majority of North Americans. In a series of essays entitled *Letters from a Farmer in Pennsylvania to the Inhabitants of the British Colonies*, Dickinson argued that the laws were an attempt to destroy Americans' rights as Englishmen, and therefore should be opposed. He supported the embargo in Massachusetts, and went so far as to condone violence as a last resort.[9]

The support of men like Dickinson emboldened the radicals. On February 11, Sam Adams drew up a circular letter denouncing the Townshend duties in the strongest of terms. Going further, he wrote that even had Parliament granted representation to the colonies, its laws would not be binding on North Americans. Although he concluded with a disclaimer of revolutionary intent, it seemed obvious Adams was willing to support this kind of a movement should the time be ripe.

Adams had gone too far. Dickinson opposed such talk, while Joseph Galloway of Pennsylvania, then emerging as a leading loyalist, spoke even more strongly against the possibility of revolution. The distinction between moderate and radical remained, and despite Dickinson's attempts to find a middle ground, was brought into even more striking contrast by the reaction to the circular letter. It would seem this was what Adams wanted, for if reform were granted, the revolution he so ardently desired might never occur. So it was that he gloated over the reactions in Parliament. Grenville called the letter "infamous," while Lord Hillsborough, who had just assumed the post of

---

8. David Stephenson. *The Townshend Alternative* (London, 1955), p. 87.

9. Hargrave. *Dickinson of North America*. II, 645.

secretary of state for the colonies, spoke in even stronger terms against
the Boston rebels. Acting swiftly, he suspended the Massachusetts
Assembly until it agreed to denounce the Adams position.

Adams and Otis couldn't have been more pleased. The legislatures
of New Hampshire, Maryland, Connecticut, Rhode Island, Georgia,
and South Carolina joined Virginia in approving the letter. Arson became common; British agents were harassed; sedition was in the air.
Even George Washington, considered a loyalist at that time, indicated
a willingness to join in violent activity if necessary to preserve his
liberties as an Englishman.[10] Men like Dickinson and Galloway, who
had supported the concept of law while opposing specific statutes,
found themselves with a shrinking constituency. The North American
embargo against British goods was thus a success. By the spring of 1768
Massachusetts appeared on the verge of rebellion. British ships were
attacked by the Sons of Liberty that summer, and additional troops
were sent from Canada to Boston to quell the disturbances. Yet they
continued, while at the same time the government in London vacil-
lated, seemingly without a sense of what was happening.

At this critical moment, Chatham resigned and was replaced by
Lord Grafton, who knew little of American affairs. He relied upon
Lord North, the Chancellor of the Exchequer, for ideas and programs
for the colonies. Grafton wanted to abolish the Townshend duties and
wash his hands of the mess, but North prevailed upon him to maintain
the tea tax as a symbol of parliamentary supremacy in colonial affairs.
Soon after, Grafton resigned, and North succeeded him as prime minister.

North's position regarding the colonies was both logical and
reasonable. He would avoid antagonizing them by rejecting regulatory
legislation, while at the same time insisting upon the principle of parliamentary supremacy. In this way London would retain the principle,
while the colonists would have the substance.[11] In practice this stance
proved unworkable, at least in Boston, where the presence of royal
troops was used by Adams and his colleagues as a pretext for more
terrorism and violence. By the winter of 1769–1770 the city's population had become polarized, with a majority supporting the Adams
camp. When in March some British soldiers, defending themselves
against an angry mob, fired upon and killed five Americans, excitement
reached a fever pitch. Even though the soldiers were acquitted of the
crime, the Sons of Liberty were able to make capital of what they
called the "Boston Massacre." The Boston fever would rise steadily in

10. Lawrence Henry. *Washington: Re-*
*luctant Rebel* (New York, 1925), p. 76.
11. Elizabeth Donner. "The Failure of
the *Via Media* in Boston in the Critical
Year, 1769," *King's University Quar-*
*terly,* CVI (Summer, 1912), pp. 1098–
1121.

the years to come, as that city became the center for rebellious activity in North America.

This polarization of sentiment not only added to the ranks of the rebels, but also led many fence-straddlers to come out in favor of the Crown. Given the choice between Adams' promises of freedom and anarchy on the one hand, and colonial regulations and order on the other, many North Americans chose the latter. The New York *Gazette and Weekly Mercury* editorialized that "It's high time a stop was put to mobbing," and similar sentiments were expressed in newspapers all along the Atlantic seaboard.[12] Just as Boston was becoming the rebel stronghold, so New York's intellectual aristocracy made its city the loyalist capital. North's firm handling of affairs, coupled with evidence of loyalism in all the colonies save Massachusetts, led the few remaining Boston patriots to rethink their position. By the summer of 1770 they had gained sufficient strength and nerve to end Adams' already enfeebled boycott of British goods. Within a year it seemed calm had returned, along with a new period of prosperity, based on close commercial contacts with Britain. Not even a mild fracas, the result of the burning of the royal ship *Gaspee*, could evoke protests from those sympathetic to the rebels. Adams, Henry, and their cohorts tried in vain to fire North American enthusiasm for sedition, but it would take more than the sinking of a ship to accomplish that task.

The rebels were more successful in 1773, when they capitalized on old fears and an admitted British insensitivity to the colonial situation, to arouse the fires of sedition once again. It all began with a surplus of tea in Britain, and the near-bankruptcy of the East India Company, some of whose warehouses were bursting with the leaf. At this time North struck upon what seemed an admirable plan, one that would benefit all who lived under the King's protection. The Prime Minister sponsored and Parliament passed the Tea Act of 1773; East India tea would be sold to the colonists at a price substantially below that of smuggled Dutch tea, but with a small tax. The Act was meant to accomplish several important goals. It would ease the Company's financial problems, please the colonists (who would now receive less expensive tea), destroy the smugglers, and force the rebels to admit that cries of "no taxation without representation" were no more than attempts to avoid paying their share of imperial costs.[13]

North's problem was his faulty assessment of North American

12. The geographic polarization of this period was one of the most striking elements of the rebellion era, and the source of New York's future political strength and the decline of Boston in the late 18th and early 19th centuries. See Bernard Lovertz. *The Rise of New York* (New York, 1886), pp. 34–37.

13. Warner Jones, ed. *Lord North's Master Plan: Genius or Ignorance?* (Mexico City, 1960) contains several informative essays on the subject, by both U.S.M. and C.N.A. historians.

conditions, and underestimation of the Sons of Liberty. Adams was both shocked and pleased at news of the Tea Act. He felt anger that Parliament had once again attempted to tax the colonies, but welcomed the chance to spark rebellion with the aid of North's flint. The Sons of Liberty gave the signal, and branches of that underground organization began their campaign against North soon after. The "Tea War" had begun, and before it was over, almost every port on the Atlantic seaboard would be involved in several violent incidents, most of them centering around "tea parties," such as that in Boston on December 15.[14] Even New York, the center of royalist strength, was seized by rebellious anti-tea forces and closed to East India Company ships. Adams' boycott was complete; not a single tea chest was opened for sale in America. By the spring of 1774 British North America was repolarized, with a larger proportion on the rebel side than even Adams had thought possible a year earlier.[15]

A similar development occurred in London, where some leading pro-American members were aghast at the destruction of property and violence in the Atlantic ports. Chatham thought the colonists' behavior in the Tea War "outrageous," and others of his party remained quiet during the debates of that spring. The King's statements on colonial affairs were applauded even by those who earlier had thought George an unwise monarch. "We must master them or totally leave them to themselves and treat them as Aliens," the King cried, and none rose to challenge the statement.[16] Instead, Parliament as a whole put aside other problems to consider what should be done to punish what North called "the haughty American rebels." A few members called for the sending of a large expeditionary force to North America, to capture the radical leaders and hang them on the spot, and then remain to teach the Americans a lesson they would long remember. Others wanted to give the Americans their freedom, to allow the Sons of Liberty to take command of North America; a few months under the control of

---

14. Even now, the Tea War is argued and debated by historians. The interests of many leading Sons of Liberty (especially John Hancock) in smuggling has been well documented, and some researchers have suggested the destruction of commerce, and not freedom, was the fear of the Sons of Liberty in this period, and it was for this reason they started the insurrection. (see Walter Brownell. *Tea and Terror: The Sons of Liberty in 1773* (Melbourne, 1954) and Robert Scott. *John Hancock: The Profiteerer and the Patriot* (New York, 1959), especially pp. 334–59). What does seem clear, however, is that the Sons of Liberty themselves were shocked at the strong public reaction against the Tea Act, and at first the public protests ran ahead of the Sons in violence and rhetoric. Dickinson, for example, opposed the Tea Act, as did others of the centrist party of 1773. Franklin Hope. *John Dickinson's Years of Trial* (London, 1917), pp. 431–33.

15. Lawrence Gilman. *Sam Adams and the Rebellion: A Study in Revolutionary Leadership.* (Mexico City, 1954), p. 101.

16. Sir James Wilcox. *Royal Leadership: George III and the Crisis* (London, 1970), p. 443.

Adams and his friends would teach the majority of radicals the value of London's rule.[17] Some—only a handful in Commons—wanted the complete leveling of Boston as a fitting rejoinder to Adams' challenge. None spoke up for North American "rights." The colonists, on the face of it at least, had challenged Parliament's right to legislate for them, and now must be shown the fruits of such violent protest.[18]

By March, 1774, the die for rebellion was cast, although few on either side of the Atlantic realized it at the time.[19] By taking the violent path, the Sons of Liberty was challenging the right of Parliament to legislate for North America, and not merely the wisdom of a particular act. A challenge on this issue united Adams and Dickinson, Henry and Galloway, while Chatham joined with North in opposing it.

Few at the time understood that the American opposition was by no means in basic agreement; Dickinson and Galloway remained true to the *Crown* while Adams and Henry, even then, were plotting an assault on royal prerogative itself. Not even North thought the rebels would go so far. Had he known this, he would have been both more concerned and relieved at the same time. For he would have perceived the ruthlessness of his enemies, and known they could not have been satisfied with anything less than complete independence. He would also have realized, however, that such a position would never attract a substantial portion of the North American population. Then, as later, the majority remained loyal to the Crown while criticizing Parliament.[20] A protest against Parliament might have succeeded in the 1770's, but any revolt against the King was doomed to failure.

---

17. *Ibid.*, p. 465.

18. Brownell. *Tea and Terror*, p. 198.

19. Lord Walter Smithies. *The Origins of the North American Rebellion* (London, 1889) remains the standard work on the subject, although some of Smithies' interpretations have been challenged. For a revisionist viewpoint, see Murray Kline. "The Myth of the Rebellion: Dorchester and Boston in the Crisis Year," *The Journal of North American History*, LI (June, 1964), pp. 430–55.

20. Adams himself later admitted this and considered loyalty to the King a problem that could not be resolved, but only overcome. Gilman, *Sam Adams and the Rebellion*, pp. 459–61. Also see Samuel Adams. *Letters of a Rebel*, 14th edition (Mexico City, 1965), pp. 865–66.

# 2

# THE REBELLION BEGINS

PARLIAMENT'S response to the colonial challenge came in March and April of 1774. Under the terms of a series of acts, Boston port was closed until the city paid for the tea the rebels had destroyed, the Massachusetts Assembly was suspended, and the royal governor's powers were expanded. During the next two months Parliament passed, and the King accepted, two additional laws. One enabled royal officials accused of crimes to be tried in Britain rather than Massachusetts, and the other authorized colonial governors to requisition buildings for the housing of troops. Finally, the Quebec Act, which enlarged upon the rights of French-Canadians and extended the boundaries of that province to include the old Northwest, was signed into law.

None of these laws was unusual in the sense that all had either been expected or had precedents in British law. Parliament had closed down British ports in the past, had revamped colonial administrations, and had for several years indicated Quebec might receive the Northwest. But the North American colonists interpreted these actions as retribution for the rebels' response to the Tea War. Charles James Fox and Burke, two of the most pro-American members of Parliament, argued that the laws punished only Boston and Massachusetts, and not other ports and colonies where similar outrages had occurred; it was unfair to make one colony pay for crimes committed in others. William Dowdeswell predicted the measures would drive the North Americans into the arms of the Sons of Liberty, and polarize Britain and North America beyond reconciliation, but his words went unheeded by an angry majority. Rose Fuller introduced a measure to repeal the Tea Act on April 15, which was defeated in Commons by a vote of 182 to 49; this was perhaps the clearest gauge of parliamentary unity against the recalcitrant Americans.[1]

1. Martin Fuller. *Rose Fuller and the Attempts to Prevent the Rebellion, including a Biography of Important Members of the House on the Eve of the Conflict* (London, 1799), pp. 19-49.

Dowdeswell's predictions were fulfilled sooner than even he had imagined they would be. On learning of the Boston Port Bill Sam Adams sprang into action, delighted at the measure and eager for war. He convened a meeting of the Massachusetts Committee of Correspondence to discuss means of retaliation, and skillfully maneuvered it into calling an all-colonial conference to decide on ways to oppose the measure. Messengers were sent to New York, Philadelphia, and other port cities with orders to contact Sons of Liberty cells there and order them into action. As Adams saw it, the way was open for war, not only against Britain and for independence, but against the North American upper classes, which were in league with London. He drew up a "Solemn League and Covenant," to be submitted to radicals in all colonies, by which they pledged themselves not to purchase British goods until Boston port was re-opened. If accepted, the embargo would harm American as well as British merchants, in effect allying them against the radicals. Then, during any war for independence that might take place, Adams would have a weapon to carry forth a social revolution as well. Although the document did not advocate class warfare as such, it seems evident that this is what Adams had in mind at the time.[2]

The New York loyalists were quick to grasp Adams' program, and swift in their opposition. They suggested the calling of a Continental Congress—which would include loyalists as well as radicals—to discuss the best means of answering the parliamentary challenge. Hopefully, they would dominate such a meeting, thus preventing Adams from having his way. Adams accepted the invitation, gambling that he would be able to influence the Congress to achieve the anti-British colonial unity he so ardently desired.

Radicals and conservatives alike planned carefully for the forthcoming congress. Jefferson, speaking for the rebels, wrote *A Summary View of the Rights of British America*, in which he denounced British rule and called for an end to Parliament's power over North America. The Virginia delegation, together with that of Massachusetts, was dominated by rebels, some of whom were openly or secretly members of the Sons of Liberty. John Dickinson, prominent in the Pennsylvania delegation, called for moderation, and was joined by Galloway and Franklin, who urged the colonists to pay the tea tax and seek an accommodation with the mother country. John Jay of New York joined

---

2. Whether or not Adams had a social revolution in mind should a war of independence occur has been a subject of debate for the past two centuries. If the rebels had succeeded in their objectives—complete independence—it is evident that an internal war would have followed, with many loyalists either exiled or killed. See Herbert Wechler. *Sam Adams' Plans: Blood and Boston* (New York, 1944).

in this plea. From the first, the division of forces was clear-cut, and on the eve of the Congress, the loyalists appeared to have a majority of delegates.

The fight began on September 5, the very day the Congress opened deliberations in Philadelphia. Charles Thomson of Philadelphia, one of the few radicals in the Pennsylvania delegation, made a speech for Adams' "Solemn Covenant," and was answered by Dickinson, who warned of the danger of sedition. A shouting match followed, with each side attempting to win the waverers to its banner. Although outnumbered, the radicals found themselves in a stronger position, due in large part to the essential moderation and willingness to compromise shown by the loyalists. Galloway and Dickinson conceded the British had treated Boston unfairly, and Galloway admitted the old ways were gone forever, and that a new compact between London and America would have to be concluded.[3] Day after day the radicals, armed with a logical program, exposed the loyalists as waverers and trimmers, and increasingly the uncommitted delegates came over to their side.

On September 17, Joseph Warren of Massachusetts introduced the "Suffolk Resolves." These statements, earlier adopted by the citizens of Suffolk, Massachusetts, declared the parliamentary actions against Massachusetts unconstitutional, urged the establishment of a revolutionary government in Massachusetts, and issued a call to arms. At first it was believed far too radical for the majority of delegates, but much to the surprise of all except Adams, the Suffolk Resolves were adopted by a slim margin.

Now the loyalists realized the essential weakness of their support, and hastened to win to their side the more moderate of the radicals. Their effort took the form of an ingenious proposal worked out by Galloway, probably with the assistance of Dickinson, known as the "Plan of Proposed Union Between Great Britain and the Colonies." The Galloway Plan was considered an attempt to reconcile all but the most ardent revolutionaries with those in Parliament who were friendly toward the Americans, but rejected any thought of independence. The plan called for the establishment of an American government (encompassing the thirteen colonies but not Canada), composed of a legislative council of representatives chosen by each colony and a

---

3. The ability of radicals to destroy moderates through the devices of oversimplification and emotionalism is best discussed in Eric Bjornson. *The Failure of The Middle: The Triumph of Radicalism in America in 1774* (London, 1965). Also see *The Radical Mind: Studies in Power* (London, 1967) by the same author. Bjornson contends that had Dickinson and Galloway been less decent men and shown the same unreasonableness as Adams and Jefferson, they could have obtained their objectives.

President General selected by the Crown. The council would have the right to legislate for internal affairs that concerned two or more colonies. Parliament would have the power of veto over its laws, but the American legislature would, in turn, be able to veto parliamentary acts pertaining to the colonies. The Galloway Plan was, in short, an embodiment of all that the Americans (except the radicals) might have desired in terms of self-government, while simultaneously maintaining the valuable ties with the mother country. A year earlier the plan might have won easy acceptance, and even in 1774, there were those who recognized its fairness and intelligence. Later on, several radicals would regret not having urged its adoption at the time.[4] But in the heat of the debate it was rejected, by a vote of six to five. A single vote would have prevented needless bloodshed, and presented London with a proposal that might have won a majority of Commons to its banner. Unlike the rebels, Galloway wished to preserve the rights of Englishmen for the colonists; he believed true liberty was possible only by accepting the English experiences.

Now the radicals presented their demands. In their "Declaration of Rights and Resolves" they argued that Americans had the rights of "life, liberty, and property," and unlike Galloway, would not accept any parliamentary controls on such rights. Referring to Commons as "a foreign power," the Declaration assumed Americans to be equals of those living in Britain, and so had the right to their own legislative body. Beyond that, the radicals did not challenge the power of the King—such an act would have been treason and recognized as such by a majority of delegates—and privately insisted they were as loyal to George III as any man.[5] The Declaration of Rights and Resolves passed with a clear majority, leaving the loyalists in despair.

Capitalizing on their victory, the radicals next obtained approval of a Continental Association, which would act as a temporary government for the colonies (although it was not presented in such a light to the more gullible delegates). Sam Adams was jubilant; he had won every major point at the meetings. John Adams, more loyalist than his cousin, now moved more clearly to the rebel camp. Peering into the future, he told Patrick Henry that "We must fight." John Adams was

---

4. John Adams, for one, wrote of his regret in 1779. "The rebellion had been brewing in the hearts and minds of Americans for a decade, and could not have been halted by mere words. But acceptance of the Galloway Plan could have channeled our energies in such a way as to enable us to achieve our goals with a minimum of effort and bloodshed. If war had come then, it would have been London, and not Philadelphia, that would answer to God for the deaths of the Rebellion." See John Adams. *Collected Works* (Mexico City, 1912), Vol. XVI, pp. 18–19.

5. Wechler. *Sam Adams' Plans*, pp. 413–19.

saddened by the thought but Patrick Henry, one of the most blood-thirsty of the radicals, spoke happily of the prospect. "The next gale from the north will bring to our ears the clash of resounding arms," he gloated, believing Boston would soon erupt and the war spread to his own colony.[6]

As the First Continental Congress drew to a close, men like Sam Adams and Patrick Henry remained cordial to their opponents among the moderates, but in private they despised Dickinson and Galloway. They could understand George III, and even agree with him when he said in November that, "Blows must decide whether they [the colonists] are to be subject to this country or independent." Such an attitude would hasten the day of revolution, for which they waited eagerly. But Dickinson and Galloway, who were still striving for a *via media* in 1774–1775, were their real enemies. Such has always been the fate of moderates; they draw the fire of both extremes.[7]

In London Lord North also strove for reconciliation, aided by his Secretary of State for the Colonies, the Earl of Dartmouth. Together with Benjamin Franklin, who, as always, maintained connections in all camps, they tried to find a way of ending the crisis. But these talks failed. Parliamentary radicals insisted on conceding every point to the Bostonians, while ultra-royalists demanded harsh measures be continued and even tightened. Charles James Fox predicted the end of the empire unless Sam Adams and his supporters were given power, while the Earl of Sandwich (then First Lord of the Admiralty) stated that the Americans were "raw, undisciplined, cowardly men," who would flee at the first shot.[8] North managed to push some conciliatory legislation through Parliament, but he was losing his leverage with the King, who considered his Prime Minister a weakling and a coward. Sandwich and his naval colleagues, along with the Earl of Suffolk, urged a hard line toward the North Americans, and at the time it seemed to make sense. What was needed in North America was a strong man, one whom Adams and his ilk knew could not be bullied into submission.

In early 1775, the King moved to implement the idea. Generals William Howe, Henry Clinton, and most importantly, John Burgoyne, were dispatched to America. Viscount Barrington was told to prepare a plan of blockade for the colonies; Colonial Allan McLean was to raise a brigade of Scots soldiers for colonial warfare. On learning of the new

6. Edgar Wainwright. *Bloody Patrick Henry: The Cromwell Who Failed* (New York, 1917), pp. 109–10.
7. Bjornson. *Failure of the Middle,* p. 199.

8. Herbert Wechler. *George III and His Circle* (New York, 1939), pp. 443–45.

hard line, Major John Pitcairn of the Boston contingent was over-joyed. For months the Redcoats of that city, not unlike the Sons of Liberty, had chafed at delay and yearned for action. Now it was at hand. Pitcairn was convinced "that one active campaign, a smart action, and burning two or three of their towns, will set everything to rights."[9] On his part, Sam Adams traveled to Lexington, a small town on the outskirts of Boston, and rallied excited and joyful Sons of Liberty to the banner of revolt. War seemed imminent by early April of 1775.

The British show of force came in mid-April. Lieutenant Colonel Francis Smith and Major Pitcairn led a detachment of troops to Lexington to take the Adams group into captivity. The rebels were warned, however, and irregulars met the King's soldiers on the outskirts of town at dawn on April 19. These "minutemen" fired on the soldiers, thus provoking the long-sought confrontation. The soldiers fell back, and after a second engagement at Concord returned to Boston. Two hundred and seventy-three soldiers gave their lives in these two engagements, while ninety-three rebels were killed. The North American Rebellion had begun.[10]

Four years after the battles of Lexington and Concord, Sam Adams and Patrick Henry would claim that they had little idea the Rebellion would begin there and then, although conceding they had worked for a break with Britain for at least a decade.[11] There is much evidence to support this contention; the Sons of Liberty were still badly organized, there was no shadow government prepared to assume leadership in the Rebellion, and not even a paramilitary operation set to go into action outside of Massachusetts. Indeed, rarely had such a struggle begun with so little preparation. The rebels had done no work at all in Canada, and had not yet prepared the general population for combat. They had poor financing and worse military leadership, and no plan of action. Sam Adams, Patrick Henry, Thomas Jefferson, and the like had proven skilled agitators, and had been able to bring the colonies to war, but had no idea as to what to do after the combat had begun. During the next three years expediency and opportunism would prove the basis of rebel plans. That the Rebellion would fail was seldom in doubt; that it lasted as long as it did was a tribute both to the ferocity of the rebels and the ineptness of early British leadership.

9. Murray Kline. "Pitcairn as a Symbol," *Britannica*, VIII (April 19, 1954), pp. 34–36.
10. Burgoyne Collins. *The Origins of the North American Rebellion* (New York, 1965), pp. 223–34.
11. Sir Evelyn Bartley. *The Treason Trials of 1778–1779: Transcripts and Records* (London, 1800), Vol. XXVI, pp. 520–22, 654–55.

Once the latter was changed, however, the conflict came to its expected conclusion.[12]

The rebels counted on dissension in Parliament to aid them in their struggle. Just as North Americans were divided on the Rebellion, so was Parliament. Colonel William Phillips wrote, "I see that so large and extensive a Continent cannot be conquered by a handful of men," while David Hartley, verging on the edge of treason, told Commons, "You may bruise America's heel, but you cannot crush its head." Such men as these were as important to the rebels as were their own troops. As Sam Adams later said, "The struggle for liberty had to be won in the streets of London, as well as in those of Boston. Parliament, as much as the Continental Congress, was to be our command point in the fight for human dignity and freedom."[13] If Sam Adams expected help from Parliament he was to be disappointed, for after Lexington and Concord those who sympathized with America steadily lost power, while the supporters of the King gained strength almost daily.

Similarly, the war party gained power in America. The Second Continental Congress met for its initial session on May 10, and it was evident from the first that radicalism was in the saddle. Now Dickinson's pleas for calmness and conciliation seemed out of place. Adams alluded to the fact that American blood had been shed. London must pay the price, he said, and that price would be paid in Redcoat gore. He did not realize at the time, however, that a subtle *coup* was being prepared even then. Men like Sam Adams and Patrick Henry were considered destructive by other radicals, who now understood the need for a common American front against the British. This could only be accomplished by new men, who would be able to win over Dickinson, Galloway, Duane of New York, and other loyalists. Thus, Adams and Henry were eased from their positions of power over the next few months, to be replaced by more able politicians; John Adams of Massachusetts, Richard Henry Lee and Francis Lightfoot Lee of Virginia, and a more subdued Thomas Jefferson were among this group of young revolutionaries. They were as forceful and politically astute as the men who a century before had followed Cromwell, and

---

12. David Wilcox. *The Lost Crusade* (New York, 1923) is the best study of rebel weaknesses. For another view, see Harmon Kennedy. *The North American Rebellion: The Crisis of Leadership* (Mexico City, 1965). Kennedy argues that with better military leadership the rebels would have won the war. Robert Graves. *Rebels in Uniform* (Cincinnati, 1945) is an excellent study of rebel leadership in war.

13. Later on, especially during the trials, there were rumors of a "rebel cabal" in Commons, which supposedly worked with Sam Adams in 1775 and plotted the assassination of the King and the establishment of a parliamentary government in Britain, all with France's help. These rumors have never been substantiated, but they persist nonetheless. See Sir Hartley McNee. *Adams and the French Conspiracy* (London, 1888), especially pp. 198–232.

equally determined in their ambitions, which were the destruction of the monarchy and the establishment of an egalitarian republic on the model of the ancient Greek city-states.

The Continental Congress's most important action was the naming of a commander for the rebel armies. At the time, a force was on its way to Canada in the mistaken hope that they would find support in Montreal and Quebec, while a ragged group of irregulars had gathered outside of Boston in preparation for a siege of that city. A man was needed to coordinate these forces and others the Congress might raise, and lead them to victory. At John Adams' urgings, Jefferson formally nominated George Washington of Virginia for the key position. Israel Putnam of Connecticut, Artemas Ward of Massachusetts, and Philip Schuyler of New York were also named, to serve as major generals under Washington.

All four of these men had fought in the French wars, while a fifth, Charles Lee, had seen extensive action in Europe and was by far the most experienced and intelligent of the new commanders. That Charles Lee was not selected for higher command, indicates the essentially political nature of the appointments. Washington was named commander because he came from Virginia, was of an important class (the planters), and considered a man of good will by loyalists as well as radicals. He was nominated by two men—John Adams and Thomas Jefferson—who though intelligent in the ways of revolution, knew nothing of war, and was approved by a Congress with a similar background. Washington had served without distinction in the Seven Years' War, losing the only battle in which he held command, and at the time of Lexington, was vegetating at his home in Mount Vernon, after marrying a wealthy widow, apparently for her money. A man of little talent and less imagination, though of great pride, Washington saw in the Rebellion a chance to make a career for himself, and so deserted his class for the sake of his ambition. Needless to say, his selection was the greatest mistake the rebels could have made. With Charles Lee as commander, the Rebellion might have succeeded in stalemating the British armies; under Washington, it was doomed to failure. The commander of the inferior rebel forces soon demonstrated an ineptness in the field and unsound training in both strategy and tactics. It would have taken a Caesar to organize the rebel armies and make a respectable showing against the well-trained professionals of Europe; instead, the Congress chose a Crassus.[14]

---

14. Washington's leading biographer, General Sir Henry Mates, claims that Washington was still learning his craft when the war ended. Given a year of experience in the field in Europe, he would have made an excellent commander. See General Sir Henry Mates. *George Washington: The War Years* (New York, 1932), Vol. II, pp. 89–98.

The loyalists made their last pleas for moderation at the same meeting that selected Washington as military commander. Dickinson wrote and introduced the "Olive Branch Petition" to the King, a request for royal restraint that included a hope the colonies might yet be reconciled with the mother country. Having won all the important battles, the radicals were willing to allow the royalists the symbols of strength, and they voted for the petition, which was sent to the King. Then Dickinson showed his ability at compromise by introducing a second resolution, "A Declaration of the Causes of Necessities of Taking Up Arms." In it he rejected independence as a goal of the contest, but stated that Americans would die before relinquishing their rights as Englishmen. The resolution carried by a large margin. It represented an important step for the loyalists, who were now willing to take up arms against Parliament to protect their rights. As for the radicals, they considered Dickinson's Declaration a weak substitute for action. Unlike him, they were prepared even then to challenge the Crown, although unwilling to let it be known to the others at the Congress. In July of 1775, then, the loyalists and radicals were joined in common struggle, but each had their own idea as to whom the enemy was. To the radicals, the only true victory would be the utter destruction of all ties with Britain; to the loyalists, British freedoms remained the goal. Had this been realized in London, much anguish might have been spared both sides in the Rebellion.

George III was not prepared to make such distinctions. The King refused to accept the Olive Branch Petition from Richard Penn of Pennsylvania, and Dartmouth sadly informed the emissary that he could not deal with an envoy of the illegal Continental Congress. Then Dartmouth himself was thrown from power, his place taken by the inept Lord Germain, whose lack of military ability was overshadowed by his willingness to follow the King's dictates. Other friends of the loyalist Americans were also replaced, as the war party gained power in London. Burke's proposed "conciliatory statement," which would have renounced British rights to tax Americans, was defeated by a vote of 210 to 105. On November 20, 1775, North was obliged to introduce a measure that provided for a naval blockade of America, the impressment of American sailors, and the seizure of American goods. It was, in effect, a declaration of war against the North Americans—all of them, royalists included. The bill passed by a wide margin. In this way, the King silenced the moderates in London, just as those in North America were either seduced or ignored.[15] The warmakers would now have their time of power, one that would last for almost three years. The

---

15. Burgoyne Collins. "The Polarization of Interests on the Eve of the American Rebellion," *London Political Review* LI (June, 1960), pp. 340–57.

moderates had less influence in this period, biding their time until they were once again needed.[16]

The radical armies were ill-equipped, untrained, and poorly-led, hardly a match in open combat for the professionals of Britain and those mercenaries hired by the Crown from the Germanies. Furthermore, the rebels lacked funds with which to carry on the fight. In order to gain military and financial assistance, the Congress was obliged to seek allies. They could best be found among the historic enemies of Great Britain, especially those nations humbled by British power in the eighteenth century. The logical allies were to be found in Paris and Madrid. Paradoxically, the North American radicals now attempted to ally their cause with that of the most reactionary governments in western Europe.

Late in 1775 Arthur Lee, the rebel agent in London, began contacting French and Spanish representatives, proposing an alliance against Britain. He and others that followed found these nations eager to re-open their old antagonisms with Britain. The Comte de Vergennes in particular encouraged such talk, and in March he approached Spanish Foreign Minister Grimaldi about the possibility of a joint Franco-Spanish effort to aid the rebels. Grimaldi showed sufficient interest for Vergennes to bring the proposal to King Louis XVI. With Louis' assent, Vergennes established a fictitious trading company, Roderigue Hortalez et Cie, through which French and Spanish aid was channeled to America. Vergennes made it clear, however, that he was not interested in aiding the Americans if their desire was to remain in some kind of restructured British Empire. Should they, however, desire true independence (naturally allied with France!) then Paris would be willing to provide any and all assistance necessary. Two conditions had to be met before an all-out effort would be made. The first of these was a promise of an American alliance with France once independence was assured. The second was some indication the rebel cause had a chance of success. The Continental Congress was willing to provide assurances for the first condition, but only George Washington could meet the second. Thus, by early 1776 the rebels attempted to win foreign support both through actions at the Continental Congress and in the field.[17]

They were more successful in the first than in the second. Separatist sentiment grew in North America in 1775–1776, the natural re-

16. James Elson. *Dickinson and Galloway in the Crisis Years* (New York, 1901), pp. 19–32; Herbert Ferrell. *The Decline and Rise of Loyalist Sentiment During the North American Rebellion (King's University Studies in History and Political Science)* (New York, 1911), pp. 11–21, 48–57.

17. Harry Forbes. *The Franco-American Alliance: Its Origins and Consequences.* (unpublished Ph.D. dissertation, Burgoyne University, 1962), especially chapters II and III.

sult of the fires of war. As bloodshed on both sides increased, the voices of moderation were either stilled or ignored; in some cases, loyalists were terrorized and forced to flee the mainland, either for Bermuda, the Indies, or Canada. Radical publications, the most important of which was *Common Sense* by British born Thomas Paine, son of a Quaker corset maker, urged the Americans to throw off all vestiges of British civilization and create a new utopia in their land. Colony after colony accepted this reasoning, rejecting their loyalist citizens and representatives and giving power to the radicals. On April 12, North Carolina's legislature voted for independence, and others indicated they would follow soon. Within weeks, talk of independence was common in Philadelphia; the Continental Congress could think of little else. The revolutionaries were now poised for their final thrust, one that would unmask their true nature and complete their break from both the mother country and America's loyalists.

On June 7, Richard Henry Lee introduced three proposals to the Congress. The first would declare the colonies independent of Britain, the second form an American government to conduct the war, and the last establish formal relations with European nations. Some loyalists protested; it was one thing to oppose Parliament, but quite another to defy the King. The radicals did not even bother to debate the point. A five man committee, consisting of Thomas Jefferson, Roger Sherman, John Adams, Benjamin Franklin, and Robert Livingston was established to draw up a bill of charges against the King and a Declaration of Independence. The former resembled the one presented to King Charles I by the revolutionaries of his day; the latter was an eloquent restatement of contemporary French radical philosophy regarding the rights of man.

The Declaration of Independence incorporated one portion designed to please those who felt the King had caused the breach in the constitution, and that revolution was not only necessary, but to be expected of free-born Englishmen. The second part seems to have been a thinly disguised play to win further support from French intellectuals.[18] In sum, the Declaration was more a political and propaganda vehicle than a serious attempt to state radical philosophy. Thomas Jefferson himself indicated some doubts as to its wisdom. In speaking to the British he said that though the two countries might be "Enemies in War," they could hope to be "in peace, Friends," while Franklin, as usual, was willing to switch sides at the slightest change in the wind.[19]

18. Reynolds Copeland. *America and the French Alliance* (London, 1924), pp. 54–58.
19. Harry Forbes. *In Peace Friends: Jefferson and the Politics of Expedi-* ency (New York, 1933) and Sir Edwin Fowler. *That Chameleon Franklin! The Life and Times of Benjamin Franklin of America and England* (London, 1800).

John Adams, in contrast, was swept away by what he considered the glory of the moment. In writing to his wife, he said he was "well aware of the toil and blood and treasure it will cost us to maintain this declaration and support and defend these States. Yet through all this gloom I can see rays of ravishing light and glory. I can see that the end is more than worth all the means, and that prosperity will triumph in that day's transactions."[20] Thus, the classic revolutionary's willingness to justify all he did by the purity of his goals. The Declaration of Independence was signed on July 2, and ratified two days later.

In this way, the radicals signaled their goals to the French and Spaniards, and now they hoped for the foreign aid which alone could enable them to achieve their objectives. But such aid would not appear until the radicals showed an ability in the field. John Adams and Tom Paine might have been able to win the battle of words, but without deeds, the words would be meaningless.

---

20. Collins. *Origin of the North American Rebellion*, p. 352.

# 3

# VICTORY IN AMERICA

WASHINGTON arrived on the outskirts of Boston in July, 1775, where he was greeted by the New England irregulars. The rebels outnumbered the British troops in the city, and had command of the heights overlooking the harbor. Yet Washington did not attack. His forces were still unorganized and undisciplined, and he lacked sufficient arms for an engagement against the well-trained professionals under the command of General Thomas Gage. On his part, Gage proved incapable of action, and refused to lead his men against the rebels. A man of common abilities and little imagination, Gage was clearly the wrong man for the position. By the time he was dismissed and replaced by General William Howe, Washington had been able to whip his men into a semblance of order. Then in January, captured cannon arrived at rebel headquarters and Washington prepared for the attack. But the battle never took place. Wisely realizing his position in the city was untenable, Howe evacuated Boston in March, taking with him some thousand loyalists who feared reprisal once the rebels took the city. Washington entered Boston in late March, amid rebel fanfare and violence against those loyalists who had remained. He had won the city without firing a shot. It was to be the only major rebel victory Washington would enjoy.

Far more important than Washington's seizure of Boston, was the failure of rebel forces to take Canada. The Continental Congress had reason to believe French Canadians would welcome rebel armies with open arms; differences with Britain had made many French Canadians sympathetic to the cause of independence, if not that of rebellion. The Collector of the Port of Quebec, Thomas Ainslie, warned London in June, 1775, that "the Canadian peasants begin to show a disposition little to be expected from a conquered people who had been treated with so much leniency by Government." When American commander Benedict Arnold entered the Canadian town of St. John's in May, he was greeted enthusiastically by the French-speaking citizens. Arnold sent word of his reception to Philadelphia, and urged the Congress to give him the men and weapons necessary to take Quebec and Montreal before winter made such an attack impossible. But New York General Philip Schuyler refused to cooperate, while the Congress seemed more intent on taking Boston than winning all of Canada. General Richard Montgomery, Schuyler's second-in-command, agreed with Arnold, but his pleas went unheeded. By the time Congress and Schuyler decided to act, the moment had passed. In late September, Montgomery received word that he could proceed to Montreal and Quebec. "A winter compaign in Canada!" he shouted. "Posterity won't believe it!" Still, Montgomery went north, while Arnold's ragged band closed in on Quebec, hounded by Indians, loyalists, and most importantly, the cold of winter.[1]

Arnold crossed the St. Lawrence on November 14, as Colonel Allan McLean and Governor Sir Guy Carleton prepared for the rebel assault. Montgomery arrived on December 2, and took command of the combined forces. The two men, probably the best field commanders on the rebel side, had reason to expect victory. "I found a style of discipline among Arnold's men much superior to what I have been used to seeing in this campaign," wrote Montgomery to Schuyler. "Fortune often baffles the sanguine expectations of poor mortals. I am not intoxicated with the favors I have received at her hands, but I do think there is a fair prospect of success."[2]

The British defenders proved tougher than anticipated, and the weather colder than the attackers could bear. Wave after wave of rebels was thrown back, as Montgomery was unable to breach the Quebec defenses. A surprise attack on December 27 failed when a loyalist learned of the preparations and informed Sir Guy. Since all enlistments ran out on January 1, Montgomery was obliged to risk an all-out attack on December 30, and the rebels approached the walls in a blinding snowstorm. It was a glorious, brave, but futile gesture. Montgomery himself was killed in the battle, and Arnold seriously wounded, while hundreds of rebels fell in bloody pools outside the city. Quebec was saved, and with it Canada. The most talented American commander was dead; the man whom Hawkes called the "Rebel Wolfe" would no longer lend his energies and brilliance to the rebel cause, while Arnold would be relegated by unimaginative rebel politicians to secondary roles.[3] Meanwhile Washington, who in taking Bos-

1. Sir Humphrey Fay. *The Canada Campaign of 1775* (Montreal, 1887), p. 860. Bamford Parkes. *Benedict Arnold: The Rebel Genius* (New York, 1965) is the best biography of Arnold.

2. Fay. *The Canada Campaign*, pp. 894–95.

3. Lord Henry Hawkes. *Benedict Arnold and the Canadian Campaign* (London, 1880), pp. iii–xii, 254–55.

ton had shown no military skills or abilities at leadership, was the toast of Philadelphia.

The scene of battle shifted to New York that summer. Washington had taken his army to the city early in 1776, and prepared to defend it against the British. The rebel leader concentrated his forces on Long Island, Bedloe (now Howe) Island, and Manhattan, in such a way as to invite easy attack from the rear. At first Howe thought Washington had some trick in mind, but later he realized this disposition of forces—dividing an already inferior army, neglecting the rear, poor discipline, etc.—was actually the result of his American counterpart's inexperience.[4] Howe's armies took up positions on Staten Island, so that by July 2—the day the Declaration of Independence was signed —he had a firm foothold and was prepared for the attack. Yet Howe hesitated, and the assault on Long Island did not take place until August 22.[5]

Howe won a victory on Long Island, as the Americans fled before the well-disciplined royal troops. Had he wished, Howe could have destroyed Washington with ease, but political considerations and his hope for a negotiated truce led him to withhold the final blow. He landed on Manhattan Island on September 15, and proceeded to force Washington northward, always believing the American would concede defeat before massive losses were incurred.

Howe's humanitarianism was misplaced, however, as Washington used the time given him to beat a hasty retreat. The rebel general mistook kindness and forbearance for weakness, and constructed a hasty fortification on the northern tip of Manhattan, where he expected his weary and dissident force to meet and defeat the triumphant, larger, and better equipped British attackers! Finally, Generals Lee and Nathanael Greene, fresh from victories in the South against General Sir Henry Clinton, prevailed upon Washington to abandon his fort and cross the Hudson into New Jersey. Still Washington was adamant, and moved into the Bronx and then Westchester before making the crossing.[6] From there he was pursued by General Charles Cornwallis across the colony and into Pennsylvania, and he crossed the

---

4. General Sir William Howe. *Memoirs of the Late Rebellion, including a diary of events and recollections of a busy life. London Antiquarian Society's Studies in Colonial History* (London, 1865), pp. 501–10.
5. Lord Henry Hawkes. "General Howe and the New York Campaign," *North American Review* (Summer, 1874), pp. 929–49. Hawkes, the most in-
fluential historian of his day, has concluded that Howe secretly sympathized with American loyalists, and hoped for a negotiated peace before a major battle had taken place.
6. Malcolm Glover. *The New York Campaign* (The U.S.M. History of the Great Rebellion) (Mexico City, 1963) Vol. III, pp. 156–69.

Delaware River to comparative safety on December 11. Washington's failure in New York convinced the more astute rebels that their cause could not prevail, and led to a general demoralization in the Congress. Had not General Lee been captured by the British on December 13, it seems probable he would have assumed the rebel command that winter.[7]

The first full year of fighting had proven disastrous for the rebels. Whatever victories they could claim were symbolic rather than substantive. The capture of Boston, for example, had little military meaning, and was recognized as such everywhere but Massachusetts. The Declaration of Independence hadn't its expected effect in the palaces of Britain's foes. The New York campaign had been a debacle, the Canadian expedition a failure. At winter camp, General Edward Grant wrote that his men were "almost naked, dying of cold, without blankets, and very ill-supplied with provisions." No munitions and men were to be sent from France, for after New York, enthusiasm for the rebel cause waned in Versailles, and a year later would vanish completely.

In early 1777, General Burgoyne spoke to North of his plan for ending the war that year. It involved a two-pronged drive from Canada and New York City to Albany, which would divide the colonies in half, and in this way, dishearten the rebels and dissuade the French from entering the conflict. Burgoyne had proposed the plan the previous year, but it had been rejected at that time. Again his plan faced opposition. Howe believed his troops could capture the rebel capital at Philadelphia without too much trouble, and this victory would end the war. It was a classic confrontation. Burgoyne argued the war was a logistical and psychological contest, while Howe considered it as a huge game of chess, which ended once you captured the enemy's capital. In this struggle, Burgoyne represented the future of warfare and the ability to adapt oneself to new circumstances; Howe, the past, with his rigid refusal to be flexible. To his credit North approved the Burgoyne plan, setting into motion the force that would end the war, and bringing into new prominence one of the most interesting figures in British history.

Burgoyne was fifty-five years old in 1777. He was still known as

---

7. Washington himself realized the war was lost in New York. In writing to a relative on December 17, he said, "your imagination can scarcely extend to a situation more distressing than mine. . . . Our only dependence now is upon the speedy enlistment of a new army." Toward this end, Washington led his troops into a series of forays against British and Hessian command posts in late December, but these were more shows of bravado than true victories, and were so recognized by the Congress and in London. Graves. *Rebels in Uniform*, pp. 435–56.

"Gentleman Johnny" to London society, a tribute to a reputation earned prior to the Rebellion. His career was filled with accomplishment and spiced with adventure. Burgoyne was an illegitimate son of Lord Bingley, Chancellor of the Exchequer under Queen Anne.[8] At the age of eighteen he purchased a commission, and three years later ran off with the Earl of Derby's daughter. Rather than being angered, Derby accepted his son-in-law and acted as his sponsor. This required considerable funds, for even then Burgoyne was a social lion. In 1741, in order to settle some debts, he sold his commission and fled to France to escape unpaid creditors. But the Earl set things right, and Burgoyne re-entered the Army in 1756, in time to participate in the Seven Years' War. Burgoyne led several daring raids on the French coast and, later on, was named lieutenant colonel of the 16th Dragoons, the famous "Burgoyne's Light Horse." His exploits in the Portuguese campaign made him as famous as a military man as he had earlier been as a rake.[9]

Burgoyne remained in the army after the war and also won a seat in Commons. While there he became interested in colonial affairs. He favored a strong line toward the colonists, voting for the Stamp Act and related measures. In 1774 he said, "I look upon America to be our child, which I think we have already spoiled by too much indulgence." But unlike the ultras, Burgoyne did not want war. "I wish to see America convinced by persuasion rather than the sword," he exclaimed.[10]

Burgoyne was sent to the colonies in February, 1775, where he first acted as Gage's second-in-command. He was the only one of what the rebels called "the triumvirate of reputation" respected for his abilities. Arthur Lee, for example, dismissed Howe and Clinton as unimaginative leaders who would give the rebels little trouble. Burgoyne was different, he said. "You will judge," he wrote, "that he is a dangerous character; and therefore be on your guard."[11]

A large part of this danger came from Burgoyne's talent at com-

8. There remains some question as to the circumstances of Burgoyne's birth. Hopkins holds to the theory presented above in Gilbert Hopkins. *Burgoyne: The Early Years* (London, 1899), pp. 5–16, while Wesley Van Luvender believed him to be the son of Captain John Burgoyne, a baronet's son. Wesley Van Luvender. *The Life and Times of John Burgoyne* (New York, 1949), pp. 19–29.
9. Michael Brown. *Burgoyne in the Seven Years' War: The Development*

of the Military Ideas of John Burgoyne, First Duke of Albany* (London, 1809), pp. 598–634.
10. Sir Edwin Colby. *The Parliamentary Experiences of John Burgoyne* (New York, 1855), pp. 346–87. Also see Clark Faulkner. *Burgoyne in Parliament: Preparation for Greatness* (unpublished Ph.D. dissertation, University of North America, 1970).
11. Maryann Benedict. *Secret Correspondences of the Rebellion* (Mexico City, 1956), p. 187.

municating with the North American moderates and attempting to understand their feelings. Long before the term was coined, Burgoyne was a master of psychological warfare, and more than any other officer able to convince waverers to remain loyal.[12] In addition, he was the only important British officer to grasp the nature of the struggle once it had begun. While Clinton and Howe insisted on using European methods in combat, Burgoyne readily disposed of earlier prejudices and tactics learned during the Seven Years' War, and adapted himself to the new military environment. In his famous "Reflections on the Rebellion," he wrote:

> Composed as the American army is, together with the strength of the country, full of woods, swamps, stone walls, and other enclosures and hiding places, it may be said of it that every private man will in action be his own general, who will turn every tree and bush into a temporary fortress, from whence, when he hath fired his shot with all the deliberation, coolness, and certainty which hidden safety inspires, he will skip as it were to the next, and so on for a long time. . . .[13]

When the Rebellion erupted Burgoyne was sent to Canada, where he served under Carleton. It was from St. John's that he embarked on his expedition to Albany.

Early in 1777 Burgoyne organized his men for the march. His "Army of Nations" included some 4,000 regulars, 3,000 German mercenaries, 650 Canadians and American loyalists, and 500 Indians. He was assured that Colonel St. Leger would drive from the west to meet him above Albany, while Howe would send help from New York City. The plan should have worked without difficulty, for the Americans were unorganized and unprepared in central New York. But Lord Germain bungled the transmission of information to the British commands, and as a result, Howe was uninformed of the final plans. On April 2, Howe sent a letter to Carleton in Canada saying he was on his way to Philadelphia, leaving Clinton in charge in the city. Because of this, he would be unable "to detach a corps in the beginning of the campaign to move up Hudson's River consistent with the operations already determined upon."[14] A copy went to Germain, who now realized his mistake. Germain sent word of this to Howe, but by the

---

12. It might be added that Burgoyne was a playwright of renown as well as a soldier and statesman. His play, "The Maid of the Oaks," was well received in the 1774 season. Had not the Rebellion intervened, Burgoyne might well have become the nation's leading dramatist. Hartley Fowler. *Burgoyne* *as a Playwright: The Last of the Restoration Writers* (Philadelphia, 1954).
13. Wesley Van Luvender. ed. *Burgoyne on War* (New York, 1950), p. 334.
14. Robert Mackreith. *Lord Howe and the Rebellion* (New York, 1965), p. 214.

time the message arrived in New York, the General was already at sea, on his way south.[15]

Unaware of these developments, Burgoyne set out on June 17. At first all went well. He captured Ticonderoga on June 30 and two days later Fort Defiance, followed by victories at Skenseborough and Fort Anne. Then the campaign ground to a near-halt, as the Army of Nations became bogged down in the forests of central New York. During this period, St. Leger's force managed to defeat rebel General Nicholas Herkimer's column, but was routed by the brilliant and erratic Arnold. As Burgoyne slogged through the woods, the expected and badly-needed St. Leger reinforcements were lost.

Now desperate, Burgoyne sent messages for aid to New York. On September 12, Clinton informed him that he would soon attack Fort Montgomery (near Peekskill) and from there take the Hudson route to Saratoga. Burgoyne replied that even greater haste was needed, and Clinton promised to speed his men northward.[16]

After collecting what meager supplies he could, Burgoyne crossed the Hudson on September 13-14. In so doing he was taking a tremendous risk, but Burgoyne was used to such dangers. Retreat was now no longer possible. Burgoyne was, in effect, wagering the Army of Nations against the rebel Gates' stronger force, his own skill against that of his American counterpart, and Clinton's abilities against the wilds of New York.[17]

By this time, Arnold's force had joined the main rebel army. Almost at once he clashed with his commander, General Horatio Gates, a political appointee like Washington, but a tough and innovative leader. Burgoyne attacked on September 18, but was forced to retreat before Gates' withering fire. Then the Army of Nations advanced toward Freeman's Farm, and once again was repulsed. Decimated and battered, the Army of Nations regrouped to hear Burgoyne's plan. Caution would have dictated retreat into the woods, but he held fast.

Awakening on the morning of October 8, Burgoyne learned his force was all but surrounded, and would have to fight its way out of a cordon of rebels. Still morale held. As one survivor later wrote, "The men were willing and ready to face any danger, when led by officers whom they loved and respected and who shared with them in every toil and hardship."[18]

---

15. Matthew Hale. *Howe and Washington: Contrasts and Comparisons* (New York, 1956), p. 187.
16. Henry Mitchell. *The Battle of Saratoga-Albany* (London, 1939), p. 98.
17. Wesley Van Luvender. *The Military Thought and Action of John Burgoyne* (New York, 1944), pp. 345-47.
18. Joanna Brooks. ed. *Men In War: Letters of the Army of Nations* (London, 1959), pp. 334-35.

Rallying his men, Burgoyne took them to Schuyler's Farm, and the next morning crossed the Fishkill River. Had Gates attacked then, he could have destroyed the Army of Nations. But he hesitated at that crucial moment, spending his time arguing with Arnold, regrouping his forces, and considering the next move. Meanwhile, unknown to the rebels, Clinton's force moved swiftly up the Hudson, and prepared to attack Gates from the rear.[19] Time was working for the British. Burgoyne knew this; Gates did not.

On October 13, Burgoyne sent a delegation to ask Gates his terms for a truce. The answer was "unconditional surrender." Burgoyne replied that he was not unwilling to admit defeat, but insisted his men be allowed to march from the field with all honors. Gates wavered; he wanted the satisfaction of receiving Burgoyne's sword on the field of battle. At the time Gates had ambitions to succeed Washington, who was in bad grace in Philadelphia. Such a victory, conceded on the field, would assure him of supreme command.[20]

As Gates hesitated, Clinton's force smashed Israel Putnam's rebel army and continued toward Saratoga. Putnam sent messengers with news of his defeat to Gates, but the men were lost in the woods, and never appeared at headquarters. By the time Gates learned of Clinton's imminent appearance, it was too late to do much about it. The rebel general was now obliged to act in an impromptu fashion. His plan was simple. The rebels would attack Burgoyne's position in force, massacring all, and then turn to face Clinton's army, which was expected in a matter of hours.

The attack came on the morning of October 21. Wave upon wave of rebels advanced on the weakened Army of Nations, and each time they were repulsed. Then, on October 22, Clinton's men broke through Gates' rear. Heartened by the sound of their comrades' bullets, Burgoyne's ragged force, now numbering less than 2,000, staged its final assault, in this way placing the now-panicky rebels in the jaws of a pincer movement. It was now Gates' turn to flee, and so he did. Within two days the rebels were on the outskirts of Albany, vulnerable to attack, unable to respond. On the afternoon of October 25, Burgoyne offered Gates a generous peace. All his troops could return to their homes, while Gates himself would be free to leave, upon his pledge never to fight again. The proposal was accepted; Gates had no

19. Mitchell. *The Battle of Saratoga-Albany*, p. 178.
20. Apparently Burgoyne, a genius in understanding the psychology of his enemy, knew of Gates' ambitions, and realized that he could play for time in this way. Field Marshall Sir Harry Dill. *The Battle of Saratoga* (London, 1888), p. 344. Also see Robert Sidney. *Horatio Gates: The Man Who Lost the Rebellion* (New York, 1970).

choice but to do so. Thus ended one of the most glorious episodes in the history of eighteenth century warfare.[21]

Burgoyne's great victory at Saratoga had been the result of many factors. Gentleman Johnny's abilities and the bravery of the Army of Nations were doubtless of great importance. Burgoyne's daring move in crossing the Hudson when he did, and his brilliance in holding Gates at bay while Clinton moved north, have become textbook cases in military academies throughout the world. This is not to say that other factors do not enter into great victories, for indeed every man's success implies the failure of another. Gates, at best an acceptable officer and at worst an amateur in over his head at Saratoga, performed at the top of his form during the battle. His was not the major failure. Rather, the rebel defeat must be rightly attributed to George Washington.

Washington had been unable to fathom the British plan of 1777. Above all, he wanted to protect Philadelphia from royal control, but it appeared Albany was also in danger and had to be guarded at all costs. Then Howe set sail for Chesapeake Bay, and Washington now knew he meant to attack Philadelphia from the south. At the time, he had sufficient rebel troops to defend only one city; either Philadelphia or Albany would have to be sacrificed. Now Washington repeated his error of the New York campaign: he divided his forces. A small detachment was sent to Albany, one too small to do much good there, but large enough to weaken Washington's main force which was stationed near Philadelphia. Then the rebel leader marched his men southward to meet Howe, who landed at Head of Elk on Chesapeake Bay on August 25.

The two armies clashed on September 11 near Brandywine Creek, and Howe easily defeated the smaller rebel army. Ten days later he won another victory at Paoli, and on September 26, Howe entered Philadelphia in triumph. After establishing headquarters in the city, Howe sent a large number of his men in pursuit of Washington and the Congress, which hastily fled the city. Howe engaged Washington next at Germantown. This time the rebel leader was able to win the upper hand; he caught Howe in a pincers movement and began to squeeze. But fate intervened in the form of a heavy fog that settled over the battlefield. While the rebels searched in vain for Howe's forces, the British regrouped and began their march back to Philadel-

21. Mitchell. *The Battle of Saratoga-Albany*, p. 209. After the battle, Burgoyne praised the rebel soldiers and their commanders. "Their quality was far better than what I had expected prior to leaving St. John's. Gens. Gates and Arnold were likewise brave and intelligent officers. May this rebellion end soon, so that we can again live in mutual friendship and respect! This would be the finest fruit of our victory at Saratoga." Van Luvender. *Burgoyne on War*, p. 476.

phia. On his part, Washington ordered his troops to winter quarters at Valley Forge. Discouraged, and by now aware of his own inadequacies, Washington learned soon after of Burgoyne's victory at Saratoga. Only a half year earlier he had sworn to defend both Philadelphia and Albany from royal troops. Now both had fallen, and before that Washington had lost New York as well.

The winter camp at Valley Forge was poorly organized and filled with dispirited men. "Poor food—hard lodging—cold weather—fatigue—nasty clothes—nasty cookery—vomit half my time—smoked out of my senses—the Devil's in it—I can't endure it" wrote one common soldier.[22] Over two thousand troops, including two hundred officers, deserted at Valley Forge. Washington thought for a moment to lift the army's spirit with a surprise attack on Philadelphia, but abandoned the plan when informed by his officers that the troops would no longer follow his orders. In the winter of 1777–78, the rebels learned the bitter implications of defeat in war.[23]

The Continental Congress had also lost faith in Washington. Even John Adams began to doubt his abilities. Benjamin Rush thought Washington was trying to rule America like a king. "All would be well had this general given us victories. Such has not been the case. Washington must be replaced, or at least given less authority over the conduct of our struggle."[24] Others spoke of replacing Washington with a more able man. General Lee had been released, and had his supporters. Colonel James Wilkinson thought highly of Gates, observing that he could not be blamed for the loss at Saratoga, which had been caused by improper support from Washington. Others spoke for Greene, Schuyler, and Arnold, but a majority could not be found for any of them.

In the end, the Congress reached a compromise. General Artemas Ward would be named chairman of a new body, the Board of War, whose members would include Washington, Gates, Lee, and Schuyler. Each general would be given command of a different theater of war. Gates, for example, would take charge in New York, while Washington was assigned Virginia and the Carolinas. On February 14, the Congress summoned Washington to its temporary quarters at York, Pennsylvania, and notified him of the change. The commander was not surprised by the confrontation, having been forewarned of it by his

22. Marvin Carleton. ed. *The Common Soldier Speaks: Voices of the Rebellion* (New York, 1954), p. 215.
23. Lord Henry Hawkes. *Peace and Victory: The Last Stage of the American Rebellion* (London, 1884), pp. 557-67.
24. Marvin Schaffer. *The Continental Congress and its Relations with General Washington in the Winter of 1777-1778* (unpublished Ph.D. dissertation, Northwest University, 1939), p. 132.

staff. In an eloquent address he admitted his failures and confessed his shortcomings. He would not oppose the decision, but rejected the southern command. On February 16, Washington resigned his commission and returned to his home at Mount Vernon. The Congress expressed its thanks for his efforts, and selected Greene as his replacement in the southern theater.[25]

By this time it was also evident that France would no longer support the Rebellion. Benjamin Franklin, the rebels' envoy to Versailles, had worked long and hard for French aid, but even he could do little after news of Saratoga and the fall of Philadelphia reached Vergennes' ears. France would support the rebels so long as they were anti-British and showed the ability to win in the field. The latter condition had not been fulfilled; France, and soon after, Spain, left Congress to its own devices.[26]

Franklin relayed this information to Congress, and recommended immediate negotiations with London for a truce, to be followed by a general peace. Without waiting for orders, he opened talks with Lord North's agent, Paul Wentworth, toward that end. While Congress awaited word from Versailles, Franklin busied himself with negotiations, so that North actually knew more of what was going on in Versailles than did the Congress.

North had never been enthusiastic in his prosecution of the war. Essentially a moderate, he viewed the conflict as both unfortunate and unnecessary. Initially, he had been caught between the extremes of men like Burke on the one side and King George on the other, each of whom seemed to have welcomed the war. By 1778, the pro-rebels had been discredited by charges of treason made in Parliament and disheartened by news of the failures at Saratoga and Philadelphia. At the same time, those who called for rebel blood were no longer as willing as they had been in 1775 to pay the price of continued fighting. The interest France and Spain had shown in the Rebellion threatened more direct attack against Britain, and American loyalty would be critical in such a conflict. All these factors, together with North's increased prestige by 1778, led the majority of Parliament to support a magnanimous peace with the rebels. Franklin had indicated privately that a generous offer would be well-received by Congress, and he expressed his willingness to serve as mediator between the two sides.

A similar development had taken place in Congress. John Adams, Thomas Jefferson, and others of their group had lost favor after Saratoga, while Sam Adams and Patrick Henry were considered little more

---

25. Mates. *Washington: The War Years*, Vol. IV, p. 560.

26. Fowler. *That Chameleon Franklin!*, p. 340.

than outright traitors by men who earlier had remained silent while they condemned Britain. At the same time, the ultra-loyalists had left America, some with Howe when he abandoned Boston, others chased by mobs who had been inflamed with the virus of independence in 1776–1777. Moderates like Dickinson and Galloway now came to the fore, and by early 1778, they had taken command at the Congress. More than ever, they were eager for peace with the mother country.

On February 16, North called a secret meeting of the Cabinet to discuss overtures to the American moderates. All present agreed that many of the laws passed prior to 1775 had been mistaken, and had served to throw their colonial counterparts into radical hands. On the other hand, too much English blood and treasure had been spent in the Rebellion to allow them to offer the Americans an easy peace. The leaders of the Rebellion must be made to answer for their crimes, but the broad mass of their sympathizers would be granted amnesty. Then North raised the problem of future governance of the colonies, and spoke highly of the Galloway Plan of 1774, by which the colonists would have control of their own internal affairs, with a parliamentary veto to prevent unwise legislation from going into effect. Over serious objections by a few members of Lords, the Cabinet majority agreed that such a plan was well-worth considering, so long as it be made to appear a British rather than an American proposal. London's acceptance of limited self-government would sit well with the moderates, win over many radicals, and succeed in mollifying the more temperate royalists in America.[27] North was able to win approval for such a plan, and on March 16 a commission, headed by the Earl of Carlisle, was sent to America to present it to the congressional moderates.[28]

By the time Carlisle had arrived at York, the moderates had taken command at the Congress, with Galloway (who returned as a delegate in January) its most influential member. Congress debated the proposals in early May in an atmosphere of fear and doubt. Most members conceded the Rebellion had failed, but they were uncertain as to the reception such a peace might receive in the country as a whole. But Congress had no choice in the matter, as the rebel armies lost more men with each passing day. On May 23, Galloway replaced Henry Laurens as president of the Congress, which four days later agreed to ask North for an armistice based on the Carlisle proposals. The Earl had been empowered to accept such a reply, and informed Howe, Clinton, and Burgoyne of the Congress's actions. Negotiations con-

27. Warner Jones. *Lord North: The British Richelieu* (Mexico City, 1958), pp. 235–37.

28. *Ibid*, pp. 239–40.

tinued for another week. On June 12, 1778, the formal articles of armistice were signed by Galloway and Carlisle. During the next two weeks the rebel commanders were notified of the fact, and most surrendered to their British counterparts. The North American Rebellion was over.[29]

---

29. King George was notified of North's plans quite early in the negotiations, and opposed them. But it soon became evident that even his supporters in Commons wanted peace, and the King reluctantly acceded to the proposal, on specific condition that the rebel leaders be brought to London to answer for their treason. North accepted this condition, although he tried to save most from their fates. Winthrop Wadsworth. *King George III and Lord North: The Struggle for the American Soul* (London, 1971), pp. 543-49.

# 4

# THE BRITANNIC DESIGN

VICTORY in the field had been a relatively simple matter; at no point did it appear the Rebellion might succeed, or the Congress win a majority of North American colonists to their banner. Far more important and difficult were the problems of peace. Moderates on both sides of the Atlantic now agreed the mother country had acted unwisely during the decade after the Peace of Paris. Had not unthinking British leaders tried to disturb the *status quo* in such a clumsy fashion, the soil so diligently cultivated by Sam Adams might never have yielded separatist fruit. Furthermore, troubles were brewing in India, where the conflict with the French showed signs of heating. This, too, encouraged the moderates to grant the Americans an easy peace so as to pacify the area.

For their part, the colonists were now more aware of the benefits of empire than had previously been the case. By 1777, moderates in London and New York openly yearned for the pre-1763 period, when "salutory neglect" was the rule, and when both colonists and British residents were united against a common foe. Men of the caliber and intelligence of North and Galloway now directed their efforts toward a restoration of the old ways, while fully aware that the events of the past five years could not be forgotten or ignored.

This attitude could be seen in the way the rebel leaders were treated. Over the strong objections of the King, North stated his intention to punish only the more prominent of the leaders, while granting general amnesty to the rest.[1] Thus, the army rounded up only those

1. The struggle between the King and North need not concern us in this narrative, but it was extremely important in the history of Britain. Prior to the Rebellion, and during its early stages, the King had effective control of Parliament by working through appointees and allies, one of whom was North himself. After Saratoga-Albany, however, the ministry began to wean itself from the King. The general sentiment that the King had acted irrationally during the war added to North's powers, as did rumors of his madness. Thus, the Rebellion had a significant constitutional effect in Britain, where the North ministry and those of his successors were far more independent than at any time since the Commonwealth. Luther Koskins, *Parliament in the Nineteenth Century* (London, 1965) and Henry Collins, *Lord North and the Rise of Parliament* (New York, 1956).

rebels who had held important leadership positions and therefore were responsible for the challenge to London and the bloodshed that followed. Of the fifty-six men who signed the Declaration of Independence in 1776, only seven were taken to London for trial and subsequently executed.[2] Another thirty-one were tried by colonial courts, found guilty of crimes against the state, and given sentences ranging from imprisonment or exile to the loss of citizenship rights. The remaining signatories, all of whom had indicated their opposition to the Rebellion by early 1778, were not even brought to trial.[3] As for the others—including the soldiers of the Continental Army—they were allowed to live as before. Indeed, North attempted to assure them in every way possible that Parliament considered them valued citizens who had been misled by false prophets. Speaking in Lords on November 12, 1778, he said:

> We have now entered into a new period of solidarity with those of our nation who live in North America. We have always considered them our cousins—nay, our brothers. Mistakes have been made in these chambers, as they have been in Boston and Philadelphia, but it will do little good to dwell on them. Instead, we must seek new ways to preserve old institutions, and this will involve a serious reconsideration of the nature of our government, and of its relations with our North American brothers.[4]

What came to be known as the "brotherhood policy" was generally successful, although loyalists in some colonies—the most important of which were Massachusetts, New York, and Virginia—did harass those who had sided with the rebels. Some one thousand lynchings took place in 1778–1779, despite all attempts on the part of the army to prevent them. Royal governers were urged to support policies of moderation, and where they failed, military commanders were empowered to countermand their orders. This in itself was a difficult task, and might have been more so were it not for the influence of Burgoyne.

In order to keep the peace, as much as prepare the way for a new dispensation, the North American colonies were divided into four dis-

---

2. This group consisted of: John Adams, Sam Adams, John Hancock, Thomas Jefferson, Richard Henry Lee, Robert Treat Paine, and Roger Sherman. In addition, Tom Paine and Patrick Henry were also put to death. George Washington was tried, found guilty, and sentenced to life imprisonment. Benjamin Franklin, seventy-three years old at the time, was not put on trial, in deference to his age, previous contributions to science, and aid in bringing the fighting to a halt. He did not return to America, taking up residence in London, where he died in 1781.
3. The most important members of this group were Charles Carroll, Samuel Chase, Elbridge Gerry, Philip Livingston, and John Witherspoon.
4. Collins. *Lord North and the Rise of Parliament*, p. 98.

tricts, each with a commanding general. Carleton was to remain in Canada, Howe went to Boston where he controlled New England, Clinton was given charge of Maryland and all colonies to the south, while Burgoyne commanded royal forces in the middle colonies from New York. Each had viceregal authority in his area, and the right to supersede civil power when and if necessary. It is generally agreed that Clinton and Howe had the more difficult posts, since rebel sentiment had been strongest in Massachusetts and Virginia. But these two men were also unfit by temperament for such roles, and pacification proceeded slowly there. Carleton, an able and sensitive commander as well as one well-versed in such matters, did a fine job in Canada, which in any case had always been strongly anti-rebel. Burgoyne, in control of a region that had been generally pro-loyalist but had large pockets of rebel forces, did a magnificent job in his command, and was easily the most successful of the four.[5]

During his four years as commanding general, Burgoyne won the affection and loyalty of those North Americans in his area. Setting up headquarters in New York, he made that city the social as well as the commercial center of North America.[6] He easily captivated the city's leading citizens with his charm and gay manner. The General even found time to write two more plays, both of which were well received not only in New York, but elsewhere in America and in London. His marriage to Mrs. Abigail Conrad, a North American who had been a known rebel sympathizer during the war, was greeted by loyalist and former rebel alike as a good omen for a new era of friendship between the English speaking peoples. "Gen. Burgoyne has come to the city and it is his," wrote one former rebel commander in 1785. "Those who only a few years ago screamed for his head, now cheer the mention of his name. The public is fickle indeed!"[7] Another, even more bitter, remarked, "Americans cannot discern the difference between jackals and lions. Now Burgoyne is greeted as the savior of the country. Had he lost at Saratoga, the public would now be cheering Gates as the father of the new nation. Such are the vagaries of fate."[8] The New York *Loyalist*, more in tune with the times, wrote in 1779, "All hail Gen. Burgoyne, whose victories have ushered in a new era for all who

---

5. Sir Douglas Carlisle. *The Four Viceroys: Burgoyne, Carleton, Howe, and Clinton* (New York, 1967), pp. 109–234, is the best short study of Burgoyne's rule in America.
6. Boston and Philadelphia, New York's most important northern rivals, fell into disfavor after the Rebellion, and went into declines. Emigration also hurt these cities, which actually lost in population

after peace. Sir Vincent Popper. *A Demographic Study of the C.N.A., 1783–1825* (London, 1954), pp. 19–27, 37–39, 154–57.
7. Alexander Hamilton. *Farewell to Change: Thoughts on Leaving the C.N.A.* (New York, 1785), pp. 14–15.
8. John Jay. *Notes on the Perfidy of Our Former Friends* (Jefferson City, 1800), p. 43.

live under the royal flag, and who has captured the hearts even of those who had fought him so bravely in the past."[9]

As the pacification and reunification of the North American people proceeded under Burgoyne's tacit leadership, the Cabinet debated the political forms to be granted the colonies. Clearly the situation of 1763 could not be revived; nor could King George's plans for imperial unity be accepted, though they played a part in the final decision. Britain as well as America wanted an end to fighting and dissension, and Parliament would reject any proposal that might lead to further warfare in America. Wisely, Lord North consulted the Americans while formulating his program. Dickinson and Galloway were summoned to London to participate in the planning. In addition, the ministry drew upon the talents of Thomas Moffat of Rhode Island, William Allen of Pennsylvania, Samuel Seabury of New York, and others of their caliber. In the end, North set forth "The Britannic Design," which was reluctantly accepted by the Crown in 1780, to be put into effect two years later.[10]

The Britannic Design had many sources. Franklin's Plan of Union, first presented in 1754, was one. Galloway's Plan of Proposed Union Between Great Britain and the Colonies of 1775 was another. The Britannic Design drew upon the ideas of statesmen like Edmund Burke and Chatham, although these men and their allies did not participate in its framing.[11] Political scientists have found in it traces of the Greek experience, Roman law, both the Old and New Testaments, and French philosophy, but much of this sophistry can be discounted. The British genius has always been based on wise improvisation and a concept of balance and continuity that has rarely been broken. Coke more than Plato, Charles II more than Voltaire, influenced the Design. This could be found in North's letter of transmission of 1780.

> The Britannic Design contains the spirit of Your Majesty's people, their aspirations and hopes. May it serve as a beacon to the world as well as a providential pattern for future growth in North America and other lands under the Crown. May it also provide a framework rather than a completed structure. We are mortals, and cannot foresee all circumstance. With this Design, we have offered a standard that our descendants may perfect.[12]

---

9. The New York *Loyalist*, April 15, 1779.
10. Sir Charles Williamson. *The Grand Design: Decision in London* (London, 1939), p. 198.
11. The literature on this subject is large and ever-growing. See Barbara Brooks. *Historians and the Britannic Design: A Study in Interpretation*

(New York, 1965), Morrow McVeigh. *The Britannic Design as Seen by Foreigners* (London, 1954), Martin Greene. *The Britannic Design: Symbol for the Age* (Canberra, 1965), and Victor La-Lumia. ed. *One Hundred Years Under the Britannic Design* (New York, 1882).
12. Collins. *Lord North and the Rise of Parliament*, p. 190.

The essence of the proposal was "confederation with federation," designed to provide the mother country and colonies with a maximum of benefits and a minimum of regulations. Under the terms of the original draft, the thirteen colonies would retain their identities and governmental apparatus. Each would have a bicameral legislature and a governor named by the Crown. In the interests of defense and growth, the thirteen colonies were to be grouped into three confederations— the Northern, Central, and Southern. These would be governed by councils consisting of one representative from each colony, which would meet regularly to legislate for inter-colonial affairs. Their presiding officers would be governors-general (who until 1808 were selected by Parliament, and from 1808 to 1844, were appointed by the royal governors of each individual colony). Each council would send representatives to the other two, and envoys to Commons, where they could speak but not vote.

This simple structure seemed wise and prudent. The individual North American, say a resident of Maryland, would still have his familiar town and county government. Over these would be the colonial legislature in St. Mary and the royal governor, and above that, the Central Confederation. Taxes, a key element in causing the Rebellion, would be levied by all three levels of government, each of which would be dominated by colonials. Parliament could vote taxes for imperial protection, but these could be vetoed by the councils if a two-thirds vote could be mustered. Maryland would raise its own militia, to serve within its boundaries. The Council could draw upon these for use in other parts of the Central Confederation, but only with the assent of Maryland's legislature. Parliament in turn could request Central Confederation troops to defend the Empire, but only after a proposal to this effect had passed the Council.[13]

This original draft, presented in 1780, was debated vigorously during that year and the one that followed.[14] Many in Parliament complained it gave the colonists the fruits of victory after they had lost the war. "Why did we fight?" asked the London *Inquirer* in 1781. "To give this rabble all they wanted, victory or no?" On the other hand, Burke and Fox praised the Britannic Design, calling it "prudent" and "generous."[15] It was known the King opposed the plan, and through his friends in Parliament, waged a struggle against it.[16]

---

13. Greene. *The Britannic Design: Symbol for an Age*, pp. 145–56.
14. Russell Snow. *Decision in London: Forging the Britannic Design* (New York, 1953).
15. Privately, Burke retained his contempt for North. "See what we have

here," he told a colleague. "The flea has given birth to an elephant." Roswell Kirk. *Edmund Burke: The Great Dissenter* (London, 1898), p. 496.
16. Wadsworth. *King George III and Lord North*, pp. 654–57.

The Britannic Design underwent changes and was amended before it emerged from Parliament and received a grudging royal seal, but its basic structure and spirit remained intact. For example, many in Lords feared the proposed Northern Confederation would prove rebellious, and suggested it be united with the Central Confederation, which would provide a necessary balance. This was done, creating the Northern and Southern Confederations, the capital of the former to be New York, while Norfolk became the capital for the Southern Confederation. It was also decided that Fort Pitt, at the junction of the Ohio, Allegheny, and Monongahela rivers, was to be the new capital for all the colonies, a place where both Councils would meet on occasion. Lords also insisted on a new royal officer who would supervise the Councils and defend British interests in North America. Thus was created the office of viceroy, named at first by the King but answerable to Parliament.[17] North was able to win approval for this office by indicating that he would name Burgoyne first viceroy. The universally popular General was not opposed by the Crown, which then tried to win him to its side by naming him Duke of Albany.

Another major problem was that of Canada's future and its place in the Britannic Design. At first, Canada was considered separately from the thirteen colonies, but moderates in Parliament—the same men who had succeeded in uniting the Central and Northern Confederations—asked for the admission of Canada to the new Confederation. General Carleton—now Lord Dorchester—had become a strong advocate for Canadian interests, and he was echoed by William Smith (who had left New York for Quebec during the Rebellion) and Francis Legge. In the end there was a compromise. Canada would come under the Britannic Design, but not as part of the Northern Confederation. Instead, the land would be divided into three additional confederations—Quebec (which included all of Canada as far west as the eastern boundary of Lake Superior), Manitoba (from there to the Pacific), and Indiana (the former Northwest Territory).[18] Nova Scotia was given a great degree of internal freedom and autonomy, more than any other part of British North America. In time it, too, would set a pattern for future developments.[19]

In addition to these changes, there were a series of minor amendments and alterations. The colonial veto of Parliament's taxes would require a three-quarters rather than two-thirds vote, the office of

---

17. Rodney Brown. *Parliament and the Cabinet in the Age of North* (London, 1911), pp. 187–89.
18. The western boundary of Manitoba was unclear, so that confederation's reach never extended to the Pacific.

19. Desmond Lefevre. *Lord Dorchester and the Britannic Design* (New York, 1945), p. 157; Davis Malone. *The History of Quebec* (Dorchester, 1967); Harold Muncrief. *Nova Scotia Forever* (London, 1959).

lieutenant-governor was provided for, and the membership of each council was fixed at a maximum of twenty.[20] Also, the institution of the Grand Council was provided for. It was merely the name for the annual meeting of the five Council representatives who met at the capital to discuss common problems, but it had no real powers until 1843.

The final version of the Britannic Design was sent to the King on January 23, 1781, and the royal seal was affixed on January 26, which has since been celebrated as Design Day. The groundwork was now set. Officials were soon after elected and designated, and preparations made for the initiation of the new governments. Finally, on July 2, 1782, Lord Albany was installed as Viceroy with Cornwallis his lieutenant. On that same day, John Dickinson assumed office as Governor General of the Northern Confederation, while John Connolly was sworn in as Governor General of the Southern Confederation. Lord Dorchester took the Oath in Quebec, while Legge became Governor General of Manitoba at North City. Pierre Concordé was sworn in at Fort Raddison, Indiana. The Assembly assumed power in Kingston, Nova Scotia. Thus was born the Confederation of North America.[21]

During the next fourteen months Albany established good relations with the governors-general, made certain the elections were held according to law, and supervised the organization of the new government at Fort Pitt. Most importantly, he was able to assure London that the C.N.A. would be a loyal and valuable part of the Empire. In this period Albany was the indispensable man. No one else had his prestige or abilities, the charm of manner that captivated even his opponents, or the trust of all. Albany had won the war for Britain and kept the Empire together. Then, as Commanding General, he had healed the wounds of war. Now as Viceroy, he established the new government and transformed the Britannic Design from a theory into a viable government. This important work was all but completed when, on September 3, 1783, Albany contracted what was first believed to be a cold. His fever continued to mount, however, and a week later Albany developed pneumonia. Bleeding was initiated to save his life, but on September 20, 1783, at the age of sixty-one, Albany died. Fortunately for the Empire, the edifice he had helped erect was secure, and would remain his greatest monument.[22] Two years later the North Americans, with Parliament's unanimous assent, changed the name of Fort Pitt to Burgoyne in his honor.

---

20. Greene. *The Britannic Design: Symbol for an Age*, pp. 254–57.
21. George Jackson. *The New Day: The First Years of the C.N.A.* (New York, 1967), pp. 145–57.

22. James Dick. "The Duke of Albany and his Doctors," *Journal of Forensic Medicine* XLIII (July 5, 1967), pp. 89–99.

# 5

# THE WILDERNESS WALK

NO survey of the early history of the C.N.A. would be complete without a discussion and understanding of the rebels' reaction to their failure. There is no way of knowing how many colonials supported the Rebellion. Estimates vary from less than one-quarter of those over the age of eighteen, to three-quarters of the population of 1777.[1] One student of the question, writing in 1832, said, "It appears the residents of the thirteen colonies were divided into three major groups, with a third of them each supporting the Rebellion, opposing it, and remaining neutral."[2] This conclusion has long since been questioned and effectively demolished, by historians on both sides of the issue.[3] Still, no other analysis has appeared to take its place, and today the general populations of both the C.N.A. and U.S.M. seem to have accepted the threefold division.[4]

What is known, however, is the reaction of the population to the Saratoga-Albany battle and its aftermath, and the actions of some in the weeks following the return of peace. News of Saratoga-Albany and Washington's loss of Philadelphia reached most colonists at the same time, and tended to reinforce each other. The general feeling was one of defeatism; few rebels believed victory possible after the double disaster. There was some talk of offering the North American colonies to Spain and/or France in return for their aid, but most rejected the idea of exchanging one form of colonialism for another. In any case, they would scarcely have received a sympathetic hearing in Madrid or Versailles. Other rebels refused to accept defeat, believing their war could be continued by irregulars operating from bases in unexplored

1. Julia Simpson. *Historians and the Demography of the Rebellion: A Case Study* (unpublished Ph.D. thesis, Queens University, 1962).
2. Sir Robert Hoskins. *Opinion on the Rebellion in the Colonies in 1775-1778* (London, 1832).
3. Herbert Rosenbaum. *The Hoskins Thesis and its Critics* (Melbourne, 1969).
4. Herbert Rosenbaum. "Contemporary Public Opinion Regarding the North American Rebellion, based on Studies in Mexico City, Boston, and New York," *Australian Journal of Political Science* LI (January, 1960), pp. 109-36.

parts of the colonies. But lacking supplies and a friendly native population, these bands soon gave up their struggle. Only in the area of New Hampshire known as Vermont and parts of western Virginia, did the irregulars show any real lasting power. The Allen brothers of Vermont were able to withstand several assaults on their stronghold, first from British troops, later on from the Northern Confederation. Their resistance lasted two generations, and as late as the 1880's, Northern Confederation representatives stayed away from the region. Similarly, the Appalachian areas of Virginia, which became a haven for many southerners who had fought in the Rebellion, were troublesome for Southern Confederation authorities. Rebel General Francis Marion joined them in 1778, and for eighteen years led the resistance. These people outlasted even the Vermonters, and to this day the "hill people" of Virginia remain an oddity, retaining many of their old ways and an abiding hatred for the C.N.A.[5]

The main body of rebels and sympathizers, however, took one of two courses. More than half (if we are to believe Hoskins as to their number) came to terms with the new government, in a way that will be discussed in a future chapter. The rest swore they would never live under what they called "Britain's yoke," and searched for a new homeland. A handful went to France, while a small group found their way to Scandinavia.

Most of the emigrants, however, rallied to a group of second-echelon Rebellion leaders. General Nathanael Greene, junior officers and politicians like Alexander Hamilton, James Monroe, James Madison and Benedict Arnold, called for a massive movement away from what Arnold characterized as "this wretched land," to a new one, "divorced from Europe's vices and America's traitors and sluggards."[6] Madison told his followers that "the torch of liberty is not affixed in any one place, but belongs to those people who hold its blessings to be worth any sacrifice necessary. The Declaration of Independence was not written only for Americans in the colonies, but for free men wherever they reside. Therefore, we carry it wherever we may go."[7] Hamilton, who had once served under Washington and had always opposed rebel persecution of loyalists, thought, "we can expect no better from those who have won the struggle than we would have meted out if the roles were reversed. The nature of man is to seek

5. Harry Content. *Never Give Up: Rebels after the Rebellion* (New York, 1950); Daniel Pitchon. *Vermont and Western Virginia in the Decades Following the Britannic Design* (Mexico City, 1965); Harvey Ritter. *Allen's Irregulars: The History of a Brave People* (London, 1967); Ralph Ocon. *The People We Left Behind: The Remnant in C.N.A.* (Mexico City, 1959).
6. Benedict Arnold. *Toward a New Jerusalem* (Jefferson City, 1800), p. 16.
7. James Madison. *The Course of Human Events* (Jefferson City, 1819), p. 49.

revenge for real and imagined wrongs. Reluctantly, then, we must move on. To stay here is, unfortunately, unthinkable."[8]

By 1779, it was evident that many former rebels would leave for a new land. The choice of this place was not difficult to make, for the only area within reasonable distance of their homes lay to the west, either in Louisiana or Mexico, both of which were nominally Spanish, or to Florida in the south, also Spanish. Florida was rejected almost at once. The Spaniards were well settled in the area, and the Seminole Indians fierce, and filled with hatred for Americans. Louisiana west of Fort Radisson was also the preserve of strong and hostile Indian tribes, as well as being *terra incognita* for the white man. The area now called Jefferson, however, was well-explored and the Indians relatively subdued at the time. The Spaniards had settlements at Espiritu Santo, San Antonio, and San Xavier which were large enough to ensure a modicum of safety and security, and yet not so strong as to prevent an American settlement in the area. Jefferson was harsh, the land not particularly inviting but many rebels believed it could be tamed. "Today we look upon this land the way our forefathers must have viewed Jamestown. Do we have less fortitude than they? We may yet make a garden of this desert,"[9] said Greene, who by year's end was recognized as the leader of the expedition.

The first emigrants from British North America left their homes in 1780. Some thousand former rebels departed from New England and the Middle colonies for central Louisiana. They reached Fort Radisson in late spring, provisioned, and then pressed on across the Mississippi. Nothing was heard from them again. Either the group was killed by the Indians, perished in the cold winter of that year, or was destroyed by some other enemy. Rumors of their disappearance reached their former homes in 1781, and discouraged others from following them into the northern wilds.[10]

A second group left from Virginia at about the same time. This expedition was far better organized, provisioned, and led, and headed toward the well-scouted area of Jefferson, rather than the Louisiana wilderness. Its leader was General Greene, with Madison, Monroe,

---

8. Hamilton. *Farewell to Change*, p. 98.
9. Richard Bennett. *Nathanael Greene: Portrait of a Founder* (Mexico City, 1929) is the best biography of General Greene. Also see Homer Conroy. *The Collected Papers of Nathanael Greene* (Mexico City, 1910) Vol. XXVI and Calvin Holbrook. *Nathanael Greene and the Long Journey* (London, 1969).
10. Speculation as to the fate of these settlers continues. See Blanche Levin-son. *The Lost Colony of Louisiana* (New York, 1967). A recent study attempts to prove the rebels mingled with the Indians, and through ethnographic techniques tries to show New England's influence thereby on the Indians of the area. Hortense Stewart. *The Lost Colony and the Shawnee: The Emergence of a New Civilization* (San Francisco, 1971).

Francis Lightfoot Lee, Arthur Middleton, and Edward Rutledge important in his councils. All but a few of the more prominent leaders came from colonies to the south of Maryland, a fact explainable by the desire of most northern rebels to find a new home in an area with a climate similar to that of New England. In addition, the trip from Virginia to Jefferson was long enough to make any but the most daring hesitate, but when the distance from Boston to Virginia was added to the total, it became awesome indeed. Nonetheless, some northerners were important in the Greene expedition, among them Alexander Hamilton, George Clymer, Benjamin Rush, and John Morton.

The first group to make the journey gathered on the outskirts of Jamestown in the late spring of 1780. Estimates as to their number differ, running as high as 5,000 and as low as 3,000, with the latter figure probably being closer to the actual count. At least three-quarters of them came from the southern states, and of this amount, half were slaveowners. Thus, there were some 500–600 slaves in the first group.[11]

The emigrants were ready to leave on June 23. Greene met with his subalterns to make last minute preparations. "We have a great duty, a responsibility I pray we can discharge," he said. "We shall be in strange lands and see strange people in our wandering. But our spirits are high and our resolve strong. Like Moses and the Israelites, we are eager for our walk through the wilderness." This group, the founders of a new nation, soon called their journey from Jamestown to Jefferson, "The Wilderness Walk."[12]

The first leg of the trek took them from Jamestown to King's Mountain, and was accomplished in a two month period. There they reorganized, and pressed on toward Baton Rouge. But the unfamiliar landscape, Indian raids, and disease took their toll, and Greene was forced to turn back and spend the winter in Charlotte.

The group set out again the following April, this time better prepared for the journey. Baton Rouge was reached in early September, but almost half the emigrants were lost along the way. Greene was unable to go on, and planned to remain in the city for the winter. This decision led to arguments, as a small number of pioneers insisted on pressing on to San Antonio, while a larger contingent indicated their intention to settle in Baton Rouge and go no further. The Wilderness Walk might have ended there were it not for the arrival of a second group in early November. This band, which had left Charleston by

11. Richard Bennett. *The First Group: Pioneers in the Wilderness* (Mexico City, 1933).

12. Wallace Gipson. *The Wilderness Walk: Greene in the Desert* (London, 1959).

boat two months earlier, numbered some 800, of whom 300 were slaves. They infused the others with a new spirit of determination, not having suffered the agonies of the long march from Charlotte.

The following April the Wilderness Walk resumed. The emigrants now numbered some 1,800, as well as an additional 200 French-speaking settlers from New Orleans. They reached San Antonio in September of 1782, and continued their journey for another 200 miles. There, with winter approaching, Greene established his camp. In honor of his former comrade and leading theoretician of the Rebellion, he called the crude collection of tents and huts Jefferson City. It was to become the capital of the new land—Jefferson—and remain such for the next generation.[13]

The settlement struggled along and had little success during its first decade and a half. A small, permanent town was constructed at Jefferson City, mostly in the Spanish style of adobe brick, with the architecture faintly reminiscent of Virginia and Carolina plantation houses, interspersed with an occasional New England frame house. The economy was based on subsistence agriculture, with every member of the community, including the very young and the aged, working in the fields. Some Virginians experimented with tobacco, but the weed would not grow well in the Jefferson soil. Nor would most of the other great southern crops prosper in the Jefferson wasteland. The settlers quickly learned how to cultivate grains and vegetables with little water, and livestock grazing became more important in Jefferson than it had been in the colonies. The institution of slavery remained, more the result of not knowing what to do with the Negroes if they were freed than because they were needed. Indeed, in the early years Madison and others urged the manumission of the slaves, basing their arguments not only on economic grounds, but as a fulfillment of the spirit of the Declaration of Independence, which by this time had taken on the cloak of holy writ. A few slaves were granted their liberty and more fled Jefferson City, and bondage, for freedom further to the west. For the most part, however, the institution remained as it had been in Virginia and other southern colonies.[14]

The death toll was heavy in these early years, but the population of Jefferson increased nonetheless. This was due to a new wave of immigration that took place after ratification of the Brittanic Design. Those in the Southern Confederation who disliked the Design were

13. David Christman. *The Founding of Jefferson City: The First Three Decades* (Mexico City, 1967), pp. 145–54.
14. Carter Wallace. *A History of Slavery in the U.S.M.* (London, 1967), pp. 17–20; Baldwin Collier. *The Lost Opportunity: Slavery in Jefferson City, 1782–1795* (New York, 1948), pp. 29–34.

tempted to leave their homes and travel to Jefferson. Interestingly enough, this group included ultra-loyalists as well as disgruntled rebel sympathizers. Few came by the land route; Greene's harsh journey had made that passage most unpopular. Instead, they purchased or hired ships to take them around Florida and from there to New Orleans or, more often, Espiritu Santo, which was but a short trip to the small settlement. The third wave, which left Norfolk, Charleston, and Savannah in 1782–83, included some 6,000 new white settlers and 1,000 slaves. During the next five years, an additional 17,000 whites and 3,000 slaves left the Southern Confederation for Jefferson City, so that by 1794 its population was well over 43,000 whites and 18,000 slaves.[15]

King Charles III of Spain knew of the settlement. Early in his reign, which lasted from 1759 to 1788, he determined to remedy the abuses then current in New Spain and transform the colony into an asset to the Crown. Under Antonio de Bucareli, viceroy from 1771 to 1779, conditions improved markedly, and New Spain prospered. Bucareli foresaw that dissident American rebels might wish to settle there, and warned the King to make preparations for their coming. But Charles, while recognizing that the rebels might pose a threat to his power in Spain, also realized that the region needed settlers; and if they became loyal citizens, they would be an asset indeed. What really saved the Jeffersonians from interference, however, was the Russian threat to Spain on the Pacific coast. Jose de Gálvez was sent to California to block the Russian advance, and did so with great skill but his efforts required most of Spain's strength in the area.

In 1787, Charles was finally aroused to move against Jefferson, but his death the following year ended not only that plan, but Spain's interest in North America. His successor, Charles IV, was an unwise and poorly-informed monarch, dominated by his wife and her lover, Manuel de Godoy, neither of whom had the inclination to continue the New Spanish reforms. Revillo Gigedo, the viceroy at the time, pleaded for help, and warned of the growing might of the Jeffersonians, to no avail. Gigedo persisted nonetheless, and was rewarded for his troubles by being dismissed in 1794, on the eve of Jefferson's greatest growth and the decline of Spanish power in North America.[16]

The seeds of change were actually sown the previous year, when a young North American, Eli Whitney, invented a new method of extracting cotton seeds from their bolls. Whitney's cotton engine—or "cotton gin" as it came to be called—enabled an operator to process

15. Christman. *The Founding of Jefferson City*, pp. 178–201.
16. Ricardo Valdez. *Mexico: The Spanish Era* (Mexico City, 1960), pp. 331–

48; Martin Wilmington. *Charles IV and Spain's Lost Opportunities in Mexico* (New York, 1959), pp. 187–90.

fifty pounds of short staple cotton a day with ease, whereas previously a trained man could do little more than a pound a day. At the time, cotton was a comparatively expensive cloth. With the invention of the cotton gin, the price of processed cotton fell, and its production and use increased enormously. The effect on the Southern Confederation was electrifying. In 1793, only 15,000 bales had been produced there; by 1795 the figure had doubled, and would double again, to 60,000 bales, by 1798.[17] But as important as cotton was to the Southern Confederation, it was more so for Jefferson, which in 1793 was still on the edge of failure.

Cotton had always grown well along the Gulf Coast, but its high cost had dissuaded Jeffersonians from its cultivation. The cotton gin changed all this. By 1795, the first gin had made its appearance at Jefferson City, stolen from the S.C. and smuggled into Jefferson City *via* New Orleans. Within months, hundreds of these gins were in production, while former Virginians and Carolinians established plantations in prime coastal areas. Jefferson's cotton production in 1793 had been less than one thousand bales. By 1795 it had reached 10,000, and in 1800 over 30,000 bales were produced. Most was processed in Jefferson, and sent to Europe for sale. The port of Henrytown, a swamp in 1790, was a bustling town of 4,000 inhabitants by 1800.[18] Jeffersonian agents were able to sell their products with ease in continental countries, and had particular success in France, where the population retained a dislike for all British and C.N.A. goods. Many of the Jeffersonians had close relations with the French during the Rebellion, and now these contacts were renewed. In addition, France favored the new colony, viewing it as a useful counterweight to British power in North America.[19]

The sudden prosperity had enormous effects in Jefferson, three of which would be of great importance in the future. The first was the beginning of a fourth wave of immigration, this one of farmers from the Southern Confederation who lacked sufficient land to expand their cotton production. In 1800, Jefferson's population reached 65,000 whites and 34,000 Negroes, and its growth continued unabated thereafter.[20]

The second effect was the revival of slavery, which in 1793 appeared on the verge of ending as a viable institution. Now the cotton

17. Confederation of North America. Bureau of Statistics. *Historical Atlas and Statistical Abstract* (Burgoyne, 1971), pp. 1098–1100.
18. United States of Mexico. *Statistical Abstract and Guide* (Mexico City, 1970), pp. 987, 1053, 1287.
19. Sir Barton McCauley. *Origins of the Franco-Mexican Alliance* (London, 1954), p. 89.
20. U.S.M. *Statistical Abstract*, pp. 809–11.

plantations along the Gulf were labor poor, and not even the increased migration of farmers could ease this shortage. The price of slaves rose sharply, in this way encouraging Jeffersonians to enter the slave trade along the African coast. A similar development occurred in the Southern Confederation, but voices were raised opposing the institution, not only in the S.C., but from the Northern Confederation and Britain itself. There was little such opposition in Jefferson, although the former residents of New England did speak out against the institution.[21]

The third effect was the formation of a new government in Jefferson. At first, politics were unimportant and given little thought. General Greene had organized a council that operated in much the same fashion as the old Virginia House of Burgesses. Representative government was taken for granted by a people long used to it in their old homes. By 1793, however, there were demands for some kind of basic law. This arose out of frictions between the New Englanders on the one hand and the Virginians and Carolinians on the other. The former group, comprising less than ten percent of the white population, claimed they were being discriminated against and afforded little say in their own future. "Without basic guarantees," said Hamilton, "the society in which we live will perish, or be doomed to constant struggle, perhaps violent as well as peaceful."[22] Madison, who had risen to prominence after Greene's death in 1790, agreed, and together the two men organized a convention to discuss a new frame of government. It should be noted that both men had earlier evinced a mistrust of popular government, Hamilton speaking of a "natural aristocracy of talent," and opposed to the "weak-minded masses," while Madison feared "the tyranny of the mob" which could be destructive of the rights of minorities.[23] Most of the members of the convention of 1793 agreed with them, with only Sam Curtis, Edwin Corbitt, Martin Collins, and William Sayre, all of whom had come to Jefferson as young men, and who had not fought in the Rebellion, speaking for democracy in an almost anarchistic fashion.[24]

21. Dana Wycliff. *The Cultural Struggle in Early Jefferson.* (Mexico City, 1910).

22. Alexander Hamilton. *Government and the Nature of Man* (Jefferson City, 1793), p. 10.

23. James Madison. *Government and the Proper Concern* (Jefferson City, 1793), p. 27. The Hamilton and Madison works were actually first presented in the journals. Later on, together with similar essays by William Duer and John Jay, they were collected in a work entitled *Federal Governance,* which Algie Baker has called "the skeleton key to the Constitutional Frame." Algie Baker. *Understanding the Constitution* (Mexico City, 1967).

24. Peter Collins. *Generations in Conflict: Republicanism vs. Anarchy in Early Jefferson* (Mexico City, 1960), pp. 190–201.

The convention was held in Lafayette in the summer of the year, and lasted two months. In this period, representatives from all segments of the population (except, of course, the Negro slaves) were heard, and all had a chance to influence the delegates. What emerged was a constitutional framework, more a collection of compromises than a rational vehicle for government. Madison led the delegates in ratifying a tripartite scheme of government, embodying separate but interrelated legislative, executive, and judicial branches. The legislature was to consist of two houses, the lower elected by all free male voters owning more than £5 in property (approximately $120). Candidates could enter the lists by presenting petitions containing the signatures or marks of one percent of the qualified voters. For election purposes Jefferson was divided into 42 "districts," with each having one representative. The upper house would be selected by the lower house during its first session, and consist of 15 men, with the understanding that no one could serve in both houses simultaneously. The term of office for the lower house was to be two years, the upper, five. All legislation would be initiated by the lower house, and passed by the upper. According to Madison's design, the lower house was called the Chamber of Representatives, the upper, the Senate.

The executive branch was selected by the Senate. It consisted of three men, the votes of two being necessary for decisions. These "governors" had authority over foreign affairs as well as the obligation to carry out legislative enactments. They were expected to have seats in the Chamber or the Senate, and Madison believed they would be the most distinguished and respected members of those bodies. The governors would also have the responsibility of nominating judges for the high courts, of which there would be seven, and these nominations would be ratified by a two-thirds vote of the Senate.

The Constitution of 1793 pleased no one completely and yet was acceptable to all. The democrats were encouraged by the Chamber of Representatives, while those who feared an excess of popular government were pleased by the methods for selecting the other governmental officers. Northern immigrants to Jefferson felt certain that one of the three governors would always be from their group; the southern immigrants were confident that two would be of their background and that they would be able to control that body. They also noted that Article VII, Section II of the Constitution, in which were enumerated the powers of the government, contained no reference to the institution of slavery, and they interpreted this to mean that the government would have no control over the blacks. The few abolitionists among the Jeffersonians of that period observed that Article XIV, Section IV, gave the government the power to "consider all problems relating to the general safety and good of the state." They hoped that, in time, this could be used as a lever to end slavery in Jefferson.[25]

The Constitution was ratified by a vote of the settlers on October 15, 1793, and elections for the Chamber were held on December 4. The Chamber met in Jefferson City on January 19, to select the Senate and establish the government. The governors were chosen on January 25. There was little contest for the posts; all knew they would be held by Madison, Hamilton, and Samuel Johnston, the last of whom had emigrated in the first wave from North Carolina, and had been a distinguished member of the Continental Congress. By February 1 all seven of the judges of the high court had been selected. The new nation of Jefferson had been born.[26]

Even then, there were to be found in Jefferson the seeds of future problems and growth. The nation would have more than adequate leadership during the next two decades. Hamilton in particular would prove a strong and resourceful executive, especially in domestic affairs. Without his skill, the new nation's financial system would have foundered and its weak and divided government fallen into anarchy. Greene is rightly considered the father of his country, but its true beginnings may be traced to Hamilton's wise leadership and influence from 1793 to 1815.[27]

It was only in the area of foreign affairs that Hamilton's advice went unheeded, and there through no fault of his own. The strong anti-C.N.A. sentiments of the Jeffersonians, begun during the Rebellion and carried with the first wave to the new land, would remain a hallmark of Jeffersonian (and later Mexican) policy to this day. Hamilton urged conciliation, not only with C.N.A., but with Britain as well. This was not to be. Instead, the government's foreign affairs came under the influence of the French party, especially Alexander Williams, Albert Gallatin, Stevens Mason, and later on, John Quincy Adams, John Gaillard, and William Crawford.

---

25. Corby Street. *Compromise and Conciliation as Factors in the Jeffersonian Constitution of 1793* (Mexico City, 1936); Martha Lamb. *The Resolution of Conflict: Constitutional Case Studies* (Canberra, 1956); Robert Wymess. *Prelude to Greatness: The Jeffersonian Constitution of 1793* (Mexico City, 1970); Max O'Connor. *The Men of Lafayette* (New York, 1960). Also see Winston Thompson. *The Flawed Design: Problems at Lafayette* (London, 1967); Martin Greene. *The Britannic Design and the Lafayette Constitution*

of 1793: *Comparisons and Contrasts* (New York, 1968); and Conrad Tracy. *Our Fathers Who Art in Lafayette* (Mexico City, 1959) for negative views of the Constitution.
26. David Christman. *The Founding of Jefferson City*, p. 362.
27. Alexander Hamilton. *Memoirs*, 3 volumes (Jefferson, 1814). George Bancroft. *Hamilton and Madison: The Grand Collaboration* (Mexico City, 1886); Edward Handleman. *The Life of Alexander Hamilton* (Canberra, 1970).

Foreign relations were extremely important to the new nation. Bounded as it was by Spanish lands, with the C.N.A. beyond and Europe hoping to gain influence in its chambers, Jefferson seemed a potential plaything for powers greater than itself. So long as this was the case, the settlers remained united, as though against a common foe. It was not enough to retain its own territory; Jefferson's leaders thought that expansion was the only method of ensuring safety. As early as 1795 there was talk of a "Greater Jefferson" which would dominate the continent.[28] The idea united the Jeffersonians for a while, but other, internal issues were also coming to the fore even then. The most important of these was ideological. Some Jeffersonians urged their countrymen to remain true to the philosophy of the Rebellion, in particular the Declaration of Independence. It had taken them to Jefferson, and there should be implemented. Generally speaking, this group was opposed to Continental Destiny and all it implied. Others, soon the majority, held the first wave had left their ideology behind when they came to Jefferson, and new theories were needed in a new land. They supported Continental Destiny and an aggressive foreign policy, as well as being highly concerned with economic development of the cotton lands. By 1797 these two groups had formed themselves into parties, the first known as the Liberty Party, the second as the Continentalists. The struggle between these factions would dominate Jeffersonian political life for the next two decades.[29]

28. Stanley Press. *The Doctrine of Continental Destiny* (Mexico City, 1965); Sir Bartley Cornwall. *Hamilton and Continental Destiny: The Lost Struggle* (New York, 1961).
29. David Christman. *The Origins of Political Parties in Jefferson* (Mexico City, 1960); Peter Collins. *The Liberty Party in Old Jefferson* (Mexico City, 1954); Soames Greeley. *The Continentalists: The Leadership and the Doctrines* (London, 1939).

# 6

# THE TRANS-OCEANIC WAR

THE events in Jefferson went almost unnoticed in most parts of the C.N.A., where the problems of adjusting to the new government and finding the proper relations with the mother country occupied the energies of the people. The residents of Indiana, Quebec, and Manitoba were scarcely affected by the exodus, since few of their number took the Wilderness Walk. Some in the Northern Confederation seemed sorry to see the former rebels and their sympathizers leave, apparently due to feelings of guilt for having participated or encouraged the Rebellion and then remaining under royal rule. In contrast, the Southern Confederation welcomed their departure, since this section had been more pro-loyalist from the start. Indeed, those who remained actually profited from the situation, since they took over the lands left by the emigrants, who rarely bothered to place them for sale, but merely abandoned their holdings to whomever would take them. Some families in both the Northern and Southern Confederations were divided by the emigration, and doubtless there was anguish, but certainly no more so than had been the case in the seventeenth century, when parts of families left England for the New World. In any case, there was no sign of either undue friendship or hostility for those who left, but rather a curiosity and interest.[1]

Albany's death left the position of Viceroy vacant, and it was widely assumed Cornwallis would succeed to the post. This would have been an unwise and unfortunate choice, since the General had few supporters in the C.N.A. North realized this, and with his usual skill convinced Parliament to select a native-born American for the post. After some discussion and a measure of grumbling, John Dickinson was chosen, and on February 1, 1784, he was confirmed in office by the royal seal, after being knighted and made a member of Lords as well.

Dickinson proved an excellent choice. Although lacking the popularity of Albany, he was an American who had participated in the

1. Ocon. *The People We Left Behind,* pp. 190–206; Katherine Rourke. *A Study of the Attitudes of the People of the* C.N.A. *Toward the First Wave.* London University Studies in Political and Social Science, Vol. LII (London, 1910).

early stages of the Rebellion, and so was able to assure many who might otherwise have gone to Jefferson to remain in the C.N.A. Sir John proved tactful at all times in his relationship with Parliament and the King, and demonstrated an unsuspected skill in dealing with the governors-general of Quebec, Manitoba, and Indiana, who viewed all those who lived in the other two confederations with suspicion. It has rightly been said that, "Albany established the C.N.A.; Dickinson assured its permanence."[2] The measure of Dickinson's political acumen could be seen in his dealings with Sir Charles Jenkinson, who succeeded to the prime ministership in 1785, and whose government was not as friendly to the North Americans as was North's. Still, the two men were able to work well together, especially during the Trans-Oceanic War, when trust and mutual respect were so necessary.

The first six years of Dickinson's administration were uneventful in Manitoba, Quebec, and Indiana, which were sparsely settled and lacked satisfactory communications with the other two confederations save through the Great Lakes and the St. Lawrence. The Northern Confederation, where George Clinton succeeded Dickinson as governor general in 1784, underwent a period of rapid economic growth. Although Boston declined as a port, much of its commerce being deflected to New York and Quebec, the shipbuilding industry of the region flourished. English investors sought opportunities to place their funds in textile mills as well, so that Massachusetts became one of the most prosperous colonies by the early 1790's. New York, with a population of almost 40,000, became the terminus of much of the export trade of the Northern Confederation, as well as the social and intellectual center of the North, surpassing Philadelphia in this respect after the Rebellion. Pennsylvania remained the bread basket of North America, and attracted one of every three immigrants to the Northern Confederation to its lush fields from 1784 to 1793. Under George Clinton's wise leadership, the Northern Confederation developed a balanced economy, with Pennsylvania wheat feeding Massachusetts industry and providing investment opportunities for New York capital. "We may thank providence the Rebellion did not succeed," said Clinton in 1790. "Cast adrift on a sea of international intrigue, we would have foundered and been destroyed. Our present prosperity can be ascribed to our harmonious relations with other parts of the Empire, and the protection of the Royal Navy. Together we control a continent, perhaps the world. Singly, we would perish before those envious of our wealth."[3]

2. Hargrave. *Dickinson of North America.* Vol. V, p. 510.
3. Joseph Clinton. *The Life of George Clinton and the Clinton Family of the* *Northern Confederation* (New York, 1882); Robert Duffy. *George Clinton: The New York Magician* (New York, 1968), pp. 332–33.

Although Connolly proved a weak reed in the Southern Confederation, that area too underwent rapid growth. Governor Theodorick Bland of Virginia dominated council meetings in Norfolk, and other governors tended to follow his lead or go their individual ways. In part, this was due to the continuing importance of Virginia tobacco to the region, but the driving force of Bland, combined with Connolly's ineffectualness, must also be considered.[4] This is not to say, however, that Virginia controlled the S.C. Rather, the situation reflected the more fractionalized economy of the area, which unlike the N.C. was not strongly united until much later. By then the pattern had been set in both confederations. From Clinton's time to the present, the N.C. was noted for strong governors-general and weak colonial governors (or "state governors" as they were called after 1810), while the Southern Confederation would rarely have a strong governor or general council, with most of the power residing in the individual states. Such a development could scarcely have been expected in 1782, but occurred with a minimum of difficulty as each confederation sought the best way to manage its affairs.

Far more serious a flaw in the Britannic Design, was the lack of inter-confederation coordination. North had expected the envoys from each branch of the C.N.A. to be welcomed in the others; such was not the case. The eastern confederations viewed the Indianans and Manitobans as barbarians, and they in turn found little in common with their more sophisticated brethren. The old antagonisms between Quebec and the N.C. remained, and were it not for the tact and skill shown by Clinton and Dorchester, war over border lines might have erupted in 1788. The N.C. also had difficulties with the Southern Confederation. Bland disliked all northerners and rejected proposals for cooperation in common causes. "Even before the Rebellion our products supported the English people of America, while our 'friends to the North' made do through piracy and other illegal acts. The Rebellion began in the North, and Northerners remain rebels at heart." So he said to the council in Norfolk in 1788, and although supposedly a secret meeting, word of it leaked to Clinton, who was enraged, and protested immediately to Connolly, who as usual did nothing. Clinton then remarked that Bland himself had fought on the rebel side, and in a fit of anger charged that "our friend from Virginia is a man of great sensitivity. He left the rebel cause only a month after Saratoga. Had the victory not been won, today he would be toasting the health of

4. Sir Humphrey Grey. *Particularism and Colonial Rights in the Southern* *Confederation* (London, 1940), pp. 119-23, 230-44.

General Gates and others of his stripe."[5] In time the heat dissipated, but difficulties between the N.C. and S.C. would remain.

Unfortunately, there was more to this rivalry than mere clashes of personality. There was, in fact, a kernel of truth in Bland's charge. The economy of the S.C. was basically agricultural and destined to remain so for the indefinite future, while that of the N.C. was increasingly based on commerce and industry. The population of the N.C. was largely Presbyterian and Congregationalist, while the Church of England held sway in all southern colonies (with a Catholic minority of importance in Maryland). One would think the religious differences relatively insignificant, while the economies of the regions would complement one another. But such was not the case. Instead, both sold most of their exports to Europe and little inter-confederation trade developed until the early nineteenth century. S.C. tobacco and N.C. industry competed for British capital in the late eighteenth century, and this too added fuel to the fires of distrust. Clinton struggled to reach accord with Bland, to no avail. "Here we are," he said in 1790, "situated between brothers in Quebec and the Southern Confederation, and both prepared to dismember us at the slightest provocation."[6]

Fortunately, the bonds of empire were stronger than Clinton supposed them to be. They would soon be tested in war, as in 1795 Britain once again clashed with France.

Historians have long differed as to the origins of the contest, and even about its name. It is still called the Habsburg War in France, the Five Years' War in Britain, and the Trans-Oceanic War in the C.N.A., the name which will be used in this book.[7] They would note that Anglo-French rivalry had been a major factor in seventeenth century European history, and regard the war as a natural outgrowth of the prior struggles both in Europe and America. Others, particularly C.N.A. historians of the early twentieth century and after, believe its origins to have been in America, and not Europe.

Whatever the case, the Paris insurrection was certainly a key element. In 1789 the city was shaken by mobs, which roamed the streets, demanding lower taxes and bread prices. Doubtless some of this was inspired by the North American Rebellion, unsuccessful though it had been. In August, the mob took control of the city, and from there marched to Versailles, apparently in an attempt to seize the King. But the government held firm, and the mob was repulsed. Then in Septem-

5. Percy Harcourt. *The Vipers in Their Bosoms: Clinton and Bland in 1788* (London, 1956), pp. 166-67, 78-79, 201-10.
6. Duffy. *George Clinton*, p. 380.
7. Artemas Kelly. *Origins of the Trans-Oceanic War* (Mexico City, 1967); Robert Seabury. *Historians and the Trans-Oceanic War* (London, 1967); Paul Mitchell. *The Jenkinson Cabinet and the Five Years' War* (London, 1958); Ferdinand Ortega. *The First World War, 1795-1799* (Mexico City, 1937).

ber, a contingent under the command of General Charles-Francois Dumouriez entered Paris and dispersed the mob, in a bloodbath known as the "Terrible September Days." Over 8,000 were killed that month, and at least twice that number fled Paris and France itself, many going to Prussia and Britain, but a handful to Jefferson. By early 1790 the rebellion was over, but a residue of distrust remained.[8]

Some of the King's ministers, such as Jacques Necker, suspected the English of having encouraged the insurrectionists. Relations with London, never good, took a turn for the worse. In late 1790 there was talk in Paris of the next round in the war between these two ancient enemies.

But war did not come at that time. King Louis XVI, a well-meaning though inept ruler, had no taste for another struggle. The King had been horrified by the Paris insurrection and fearful during the march on Versailles. Now that the country seemed calm once more he had no intention of embarking on new adventures. As long as he had power, Europe would remain at peace.

On September 23, 1793, the King traveled from Versailles to a hunting lodge. The front wheel of his carriage hit a rock in the road, causing the coach to pitch to one side. Louis' head struck an ivory handle, causing him some pain but apparently little else. Two hours later, while alighting from the carriage, he fell to the ground, dead from the head injury.

The King's sudden demise (he was only thirty-nine years old at the time) caught Paris by surprise. His son was elevated to the throne as Louis XVII, with Queen Marie Antoinette as his regent.

Almost overnight, France's foreign policy underwent a great shift. A Habsburg who had never been popular in the Bourbon court, the Queen now looked eastward for support. Marie Antoinette sent an emissary to Vienna, where he met with representatives of Emperor Francis II. Messengers traveled back and forth between Versailles and Vienna that winter, and in April of 1794 the Queen and the Emperor concluded a secret treaty, under the terms of which both agreed to a coordinated attack on Prussia, and division of the country after victory. The secret was badly kept, however, and news of it reached London by August. Jenkinson swiftly sent envoys to Prussia to warn Frederick William II of the coming attack and to offer aid. Prussia, together with several minor German states, signed a treaty of alliance in December, and so were prepared for the attack when it came the following April.[9]

---

8. Hector Pavelle. *Paris During the Insurrection* (London, 1956); Lafayette Ortega. *The Paris Insurrection as a Factor in European and American History* (Mexico City, 1970).

9. Pierre Clouzot. (trans. by Martin Corn) *European Diplomacy on the Eve of the Habsburg War* (London, 1939), pp. 203–56.

At first all went well for the French and Austrian armies, as Dumouriez and Ney attacked from the west and the Austrians advanced toward Berlin and seized Silesia. Now Marie Antoinette moved to solidify her grip on the continent. Her agents in Madrid contacted King Charles' ministers and warned of France's displeasure with that monarch's apparent friendship with Britain. Simultaneously a French army was sent to the Pyrenees, as though poised for attack. Charles had no choice; he asked Versailles for a treaty of friendship, and one was signed on April 12, 1795. In effect, France now dominated Spain. In all but name, Marie Antoinette had united the two countries, thus realizing the dream that had eluded Louis XIV.

A frightened Queen Maria I of Portugal appealed to London for assistance, if and when the Franco-Spanish forces attempted to seize her country. Jenkinson assured the Queen that the ancient Anglo-Portuguese ties were intact, and began preparations for war by enlarging the military and naval budgets and adding new men such as William Pitt and Charles James Fox, to his Cabinet. Then, without waiting for additional provocations, Jenkinson asked for war on August 23, 1795, thus beginning the next stage in the Anglo-French confrontation.[10]

Details of the European war need not concern us in this book. Suffice it to say that Jenkinson sent troops to Portugal and Prussia as well as instituting a blockade of the continent. The war in Europe dragged on, as Prussia revived and fought off the invaders successfully, but lacked the power and men to mount invasions of France and Austria. More important than this, however, was the war in America.

News of the fighting was greeted with cheers in New York, Norfolk, and Fort Radisson, though with less enthusiasm in Quebec and North City, where pro-French proclivities were not yet dead. The Americans were particularly delighted to learn of the Franco-Spanish alliance, for this would give them an excuse to seize the Floridas and Louisiana, which in 1795 had been areas of friction between the C.N.A., especially between the S.C., and Spain. For the past three years Georgians had invaded the Floridas regularly in search of marauding Seminoles, whom the Spaniards were unable or unwilling to control. Madrid issued regular protests, and in 1794 had gone so far as to send troops into Georgia in retaliation. Now the Georgians had an excuse to take the region, and they promptly dispatched an army under the command of Colonel Richard Tomkinson to wrest it from the Spaniards and their Indian allies. The campaign was swift and brutal. Although more than 300 Georgians died in Florida, they massacred the Seminoles and crushed the Spaniards. Within a year the Flori-

---

10. Mitchell. *The Jenkinson Cabinet and the Five Years' War*, pp. 300–10.

das were in Georgian hands, and that colony annexed them without waiting for permission from the Southern Confederation, Viceroy Dickinson, or Parliament.[11]

In much the same way, Indianans had designs on the area bounded by the Mississippi and Missouri Rivers which was rich in fur-bearing animals. Similarly, the Carolinas and Georgia hoped to take New Orleans and the lower Mississippi; New Orleans for its port facilities, and the Mississippi so that commerce from Indiana could be sent to S.C. ports instead of going to the N.C. The Carolinians did not wait for a formal declaration of war before crossing the Mississippi, and together with the Georgians, planned an attack on the fortified installations at New Orleans.

The initiative for the New Orleans expedition came from Governor Bland, however, who urged Connolly to send troops from other S.C. colonies to join the Carolinians and Georgians in their campaign. In the end, a united S.C. army, led by General Edward Curtis of Georgia, was formed for the expedition. Curtis was to take the land route across Georgia, while a British naval force led by Captain Horatio Nelson would carry Cornwallis' British troops by sea to the port. The campaign went off without a mistake, and New Orleans fell with little resistance on October 1, 1797. Then Nelson and Curtis combined forces and went up the Mississippi, left their ships at Fort George, and swept the area clean of hostile Indians and Spaniards. By the late summer of 1798, all of North America east of the Missouri-Mississippi waterway was in C.N.A. hands.

The Jeffersonians also benefited from Spain's misfortunes in selecting the wrong ally in the Trans-Oceanic War. Although the Jeffersonians had little sympathy for the British or North Americans, they recognized the war as an opportunity for expansion, and they seized upon it. Despite the strong opposition of the Liberty Party, the Continentalists led Jefferson into the war, although without a formal declaration. Governor Hamilton resigned his position and took command of the small but tough Jeffersonian army. His objectives were simple. Two armies would be formed, one to penetrate as far eastward toward New Orleans as possible, while the other would drive toward the Rio Grande. General Jacob Mellon took charge of the eastern army, and taking a coastal route, reached within twenty miles of New Orleans by May 14, 1796. Then, leaving Major Andrew Jackson in charge of affairs in the east, he took the bulk of his forces and joined Hamilton,

---

11. Parliament later agreed to the annexation, which made Georgia the largest and most powerful colony in the Southern Confederation. Within a generation Georgia would dominate the S.C., taking the lead from Virginia.

Beauregard Hopkins. *The Pearl of the Southern Confederation: Life in Early Georgia* (Atlanta, 1906); Bernard Telford. *Georgia and the Rise of the S.C.* (Mexico City, 1965).

who had already begun his drive to the river. The combined forces reached the Rio Grande in April of 1797, having suffered more casualties through accidents and disease than from Spanish bullets. By war's end, Jefferson was a major North American nation, and the price paid for such status was low indeed.[12]

As early as 1797 France sent out feelers for peace, but Jenkinson and Pitt rejected them at first, awaiting the time when the Franco-Austrian alliance would be shattered and its armies completely destroyed. Such was the case by late 1798, and at that time serious negotiations began. On March 1, 1799, the articles of peace were signed in Aix-la-Chapelle. Under the terms of the treaty, Prussia would receive Austrian land to the east and would join with her western German allies to form the Germanic Confederation, to be headed by King Frederick William I.[13] Charles of Spain was deposed, and replaced by the aged Prince Ferdinand of Prussia, the great uncle of Frederick William I, who took the title of Ferdinand II and initiated a Hohenzollern dynasty in Spain. France was made to pay an indemnity to Britain, but little else. The country was in poor condition in 1799, and Jenkinson feared that revolution might result if Louis XVII were severely humiliated. Indeed, as the diplomats met to discuss terms, a revolt began in Paris which had to be put down by British and Prussian troops. They remained there after the war, and Louis XVII became, in effect, a puppet whose strings were pulled by statesmen in Berlin and London.[14]

Although the Five Years' War ended in Europe in 1799, the Trans-Oceanic War continued. The Indianans and the Southern Confederation continued to seize Spanish lands in Louisiana, while Jefferson consolidated its gains and considered a crossing of the Rio Grande. At the same time, revolution erupted elsewhere in Spanish America. Jose de Conslaves, Martin Obregon, Carlos Gomez, Fernando de Abruzzo, and Jose Flores organized their forces in South and Central America and by 1805 had thrown the last Spanish viceroy out of their lands. There were slave rebellions in the Spanish Caribbean islands, and several republics established in 1804, but within two years the white planters had taken power, instituting their own regimes.

Events moved swiftly in New Spain in this period. Revillo Gigedo called for an uprising against Charles in Mexico, and thousands flocked

12. Henry Miles. *Jefferson in the Trans-Oceanic War* (Mexico City, 1956), pp. 337–89.

13. Not to be confused with his great-grandfather, King Frederick William I of Prussia, Frederick William I of the Germanic Confederation ruled from 1799 to 1840. He had been crowned Frederick William III of Prussia in 1797, and as such had led Prussia during the last stages of the Five Years' War and helped formulate the peace treaty.

14. Charles Agissiz. *The King on a String: The Last Years of Louis XVII* (London, 1956).

to his banner. Miguel Hidalgo y Costilla, a former priest, led the revolutionary army, whose slogan was "Mexico Libre y Siempre." The revolution was successful, and on March 17, 1805, the Republic of Mexico was proclaimed in Mexico City, as the last Spanish soldiers left America by ship. Gigedo headed a provisional government, promising to draw up a constitution which recognized the rights of "liberdad y vida." Indians would receive the lands taken from them by the Spaniards, slavery would be abolished in fact as well as in theory, and civil rights would be guaranteed by the state. The most contentious right, however, was that of religious freedom. Many priests had joined in the rebellion; and they now rejected the idea that the Catholic Church would be only one among many in the new nation, without special privileges. This problem could not be resolved, and in 1806 the Mexican Civil War began, one that would last for more than a decade and was not resolved until the Jeffersonian Intervention.[15]

In a sense the Trans-Oceanic War never truly ended, but has continued in South and Central America to the present day. The victors in Europe were Britain and Prussia. Austria would count for little in the nineteenth century, while France would remain a second-class power for a generation. The new Germanic Confederation would come to dominate central Europe; Jenkinson was wise in not accepting continental territory for Britain, although he could have had it for the asking in 1799. Far more significant was the impact on Spain, now clearly in the backwash of world politics, the nation humiliated, her empire lost. The successor states of South America would be embroiled in petty wars that last to this day, and would never fulfill the promise predicted for them by Obregon and Abruzzo. Mexico seemed no different from the others, although she would suffer a shorter life than most, and paradoxically become a major power as a result. As Carlos Ortez put it, "the Trans-Oceanic War was won by two nations, and neither of them European in thought or mold. The Confederation of North America emerged from the conflict a major power, even though divided internally and still seeking its national soul. Jefferson, on the other hand, was able to catch a glimpse of its destiny, but still lacked the power to carry it out. The war began as a conflict between Britain and France for the past; it ended with the seeds being sown for the future, with the C.N.A. and Jefferson the keys to the nineteenth century and after."[16]

15. Carl Ortez. *The Mexican Civil War* (Mexico City, 1960).

16. Carlos Ortez. *America and the Struggle for the World* (Mexico City, 1970), p. 8.

# 7

# THE ERA OF HARMONIOUS
# RELATIONS

To the North American of 1810, the world must have appeared quite different from what it had been only thirty-five years earlier. In less than four decades the continent had undergone the Rebellion, the organization of the C.N.A., the Wilderness Walk and the formation of Jefferson, and finally the Trans-Oceanic War. Now the continent was at peace; the times of great change seemed over. So they were. The next three decades were generally without foreign conflict, although the seeds of future troubles were germinating. From 1810 to 1837, however, peaceful means would be found to assure continuity and growth in the C.N.A. The period is still called the "Era of Harmonious Relations" by some historians, although most now realize that conflict did exist, and more was yet to come.[1]

The War had added a new confederation to the C.N.A.; Vandalia, formed of the lands ceded by Spain, was bounded by the Mississippi to the east, the Arkansas to the south, and Manitoba's southern boundary to the north. The western boundary was uncharted, the subject of conflicting claims. But in 1810 few gave the matter much thought, for the population of the new confederation was fewer than 2,000 whites.[2]

Quebec and Manitoba caught a glimpse of their economic destinies in this period. Neither confederation was able to attract many settlers or compete with the N.C. in agriculture or industry. Quebec

---

1. The seminal work on this period is Howard Pugh. *The Era of Harmonious Relations* (New York, 1890). For thirty years the Pugh thesis was generally accepted. Then Philip Key's *Internal Dislocations in the Early Nineteenth Century* (London, 1921) appeared, to question the validity of Pugh's sources. Howard Tracy. *Vipers in the Garden: Party Struggles in the Era of Harmonious Relations* (New York, 1930)

demonstrated that political maneuverings were far more important than Pugh had assumed them to be, and stressed the economic problems more than had his predecessor. Martin Kleberg. *The Pugh Thesis Revisited* (New York, 1961) has shown that some of Pugh's conclusions were valid, although his sources were shoddy.

2. David Lea. *The Birth of Vandalia* (Galloway, 1951).

would soon become an economic colony of sorts for the Northern Confederation, and be part of that state in all but name. This caused deep resentment, especially among the French-speaking inhabitants, who had never fully accepted English rule after the Seven Years' War and were always wary of the C.N.A. Now they saw Quebec suffer the double humiliation of being controlled by English-speaking politicians ruling from Quebec City, and economically, by N.C. merchants and industrialists concentrated in New York.

As early as 1800 there had been discussions of secession among the French population, but little had been done about it during the war. By 1810, however, the talk had been translated into action. Under the leadership of Paul Cerdan and Pierre Ribot, the dissidents organized the Free Quebec Party, which demanded full recognition of French Quebec's autonomy in the confederation's internal affairs. The party did not go so far as to seek separation, and Ribot in particular repeatedly affirmed his allegiance to the C.N.A.[3]

For the moment, then, the English-speaking citizens of Quebec tended to dismiss the Free Quebec movement as a crank organization that would never amount to much, and they turned to other issues. Some saw their confederation's future in industrialization, increased commerce, and the development of the north country. This program would require much capital, most of which would come from London and New York. Thus, they called for strong imperial ties and full partnership in the C.N.A. By 1811 this group, centered in Quebec City and including its wealthiest citizens, formed the Progress Party, which was more commonly called the Liberal Party.

Their opponents saw a different future for Quebec, based on the land, which was rich and well suited to agriculture and animal husbandry. These individuals saw few benefits in industrialization. Furthermore, if that route was accepted, it would mean domination by London or New York, and both cities were hated and feared, as were all urban centers. They saw the Liberals as agents of foreign powers, who would cooperate with strangers to exploit their brothers. To combat them, they organized the Farmers Congress, which had its first meeting in Montreal in 1812, and which was transformed into the Conservative Party the following year.

As might be expected, the Conservatives appealed to farmers, some urban workers who opposed their employers, and small businessmen fearful of being engulfed by their larger competitors. The anti-

---

3. Although it was not known at the time, Ribot planned violent action to overthrow the government as early as 1812. Realizing his group was a minority, he spoke softly in public while organizing the resistance. Pierre Ribot. *My Life and Works* (London, 1829); Thomas Taggert. *Ribot of Quebec: Patriot or Demagogue?* (New York, 1954).

New York and anti-London sentiments of the Conservatives made them natural allies of the Free Quebec coalition, and also the target of charges made by Liberals of sedition and disloyalty. But when the Conservatives won the state elections of 1814, they proved moderate, and gave no comfort to Ribot and Cerdan, after which the Free Quebec movement turned to terrorism and sporadic violence. Neither party was able to deal effectively with the problems, which remained the *leit-motif* of Quebec's politics for the next half-century.[4]

Little may be said of Manitoba in this period. Her grain fields would soon be recognized as among the finest in the world, but until better means of transporting grain from field to city were found, this mattered little. The completion of the first railroad from Port Superior to North City in 1855 would change that state's future dramatically, but even before then it attracted settlers from the N.C., S.C., and Indiana who sought cheap, good land and were willing to accept isolation as the price for it. Many Englishmen also came to Manitoba, and were not disappointed by what they found.

The population of Manitoba was homogeneous; there was no group seeking to industrialize the area or promote plans to lead in directions other than the pursuit of land and grain. As a result, Manitoba was called "the land without politics" in the first half of the century. Madame Floride Quesnay, visiting Manitoba in 1850, called it a "dull paradise," and her hosts in North City considered it a compliment. Manitoba would not figure importantly in the politics of the C.N.A. for a century, and did not seek the kind of power so prized in the S.C. and N.C., and even in Indiana. For this reason it attracted those North Americans disillusioned with life further south and east, and became a haven for farmers, religious sects, utopians, poets, and the discontented of the other states.[5]

Indiana was the fastest growing state in the period from 1810 to 1840. Its population in 1810 was barely 250,000; by 1820 it had reached 900,000, and rose to 1.7 million in 1830, and 3.5 million in 1840.[6] Michigan City, which was a swamp in 1810, had 500,000 inhabitants by 1840, was the fifth largest city in the Confederation, and its most rapidly growing urban complex. Kent and New Boston were rising industrial and commercial centers, while Burgoyne was not only a lively capital, but a busy port as well. Visitors complained the Indiana cities were rustic and lacked culture, especially when compared to

---

4. Etienne Bayard. *The Sputtering Fuse: The French Question in Quebec in the Nineteenth Century* (Quebec, 1967).
5. Floride Quesnay. *Travels Through the C.N.A.* (London, 1854), p. 133;

Thomas Irwin and Donald McLean. *Manitoba: Athens of the North* (New York, 1966); Donald McLean. *The Rise of Manitoban Nationalism* (New York, 1970), esp. pp. 167–240.
6. C.N.A. *Statistical Abstract*, p. 788.

New York and Norfolk, but they had a vitality absent in the eastern cities. This was due in part to the diversity of the state, which had attracted S.C. immigrants to its southern counties, and former Pennsylvanians and New Yorkers to the northern ones. Michigan City was dominated by people from the older states, who were drawn there by promises of commercial and mercantile wealth as well as that of excitement and challenge. By 1830, St. Louis resembled a smaller, less sophisticated version of New Orleans, while Michigan City had many of the characteristics of New York. Both had one feature missing in the urban centers of the S.C. and N.C.; exterior forts were found around most Indianan cities in this period, evidence that the Indian threat still existed.

The coming of large numbers of white settlers caused consternation among the tribes of Indiana, especially the Shawnee, Iowa, Missouri, Osage, and Dakota. By 1803, these tribes and others were united behind Shawnee Chief Tecumseh and his brother, the Prophet, and were determined to protect their land against the invaders. A "pact of union" and political organization had been erected by 1808, and the following year saw the emergence of a major Indian army. It was this force, led by Tecumseh himself, that crushed General William Henry Harrison at the battle of Twin Forks in 1810, and then wiped out the Indianan army at Bloody Creek the following year. By 1814 Tecumseh was actually threatening to destroy the capital at Burgoyne, and Harrison, now Governor of Indiana, was obliged to call upon the Confederation for military assistance. Detachments from the N.C. and S.C. arrived in the summer of 1815, and under Harrison's guidance, proceeded to attack the Indians. Tecumseh was forced to retreat, but was never defeated in open battle.[7] Not until the 1850's would the Indian threat end. For the next four decades no major decision could be made by an Indianan governor, without taking into consideration the Indian reaction.[8]

If the Northern Confederation lacked Indiana's rapid demographic growth, the idealism of Manitoba, and the political intrigue of Quebec, it ran a close second to all in these areas, as well as being the most industrialized state in the Confederation. Like Indiana, the Northern Confederation had large deposits of raw materials, a hardworking population, and good political leadership from 1810 to 1840. Thus, it attracted immigrants from Europe in large numbers, while not

7. Henry Brand. *Tecumseh and the Indianan Wars* (New York, 1970); James Paulding. *One State, Two Nations: Indianan and Indian* (New York, 1967); William Henry Harrison. *The Autobiography of William Henry Harrison* (Burgoyne, 1840), pp. 540–689.
8. James Paulding. *The Indian Question in Indianan Foreign Policy* (New York, 1959); James Barrett. *Counting the Cost: The Legacy of Tecumseh* (Mexico City, 1960).

suffering losses due to military clashes with the Indians. The N.C. had a population of well over 3.6 million in 1810, which rose to 4.5 million in 1820, 6.8 million in 1830, and 9 million in 1840.[9] By then New York was the largest city in the Empire, dwarfing even London. It was a larger commercial center than either London or Amsterdam, it boasted more theaters than any city in North America, and was the financial capital of the hemisphere. Boston continued to stagnate, but Philadelphia underwent a renaissance, becoming the literary and artistic capital of the N.C. All three cities had major universities and laboratories, and the educational level in the N.C. was clearly the highest in the Confederation.

The N.C. prospered mightily in this period. The coming of the railroad in the early 1820's is given the credit for sparking the boom. Financed at first from London but soon from New York as well, entrepreneurs built lines to every corner of the Northern Confederation, reaching into the S.C. and Indiana by 1831, and terminating in Michigan City by 1836. It was the railroad that tied Indiana to the N.C. by ribbons of steel, just as the Missouri-Mississippi connected the Southern Confederation to that central state. The port city of St. Louis and the rail town of Michigan City thus became rivals for Indiana leadership, the result of linkages to the two larger confederations to the east.[10] By 1837 it was clear that the contest had been won by the N.C., which was beginning to dominate business in every corner of the C.N.A. Space does not permit a lengthy exposition as to the individual accomplishments of N.C. businessmen, but note should be taken of the role played by Cornelius Vanderbilt in the construction of the Northern Confederation Central Railroad, which had lines into Michigan City to the west, Portland to the north, Norfolk to the south, and a fleet of trans-oceanic cargo vessels which gave him domination of the Atlantic seaways. Malcolm McGregor, a Scots immigrant who arrived in America soon after the Rebellion, was destined to control a major industrial complex centered in Philadelphia, but financed from New York, which contained iron foundries, mines, and even mercantile establishments. "McGregorization" became a common word in the 1830's, standing for the accumulation of large firms and the domination of whole areas by a single man. In banking there were Junius Morgan, Jacob Little, Henry Cowell, and Samuel Slocomb, who along with such older men as Ezra Hopkins and Homer Young erected large and powerful banks along Broad Street in New York, the financial capital of North America. Morgan's Bank of New York opened its first Lon-

9. C.N.A. *Statistical Abstract*, p. 799.
10. Robert Small. *The Role of the Railroad in the History of the Northern Confederation* (Mexico City, 1960);

Andrew Sloan. *The Colossus of the East: The Rise of the Northern Confederation* (New York, 1952).

don branch in 1819, and within twenty years became a major factor in imperial as well as in North American banking, often working in conjunction with the Rothschilds. Little, one of the most daring businessmen of his day, had extensive interests in the Southern Confederation, and was often portrayed as the power behind the Country (Liberal) Party in Norfolk. Cowell's Fidelity Bank became the financier for the Vanderbilt lines, while Hopkins' Manhattan Bank financed his rivals. With reason, S.C. businessmen complained that, like their counterparts in Quebec, they were under the control of "the New York interests."[11]

Despite financial panics and depressions from 1815–19, 1829–31, and 1837–40, N.C. prosperity grew at what seemed a geometric rate. The statistics indicate the magnitude of the accomplishment.

*Selected Northern Confederation Statistics, 1810–1840*

| YEAR | RAILROAD MILAGE | EXPORTS (MILLION N.A. POUNDS) | IMPORTS (MILLION N.A. POUNDS) | IRON ORE (1,000 TONS) | BANK CAPITAL (MILLION N.A. POUNDS) |
|---|---|---|---|---|---|
| 1810 | 0 | 15 | 60 | 60 | 10 |
| 1815 | 0 | 20 | 71 | 91 | 21 |
| 1820 | 0 | 40 | 103 | 187 | 36 |
| 1825 | 156 | 71 | 128 | 240 | 59 |
| 1830 | 967 | 85 | 137 | 258 | 88 |
| 1835 | 2,009 | 101 | 151 | 365 | 121 |
| 1840 | 4,448 | 115 | 179 | 457 | 130 |

Source: C.N.A. *Statistical Abstract*, pp. 543, 687, 1179.

Statistics cannot fully indicate social progress, however, since they rarely reflect social unrest. The Northern Confederation had its share of difficulties in this period, the natural result of growth and dislocation concomitant with the rise of an industrial state.

The textile factories of New England, the iron foundries of Pennsylvania, and the railroad yards to be found throughout the N.C., employed large numbers of manual workers. Although better paid than their English counterparts, these men and women did not receive a large share of the fruits of their labor, and what was more, they knew it. The small businessmen, unable to compete against the large combines put together by McGregor and men like him, were not to share fully in the prosperity. When McGregor's Society for Industry came

11. Albert Todd. *Industry and Commerce in the N.C.: 1810–1840* (New York, 1943); Martin Denny. *The Northern Confederation in the Era of Harmonious Relations* (New York, 1967).

into an area, its competition either joined with it on disadvantageous terms or was destroyed, and this created a class of discontented, middle-class merchants and industrialists. Bankers in Philadelphia and other cities resented control from New York; farmers saw in the coming of industry their own destruction. Among groups like these arose a strong desire either to control or destroy the new industrial state being created in the Northern Confederation.[12]

From 1809 to 1813 the Northern Confederation Council was dominated by a group of delegates who largely represented the agrarian and small business interests. There were no parties in this period; none seemed necessary. Then, beginning in 1814, pro-big business delegates made their appearance. These men sponsored measures for high tariffs, aid to manufacturers in the form of subsidies, and laws making it easier to create private banks. By 1820, they had sufficient strength to form their own political party, called the Liberals, and their power was such that they were able to place their nominee, Daniel Webster, as Governor the following year. Webster was a skillful politician and a master manipulator. During the next two years, he steered through the Council the Tariff of 1822 (the highest up to that time); the Bank Bill of 1822, which lowered the standards for the establishment of banks; the Internal Improvements Bill of 1823; and the Harbors Act of 1823, a measure designed to improve New York and Boston ports with Confederation grants. The crowning touch was his establishment of the Bank of the Northern Confederation, a central bank modeled on the Bank of England, which had the power to manipulate the currency, usually to the advantage of the industrial class.[13]

Webster's successes led to the formation of a rival political party, called the Whigs, or more commonly, the Conservatives. From the first the Conservatives were poorly organized and without a clear-cut philosophy of their own, aiming instead at the destruction of the Liberals. The farmers who provided the backbone for the Conservatives had little in common with the urban workers and small businessmen who were also in their ranks, but could agree with them that the Liberals represented a threat to their way of life.

The Conservatives took control of the Council after winning the elections of 1825, but having done so, were unable to put forward a rational program or organize their forces to continue receiving popular support. Their manipulation of the banking system was a major cause

12. Burgoyne Garner. *Origins of the Conservative Party in the Northern Confederation* (New York, 1929); James McCormick. *The Anti-Liberals: Their Origins* (New York, 1967).
13. Daniel Webster. *The Program for Progress* (New York, 1838), pp. 109–138; Thomas Rivers. *Daniel Webster and His Confederation* (New York, 1970); James Ripley. *The Webster Legacy: The Creation of an Industrial Commonwealth* (New York, 1967).

of the 1829–31 depression, after which the Liberals won a majority in the Council. Conservative Governor Martin Van Buren was now replaced by Webster once again. Thus, the political life of the N.C. was paradoxical. The Liberals were a minority party with a distinct philosophy and vision of the future, capable of formulating and carrying through a clearly defined program. The Conservatives were a majority party, but because of loose organization and conflicting elements could not take advantage of their brief moments of Confederation power. With a responsible minority and an irresponsible majority, political life in the Northern Confederation was both dangerous and shaky.[14]

It was also frustrating, particularly for the small farmers and unskilled workers, many of whom were Conservatives. After the 1829–31 depression, both groups turned to non-political avenues to redress grievances. The workers organized the Grand Consolidated Laborers' Union, which pressed for better living conditions and wages, and called for a radical transformation of society in which the workers would control the factories and railroads. The farmers wanted currency inflation, an end to the Bank of the Northern Confederation, and anti-creditor laws, and toward these ends, they formed the Freeholders' Alliance. Both also engaged in political activities, at times within the Conservative Party, but most of the time on their own. Each was capable of violence, as was shown during the wave of strikes in 1834 and the assassination of Webster by Matthew Hale, an embittered bankrupt worker, in 1840.[15] The Northern Confederation was able to survive such violence, but the threat of insurrection was never absent.

The Era of Harmonious Relations saw impressive growth and apparent prosperity in the Southern Confederation, but as in Quebec, Indiana, and the Northern Confederation, beneath the shiny facade lay several serious problems that went unresolved.

The facade itself was constructed of cotton, which was also the heart of the S.C. economy. Production, acreage, and other related statistics rose sharply from 1810 to 1837, but at the same time, so did total indebtedness, investment in slaves and the slave trade, and—after 1839—manumission fees. The S.C. could rightly claim to be the most valuable part of the C.N.A. in terms of earnings of foreign currencies. While the Northern Confederation ran a perennially unfavorable balance of trade from 1810 to 1838, S.C. cotton exports alone provided more than adequate funds to pay for their own state's imports. Pros-

14. Thomas Ripley. *The Political Structure of the Northern Confederation in the Mid-Nineteenth Century* (New York, 1967); Hugh Scott. *Giant in Chians: Van Buren and the Conserva-* *tives* (Mexico City, 1960).
15. Andrew Shepard. *The Northern Confederation in the Violent Years, 1835–1839* (New York, 1945).

perity could be seen in the brilliant social scene in Norfolk, Charleston, and Cornwallis, the impressive plantations of Virginia and the Carolinas, and the huge estates of Georgia. There was, too, the large, modern, and well-equipped S.C. Navy; in 1830 it was second only to that of Britain in size, and was generally considered the best in the world in terms of efficiency and power. To the casual observer, the S.C. appeared the most powerful state in the C.N.A., and its natural leader.[16]

### *Selected Economic Statistics, Southern Confederation, 1810–37*

| YEAR | COTTON PRODUCTION (1,000 BALES) | SLAVES (1,000) | FREE POPULATION (1,000) |
|------|------|------|------|
| 1810 | 180 | 590 | 2,998 |
| 1815 | 249 | 619 | 3,267 |
| 1820 | 408 | 770 | 3,498 |
| 1825 | 540 | 832 | 4,003 |
| 1830 | 759 | 1,098 | 4,443 |
| 1835 | 998 | 1,348 | 4,972 |
| 1837 | 980 | 1,449 | 5,369 |

Source: C.N.A. *Statistical Abstract*, pp. 554, 890, 1253.

Behind what one historian has called "the cotton curtain" lay deep problems, however, and apparent strengths were actual weaknesses. The cotton culture was hard on the earth and on men. By 1831 the S.C. was running out of good cotton land, and much of the soil along the eastern coast was already eroded, producing poorer crops each year. Virginia, the leading producing area in 1818, was the first to fall behind, and then came declines in the Carolinas. After 1825, only Georgia showed substantial increases every year, and that colony became the key to the S.C. late in the decade. But even Georgia had problems, as by 1837 the last great area for cotton culture had been taken, with no more acreage in sight. In that year, too, Jefferson passed the S.C. in total cotton production, and the price of its product was slightly below that of the S.C. Cotton was still the major C.N.A. crop and earner of foreign currencies, but its days as such were numbered.[17] Caught between the fast-rising industrial giant to its north and the vigorous Jeffersonians to its west, the Southern Confederation

16. Sir Joshua Hendly, writing of his travels through the S.C. in 1833, said, "The people are cultured and friendly, the land is rich, and the climate near perfect. The Southern Confederation seems destined to control the continent, and become the rival of the most powerful states of Europe." Sir Joshua Hendly. *Travels Through the Southern Confederation in the Winter of 1833* (London, 1835), p. 593.
17. John Snodgrass. *Cotton as a Factor in the Southern Confederation* (New York, 1965), pp. 147–49.

was a rich but troubled state by 1837, and suffered greatly in the depression of that year.[18]

Cotton required large numbers of slaves for its cultivation, and the slave population of the S.C. rose sharply from 1810 to 1836. In the former year, one of every six people in the S.C. was a Negro slave; by 1836, the ratio was slightly less than one in four. Slave insurrections had become commonplace, with over six hundred individual uprisings recorded from 1810 to 1836. The most important of these, Howard's Rebellion, struck every major plantation in the Carolinas and Virginia in 1815, and wiped out property valued at N.A. £ 20 million before the leaders were captured and killed. John Howard, an illiterate Virginia slave, vowed to kill every plantation owner or die in the attempt. He failed, but his example was followed by others. The Levering Conspiracy, led by Martin Levering and Sam Peck, two Georgia slaves, caused great consternation in 1821, and the Insurrection of 1829 resulted in the deaths of over 3,000 Negro slaves and 1,400 whites.[19] By 1832, many slaves refused to work in the fields, and large plantations became armed camps as the use of private armies grew.

Most S.C. leaders called for increased force to control the slaves, but a few thought emancipation might be a better solution to their problem. "Would that we were rid of the accursed Negroes," wrote Sir Malcolm Smith in 1834. "All would agree they are not worth the trouble of keeping. But we cannot kill them, or send them to Africa or Jefferson, or free them at present, for to do so would be to invite reprisals and perhaps destruction. The problem does not admit of resolution, but a cure must be found."[20] Smith went on to note that the S.C. Navy, the pride of the state, served no real purpose beyond protecting the slave ships and helping put down insurrections. The S.C. Army, already the largest in the C.N.A. and growing yearly, was necessary for the same reasons. The military budget was enormous, and the costs in terms of property losses due to insurrections was incalculable but surely its equal. The S.C. earned large amounts of money through cotton sales, but these profits were being used to create a police state, not to enrich the lives of the planters.

Some, like Alexander Stewart and Theodore Bailey, recognized this paradox as early as 1821, and organized the Anti-Slavery Society in Norfolk to find a solution to the problem. At first the Society attracted few supporters, but after the Levering Conspiracy, more joined. In 1825 the Anti-Slavery Society combined with other groups to form

---

18. *Ibid.*, pp. 243–48.
19. Theodore Holmes. *Slave Rebellions of the 1820s* (New York, 1945); Ricardo Rodriguez. *Slavery as an Issue in the Southern Confederation* (Mexico City, 1970).
20. Sir Malcolm Smith. *An Address to the People of the Southern Confederation* (Norfolk, 1834), p. 9.

the Southern Union, which was designed to unite all S.C. citizens opposed to slavery in a party dedicated to that end. The Southern Union was a success, and shattered political life in the Confederation.[21]

Prior to 1825, the S.C. had two major political parties, almost equal in size and power. The Country Party (Liberals after 1819) consisted of wealthy plantation owners, their allies in the cities, and professional men in most parts of the S.C. It supported low tariffs, improvements of waterways, and a large navy to protect the slave trade. The Farmers Party (Conservative after 1820) included small farmers, workers, and the few freed slaves. It called for higher tariffs, subsidies to industry, a limit to the size of plantations, and smaller expenditures for the armed forces. Neither party showed much concern about the slavery issue until the rise of the Southern Union, but that organization's power and support was such that both were obliged to respond.

The leader of the Liberals was John Calhoun of Georgia, who in 1829, in the wake of the Insurrection, delivered his famous Defense of the Realm speech in Norfolk. Calhoun began by noting that without cotton, the S.C. would be a poor and backward area. Slavery might have been a mistake, he conceded, but now it was a fact, and had to be accepted as such. "Those who call for an end to slavery, offer us no way of accomplishing such a desired end. Jefferson will not purchase them; that nation has a surplus at present. They cannot be sent back to Africa; no nation has that many ships. Nor can they be massacred; our esteemed friends would not go so far, and neither would any sane or humane man. We cannot give the slave his freedom, for without the restraints of civilization they would either destroy themselves or us. No, gentlemen, the institution must remain as it is." Calhoun then went on to suggest an alliance of like-minded men in the S.C., N.C., and Indiana. "Ours is not the only state with such difficulties, and our critics elsewhere had best cleanse their own stables before turning to ours. What of the Indians of Indiana? The common laborers of the Northern Confederation? And the French-speaking population of Quebec? Surely they have complaints as worthy, if not more so, than the Negroes of the S.C. I would submit that the average slave in Georgia is far better off than his counterparts elsewhere in the Confederation of North America, or indeed, the world." Calhoun ended his address with a call for unity among the Liberal Parties of all the states, to defend the *status quo* against its enemies.[22]

Calhoun's plea was rejected by Willie Lloyd of South Carolina,

21. George Caldwell. *Free Men in a Slave State: The Origins of the Southern Union* (New York, 1964).

22. John Calhoun. *Defense of the Realm and Other Essays* (Norfolk, 1845), pp. 23–40.

leader of the Conservatives. First Lloyd noted that Calhoun's depiction of the benefits of slavery did not fit the facts. "Slavery is the bane of our state," he concluded, "bleeding us at every occasion, destroying the fabric of our society, and making our slave and slaveholder alike less than men." Lloyd also denied that freedmen would necessarily revolt; such had not been the case among those few who had already obtained their freedom. Calling for an alliance with the Southern Union and the abolitionists of Britain, he claimed that "only through freedom for all can our state survive."[23]

The Liberals won the election of 1833, and Calhoun became Governor-General as well as Governor of Georgia. But the Conservatives regrouped, and by 1836 appeared on the point of success. It was then that the disastrous financial crisis of '37 struck, affecting every citizen and slave, Indian and worker, in the C.N.A.

---

23. Ernest Passman, *Lloyd of Carolina: A Political Biograph* (New York, 1965), pp. 156–57.

# 8

# THE CRISIS YEARS

LATE in 1835 London was hit by a financial crisis. The house of
Baring had overextended itself in India and the Near East, and
found itself in a precarious position. Investments in France were jeop-
ardized by an economic slowdown there, while Britain itself was in the
midst of a minor depression. All of London realized that several major
banks were insolvent, and this led to a panic on Lombard Street. Then,
on October 14, the Barings closed their doors, precipitating the worst
banking crisis Britain had ever witnessed. Before it was over, a dozen
private and public banks had shut down, and were it not for the skillful
use of Bank of England resources, the nation might have been bank-
rupted. As it was, the Liberal government of Prime Minister Lord
Thomas Tillotson was overthrown, and after new elections, replaced
by a Conservative-Reform coalition with Lewis Watson as Prime Minister.[1]

At first the London crisis did not effect the C.N.A. Then, in early
1836, British investment capital ceased entering New York, and the
banks there found themselves in danger of collapse. Always poorly
capitalized and rarely prepared for less than prosperity, the New York
financiers had had little experience with times of trouble. The Peoples'
Bank was forced to close its doors in March, and others followed, as
panic grew daily. The Manhattan Bank, the city's fourth largest, declared insolvency on April 15, and the rout was on in earnest. On
May 1, Jacob Little closed down his office and fled to Mexico. Soon
after is was discovered he had embezzled more than N.A. £20 thousand from his firms, many of which were in the S.C.[2]

The financial paralysis in New York quickly spread throughout
the Northern Confederation, where capital-short firms closed by the

1. Arthur Watkins. *The Baring Crisis
of 1835* (London, 1910); George Andrews. *Business Cycles in Nineteenth
Century Britain* (London, 1959), pp.
281–310.

2. Paul Brooks. *Jacob Little and the
Panic of 1836* (New York, 1967);
Esther Kronovet. *New York in the
Crisis Years: 1836–1837* (New York,
1960).

hundreds. Unemployment grew steadily in the Massachusetts manufacturing centers as well as the Pennsylvania foundries and mines, and in the port cities of New York and Philadelphia. Indiana agriculture and industry, financed in large part from New York, felt the effects of panic, and by early 1837, that confederation too was in serious economic straits. The Southern Confederation also suffered, but not so much as her sister confederations. Although the price of cotton declined, sufficient demand existed to enable the plantation owners to survive the debacle. However, in the S.C. as elsewhere, good times were over and a period of hardship began. Dramatically and harshly, the Era of Harmonious Relations ended, to be replaced by a time of troubles, social unrest, and threats of rebellion.[3]

The situation was bad in Indiana, where the general economic malaise was complicated by an Indian uprising led by Chief John Miller, a Christianized Osage who claimed to be both the Messiah and the ghost of Tecumseh. Miller promised a new heaven on earth, to come after the destruction of the whites, whom he claimed were agents of the devil. Thousands of Indians flocked to Miller's banner, and he began his "crusade" in 1839 by attacking Michigan City, seizing it on July 21 after a bitter two-week battle, and putting to death some 5,000 of its inhabitants.

News of the Michigan City massacre spread quickly, and reached Burgoyne within days. Viceroy Sir Alexander Haven called a hasty meeting of the Grand Council, which met on August 15 to deal with the uprising. All states agreed to the formation of a C.N.A. army to march on Michigan City and defeat Miller. One was organized, under the command of General Winfield Scott of Indiana, who himself had been a resident of Michigan City. Scott led his soldiers through the state with great determination, arriving at Michigan City on October 18, and engaging Miller's men the following day. The battle was short and brutal. Scott's army overran the inferior Indian force with ease, and proceeded to butcher the entire group, including Miller, in what was the most savage act of retribution in Confederation history.[4] The nation was shocked, but Scott emerged from the conflict a hero, and the massacre at Michigan City had been avenged.

Rebellion and bloodshed also struck Quebec. Louis Papineau, the leader of the French community, organized a resistance group known

---

3. Lady Jane Hargrove. *The Flaw in the Design: Suffering During the Crisis Years* (London, 1899).
4. At the official inquiry into the Battle of Michigan City, Scott stated he had attempted to restrain his troops, but they would not listen to him. Others claimed he had asked his officers to bring back no prisoners. The public chose to believe the latter story, although the court acquitted Scott of any wrongdoing. Colonel Harry Warner. *The Michigan City Inquiry: Scott and the Nation* (New York, 1906); Frank Cockrill. *What Happened at Michigan City?* (London, 1968).

as the *Patriotes*, which blamed the financial disaster on the New Yorkers and demanded a complete separation from the Confederation.
There had been earlier attempts at secession, but none had been taken
seriously or was well-organized. Paul Cerdan sought to rally the
French-speaking citizens during the Trans-Oceanic War, and Ribot
wrote of the need for separation as early as 1812.[5] Neither had much
success; Cerdan and Ribot were dull men, lacking glamour and the
kind of magnetism so admired in the French community. Such was not
the case with Papineau, who though quiet, inspired confidence and a
belief in his cause. In 1839, Papineau raised the *Patriote* flag in Mont
Michel and issued a call to arms. Some 3,000 men rallied to his banner,
and an additional 800 came from Nova Scotia. Together they descended on Quebec, and on September 21, entered the city. Governor
Henry Scott was prepared for the assault, and Papineau was met with
"a wall of lead and iron" as he entered the main gates.[6] Within an hour
the attackers had been crushed. The Papineau revolt ended as dramatically as it had begun, but fear of future insurrections remained.

The Northern Confederation was also visited by violence, of a
more sweeping but less dramatic variety. Just as the Indians in Indiana
and the French in Quebec considered themselves despised minorities,
so many urban workers and small farmers felt bypassed by the rapidly-
growing industrial civilization then being created in the cities. In 1826
a group of textile workers in Andersontown, Massachusetts, attempted
to form a trade union which would give them some power and leverage to use against the manufacturers. The organization was flabby, and
management reaction was strong and swift; the effort failed. During
the next decade other groups organized unions. Some were to include
all workers in a single factory, while a few—most notably the cord-
wainers, iron workers, and copper workers—were geared to fill the
needs of mechanics in special trades. Generally speaking, the former
group failed, while the skilled workers had a measure of success in
local bargaining.[7]

In 1835 Franz Freund, a recent immigrant from Austria, attempted to organize all workers in what he called "The Grand Consolidated Union of Producers." The Consolidated was to work for a more
liberal franchise which would enable workers to elect representatives
to the legislature, and perhaps, in time take over the governorship. In

5. John Reynolds. *Background for Rebellion: Quebec, 1800–1838* (New York,
1956).
6. Papineau, who died in the charge,
had not expected such massive opposition. His last words were, "Our cause
is just and will prevail. But flesh and

blood can do little against a wall of
lead and iron." Francois Papineau. *My
Father: His Cause Was Just* (Mexico
City, 1854).
7. William Reuss. *The Origins of
Unionism in the N.C.* (New York,
1950).

addition, Freund called for government regulation of key industries such as shipbuilding, railroads, and textiles, and heavy taxes on profits, the moneys to be used to improve the living standard of the workers. Freund called his proposal the "Two Pronged Fork." "The history of unionism in the past has shown we have little power in the face of determined opposition. The government, however, may be made a stronger tool than the old unions. We must take control of the government, and through it the factories, and in this way, we may live as human beings rather than as cattle."[8]

The Consolidated had little success at first. Freund was scholarly rather than dynamic, and his foreign accent aroused mistrust in worker circles. Had not the depression occurred when it did, the Consolidated would have doubtless failed. But massive unemployment, the inability of Governor Webster to instill confidence in the N.C., and growing hardship in urban areas gave the Consolidated a new lease on life. By 1839, the Consolidated had branches in every big city, and organizers in every major firm, and had even formed a political party, the Laborers' Alliance, which campaigned vigorously for local and state candidates in the election of 1839.

The election resulted in a decline in Liberal strength, but Webster was able to win a new vote of confidence and remained as Governor. Now the Laborers' Alliance joined with the Conservatives in opposition, and Freund sought passage of measures to alleviate suffering among his workers. But the distress was so great that many members of the Consolidated turned to more direct action. Taking the name of the Sons of Liberty, they went underground, and embarked on a program of terrorism against elected officials and manufacturers who cut wages and employment.

In the summer of 1840, the state was hit by a massive general strike, and several cities were dominated by mobs as Webster lacked sufficient troops to put them down. Then, on September 4, a radical worker by the name of Matthew Hale stabbed the Governor while he walked from the Hall of Justice to his home. Webster died three days later, and this became the spark that ignited the reaction. Private armies hired by manufacturers descended on Consolidated headquarters throughout the Confederation, killing and burning as they went. Henry Gilpin, who succeeded Webster, supported the repression, saying that "there is no room for violence in the N.C., but the situation is so critical that strong measures are needed."[9] Together with the N.C. Army, the private forces all but destroyed the Consoli-

8. Franz Freund. *The Work of Three Decades.* 2 vols. (New York, 1869), I, 452.

9. Henry Gilpin. *No Apologies Are In Order: My Term as Governor* (New York, 1860), p. 333.

dated and the Laborers' Alliance, many of whose leaders fled to avoid capture, and some of whom eventually emigrated to Jefferson City.

By March, 1841, the N.C. had suffered over 40,000 dead and 78,000 wounded, but peace had been restored. For the next three years Gilpin ruled the Confederation with an iron fist, suspending the Britannic Design in the name of safety. Not until the election of 1842, when a newly-revived Conservative Party won a sweeping victory at the polls, did the repression end. The new Governor, John Dix of New York, promised an administration of "healing and humanitarianism, in which the rights of all will be protected."[10] By then, too, the depression was over, and the demands of workers not as violent as they had been previously.

The Confederation had survived its worst crisis, but historians still debate the appropriateness of the Gilpin policies. All would agree, however, that his swiftness in response saved the N.C. from anarchy. His supporters view Gilpin as the savior of his state, and the father of the Burgoyne Conference. Gilpin's detractors note that the N.C. never regained its lost freedom, despite the attempts of Dix and his successors to restore the *status quo ante bellum*. The Northern Confederation would grow and prosper, but a price was paid for this prosperity. Of all the states, the N.C. had the worst record of violation of civil liberties and the most internal turmoil, and this too was part of the Gilpin legacy.[11]

The Crisis Years had their greatest effect on the Southern Confederation. In a way this was paradoxical, because change there was not accompanied by violence or caused by fear. No S.C. city had been in flames; what little bloodshed did take place was minor and required no massive outpouring of troops. More than one student of the subject has concluded that it was precisely this lack of bloodshed and fear that made change in the Southern Confederation possible. On the other hand, the echoes of this reform movement resound to this day, not only in the S.C., but throughout the Confederation and the world.

As has been mentioned, the price of cotton declined at the beginning of the Crisis Years. The large plantations were strong enough to

---

10. William Cocke. *John Dix: The Great Healer* (New York, 1905), p. 149.
11. The standard work in the field is Henry Gibbs. *The Gilpin Legacy* (New York, 1889). William Cocke's *Caesar in Broadcloth* (New York, 1910) is the strongest critique of the Gilpin administration and a scurrilous attack on the man. George Loring's *The Right Man: Gilpin in Command* (London, 1956) tends to exaggerate the Governor's abilities. Unfortunately, after more than a century, we still lack a "standard biography" of this important and complex man. See Henry Murray. ed. *Gilpin and Historians* (New York, 1970), for the most recent scholarship in the field.

survive bankruptcy, but the leveling off of the economy caused many problems related to the institution of slavery. Since the plantations were no longer expanding and production had stagnated, fewer slaves were needed than before. Owners of slave ships, with large capital investments both in vessels and African outposts, were now faced with a sharply declining price for slaves. A prime field hand, who went for N.A. £150 in the spring of 1835, sold for N.A. £30 by October, 1837. The best estimates we have for the cost of acquiring a slave in Africa and shipping him to the S.C. is N.A. £21. The price of slaves in the Norfolk market fell below that figure in February of 1838, rose slightly in April, and then declined to N.A. £19. By that time it was difficult to sell slaves at Norfolk or Jamestown, or even at Sparta in Georgia, since they were a glut on the market. Hatch and Sons, the major importer of slaves for the S.C., went bankrupt that year, and most others followed. The slave trade, once a flourishing business in the S.C., ground to a halt in 1839, and giant fortresses strung along the Slave Coast of Africa were abandoned.[12]

The situation became critical on some plantations, where the owners had to meet heavy overhead costs while at the same time receiving lower prices for their product. Most survived by cutting back on cotton production and turning their attention to vegetables and grains. Each plantation came to resemble a miniature feudal state by 1838, as commerce ground to a halt and its inhabitants had to accept a lower economic level than before.[13] The times were not so hard as to cause panic and despair, but sufficiently harsh to force the planters to take a long, hard look at their situations.

The largest investment for a plantation owner was his slaves. A person with 200 slaves in 1835 could reckon their worth to be in excess of N.A. £30,000, and himself a rich man by S.C. standards. By 1838 this investment was worth less than N.A. £4,000, and the planter would have come to realize the dangers inherent in such an investment. At the same time, the slaves were consuming more food and clothing than they produced in terms of pounds sterling. Clearly, slavery was a losing proposition, and the planters were open to suggestions as how to best rid themselves of this albatross.[14]

As before, Calhoun rose to defend the institution. He warned his countrymen to avoid quick decisions and harsh remedies. Speaking in

12. Roscoe Symes. *The End of the Slave Trade* (Norfolk, 1904); H. C. Hartwick. *Black Skin and Red Ink: Profits in the Slave Trade, 1820–1840* (New York, 1967), pp. 109–13, 145–46, 208–18.

13. Arthur Ruppert. *Georgian Feudalism* (New York, 1910).

14. Hartwick. *Black Skin and Red Ink*, pp. 339–43.

Sparta in August of 1838, Calhoun reminded his listeners of economic conditions only four years earlier, when slaves fetched a premium price on the market, and produced far more than their cost for their owners. The slowdown in business activity was surely temporary, he claimed, and would pass before long. If the S.C., in one way or another, tampered with the institution of slavery in the hope of alleviating its problems, it would rue the day for decades. "What kind of a people are we," he asked, "to be frightened into bartering away our way of life in a moment of temporary despair? Change the basic relationship between master and slave, and you will create an atmosphere of confusion and anarchy in our land that will never pass, and our decisions will haunt our ancestors to the end of their days."[15]

Lloyd responded effectively to Calhoun's charges. He wisely chose to forego the pleasure of reminding the S.C. that he had predicted disaster related to slavery a decade earlier. Instead he attempted to calm the fears of those who saw in manumission the end of civilized life in the Confederation. "What is the essential difference between the relationship of master and slave on the one hand, and that of employer and laborer on the other?" he asked. His answer was short and to the point. "In the former case, the master is obliged to bear all of the responsibilities for the well-being of his property without being assured of a fair return on his investment. The employer, on the other hand, may actually pay less for his worker than does the slaveholder, and may rid himself of the worker when it suits his need or mood." With this, Lloyd called for the manumission of slaves within a period of ten years, the costs to be born by the central government.[16]

A combination of factors and events led to the adoption of the Lloyd proposals. In the first place, his speech was cheered throughout Britain, where for many years abolitionists had fought to end slavery. By 1835, they had achieved some power within the Tory Party and were prepared to use their leverage. When, in 1839, the Tories attempted to put through important banking and tariff legislation to end the depression, the abolitionists refused to vote for the measures unless the party as a whole came out in favor of manumission. This was agreed to, and Sir Duncan Amory, the new Prime Minister, called for an end to slavery in all areas of the Empire, promising financial as well as administrative aid in manumission programs.

Those in the S.C. who opposed slavery, but did not know how to finance manumission, were now given the weapon with which to at-

---

15. Frank Stroud. "Calhoun in Defeat: The Lost Cause of '39." *Annals of the Southern Confederation.* Vol XXXVI, No. 5 (April, 1889), pp. 90–92.

16. John Pritchard. *William Lloyd: The Southern Emancipator* (New York, 1956).

tack the slaveholders. In 1840, Lloyd proposed the payment of N.A. £35 per slave to any and all slaveholders who would accept the price, the money to be raised through the sale of "manumission bonds" both in the C.N.A. and Britain. This offer was to be open until January 1, 1842, after which time all slaves would be freed, with the payment of N.A. £32 per slave made to the owners. The Lloyd bill provided for the gradual education of the former slaves, and in other ways arranged for their incorporation into white society. A little noticed clause, inserted by James Philipson, stated that freedmen would be bound to their plantations until their period of education was over. In time, of course, the "free bondage" proposal would become the key to the whole program, and provide the S.C. with a new form of slavery, more subtle but just as exploitive as the old, which lasted for another two generations.[17]

After bitter wrangling and amid warnings of doom, the Lloyd bill passed the Council and was ratified by the Viceroy on May 16, to go into effect immediately. During the week prior to the signing there was talk of revolution and anarchy in the S.C., but the day came and went with little dislocation. Within six months, fully half the planters had accepted the manumission program, and before the deadline of January 1, 1842, almost all the slaves had been granted their freedom.

There was much celebration in abolitionist circles in London at news of the passage of the Lloyd bill, and the S.C. was viewed as an enlightened and progressive state. Not for many months would the London abolitionists grasp the meaning of the change in America. Few slaves who were granted their freedom were permitted to leave the plantations. Even had this not been the case—had the planters been willing to allow their former slaves complete and unqualified freedom —they would have remained on the plantations. The depression was still effecting the S.C. in 1841, and there were few jobs to be had in the coastal cities, or even in the Northern Confederation, had the freed slaves been able to migrate to that area. In the words of a major historian of the abolitionist movement in the Empire, "The Southern Confederation slaves exchanged one form of slavery for another. Prior to passage and enforcement of the Lloyd bill the slaves knew what their status was, and were able to mount impressive revolts against the system. Now that freedom was theirs in form, if not in fact, there seemed no reason for revolt. Thus, the planters, many of whom had opposed manumission, now found themselves with more money than they had had since 1835, less responsibility, and for the first time in a century, without the fear of slave revolts. One might easily say that

17. *Ibid.*, pp. 643–48.

the Lloyd bill did not grant freedom to the slaves, but rather to their masters."[18]

By the summer of 1841 it was clear the four major states of the C.N.A. had suffered much in the depression, and that all had or could expect similar problems in the future. Calhoun had failed to convince the planters of his state of the correctness of his proposals, but the ideas first set forth in 1829 in his Defense of the Realm speech had proven an accurate and important analysis of the problems of the entire C.N.A. The Indians of Indiana, the French-speaking population of Quebec, the workers and small farmers of the N.C., and the newly freed Negroes of the S.C. were indeed common threats to the existence of ruling groups in all states.

With this in mind, the leaders of the Liberal parties in the four confederations met at a convention in Concordia, North Carolina, in July of the year to map out a joint strategy. Led by Calhoun, General Scott, and Gilpin, the delegates quickly agreed that each must take a concern with affairs in the other states, and that a threat to one represented a threat to all; if nothing else, unity had resulted from the Crisis Years. The delegates also concluded that the Indiana experience could easily be duplicated elsewhere, and that a strong C.N.A. Army would be needed in the future. The economic difficulties of the Crisis Years were discussed, and the delegates agreed to the necessity of a common currency and inter-related banking system. Other matters—postal service, the problems of passports, etc.—all pointed the need for a more cohesive state. The Concordia meetings resulted in a greater show of unity than had ever existed in the C.N.A., and from that town, in August of 1841, came the call for amendments to the Britannic Design, which would result in a closer union and a more centralized nation.[19]

On learning of the Concordia meeting, Conservative Party leaders held a convention of their own, which met in Brant, Indiana, in September. Delegates from the four states were there, led by Charles Lefort of Quebec and Freund and Dix of New York. Like their Liberal opponents, they agreed on the need for greater unity. Freund in particular stressed the solidarity of workers and freed slaves. "Color and status have divided us in the past," he told the delegates. "Common persecution and suffering will unite us in the future." The Brant meet-

---

18. John Harnett. *A History of Slavery in the Southern Confederation* (London, 1935), pp. 879–80. It should be noted that the same phenomenon took place in the West Indies, where the slaves were also granted their freedom. Not for another generation would the West Indies freedmen begin to leave the sugar plantations and seek independent employment in the towns and factories. José Delgado. *The West Indies Freedman: A Case Study in Manumission* (Mexico City, 1967).

19. Alex Prentiss. *A More Perfect Union: The Concordia Accords* (New York, 1967).

ings, which concluded in October, also resulted in a call for a more united and stronger C.N.A. Thus, both segments of C.N.A. society were able to agree on a vehicle for change, even though they disagreed about who would occupy the driver's seat and where it would go.[20]

Viceroy Haven was informed of these desires in November, and agreed to submit them to the Crown. In London, Prime Minister Amory indicated sympathy for the proposals, as did Queen Victoria. Discussions were opened in the House of Commons on the subject in January, 1842, and the Government gave its assent to the convening of the C.N.A. Grand Council to consider amendments to the Britannic Design. The meetings were held in Burgoyne in June, and lasted three months, during which time the Liberals and Conservatives regrouped into the Unified Liberals and National Conservatives. Lloyd became the spokesman for the latter party, while General Scott was the major Unified Liberal leader. Although these two men differed on programs, they were able to work well together in formulating amendments, which were accepted by large majorities of the delegates.[21]

The amendments were few in number but far-reaching in importance. The first concerned the Grand Council, which was transformed from a high-toned social club into a powerful legislative instrument. There were to be 150 members of the revamped Grand Council, selected by popular vote of the citizenry every five years, and more frequently if a special election should be called by the Governor-General.[22] In addition, a Confederation Senate was created, which would act in a manner similar to the House of Lords. It would represent the confederations, with each having five members, but have little power.[23]

The second amendment revised the office of governor-general, which in the past had been little more than a figurehead position. Now the governor-general would be selected by a majority vote of the Grand Council, and would serve so long as he retained the confidence of that body. If no candidate had a majority, the Grand Council would continue to vote until one was achieved. In the interim, the Viceroy would serve as acting governor-general. Since it was expected that the governor-general would be the head of his party, and that his party would control the Council, he would be a powerful figure indeed, somewhat similar to the United Kingdom Prime Minister. The office

20. Francis James. *Decision at Brant* (Mexico City, 1967).
21. Dickinson Letts. *Origins of the Two Party System* (New York, 1923).
22. At first the qualifications were such as to allow the vote only to landholders. But this was changed in the Reform Bill of 1869 and subsequent measures, so that by 1898 the franchise was open to all males. Women received the vote in 1908.
23. Letts. *Origins of the Two Party System*, p. 292.

of viceroy would be retained, more as a symbol of the C.N.A.'s ties with Britain than anything else.[24]

Other amendments dealt with the C.N.A.'s relation to the mother country, affirmed Britain's right to call upon C.N.A. troops to defend the Empire, and maintained the established Anglican Church in the nation. These too were accepted without much debate, although there were some protests against the Church amendment.[25]

The Burgoyne Conference was an amazing meeting in many respects, as were its results and their ease in passage. The Queen and Amory both indicated their trust in the C.N.A. by raising few objections to the amendments; never before or since has an empire so willingly given its subjects such a degree of autonomy. It was another sign of Britain's maturity, and did not go unappreciated in the C.N.A., where loyalty to the Crown became even stronger. Three generations under the Britannic Design, and common problems during the depression, had united the C.N.A.'s peoples and strengthened the bonds with Britain. Then, as never before, they were a nation, rather than a mere conglomeration of peoples. "Prior to the Burgoyne Conference, the initials C.N.A. stood for the Confederation of North America; afterwards, they symbolized the Concord of North Americans." With these words, Fanny Lever indicated the importance of the Burgoyne Conference in C.N.A. history.[26]

Plans for revamping the Britannic Design began when the C.N.A. was still in the grips of depression; the amendments were accepted at a moment of renewed prosperity. Ironically, this was not the result of any legislative enactment, but rather the forces of nature.

The summer of 1841 was unusually harsh in continental Europe. Snow fell in Paris that June, and in Berlin in July. The frost was particularly severe in Russia throughout the summer, so much so that peasants believed the world was coming to an end, and many killed themselves in fits of religious frenzy that August.

The early winter of 1841 had its effects, too, on Europe's harvests, crippling all countries in a broad band from Ireland to the Urals. Europe turned to the C.N.A. for foodstuffs that autumn, and, in particular, to the wheatfields of the Northern Confederation and Indiana. North American wheat saved the lives of hundreds of thousands of Europeans during the winter and spring of 1841 and 1842. At the same

24. Prentiss. *A More Perfect Union*, p. 490.

25. The Anglican Church amendment was repealed in 1888, and while Britain can still call upon the C.N.A. for military help, she has never chosen to exercise this right, not even in the darkest days of the Global War.

26. Fanny Lever. *The Second Britannic Design* (New York, 1850), p. 56; Adolph Anderson. *The Rise of C.N.A.* (London, 1967); Valentine Edwardson. *The Burgoyne Conference of 1842.* University of Canberra Studies in Political Science. Vol. XXVI. (Canberra, 1960).

time, the funds paid for the grain restored liquidity to the C.N.A. banks, and this was quickly transmitted to the rest of the economy. By late 1842, it was evident that prosperity had returned to the C.N.A., and indeed to the western world as a whole. The six years of crisis and depression had ended, and as the C.N.A. surveyed the scene in 1842, it could see a strengthened land, which had transformed itself from a loosely-tied confederation into a strong nation. Slavery, an institution that had earlier seemed forever fixed in the S.C., had been ended, even though replaced by a more subtle form of servitude. Two major political parties, the Unified Liberals and the National Conservatives, had replaced the state parties of the pre-depression era.

General Scott campaigned against Governor Lloyd in the national elections of 1843. Lloyd called for a broad program of social reform, while Scott stressed the opportunities of the frontier and opposed what he called "Conservative paternalism." The return of prosperity, continued fear of insurrection, and increasingly poor relations with the Mexicans, resulted in a Unified Liberal victory at the polls, and with it the selection of Scott as the first Governor-General under the revised

*Party Strength in the First Grand Council, 1843*

| STATE | PARTY LOYALTY OF COUNCILMEN | |
| --- | --- | --- |
| | UNIFIED LIBERAL | NATIONAL CONSERVATIVE |
| Northern Confederation | 31 | 13 |
| Southern Confederation | 18 | 12 |
| Quebec | 9 | 15 |
| Indiana | 17 | 7 |
| Manitoba | 9 | 10 |
| Vandalia | 7 | 2 |
| | 91 | 59 |

Source: New York *Herald*, February 15, 1843.

Britannic Design. In speaking to the nation after his victory, Scott urged good will and predicted a glowing future for the C.N.A. Warning of dangers from Mexico, he nonetheless assured the people that "We are strong enough to defeat any enemy." He ended with the stirring words, "Now we are one. Our nation has survived a period of trial, and is stronger than ever before. There is no distinction between Indianan and Northern Confederationist, no disharmony of interests between Quebec and the Southern Confederation. These four states will help develop Manitoba, already a rapidly growing part of the Confederation. And all will defend Vandalia against those who would threaten her integrity. Now we are one."[27]

27. John Pritchard. *He Was First! The Governorship General of Winfield* Scott (New York, 1960), p. 209.

# 9

# THE UNITED STATES
# OF MEXICO

ON April 14, 1806, a detachment of Mexican soldiers surrounded Cuautla, apparently in search of several priests who were leading guerrilla activities in the area. As they entered the town, the soldiers encountered gunfire on two sides. Within minutes, forty-two Mexican infantrymen lay dead and wounded in the plaza. The Mexican Civil War had begun.

Initially, the war pitted those in Mexico City, who hoped to make Mexico a secular state, against a priestly faction which wanted the Catholic Church to have a strong voice in the government. José Morales, a full-blooded Indian who was the leader of the government forces, was a well-known, former college professor. He had been inspired by the rebels of North America, and in 1804, had joined Gigedo in his revolt against Spain. His arch-enemy, Miguel Hidalgo y Costilla, had been considered the "conscience of the revolution" in 1804, and at that time, the two had been good friends. Then, when Morales insisted on the separation of church and state, Hidalgo took his forces to the hills; his "army of clerics" controlled a good deal of northern Mexico by 1806, as well as having allies throughout the rest of the country. It was a Hidalgo contingent that was responsible for the successful ambush at Cuautla, which became the signal for uprisings elsewhere.[1]

The guerrilla attacks continued for twelve years, but were not truly disruptive of life or commerce. Hidalgo lacked sufficient men and material to mount a large-scale offensive against Mexico City, and was forced to rely upon hit-and-run tactics. After his death in 1809, the army of clerics was headed by Simon Figueroa, a man of great ego but small ability at war. Figueroa issued wordy broadsides against the enemy, but did little else. He was, however, a genius at concealment, and the government troops were unable to destroy the army of clerics,

---

1. Ortez. *The Mexican Civil War*, pp. 224–26.

who could melt back into the population, only to surface periodically for espionage and nuisance raids. Morales compared these attacks to the stings of mosquitoes which, though troublesome, could be born by a patient man.[2]

By 1815, however, Morales' patience was at an end. Determined to put a stop to the guerrilla activity, he issued warnings to the population that anyone found aiding the hidden clerics would be executed summarily. Then the *federales* from Mexico City entered the country's urban centers and embarked on a program of terror, killing wherever they went, excusing their actions as necessary in the light of Figueroa's provocations. The deaths reached a peak in March of 1816, when Figueroa claimed that over 5,000 peasants—men and women having no connection with the Civil War—were killed by the *federales*. He appealed to the outside world for aid in stopping the bloodshed. "In the name of humanity and the Holy Church," read one demand, "the people of Mexico must be freed from the tyranny of the murderous, immoral butchers of Mexico City."[3]

Figueroa's pleas went unanswered in Europe. Mexico seemed far away to the Continent concerned with talk of a new war between Austria and the Germanic Confederation. The C.N.A. similarly had become isolationist in this period. Only a few men, the most notable being Henry Wilkins of Georgia, thought the Confederation should intervene in the Mexican Civil War. A young Daniel Webster was intrigued by the possibility of war, but rejected the idea after some thought. Writing to his wife, he said, "Who knows what could come of our interests in Mexico? Four, perhaps even six, new states could be added to the Confederation if we joined to rid that unhappy land of those evil men who now control it. All the civilized world would applaud our entry on the side of Figueroa; none would complain if we made Mexico part of the C.N.A. after Morales was defeated. But what North American would bear the cost of such a campaign? How would we raise an army? Intervention in Mexico would suit Confederation interests, but unfortunately is impossible."[4]

Only Jefferson showed a keen interest in such an intervention. That nation had a long common border with Mexico, the Rio Grande, and a deep, personal interest in the fighting. Jefferson was already a large nation, and soon would equal the Southern Confederation in cotton production. Its small population was vigorous and expansionist, appetites in Jefferson City having been whetted by the Trans-Oceanic War.

---

2. José Morales. *My Cause Is Mexico.* 4 ed. (New York, 1902), pp. 339-48.
3. Simon Figueroa. *La Vida de Libertad (The Life of Liberty)* 13th ed. (London, 1955), p. 490.
4. Rivers. *Daniel Webster and His Confederation*, pp. 145-50.

Jefferson still had vast areas of open land, so its leaders could not claim that expansion was necessary for the national good. Still, Hamilton called for "continental destiny" in 1815. Viewing events across the river, he noted that as the Mexicans were unable to solve their problems, intervention was necessary to stop the bloodshed. "Then, at peace and under proper supervision, the land may prosper. Mexico is rich in minerals, has soil suited to cotton, and may flourish, given wise government." Even then, it was clear Hamilton meant Jeffersonian management; the words could hardly be misconstrued.[5]

In 1815, Hamilton sent John Quincy Adams to Mexico City to seek recognition for his nation.[6] Morales, who himself had grandiose visions of a Mexican nation stretching from the Pacific to the Mississippi, refused to meet with Adams, sending instead his young secretary, Pablo Gonzales, to greet the Jeffersonian. Apparently Adams and Gonzales had words, for the next day the *Diario de Mexico* published a bitter denunciation of Jefferson in general and Adams in particular. With great difficulty and some threat to his life Adams left Mexico, and arrived in Jefferson City a month later to tell Hamilton of what had transpired.[7] Hamilton immediately met with the two other Governors, who at that time were John Gaillard and James Monroe, and discussed the rebuff.[8] Together they agreed to issue a declaration of war, the cause to be an insult to Jefferson and the continued violence in Mexico.

On May 16, 1816, Hamilton addressed the Chamber, with Monroe and Gaillard on either side. "We fight for civilization," he told the representatives. "We cannot permit the slaughter of innocents to continue. Even now blood flows through the streets of most Mexican towns and cities, her villages are in flames, and her people oppressed. We go to Mexico not as conquerors, but as friends, to end this destruction which has been allowed to continue for too long."[9]

In 1816 the population of Mexico was some 3 million, while that

5. Greeley. *The Continentalists*, pp. 330-35.
6. Mexico never recognized Jefferson, claiming it to be part of New Spain, and therefore devolving to Mexico when that nation was born. In sending Adams on his journey, Hamilton claimed he wanted to normalize relations with Mexico. Publication of the Adams diary in 1856, however, proved that Hamilton wanted the mission to fail, thus offering an excuse for a war declaration. John Quincy Adams. *The Diary of John Quincy Adams* (Mexico City, 1856), Vol. 3, pp. 192-245 passim.
7. Thomas Mifflin. "The Adams Mission and its Consequences," *Journal of Mexico*, XXXVI (June, 1934), pp. 111-28.
8. Apparently Monroe was told of Hamilton's plans, and knew of his hopes for a failure of the Adams mission. Gaillard was not privy to such information, and supported the war for patriotic reasons. When he learned of this deception, Gaillard resigned his post and joined the Liberty Party. Lewis Reins. *John Gaillard: Nobility in Chains* (Mexico City, 1943), pp. 438-59.
9. Alexander Hamilton. *The War With Mexico* (Jefferson, 1818), pp. 39-41.

of Jefferson was less than 130,000. The Mexican Army was experienced, and numbered 85,000. Jefferson's citizen militia had fewer than 25,000 whites and 980 slaves, who served in supporting roles. Moreover, the Jefferson army and leadership had not been tested by the fires of war; a few skirmishes in the Trans-Oceanic War and against the Indians were all the army had to its credit. Given these facts, Hamilton's declaration of war seemed foolhardy when viewed from Burgoyne or London.[10]

It was soon evident, however, that the small, tough Jeffersonian army was more than a match for the Mexicans. There were several reasons for this. In the first place, a large portion of the Mexican army was busily engaged in fighting Figueroa and his clerics, and never met the Jeffersonians in combat. The Mexican army was well-trained, but its morale was low after a decade of civil war. On their part, the Jeffersonians were resourceful, well-equipped, and blessed with capable leaders. Colonel Andrew Jackson, a veteran of the eastern campaign of the Trans-Oceanic War, proved his genius in several battles early in the war. When General Horatio Conyers, the leader of the Jeffersonian brigades, was killed in the battle of the Rio Grande during the first week of the war, Jackson took charge of the army, and inspired it to march to Mexico City. He defeated the Mexican General Carlos Mejía in the battle of Seven Forks in November, after which the road to Mexico City was open. On February 6, 1817, the Jeffersonians, now joined by the army of clerics, marched into the capital. The campaign had lasted eight months, and resulted in the deaths of fewer than one thousand Jeffersonian troops.[11]

Later on, Figueroa would assert that the Jeffersonians could not have won a single battle without his aid, but, at the time, he had nothing but praise for the invading army. He heaped rewards on Jackson, who, in turn, supported the Figueroa claim to the presidency. Morales, who died a natural death two months before the end of the war, was now relegated to the position of villain, and statues of him were ripped down and destroyed. For years the clerics and their supporters had been oppressed by the *federales*, and now they sought and found revenge. Mexico underwent the worst purge in the continent's history during the first three months after liberation. All those who had even the remotest connection with the Morales regime were hunted down, tried by hastily assembled courts, and executed. Figueroa claimed he could do nothing to stop the blood bath, but, in reality, he encouraged it. Jackson recognized this, and in June, stepped

---

10. Clark Croly. "Contemporary Opinion of Jeffersonian Strength Before and During the Mexican War," *Journal of Mexico*, LI (January, 1948), pp. 23–49.

11. Leland Commons. *Jackson and the Mexican Campaign* (Mexico City, 1951).

in to take command of the country. Leading a small force of Jeffersonians to the presidential palace, he placed Figueroa under arrest and
named himself provisional president of Mexico.[12] Then the Jeffersonian army, cooperating with dissidents and moderate *Figueroaistas*,
ended the killings. For the first time since the Republic had been
established in 1805, Mexico was at peace. But the nation's future was
still in doubt.

Hamilton made no secret of his plan to unite Mexico and Jefferson, and the Continentalist Party supported him in this desire. "We
must not shrink from our destiny," he told a crowd at Lafayette in
May. "Jefferson must lead the peoples of Mexico to greatness, and will
do so through sacrifice and prudence."

Even as he spoke, the Liberty Party rallied to oppose him. Led by
Gaillard who had defected, William Bibb, and Eligius Fromentin, they
prepared to challenge Hamilton and Monroe in the gubernatorial elections of that year. Hamilton selected Jackson to fill the vacancy caused
by Gaillard's resignation, and prepared to do battle at the polls. He
died a week before election day, however, and the Continentalists, in
disarray, replaced him on the ballot with Josephus Carter, while Jackson, leaving Colonel Barton Kelly in Mexico City as his deputy, hastened to return to Jefferson City.

The election of 1818 took place before Jackson could arrive at the
capital. The combination of Jacksonian glamour and the memory of
the departed Hamilton, added to the fantasies of great-power status,
led to a Continentalist sweep in October. The Jackson-Monroe-Carter
government took power in December, with Monroe the senior executive, but Jackson acknowledged as the leader of the executive
branch.[13]

Andrew Jackson was clearly one of the most important figures in
nineteenth century history, as well as the "third founder" of his nation.[14] He had all the dash of Burgoyne, the ability to make difficult
decisions forcefully that characterized Hamilton, and the personality
and charisma of Lloyd. For two decades he dominated his country's
political history, reshaping the small, tough nation he founded into the
great power it was when he died. "Greene was intelligent, Hamilton
was magnificent, but Jackson was superlative," was the judgment of
one historian,[15] while another thought Jackson to be "the leading

12. Albert Hawes. *Jackson of Mexico: A Hero's Story* (Mexico City, 1956), pp. 420–32.
13. George Tinker. *The Monroe-Jack-son-Carter Administration* (New York, 1967).
14. The "first founder" was Greene, while Hamilton was considered the "second founder." Alice Rich. *Jackson: The Third Founder* (Mexico City, 1967).
15. Miles Vining. *Andrew Jackson: A Study in Courage* (Mexico City, 1970), p. 598.

figure in a century of talent."[16] On the other hand, he was also called "the greatest slaver in human history,"[17] and the man who "caused more misery than any person since Genghis Khan."[18]

Andrew Jackson was born in the Carolina area of the Southern Confederation in 1767. As a child during the Rebellion, he was held captive by the British and confined to a stockade, an event he never forgot and an insult he never forgave. Jackson would remain strongly anti-British for the rest of his life, and in practical terms this meant unalterable opposition to any friendly contacts with the C.N.A.

Jackson was only thirteen years old when Greene organized the Wilderness Walk. He persuaded the John Collingswood, a Virginia family that was making the trip, to take him along. Collingswood allowed Jackson to join his wagon, and came to consider the young man as a son. Jackson aided Collingswood on his plantation, which was twenty miles north of Arnold, and by the time he was twenty-five was in charge of the place, which included 200 slaves. Later on Jackson was elected district judge, representative, and mayor of Arnold. He also joined the militia, serving briefly in the Trans-Oceanic War and then becoming commander of the 14th Dragoons, considered the cream of the Jeffersonian Army. His exploits in the Mexican War have already been discussed. In 1819, when he took the oath as second governor, Jackson was fifty-one years old, a tall, vigorous man, capable of flying into swift rages, but at the same time well-known for his tenderness toward children and his deep love for his wife, Sarah, who was Collingswood's youngest child.[19]

From the beginning it was evident Jackson had no intention of relinquishing Jefferson's position in Mexico, and that he would attempt instead to solidify his grip on that country. During the first year of the Monroe-Jackson-Carter Administration, however, Jackson was content to remain in Jefferson City, increasing his power and support, and organizing for the future. By 1820 he was in full command of the government, with Carter satisfied to take care of administrative details while Monroe was charged with the problems of foreign affairs.

On February 1, an insurrection erupted in Mexico City, as former Morales supporters tried to overthrow the provisional government. The *coup* was aborted with ease, but Jackson thought it necessary to go to Mexico City himself to oversee the situation. He arrived there on May 4, and took up residence in the presidential palace. A month later, he sent word to Jefferson City that he would remain in Mexico until

16. John Heflin. *The U.S.M.: The Second Stage* (New York, 1959), p. 308.
17. Archie Jenkins. *The Last to Go: U.S.M. Slavery* (London, 1949), p. 617.
18. James Strawbridge. *Butcher Jackson* (New York, 1961), p. 2.
19. Albert Hawes. *Jackson the Man* (Mexico City, 1952).

relations between Jefferson and the conquered area had been "made more reasonable than they are at present." Speaking through Carter, he asked for a new constitutional convention, from which would emerge a permanent union of Jefferson and Mexico. As might be expected, the Liberty Party strongly opposed this move, but lacked the votes to prevent it. On June 15, the Chamber accepted Jackson's proposal in principle, and then voted to dissolve, to be regrouped on September 22 as a constitutional convention in Mexico City.

The Mexico City Convention of 1819 included not only Jeffersonians, but former Figueroaistas who supported Jackson, non-voting delegates from the Indian tribes, and observers from other Mexican factions. None except Monroe and Carter seemed to know what Jackson planned for the Convention, but all agreed he could have almost anything he wanted—perhaps even a monarchy.

Eschewing all pretense and politicking, Jackson addressed the Convention in blunt terms on September 28, and in a series of swift sentences outlined his proposals. In the first place, Mexico and Jefferson would be united as a single nation; under no circumstances would the Jeffersonians leave the conquered land, but on the other hand they did not mean to stay as occupiers. Secondly, Jackson meant to preserve local customs whenever possible; the new government would not try to shape the Mexicans into the Jeffersonian mold. When asked whether this meant the new nation would be bilingual, Jackson said it did. Slavery would be guaranteed in the nation, which would also maintain a strong army and navy and be headed by a strong executive. Having said this, Jackson turned and walked from the platform without looking back. That night, at a dinner, he offered a toast. "Gentlemen," he said, "I give you the United States of Mexico." Even then, it was assumed the delegates would hasten to do Jackson's bidding, and so they would.[20]

The United States of Mexico, as organized at the Mexico City Convention, consisted of six states, of which only Jefferson had a dominant Anglo-Saxon majority. The others, carved from Mexico, were: California, Arizona, Mexico del Norte, Durango, and Chiapas. Each would have a regional capital which were (in order) San Francisco, Sangre Roja, Conyers, Torreón, and Palenque. In addition, there was the capital district, Mexico City, which would be the center of the new nation and the seat of its administrative apparatus.

The power distribution in the new government may best be discussed under two headings: the states and the central government on

20. Pedro Cordovan. *Jackson at the*     (Mexico City, 1962), pp. 293-304.
*Convention: The Strokes of Genius*

the one hand, and the executive and legislature in Mexico City on the other.

Each state was instructed to hold elections and draw up its own "charter." There were, however, several limits on their freedom, some of which were outlined in Jackson's September 28 address. In addition to accepting slavery, the states had to include strong guarantees of property rights in their charters, and statements that any law passed by a state legislature could be superseded by federal law or executive action. All cases tried in state courts could be appealed to the Mexico Tribunal, a type of supreme court. Finally, all taxes would be levied and collected by the central government, to be redistributed to the states according to need. Naturally, no state was permitted an armed force other than the local police. Thus, in spite of Jackson's pledge to protect local customs and traditions, it was evident from the first that the state governments would have little power.

Each state was permitted to formulate its own relationship to established religion, with the understanding that all religions would be free to function. Although this provision was opposed by the Catholic hierarchy and many Figueroaistas, it came to be accepted, especially when Chiapas, Durango, and Mexico del Norte wrote charters granting the Catholic Church special rights.

The central government consisted of three branches, and in general resembled the Jeffersonian forms. But there the similarity ended. Instead of a tripartite executive, there would be a single person selected, to be elected by the Senate for a six year term. The executive, known as the President, would have the power to call new elections when he felt them necessary, be commander-in-chief of the armed forces, and have a veto over laws passed by the legislature, which could be overridden by a two-thirds vote.

The legislature, known as Congress, consisted of two houses, the upper (Senate) representing the states, the lower (Assembly) based on a complicated formula but essentially representing the people.

There would be four senators from each state, selected by assemblies of the states by whatever means they thought best. The Senate would have the right to introduce bills relating to external affairs, and would also act as a consultative arm of the presidency. The Assembly consisted of one hundred representatives, reapportioned among the states every ten years. Only free men were permitted to vote, and since peons were not considered free under Mexican law, this limited the franchise to a virtual handful of people, at least in the early years. Because apportionment was based on free population, it meant that Jefferson, with a small population, would have thirty-four seats in the 1820 Assembly, while the other states, with over ten times the Jeffersonian population, would have the remainder. The Assembly would introduce all domestic legislation, but a measure would have to pass two times, at a six month interval, before being sent to the Senate for consideration. Thus, the Assembly was clearly in a subordinate position to the other branches of government.[21] Furthermore, all governmental deliberations would be held in English, and this would prevent many important Mexicans from taking seats or participating fully in the first few years.

The judicial branch, the Mexico Tribunal, consisted of seven men; to qualify for a position required previous service either in the presidency or the Senate. They were chosen by the President and ratified by a majority vote in the Senate. The judges had life tenure unless suspended from office by a three-quarter vote of the Senate.

Opposition to the new constitution centered in the Liberty Party and the non-voting delegations. Gaillard argued that the Jeffersonians, having conquered an innocent people through subterfuge and force, now intended "to give tyranny the mask of republicanism." Bibb called for a more representative and powerful Assembly, while Fromentin thought the president "would be monarch in all but name, and that may follow in time." Augustín de Iturbide, a well-regarded former soldier and cleric who had fought alongside Figueroa and was now a leader of the church faction, was equally critical, but he recognized that Jackson could not be stopped, and tempered his observations with praise of the Jeffersonian, hoping to be included among his advisors. Similarly, representatives of the Navaho, Apache, Crow, and Mohave tribes tended to side with Jackson, while the more southerly Tlaxcalan, Tamualipec, Concho, and Opata were more outspoken in opposition.[22] In time Jackson would reward his followers and punish his opponents.

These critics did not prevent Jackson from having his way, and the Mexico City Constitution was ratified by the delegates with only a few minor changes. Then preparations were made for state and congressional elections, which took place on July 18 and August 12, 1821. The Continentalists were well organized and ably led by Jackson, while the Liberty Party, though attracting a majority of Mexicans to its side, did not have many registered voters in their corner. As a result, the Continentalists took command of the Assembly by a margin of 68 to 30 (with two members of the Indian Party elected from Mexico del Norte), and of the Senate, by a margin of 18 to 6. On September 5, the Senate elected Jackson first President of the U.S.M.

21. Curt Reinech and Henry Collins. *The Mexico City Constitution: An Analysis and Interpretation* (Mexico City, 1959).

22. Albert Hawes. *Jackson and the Mexican Indians: Partners in Opportunity* (Mexico City, 1958).

The vote, which was secret, was 21 to 3. Thus, three members of the Liberty Party, which strongly opposed Jackson, voted for him. Never again would party lines be breached in this fashion; one of the first laws passed by the legislature provided for open elections for the president.[23]

Jackson took office immediately, and surprised the nation by offering cabinet posts to Fromentin as well as to Iturbide, Chief Henry Smith (a Christianized Apache), and Miguel Montez, a leader of the Moralistas, a strongly anti-Jeffersonian group in Mexico City (not to be confused with a later group of the same name). Fromentin and Smith refused the nominations, but Iturbide was named Secretary for Religions while Montez became Secretary for Indian Affairs. Neither post was considered important, but were symbolic of Jackson's interest in creating a united nation of the two parts of the U.S.M.

For the next eighteen years, Jackson would lead his nation with vigor, and rule with an iron hand. His critics may have charged him with being anti-democratic and a despot, but they could not deny that he obtained results. On the other hand, the tradition of strong presidential leadership that Jackson established would haunt the U.S.M. for the rest of its existence.

---

23. Archie Jenkins. *And So We Began: The First Days of the United States of Mexico* (London, 1951).

# IO

# THE TAKING OF THE WEST

FROM the first, it was evident that Jackson meant to be an activist and expansionist President. His early career, his identification with the Continentalists in general and Hamilton in particular, and finally, his active role in forging the new Constitution, were the first steps in leading the U.S.M. into a period of national greatness.

An important part of his overall plan was to move the capital from Jefferson City to Mexico City, from a town dominated by the sons of the American rebels, to a large city with a majority Mexican population. The former Jeffersonians would be only a small minority in such a setting, open to obvious dangers of *coups* and the more insidious ones of acculturation. In changing the name of the state, he again demonstrated his vision; as conqueror, it had been assumed that Mexico would be submerged in Jefferson. Instead, Jackson adopted for his country, the name of the foe. To many, the concession seemed out of character; later on, it would be realized that this was Jackson's master stroke.

With remarkable foresight, Jackson knew that to have a nation of Mexicans controlled by a numerically smaller, though more energetic group like the Jeffersonians, would do damage to the best qualities of both peoples. In such a situation all Mexicans would be reduced to the status of a permanently occupied people. In time, this would lead either to rebellion or despair, and, in either case, the Jeffersonians would be the losers. Jefferson itself had too small a population to put down repeated insurrections, while a population of Mexicans without hope would be an insurmountable burden to the new state. Thus, Jackson gave the Mexicans genuine hope of a better future; he extended a modicum of power to a number of the Mexican and Indian leaders, intending to use them to control their own populations. As we shall see, he was generally successful in this policy.

By the same token, had Jackson incorporated Mexico into some form of "Greater Jefferson," the effect on the sons of the American rebels would have been shattering. Already, the Jeffersonians had compromised the philosophy that had taken them on the Wilderness Walk by becoming a nation based on a slave economy. Writers like Carl Markham and Frederick Reilly had attempted to rationalize slavery as part of the democratic tradition. They had not been wholly successful in their efforts, but on the eve of the Mexican War, Jefferson was well on the road to becoming a slave nation.[1] Greene had seen Jefferson as a new Athens; in reality, it more closely resembled Sparta. The war had served to increase Jeffersonian militarism and reinforce the white population's belief in its innate superiority, its destiny to rule over an "inferior" people.[2] By moving the capital to Mexico City, and calling the new nation the United States of Mexico, Jackson was serving notice to his countrymen. The enlarged nation would not be merely an extension and elaboration of Jeffersonian society, but would include Mexicans in significant roles, and Mexican and Indian ways would be accepted and valued.

It should be noted that little internal migration took place in the U.S.M. until the late nineteenth century. Thus, only Jefferson and, later on, California had significant Protestant populations; to this day, Jefferson remains the only one of the original six states with a Protestant majority. Jackson's perennial claim that the U.S.M. had little religious bigotry was true, but was more the result of fear than conviction. Faced with a huge Catholic majority, it was only natural the Jeffersonian Protestants would demand separation of church and state and religious freedom for all.

It is doubtful that any other man, Hamilton included, could have obtained Jeffersonian acceptance of the new nation, one which implied a partnership with brown-skinned peoples. Had his own party had its way, the new nation would have quickly become a totalitarian state controlled by the white Jeffersonian minority. Under Liberal leadership, the Mexicans would have controlled the nation, and the U.S.M. of 1850 might have resembled New Granada, Brazil, or the Argentine in its lack of progress and stability. Even with the acceptance of Jackson's program the nation had many problems; without his vision, the nation could not have survived a generation.

This is not to imply that Jackson believed the colored races the equal of the Caucasian. To the contrary, he told a close friend, Malcolm Brayback, that "If one people and race are to rule this land, it must be the Jeffersonians and the whites. This is not so because I happen to be of these peoples, but rather because only the Jeffersonian whites have the abilities, intelligence, and vigor for the task."[3] Jackson

---

1. Carl Markham. *The New Athenians* (Jefferson, 1820); Frederick Reilly was editor of the Jefferson *Argus* from 1818 to 1843. His writings may be found in Theodore Follows. ed. *Reilly: The Giant* (Mexico City, 1901).

2. See Reilly's editorials for June, 1819, in *Ibid*, pp. 56–79.
3. Malcolm Brayback. *Conversations with President Jackson: A Record of My Friendship with the Father of Our Country* (Mexico City, 1855), p. 294.

made no secret of his dismay of what he called "Mexican slovenliness."
He found the population "apparently unwilling or incapable of firm
action," while the Indians seemed to him "unable to adjust to the kind
of world we are living in at the present time. They are at the same
level of accomplishment as when Columbus first landed here. I do not
expect to change them."[4]

This did not mean, however, that Jackson would allow the Mexicans and Indians to be reduced to the level of slaves, used in the same
fashion as were the Africans in Jefferson. The President had a low
opinion of the Jeffersonian Negroes and their heritage, while he had
some admiration for aspects of Indian and Mexican culture. He conceded the Indians to be good fighters, and encouraged them to join the
Mexican army; the Negroes, he said, "are sluggish and quite simple,
good for nothing but field labor."[5]

Jackson divided the Mexicans into two groups. The largest of
these—the one that came to be known as "Mexicanos"—consisted of
Mexican Indians, usually Spanish-speaking, at times pagan, who were
centered in Chiapas and Durango. They had been exploited since the
Spaniards had arrived, and in New Spain were in a state of semi-bond-
age. The second group were the "Hispanos," descendants of the Spaniards who had conquered Mexico in the sixteenth century and who had
ruled the nation ever since. Jackson told Brayback, "In the veins of
some Mexicans flows Spanish blood, and glimpses of the conquistador
may be seen from time to time."[6] Jackson either did not know, or
refused to believe, the Hispanos and Mexicans had intermingled for
more than two centuries, and that few Hispanos could claim to be
"pure blooded" in his sense of the term. Nevertheless, he did make the
distinction, and attempted to form an alliance with the Hispanos, if not
for what he called "the future of civilization," for the obvious fact that
the "Anglos" of Jefferson needed allies, and the Hispanos were the
most obvious of these. Thus, the Anglo-Hispano alliance which controlled the U.S.M. through most of its history, and which created its
dominant culture, was fashioned in the Jacksonian era.

To men of the late twentieth century, Jackson remains an enigma.
In his attitude toward the Indians and Hispanos he represented the
most humane and Christian views that could have been expected from
a Jeffersonian, and for which he received much criticism from leaders
of his own party. On the other hand, Jackson was a staunch defender
of slavery, not only on economic grounds, but due to his utter disre-

---

4. *Ibid*, pp. 372, 397.
5. Speech at Seven Forks, May 8, 1837,
in Jefferson *Tribune*, June 2, 1837.

6. Andrew Jackson. *Our People: Views
and Observations* (Jefferson City, 1841).

gard of the Negro as a human being. Few Jeffersonians would have supported his aborted attempt in 1824 to enslave all free Negroes, even had it come to a vote; Jackson later observed that the one piece of legislation he was never to win, but which he felt necessary to Mexican greatness, was his 1826 bill to enslave all those who had more than one Negro grandparent.[7]

Always a man of paradoxes, Jackson set out to create a multiracial state a century before any other nation would make the attempt, but at the same time was adamant in his defense of slavery. When intellectuals in the C.N.A. sent a delegation to Mexico in 1841 to win support for manumission of the Jeffersonian slaves, they met with the aged Jackson, then in retirement at the age of seventy-six, and in the last year of his life. Journalist Carter Martin noted that Mexico was the only western nation that still maintained slavery. He voiced the hope that this "blot on civilization will soon be removed." Jackson shook with rage, but composing himself quickly, he turned to Martin and said, "Sir, ours was a nation of diverse peoples at a time when yours was the leading defender of slavery. We have men of color in high government posts at the present time, and we honor them as we do all men of talent and accomplishment. But we do not believe the African capable of freedom, and so we keep him in a state of benevolent slavery. And what have you done in the Southern Confederation? You claim to have given the Africans their freedom but in fact, have kept them in slavery. The difference between the Mexicans and the North Americans is that you are a nation of hypocrites, while we have the courage of our convictions and are men enough to say what we believe." Then, as though to finish off the shocked North American with a rapier rather than a saber, Jackson noted that "Not one of you is a man of color. Do not even you gentlemen have the desire to mingle with the Africans whom you profess to love? A similar delegation as yours, composed of Mexicans and visiting the C.N.A., would have included Indians and others of color. It is Mexico, and not North America, where the descendants of Jefferson and Adams reside. And we, not you, maintain the hope of human equality for all those whom God has given a soul."[8]

It is necessary to understand Jackson's attitude on racial questions to appreciate his programs and their successes during his administration. Also noteworthy is the fact that his views were well known prior to his becoming president, and that he never significantly changed them. Indeed, this major political figure was unusual in his directness,

7. *Ibid*, p. 849.
8. Carter Martin. *Visits to Strange*     *Lands: My Struggle for Peace and Justice* (New York, 1865), pp. 319-28.

and appeared to lack the subtlety and sophistication historically associated with prominent politicians.[9]

Jackson spent his first year in office organizing the government and assuring a smooth operation of the Constitution. Within a few months, all Mexico knew the government was in full control. Bandit groups that had dominated the Yucatan and Baja California were ruthlessly exterminated. Governor Victoriano Carranza of Chiapas, who had raised his own militia and tried to collect state taxes, was summoned to Mexico City and subjected to one of the President's blistering lectures; he returned to Palenque a subdued and cowed man, never to attempt an independent role again. When Senator Thomas Hinds of Mexico del Norte refused to pay a questionable federal tax, Jackson sent troops into the legislative chambers and had him arrested while in the midst of delivering a speech. Opposition newspapers, among them the Mexico City *Journal*, the Torreón *Liberdad*, and the San Francisco *Sun*, were closed down on the President's orders, and allowed to reopen only after admitting to having printed false stories about federal abuses.

Jackson explained that such power displays were necessary to convince the Mexican people that their government was indeed capable of ruling the vast lands under its control, but the Liberty Party called him a dictator and violator of all that Jefferson had ever stood for. Significantly, however, Jackson attempted to muzzle his political opponents only rarely. Governor Leslie Folger of Jefferson, leader of the Liberty Party after 1824 and Jackson's opponent in the 1827 election, was guilty of the most flagrant lies regarding Jackson's personal life and wealth, but the President never moved against him. Senator Albert Burley of California, who later charged Jackson with taking ten percent of all federal receipts to use for his own purposes (a charge he later withdrew), was likewise ignored, although for a while he had a powerful following. Jackson's supporters claimed for the President an innate love of democracy and belief in the desirability of a responsible opposition; his critics felt the President considered men like Burley and Folger beneath contempt, and not worthy of his attention.[10]

On February 24, 1823, Jackson announced that he would embark

9. Some historians and biographers credit Jackson's personality not to simplicity, but to arrogance. Richard Harrison, in his Cox Prize biography, *Jackson the Man* (New York, 1967) wrote that "Jackson was the most arrogant man the continent has produced. Others had the grace to hide their contempt for inferiors. Not so with Jackson, who never felt it his obligation to suffer fools. . . . The President combined all the power of a rhino with that animal's tact."

10. It should be mentioned, however, that Jackson's last words were: "My only regret is not having choked Burley and Folger to death. It would have given me great pleasure." Hyman Lichtenstein. *On the Seventh Day He Rested: Jackson in Retirement* (Mexico City, 1969), pp. 56–62.

on a "grand tour" of the nation that April. His itinerary would begin in the far south, then go to Jefferson, and from there across to San Francisco. He announced there would be major addresses before each state assembly as well as visits to Indian areas in Mexico del Norte and Arizona. He would be accompanied on his tour by Secretary of the Exchequer John Berrien, Secretary of Indian Affairs Miguel Montez, and Secretary of War Arturo Aragon. In his absence, Secretary of State Adams would assume additional administrative powers, although it was understood by all that, in Jackson's words, "Where I am, there is the capital."[11]

The grand tour was a resounding success. In Palenque, the President promised a program of internal improvements that would ease misery in all Chiapas. Durango Governor Alberto Rias' attempts to introduce cotton culture were encouraged by the Torreón address. Jackson received a tumultuous greeting in Jefferson City, one that moved him visibly. While there, he compared Jefferson's prosperity to that of the Southern Confederation, much to the disfavor of the latter. Then on to Sangre Roja and Conyers, where he spent much time in inspecting the land and speaking to the Indians. But the highlight of the trip came in San Francisco where, on Christmas Eve, he spoke of the U.S.M.'s future. "I ask Californians to join in our quest," he said, adding that in the "voyage through time and space" California may have "the greatest frontier of all the Mexican states." Secretary of War Aragon told the press that Jackson was referring to the agricultural potential of the state; but to others it seemed Jackson was already seeking new conquests, perhaps at the expense of the Russians, who shared the common frontier with California to the north.[12]

Jackson arrived in Mexico City on February 5, after ten months of travel. A week later, he addressed the Congress to tell them of his findings. Those assembled expected to hear homilies of the greatness of the new nation, and vague generalities about its future. Instead, Jackson spoke in specifics, concentrating on the economic potential of the states, and in particular of Mexico del Norte and Arizona. Thus it became clear why Jackson had taken Berrien, Montez, and Aragon on the grand tour.

The President noted that the U.S.M. was a large country with a small population, and that much of it remained unexplored and undeveloped. Some citizens, most notably the Jeffersonians, had made good use of the land and were comparatively wealthy, but bleak poverty existed in Chiapas, Durango, and parts of the capital district. California

11. Brayback. *Conversations with President Jackson*, p. 495.
12. At least one scholar believes Jackson was not referring to the Russians in this speech, but instead to expansion across the Pacific. See Jethro Stimson. *Jackson and the Pacific Dream* (London, 1950).

was already becoming an important agricultural state, but Mexico del Norte was occupied by a handful of Indians who were not developing that district's economic possibilities. Yet, said Jackson, "our land is rich, our bounty great." He went on to discuss the mineral wealth of Durango, the agricultural potential of Chiapas, and the unknown frontier in Mexico del Norte and Arizona. All these regions held the promise of wealth for intelligent and energetic young people, whom Jackson urged to go to the areas and become pioneers. Obviously speaking to the Jeffersonians, he said, "Go to these new frontiers, just as our forefathers came across the unknown wilderness, and like them, you will find a new Jerusalem." These words and others like them indicated the direction of Jackson's proposals, and his hope for the U.S.M.'s future. The President would keep his earlier pledges. Each state would have control over its internal affairs, and a partnership of the peoples of Mexico was to be created. Now he indicated his desire to have the Jeffersonians settle in the other states, presumably to assume leadership there, and become the senior partner in the U.S.M.

Jackson next discussed his proposals for the economy. As far as he could see, Mexico had been destined by nature for agriculture and mining. The cotton culture of Jefferson would be spread wherever it could take root, while the peoples of other states would be encouraged to produce foodstuffs, in particular grains. Those states unable to do so, would look elsewhere for their products. Durango's copper mines would be reinvigorated, while a large-scale development program would be undertaken in Chiapas, where Jackson thought indigo, rice, and sugar might become important crops. He also believed more silver might be found in Chiapan mines.

Such a program would require large amounts of capital and dictate a particular kind of trade policy. Jackson told the legislature that "several friendly nations have indicated interest in participating in Mexico's future." Within days it was learned that France had decided to lend the government $4 million, with more to come later on. In addition, several French bankers had formed a consortium to invest in Mexico. Dutch, German, and Swedish investors made their appearance later on, but the scene was always dominated by the French. "We have many common interests with our French brothers, whose concern with our cause goes back to the Rebellion," said Jackson.[13]

Jackson remained pro-French for the rest of his life, but would not sacrifice Mexican needs to this friendship. Instead, he planned to

---

13. Even then, Jackson meant to use France to further his programs, but he had no illusions regarding his ally. "We are with the French because they are with us," he told Brayback. "When our interests change, so will our friendships. I would make a pact with the devil if it would enable us to double cotton production." Brayback. *Conversations with President Jackson*, p. 729.

use the French as a weapon in his drive to make the U.S.M. a major power. Fortunately, France's needs paralleled those of Mexico. King Louis XVIII was strongly anti-British, while Jackson's Anglophobia and hatred for the C.N.A. were legendary. Just as France opposed Britain in Europe, so the U.S.M. saw in the C.N.A. its natural rival. Thus, an alliance of convenience was formed, which in time would ripen into one of respect and affection as well.[14]

Jackson planned to use the French and other loans to enlarge the harbors at Tampico and Henrytown, construct a national road to connect all the states, and encourage agricultural programs in Chiapas and Durango. Under the terms of the Hagen bill of 1825, every settler who came to these states would be granted 250 acres of land outright on the understanding that he would produce crops for three successive years. The government gave bounties for the production of indigo and hemp, and in time added other tropical and semi-tropical products to the list. In every way possible, Jackson bent his efforts to develop Chiapas and Durango, but little progress could be seen until the 1830's, when the first group of Jeffersonian pioneers began to make their impact felt.

Durango would not become self-sufficient until the late nineteenth century, and even now Chiapas is the poorest of the Mexican states. But progress there was notable in the second half of the century. Starvation in southern Chiapas, once a common occurrence, was virtually eliminated. But these two states had to pay a price for their increased prosperity. The Jeffersonians brought slaves with them to Chiapas and Durango, and affixed upon these states the same kind of labor system that had existed in their old homes, with one significant exception. In Jefferson there were two major groups—whites and blacks. In Chiapas and Durango, the majority remained Indian and people of mixed blood. Unable to join with the Anglo-Saxons, and unwilling to become identified with the Negro slaves, the old residents of these states tended to withdraw from the newcomers and form a separate though parallel society of their own. Thus, in Chiapas, two nations existed side by side, with little contact between them.[15]

Another part of the Jacksonian economic program worthy of comment was his tariff and banking policies. Jackson believed in the ideal of free trade; he found in the 1820's that he was able to put it into

14. Henri de Amory. *The Ghost of Lafayette: The Franco-Mexican Alliance* (Mexico City, 1959).

15. This division in Chiapas began to break down in the late nineteenth century, when the native Mexicanos were wooed by both white and black leaders. The Anglo-Saxons needed the Mexicanos to aid them in putting down slave insurrections, while the Negroes attempted to find a common cause with the Mexicans on the basis of both being subjected to racial humiliations. Torn between the demands of economic well-being and racial justice, the Mexicanos divided into two factions, each at war with the other as well as with the other groups in the state.

practice. Since Mexican cotton could compete in price with cotton from any other country (including the C.N.A.), it found a ready market abroad. Similarly, when Chiapan indigo production was established, that plant, too, was of a high grade and low price. Mexico was able to achieve a favorable balance of trade by using funds gained from cotton and indigo sales to purchase whatever mechanical equipment it needed. In addition, the continuing stream of French investments assured Mexico of sufficient capital for Jackson's ambitious road-building program.

This balance of trade situation also enabled the President to indulge another of his beliefs. Since his earliest days, Jackson had been distrustful of banks, and unwilling to accept paper when gold or silver was available. For a while, the President experimented with a bimetallic standard, with paper money used only for inter-bank transactions. But this proved unworkable, especially after Durango's silver mines began full operations in 1829, thus upsetting the ratio. Within a few years, Jackson became convinced that the nation would need a more elaborate monetary system, and he grudgingly conceded that paper money would be necessary. With this in mind, he acceded to the establishment of the Bank of Mexico, a central bank on the French model, which became the government's depository and acted as its fiscal agent. The B.M. had the right to issue paper money against gold and silver deposits, as well as bills-of-trade and other commercial paper. It was charged with the task of maintaining the gold-silver ratio and making certain the flow of capital into the various states was both smooth and beneficial. Thirty percent of the B.M.'s stock was taken by the government, with the other seventy percent sold to private investors. By 1835, almost forty percent of the stock was in the hands of the French government or French citizens. Jackson was unhappy with this situation, but recognized its benefits. Bank President Henry Aikins, noting the situation, remarked that "we are like two men in a boat. If we sink, so do they. This alone would suffice to cement relations with our French friends."[16] So it did. By that time Tampico and Vera Cruz had substantial French business communities, while other leading cities had also taken on a French atmosphere.[17]

Jackson won re-election with ease in 1827. Indeed, so popular was

---

16. Alexander Harper. *Banking Policies in the United States of Mexico During the Aikins Years* (Mexico City, 1950), p. 148.
17. The reader should not be tempted to consider the U.S.M. and the C.N.A. as mere extensions of France and Britain, however. While it is true European historians tend to view the two nations this way, at least insofar as nineteenth century developments are concerned, the evidence is that both nations followed independent policies as early as 1835. John Perkins. *Britain, France, and the North Americans* (London, 1945); Consuela Strong. *Separate and Equal: Mexico and France in the Early Years* (New York, 1940).

the President that the Libertarians put up no candidate to oppose him. The situation was different by 1833, however. By that time problems had emerged in the U.S.M., and an opposition alliance was there to threaten the Continentalists in Congress.

Several developments enabled the Libertarians to increase their power during Jackson's second term. The new nation's prosperity made it possible for many Mexicanos and Indians to leave the farms and plantations, form small businesses, find employment in the export trade, or work in the new textile factories the French had opened in Jefferson, Durango, and Chiapas. No longer peons, the Mexicanos and Indians now had the vote, and most tended to join the Liberty Party. The increase in the "free" population also resulted in a redistribution of seats in the Assembly, so that Jefferson's representation was lowered, while that of Durango, California, and Chiapas was increased.

Then there were the slave revolts. Jackson refused to recognize this problem, but during his second term, there had been at least a dozen major rebellions in Jefferson, all of which were put down swiftly and brutally. Jackson told Montez that the revolts had been caused by infiltrators from the Southern Confederation, and on two occasions sent strongly worded notes to Norfolk on the matter. Relations between Mexico and the S.C., never good, almost reached the breaking point in 1832, and this, too, provided ammunition for the Libertarians. Few Mexicanos wanted a conflict, from which they could gain little. But the war would have been popular in Jefferson, the center of Continentalist strength. Thus, foreign policy was also a determinant in the 1833 election.

A small group of Jeffersonians opposed Jackson's agricultural policy that year. By 1833, it was evident that the C.N.A. was rapidly industrializing. This was on the eve of the great panic and depression, at a time when optimism reigned, and the budding Jeffersonian industrialists wanted their nation to take the lead in this field. Jackson's low tariff policies, his blindness to the railroad's potential, his unwillingness to support the Sprague bill (which would have authorized a search for iron and coal in Mexico del Norte and California), and the pro-agrarian stance of the Bank, all added to their discontent. Under the direction of George McDuffie of Henrytown, these former Continentalists had broken with Jackson in 1832 to form the Progress Party, and soon after joined the Libertarians. They provided that party with experienced leadership and funds sufficient to wage a spirited campaign in 1833.

The Libertarians made impressive gains that year. The new Assembly had 53 Continentalists and 46 Libertarians (with one member of the United Indian Party, who voted with the Libertarians). Now the

Libertarians organized for the presidential canvass by putting pressure on senators, who by that time voted openly and followed party discipline, but were free to select from among the several candidates their party offered.

The Libertarians had several candidates in 1833, but by late February the field had narrowed to three, and of these, Miguel Huddleston of Durango, a Senator for the past six years, had the most support.

Huddleston's ancestry was Jeffersonian. His parents had taken the Wilderness Walk with Greene, and settled in western Jefferson, where Thomas Huddleston soon became a leading planter with interests in the slave trade as well. Michael Huddleston was born in 1795, and was raised with his three sisters on the plantation, where he prepared to take charge after his father's retirement. When the Mexican War erupted, Michael was twenty-one years old, an intense nationalist, and a rising member of the Continentalist Party. He joined Jackson's army and was at his side when the General entered Mexico City in 1817. At the time he had contempt for the conquered people, whom he considered "only a trifle better than our slaves."[18]

Within a few weeks Huddleston discovered Mexico was a far more complex place than he had imagined. Also, he had a certain sympathy for Mexican culture, a liking for Mexico City—which was a more refined center than any Jeffersonian city he had known— and admiration for a few of the Mexicans with whom he came into contact. Then he met Consuela Venegas, the daughter of a deposed Hispano official, and they fell in love. The two were married in 1819, in a ceremony that shocked the Jeffersonian community in the capital. Not only did Huddleston convert to Catholicism, but he changed his name to Miguel, symbolizing his acceptance of the Hispano culture.

Huddleston did not return to Jefferson; to do so would be to invite rebuffs from his former friends. Instead, he settled in the capital, entered the cotton factoring business, and soon amassed a fortune. Living in a hacienda in nearby Pimintel, he was able to run for office in the Durango legislature, and was elected in 1822. His rise in politics was rapid. Huddleston entered the Mexican Senate in 1827, and soon became a leader of the Liberty Party caucus. Within six years Huddleston was recognized as the most talented politician in the party, as well as its best hope for future power. He also personified what many thought would be the U.S.M.'s future—the union of Anglo and Hispano strains to produce a new type of individual and culture. As such, he was carefully watched.

---

18. Fernando de Durán. *La Vida de Miguel Huddleston* (Mexico City, 1909), p. 98.

Huddleston showed proper respect for his elders, and was considered a particular favorite of Arthur Younger, minority party leader in the legislature. It was expected that Younger would be Jackson's opponent in 1833, and he was prepared for that thankless task. Then, as it seemed the Libertarians might win, Younger stepped down and threw his support to Huddleston. "I am sixty-six years old," he said, "and have amassed that many years' worth of enemies. I would have made the stand to offer voters an alternative to Jackson, and for no other reason. But now it appears the people of Mexico are ready to overthrow the tyrant, and they need a potential president, and not only a symbol. Therefore, I hereby support Huddleston."[19]

Not all Libertarians accepted Younger's choice. Douglas Watson of Chiapas, a wealthy planter who had relocated there after the war and then entered the Senate, campaigned for the designation, as did Henry Morris of Jefferson, who represented the old guard in the party. At a stormy meeting of the Libertarian caucus these two united in an attempt to reject Huddleston, but failed. In the end all the Libertarians voted for Huddleston, thus setting a pattern that would not be broken. Jackson won the election of 1833 by a margin of 18 to 6, but in Huddleston the nation had the kind of man who could take over after the old President was gone. Continentalist Senator John Shelby of California voted for Jackson, but recognized the meaning of the Huddleston phenomenon. "Huddleston was defeated by a phantom, not a man," he said years later. "We cast our ballots in '33 for the ghost of '17, not the man who stood before us."[20]

Huddleston took his defeat in good grace, and prepared for the election of 1839, when he knew Jackson would step down from office. There seemed no Continentalist capable of defeating him then.

Jackson's third term was both a success and disaster. Most historians—even the pro-Jacksonians—would agree that the aged President bore only indirect responsibility for the successes, while his handling of state affairs, especially during the last half of his third administration, was weak.[21] In the words of his close friend, "Jackson

19. Miguel Huddleston. *Portrait of the Founder: Arthur Younger of Mexico del Norte* (Mexico City, 1855), p. 293.
20. William McMullan. *A Half Century of Life and Labor* (Mexico City, 1869), p. 520.
21. Harrison claims Jackson's personal difficulties, especially the death of his wife in 1836 and a bout with typhoid fever in 1837, were the major causes of his weakness. Harrison. *Jackson the Man*, pp. 529, 546. Other biographers

consider the changing events of the third term too much for a stubborn old man to handle. Hawes. *Jackson of Mexico*, p. 598. In Vining. *Andrew Jackson*, pp. 440-56, we find a man in the grips of a severe psychological problem, while in Strawbridge. *Butcher Jackson*, pp. 444-56, we read of a president who merely carried out the program he had always pledged himself to, in that way wrecking any hope of internal harmony in the U.S.M.

dominated the scene during his first two administrations, and clearly controlled events. Then came the news from California, followed by repercussions in Arizona and the north country. After that, events controlled Jackson."[22]

22. Brayback. *Conversations with Jackson*, p. 801.

# II

# CALIFORNIA GOLD

THE financial crisis and depression that began in 1837 took its toll in the U.S.M., but that nation was less affected by the disaster than was the C.N.A. The Bank of Mexico was firmly established by then, and Aikins was able to rush reserves into the breaches when they appeared. From 1837 to 1841, not a single major Mexican bank failed due to lack of central bank support.[1]

The U.S.M. economy was also able to rebound quickly from the blow. Many cotton farmers turned to foodstuffs until the price rose once more. Although slave prices declined worldwide and resulted in the ending of the institution in the S.C., it merely meant a short-lived closing of the slave markets in Jefferson City and Quatros Hermanos; these revived by 1842 and afterwards did better business than before.[2]

France continued to purchase Mexican cotton in the crisis years, but at a lower price than before.[3] French loans, which had sustained

1. William McCoy. *Great Central Bankers of the Nineteenth Century* (London, 1929), pp. 195–269.
2. According to Arthur Wing, "Jefferson had a 'stockpiling problem' in the 1837–1841 period, but this was as common for businessmen then as it is now. After 1841 the 'inventory' had to be worked off, which took five years. At that point the market stabilized and prices began to rise." This quotation is from Wing's manuscript, "The Business of Slavery and the Slavery of Business," which may be found in an unpaginated volume, *Occasional Papers of Arthur Wing*, on deposit in Mexico State University. The volume, which is in typescript, is undated, but appears to have been collected around 1900. Nothing more is known of Wing, apparently a student in the classes of Professor Hiram Garnett, who was at the University from 1889 to 1905, and who trained an entire generation of Mexican historians of slavery. Wing is not mentioned in Hiram Garnett. *Fruitful Years and Good Friends* (Mexico City, 1907), and his identification remains a mystery to this day. Yet his writings, which have only recently been discovered and are now in preparation for publication, offer one of the clearest and most interesting analysis of slavery we have. Montgomery Cochran, provost of Mexico State, is preparing the first volume of his writings, and promises to have them ready for the publisher by January, 1974. Meanwhile, see his article, "The Students of Hiram Garnett, Including a Special Note as to the Identity of Arthur Wing," *Mexico City Journal of Local History*, XXVI (January, 1968), pp. 89–108.
3. McCoy. *Great Central Bankers*, p. 288.

Jackson's internal improvements programs, came to a halt, and half-built roads had to be abandoned. This was probably for the best; the railroad had made such roads obsolete, and it was only Jackson's bitter hatred of the "iron monsters" that had kept them from Mexico in the past.[4] Similarly, other Jacksonian plans, such as a canal across Chiapas and the irrigation of desert lands in Mexico del Norte, also economically unwise and in any case beyond the technology of that period, were abandoned.

Not only did the Mexican depression end earlier than the world-wide depression, but it did so in a more dramatic fashion. On February 2, 1838, Hernando Montez, a subsistence farmer in Santo Tomás, California, found small nuggets of gold in a creek that ran through his farm. Word quickly spread through the community, and dozens of gold-seekers appeared at the creek in mid-February to pan for the metal. By April, the rest of California had heard of the Santo Tomás discovery; the news reached Mexico City in early May, and the Atlantic coast cities of the C.N.A. by June. All the world knew of the California gold that summer, and it seemed everyone wanted to go to the "golden land" and pick nuggets from the streams.[5] At that time, however, few could afford the trip. But after the economic recovery of 1840–1841, thousands flocked to California by whatever means possible, and the gold rush was on in earnest.

Jackson was surprised and amazed by the discovery, and at first did not know what to do about it. He recovered quickly, and in September, 1838, sent a large part of the Mexican Army to California, where it joined with the California police in sealing the area off to outsiders. "This is Mexican gold," said the President, "and will be used to serve Mexicans. All others will be given a clear notice. Leave or be shot."[6]

By the time prospectors from Indiana and Vandalia had arrived at the California border, the Mexican police had the gold fields closed off, and the North Americans were faced with three alternatives: they could remain in Arizona and seek their fortunes there; return to the C.N.A.; or attempt to sneak through the "grey cordon" of Mexican soldiers. Many returned home, but a large number managed to bypass the soldiers and descended upon Santo Tomás and the vicinity. Others followed, usually bribing members of the army. Indeed, hundreds of soldiers deserted and they, too, became prospectors. Gold fever, of an unprecedented nature, hit the U.S.M. The nation would not recover from the disease for a generation.

Within five years, California, in 1837 an out-of-the-way state in-

---

4. Edwin Radcliffe. *Jackson the Econo-mist* (London, 1960), p. 390.
5. Walter Ramspeck. *The California Gold Rush of '39* (New York, 1956).
6. Radcliffe. *Jackson the Economist*, p. 399.

habited by farmers and a few merchants, had become the second most populous state in the U.S.M. In 1837, cotton had been the U.S.M.'s most important product. By 1844, gold had surpassed it in total value, and even the plantation owners were talking about leaving their fields for California.

### Selected California Statistics: 1838–1848

| YEAR | POPULATION | GOLD PRODUCTION (IN THOUSANDS OF FINE TROY OUNCES) |
|---|---|---|
| 1838 | 45,000 | 5 |
| 1839 | 47,000 | 486 |
| 1840 | 106,000 | 1,260 |
| 1841 | 198,000 | 1,320 |
| 1842 | 258,000 | 1,334 |
| 1843 | 407,000 | 1,293 |
| 1844 | 598,000 | 1,592 |
| 1845 | 665,000 | 1,929 |
| 1846 | 712,000 | 2,004 |
| 1847 | 902,000 | 1,892 |
| 1848 | 1,110,000 | 1,692 |

Source: U.S.M. *Statistical Abstract*, pp. 928, 1056.

The gold rush of 1838 and after was the most significant event in Mexican history since the inauguration of Jackson, and some would say it even transcended the founding in importance.[7] Few in the U.S.M. were unaffected by the discoveries, which radically transformed the nation in all of its aspects.

The most obvious changes were economic in nature. California, the far western part of the country, was isolated from the rest of the U.S.M. Although the port facilities at San Francisco and Puerto Hancock were sufficient for the needs of gold traders, transportation from there to the Gulf ports was difficult and costly, while transfers to Chiapas through Villera and across the waist of southern Mexico was a dangerous undertaking. Thus, Jackson was forced to concede the necessity of a railroad. A group of French and Jeffersonian businessmen, headed by Maurice Duforge and Jethro Baker, organized the Jefferson and California Railroad Company in 1838, and received government support that same year in the form of land grants and subsidies. The first rails were laid in Henrytown on February 4, 1839, while a second crew began construction in San Francisco on April 11. French engi-

7. Evans Craford. *California Gold: Its Impact and Implications* (Mexico City, 1894).

neers supervised construction on both ends; French iron, and later steel, made the feat possible. The J and C Railroad could not be completed until 1848, by which time the California gold rush was almost over. But it did open the Far West to settlement, and without it, the westward drive of the Jeffersonians would have been crippled.[8]

A second major transformation could be seen in the foreign trade picture. Prior to 1840, cotton had dominated Mexico's exports, with other agricultural products following. Mexico had some textile factories, mines, and light manufacturing, but was basically an agrarian nation, founded on rural values and slavery. The gold rush altered all this. The transportation boom, sparked by the organization of the J and C Railroad Co., led to the formation of other railroad and steamship firms. This increased the need for iron and coal, which were imported in large quantities from France.[9] It also encouraged former gold prospectors, who realized the California bonanza was almost played out, to seek mineral wealth in other parts of the U.S.M., and, in particular, in Arizona and Mexico del Norte. Insufficient iron and coal for Mexico's needs were found, although California, Mexico del Norte, and Jefferson did, in time, organize respectable industrial complexes. But Mexico del Norte, parts of northern Jefferson, and northern Arizona were found to be rich in non-ferrous metals, especially copper, zinc, and lead. Sulfur was found in Durango and southern Jefferson, while fertilizers were apparently deposited in all parts of the U.S.M.[10]

The discovery of these mineral storehouses had their effects on foreign trade. Henrytown, which had begun its history as a cotton port and then became the terminus for the gold trade and "doorway to California," now developed into a center for the export of all kinds of minerals, as well as a shipbuilding, insurance, and banking complex.[11] Tampico also grew rapidly in the 1840's and 1850's, and would soon be the rail hub of Durango, Chiapas, and the capital district. More than any other Mexican city, it had the French flavor, as French traders and investors made it the principal place for their activities.[12] On the other

---

8. The last of the western nations to begin railroad construction, Mexico soon became enraptured by the "iron horse," and by 1875 had more railroad miles *per capita* than any nation in the world. David Gould. *Gold and Railroads, Profits and Losses* (Mexico City, 1948) notes that Mexico spent more on railroads from 1842 to 1875 than it extracted in gold from California. "Thus was California gold transmuted to Mexico del Norte iron and Jefferson steel."

9. Jackson refused to purchase iron and coal from the C.N.A. or Britain, even though the price was always lower.

10. Barbara Hoover. *The Role of Mineral Investigations in Mexico del Norte, Arizona, and Jefferson During the 1840s and 1850s* (unpublished M.A. thesis, Jackson University, 1962).

11. Paul Murphy. *New York of the South: The Rise of Henrytown in the 1840s and 1850s* (Mexico City, 1967).

12. Sylvia Spinner and Andrea Small. *Views of Tampico: Being an Investigation of the Growth of Our City* (Tampico, 1940).

hand, San Francisco's greatest growth would come later on, and Puerto Hancock stagnated after the gold rush was over. Finally, Jefferson City actually lost part of its population, as did other cities in the cotton region in Jefferson.

The decline of cotton was a major result of the mineral discoveries. The textile industry was beset by problems in this period, which combined to force cotton into a secondary role in Mexico's economy. There was, of course, the old competition from the Southern Confederation, to which was now added the production of Egypt, India, and South America. The result was a cotton glut that lasted for more than thirty years. Its effects were first seen in the late 1830's, but at that time it was assumed to have been the consequence of the worldwide economic crisis. Consumption picked up in the early 1840's, but the cotton price continued to decline, falling from over twenty-five centavos a pound in 1837 to less than half that in 1846, before leveling off. Jackson claimed the situation was temporary, and proceeded with the introduction of cotton culture in Chiapas, Durango, and other states. But these efforts failed, and by 1844 only Jefferson produced cotton in any substantial amounts.

The double blow of California gold and the decline of cotton caused tremors to develop in Jeffersonian society. Formerly the richest of the states, the one that provided leadership for the others as well as capital, Jefferson now fell to second place behind California in population, while its cities lost inhabitants and prestige, wealth and culture. More important, the Jeffersonian leaders suffered a "loss of nerve." The world decline in cotton was uncomprehensible at first to men who had based their entire lives on the "white gold."[13] Their immediate reaction was one of disbelief; some Jeffersonian Continentalist leaders went so far as to claim the decline had been organized in the Northern Confederation, and they called for war against the C.N.A. to rectify the situation. Then, upon more sober reflection, the Jeffersonian planters decided to expand their acreage in order to maintain their income. This meant a heavier capital investment in slaves and land-clearing, at a time when the moneys might have been employed more usefully and profitably. By 1845, when the planters finally realized that their decline was not a temporary phenomenon but a more lasting one, they were already weakened, decimated, and too late to share in the western bonanza.

The old Jeffersonian cotton aristocracy also suffered a major political blow in the 1839 presidential election. As expected, the Liberty Party nominated Miguel Huddleston, who had spent the previous six

---

13. Frank Dana. *The Cotton Culture of*   (Mexico City, 1967), pp. 486-90.
*Jefferson: White Gold in the Sun*

years organizing the party on the local level in order to capture control
of the Senate. By 1837 each state, with the exception of Jefferson, had
instituted a system whereby senators were elected directly by the
general public; Huddleston's organizing brilliance was such that, by
1838, the Liberty Party controlled the upper house, a situation that
seemed to guarantee him election to the presidency the following
year. Huddleston's platform was simple and straightforward, and was
symbolized by his slogan, "Progress Together." Huddleston would
work for equal rights for all free Mexicans, an end to discriminations
against Mexicanos and Indians, the channeling of California gold into
internal improvement projects in Chiapas and Durango, and the encouragement of native industry.

Jackson himself could find little to quarrel with in such a program, and recognized that Huddleston was seeking to win Continentalist as well as Liberty votes in the forthcoming election. On the other
hand, there were differences between the two parties. Whereas the
Continentalists were pro-French and had allowed a good deal of Mexico's development to be directed from Paris, Huddleston was more
independent, and even went so far as to express the hope that relations
with the C.N.A. could be improved. Furthermore, Huddleston's program was not geared to the needs and desires of the Jeffersonian
planter aristocracy, but rather to the Hispanos and Mexicanos of California, Arizona, and other rapidly-growing states of the West. Significantly, however, Huddleston said nothing of slavery, even when
pressed to do so by his own followers and Continentalist spokesmen.
On those rare occasions when he discussed slavery openly, he indicated
that he would allow the institution to remain where it was, and would
do nothing on the federal level to disturb it in Jefferson. However,
Huddleston noted that each state had the right to pass labor laws, and
could do so in such a way as to discourage the entry of slaves. Jackson,
who though not a candidate but still active politically, was enraged,
and attacked Huddleston publicly, saying that the Constitution guaranteed slavery, and that to attempt the institution's destruction would be
to violate the law. To this Huddleston replied that he would not try to
destroy slavery, but merely control it. The distinction (if there was
one) was lost on the Jeffersonian aristocracy, and that segment of
U.S.M. society was strongly opposed to Huddleston in 1839.

The Continentalists' candidate was John Mason, a former Jeffersonian planter who had managed to get to California during the early
days of the gold rush and had amassed a fortune. Although sympathetic to the Jeffersonian problems, Mason had no slaves of his own, or
indeed any connection with the Jeffersonians. Calling himself "a Californian, by God, and proud of it!" Mason stood for a continuation of
Jacksonian policies but at the same time, like Huddleston, took cogni-

zance of the problems of the West. He, too, called for more independence from France and assistance to the poor of Chiapas and Durango, as well as the development of Arizona, but said little of Jefferson and its problems. Thus, Mason attempted to straddle both the issues and the parties, but in the end managed to displease both segments of the electorate. The Jeffersonians considered him a turncoat, while the Mexicanos looked upon Mason as an interloper and pretender.

Despite this, party discipline held in the Senate. In 1839, as a result of the election, the Liberty Party had seventeen senators while the Continentalists had the remaining seven. The final vote was along party lines; for the first time in Mexico's history, the political parties were strong enough to overcome the traditional independence of the Senate. Thus, Huddleston became the second president of the U.S.M., which now passed to Libertarian control.[14]

Despite widespread Continentalist fears, especially in Jefferson, Huddleston preserved many Jacksonian programs, and there was a continuity in governance. In his inaugural address, Huddleston said, "Progress Together is not a mere slogan, but the true goal of this administration. We have prospered in the past, and will continue to do so in the future. But this progress must be made together. All Mexicans must make their contributions and receive their fair share for work performed. Mexicano and Anglo, Indian and Hispano, are all equal and together in their efforts. Whether a man's origins can be traced to the Wilderness Walk or to the Conquistadores is of no importance today. He is not a dweller in the past, but in the present and the future. Viva Mexico! Long Live the U.S.M.!"[15]

Contrary to the expectations of his more ardent followers, Huddleston did not expel the French or seize control of the gold mines. Instead, he retained his French bankers and assured the miners they would not be interfered with by the federal government. There was a shift of public works to Chiapas and Durango, while Huddleston promised a future railroad to Baja California, and a survey as to the feasibility of a canal through Chiapas. As for Jefferson, he said and did little to or for that state, as though willing to permit natural factors to take their effect. Nor did he mention slavery, thus disappointing the growing number of abolitionists in Durango and other states, as well as their counterparts in the C.N.A. and in Europe.[16] While Huddleston's restraint was noted in Jefferson and ended some wild talk of secession there, it did little to alleviate the state's basic problem, and Huddle-

14. Martin York. *The Election of 1839* (Mexico City, 1970), pp. 485–506.
15. Paul Murphy. *Together Forever: The First Years of the Huddleston Ad-* *ministration* (Mexico City, 1962), p. 102.
16. Jack Hollenberg. *It Began in Triumph: Huddleston in 1841* (London, 1962).

ston's attitude indicated that he would not use the powers of his office to assist the Jeffersonians. This would have to be done by the Jeffersonian aristocrats themselves.

During the next three years the Jeffersonian Continentalists attempted to solve their problems by increasing the land under cultivation and refining cotton-production techniques, but the world price of cotton continued to fall. The Continentalist party was in disarray, deeply pessimistic about the future, when they gathered in Henrytown on May 5, 1843, to hold their annual convention. Senator Peter O'Gorman gavelled the meeting to order; his speech on the problems of Jefferson threw the convention into a deep gloom. "Our land is leeched of its vitality," he concluded, "and our people of their soul." The next day, former Secretary of Agriculture Homer Brown made an unconvincing speech in which he predicted a rise in cotton prices, which only served to remind the Continentalists of better days prior to the gold rush.

Everything changed on the third day, however, when a Hispano, Assemblyman Pedro Hermión of Lafayette, was given the rostrum. Hermión was little known outside of Lafayette, where he was considered a hard-working politician, used by the Continentalists to placate the growing Hispano minority in the city. But the thirty-two-year old Hermión was an ambitious man who recognized the absence of leadership in the Continentalist Party, and felt that a person with his background might be the best person to provide it. With this in mind, he had pleaded with O'Gorman for the opportunity to speak to the Convention "on the problems of my people in Lafayette." Feeling that such an address could do no harm, and faced with a dearth of speakers in any event, O'Gorman agreed.

On May 7, Hermión faced the assembled delegates of Jefferson at a crucial period in the party's fortunes. These people did indeed want leadership, but they were not disposed to accept it from a Hispano from Lafayette. With this in mind, Hermión opened his speech with a charge. "Our party," he said, "has been at different times accused of weakness, wrong-headedness, and incivility. We have been called slavers, tyrants, yellow dogs, and scorpions. But we have never been accused of blindness or lack of daring. I charge, gentlemen, that our opponents are wrong. We are not scorpions or yellow dogs, tyrants or weaklings. But we are blind and have lost our ability to meet challenges. And the fault, my fellow-Continentalists, is with you, the people I see before me. It is people such as you who have brought our party to its present sorry state."

With this charge, the delegates, for the first time, showed signs of life. They attempted to shout the speaker down, hurling epithets at him, such as "greaser," "Mexican chico," and "traitor." Hermión stood his ground and remained silent, waiting until the jeers ended. Then he raised his hands and said, "You have just given the world another example of this blindness of which I speak." More roars followed, a few delegates moved to leave the hall, but Hermión continued to speak, and his powerful oratory finally imposed silence on the hall.

> Our party built this nation. Our party led it through its most difficult years. Our party was responsible for the gathering of the wealth in California, for the lifting of oppression in Chiapas, for the beginnings of explorations in Arizona and Mexico del Norte. Our party, our President, led the way for harmonious racial relations in the capital district. Our party has made the U.S.M. a major world power. And now our party is in despair, not because of any failing of the party or its leadership, but because of events our party could not control, the price of cotton has fallen a few centavos. Our party has not been built on cotton, but on men! And men, not cotton, will bring our party to greatness once again.

Now the shouts were of approval. Hermión had succeeded in rousing an audience that was ninety percent Anglo.

> Our past has been glorious, and we need not apologize for anything we have done, to any man, be he Mexican or North American, English or French. But a party lives in the present, and not in the past, and we must direct ourselves to these tasks, and not with the current Paris or Liverpool or New York cotton quotations. Greene was not concerned with such matters, nor was Hamilton or Jackson. They were men involved with men, and not with dolares and centavos. And the program for the future is so obvious that it begs for recognition. That is why I say we are blind, and it is for this program that I will speak.

Now the audience was completely quiet, as old Jeffersonians who had fought side by side with Jackson strained to listen to a Hispano whose father had died opposing Jackson at the battle of Seven Forks.

> For too long we in Mexico have forgotten our heritage and roots. As President Jackson once said, "In our veins flows the blood of rebels and conquistadores." Yet all we talk of today is gold and cotton, as though such commodities could purchase national greatness and honor. Nor should we forget the threats to our land from abroad. Russia looks longingly at California, Spain dreams of a new empire in the Americas. And most of all, the Confederation of North America threatens our very existence. Along the Mississippi and Arkansas, in the Gulf of Mexico and the west Atlantic, we face the North Americans, who hunger for our lands and wealth.

The Continentalists, founded as an expansionist party by men who had lost the Rebellion and had never forgotten it, were now asked to pledge themselves to a conflict with the C.N.A. They interrupted

Hermión's speech with cheers and whistles; the same men who minutes before called for his head, now came to look upon him as a leader. Then Hermión concluded his address in a memorable fashion.

> In Mexico del Norte the Mexicanos have a game—some call it a sport. The peasants put two scorpions in a large bottle, and then take wagers as to which will win the struggle. Slowly the scorpions circle each other, until one lashes out at the other, and strikes him dead. So it is on our continent. On first glance it appears North America is a large place, with room enough for all. But the C.N.A. and the U.S.M. are both inhabited by aggressive and expansionist peoples. Within a few years this great expanse will seem small indeed, as we meet in the waters of the Gulf and along the Jefferson-Vandalia border. At this point the scorpions will meet in combat, with only one the victor. I mean that victor to be Mexico, and I believe only the Continentalist Party, revived and restored, can lead the nation to such a destiny!

The convention exploded into a roar of approval as Hermión stepped down. His speech had lasted only fifteen minutes. But in that time, Hermión had given the Continentalist Party a new program and a new leader. The men whose fathers had followed Greene and Hamilton, and who themselves had supported Jackson, now turned to the young Hispano as the hope of the party.[17]

Hermión, the acknowledged leader, now began to make plans for the 1845 elections. He gained a Senate seat in 1844, and from his office in Mexico City took command of the anti-Huddleston forces. Onlookers thought the contest between the two men both exciting and bizarre. "We face the prospect of choosing between two unusual men," wrote Senator Hernando Montoya of Chiapas. "On the one side we have an Anglo who has accepted Hispano ways and has a Hispano wife, and who leads the forces of reform and change. On the other we find a Hispano who has become the savior of the Anglo party, and who stands for the kind of aggression his father and people have always opposed."[18]

Huddleston read the speech and soon learned of its impact. He immediately denounced Hermión's view of the U.S.M. and its future. "We have troubles enough in our own land without seeking new ones

---

17. The most accurate text of the speech may be found in the Jefferson *Patriot*, May 8, 1842. A different, more grammatical copy is in the Mexico *Gazette*, May 15, 1842. There is justification to believe the Continentalists altered the text to make it more palatable to the Anglos. James Boatwright. *Pedro Hermión: A Hero in His Own Land* (Mexico City, 1954); Herman Muller. *Hermión of Jefferson: Patriot or Traitor?* (Mexico City, 1969). For a C.N.A. view, see Janet Holt. *Demagogue and Dictator: The Life of Pedro Hermión* (New York, 1954).

18. Hernando Montoya. *Strange Places and Strong Men* (Mexico City, 1857), p. 92.

abroad," he told a group of reporters. "Mexican gold and silver will be used for the benefit of all, not the destruction of property and the murder of men." But privately Huddleston conceded Hermión had struck a raw nerve. The U.S.M. had more than its share of firebrands and warhawks, from the Anglos of Jefferson to the young chiefs of Mexico del Norte and Arizona, to the Hispano upper class of Durango and the capital district.

Meanwhile, Huddleston continued to strive for unity. The task was not easy. His program of bringing harmony to the four groups— Mexicano, Hispano, Indian, and Anglo—proved a failure; tensions between them, which had been softened by Jacksonian prestige, now came into the open, and each blamed Huddleston and the Liberty Party for injustices, real and imagined. The Hispanos claimed California gold was being used to enrich "Huddleston's Anglo friends," while the Indians and Mexicanos were chagrined at "the President's lack of interest in our problems." On their part, the Anglos of Mexico City found it difficult to trust a man who had converted to Catholicism and had taken a Hispano wife. None were satisfied with Huddleston's temporizing on the slavery issue or the question of French influence in Durango, California, and the capital district.[19] Furthermore, there were charges of misappropriation of funds, many of which revolved around Secretary of Finance William Wilson, and although none were ever proven true, several minor officials in the customs and treasury were convicted of theft and accepting bribes.[20]

But Huddleston's major problems lay in his own personality, and in his foreign policy. He was by nature a compromiser and conciliator, a fine and decent man of good will who might have been a successful leader in Manitoba, Vandalia, or even in the Northern Confederation. But the Mexicans liked their presidents with the fiery ways of a Jackson, or the pioneering fervor of a Hamilton. Huddleston notably lacked the charisma to hold the fickle public in times of stress.

Huddleston's second problem lay in the area of foreign policy. Ever since its founding, the U.S.M. had been anti-C.N.A., and the North Americans had returned the hatred. Viceroy Sir Alexander Haven of the C.N.A. had characterized President Jackson as "a thoroughly rotten person.[21] Like most North Americans, he thought the election of Huddleston a good sign, and Haven was able to persuade Governor Webster to represent him at the Mexico City inauguration

19. Hollenberg. *It Began in Triumph*, pp. 397–401.
20. Paul Murphy. *Ants in the Sugar: The Problem of Honesty in the Huddleston Administration* (Mexico City, 1960), pp. 500–503.
21. William Cocke. *Sir Alexander Haven: Proconsul in the Wilderness* (London, 1910), p. 392.

in 1839.[22] Then, when Scott was elected Governor-General in 1843, Huddleston sent words of greeting to his C.N.A. counterpart, and dispatched Secretary of State Isaac Shelby to Burgoyne to represent Mexico at his investiture. There is reason to believe both Huddleston and Scott hoped for a bettering of relations between their countries, although neither man discussed it publicly.[23]

The cause of this silence rested more with the disputed riches discovered in the Rockies in the 1840's, than with past bitterness about the North American Rebellion. Copper was discovered in Mexico del Norte in 1843, and silver early the following year along the Mexico del Norte-Vandalia border. Thousands of miners, knowing the best gold claims in California had been taken, rushed eastward to the new diggings. Others arrived from Jefferson, some the sons of planters who realized that cotton would not recover in price during their lifetimes. Some twenty thousand left the N.C., the S.C., and Indiana for the Vandalia western border, and that state suddenly became the focus for emigration from others who were still recovering from the depression.

Although the mineral deposits were not as rich as people of the time believed them to be, the search for them was as feverish as had been that in California. Moreover, the situation was complicated by the uncharted border between Mexico del Norte and Vandalia, which had been a source of trouble since the end of the Trans-Oceanic War. Both Mexico and the C.N.A. produced evidence to substantiate their claims, and each rejected the maps of the other. The disputed area, more than five million acres in size, contained some of the wealthiest silver deposits in America, and this served to make the problem even more serious than it might otherwise have been. By 1845, open war had erupted between Mexicans and North Americans in the Broken Arrow region, while guerrilla activity from both sides laid waste to the more southerly towns of Morales and Kinsey. From February to June, 156 Mexicans and 197 North Americans were killed, and cries for revenge were heard in Mexico City and Burgoyne.[24]

Neither Scott nor Huddleston wanted war, and both sought some way out of the crisis. In April, both executives agreed to arbitration by a three-nation panel, consisting of the Germanic Confederation, Spain, and the Netherlands, but this arrangement misfired, as Spain refused to serve at the last minute, and no other nation could be found that would

22. Indirectly the Mexico City mission resulted in Webster's death. His assassin, Matthew Hale, was an ardent abolitionist as well as a labor agitator, and considered the visit proof of Webster's sympathy for slavery. Sylvia Spinner. "Matthew Hale and the Assassination of Daniel Webster: A Contrast in Character," *Essays in Radical History*, III (1954), pp. 34–65.

23. Martin York. *Huddleston, Scott, and the Rapprochement of 1844* (Mexico City, 1929), pp. 299–309.

24. Lord Henry Hawkes. *Logistics and Tactics in the Border War* (London, 1888), pp. 539–42.

satisfy both Huddleston and Scott.[25] Alternate plans, including a division of the disputed territory, also failed. Both men knew their nations wanted war, and neither could do anything to prevent it.

The situation was complicated by the imminence of the Mexican senatorial elections. As expected, the Continentalists selected Hermión as their candidate for the presidency, while Huddleston stood for a second term. True to form, the President conducted a calm, intelligent campaign. He stressed the rising wealth of the nation, the growth of accord between the races (which, unfortunately, was not true), the expansion of Mexican foreign trade, and his social welfare schemes in Chiapas and Durango.

### The Mexican Elections of 1839 and 1845

| STATE | SENATORS IN 1838 | | SENATORS IN 1845 | |
|---|---|---|---|---|
| | LIBERTY | CONTINENTALIST | LIBERTY | CONTINENTALIST |
| Jefferson | 0 | 4 | 0 | 4 |
| Mexico del Norte | 2 | 2 | 0 | 4 |
| Arizona | 3 | 1 | 2 | 2 |
| California | 4 | 0 | 2 | 2 |
| Durango | 4 | 0 | 3 | 1 |
| Chiapas | 4 | 0 | 3 | 1 |
| | 17 | 7 | 10 | 14 |

Source: Mexico City *Tribune*, August 14, 1845.

In marked contrast, Hermión spoke only of what he called "the coming struggle for the continent." He called upon all Mexicans to remember their long enmity with the North Americans, the riches of Mexico del Norte and, most importantly, the "martyrs of Morales." The Continentalists ran a shrewd campaign, playing down the racial questions in the western states, while in Jefferson, they harped on fears of slave insurrections. Finally, they asked the Mexican people to "be true to the memory of Jackson," who had died little more than three years before. A combination of these factors, plus the release of news of further fighting the week prior to election day, led to a Continentalist victory.[26]

---

25. Recent research in the Scott papers has clarified the Spanish role in the negotiations. King Miguel at first agreed to be party to the arbitration, but then learned Huddleston and Scott intended Spain to state specifically where the line had been drawn after the Trans-Oceanic War. Since to do this would risk bad relations with either the C.N.A. or the U.S.M.—or both—the King refused to cooperate. See Adlai Groggins. "New Revelations from the Scott Papers," Burgoyne *Herald and Times*, January 14-18, 1971.
26. Harper Reichart. *The Election of 1845: The Mandate for War* (Mexico City, 1956).

The Continentalist victory was seen in the C.N.A. as a mandate for war. Scott ordered a mobilization of the army and the stationing of additional troops in Vandalia and along the western boundary of the Southern Confederation. On his part, Huddleston did nothing; during the three weeks between election day and the first meeting of the new Senate, at which time Hermión was certain to be selected his successor, he remained at his hacienda and "awaited fate."[27] As for Hermión, flushed with success, he met with Continentalist Party leaders in Mexico City and prepared to assume leadership of the U.S.M. In late August and early September, 1845, war hung heavy in the atmosphere of Burgoyne and Mexico City.

---

27. Jack Hollenberg. *It Ended in Tragedy: Huddleston in 1845* (London, 1966), p. 520.

# 12

# THE ROCKY MOUNTAIN WAR

GOVERNOR General Winfield Scott of the C.N.A. had little taste for war, which he called "the worst form of human activity."[1] It was, of course, his military background and his success during the Indiana insurrection of 1839 that had made his political career, but his real interest lay in economic affairs, particularly the development of Manitoba and Vandalia. During the first year of his administration he introduced a series of homesteading laws, and actively encouraged Europeans to settle in the western states. He helped form the New York, Michigan City, and Pitt Railroad, which was designed to connect all major cities across the C.N.A. through a system of feeders, and which was financed by Northern Confederation and British funds. At the same time, he urged formation of a similar north-south linkage, the Quebec and St. Augustine, which never came to fruition. New banking legislation was passed to ensure the stability of each state's banks, and Scott planned, as well, a central bank along the lines of the Bank of England. It was from projects such as these that the Governor General had to turn as war with Mexico threatened.

As we have seen, Scott attempted to cooperate with Huddleston in preventing the war, but there were elements within his own party that opposed him. Minister of War Henry Gilpin, whom many believed was more influential in Unified Liberal party circles than the Governor-General, called for a contest with the "anarchists and half-breeds of Mexico." He began to pressure Scott to consider a surprise attack against Tampico and Jefferson City soon after Hermión's *Scorpions in a Bottle* speech. Even as Scott strove valiantly for continuing negotiations, Gilpin increased the pressure for a declaration of war. The Governor-General sought National Conservative support for his peace program, but although Lloyd was sympathetic to his problems, he refused to give aid and votes. "If Scott cannot control his own party, he should resign and allow Gilpin to take command. Better still, let him call a new election, so that the people may judge his party on

---

1. Groggins, ". . . the Scott Papers," Burgoyne *Herald and Times*, January 15, 1971.

the record."[2] Lloyd's attitude was understandable, though unfortunate. Within the year the opposition leader would come to regret his refusal to give Scott the support he so badly needed.

The war party increased in power after the Continentalist victory in the 1845 elections. Now that Hermión was to become the next President of Mexico, war seemed inevitable. On August 28, Scott called a secret meeting of his Cabinet to discuss the foreign policy situation. There he issued a moving plea for further negotiations, but Gilpin managed to rally a majority of the eleven man cabinet to support a war declaration.

Now Scott was faced with a problem: resign and allow Gilpin to become Governor-General, or accede to the will of the party and accept war. At this time, Scott chose the latter course of action. The following day, Gilpin sent word to his field commanders to make final preparations for a Mexican attack, and to have the troops put on a war footing.[3]

Hermión took office as President of the U.S.M. on September 6, 1845. "We do not want war with any nation," he told the public in his inauguration speech, "but we do not shrink from action when it is necessary. We know what is ours, and we mean to keep it."[4] Significantly, Hermión ordered negotiations to continue with the C.N.A., and in a message to Scott, indicated in diplomatic tones, surprisingly uncharacteristic of the man, that he would continue the search for peace "in the spirit of my predecessor."[5]

Scott called a second special Cabinet meeting on September 11 to hear the Hermión message. He sincerely believed Hermión wanted peace. Then, as the Governor-General prepared to ask for a vote on a war declaration, Captain Nathan Rusher, Gilpin's *aide*, broke into the room with news of a clash between C.N.A. and Mexican troops in the disputed area. The battle had taken place on September 4, or the day before Hermión's selection as President. Clearly the attack, if ordered from the Mexican side, must have come from Huddleston, and this was unthinkable. More likely, it was the result of tensions that had been building for the past year, a stray encounter between squads of troops. There are those who believe the attack came from the C.N.A. side, but this has never been proved.[6]

2. Passman. *Lloyd of Carolina*, p. 360.
3. John Pritchard. *The First Shot: Origins of the Rocky Mountain War* (Mexico City, 1958), pp. 80–83.
4. Boatwright. *Pedro Hermión*, p. 299.
5. Pritchard. *The First Shot*, pp. 189–91.
6. There is evidence that Gilpin ordered an attack, but several recent works conclude that his orders, poorly worded, were misinterpreted by field commanders. In any case, most historians now believe the Mexicans, acting without orders from Mexico City, fired the first shot. Gilpin. *No Apologies*, p. 504; Cocke. *Caesar in Broadcloth*, p. 403; George Loring. ed. *Origins of the Rocky Mountain War* (London, 1969).

In the weeks that followed, diplomats in Mexico City and Burgoyne strove to find a formula that would prevent a war declaration, while at the same time couriers scurried between the two capitals, to little avail.[7] Meanwhile, military activity in the disputed zone increased in intensity and regularity. Without a declaration of war—without even knowing which side was responsible for the first shot having been fired—the Rocky Mountain War had begun.

On the face of it, the C.N.A. appeared better prepared for war than the U.S.M. In 1845, there were some 24 million North Americans and only 16 million Mexicans, of whom 200,000 were slaves. The C.N.A. was assured of British support, and in 1845 the United Kingdom was the most powerful nation in the world; Mexico retained her friendship with France, but King Henry V was in no position to help the Mexicans, being involved in difficulties with the Germanic Confederation at the time. The C.N.A. fleet was second only to Britain's in 1845, and was able to blockade Mexico with ease, while the Mexicans had only a small navy, and most of it was destroyed in the first two years of the war. In the Northern Confederation was the world's second largest concentration of industrial might (which by 1849 would become the leading industrial complex in the world); Mexico's industry was still undeveloped, although the nation never lacked for sufficient arms. The internal transportation of the C.N.A.—roads, rivers, and railroads—was superior to that of Mexico, which still relied heavily upon the outmoded Jacksonian road system. On the eve of war, the C.N.A. had 500,000 men under arms, and would raise an additional million before the fighting was over. In contrast, the Mexican Army numbered 200,000 in 1845, and would never rise above 650,000.[8]

But Mexico was not without assets of her own. Jackson's economic policies may not have served the country well, but his program of cooperation with Hispanos and Indians bore fruit, and both groups fought well during the war. The slaves were kept under control, usually by brutal methods, including genocide.[9] The French Canadians, in contrast, saw in the war a chance to assert their individuality, and under the leadership of Charles de Frontenac raised the *Patriote* banner and demanded independence. A sizable number of Indiana Indians de-

7. "It is interesting to speculate what might have happened if Mexico City and Burgoyne had been connected by telegraph in 1845. If one had existed, the war might not have taken place. But Aaron Garfield's invention did not come until the following year, and the capitals were not connected by wire until 1876." Pritchard. *The First Shot*, p. 199.

8. General Wesley McDougall. *The Relative Strengths of the C.N.A. and the U.S.M. in the Rocky Mountain War* (London, 1911).
9. The genocide charges are documented in John Reynolds. *The Shame of Western Civilization* (New York, 1960), especially chapters III and IV.

serted the C.N.A. and served in the Mexican armies. Freedmen in the S.C. used the war as an opportunity to declare their rights as citizens, refusing to serve until their demands for equality were met. The N.C. was struck by a wave of labor stoppages and anti-draft riots in 1848 and 1849, which crippled the war effort. The C.N.A. used more troops to keep the peace at home than to fight the Mexicans for much of the war.[10]

Since most of the fighting took place on Mexican soil, Hermión's soldiers had the advantage of knowing the terrain. Time and again the North American troops froze to death, starved in the mountains, or were lost in the vast expanses of Mexico del Norte; at least 80,000 died this way. Another 10,000 died of disease during the ill-fated Durango campaign. Finally, the Mexicans had better field commanders than the North Americans; Homer, Chapin, Lodge, and Williamhouse were no match for Hernandez, McDowell, Running Deer, and Doheny. Hermión had the good sense to give his commanders a free hand; Scott continually second-guessed his military chiefs, usually to their misfortune and detriment.[11]

The war itself need not concern us in this history; it has been covered brilliantly by others, and may be studied in innumerable books and articles.[12] There were three stages to the war proper—1845–48, 1848–51, 1851–53. At first the advantage lay with the North Americans, as the Mexicans withdrew along the Vandalia border. By January, 1846, General Philip Lodge's N.C. forces had cleared the last Mexican from the disputed territory and poised to invade Mexico del Norte. His army and that of General Harry Chain of Indiana entered Mexico del Norte in March, vowing to reach Conyers by September, In late August, however, the Mexicans, led by Chief Running Deer's Cheyennes, met the North Americans at Arroyo de Dios and won a great victory, killing 10,000 of Lodge's men before the North Americans left the field. Lodge returned to Mexico del Norte the following year, and again was defeated. Not until 1848 did the C.N.A. abandon the drive on Conyers.[13]

In March a Southern Confederation force, with a large Negro contingent, massed at Port Ashly some hundred miles north of New Orleans, and the following month launched an attack on Jefferson.

10. Samuel Collum. *The Home Front: A History of the C.N.A. in the Rocky Mountain War* (New York, 1967), pp. 338–40.
11. Frank McKinley. *Winfield Scott and the Sin of Pride* (Mexico City, 1957).
12. United States of Mexico, Department of War. *The History of the Rocky Mountain War.* 29 volumes (Mexico City, 1910–1925); Confederation of North America. *The Rocky Mountain War.* 37 volumes (Burgoyne, 1888–1899). Also see Ellsworth Crown. ed. *A Bibliography of the Rocky Mountain War* (New York, 1966).
13. General Sir Hugh Brandon. *The Lodge Campaign of 1845–48* (London, 1882).

Although Colonel Martin Washington's Fifth Alabama Horse was able to crack Jeffersonian lines, the invaders were repelled after two weeks of bitter fighting. Soon after the Jeffersonians stationed strong patrols along the Mississippi, and although other attempts were made to cross, all failed.

A North American force landed at Tampico on July 8, 1846, secured the city, and under the command of General Herbert Williamhouse began the drive to Mexico City. Hermión dispatched the district guard under the command of Major Michael Doheny to the Tampico Road to intercept Williamhouse and hold him there until reinforcements arrived. Not only did Doheny stop Williamhouse; he was able to counterattack, forcing the North Americans to retreat. More North Americans landed but Doheny, now promoted to General, kept the far superior force contained. Finally, on March 5, 1848, Williamhouse withdrew from Tampico, and Doheny entered the city in triumph.[14]

During all this, peace negotiations were conducted in Paris and London, but little progress was made until 1848, when it appeared a stalemate had been reached. C.N.A. negotiator James Buchanan suggested an armistice based on *status quo ante bellum*, with an election to be held in the disputed zone to determine which nation would control it. Mexican envoy Carlos Franklin consented, and by November it seemed peace might be secured. But the two men could not agree on the mechanics for the election or the zone's status prior to the election. Negotiations broke down in January, 1849, and the war continued.[15]

In March, 1849, General David Homer led a large C.N.A. force westward from Fort Webster. At first it seemed his destination would be Conyers, and Running Deer deployed his troops to meet the expected attack on the Mexico del Norte capital. But Homer did not turn southward, instead he continued until he reached Mendoza, one hundred miles within the Arizona border, where he made winter camp in October. By then it was clear that Homer was not following in the path of Lodge, but instead was driving toward San Francisco, in an attempt to cut the U.S.M. in two. That winter the California brigades, led by General Franco Hernandez, moved to the Sierra Madre foothills, and prepared to cross the Rockies in the spring to head off the Homer attack. Thus began the second phase of the war.[16]

From 1849 to 1852 fighting centered in the Rockies, and involved direct confrontations between major elements of both armies. Homer led his men through Williams Pass in June, moving slowly in order to avoid ambush. Hernandez awaited him on the other side, where the

---

14. Edgar Almond. *Michael Doheny: The War Years* (Mexico City, 1969).
15. James Buchanan. *The Paris Mission* and *Other Episodes* (New York, 1868).
16. C.N.A. *The Rocky Mountain War*, Vol. 10, pp. 492–506.

battle of San Fernando took place on July 5–7. This was the last field battle of the war, and it ended in a draw, with both armies retreating. The Mexican force lost 4,500 men in the encounter; Homer's losses were more than 5,400.

Even as Hernandez awaited Homer's attack, Hermión made plans to free his most successful General for the western campaign. In March, 1850, Doheny gave control of the capital district forces to Colonel Andre Montez, and taking command of a newly formed army, headed toward the Rockies, where he arrived in mid-June. His plan was obvious; Doheny would await Homer's return from California, and then trap the C.N.A. force in the mountains for the winter, where the soldiers would die of starvation or freezing.

The scheme would have worked had not Scott learned of it. Swiftly he ordered Gilpin to prepare for the relief of Homer's army, and the Minister sent word to General FitzJohn Smithers of the Southern Confederation militia to move westward. But the message was lost in transmission, and by the time Smithers was able to move to assist Homer all hope for the C.N.A. Rocky Mountain force was gone.

Still, the S.C. militia made a valiant effort to arrive in time to prevent the anticipated slaughter, and in one of the most dramatic events of the war, the army pushed on, always moving, until it reached the Arizona town of Bald Eagle, which guarded the Williams Pass. Smithers leveled the city in two days, and then continued on to the eastern end of the pass, reaching it in mid-November, as the snows began to fall, and as Hernandez on the western end of the pass and Doheny on the eastern end began to squeeze Homer's tired force between them. Without waiting, Smithers entered the pass, hoping to destroy the Doheny army, and so open a path for Homer and his men. The plan failed, as Doheny's Indian regiments withstood three furious Smithers attacks.

None of the generals would withdraw from the mountains; to do so would be to admit defeat. During the next five months, 140,000 C.N.A. soldiers and 97,000 Mexicans slogged through the snows, attempting to destroy each other. "It was the most senseless battle in the history of warfare," wrote Sir Wesley McDougall. "Never before or since have so many brave died for so foolish an objective. Pride, and nothing else, dictated the retention of the Rockies."[17]

In late March, 1851, the first stragglers emerged from the Williams Pass. Others followed in April. Only 27,000 C.N.A. soldiers survived the winter, and 31,000 Mexican troops remained alive. All four

---

17. General Wesley McDougall. *The Lessons of the Rocky Mountain War* (London, 1914), p. 620.

generals—Doheny, Hernandez, Smithers, and Homer—died in the mountains, the first three of the cold, and Homer by his own hand.[18]

By mid-summer, news of the results of the Rocky Mountain campaign of 1851 had reached Mexico City and Burgoyne, and from there was relayed to the cities and towns of the U.S.M. and the C.N.A. By that time, both nations were ready for some kind of negotiated peace. Still, there were those in power in Mexico City and Burgoyne who wanted to fight on to the end, convinced their country would win not only a major victory, but a continent as well.

C.N.A. Minister of War Gilpin was notable among them. He broke with the Government in 1849, charging Scott with incompetence and a lack of dedication to the fighting men. This split in the Unified Liberals brought about a political crisis in April, as Gilpin joined with Lloyd in a no-confidence motion. But Scott refused to call an election, and spent the next three weeks trying to form a coalition government. The attempt failed, and when Gilpin supporters voted to expel him from the party, Scott finally conceded defeat and resigned his post.

Lloyd demanded a new election, but moving swiftly, Gilpin took command of the party apparatus, was selected as Governor-General, and formed a cabinet including some pro-war National Conservatives. The Gilpin government received a vote of confidence on May 15, by the narrow margin of 78–72.

Gilpin promised the country to bring the war to a close through "a massive assault on the Mexicans, who shall not rest from our blows."[19] The Rocky Mountain campaign of 1849 had been Gilpin's idea, and its failure was blamed on him. Gilpin rejected the notion that the C.N.A. had suffered a disastrous defeat, however, noting that "Our nation can afford to lose men; the Mexicans cannot. We shall grind them to dust."[20] Gilpin attempted to rally his forces in 1852 and make another assault on the Williams Pass, but mutinies in the field, troubles at home, and a growing rejection of the war throughout the C.N.A., led to his decline. The Gilpin government's term ended in February, 1853, and new elections took place that month.

Neither Gilpin nor Scott stood for office that year; the Unified Liberals passed to a new generation of leaders. Councilman Bruce Harrison of the Northern Confederation, who had served as Minister of State in the Scott cabinet before resigning in 1839 in protest against the war, now took command of the Liberal party. Harrison called for a

---

18. Even today, visitors will come across military hardware in the snows, and from 1968–1971 more than ten bodies a year have been found, some in remarkable states of preservation.
19. Burgoyne *Times*, May 20, 1849.
20. Burgoyne *Times*, December 3, 1852.

gradual withdrawal from the Rocky Mountain area, and a "peace with dignity," to be negotiated with the Mexicans. Lloyd, who had been on all sides of the issue since the war began, was unacceptable to young National Conservatives, and he was replaced at the party caucus by William Johnson, an aged Councilman from Manitoba, who had been against the war from the first. Johnson called for an immediate halt to the fighting and a unilateral withdrawal of C.N.A. forces from Arizona, which would be followed by a peace conference to determine the fate of that part of northern Mexico del Norte still in C.N.A. hands. As expected, the National Conservatives won an easy victory, and on February 16, Johnson took command in Burgoyne, at the head of a peace cabinet.[21]

### Results of the C.N.A. Election of 1853

| STATE | PARTY AFFILIATION OF COUNCILMEN | |
| --- | --- | --- |
| | UNIFIED LIBERAL | NATIONAL CONSERVATIVE |
| Northern Confederation | 12 | 32 |
| Southern Confederation | 15 | 15 |
| Quebec | 2 | 22 |
| Indiana | 17 | 7 |
| Manitoba | 4 | 15 |
| Vandalia | 9 | 0 |
| | 59 | 91 |

Source: New York *Herald*, February 16, 1853.

Similar, though more dramatic events, took place in the U.S.M. At first Hermión was a popular leader, especially after news of the border warfare reached Mexico City. Hermión claimed Mexico del Norte had been invaded "in the night, in secret, by men who dare not face us in the open," and he called upon all Mexicans to join in the struggle for "national honor."[22] The President's support reached a high point when Running Deer defeated Chapin in the Battle of Arroyo de Quatros Hombres, after which even the Liberty Party leaders joined in advocating the war. Only Huddleston, now in retirement, spoke out against the conflict, charging Hermión with having exaggerated the border fighting out of proportion, and calling for a cease fire and immediate negotiations with the C.N.A. Secretary of War Yves St. Just labeled Huddleston "a man who is not really a Mexican, or even a Mexicano, and whose heart may still be found east of the Mississippi,"

21. Winsor Watkins. *The Late Bloomer: William Johnson and the Election of 1853* (New York, 1969).

22. Muller. *Hermión of Jefferson*, p. 492.

while Senator Joseph Marro of Mexico del Norte went further, calling Huddleston "a traitor, pure and simple."[23] A statue of the former President in Constitution Square was blown up, and Hermión had to send a squad of men to protect his predecessor from angry pro-war mobs.

The situation changed drastically in 1851, as the tragedy of the Rocky Mountain campaign dawned on the peoples of the U.S.M. Now it appeared the war could not be won, and might even be lost. Seeking a scapegoat, the Mexicans turned on their President, who only a few months before had been compared to Jackson. All his efforts to reassure the nation failed miserably. The Liberty Party, which in 1849 had little hope of ever returning to power, now spoke confidently of a victory at the polls that autumn. Several attempts were made on Hermión's life, and the President was unable to leave the palace without a large contingent of armed guards. By June it seemed that the U.S.M. was on the verge of dissolution, as open warfare between peace advocates and Hermión supporters was reported in all states.

On June 19, the President appeared before the Congress to deliver a special message. Some thought Hermión would announce his resignation, or at least withdraw from the coming political contest. Instead, the President strongly defended his war policies, castigating his enemies as "turncoats, fair weather friends who run at the first sign of problems." The war would continue, he said, "until we drive the last North American from our soil, and then we will march upon Burgoyne, and I will personally dictate peace terms to Gilpin and his jackals." As always, Hermión was a forceful speaker, and the legislators seemed to follow his every word. At first they were silent, with a few openly defiant of the President, but soon they began to interrupt the speech with applause. Toward the end they were openly enthusiastic, and when Hermión closed with the words, "We shall never give up! Our Cause is just!" half the Congress rose and gave the President a standing ovation. Hermión's 19th of June speech, in which he turned the tide of congressional opinion in his favor, ranks with the *Scorpions in a Bottle* speech that nine years earlier had propelled him to national prominence.[24]

Hermión's victory was short-lived. As the President bowed to the applause, a shot rang out from the balcony. An onlooker, Emiliano Zangora, once a member of the Hermión guard, had shot his former hero in the back of the head, and the President died instantly. Zangora ran to the back of the hall, shouting, "Viva Huddleston y Paz," but before he could escape he was gunned down by the Congressional

23. Philip Wright. *The Marroista Interlude: The Decline of Liberty in Mexico* (Mexico City, 1952), p. 176.

24. John Conroy. *The Rhetoric of Pedro Hermión: A Study in Mob Psychology* (London, 1970), pp. 309-28.

*For Want of a Nail*

guard. Within the space of less than one minute the destiny of the war—and indeed of Mexico itself—had been altered.[25]

The Hermión assassination shocked Mexico. Men who only a day earlier had called the President a butcher and tyrant, now viewed him as a saint and martyr. A "Hermión-craze" swept over the land; pictures of the dead President appeared in every shop while towns renamed themselves in his honor.[26] For almost a month all other happenings—the war and election included—were forced to the background as the nation went on a binge of soul-searching and mental flagellation.

Meanwhile, preparations for the congressional elections proceeded apace. There was little campaigning that season, as no politician wanted to be branded as "a profit seeker in a mourning nation." Despite this, there was no need for any voter to go to the polls uninformed, for both parties made their positions fairly clear through the political newspapers.

The Continentalists ran on Hermión's memory; for the first time, even Jackson was eclipsed in political rhetoric. But it was a Hermión few would have recognized only a month before. Senator Raphael Blaine of Arizona, former Secretary of State and now Acting President, was chosen to lead the Continentalists; he spoke of the dead man as "a true lover of peace, who went to war sadly, and only when his nation was threatened." Blaine (who always had doubts about the war) claimed Hermión had been seeking peace at the time of his death, and

---

25. At first it was assumed Hermión had been assassinated by a cabal headed by Huddleston, but the former President was cleared of any wrongdoing by the Fuentes Commission, established by the Congress to investigate the matter. The Commission concluded that "Our leader was killed by a single assassin, operating alone, apparently half-crazed . . . the assassin Zangora was a disappointed former guard, who being rejected for promotion for good and sufficient reason, vowed to take revenge on the man whom he had once admired, but who now seemed to have rejected him." The United States of Mexico, Congress, *Commission to Inquire into the Assassination of President Pedro Hermión: Final Report* (Mexico City, 1852), p. 820. To this day, however, there are those who believe Huddleston organized the killing, while a second group believes it to have

been originated in Burgoyne. See Samuel Menzer. *The Huddleston Conspiracy: The Brown Menace of 1851* (London, 1970) and Joan Kahn. *The Unknown History of the Hermión Assassination: The Gilpin Connection* (New York, 1968).

26. There have been few phenomena comparable to the "Hermión-craze." A group of his supporters went so far as to petition the Pope to beatify Hermión, in preparation for sainthood, and steps in this direction were actually taken. Towns in France, the Netherlands, and even Russia were renamed for him. The most amazing part of the Hermión-craze, however, was the appearance of two men, Cabral Fernandez and José Torres, who in 1859 claimed to be the illegitimate sons of the dead President. Margaret McQuire. *The Hermión-Craze: Mass Delusion in Mexico* (London, 1910).

he—Blaine—would continue that quest. It was a rather foolish and desperate move. Realizing the war was still unpopular even though Hermión had been all but canonized, Blaine attempted to wed memories of a warrior President to a peace platform. The voters saw through this device, and by Election Day Continentalist credibility had been shattered.

Normally the Liberty Party would have selected Huddleston as its leader, but the former President, under suspicion of being implicated in the assassination, could not hope to make the race, and for that matter had earlier indicated an unwillingness to reenter politics. The Libertarians, so strong before the Hermión assassination, were now charged with being the party of treason, and had to move cautiously in order to avoid any appearance of disloyalty.

After serious deliberation the party selected Assemblyman Hector Niles of California, a quiet man, who was believed to be a mild opponent of the war, but who had participated in few of the debates of the previous year. Niles was considered an expert on economic matters, and had spent most of the war as head of a special committee in charge of armaments. He prided himself on being a meticulous worker, a family man, and a good businessman. Blaine called his opponent "The Faceless Wonder of San Francisco," and alluding to his hobby, stated that Niles was "the best butterfly collector Mexico has ever seen, but this is no recommendation for the presidency." On his part, Niles said little during the campaign, except to pledge himself to end the war "in such a manner as to preserve our integrity and honor."[27]

In 1851, the voters were forced to select between the confusing candidate of the war party and the unknown Californian offered by the Libertarians. There were no Jacksons, Huddlestons, or Hermións to consider; both party leaders were drab and lacked glamour. But the war remained a running sore, and Niles seemed better equipped than Blaine to end the fighting. For this reason, the Libertarians did well in both the congressional and state elections in 1851. In the words of Senator Marro, "We did not vote for a man who would lead us to greater glory, or for a man who could inspire Mexico with dreams and visions. Nor did we have the choice between reasonable programs, for none were set forth by Niles or Blaine. But the people were tired of war, and this decided the contest."[28]

Niles won an impressive victory in 1851, although the division in the new Assembly was far closer than that indicated by the state and Senate elections.

27. Carlos McBride. *The U.S.M. Elections of 1851: The End of an Era* (Mexico City, 1960), pp. 119–65.

28. Joseph Marro. *In the Service of Mexico* (Mexico City, 1871), p. 181.

## The Mexican Elections of 1851

| STATE | SENATE LIBERTY | SENATE CONTINENTALIST | ASSEMBLY LIBERTY | ASSEMBLY CONTINENTALIST |
|---|---|---|---|---|
| Jefferson | 2 | 2 | 9 | 15 |
| California | 3 | 1 | 18 | 11 |
| Durango | 3 | 1 | 13 | 11 |
| Chiapas | 3 | 1 | 5 | 4 |
| Mexico del Norte | 2 | 2 | 4 | 3 |
| Arizona | 2 | 2 | 3 | 4 |
| | 15 | 9 | 52 | 48 |

Source: Mexico City *Tribune*, August 14, 1851.

On September 5, 1851, Hector Niles took the oath as the fourth President of the U.S.M.[29] His address was short and to the point. Niles pledged himself to the search for an end to the war. "Let there be peace," he told the throng outside the presidential palace. With this, Niles set about liquidating the legacy left him by Hermión and Blaine, and began by offering to meet Gilpin "at a place of the Governor-General's choice, where we may end this sad conflict in good will."[30]

---

29. In some tabulations, Blaine is considered the fourth president, and Niles the fifth. Since Blaine was actually "acting president," however, most historians do not count him in their tabulations.

30. David Marks. *Hector Niles: The Mexican Augustus* (Mexico City, 1949).

# 13

## The C.N.A.:
## THE CORRUPTION
## OF PROGRESS

IMMEDIATELY after he assumed office, President Niles ordered the army to cease all offensive operations and concentrate, instead, on guarding land already held. In effect, this meant abandoning all the disputed zones, almost half of Mexico del Norte and a small section of northern Jefferson to the North Americans. Governor-General Gilpin interpreted this policy as an admission of weakness, and during the third and last stage of the war sent his armies against U.S.M. fortifications time and again. The U.S.M. line was never breached, however, and new invasions of the Mexican Gulf coast were also failures, as was Commodore Daniel Hanson's daring run around Tierra del Fuego, which ended with an attack on San Francisco. Then, in 1852, came the last assault on the Williams Pass, led by General Herkimer Ware and foiled by Colonel Miguel Fernandez and Chief Brave Eagle. By the time the Gilpin government fell in February, 1853, Niles' patient, defensive program had salvaged the military situation he had inherited from Hermión and Blaine. Gilpin's successor in the C.N.A., William Johnson, was a moderate like Niles. On April 15, he informed Niles that he would accept the offer of negotiations made by the President two years earlier, and suggested the Hague as the best place for preliminary discussions.

The first session of the Hague peace conference took place in June. Senator Frank Rinehart of Arizona, the chief Mexican negotiator and his C.N.A. counterpart, Minister of War John Wolff of Indiana, arranged for the resurrection of the 1845 arbitration panel which consisted of the Germanic Confederation, the Netherlands, and Spain, which met that November.[1] Meanwhile, both countries accepted a

---

1. Peace would have come in any case in 1853, since neither the C.N.A. or Mexico wanted to continue a fruitless war. But the event that triggered the particular method by which peace came was the death of King Miguel of

cease-fire, to begin on August 1, with each army withdrawing ten miles so as to form a new neutral zone that ran the length of the continent.[2]

The panel did not return with a final report until June 15, 1855. Under the terms of the agreement, a small part of Mexico del Norte would be annexed to the C.N.A., but would be done not as a result of the fighting, but rather because the North Americans should have received the land under the terms of the Treaty of Aix-la-Chapelle of 1799.[3] The C.N.A. would pay the U.S.M. N.A. £2.5 million in indemnities "for slaves who left the United States of Mexico to take residence in the Confederation of North America, and who for reasons of their amalgamation with the general population cannot be found and returned."[4] No mention was made of the causes of the war; blame for the first shot was not fixed. Mexico and North America accepted the findings, and the treaty was signed in the Hague on August 7, 1855. By then both nations had already turned to peaceful pursuits, and the signing, though celebrated, did not create as much excitement as might have been expected.

The C.N.A. emerged from the war a major industrial power. North America surpassed the United Kingdom in coal production in 1850, in railroads in 1852, and in manufactured goods in 1853. Economists have concluded that the C.N.A.'s growth had been the result of massive infusions of foreign capital and wise fiscal and monetary policies, while the war itself hastened industrialization.[5]

The keys to rapid industrial growth were British investments, and the transfer of imperial economic power from Europe to North America. The higher interest rates in North America, the lure of new enterprises and plentiful raw materials, and the initiative and vigor of the London business aristocracy were all important factors. Credit must be given, too, to Governor-General Johnson, who recognized

Spain in 1851, and succession by his brother, Ferdinand VII, who was eager to be a party to the negotiations, which he felt would add to his prestige. Frank Taft. *The End of the War: The Hague in 1853–1855* (Melbourne, 1967).

2. The only exceptions to this were the Mississippi and Arkansas River boundaries.

3. This clause was inserted as a face-saver for Mexico. Now Niles could claim he did not concede North America an inch of territory. Marks. *Hector Niles*, p. 250.

4. This too was a face-saver, since only a few slaves managed to escape from Jefferson. The money was really to pay for the loss of disputed territory. Taft. *The Ending of the War*, pp. 300–11.

5. Simon Rabbino. *The Impact of the Rocky Mountain War on the North American Economy* (London, 1967). Rabbino holds that the war stimulated North American industry and so was responsible for the great boom of 1855–1880. On the other hand, Philip Bullard, "New Perspectives on North American Economic Growth During the Rocky Mountain War," *London Economic Review*, Vol. XXVII (June, 1970) pp. 435–56, holds that the war actually retarded industrialization in the C.N.A.

## Selected C.N.A. Statistics, 1840–1878

| YEAR | STEEL (1,000 TONS) | ANTHRACITE COAL (1,000 TONS) | RAILROADS (MILES) | FOREIGN INVEST- MENTS (MILLIONS N.A. £) | GROSS NATIONAL PRODUCT (MILLIONS N.A. £) |
|---|---|---|---|---|---|
| 1840 | n.a. | 1101 | 4448 | 5 | 1419 |
| 1845 | n.a. | 2230 | 4879 | 19 | 2420 |
| 1850 | 2 | 3854 | 8793 | 18 | 2945 |
| 1855 | 10 | 7902 | 11980 | 19 | 3298 |
| 1860 | 68 | 10980 | 16486 | 29 | 4765 |
| 1865 | 104 | 12042 | 21095 | 22 | 5762 |
| 1870 | 298 | 17960 | 32768 | 52 | 7982 |
| 1875 | 359 | 22324 | 52689 | 106 | 9802 |
| 1878 | 562 | 28794 | 52689 | 259 | 12938 |

Source: C.N.A. *Statistical Abstract*, pp. 543, 592, 796, 2320.

that the C.N.A. was rich in raw materials but in need of capital to develop them. Even while peace negotiations were taking place in the Hague, Johnson sent Minister of State Montgomery Harcourt to meet with Prime Minister John Temple to encourage British investment. Temple was intrigued with the idea, and used his connections in the City to persuade several leading bankers to make a survey of opportunities in North America. With the exception of three years (1861–63) when the United Kingdom suffered an economic recession, total British investment in the C.N.A. increased in every year from 1855 to 1880.[6]

The opening of North America to massive British investment also provided a spur to British emigration to the C.N.A. Beginning in 1855, a new group of British subjects joined the Irish wave, which had scarcely subsided, even during the Rocky Mountain War. Others followed, as the C.N.A. became the Mecca for the more enterprising workers and farmers of northern Europe.

In this period, the population center of the C.N.A. shifted considerably, as did the relative strengths of the states. Disillusionment with the war led thousands to relocate to Manitoba, and others came as railroad linkages with Indiana made its wheatfields more inviting. That confederation's population, less than 100,000 in 1840, rose to a million by 1855, and 4 million by 1880. Manitoba remained "a grassy paradise," however, and despite the fact that it provided two governors-general for the nation, the Confederation remained essentially apolitical.

---

6. Simon Rabbino. *The Invasion of the Pound: British Investments in the* C.N.A. *from 1840 to 1880* (London, 1965).

*For Want of a Nail*

## C.N.A. Population Statistics, 1840–1880
### (IN THOUSANDS)

| YEAR | IMMIGRANTS BY COUNTRY OF ORIGIN | | | TOTAL C.N.A. POPULATION (IN MILLIONS) |
| | UNITED KINGDOM | IRELAND | OTHER EUROPE | |
|---|---|---|---|---|
| 1840 | 2 | 28 | 85 | 20.6 |
| 1845 | 24 | 39 | 101 | 24.3 |
| 1850 | 88 | 58 | 92 | 29.0 |
| 1855 | 143 | 72 | 83 | 33.5 |
| 1860 | 89 | 75 | 62 | 38.4 |
| 1865 | 116 | 83 | 71 | 43.8 |
| 1870 | 107 | 65 | 62 | 47.2 |
| 1875 | 98 | 82 | 57 | 53.9 |
| 1880 | 123 | 94 | 67 | 60.2 |

Source: C.NA. *Statistical Abstract*, pp. 98, 382.

Vandalia enjoyed a period of phenomenal growth from the end of the war to the 1880's. In the beginning it attracted miners, railroad builders, and those in related industries as well as wheat farmers. Then, as the silver mines petered out, a boom in copper, connected with the development of the electrical industry, began. Finally, Vandalia drew hundreds of thousands of small subsistence farmers from the other confederations and Europe. The Vandalian population, less than 80,000 on the eve of the Rocky Mountain War, was over a half million by 1850 (part of this increase, of course, was the result of annexation). The census of 1870 credited Vandalia with 4.5 million inhabitants; in 1877 the number was estimated at 6.8 million, and was still increasing at a rapid rate.

This fast growth created problems of administration, and in addition, there were conflicts between miners and farmers, immigrants and native-born Americans, settlers from Indiana and the N.C. on the one side and the S.C. on the other. Because of this, all members of the Grand Council but four recommended the division of the confederation. Governor Hiram Potter also supported division, which was accomplished in 1877. Northern Vandalia (the area north of the 40th parallel) contained the mines, many foreign-born and Indiana-N.C. settlers, and wheatlands, while Southern Vandalia had almost all the S.C. immigrants, the richest farmlands in the region, and the largest proportion of Negro North Americans in the C.N.A.[7] Galloway re-

---

7. David Lea. *Vandalia in the C.N.A.: A History* (Galloway, 1946), pp. 365–68; Martin Kleberg. *The Politics of Vandalian Separation* (New York, 1957). Potter's support was based in part on the fact that Vandalia would receive, through separation, the equivalent of five additional Senate seats.

mained the capital of Northern Vandalia, while Fort Lodge became the capital of Southern Vandalia.

Quebec was the only state to decline economically in the quarter of a century following the end of the war. There were political, cultural, and social reasons for Quebec's stagnation, as well as the economic problems endemic to that state.

Quebec had always been an uneasy member of the C.N.A. With a large, French-speaking population, a strong Catholic Church, and an economy based on subsistence agriculture, it had more in common with Durango and Chiapas than with English-speaking, Protestant Indiana or the Northern Confederation. During the war, many in Quebec made no secret of their pro-U.S.M. sympathies, and a few went so far as to demand independence from the C.N.A. Charles de Frontenac revived the *Patriote* movement as a terrorist organization. From 1855 to the time of his capture in 1864, de Frontenac killed some 3,000 of the English-speaking citizens of Quebec. His opponents responded in three ways. Some capitulated to the night bandits, paying sums of money for "protection," which were used to purchase supplies for the rebels. Others relied on the Quebec police to capture the *Patriotes*, and when the police failed to uncover them, formed a rival organization, the "Anti-Papists," which burned Catholic churches, killed French-Canadians, and in their own way were as brutal as the *Patriotes*. By 1858 many took the third alternative: emigration. During this period, over half a million residents of Quebec left their homes to relocate elsewhere. Most of the English-speaking people went to Massachusetts, Indiana, and Vandalia, while the French-speakers journeyed further, many to New Orleans, some to the U.S.M., and at least 500 to France. Since few Europeans or North Americans found Quebec inviting, the state's population actually declined, falling from 5.9 million in 1855 to 4.8 million a decade and a half later.[8]

European and North American investors, too, found little to attract them to Quebec. With an insurrectionary confederation, a generally unskilled population, and few known natural resources, it became the backwash of the nation and its greatest failure. Quebec would not turn the corner until the early twentieth century, and to this day remains the most undeveloped part of the C.N.A. As Etienne Bayard put it, "If Manitoba is the C.N.A. garden, Vandalia its granary, and the Northern Confederation its workshop, Quebec is the slum of the naion."[9]

During this same period, the three older confederations of the C.N.A.—the N.C., S.C., and Indiana, also became the nation's most

8. Etienne Bayard. *The Decline of Que-*    9. *Ibid*, p. 521.
*bec* (New York, 1965), pp. 442–43.

prosperous ones, although each had problems associated with growth
and change. In addition, they grew closer together culturally and socially, so that a New Yorker would feel comfortable in Michigan City
or Norfolk, while he would be out of place in Galloway and decidedly
uncomfortable in Quebec City.

The reason for this was the leveling nature of industrialization,
and the ease of transportation from one confederation to the other. By
1860, it was possible to travel efficiently and inexpensively from almost
any town in the eastern C.N.A. to any other, while goods were trans-
ported with equal ease. The Tennessee River area of Georgia, the
Michigan City region of Indiana, and the capital district around Burgoyne were all major steel-producing locations by 1870, and fabricat-
ing plants, mills, and rail terminals surrounded the vast beds of ore and
coal. New York, New Orleans, and Charleston became huge cities,
each dwarfing their European counterparts. North American universities, the most famous of which were Burgoyne, Harvard, Northwest,
Kings, Georgia, and Webster, produced more graduates than all of
Europe combined. C.N.A. medical standards were the highest in the
civilized world by 1870, and North American engineers, the most innovative. The period which began with the signing of the Hague
Treaty and ended with the economic collapse of 1880, saw the C.N.A.
take the technological lead in the world. Scarcely an important invention or technique of this era did not appear first in the C.N.A., was not
the product of C.N.A. laboratories, or was not refined by C.N.A.
manufacturers.[10] In writing to the Queen during the last days of his
North American tour of 1860, Prince Albert said, "If one had to pick
a place to live in the seventeenth century, it would be France. In the
eighteenth century, London was the center of the world, a position it
held when we first met. Now the flag of civilization has been passed
to the North Americans. During the last two months I have seen the
shape of the future; it is here, in this wonderful land."[11]

Much more would come in the next decade. A North American,
Henry Woodhouse, discovered the furnace method of steel production
in 1850; it was refined by another American, Milton Rommell, and
turned into big business by yet a third, Edwin Bromfield, who in 1871
organized North American Steel Corporation, which within fourteen
years outproduced all of Britain's mills. Benjamin Stilton, a Burgoyne
professor, discovered petroleum in western Pennsylvania in 1855;
Edgar Van Dant, a North American engineer, unlocked the secret of
the petroleum molecule and made possible its inexpensive reduction to

10. Robert Sobel. *The Epic Age of North American Industry* (Melbourne, 1960).
11. Sir John Welles. *A Love That Never Died: The Letters of Queen Victoria and Prince Albert* (London, 1935), p. 820.

lubricating oil, grease, kerosene, and vulcazine; John Rockefeller organized Consolidated Petroleum of North America, a gigantic trust which controlled over ninety percent of the C.N.A.'s petroleum supply by 1880. Building upon the work of his predecessors, Thomas Scott put together the Grand National Railroad, which by 1880 controlled 18,000 miles of track. Another rail tycoon, Andrew Carnegie, organized a rival line, the North American United, which owned 22,000 miles of track in 1880. Between them, Carnegie and Scott dominated rail transportation in the eastern C.N.A., and through good management and intelligence gave the nation the cheapest and most efficient lines in the world. Carnegie was the first to introduce sleeping and eating cars, air brakes, and carriage feeders; Scott was responsible for refrigerated cars, automatic switches, and the rationalization of gauges in 1878.[12] Others—Ralph Davis in ocean transportation, Gail Borden in food packing, Philip Peabody in chemicals, and Samuel Holt in textiles—led in their fields.[13]

The most innovative of all North Americans made his impact felt toward the end of this period of great growth. Thomas Edison, born in Indiana in 1847, perfected Aaron Garfield's telegraph when only twenty years old, thus making long distance transmission possible. Forming his own company, National Union, Edison won the contract for the construction of the Burgoyne-Mexico City linkage, which was completed in 1876.[14] During the next thirty years Edison invented a workable electric light bulb (National Electric, a subsidiary of National Union, electrified Burgoyne in 1880); a radio; a phonograph; a telephone; and motion pictures. "To whom shall we compare Edison?" asked the Queen in 1898. "There is none who has contributed more to the betterment of mankind than this wonderful man."[15] Even as the Queen spoke, Edison was working on still other, more amazing inventions. He would invent vitavision, the locomobile, and the airmobile between 1898 and his death by accident in 1903, when he was only fifty-six years old.[16]

North American politics were as bland as the nation's economic development was rapid. It was, as one writer called it, "the era of faceless men."[17] No Governor-General who served from 1853 to 1878 was either memorable or forceful in his programs.

12. John Flaherty. *Builders of North America* (London, 1967); Bernard Sennett, *The Growth of the North American Steel Industry* (New York, 1970).
13. James Queen. *North America's Age of Genius: 1855–1880* (London, 1959).
14. Horace Medill. *The American Da Vinci: Edison and His Works* (New York, 1954).
15. Sir John Welles. *Queen Victoria's Table Talk* (London, 1929), p. 204.
16. Philip Davis. *Second But To God: The Works of Thomas Edison of Indiana* (New York, 1911); George Ryder. *And There Was Light!* (New York, 1962).
17. Lewis Duane. *The Era of Faceless Men: The C.N.A. from 1845 to 1880* (New York, 1931), pp. 11–12.

Both the Liberals and Conservatives[18] realized the nation was in the midst of great growth, and neither wanted to take actions that might interfere with it. Each agreed to a policy of isolationism, reflecting the nation's mood after the war. Generally speaking, the Liberals became more allied with the rising industrial class than had previously been the case, supported high tariffs and hard money, and opposed national economic controls. The Conservatives remained the party of small businessmen, farmers, and moderate reformers. The party favored lower tariffs and were more willing to legislate economic controls than the Liberals. But such distinctions meant little in practice, for neither party had capable men willing to present such programs to the Grand Council and fight for them there. Finally, both parties were corrupt in this period. With few exceptions, leaders of both parties also held positions with outside interests, received "favors" from "sponsors," and tended to vote in their interests. Venality and cynicism ruled in Burgoyne, no matter which party held power.[19]

William Johnson was the shining exception. The Manitoban ended the war as promised, encouraged foreign investment, and presided over the beginning of the age of prosperity that came with the peace. Then, in August of 1856, after having signed the Hague Treaty, Johnson announced his retirement, and the Conservative caucus ratified his selection, Whitney Hawkins of Indiana, as the next Governor-General. Hawkins had served as Minister of the Exchequer in the Johnson government, was a capable financier, an able Cabinet member, but a man who had little experience in day-to-day politics. He was soon faced with hostile and ambitious rivals within his own party. In addition, Hawkins made a number of poor selections for his Cabinet, most notably Bruce King, Minister of Resources, who in the next two years stole more than N.A. £500,000 from the government and took bribes for twice than amount.[20]

The Conservatives were in disarray and disrepute by the time the 1858 elections were held. Hawkins insisted on leading the party, asking for vindication to "carry on the programs and policies of William Johnson." The Liberal caucus selected Councilman Kenneth Parkes of the Northern Confederation as its leader. Parkes had seen duty in the Rocky Mountain War, serving as Chapin's *aide* in 1846 and later on as

---

18. Without fanfare, the two parties simplified their names during the election campaign of 1853, to Liberal and Conservative.
19. Franklin Packard. *Plenty for Everyone: Corruption in the C.N.A. in the Age of Prosperity* (New York, 1950); Richard Maxwell. *The Prostitutes of Burgoyne: Conservative and Liberal in the Glory Years* (Mexico City, 1967); Simon Hall. *How Much?* (New York, 1890); Leland Turner. *Three Bags Full: The King Conspiracy* (New York, 1970).
20. Milton O'Casey. *The Hawkins Administration* (New York, 1953).

military governor of the conquered Mexico del Norte lands. He had been elected to the Grand Council in 1853, was known as a lady's man, and had connections at the Scott interests and other large corporations. He was also a skillful politician and a fine orator. Parkes' campaign was well-organized, while Hawkins scarcely spoke to his own leaders; the Liberals released new information regarding the King scandals just before Election Day, which hurt Hawkins.

### Results of the C.N.A. Election of 1858

| STATE | PARTY AFFILIATION OF COUNCILMEN | |
| --- | --- | --- |
|  | LIBERAL | CONSERVATIVE |
| Northern Confederation | 35 | 9 |
| Southern Confederation | 13 | 17 |
| Quebec | 8 | 14 |
| Indiana | 10 | 14 |
| Manitoba | 5 | 16 |
| Vandalia | 7 | 2 |
|  | 78 | 72 |

Source: New York *Herald*, February 16, 1858.

The councilmanic races were close, and Parkes might not have won were it not for wholesale vote-buying in the Northern Confederation, the bribing of two Vandalian councilmen, and Liberal threats to disclose thievery on the part of five Indianans.[21] It was the most corrupt election the C.N.A. had seen up to that time; more would follow.

The Parkes administration was thoroughly pro-big business. The Hawley Tariff raised rates to new highs; the Bank of North America was transformed into a central bank, under the control of New York and London financiers; the Grand Council voted new appropriations to assist the railroads and lowered taxes on large enterprises; almost every post in the national government was for sale, and many were bought by big businessmen. In this period, too, the Northern Confederation legislature was dominated by "big money and railroads," and large slices of Vandalia were given as "gifts" to friends of Governor-General Parkes. Yet throughout all this, Parkes remained personally popular; he won a major victory in 1863, when the Liberals increased their margin in the Grand Council from 78–72 to 89–61, with the additional votes coming from purchased elections in Vandalia and Indiana. Parkes himself became a wealthy man during these years; although

21. Sidney Bostwick. *Every Man Has His Price: The Elections of 1858* (Burgoyne, 1958).

the size of his fortune was not known until after he died in 1878, at the time its was estimated to be well over N.A. £700,000.[22]

Parkes announced he would not seek a third term, and that "Liberals throughout the land shall be allowed to select the next governor-general in an open convention." Thus, the party caucus, long considered corrupt, was now replaced by a convention of delegates from all parts of the C.N.A., most of whom were equally venal and more easily bought. The result was as expected. The delegates, all well-paid and instructed, selected Parkes' protégé, Victor Astor of the Northern Confederation, as their leader. Astor, who had served as Governor of the Northern Confederation, had his master's charm and political acumen, as well as his penchant for enriching himself at the public's expense. He pledged to the cheering convention, "To carry on the fine work begun by Kenneth Parkes, and to bring our nation to new heights of glory and respect among the peoples of the world." Some thought they saw in Astor's speech a hint of a more aggressive foreign policy. Such was not the case; Astor had not seen the speech—which had been written by party boss William Conrad—prior to delivering it to the Burgoyne Convention.[23]

At the rival Conservative convention in New York, the party's leaders harangued the delegates about the corruption of the Liberals, their alliance with big business, and the need for reform. In truth, however, most of the speakers were concerned with getting their own share of the spoils. If the Conservatives were more honest than the Liberals it was due less to innate purity than to the lack of opportunity.

After bitter squabbles, the Conservatives selected Councilman Herbert Clemens of Indiana as the party's standard bearer. Clemens had served as a major in the war and afterwards returned to Michigan City, where he opened a dry goods establishment that soon became the largest in the state. Personally wealthy, he could not be accused of wanting office for gain. Clemens appeared rough-hewn, simple, and honest. "I shall do what is right," he told the delegates, "and will do so with dispatch, honestly and openly." Clemens then poured a good part of his personal fortune into the race, and stressing the corruption of his

22. The actual Parkes estate was valuted at N.A. £2,454,650. It should be remembered, however, that Parkes made an additional fortune by going into business after leaving office, and that much of his estate was hidden, and not reported in the final will. Leland Turner. *The Tin Cup Governor-General: The Parkes Estate* (New York, 1967).

23. It should be noted that Astor was also the owner of at least fifteen houses of prostitution in New York and Philadelphia. He freely admitted this in 1872, noting that "a little fun did no one harm." Milton O'Casey. *I Never Told a Lie: The Political Career of Victor Astor* (New York, 1950), pp. 336–407.

opponent (while purchasing votes himself) won sufficient ballots to become the next governor-general.[24]

Clemens' first administration was, indeed, reform-minded. Out of office for ten years, the Conservatives intended to make up for lost time. They punished those businessmen who had allied themselves with the Liberals, and sought "favors" from their opponents. This meant Clemens' supporters tended to be middle-sized companies, more often from Indiana and the Southern Confederation than from the Northern Confederation. This, and the fact the Conservatives were less open in their corruption, gave the Clemens government an undeserved reputation for honesty.

## Results of the C.N.A. Elections of 1868

| STATE | PARTY AFFILIATION OF COUNCILMEN | |
|---|---|---|
| | LIBERAL | CONSERVATIVE |
| Northern Confederation | 33 | 11 |
| Southern Confederation | 9 | 21 |
| Quebec | 8 | 14 |
| Indiana | 11 | 13 |
| Manitoba | 2 | 19 |
| Vandalia | 2 | 7 |
| | 65 | 85 |

Source: New York *Herald*, February 15, 1868.

All the major Clemens reforms, however, were self-serving. The Reform Act of 1870, for example, which reapportioned the Council, added seats for the Northern Confederation, Indiana, and Vandalia, while the Southern Confederation, Manitoba, and Quebec lost seats. At the time this seemed disinterested, since the S.C. and Quebec were both strongly Conservative, while the N.C. and Indiana had powerful Liberal parties. "As I said before, we must do what is right, not what is expedient," said Clemens. In fact, new districts were so drawn as to dissipate Liberal votes and assure a larger delegation of Conservatives from each confederation than would have been the case had the reforms not taken place.[26]

The elections of 1873 were the first to be conducted under the redistricting. They saw the appearance of the first major third party in

25. Arthur Kurtz. *Clemens of Indiana: Pirate with a Clerical Collar* (New York, 1960), pp. 420–36.
26. Theodore Kirk. "An Analysis of the Redistricting Bill of 1870, and its Implications in Indiana, the Northern Confederation, and the Southern Confederation, with a Note on Vandalia." *The Journal of Politics*, January 12, 1970, pp. 21–34.

C.N.A. history, the People's Coalition, which ran candidates for confederation and local office, as well as a full slate for the Grand Council. The People's Coalition proved the surprise of the decade by taking command of the legislatures in New Hampshire, North Carolina, and Virginia, where they displaced the Conservatives, and electing ten members to the Grand Council. Clemens won a second term easily, but the People's Coalition was the greatest victor in the 1873 election, and the clearest sign that all was not well in the nation.

### *Results of the C.N.A. Elections of 1873*

| STATE | PARTY AFFILIATION OF COUNCILMEN | | |
| | LIBERAL | CONSERVATIVE | PEOPLE'S COALITION |
| --- | --- | --- | --- |
| Northern Confederation | 34 | 10 | 1 |
| Southern Confederation | 7 | 17 | 5 |
| Indiana | 8 | 17 | 4 |
| Vandalia | 9 | 12 | 0 |
| Manitoba | 5 | 8 | 0 |
| Quebec | 0 | 13 | 0 |
| | 63 | 77 | 10 |

Source: New York *Herald*, February 15, 1873.

# 14

# THE PEOPLE'S COALITION

T HE dramatic emergence of the People's Coalition and its immediate success in the 1873 elections were a direct reflection of the
discontent that existed in the midst of prosperity.[1] To be sure, any educated person realized the nation had its share of internal problems. The
events of the Crisis Years, the Quebec turmoil, the riots during the
Rocky Mountain War—all were symptomatic. Far more serious in the
1870's, however, was the complex of problems resulting from the nation's successful industrialization. Unperceived by most North Americans, industrialism had created a new kind of society, one that could be
discerned in embryo prior to the War, and which now emerged full
blown.

In 1870—the same year North American Steel Corporation and
Imperial Dry Goods were formed, and Rockefeller entered the petroleum business as incorporator of Pennsylvania Petroleum—North
America exported more finished, manufactured goods than agricultural
products. For the first time, the industrial sector outdid the cotton and
wheat fields in value of exports. Never again would agriculture be as
important in the C.N.A.

The 1870 census showed that 71.9 percent of North Americans
lived in rural areas, with the rest residing in urban centers with populations of 50,000 or more. That same year only 57.3 percent of Northern
Confederationists lived on farm regions. The 1880 census placed 65.5
percent of North Americans in rural areas; it also showed that 48.8
percent of Northern Confederationists lived in rural areas. Thus, the
N.C. had become a primarily urban confederation during the late
1870's. Not until 1900 would Indiana become predominantly urban,

---

1. Actually, the first meeting of a local
political organization calling itself the
People's Party took place at Fort Ras-
musson, Quebec, in 1856, but this group
had no direct connection with the
People's Coalition of 1873. At least
fifteen confederation groups claimed to
have been the founder of the Coalition.
Most historians agree that it began in
Norfolk in 1869, but that the ideals on
which it was based spread independent
of the organization. See Julius Carter.
*The People Want Bread: A History of
the People's Coalition* (New York,
1937), pp. 88–97.

and the others (except Manitoba and Southern Vandalia) would follow in the next generation.[2]

In 1860 there were approximately 3.3 million Negro North Americans, roughly ten percent of the population. Of these, 74.6 percent lived in the S.C., and more than half were still bound to the soil. Prosperity, inexpensive transportation, and harassment had led many Negroes to leave their homes and head west across the Mississippi. According to the 1880 census, Southern Vandalia had 2.2 million Negroes out of a C.N.A. black population of 5.9 million.[3] Since Southern Vandalia had a total population of only 3.2 million, it may be considered to have become a "black confederation" by that time. Southern Vandalia had excellent farms, good river and rail transport, and a satisfactory climate. The Negroes there prospered, and although there was little racial mixing in 1880, there was also no important friction between the races. Burgoyne Willkie, the son of a manumitted slave and a self-taught lawyer, was elected first Governor of Southern Vandalia in 1887, on a vote which divided along racial lines. But Willkie proved a capable and fair administrator, and he received over thirty percent of the white vote when he ran for re-election in 1892.[4]

Fears that Southern Vandalia would in time become a "black Quebec" proved groundless. The state's loyalty to the nation was never in question, even when talk of secession began elsewhere.[5] But the racial question persisted in other parts of the C.N.A., and remained a burning question in the S.C. and N.C. This too was a problem created by industrialization, for those Negroes who left the S.C. for the N.C. after 1855 were drawn there by jobs in the cities, where they mingled with immigrants and native Northern Confederationists, neither of whom had any love for those whom they called "the black apes" and "the niggers."[6]

In 1860, no North American firm was capitalized at more than N.A. £20 million. By 1869, there were eleven firms capitalized at over

2. Confederation of North America. Department of Statistics. *The Census of 1870* (Burgoyne, 1872), p. 1045; Confederation of North America. Department of Statistics. *The Census of 1900* (Burgoyne, 1901), pp. 335, 465, 658, 997, 1476.

3. That same year the S.C. had 1.1 million Negroes, the N.C. 1.0 million with the remainder scattered throughout the rest of the nation.

4. Burgoyne Willkie. *Good Friends and Fair People* (Fort Lodge, 1895). Willkie was never accepted socially by the Southern Vandalian whites. The

confederation had an interesting form of self-segregation, which Willkie chose to ignore. Today Willkie is considered a tool of white oppressors by many militant Negroes, while at the same time honored by whites as a great man. Chester Winslow. *Willkie and the Rise of Black North America* (New York, 1969), pp. 88, 104, 245.

5. Stewart Hoskinson. *The Loyal Americans: The Negroes of Southern Vandalia* (New York, 1962).

6. Chester Winslow. *The Race Problem in the N.C.: 1857–1892* (New York, 1965).

N.A. £34 million. The first N.A. £50 million firm, North American Steel, made its appearance the following year. In 1878 there were nine North American firms capitalized at more than N.A. £60 million.[7]

At the time of the Hague Treaty of 1855, approximately 90 percent of all mercantile and manufacturing business done in the C.N.A. was handled by firms with twenty or fewer employees; by 1878, 74 percent was handled by companies employing over one hundred men and women. In 1855 every confederation had major banks able to finance local business; by 1878, the nation's five largest banking organizations were in New York City, and of the top twenty banks, only two were in Michigan City and one in Norfolk. One small area in New York, Broad Street, financed most of the business in the C.N.A. Of the one hundred leading North American corporations (banks and railroads as well as manufacturing enterprises) seventy-nine had headquarters in New York, and an additional eleven were to be found in Philadelphia and Boston.[8]

Some may see in these facts and figures a picture of a vital and growing people, moving rapidly toward an industrial society. This was true, to be sure, but the changes also brought many problems in their wake. The rapid growth of the cities created large slum and ghetto areas. By 1868 gangs had formed in New York, Philadelphia, and Michigan City, usually based on ethnic origin or race, and the police were barely able to prevent conflicts between them. One predominantly Irish gang, the Merry Walkers, seized City Hall in New York and held it for two weeks in 1869 before the state militia could dislodge them. The Merry Walker insurrection sparked other, similar movements throughout the cities of North America, so that urban, middle-class citizens went literally in fear of their lives.[9]

Then, too, there was the problem of wages. The old unions of pre-Rocky Mountain War days proved incapable of bargaining effectively with the large corporations that had emerged in the 1860's and after. Although productivity rose dramatically, wages did not, and this resulted in widespread urban unrest. The Grand Consolidated Union, which had never been strong or well-led, was now replaced by three different kinds of organizations, each with its own set of leaders and philosophy, and which vied with one another for support among the working class, especially in the Northern Confederation.

The first and most important group of new unions drew its members from the skilled trades. Its beginnings were on the railroads,

7. Robert Sobel. ed. *A Statistical Survey of North American Business, 1855–1910* (New York, 1957), pp. 452, 758, 1087.

8. *Ibid*, pp. 332, 654, 879, 1103.
9. Edward Hetherington. *Urban Riot: The N.C. Cities in the 1870s* (London, 1956).

where the engineers formed the Consolidated Engineering Fraternity in 1857. This was followed by unions of switchmen, yardmen, and dispatchers. In the steel industry there were foremen's unions, and organizations for pourers, keymen, and mechanics; along the docks there were loaders' and warehouse managers' unions, and similar groups in other trades. These unions came together in 1874 in the Mechanics National Union, which was organized by Michael Harter of the Yardmen. Generally speaking, the M.N.U. worked for higher wages, better working conditions for its members, and a share in the profits for supervisory personnel. The M.N.U. was also strongly in favor of laws to restrict immigration, high tariffs, and stronger police forces to put down urban insurrections. Although management resented the M.N.U., it found the unions fairly easy to work with, and by 1880 the organizations of skilled workers had been incorporated fairly well in the industrial complex.[10]

The second type of union was that composed of all workers in a single industry or factory. In 1861, William Richter brought together the tobacco workers in such an organization, and others followed in the next decade. Often these industry-wide unions clashed with the M.N.U.; in 1869, the M.N.U. and the dockworkers union both tried to organize along the New York piers and a labor war erupted which ended with police intervention and the subsequent victory of the Mechanics National. Learning from this lesson, the industry unions met in Philadelphia in 1870 to form the Consolidated Laborers Federation, which by 1874 had over half a million members. In general, the C.L.F. worked for industry-wide bargaining, recognition of themselves as sole negotiating agents, and political action, as well as higher wages. In 1873 many C.L.F. locals worked for Conservative Party candidates, but as we shall see, the national organization allied itself with the People's Coalition.[11]

A relative handful of workers were attracted by still a third union, the United Workers of the World. The U.W.W., headquartered in New York, denied the value of higher wages and better working conditions to solve the basic problems posed by a capitalist system. The only way to distribute the products of the factories equitably, they claimed, was for the workers to rise up, overthrow the industrialists, and run the factories themselves.[12] To this end, the U.W.W. refused

---

10. Max Finnigan. *Organizing the Elite: A History of the M.N.U.* (New York, 1968).
11. Howard Hopkins. *Saints in Overalls: The Consolidated Laborers Federation in Confederation of North American History* (London, 1955).
12. Many of these ideas were first put forth by a German philosopher, Karl Marx, whose major work, *The Anatomy of Capitalism*, had influence among the socialists of the 1870's and after. See Hendrick Petersson. *The Philosophy and Works of Karl Marx: His Epistemology, Ontology, and Gestalt* (London, 1943).

to join with either the Liberals or Conservatives, and even found the People's Coalition "overly sentimental." Led by a German immigrant, Daniel Schwartz, the U.W.W. had some impact on those industries that hired many new Americans, and appealed strongly to militant Canadians. By 1878, the U.W.W. had joined with the *Patriotes*, and soon after all but disappeared from view in the other states.[13]

The rapid industrialization of the C.N.A. had a still greater effect on farmers, especially the cotton barons of the Southern Confederation. Even before the Rocky Mountain War the planters had begun to price themselves out of the market, and after the Hague Treaty, as Jefferson cotton once again reached the marketplace, the Southern Confederation found its product less in demand each year. High labor costs, leached soil, and a general lack of interest in cotton by the younger generation, added to foreign competition, caused many plantations to convert to other crops, while others simply went bankrupt, and were later subdivided into small farms. In the 1830's, "white gold" was the key C.N.A. product; by 1870 it was relatively unimportant, as the S.C. itself was swept up in the industrial revolution, and population became concentrated in the Tennessee River area of Georgia (especially the cities of Lloyd, New Birmingham, and Clyde).

Once a Liberal stronghold, the Southern Confederation now became increasingly Conservative, as the Tennessee Valley workers, whose wages were generally lower than those of N.C. workers, demanded equality. The party of John Calhoun, based as it was on the plantation owners, seemed an anachronism in the 1870's, while that of Lloyd was able to adjust to the new conditions. As early as 1868, the Conservatives put themselves forth as the party of the "New Southern Confederation," by which they meant "the laborers, the businessmen, and the merchants." In disarray, the Liberals attempted for the first time to make an appeal to rural Negroes. This failed, but even had the Liberals succeeded, the emigration of Negroes to Southern Vandalia and the N.C. would have made such an alliance of white and black farmers a permanent political minority. As rural population and income declined while that of urban centers rose, the farmers and former plantation owners of the S.C. were ready for a new political organization.[14]

Looking upon the Conservatives as their natural enemies and the Liberals as a party that lacked relevance, younger Negro and white farmers, together with several now-impoverished plantation owners, united in the People's Party of the Southern Confederation in 1869.

13. Max Finnigan. *While the Iron Is Hot: The Early Years of the U.W.W.* (London, 1970); Wayne Carton. *Brothers in Oppression: The U.W.W.* and the Patriotes (Mexico City, 1950).
14. Martin Tucker. *The Rise of the New Southern Confederation* (New York, 1960).

The Party's goals were simple. It would work for a heavy business tax, the proceeds to be used to revive agriculture. Government banks would be established to offer farmers low interest loans; government would guarantee the price of cotton; and finally, the railroads, turnpikes and canals would be placed under the control of a state agency which would determine rates.[15] These four points, known as the Norfolk Resolves, became the basis of the People's Party in the S.C.

On learning of the new organization, workers and farmers from other states rushed to form branches. The impetus in the N.C. came from Richter and the Consolidated Laborers Federation, although thousands of small businessmen, squeezed by the new industrial giants and the railroads, also joined. In Indiana, wealthy wheat farmers, who felt themselves victimized by N.C.-controlled banks and railroads, also formed units of the now-renamed People's Coalition. Radical intellectuals from Manitoba, struggling pioneers of Northern Vandalia, and the lower classes in almost every part of the nation were attracted to the new party. The only exceptions were the French Canadians and the immigrants, the former because the People's Coalition seemed uninterested in destroying the nation politically, the latter because the Norfolk Resolves said nothing of their plight. Indeed, as it grew in strength, the People's Coalition added hatred of the newcomers to that of big business. "The capitalists of the Northern Confederation are controlled from the City in London," said Matthew Ruffin, one of the Coalition spokesmen in 1878, "and so are the slumdwellers, who have been sent here to aid their masters in making the C.N.A. a colony in fact as well as in theory."[16] Although receiving much support from laborers, the Coalition was strongly anti-urban, issuing strong blasts against the political machines, most of them Conservative, which controlled the cities. These attacks led to a flocking of immigrants to the Conservative Party, and added to the older organization's strength.[17]

All three parties held conventions in 1878. The Liberals gathered in Philadelphia in a mood of despair. They had been out of power for ten years. During that time the scandals of the Parkes administration had been made public. Parkes had died a week before the convention, and news of his will was on the front pages of most newspapers, reminding voters of their corrupt former governor-general. Astor was hardly the kind of man to lead the party, especially since he had not only retained ownership of his houses of prostitution after their dis-

15. Max Finnigan. "The Origins of the People's Party, and the Writing of the Norfolk Resolves." *The Journal of Politics*, December 4, 1958, pp. 934–57.
16. Julius Carter, ed. *Voices of Reform and Bigotry: The People Coalition Speaks* (New York, 1940), p. 192.
17. William English. *New Friends in an Old Bed: The Immigrant-Conservative Alliance of 1878* (New York, 1969).

closure in 1872, but had actually added to their number.[18] There were, however, several candidates anxious for party leadership. Councilman John Runk of Georgia was a handsome man, a good speaker, and had a generally reformist record in the Grand Council. But Runk had been an admirer of Calhoun, and could not hope for Negro votes or those of their allies. Former Governor Claude Baldwin of Indiana, a man who had been elected twice in a Conservative state, also offered himself for consideration. Baldwin was corrupt, however, and what is more, all the C.N.A. knew it. Finally, there was Councilman John McDowell of Manitoba, who had all the assets and liabilities of most of his confederation's political leaders. He was personally honest and outspoken, a reformer, and a competent legislator with few enemies. McDowell was also unknown in most of the rest of the nation and had little identification with either the old, corrupt politics of the 1870's or the new reformism of the Coalition. Still, McDowell was the most attractive leader the Liberals could find, and the party selected him as its spokesman, without much hope of having him elected.

The Conservatives was a different party in 1878 from what it had been five years earlier. Many reformers had deserted to the People's Coalition, but their places had been taken by English and Irish immigrant spokesmen, urban machine leaders, and some Liberals who had been affected by the reform wave, but were not yet ready to join the Coalition. Clemens was at the Michigan City Convention to lead the party, but announced he would not accept another term. His administration had been relatively free of scandal. Clemens had done a good job in welding together a coalition of small businessmen, farmers, and Negroes, although many Negroes had already been attracted by the Coalition, while the workers, always uneasy in the two major parties, were also drawn to the new organization. On the surface the Conservatives appeared strong, but underneath there were elements of weakness. On specific orders from Clemens the party selected Governor Joseph Fellows of Indiana as its leader, and the nominee pledged himself "to the continuation of the prosperity we have enjoyed for the past decade."[19]

The People's Coalition gathered in New York in 1878 for a wild, disorderly meeting. Whatever plans had been made prior to the convention were forgotten after the first day.[20] Instead, the majority of

18. O'Casey. *I Never Told a Lie*, p. 472.
19. Edwin Doe. *The Last Days of C.N.A. Conservatism* (Burgoyne, 1952).
20. Writing in the New York *Herald*, an unnamed reporter viewed the convention as "a combination circus-revival meeting-German wedding-Irish wake, managed by people who are novices at this sort of thing, and attended by some of the strangest characters ever to be seen in C.N.A. politics." New York *Herald*, January 4, 1878.

delegates chanted and hooted, screamed and danced, as older politicians, some of them refugees from the two major parties, looked on in wonderment and horror. In the end, however, they did transact convention business, but here too the People's Coalition did it in an unusual manner. "It would scarcely be democratic to select a 'leader,'" screamed Nathaniel Teller of Northern Vandalia. "The people do not need one, since they can trust themselves to run their own affairs." Edward Dietrich of the Northern Confederation suggested the Coalition name no single person for the governorship-general, but have the strongest candidates possible stand in each state, and then, if the Coalition was sufficiently strong to do so, have a new convention after the election to determine which of the councilmen should become the next governor-general. It was a unique, rather appealing idea, but it did not take into consideration the tradition-minded North Americans who would resent the Coalition suggesting it "buy an unseen dog." The plan was adopted, however, and amid the cheering of the delegations, leaders of the Consolidated Laborers Federation entered the hall, and Richter himself pledged his support for the People's Coalition.[21]

The brief campaign that followed saw some of the most vicious and underhanded politicking in C.N.A. history, as Liberals and Conservatives alike warned workers and farmers of dire happenings should the Coalition win the Grand Council majority. Several Coalition candidates in the S.C. were waylaid and beaten badly; in Indiana, Coalition headquarters was burned to the ground; in New York, Richter was seized by unknown people and held until after the election, the C.L.F. being warned that "Your leader will die if the Coalition wins in the Northern Confederation."[22]

The violence was started by the Liberals and Conservatives, but, toward the end of the campaign, the Coalition retaliated. In the end, all three parties were guilty of undemocratic and murderous activity as the public watched in shock and disbelief. A wave of middle-class revulsion against the killings and desecrations swept the land, and voters turned to the candidate who seemed most likely to restore harmony.

McDowell, hitherto a probable poor third in the election, awoke the morning of February 16 to find the Liberals with a plurality in the new Grand Council. Immediately, he was besieged by politicians of all three parties, discussing deals that would give him a majority in the governorship-general balloting. But McDowell refused to concede anything to the Coalition or Conservative councilmen who approached him. "Let each man vote his conscience," he is reported to have said.

---

21. New York *Herald*, January 5, 1878; New York *Times*, January 6–7, 1878; Philadelphia *Messenger*, January 6, 1878.

22. William Harris. *The Bloody Ballot: The C.N.A. Elections of 1878* (New York, 1943).

### Results of the C.N.A. Elections of 1878

|  | PARTY AFFILIATION OF COUNCILMEN | | |
|---|---|---|---|
| STATE | LIBERAL | CONSERVATIVE | PEOPLE'S COALITION |
| Northern Confederation | 28 | 7 | 10 |
| Southern Confederation | 7 | 13 | 9 |
| Indiana | 9 | 10 | 10 |
| Northern Vandalia | 5 | 5 | 1 |
| Southern Vandalia | 3 | 6 | 1 |
| Manitoba | 9 | 2 | 2 |
| Quebec | 1 | 6 | 6 |
|  | 62 | 49 | 39 |

Source: New York *Herald*, February 16, 1878.

McDowell won the election on the seventh ballot, when sufficient moderates from both the Coalition and Conservatives switched their votes. He could truly tell the nation, "I come to this office without a single pledge to any man."[23]

### Grand Council Votes for Governor-General in 1878

| CANDIDATE | BALLOT | | | | | | |
|---|---|---|---|---|---|---|---|
|  | FIRST | SECOND | THIRD | FOURTH | FIFTH | SIXTH | SEVENTH |
| McDowell (L) | 62 | 62 | 62 | 62 | 74 | 73 | 89 |
| Fellows (C) | 49 | 49 | 49 | 49 | 45 | 46 | 37 |
| Ruffin (PC) | 20 | 30 | 39 | 39 | 30 | 28 | 12 |
| Teller (PC) | 19 | 9 | 0 | 0 | 1 | 3 | 12 |

Source: New York *Herald*, February 22, 1878.

Whether because of conviction or political shrewdness, Mc-Dowell's first two years were overwhelmingly successful, and the new executive proved a most effective politician. McDowell secured passage of a series of laws in 1878–1879 that did much to quiet Coalition demands. The Railroad Control Commission Act of 1878 established a regulatory body for the nation's railroads, which had the power to investigate complaints and make recommendations for rate adjustments. The Williamson Anti-Monopoly Act gave the Minister of

---

23. It should be noted, however, that McDowell didn't have to make such deals, because his election was all but certain at the time. Thus he won the reputation for honesty without having to pay the price of a loss. See Worthington Fowler. *John McDowell and the Fruits of Reform* (New York, 1899); Reuben Fenton. *McDowell: Appearance and Reality* (New York, 1957).

Home Affairs the right to prosecute any large corporation or railroad "engaged in unfair or unethical practices." The Civil Rights Act of 1879 guaranteed for all C.N.A. citizens "the full protection of law in their public pursuits"; while the Morgan Act "encouraged management and labor to reach equitable solutions to their common problem." All these enactments were cheered by the reform elements, while the big businessmen and bankers realized that few of the measures had effective enforcement provisions. Thus, McDowell achieved a reputation as a reformer without having to pay the price of business opposition.[24]

One area in which the reality and appearance were the same, was that of honesty in government. True to his promise, McDowell ran an honest administration. In 1878, he organized the Confederation Bureau of Investigation to supervise the various agencies of the national government. The C.B.I. did its work well, rooting out dishonest men and their allies. McDowell received much public support for the C.B.I.'s investigations, and for every enemy he made, he won the admiration of hundreds of voters.[25]

McDowell was riding the crest of his popularity when the world depression of 1880 hit the C.N.A. Like the crisis of the mid-1830's, the depression had its origins in Europe. In 1878, the long-simmering tensions between the Germanic Confederation and France finally erupted. For the past two decades Germany had undergone rapid economic growth, surpassing France in almost every industrial category. Then, in 1870, German King Frederick William V embarked on a large-scale naval construction program, and three years later, German merchants began to invade French markets in Africa and Asia. To this were added longstanding disputes over border regions in Europe. Inevitably, war came in the late autumn of 1878. King Frederick William claimed the French had fired the first shot, while King Louis XX of France blamed the Germans. In truth, both nations wanted war, and were eager for the conflict when it came.[26]

The war, though expected, took Europe's bankers by surprise, since few thought it would come before the spring of 1879. Immediately panic struck the money markets in Paris and Berlin, and was transmitted to London and New York. But the latter two markets recovered within a week, and the monetary crisis eased soon after. To all outward appearances, then, the Franco-German War would not affect the English-speaking world.

---

24. Fowler. *John McDowell*, pp. 332–38.
25. Fenton. *McDowell*, pp. 119–82.
26. Heinrich Himmelstein. *The War for the World* (London, 1907); Yves Marchand. *The Coming of the Franco-German War* (London, 1965).

But it did affect the Empire. Prime Minister Geoffrey Cadogan, ever mindful of the possibility of a general war, ordered a mobilization of the army and doubled the naval appropriations in 1879. Within a year, Britain was on a war footing, prepared for whatever might come.

Higher taxes, fear of war, increased interest rates in Britain—all served to discourage further investment in North America. Beginning in early 1879, British bankers began to call in their C.N.A. loans, and new investment fell sharply. By year's end, more money was leaving North America than was coming in, and withdrawals reached flood tide in January, 1880.

### *New Foreign Investment in the C.N.A., 1877–1882*
#### (IN MILLIONS OF N.A. POUNDS)

| YEAR | BRITISH INVESTMENTS | OTHER FOREIGN INVESTMENTS | TOTAL |
|------|---------------------|---------------------------|-------|
| 1877 | 30.7 | 9.2 | 39.9 |
| 1878 | 36.5 | 6.2 | 44.7 |
| 1879 | 10.2 | 2.1 | 12.3 |
| 1880 | −22.4 | −6.4 | −28.8 |
| 1881 | −26.0 | −3.1 | −29.1 |
| 1882 | −10.3 | −1.3 | −11.6 |

Source: C.N.A. *Statistical Abstract*, p. 796.

The C.N.A. banks attempted to cover British withdrawals for the first three months of 1880. Then, in April, the Northern Confederation Trust closed its doors and announced its insolvency. The following week, North American Steel announced it would close down two mills due to lack of capital. National Electric, which had just completed the electrification of Burgoyne, declared bankruptcy in May, setting off a panic that struck every confederation.

Thus was ushered in a two and a half year financial crisis which was far worse than that of the 1830's, since the economy of the 1880's was so much more complex. The crisis ended the harmony of the McDowell administration, and turned the hopes of the past two decades into despair. Like the Crisis Years, the Great Depression brought fears of insurrection and radicalism in the C.N.A.[27]

27. Arthur Watkins. *The Great Depression of 1880–1883* (London, 1915); Sir Monte Barkins. *Long-Term Dislocations in the C.N.A. Economy in the Great Depression* (London, 1970).

# 15

# RECOVERY AND PROGRESS

THE United States of Mexico was able to recover from the scars of war within a few years of the Hague Treaty, but not so dramatically as the C.N.A. The nation was wracked by recriminations against what Continentalist leader Benito Calzón called "the betrayal of the memory of Pedro Hermión." Calzón argued that President Niles had "bartered away our birthright in Mexico del Norte for a questionable peace with a dastardly foe."[1] In fact, the overwhelming majority of Mexicans were happy to see the long war ended, but sought a scapegoat for the supposed defeat. Had Hermión lived, in all probability, he would have been castigated as an overly ambitious demagogue who was responsible for the loss of 90,000 Mexican lives in a fruitless and senseless war. When Hermión had come to office in 1845, the nation had been rich and optimistic; the Mexico of 1855 was bankrupt and in the depths of despair. Niles had been responsible for none of this; indeed, he had ended the disastrous war on most advantageous terms. Nonetheless, he reaped the whirlwind sown by his predecessor. Ironically, Hermión was politically deified, while the unhappy Niles was afraid of leaving the presidential palace for fear of assassination attempts.[2]

From 1855 to 1857 Niles valiantly struggled to return to Mexico a measure of its pre-war prosperity. As before, the French were willing to cooperate, advancing long-term loans at advantageous interest rates, to a nation King Louis XIX had come to look upon as his protégé. The combination of French money, a resurrected cotton-export program, continued exploitation of the mining sector, and the first dividends from the generation-old development programs in Chiapas and Durango, helped raise the U.S.M. to its pre-war economic level by 1858. A considerable factor, also, was the vitality of the Mexican people—

---

1. Hector Corazón. *The Vida y Obras de Benito Calzón de Durango* (Mexico City, 1962), pp. 49, 106.

2. Simon Rabbino. *Except in His Native Land: The Irony of the Niles Presidency* (London, 1970).

Anglos, Hispanos, Indians, and Mexicanos alike—who sacrificed will-ingly to restore the nation to its former stature.

Not recognized or appreciated at the time, was the skillful leader-ship of President Niles. Even before the Hague Treaty was ratified, Niles had ordered Secretary of Home Affairs Fidel Sonora to "make an inventory of assets and liabilities, to determine where we stand." Sonora was able to report that conditions were better than had been believed. The war had barely touched the developed parts of the na-tion, having been fought primarily in the northern reaches of Mexico; indeed, Sonora recommended federal aid only to the Indian tribes in Mexico del Norte and Arizona who had suffered most from the war. All seemed well in California, Jefferson, Durango, and Chiapas. Most important, gold production had remained stable during the war, and since little had been shipped to Europe for sale, the reserves provided the nation with reconstruction capital.

### Selected U.S.M. Statistics, 1840–1870

| YEAR | GROSS NATIONAL PRODUCT | FOREIGN DEBT & INVESTMENTS (IN MILLIONS OF DOLARES) | IMPORTS | EXPORTS |
|------|------|------|------|------|
| 1840 | 304 | 30 | 42 | 35 |
| 1845 | 348 | 24 | 47 | 45 |
| 1850 | 398 | 110 | 62 | 20 |
| 1855 | 388 | 122 | 82 | 22 |
| 1860 | 354 | 134 | 114 | 69 |
| 1865 | 586 | 85 | 100 | 98 |
| 1870 | 701 | 89 | 119 | 122 |

Source: U.S.M. *Statistical Abstract*, pp. 109, 539.

The war had caused a shortage of cotton in Europe, and Jeffer-son's planters received a new lease on life. During the first post-war decade, that state would compete with the S.C. for domination of Europe's cotton market, usually with great success. For the first time in a generation, Jefferson's remaining cotton aristocrats tasted pros-perity. But the cotton economy of the late 1850's was quite different from that of a generation earlier. The beginnings of mechanization were evident, and machines, each able to replace dozens of slaves, had made their appearances. Once the key to cotton culture, the slave, by 1860, was an uneconomic and embarrassing relic.

As plantation owners spent profits and borrowed money to pur-chase new equipment, the demand for and price of slaves stabilized, and then declined. The plantation owners would not consider manumission—the idea of living among freed Negroes was repulsive to the average Jeffersonian of that day—but little effort was made to capture escaped slaves if the owners felt they would eventually cross the Mississippi into the C.N.A. Almost by tacit agreement, slavery declined in Jefferson, although neither Jefferson City or Mexico City would admit the fact.[3]

Another factor in Jefferson's economic growth was the discovery of petroleum in the Tiempo de Dios area in 1863. At the time, it was believed the Jefferson discovery was minor compared with the oil found in the N.C. and of the enormous Indiana wells, then the leading producers of petroleum in the world. In 1865, Jefferson produced only 10,000 barrels of petroleum while Indiana totalled 2 million. But as the Jeffersonian fields were explored more fully, the Mexicans came to realize the entire state was floating on a sea of oil, and French and Jeffersonian businessmen rushed to stake claims. In 1870, Jefferson produced 2.1 million barrels against Indiana's 5.2 million; in 1875, both produced approximately 8.4 million. Jefferson went into the lead the following year, outproducing Indiana 8.9 million barrels to 8.8 million, and would never again relinquish the advantage.[4]

---

3. Jefferson's treatment of slavery was unique. At the end of the war, the state had some 150,000 slaves, with another 50,000 or so in the other states. The average price of a healthy, adult field hand, age 25, in 1856, was around one hundred dolares, so that the total Jeffersonian investment might be figured at some $15 million. But this is deceiving, for no other nation in the western world had slavery at the time, and so the slaves could not have been disposed of outside Mexico's borders. Realizing this, the planters were willing to see their slaves depart rather than face the alternatives of keeping them as economic chattel, or giving them freedom and allowing a potentially dangerous, large ex-slave population to live among them. Some scholars have claimed that Jefferson's solution was both open-handed and humane. Such was not the case. It was widely recognized at the time that the planters were simply following the course of least resistance by allowing their slaves to depart the way they did. By 1890 there were only 50,000 slaves in Jefferson, and another 50,000 elsewhere in the U.S.M. Although the average female slave produced 3.6 children from

1890 to 1920, the slave population of 1920 was only 103,000. Since the death rate declined in this period, it may only be assumed that most of the slaves crossed the Mississippi into Southern Vandalia. This is an almost blank subject in the histories of both countries, not through design, but rather because the C.N.A. and U.S.M. chose to ignore the one-way traffic. The best study of this subject is Luther Moltke. *Across the River Jordan: The Slave Trade and the Vandalia Trek* (Mexico City, 1950); William Matthias. *Like an Old Shoe: The Decline of Slavery in Jefferson* (Mexico City, 1961). The Revisionist school is best represented by Harley Crawford. *The Triumph of Humanism in Jefferson, 1855–1880* (Mexico City, 1969). For the views of "the Emancipator" on the subject, see Emiliano Calles. *The People and the Nation* (Mexico City, 1931), pp. 23–55. President Calles was the only major public figure ever to write extensively of the history of the Mississippi crossings, and did so after referring to secret Mexico City archives.

4. Frederick Montgomery. *A Short History of the Mexican Petroleum Industry* (London, 1951).

Jefferson's cotton aristocrats, who had undergone a remarkable resurrection, were now joined by a new leadership group, the petroleum millionaires. Each had its own set of interests and objectives, and their clash would determine the state's future and, ultimately, that of the nation. For the time being, however, Petroleum of Mexico, formed by Monte Benedict in 1874 (with 29 percent of the stock controlled by a Paris banking consortium), was the leading corporation in Mexico in terms of assets, sales, and profits, dwarfing even Van Dant's Pennsylvania Petroleum Corporation. Indeed, it was the P.M. challenge that led to the formation of the North American giant, Rockefeller's Consolidated Petroleum, which was incorporated in 1875.[5]

California also underwent an important economic change in the two post-war decades. By 1858 gold production was clearly on the decline, with only 875 thousand ounces being shipped; never again would California produce more than 850 thousand ounces a year. The state no longer attracted miners, who went instead to the silver and copper fields of Mexico del Norte and Northern Vandalia. Many remained, however, entranced by California's excellent climate and good soil. After the war, a fast-growing fruit and vegetable industry sprang up in the northern part of the state, and by 1860, California wines, dried fruits, and tinned vegetables were a significant part of the economy. Mining camps now become ghost towns, as large plantations became more common. Writing of California's agricultural regions in 1877, Charles Nightingale observed, "This state has all the qualities of Manitoba with a far more salubrious climate than that northern paradise. The land is rich, the people friendly, the prospects inviting. Heaven, thy name is California!"[6]

California's major problem was transportation. Far from the other population centers of the U.S.M., and separated from Hawaii and Asia by a large ocean, it had become more self-reliant than most states; the completion of the Jefferson and California Railroad in 1848 provided the state with a link to the rest of the U.S.M., but the single-track line was inadequate for the bulky shipments of farm products from southern California, and the railroad only served Arizona, Mexico del Norte, and Jefferson, lacking spurs to Durango, Chiapas, and the Capital District. These regions were reached by steamships from San Francisco and Puerto Hancock, which travelled to several west coast ports in Durango and Chiapas, and from there by road to the interior. What was lacking was access to the Gulf ports and to Europe, and in 1863 plans were advanced to remedy this situation.

---

5. Ralph Taft. *The Keystone: Petroleum of Mexico* (Mexico City, 1955), pp. 114–21.

6. Charles Nightingale. *An American Journey: Views of Mexico and North America in 1877* (London, 1880), p. 338.

Bernard Kramer, a German miner who had travelled all over the world searching for wealth, had arrived in California at the height of the gold rush. He had failed to make his fortune in the streams and mines, and had turned instead to the supply business. In this way he amassed a fortune, and soon became one of the wealthiest citizens of the state. In 1865, he and a group of friends formed the Kramer Associates, whose purpose was to "explore means by which the system of transportation within California, and between California and the rest of the world, might be bettered."[7] The Associates, with twenty-six members, each of whom contributed $200 thousand for a share, hired Courtney Wymess, California's leading mining engineer, as its advisor, and mandated him to begin surveys at once. Wymess did so, and in 1866 offered two suggestions to the Associates. The first involved the construction of a new railroad across the southernmost part of Chiapas, with ports on either end. California-based ships would unload their cargoes on the Pacific side, where they would be reloaded on railroad cars for the trans-Chiapan trip. Then the process would be repeated on the Gulf coast. Wymess would not recommend this plan, however, since the costs of shipments would be prohibitive, assuming the ports and railroads were ever completed.

Instead, the engineer urged support for a second plan, one that would involve the construction of a canal across the narrowest part of Chiapas, the Isthmus of Tehuantepec. The land was hilly in the region, alive with tropical disease and unfit for human habitation; but Wymess thought a series of locks would overcome the irregular landscape, and that a massive cleaning up operation would make that part of Chiapas livable. Once the project was completed, goods could pass from California to the Gulf far more inexpensively than they could by railroad and port.[8]

Kramer rejected the proposal, but did not forget it. He now became interested in Chiapas and lands to the south, especially Guatemala and New Granada. For years these two nations, both politically unstable and economically backward, had fought over possession of the Isthmus of Panama, a narrow neck of land between North and South America. Although the Panamanian climate was poor and the terrain rough, a canal through the region would be only one quarter the length of the Chiapan cut. Kramer thought this the best route. He had already begun making plans to approach both governments when

7. Stanley Tulin. *The Kramer Associates: Its Origins* (London, 1965), p. 97. Kramer Associates initially invested in railroads, dry goods, and canning. Later on it became involved in other aspects of economic life with the exception of cotton and petroleum. Most of the material in this book concerning Kramer Associates has been derived from the files of Stanley Tulin, and is reprinted with his permission.

8. Courtney Wymess. *Remaking a Continent: My Life and Work* (Mexico City, 1892).

Wymess informed him of a second, more advantageous route. This one ran through uncontested Guatamalian territory. Although twice as long as the Panama route, the Guatamalian land was relatively flat, and part of the route would go through Lake Hernandez, a large body of water which could be dredged to provide convenient mooring facilities. At Wymess' insistence, Kramer sent his representatives to survey the area secretly. Their report confirmed his judgement.[9]

Once assured of its practicality, Kramer became impatient to begin work on the canal. He told his colleagues, "We shall go through Guatamala. Nothing can stop us now."[10] In March, 1867, Kramer journeyed to Mexico City to meet with Senators Alberto Gomez and James FitzHugh, to enlist them in his cause. Since both owed their elections to the Kramer Associates, the task was not difficult. The two men then spent the next few months endeavoring to convince the executive branch to support Kramer's plans. As we shall see, the task was not difficult.[11]

The great petroleum boom, the development of California agriculture, and the drive for a Guatamalian canal would change the face of Mexican politics, but all of this was in the future in 1857, when Niles led the Liberty Party to the polls. The President tried to campaign on his record. He had ended the war and led Mexico on the road to economic strength. On the face of it, he had done a creditable job, and ordinarily might have expected re-election by a record majority. But 1857 was not an ordinary year. Memories of what the citizenry considered a defeat in war, the continuing glorification of Hermión, and the presence of new, attractive, Continentalist leaders combined to defeat Niles at the Senatorial election.

The new faces were those of Senator Finley Kenworthy of Jefferson, Senator James FitzHugh of Durango, and Governor Arthur Conroy of Arizona, all of whom had been identified with Hermión in one way or another. In the end, Conroy, backed by Jeffersonian cotton money, won the designation of the caucus, and he went on to defeat Niles with ease in the election.

Conroy was a mild-mannered individual, who had served as Hermión's political advisor prior to, and in the first stage of, the Rocky Mountain War. At that time he had left Mexico City to run successfully for the governorship of his native Arizona, with Hermión's public blessing. Actually, Conroy had left the government because of

---

9. There is reason to believe Wymess was in the pay of Guatamalian politicians eager to reap benefits from a canal. See Herbert Clark. *The True Story of the Kinkaid Canal* (Mexico City, 1889); Winston Revell. *Wymess,* *Kramer, and the Big Ditch* (New York, 1968).
10. Tulin. *The Kramer Associates,* p. 206.
11. Clark. *The True Story of the Guatamalian Canal,* pp. 338–42.

his opposition to the war. Later on, it was discovered Conroy had urged Hermión to try to solve his differences with the C.N.A. through negotiations. It was Conroy, for example, who had been responsible for the surprising moderation of Hermión's inaugural speech of 1845. When war came, Conroy was suspected—rightly so—of being less than enthusiastic. Had he not left the government, Hermión would surely have found some way to ease him out. At the time of the election, however, Conroy ran for the presidency on the record of his friendship with Hermión, and on his own competent record as governor of Arizona.[12]

### The Mexican Elections of 1857

| STATE | SENATE | | ASSEMBLY | |
|---|---|---|---|---|
| | LIBERTY | CONTINENTALIST | LIBERTY | CONTINENTALIST |
| Jefferson | 1 | 3 | 4 | 20 |
| Mexico del Norte | 1 | 3 | 2 | 5 |
| Arizona | 1 | 3 | 2 | 5 |
| California | 2 | 2 | 15 | 14 |
| Durango | 2 | 2 | 12 | 12 |
| Chiapas | 3 | 1 | 6 | 3 |
| | 10 | 14 | 41 | 59 |

Source: Mexico City *Tribune*, August 15, 1857.

Although a Continentalist, Conroy did not favor a vigorous foreign policy. Like his C.N.A. counterpart, Governor-General Parkes, Conroy was content to restore the country internally and forego the luxuries of empire building. Unlike Parkes, however, he was scrupulously honest and genuinely tried to be fair to all factions in Mexican politics. During his first term in office, Conroy won legislative approval for measures to establish a Control Commission for the railroads; a Harbors Act to widen and dredge ports along both the Pacific and Gulf coasts; and bills to make elementary education compulsory in all the states.[13] Conroy also raised the level of the diplomatic corps, tried to better Mexico's relations with Britain and the Germanic Confederation, while at the same time reassuring France of his continued friend-

---

12. Harper Reichart. *The Quiet Messiah: Arthur Conroy of Arizona* (Mexico City, 1952).
13. The education bill was later declared unconstitutional, but during the next ten years each state passed a similar law, and so Conroy's intent was served. Millie Fernandez. "The Growth of Elementary Education in the U.S.M. Under the Conroy Administration." *Journal of Education in Mexico*, XXVI (December, 1953), pp. 464–87.

ship. His successful leadership enabled the Continentalists to win an impressive victory in the Senatorial races in 1863, and Conroy was returned to the presidential palace for a second term.[14]

Conroy's second administration was as reformist as his first; some of his own colleagues called the President a radical. Soon after the election he spoke before a special session of Congress and asked for new reforms.

> Although the *rationale* for our Constitution was sound, and it remains a beacon to the world, it is in need of repair so as to better meet the challenge of the last half of the century. Consider, if you will, the nature of our land when Jackson assumed power. Our founder led a nation of disparate peoples, speaking different tongues, and existing in stages of development ranging from industrial to primitive. The Indians and Anglos were enemies, and both distrusted the Mexicanos, while the Hispanos were uncertain as to their role. The new nation had a population of only 3.3 million, most of whom were engaged in farming. They lacked even the most primitive forms of long-distance communication and transportation. For that kind of land, the Constitution was well-suited, even inspired.
>
> Conditions have changed considerably in the last forty-four years. There are some 30 million of us today, and within six years, all should be literate. We have come through a major war with honor. Our communications and transportation are the envy of the world, as are our cotton fields and mines. While differences between our peoples remain, they are far less important than they were in Jackson's day. In truth, Mexico has shown the world that origins and religion are no barrier to public service and personal success.

Most congressmen had heard such talk before, and Conroy's words, spoken in his nasal twang, made the words appear even more commonplace. Then the President startled his listeners by coming to the crux of his address, and even those who had tarried in the lobby to smoke and pass the time of day, rushed to the chamber to find out what caused the buzzing among the congressmen.

> It is for this reason I have called you here today. We must modernize our basic law. We will not change its spirit, for to do so would be both rash and unwise. Instead, we shall broaden its scope while retaining its focus.
>
> Therefore, I recommend two basic changes in the method by which we select our leaders. The first involves the president. At the present time he is selected by a senatorial vote. This cumbersome apparatus, so useful in the past, should be altered so as to make the president more

---

14. Reichart. *Quiet Messiah*, pp. 520–34.

the selection of *all* the people, and not just the choice of a small group. What I would recommend, then, is that the president in the future be selected by a majority vote of all the qualified citizens of our nation. Should no candidate receive a majority, then the Senate may select the president among the leading two contenders for the post.

My second proposal is for senators, in the future, to be selected in the same manner, with the state legislatures choosing from among the two leading contenders, should no individual receive a majority in the balloting. Of course, this is not a matter for us to decide, but for the states, and I hope each will consider this proposal seriously, for to accept it would be to reaffirm our confidence in the wisdom and patriotism of our citizenry.[15]

To some, the Conroy proposals seemed radical, and if accepted, destined to change the face of Mexican politics. Then Continentalist leaders in the Assembly began to seek out their fellows, and amplify and interpret the President's address. They noted that pressures for "a more democratic method" of selecting officials had been building in the states, especially in Chiapas, Durango, and Mexico del Norte. The Conroy proposals would head off a protest movement before one could be organized. Furthermore, the proposals would not change the present methods as much as they would appear to do at first blush. Jefferson and California, the states with Anglo majorities, were also the most populous, and would surely dominate any general election. Hispanos controlled Durango, and they tended to vote with the Anglos. The Indians of Mexico del Norte and Arizona had received many benefits from the central government, and their votes, too, were "safe." Fears that Mexicanos from Chiapas (the third most populous state in 1862) would take control of the nation were thus groundless; since a candidate would require a majority to be elected, and since more often than not, party discipline would hold and the two-party system remain, this too would serve as a brake on future problems.

As a result of skillful politicking and the support of the Liberty Party's legislative leaders, Conroy was able to obtain passage of the amendment in 1864. He also persuaded Congress to accept a redistricting plan for the Assembly, to go into effect after the 1870 elections, by which a state's representation would be based on its voting population. Finally, Assembly-passed bills would require only one vote, and not the two provided for in the 1819 Constitution. These measures, also in the form of amendments, were passed in 1865. Together, the three constituted the most important political reform in the nation since the time of Jackson. Although, in fact, they did little to change the actual power structure in the U.S.M., they did manage to still cries of protest

---

15. Mexico City *Record*, November 11, 1863.

and calls for reform that were heard in all parts of the western world in this period.[16]

The President's reformism did much to dispirit Liberty Party leaders, who had tried for years to bring about the same changes Conroy had accomplished in two. Niles applauded his rival, but others were not as magnanimous as the former President. "Under the guise of reformism, this man had managed to solidify his class's control over the nation. We are doomed to many more years of Conroyism, unless the people wake up to what this Machiavelli has done to deceive them," exclaimed Senator Carlos Concepción of Chiapas, a Mexicano who was the leader of the Libertarian radicals.[17] Conroy's own Continentalist Party, however, was not altogether happy with the changes. The Party's leader in the Senate, Oscar Barkley of Jefferson, refused to vote for the measures, as did five other Continentalists, and without strong Libertarian support, the Conroy proposals would never have passed.

By late 1866, indeed, it was evident Conroy was no longer in control of his own party. Senators Barkley and Omar Kinkaid of California now dominated the Continentalist caucus. They had gained their power partly through political skill, partly due to sincere opposition to the Conroy proposals, but mostly because large amounts of money had been deposited in the bank accounts of those Continentalists who could be bought. The Conroy administration, which had been scrupulously honest, was now being undercut by Monte Benedict and the Jefferson oil interests who had joined forces with Kramer Associates of California to take control of Mexican politics. By 1866 they seemed invulnerable.[18] ·

---

16. Conroy's hope for state actions to liberalize the election processes for senators was not realized during his administration, but starting in 1876, the states began to pass direct election laws. The last of these, that of Jefferson, was passed in 1892. Reichart. *Quiet Messiah*, pp. 600–11.

17. Herbert Brinkerhoff. *Mexico's Political Revolution* (New York, 1964).

18. Thomas Mason. *The Jefferson-California Axis of 1866–1876* (London, 1968); Mortimer Dow. *The Giants of Mexico: the Political Maneuverings of Kramer and Benedict in the Industrial Era* (Mexico City, 1950); Herbert Brinkerhoff. *The Price of a Man: Oil and Produce in Mexican Politics* (Mexico City, 1970).

# 16

# THE KINKAID INTERLUDE

THE alliance between Kramer Associates of California and the Jefferson petroleum interests developed naturally and out of an area of mutual concern. Kramer Associates wanted a canal through Guatamala; Monte Benedict's group suspected the region was rich in oil. Both leaders were Continentalists, not only by birth and status, but by conviction. In 1866, both Benedict and Kramer gave speeches in their own states calling upon the people of Mexico to realize their destinies through territorial expansion. Benedict was cautious. "The lands to the south are veritable storehouses of raw materials, but the peoples of these nations lack the resources to extract them. We in Mexico have these resources. A marriage of their land and our people would surely benefit all."[1] Kramer was more direct. "When a backward people encounter one with vigor and determination, they must succumb. This is the law of nature, and of nations."[2]

Finally, both Kramer and Benedict were Anglos, determined their people would retain leadership in the U.S.M. Benedict disliked all men of color, and even disdained contact with Hispanos, leaving such matters to subordinates. Kramer, on the other hand, had been raised in a polyglot culture, and was used to mixing with all kinds of people. Kramer Associates included five Hispanos, one of whom was Kramer's brother-in-law, and as Kramer crudely remarked, "It's the color of a man's money that interests me, not that of his skin."[3] This attitude kept a close personal relationship from developing with Benedict and other Jeffersonians of his persuasion, but it did not mean Kramer consorted regularly with men of color. He tended to judge a person by the amount of money he had earned and the power he had accumulated, and in California, the money and power belonged to the Anglos and, to a lesser extent, the Hispanos.

To Benedict and Kramer, Hermión had appeared a superlative

1. Jefferson City *Tribune*, March 12, 1866.
2. Stanley Tulin. *He Straddled the*
Continents: The Life of Bernard Kramer (London, 1960), p. 189.
3. *Ibid*, p. 258.

leader and a man of vision. As young men both had fought in the war. Benedict had been with Doheny when he had marched from Mexico City to Arizona in 1850, while Kramer had been a major in Hernandez' California brigades.[4] They had supported Conroy in 1857, considering the Arizonan a worthy, if lackluster, successor to the Hermión tradition. But when Conroy put forth his reformist proposals in 1863, both men lost faith in his administration, and when the amendments were accepted, they realized their groups would have to play a more important political role than they had in the past. By 1863, Benedict exercised control of the Jefferson Continentalist Party through Senator Barkley, while Kramer's satellite in California was Senator Omar Kinkaid. Conroy had earlier indicated he would not seek a third term, but by 1867 the question was academic, for by then he had lost control of his own party.

The Continentalist caucus of 1869 had to choose between two candidates. Conroy supported Secretary of State Lorenzo Diás of Durango, while Kinkaid was the candidate of the Kramer-Benedict axis. Conroy had expected a struggle for the nomination, but when Kinkaid won easily on the first vote he exclaimed, "I knew Kramer had power, but I did not realize its extent."[5]

The Libertarians caucused at a time when they, too, were in the midst of political change. Senator Conceptión had ambitions for the nomination, claiming that under the new amendments, a Mexicano from Chiapas might garner sufficient support to win the election. But Conceptión had no support among the party's leaders, and in any case, the Libertarians were not yet ready to unite behind a Chiapan, much less a Mexicano. Some maneuvering behind the scenes took place, and on the third day the party announced its selection of Governor Henry Colbert of Mexico del Norte as its candidate. Colbert was a colorful character, one of the few Libertarians who had supported the Rocky Mountain War, and who now called for the return of the "lost provinces." He too had ambitions regarding expansion to the south, and in his acceptance speech spoke of "the fulfilment of our territorial destiny."[6] Thus, both the Libertarians and the Continentalists put forth expansionist candidates in the first elections under the new amendments.

There was far more electioneering in 1869 than at any other time prior to that date. Kinkaid's picture was plastered over walls in every city and town, and a small army of speakers was recruited to harangue the crowds for the Continentalist nominee. Lacking sufficient funds for

---

4. The two men might have met during the 1850 fighting, but neither had any recollection of a meeting.

5. Reichart. *Quiet Messiah*, p. 620.
6. Ferdinand Marcos. *Henry Colbert* (New York, 1956), p. 207.

such an operation, Colbert contented himself with advertisements in leading newspapers and the work of his supporters in each of the states. The election ended in a victory for Kinkaid, but the vote was closer than Benedict or Kramer had expected.

### The Mexican Elections of 1869

| STATE | KINKAID (C) | COLBERT (L) |
|---|---|---|
| Jefferson | 1,045,529 | 562,489 |
| California | 952,036 | 634,768 |
| Chiapas | 458,297 | 739,657 |
| Durango | 397,923 | 426,870 |
| Arizona | 204,356 | 223,426 |
| Mexico del Norte | 192,554 | 213,960 |
| | 3,250,695 | 2,801,170 |

Source: U.S.M. *Statistical Abstract*, p. 112.

Since the 1869 election was the first under the new amendments, it was an awkwardly-run affair, and even before it was over, politicians of both parties realized certain changes would have to be made in the future. For example, the elections were held in mid-August, as before, while the party caucuses met in late July. This left only two weeks for electioneering, a satisfactory period at a time when presidents had been selected by senators, who themselves had over four months in which to campaign, but insufficient time to mount a major electoral effort for a nationwide campaign. Thus, both parties agreed to hold their nominating meetings in late April, at which time senatorial as well as presidential candidates would be considered and ratified. The small caucuses were to be broadened to include delegates from all states meeting in open convention. This probably resulted from the good reception the C.N.A. conventions of 1868 had received; the Mexican politicians decided to follow the lead of their North American counterparts.[7] These changes came naturally and over a period of time, being suited to the needs of the people, and not the result of philosophical considerations.

The election of 1869 brought into the open a fact Mexico's politicians had long realized but of which they had seldom spoken. Jefferson and California, both controlled by Anglos and their Hispano friends, were clearly Continentalist, while Chiapas, and to a lesser extent Durango, which had a large Mexicano majority, were Libertarian strongholds. Arizona's Indians, who had received many favors from the Continentalists in the past, tended to vote with that party; the

7. Mason. *The Jefferson-California Axis*, pp. 416–23.

Indians of Mexico del Norte, who felt the Libertarians had betrayed them by ceding land to the C.N.A., also voted Continentalist. But the Mexicanos in both states were in the Libertarian camp. Ironically, the Anglos had by this time raised Jackson, Hermión, and to a lesser extent, Hamilton, to the status of party saints, but the men whose ancestors had made the Wilderness Walk appeared to have forgotten the events that had made the journey necessary. The leaders of the North American Rebellion—Sam and John Adams, Patrick Henry, and John Hancock—were now Libertarian heroes. Even Jefferson was ignored by the Anglos of the state named in his honor, but was quoted at length by Mexicanos of Chiapas and Durango. A little less than a century after Burgoyne's victory at Saratoga, the heritage of the Rebellion was remembered by the Mexicanos, but forgotten by the descendants of the men who had fought alongside Washington, and who had written the Declaration of Independence.

President Kinkaid came to office with a host of friends and the good will of even his enemies. For the past three years he had worked with Barkley in the Senate to frustrate Conroy's reformist programs, but it was Barkley who was blamed for manipulations, while Kinkaid came to be considered an "honest broker" between reformist and conservative factions. Kinkaid realized that he owed his election to Kramer and Benedict, and that they had more power within the party than he did himself. On the other hand, Kinkaid was personally honest, and wanted to be a truly independent leader. "Mexico needs a president who will rise above party and faction, and judge each issue on its merits," he told reporters in 1869. "I intend to be that kind of leader."[8]

As it turned out, Kinkaid and his sponsors thought alike on most issues and agreed on many programs, although Kinkaid came to those conclusions on his own. In this way he served Kramer and Benedict even better than if he had been bought. Thus, like the real party leaders, Kinkaid was an expansionist, an admirer of Hermión, and a man dedicated to a "vigorous policy in the South."[9]

Soon after taking the oath of office, Kinkaid opened negotiations with Guatamala concerning rights to construct an inter-oceanic canal. Guatamalian dictator Miguel Rubio had earlier indicated that he was favorably inclined to the Kramer Associates' venture, and it now surprised Kinkaid to learn that Rubio was planning to sign over rights to a canal to a group of German financiers, backed by King Frederick William himself. The idea of having Germanic influence exerted in Mexico's southern neighbor shocked both Kramer and Kinkaid. The president asked Minister to Guatamala José del Castillo to inform

---

8. Mexico City *Journal*, November 4, 1869.
9. John Robinson. *The Kinkaid Presi-* *dency and the Men Behind It* (London, 1950), p. 159.

Rubio of his "sadness at learning of this plan, and hope that further talks between our two nations may result in a more satisfactory solution to the canal problem."[10]

Kramer didn't bother with such niceties. Without discussing the matter with Kinkaid, or even informing his Jeffersonian partners, he acted. On March 9, 1870, a revolution erupted in Guatamala City, led by Vincenzo Martinez, a Senator who had long opposed the Rubio regime. The dictator was forced to flee four days later, and Martinez took office as "provisional president," swearing to hold elections, "as soon as it is humanly possible." The elections never took place. It was learned soon after that the Martinez *coup* had been planned in San Francisco, provisioned from Puerto Hancock, and financed by the Kramer Associates.

Martinez signed over rights to a canal to Kramer on April 20. It was widely believed throughout Europe that Kinkaid had been behind the *coup*, and that Guatamala had now become a dependency of the U.S.M. This assessment was not accurate. In fact, Guatamala was now a subsidiary of the Kramer Associates.

Mexico extended recognition to the new government on March 16, and Kinkaid's relations with Martinez were correct, if not cordial. The canal zone, which was mapped out in June and assigned to the Kramer Associates in September, was still to be part of Guatamala, although in fact the Associates' small private army patrolled the area and there were few signs of a Guatamalan presence in the ten-mile wide zone. Wymess arrived in New Cordoba, near the Pacific end of the zone, in April, and supervised the surveys and organization of the work teams. He entered upon his work with gusto, and confidently predicted the canal would be completed by January 1, 1874. Wymess did not realize the difficulty of his task, especially the problems of disease and sanitation. The canal would not be completed until 1878, and would not earn money for its owners until 1885.[11]

Although the Kramer Associates owned the canal zone, Benedict and the Jeffersonians were not forgotten. Membership in the group was now increased by sixteen, to a total of forty-two, and all the new shares were sold to the Jeffersonian petroleum interests at the original price of $200 thousand a share. In return for this concession, Benedict united his interests to form the massive Petroleum of Mexico Corporation, which was capitalized at $200 million. The firm's underwriting was complicated, being devised by Benedict's Paris bankers. Original investors were to purchase bonds, and would receive common stock as

---

10. Tulin. *He Straddled the Continents*, pp. 329–39.

11. Wymess. *Remaking a Continent*, pp. 433–39.

a bonus. Under the terms of the original agreement, the Paris group purchased slightly less than $60 million worth of bonds for 29 percent of the new firm's stock, Kramer Associates received 20 percent of the stock for $40 million, while Benedict's group retained 51 percent, which it received in return for the properties surrendered to form the new company. Since their stock was worth $80 million at the time, and the Petroleum of Mexico securities they received in exchange were valued at over $100 million, they too benefited from the transaction. It was the first major exercise in the creation of money through financial manipulation.[12]

Benedict suspected petroleum might be found in the zone, and his engineers instructed Wymess to prospect the area. None was found, but as the canal progressed, Benedict's attention was increasingly directed toward the southern states, and his teams made exploratory drillings in eastern Chiapas and Durango. The first important strike was made near Minatitión in Chiapas early in 1880. Then, later in the year, petroleum was found on the outskirts of Tampico and between that port and Reynosa in Durango. Benedict and Kramer were jubilant. The discoveries enabled PM to borrow additional capital at a time when such loans were hard to get.[13] In addition, sales of drilling rights made many poor farmers paper millionaires overnight. Of course, few were able to survive the next decade, but those who did became economic powers in their states.[14]

Kinkaid's first term was judged a success, both by contemporaries and historians. The President did not sponsor much in the way of legislation, concentrating instead on solidifying his power within the Continentalist Party, and organizing the party's machinery in the states. Kinkaid spoke on several occasions of the Gulf being a "Mexican preserve," looked longingly at Hawaii and Alaska, and increased the size of both the army and navy "to protect Mexico against her enemies." Relations with the C.N.A. were satisfactory, since despite Kinkaid's talk and gestures, he, like Clemens, was more interested in domestic affairs than in a revival of old animosities.

The Continentalist caucus of 1875 renominated Kinkaid by acclamation. The party's platform called him "a man of vision when others are blind," and called for "a continuation of prosperity and progress." There were complimentary references to the canal, "which will serve

12. Robert Sobel. *Men of Great Wealth: Operations of the Kramer-Benedict Combine* (Melbourne, 1956), pp. 154–69.
13. Money had become increasingly scarce by 1880, and prior to the Chiapas strikes it seemed PM might not be able to float additional bonds, in which case the company might have collapsed under its already heavy debt burdens. *Ibid*, pp. 200–10.
14. Charles Winslow. *Peasants in Brocade: The Oil Millionaires of Chiapas and Durango* (New York, 1962).

to bind our nation's peoples even more closely together than they are at present," and talk of "our mission in the Caribbean."[15]

The Liberty Party's caucus was rough and divisive. Colbert was there and had hopes for renomination. He spoke of "regaining the lost regions of Mexico del Norte," and chided the President for his lack of vigor in foreign affairs. He also called for political control of Guatamala and strong actions against the Russians, "who even now are threatening the borders of California." But such words had little meaning for the majority of delegates; Colbert was never in serious contention for the nomination.[16]

By the third day two men stood out from the rest, and the caucus divided between them. The first was Senator Concepción of Chiapas, who still railed against what he called "reformism without change." Concepción, the first Mexicano to be seriously considered for the presidency, was colorful, handsome, and at the age of fifty, in his prime. He spoke English with a decided accent, was a devout Catholic, and in the past had spoken contemptuously of the Anglos. Concepción had formed alliances with some of the more radical Indian tribes in Mexico del Norte and Arizona, had taken up the cause of small farmers in California who felt victimized by the Kramer Associates, and criticized the relation between Mexico City and Guatamala as being one between "thief and assassin." "If I am defeated at this caucus," he said, "it will be because of my race and the opposition of powerful interests opposed to the well-being of all Mexicans." Concepción spoke too of "Mexico's wealth having fallen to a few, while the rest of the nation remains in chains." Talk such as this won Concepción many ardent followers among the party's radical fringe, but alienated the mainstream Libertarian voters.[17]

Concepción's rival was Governor Thomas Rogers of Arizona. Rogers was a dynamic, forceful, and reformist leader of his state. Under his administration, mine-safety laws were put into effect, the nation's first accident and unemployment compensation laws were passed, and a controversial tax on corporations was being considered. Rogers was also a life-long opponent of slavery. "If I become president," he said, "I shall destroy this evil, root and branch." He sympathized with the plight of the Mexicano, and pledged himself to "bring all Mexicans to full citizenship." Unlike Concepción, however, Rogers believed in the capitalist system, would not advocate radical

15. Mexico City *Journal*, April 23, 1875.
16. Four years later it was discovered that Benedict money supported the Colbert candidacy. But there is reason to believe Colbert was ignorant of the fact at the time. Mason. *The Jefferson-California Axis*, p. 483.
17. Mexico City *Journal*, April 30, May 3, 5, 1875; Mexico City *Times*, April 30, May 2, 1875.

change, and refused the help of "those who would destroy, not create."[18] It seemed clear to all present that Rogers meant Conceptión when he spoke of such individuals.

Rogers won the Libertarian nomination on the second ballot. He did so with the support of the party's Anglos, moderate Mexicanos, some Indians, and most of the Hispanos. Immediately afterwards he made the customary appeal for party unity, but Conceptión was not there to hear it. The Mexicano leader had walked out of the convention in disgust. The following day he announced he would form a new party, to be called the Workers' Coalition, and would oppose both Rogers and Kinkaid at the polls that August.[19]

The campaign of 1875 was bitter and divisive. Conceptión became more radical and aggressive each day. He refused to appear in Anglo areas, called for a "union of Mexicanos against our oppressors," and demanded the nationalization of Kramer Associates. By late July he was speaking in Spanish most of the time, and on one occasion, called for the "removal of those who stole our country from us." It was clear later on that Conceptión had given up hope of winning the election, and was laying the groundwork for a revolutionary organization that would begin operations after the election.

As expected, Rogers stressed the same problems he had dealt with as governor. He outlined a program of social insurance and aid to education which he would support if elected. Rogers would also end slavery by constitutional amendment, investigate big business (by which he obviously meant the Kramer Associates), and "redirect our effort toward making a better Mexico, for all Mexicans." On the one hand, he criticized Conceptión for "having lost faith in our people, and substituting force for reason," while on the other, Rogers lashed out at "the plutocracy of the Constitutionalists, and the hypocrisy of a President who is on a leash, but does not know it, or does not care."

Kinkaid did little electioneering, relying instead on an army of paid workers who spread his message through the states, and who urged people to "vote for the man who has made Mexico great." "If you are more content today than you were six years ago, the credit must go to President Kinkaid, and recognition of the fact should be made at the polls." This seemed a veiled appeal to Anglos, and it was, for that group more than any other had prospered during the Kinkaid presidency. More direct was the speech of a Kinkaid supporter in Jefferson. "If Kinkaid loses, then it will no longer be safe for an Anglo

18. Mexico City *Journal*, April 29, 30, May 2, 3, 1875; Mexico City *Times*, April 30, 1875; Sangre Roja *Voice*, May 2, 3, 4, 1875.

19. Robert Kerr. *Carlos Conceptión and the Birth of the New Radicalism* (New York, 1960), pp. 223-30.

to reside anywhere but in Jefferson and in parts of California. Our nation will be in flames. The work of a half century and more will be destroyed by either a half-crazed Mexicano or a well-meaning but lunatic reformer."[20]

### The Mexican Elections of 1875

| STATE | KINKAID (C) | ROGERS (L) | CONCEPCIÓN (WC) |
|---|---|---|---|
| Jefferson | 1,198,908 | 492,354 | 135,666 |
| California | 1,282,034 | 436,059 | 168,398 |
| Chiapas | 297,843 | 500,945 | 213,487 |
| Durango | 343,465 | 405,658 | 164,565 |
| Arizona | 243,235 | 287,502 | 18,768 |
| Mexico del Norte | 205,398 | 210,303 | 18,003 |
| | 3,327,418 | 2,332,821 | 718,887 |

Source: U.S.M. *Statistical Abstract*, p. 112.

As expected, Kinkaid was re-elected, and by a good majority; in fact, his total was more than he had received in 1869, while Rogers received 470,000 fewer votes than Colbert had when he lost six years before. The fact that the radical Concepción won more than 718,000 votes, well over all expectations, was mitigated by the fact that almost a third of his total came from Chiapas, and that his strength in Durango, Jefferson, and California was concentrated in Mexicano areas. His much-vaunted appeal to the Indians failed, as they remained true to the Liberty Party and Rogers. Nonetheless, Concepción had every right to claim a "moral victory" in the election. "We have shown the plutocrats of Mexico City and Paris that we are united. We have been heard. We will be heard in the future. Mexico will shake to the sound of our voices, united in the cause of justice. God is speaking to us today, just as he spoke to Patrick Henry and Thomas Jefferson, to Gigedo and to José Morales when he first dared defy the might of the white devils of Jefferson. The Workers' Coalition is dead, killed by the cynics of the north. Long live the Moralistas!!"[21] Then Concepción and his key lieutenants vanished into the western Sierra Madre, to begin a guerrilla campaign aimed at the destruction of the government.

Rogers took his defeat in good grace, sending Kinkaid the customary message of congratulations. But he was not finished with politics. Within three months of the election, Senator Hiram Green of Arizona stepped down, and Governor William Simmons named Rogers as his

---

20. Felix Lombardi. *The Three-Cornered Hat: Conception, Kinkaid,* *Rogers, and Election of 1875* (Mexico City, 1955).
21. Kerr. *Carlos Conception,* p. 365.

replacement. Now Rogers took command of the Libertarian delegation in Congress, and from there prepared to wage legislative war against Kinkaid.

The bitterness of the campaign had shaken Kinkaid out of his former smugness and self-satisfaction. Now he truly realized there were internal problems to be solved before foreign adventures could be considered. He had also come to understand how he had been used by Kramer Associates in the past, and was determined to break with the group. Beginning in 1876, the President attempted to lead his party in a reform effort, including greater controls over railroads, a program of aid to farmers, and the beginnings of a social welfare program. Again and again, Kinkaid spoke of his predecessor, Arthur Conroy, and indicated his desire "to complete the reforms begun by that great Arizonian." Since Conroy had been a close personal friend of Rogers, he was able to bring these two men together. Rogers cooperated whenever he could with the President, often losing support by so doing.

"Country before party," which had become Rogers' motto, won him the gratitude of Kinkaid and the Continentalists and the admiration of independents, but cost him dearly in his own party. As Concepción's raids began in earnest in 1877, there was some talk of Rogers becoming Kinkaid's Secretary of State, and rumors of Kinkaid supporting Rogers in the 1881 elections. None of this was true, but both men, each a believer in the Constitution and a united Mexico, worked together to preserve the nation against a force that could destroy it.[22]

Kinkaid's reforms were accepted, although Kramer opposed them and was able to win a majority of Continentalists to his banner. But Rogers' supporters in the Liberty Party, together with Kinkaid's in the majority party, had sufficient strength to pass the Thomas Railroad Reform Act, which placed the lines under a government commission which set rates and determined future expansion. Then the coalition passed the Keefe-Wilkinson Social Insurance Bill, which set into motion the machinery for a program of health and sickness benefits; and the Fernandez Tax Reform Bill of 1878, which placed a tax on corporations. The last of these measures was declared unconstitutional by the Mexico Tribunal, but the first two became the cornerstone for what Kinkaid called "an epoch of reform."

Kramer, Benedict, and the Jefferson-California axis of industrialists and planters were able to block Kinkaid's reform measures in 1879, but it was evident they could not do so indefinitely. In the next two years, Rogers won the support of the Jefferson cotton planters,

---

22. There are letters between the two, twenty-six in all, written from December 14, 1878 to June 12, 1879, in which they discussed a variety of subjects, but nowhere did Kinkaid write of the possibility of such support. See *Kinkaid Papers*, folio 2435.

who came to view Benedict as their natural enemy, and they were willing to finance Rogers' 1881 campaign.

Kinkaid may have harbored thoughts of standing for an unprecedented third term. Not since Jackson had a Mexican president seemed so near that goal, but Kinkaid kept his own council. His every action was watched with interest, but his ideas will never be known. On December 7, 1879, President Kinkaid was killed by a bomb thrown in his direction during a parade.

The thrower was never found, and to this day we cannot know for certain whether or not Kinkaid was the target, although it may be assumed such was the case. Rogers blamed Conceptión for the deed, while the radical leader, through his spokesman, denied the charge, claiming to know for certain the plot had been hatched by Kramer and Benedict. For their part, the two businessmen offered a million dolares reward for information leading to the conviction of the assassin. Kramer renamed the newly-opened Guatamala Canal the Kinkaid Canal, and endowed Kinkaid University in the President's home town. Like others, he had his idea as to the identity of the killer, and he was said to have told a friend that only one person could benefit from the death, "and that is Rogers."[23]

When Hermión had been shot twenty-eight years before, the nation had entered a period of deep mourning, even in the midst of war. Kinkaid was mourned, but not with the same depth of feeling. The late President lacked Hermión's warmth, and was already quite old (sixty-three), whereas Hermión had been in the prime of life. Then, too, Hermión had died when the U.S.M. was engaged in a war, and this had served to unite the nation. At the time of Kinkaid's assassination, the nation appeared on the verge of some kind of civil confrontation, and the President's death seemed a disturbing omen of coming insurrection.

A confused and disturbed Senate met to select an acting President on December 9. Although there was some party and partisan manipulations, the senators genuinely wanted a person who would heal the divisions in the country and assure a continuation of constitutional government. None could be found, however. Only a few days earlier Rogers had seemed Kinkaid's logical successor; now he was a suspect in

23. Frank Howard. *The Strange Death of President Kinkaid* (New York, 1888); Samuel Menzer. *Who Killed Kinkaid?* (London, 1967); David Green. *A President Dies: The Assassination of Omar Kinkaid* (New York, 1960). The classic work remains the United States of Mexico, Congress. *Report on the Death of President Omar Kinkaid.* 7 vols. (Mexico City, 1880). Joan Kahn, in her *Secret History of* the Kinkaid Assassination (New York, 1970), holds the plot was hatched in the C.N.A., but there is little evidence to support her thesis. In 1905, a Mexicano peasant, Carlos Feliz, told a Mexico City *Herald* reporter that he had thrown the bomb, and at the time was a member of a Moralista band. But there is no supporting evidence for his tale. Mexico City *Herald*, June 5, 6, 18, 1905.

the assassination. Just as Hermión's death had ended Huddleston's political career, so Kinkaid's crippled that of Rogers.

But Rogers would not withdraw, or concede defeat. Instead, he rallied a portion of the Libertarians and a handful of Continentalists to support his candidacy. He had a plurality of the Senate, but clearly no chance of winning. Several ballots took place before this could be known, however, and by then, Rogers was prepared to compromise.

In the end, the Senate selected Senator George Vining of Jefferson, a sixty-seven year old Continentalist, whose age was dramatized by the fact that Alexander Hamilton had been his godfather. Vining was an unambitious man, who accepted the post only for the sake of unity. The real power in the government would be the Secretary of State, and the nation was surprised when Vining named Rogers for the post.[24]

The new government was sworn in on December 11. No one expected much of what was already being called "the Vining Interlude." Instead, politicians looked forward to the conventions due to be held in less than a year and a half, at which time Rogers was expected to make the race. Before then, however, Mexico, the continent, and the world would be shaken by a series of events that would make Kinkaid's assassination seem a minor incident.

---

24. Robert Kerr. *The Life and Times of George Vining* (New York, 1955); Francis McGovern. *They Stuck in Their Thumbs! The Selection of Vin-* ing (London, 1967); Earl Watson. *The Right Man: The Vining Administration* (Mexico City, 1943).

# 17

# THE BLOODY EIGHTIES

IT is impossible to determine when the Bloody Eighties began, the exact causes, and why it was manifested in different ways throughout the western world. Certainly there were connections between events in France and the Germanies; between Britain and the C.N.A.; and between the C.N.A. and the U.S.M. The dislocations of war and the demands of a superheated economy helped cause the crises, but most of them had roots extending into the eighteenth century and beyond. It would appear that a superstructure had been erected on a foundation incapable of supporting it for long. Many years after the builders had left and the population considered the edifice to be a landmark that would last forever, the flaws in the foundation began to show, and parts of the building crumbled. Such a tragedy would not be the fault of those who first set down the foundation—it was not designed for the purpose it later filled—and those who erected the superstructure could prove their building was soundly designed. But they were not meant to go together, and so the project ended in disaster.

So it was with the problems that surfaced in the 1880's. Western industrial society, which only a few years before seemed confident, progressive, and destined for remarkable gains, had been the creation of capitalism. It was held together at the interstices by businessmen, bankers, managers, and the like. It was fueled by engineers and scientists, explained by philosophers and professors, and glorified by believers in a new cult of progress who took some of their ideas from the biological discoveries of Alfred Russel Wallace and Charles Darwin. But this society was constructed on an improper foundation, that of feudalism. Side by side with the men and institutions of the late nineteenth century, were individuals whose lives and values were those of an earlier period. Such people distrusted the complexities of capitalism, considered its wonder-workers either wizards or devils, viewed progress as an abomination against God, and would, if they had the power, destroy the machines, laboratories, and chanceries of Europe and America.

Others, more important in influence and numbers, would not destroy the present and abandon the future, but change the institutions of feudalism in order to better equate social forms with economic reality. Erich Neiderhoffer called for the gradual purchase by workers of their plants, so that "no one would be an exploiter, everyone would be an exploiter." Leon Martell thought a political union of producers could exert sufficient strength to force governments to be responsive to the needs of workers and marginal farmers. Karl Marx believed workers would have to develop a greater class consciousness, then unite, destroy private ownership, and form a government of their own, in which "the materials of life belong to all who live."

In America, Franz Freund began a labor movement which, in varying forms, was duplicated throughout the West. Waldo Turner wrote that "the new order is corrupt, and the old is decayed. There is no hope for either." Turner and his followers (who came from Europe and South America as well as from Turner's own C.N.A.) left their homes to travel to Manitoba, where they formed "The New City of God" in the wilderness, a society based on mutual respect, sharing, and free love.

Otto von Kelsing disdained Turnerism as "romantic nonsense," but he recognized its appeal. "In the past we were united under a common church," he wrote. "The efficacy of that Church is gone; the world cries out for new churches." Kelsing believed nationalism would be "the church of the future," and he called for a union of all peoples within discernible geographic bounds, "with a belief in a common future," to unite "in brotherhood, sharing the fruits of the soil with others of the same nation." There were many other philosophers and theoreticians to attempt solutions of the problems of the time, and in the Bloody Eighties many received not only followings, but power as well.[1]

Of course, all of these men were as much a product of the society they criticized as were Rogers, Edison, Clemens, and Kramer. They lived at a time when every problem appeared capable of solution, and so they put forth their own nostrums to cure ills which had bedeviled mankind since the world began. The problems, in fact, were far more complex than they could imagine. The mechanists among them thought that by changing a few basic institutions, the world would become perfect, but they did not consider the more subtle problems of changing human nature and the people who accepted the institutions.

---

1. The bibliography on this issue is large and complete. See Harvey Forrest. ed. *Philosophers of Crisis* (London, 1958); Malcolm Hershkovitz. *Socialists and Society* (New York, 1960); Robert Grady. *The Age of Neiderhoffer* (New York, 1965); Waldo Turner. *Utopia Across the River* (New Jerusalem, 1903); Frank Wilkerson. *Reaping the Whirlwind: The Crisis Philosophers of the Late Nineteenth Century* (London, 1970).

The vitalists claimed man was evolving toward perfection, and some of them—Harding, Watson, Clinton—believed they could speed up the process. But they, too, failed when it came to functioning on an individual basis. Understanding comes before solutions, and the reformers of the late nineteenth century seem today to have lacked a proper understanding of the nature and causes of the problems of their time.[2]

Many historians believe the problem first made its existence known in the North American Rebellion. One has only to read the words of the Declaration of Independence, *Common Sense*, the last letters of John and Sam Adams, and *Apologia* by Jefferson to see the germs of these future ideas. The works of such diverse men as Neiderhoffer, Turner, and Marx can be traced to the North American rebels, and the crisis philosophers of the late nineteenth century usually credit them with part of their inspiration.

This was partly so because, by then, the historiography of the North American Rebellion had taken a new turn. Earlier scholars had stressed that part of the Rebellion's philosophy which demanded the rights of Englishmen for all those living under the flag. But the rebels had also philosophized about the rights of *man*, and the foremost of these were "Life, Liberty, and the Pursuit of Happiness." To the revisionists, the key word was "liberty," for by it Jefferson seemed to mean the right of *all* men to cast off old institutions. Jefferson and other rebel leaders had written often of the need for equality; and although they did not free their slaves, many indicated they would do so after the Rebellion. They appeared to believe workers should have the right to receive a fair share of the goods they produced; they distrusted both big government and large-scale businesses. They firmly believed in the brotherhood of man and the fatherhood of God.

Had the rebels succeeded in winning their struggle, they probably would have created a confederation of small communities, based on farming, in which all would share the products of the group and contribute what they could to the common store. This confederation might have become, in Jefferson's words, "a beacon to all people in all parts of the world," and the excesses of the industrial revolution might have been spared humanity in the nineteenth century. Such bloody conflicts as the Rocky Mountain War and the Mexican War, the Trans-Oceanic War and the European conflicts, would have been prevented —or so the scholars of the late nineteenth century seemed to believe.

2. The author would be the first to concede that his view too has been formed by his background and prejudices. In this chapter I hope to act as a critic, aware that future historians will operate on me the way I have operated on others. The dilemma is discussed fully in Arthur Vendergrift. *The Faiths of Historians* (London, 1959), pp. 227–57.

According to them, the Rebellion's failure caused the loss of a golden age of mankind.[3]

But the rebels lost their struggle, and in so doing, dispirited like-minded groups elsewhere in the western world. The Rebellion, according to some historians, alerted the old regimes in Europe to the dangers of revolt, and so was an important factor in the brutal crushing of the Paris insurrection of 1789 and other uprisings of the period.[4]

A newly-aware old regime now took command of the technological and scientific forces then at work in the world. Monarchy was preserved, as the nobles formed alliances with businessmen in most western European nations. In America, both the C.N.A. and the U.S.M. put into office men who had close relations with the business community. Despite talk of reform and government control of business, capitalism flourished. The society of the third quarter of the century was one in which an increasingly smaller number of people in Europe were receiving an increasingly larger reward from the economy, while most of the workers received only a bare subsistence.

Conditions were better in the C.N.A., where a genuine reformism in the union movement, in politics, and in local and state governments could be discerned. In addition, the C.N.A. had a chronic labor shortage, and so its workers were always among the best paid in the world. Thus, the laborers were given a stake in the system, and so were less revolutionary than they were in other parts of the world.[5]

The U.S.M. was an anomaly in this period. Based on the Jeffersonians, but with a majority of non-Anglos; led by a people who came out of the North American Rebellion to found a land based on Jeffersonian ideals, but who still practiced slavery; the most rapidly industrializing nation in the world with the exception of the C.N.A., and yet one in which Mexicanos were still living in a feudalistic economy, it had at once the most imposing superstructure and the most rotten foundation in the western world. Kinkaid's assassination and Concepción's guerrilla brigades were major symptoms of the nation's problems. The growing power of the Kramer Associates and Petroleum of Mexico was another, while the desire of the Continentalists to engage

3. We can never know what would have happened in such an eventuality. To be certain the reader understands the author's view, allow me to reiterate what in earlier chapters may have been only implied. My own feeling is that a rebel victory would have signalled the beginning of an age of anarchy, in which western civilization might have been crushed. In this section I am trying to present the opinions of others as fairly as I can.

4. Reynolds Copeland. *The Legacy of Failure: Europe and the Rebel Defeat in British America* (London, 1929).

5. This evaluation excludes Quebec, of course, and that state remained one of frustrated ambitions and sadness. Carter. *The People Want Bread!*, pp. 409–14.

in overseas expansion at a time when the nation had forgotten its domestic problems was a sign of future trouble.

Mexico had one of the highest literacy rates in the world in 1880, the result of Conroy's educational reforms. It led the world in the granting of social insurance and labor benefits, which had been accepted by both the Continentalists and the Libertarians. But these and other reforms had been granted by reformers to their people, and not fought for and won by the people themselves, as had been the case in the C.N.A. The non-Anglo population of Mexico had grievances and solutions, but the grievances were theirs, while the solutions had been imposed on them by Anglos and their Hispano cohorts. By 1880 the Mexicanos, oppressed lower-class Anglos, some Indians, and a majority of the slaves were ready for revolution; they were sufficiently educated to realize their problems, were aware of the growing disparity between them and the Anglos, and were disillusioned with political solutions. The nation was a veritable tinder box, but this was not realized until Kinkaid's assassination and the withdrawal of Concepción from politics.[6]

The Bloody Eighties did not begin in the U.S.M., however, but in France, in the aftermath of the Franco-German War. From the first, the French armies proved no match for the better-organized and equipped Germans. By 1879 two German armies had surrounded Paris, while France's overseas markets and possessions were all in the hands of German sailors and merchants. A series of what appears to have been spontaneous riots erupted in Paris in November, and the government lacked the power to control them. By early December anarchy ruled the city. Louis XX lost his nerve, and in a dramatic speech, announced the beginning of formal negotiations to end the war and his own abdication in favor of his son. The newly crowned young Louis XXI was considered a reformer, but the Paris mobs would have none of this. On December 25, Christmas Day, 1879, protesters stormed the palace, seized the royal family, and put the new King, his unhappy father, the queen mother, and the three princesses to death.

German troops entered Paris on December 27, and were welcomed by middle-class merchants who viewed them more as saviors than conquerors. Within days, however, two regiments had joined the rioters, and by mid-January the invading army was demoralized and radicalized. Now the uprisings spread to the German Confederation, from there to Austria, and then to the Italian kingdoms. Every major European capital was in shambles with the exception of St. Petersburg and London, both of whom were protected by loyal troops.[7]

6. Arthur Watkins. *Mexico on the Eve: Society in the U.S.M. in the 1870's* (London, 1920).

7. Zelda Carmichael. *The Flames of February: Europe in the Winter of 1880* (London, 1967).

The objectives of the terror were at first unclear. The rioters seemed intent on destroying all they could find. Later studies indicate that there was surprisingly little looting, except in Marseilles, Hamburg, and Vienna. Also, the mobs were leaderless for the most part, or if they did have organizers, they were local farmers and workers with little in the way of ideological baggage, but eager to obliterate every vestige of the old regime.[8]

Europe's governments were able to quell the riots by March. France remained leaderless until late autumn, however, as no government—not even one established by the German puppets—was able to achieve the confidence of sufficient people to assume command. By that time, the rebels had found *rationales* and leaders for their protests. Léon Gambetta was able to form a socialist government in Paris, which by 1884, had control over most of France. Gambetta, who had been influenced by the writings of Erich Neiderhoffer, called for the distribution of equity ownership of France's industries to the workers, and the expropriation of unused private and Church lands, which would be distributed to farmers. As might be expected, the monarchists and others of the *ancien regime* protested, and rallying behind the exiled pretender, Charles X, called for a return to the pre-war government. These two forces would struggle against each other for the next quarter of a century, and in the process, cause the decline of France.

The German Confederation remained under the leadership of the Hohenzollerns, although a new party, the Free Germans, made its appearance, and under the leadership of Karl Ollenhauer was able to force some moderate reforms through the Diet. The other continental nations followed the French example, and so the Germanic Confederation became the only major power in Europe with the exception of Russia and Britain.[9]

Russia was able to survive due to the strength of its army and the backwardness of its population. Britain had the ability to absorb much of the revolutionary protest into conventional politics. British reformers joined the Whigs, which in 1885 was the minority party, but whose reform program won them power in that year. Under the leadership of Prime Minister Richard Cross the Whigs sponsored and passed the Great Reform Bill of 1886, which enlarged the franchise, redistributed seats in Commons, established social insurance, and set into motion plans for a redistribution of equity in large corporations. These programs were grudgingly accepted by Britain's business leaders, although J. P. Morgan and Shawcross Finlay led a determined op-

---

8. Erich Neiderhoffer. *My People, My Life* (London, 1890).
9. Zelda Carmichael. *In the Wake of the Red Witch: Reform in Europe in the 1880's* (London, 1970).

position to the nationalization of the banks and managed to delay it for seven years.[10]

Despite these changes and reforms (some conservatives would argue that it was because of them), revolutionary activity continued. The fighting in France would not end until 1892, and then only for a few years. When Charles X landed at Calais in 1895, civil war erupted, and would decimate the population within a generation. Similarly, much of central Europe was victimized by bands of roving marauders, who stole, raped, and destroyed as they went. Only in parts of Germany were they controlled, and even there people were not safe in their houses. The Russian response, though late in coming, was extremely violent and bloody. In 1888 there was an uprising in Moscow and another in St. Petersburg, which the government believed to be the work of French radicals who had entered the country and were being protected by their Russian counterparts. Czar Nicholas II ordered his secret police to put down the insurrection, and they did so with brutal thoroughness. Within the next five years, over two million Russians had been put to death by the police or the army[11] and another 80,000 sent to Kamchatka and the prison camps.

The insurrections created economic chaos in continental Europe, so that the standard of living declined sharply in all countries, with the worst conditions being those of Austria and the Italian kingdoms, while Britain and the Germanic Confederation had the fewest problems. Hundreds of thousands of homeless people, fleeing from persecution by revolutionaries or leaders of the old order, criss-crossed the continent, searching for peace and work. Few such places existed in the Europe of the 1880's. Some were able to cross the Scandinavian, Spanish, and Swiss borders to find a measure of safety, although there was little in the way of work for the immigrants. By 1885, these countries closed their borders to newcomers, and others followed suit. Many middle-class French families, eager to settle in Britain and possessing skills and money, were rejected, as British workers demonstrated against the foreigners and warned of an uprising should they be permitted to enter the country. Some 50,000 were allowed to settle in Ireland, however, along with an additional 65,000 Germans, Austrians, and Italians, all of whom had sufficient capital to support themselves for the first year of their stay.[12]

The greatest migration, however, was to non-European nations. Hundreds of thousands of poor Russian peasants, many of them Jews,

10. Werner Hiedi. *The Making of a Bank: The History of the Morgan Bank of London* (London, 1939), pp. 226-29.
11. Ferdinand Rainy. *Nicholas II and the White Terror* (New York, 1955).
12. George Schultz. *The Great Migration: The Dispersion of the 1880s* (London, 1963).

crossed the Turkish border, and some eventually found their way to North Africa, where a large Russian community was formed by the turn of the century. Some Germans went to Iceland, and a hardy few to Greenland. There was a large-scale migration of Italians to South America, especially to Brazil and the Argentine. Some 47,000 people left the Netherlands for South Africa, where they reinforced an already thriving settlement at the Cape. But the most interesting population shift was to the nations of the British Empire. Wealthy, talented, and ambitious French, Dutch, and Italian men and women went to Australia, and some continued on to New Zealand. Others, including many Englishmen, went to Kenya and Uganda in eastern Africa. Some 10,000 Londoners resettled in Bermuda, the Bahamas, and other British islands in the western Atlantic and Caribbean. But the most desirable goal of all was Manitoba.

Ever since the founding of the C.N.A., Manitoba had been considered a rustic paradise of sorts, a place where people might vegetate, achieve some measure of prosperity, but a confederation which "history was passing by."[13] This situation and reputation had hitherto made Manitoba the goal of dreamers and visionaries, not men of ambition. But during the 1880's, when it seemed the very fabric of western civilization was being destroyed, Manitoba's reputation made that confederation a magnet for some of the most talented people in the world. Manitoba was difficult to reach, however, and many turned back before they got there. Others settled in the eastern parts of the C.N.A., while a few went on to the more accessible parts of the Vandalias, especially Northern Vandalia's Fowler region. In all, some 1.5 million immigrants arrived in the C.N.A. from 1880 to 1882, at which time further entry was prohibited. An additional 100,000 arrived in Mexico in this period, but then that country, too, turned its back on Europe.[14] Each had good and sufficient reason for so acting. Both the C.N.A. and the U.S.M. had major problems in the early months of 1882, and there was talk of dissolution in government circles in Burgoyne and Mexico City.

13. Irwin and McLean. *Manitoba*, pp. 205, 239–43, 340–42.

14. Schultz. *The Great Migration*, pp. 364–66.

# 18

# AN AGE OF RENEWAL

JOHN McDowell's Liberal government was well-established and firmly in control of the C.N.A. when the Great Depression struck. McDowell had come to office as a result of the appearance of a strong third party, the People's Coalition, which had gained far more supporters from the Conservatives than it had from the Liberals. Still, McDowell was the first Governor-General to take office without a majority in the Grand Council, and at the time of his nomination had been virtually unknown outside of Manitoba.

In his first year in office, McDowell had been able to take command of the political reform movement that had preceded him. He managed to placate the more moderate Coalitionists by advocating and passing what appeared a major reform program. On the other hand, he won Conservative support by rejecting the more radical demands set forth by the Coalition.

### Composition of State Legislatures, 1878 and 1879

| STATE | 1878 | | | 1879 | | |
|---|---|---|---|---|---|---|
| | LIB. | CONS. | P.C. | LIB. | CONS. | P.C. |
| Northern Confederation | 59 | 26 | 46 | 57 | 18 | 56 |
| Southern Confederation | 23 | 61 | 52 | 21 | 69 | 46 |
| Indiana | 20 | 25 | 19 | 31 | 23 | 10 |
| Northern Vandalia | 19 | 21 | 4 | 24 | 17 | 3 |
| Southern Vandalia | 24 | 54 | 7 | 30 | 50 | 5 |
| Manitoba | 25 | 15 | 9 | 31 | 11 | 7 |
| Quebec | 8 | 38 | 32 | 10 | 33 | 35 |

Source: Albany *Gazette*, November 11, 1879.

The 1879 state elections appeared to confirm what Burgoyne politicians had suspected for a year. The People's Coalition seemed to have reached its crest, making gains only in the Northern Confederation and Quebec, while the Conservatives were losing power in all states except the Southern Confederation, and even there, the gain was destined to be temporary.[1] In 1878, the Conservatives had controlled five confederation legislatures against the Liberals' two; in 1879, as a result of the confederation elections, the totals were Liberals four, Conservatives two, and People's Coalition one.

It would appear, then, that the reform wave of the late 1870's and its manifestations within the political arena had resulted in a new party structure. The Conservatives, who had been so powerful prior to 1878, were now sharply declining; its reformers entering the P.C., its moderates joining the Liberal Party. The party which had given the nation such men as Willie Lloyd, William Johnson, and Herbert Clemens, was now relegated to the role of a balance wheel between its more reformist and radical adversaries.[2]

This development should not have been surprising. The party had stagnated during the Clemens administration, while the Liberals had been able to capitalize on Conservative mistakes. McDowell proved able to lead his party into the reform era and so capture the support of moderates and advocates of "celan government"; the P.C. was effective in its appeals to the C.N.A.'s more radical elements. The Conservatives were left with a holding operation in the S.C., and aged, declining, and usually corrupt politicians in the other states. The party would linger on, but to all intents and purposes, had lost its power by 1881.[3]

McDowell delivered the final blow to the Conservatives by the way he handled the Great Depression. When the British banks began calling in their loans in 1879, the Governor-General ordered the Treasury to make deposits in key financial institutions throughout the nation, thus assuring their liquidity. This won him the applause of the business community, while at the same time the workers and farmers appreciated this bulwark against foreclosures and high interest rates. When despite this, several large corporations, including National Electric, declared bankruptcy, McDowell arranged for an emergency loan fund, to be administered by the newly-created National Financial Administration, to be used to help them recover. Under the leadership of Howard Carson, the N.F.A. made 354 loans totalling more than N.A. £3.5 million during the 1880-1884 period. Carson's intervention was credited with the resurrection of the Northern Confederation Trust

---

1. Ironically, the growth of Conservative strength in the Southern Confederation was due primarily to the growing political awareness of the Negroes, who now gave their full support to the party of Willie Lloyd. But this new awareness in politics came too late to save the party, for the great exodus of Negroes to Southern Vandalia continued, and once there, the newcomers would often vote Liberal. Marshall Butler. *The Paradox of the Black Vote* (Burgoyne, 1955), pp. 338–43.

2. Fowler, *McDowell*, pp. 487–89.

3. Reuben Fenton. *And Close the Door: The Decline of C.N.A. Conservatism* (New York, 1955).

Company, the saving of North American Steel, and the prevention of a wave of foreclosures in Michigan City. This, too, won him the applause of businessmen and workers alike. The C.N.A. Businessmen's Association, the most powerful organization of its kind, called McDowell "the strongest and wisest leader our nation has ever had," while Carl Bok, president of the Mechanics National Union, foreswore that organization's customary political neutrality to offer McDowell "the support of our members throughout our land, and this definitely extends to the political campaign of 1883."[4] McDowell also helped farmers through the establishment of the Rural Credit Association, headed by Senator Clifford Brinton of Indiana. The R.C.A. was empowered to grant loans of up to N.A. £400 to farmers whose holdings were endangered by foreclosures, but who had sufficient collateral to have gained loans in more normal times.[5]

While laying the groundwork for domestic recovery, the Governor-General strengthened the ties of Empire. Working in conjunction with Prime Minister Geoffrey Cadogan, he called an Imperial Conference, which met in London in 1881 to discuss common problems. The participants agreed to maintain free trade between the member nations; affirmed their loyalty to the Queen; established the Imperial Monetary Fund (which had the power to make low-interest loans to member governments); and initiated discussions as to the creation of a common defense force. The Second Imperial Conference, which increased the lending power of the I.M.F., met in New York, and this was considered a McDowell victory, and a sign of rising C.N.A. prestige.

McDowell accomplished all his reforms without a preconceived plan, meeting each crisis as it came. His flexibility, his talent for making the average North American believe he understood his problems and would do something about them, and his skill at political maneuvering, made McDowell a difficult target for his opponents. The only major criticism of McDowell could be that the Governor-General was an opportunist, a trimmer, a person whose only real dedication was to maintaining his personal power. These criticisms began to mount in intensity as the 1883 elections approached. Aware of this, McDowell spoke to the nation on the subject in a New York address of October 11, 1882. Toward the end of the speech, the Governor-General spoke of his philosophy, ambitions, and future programs.

> We are living at a time of momentous change, one which has seen the decline of monarchies and the end of empires we once thought immortal. The faiths and truths of yesterday seem outworn and curiously

4. Abner LeFevre. *The Age of Renewal: The First McDowell Administration* (New York, 1968), pp. 138–68.
5. *Ibid*, pp. 184–86.

meaningless. Our way of life is being threatened as never before. Yet we hold on, we organize, we persevere. We shall pass through this dark corridor, just as we did the Rebellion, the Crisis Years, and other times of distress. Our fathers had problems, which they solved. Ours may appear greater than theirs, but so are the resources we command. Even now our problems are being resolved, our wounds healed, our nation renewed. More will be needed before we achieve our ambitions, and we shall sacrifice much in order to save; we must change in order to preserve.

This administration has done much to preserve the North American farm, the North American business firm, the North American banking system, and has succeeded in all its efforts, as the N.F.A. and related agencies prove. But more must be done in the future. Every North American has the right to hold a job, to a fair wage, to a fair return on his investment, to a decent place in which to live, to security in his home, to the knowledge that his government knows of his needs, and is prepared to help him help himself. Few of these goals have been reached, and some may appear impossible of achievement in our life-time. But we must make the effort. For this reason, I call upon all North Americans to undertake a time of soul-searching, to go into the Wilderness and then return, better prepared and more willing to work for a better nation and world. North America is in the midst of its Age of Renewal, from which it will emerge greater and more powerful than before.[6]

The speech was much discussed and analyzed. To those who heard it, McDowell seemed to be saying that more widespread reforms were needed. Others noted the Governor-General also spoke of the need for North Americans "to work for a better nation and world." Did this mean McDowell had international ambitions? The fact the Second Imperial Conference had been held in New York was viewed by some as a sign that the leadership of the Empire was passing to the C.N.A., and with it, new international responsibilities. When questioned about this point later on, the Governor-General was vague and evasive; clearly the words were no accident, and had portents for the future.

More significant for the time being, however, was McDowell's indication of a desire to move more rapidly and differently in the reform field. What did he mean, however, by saying the government should help people help themselves? In the past, the government had intervened in the economy only in a regulatory sense, and never as a direct participant. Did McDowell intend to change this in the future? Again, the Governor-General evaded questions on this and related points, deliberately leaving himself as many options in the future as possible. The Age of Renewal was not, as was believed at the time, a

6. New York *Herald*, October 12, 1882.

blueprint for a new society, but rather a catch-all for any future programs the Governor-General might deem necessary.

The Conservatives charged McDowell with radicalism, with attempting to destroy the rights of the individual, and with the desire to become a tyrant by catering to the whims of the multitude at a time of great distress. "Such talk is not only dangerous, it is cruel," said Theodore Lindsay, publisher of the New York *Herald* and a power in the Conservative Party. "Our country is in grave danger. We have more than one million men out of work, our factories are operating sporadically, our trade is declining, and there are revolutionaries at work in all the states. And the Governor-General talks of progress, of his accomplishments, and of his plans for the future! Any more such plans, and we shall have no future, but go the way of France and Austria into national oblivion!"[7] Lindsay urged the nation to reject McDowell's leadership, and elect instead, "a man who will recognize the old values of our nation, those cherished by Burgoyne and Dickinson, and not be moved to accept every nostrum that comes along." By then it was clear Lindsay considered himself that man.

The People's Coalition had a clearer concept of the meaning of the Age of Renewal. Although the party had been disappointed by the results of the 1879 state elections, its leaders believed the nation was now ready for a thoroughgoing reform program, one similar to that of France. As early as 1880, P.C. leaders in the Grand Council had challenged McDowell as "a tool of the big banks, the big corporations, the reactionary unions," and claimed that he, like other "politicians of the past," was offering the people "the form of change, but not the substance."[8] As they saw it, the Age of Renewal proved McDowell recognized their strength, and was now moving to seize the initiative from them by offering the public "more of the same placebos, when the body needs stronger medicines than ever before." The P.C. called for a version of Neiderhofferism—a guaranteed wage for workers, government support for farm prices, and "solidarity with our brothers across the seas." In response, McDowell talked of the need for fairer wages, guaranteed employment, and unity with the Empire.

P.C. leaders also noted that McDowell's program was designed to aid business as well as workers. The Governor-General would guarantee the capitalist a "fair return on his investment," leaving the meaning of "fair" to be determined at a later time. Finally, the People's Coalition feared McDowell was planning an assault on freedom and the rights of free speech generally, by stressing the need for "security in the home." At the time, the C.N.A., like all the western world, was

---

7. New York *Herald*, November 1, 8, 1882.

8. *The People's Voice*, September 5, 1880, January 18, 1881, February 1, 1881.

plagued by looters, rioters, and the like, although it was far less serious in North America than elsewhere. Now McDowell pledged himself— the P.C. accused—to repression. The fact that the Governor-General had doubled the size of the Confederation Bureau of Investigation and had named Colonel Mark Forsyth, a well-known believer in a tough law-enforcement policy, as its chief, was of deep concern to P.C. leaders, just as it was applauded by the middle class throughout the C.N.A.[9]

During the three months between the Age of Renewal speech and the 1883 elections, McDowell travelled to Indiana, the S.C. and the N.C., delivering speeches on the subject of reform. Meanwhile, the Liberal Party in the Grand Council introduced a series of measures designed to implement some of his programs. These bills were poorly drawn and managed. Even if the Liberals had enjoyed a majority in the Council, they would have had difficulty in passing; as it was, they all failed to gain acceptance, being defeated by an alliance of Conservatives and Coalitionites. Little did the two parties realize that by so doing, they were falling into McDowell's carefully laid trap.

On January 8, 1883, in a speech in Burgoyne, the Governor-General lashed out at those "men of the past and radicals who would destroy our future, who have hindered every attempt at justice I have made in the past five years." He then ticked off a list of the bills rejected at the last session of the Grand Council. "Each of these measures was designed to better the lot of our people. Each, if passed, would have alleviated misery, created jobs, raised wages, or provided cleaner and better places in which our people could live and work. But they have been rejected by the merchants of fear and hate. The people know who their enemies are, and the people will reject them at the polls in February."[10] It was thus that the Governor-General opened the political season of 1883, and did so in a most spectacular manner.

The Liberal Convention was a happy affair, in marked contrast to the despair of five years before. In 1878, the party suspected it had lost both its appeal and relevancy, but after the successes of the McDowell administration the Liberals not only expected to win the election in 1883, but capture a majority in the Grand Council. McDowell was selected party leader by acclamation, and pledged himself to the "creation of The Age of Renewal in North America, one that will bring benefits for all citizens, in every part of the nation."

Still dismayed by their losses in the 1879 confederation elections, and municipal and local defeats in 1880 and 1882, the Conservatives met in New York at a time when party fortunes seemed low. The

9. Barbara Montez. *A History of the People's Coalition* (London, 1960), pp. 375–98. Hector Welles. *The Peoples'*

*Coalition During the Great Depression* (London, 1967).
10. Burgoyne *Times*, January 9, 1883.

once-mighty coalition that had controlled the Grand Council during the Clemens decade was now shattered. The reformers had been attracted to McDowell; "clean government" advocates had been shocked away from the Conservatives by the party's corruption; the memories of Willie Lloyd were insufficient to retain Negro votes so long after that statesman's passing; radicals and extremists had been drawn off by the People's Coalition; and middle class businessmen, formerly the bulwark of the Conservatives, had fled to the Liberals for protection. The Conservatives retained their popularity only among the recent immigrants, who were not opposed to the way power was distributed (and so would not join the P.C.), but who found all positions closed to them held by Liberals. The large increase in immigration from 1880 to 1883 encouraged Conservatives somewhat, but the party's leaders knew that most of the newcomers would not or could not vote, and that once they were able to adjust to life in the C.N.A., they would more often than not go over to the Liberals.

So it was that a dejected Conservative Convention looked over its hopefuls. Even there, the signs of decline were to be seen. Four men, three of them councilmen, put themselves forth as potential party leaders. Each was over sixty-five years of age, while their ideas and rhetoric were that of the pre-Clemens era. The fourth, Theodore Lindsay of the New York *Herald*, was only thirty-eight. He was brilliant, dynamic, and one of the most influential men in the C.N.A., but Lindsay also lacked political experience, had a reputation for supporting crank causes, and was unpredictable. Even so, the publisher won the nomination and swore "to carry the message of the New Conservatism to every part of the Confederation, and before I am done, the people will know of our dangers and how McDowell has deceived them, of their own hidden resources, and of the government's attempts to steal them from their rightful owners." It was a strange, often contradictory speech, but Lindsay spoke well, and the delegates applauded with as much verve as they could muster.

The People's Coalition held its convention in Boston (some suggested to indicate their relationship with the rebels of the 1770's). Five years before it had been a new, untested party, with romantic and impractical ideas as to how best run a campaign. Now the Coalition could smell victory, and more prudent leaders took the tiller to steer it to a Council majority.

The most important of these was Ezra Gallivan, who at the age of thirty-three, had just been elected mayor of Michigan City. Gallivan was the son of Patrick Gallivan, an Irish immigrant who had come to the C.N.A. soon after the Rocky Mountain War, hoping to strike it rich in the Vandalia copper fields. The elder Gallivan never reached Vandalia, stopping instead in Michigan City, where he found employment as a railroad yardman. He had a talent for and an interest in railroads, as well as a fine native intelligence. These, coupled with good fortune, enabled Gallivan to rise quickly at the Indiana Northern, and by 1861, he became its president. With the help of two lawyers, Martin Kelsony and Abraham Lincoln, Gallivan was able to extend the line into Manitoba to the northwest and later on, to Southern Vandalia. His was the first railroad to join with the Mexican lines, in this case the Jefferson and California, and Gallivan was as much the king of the western roads as Scott and Carnegie were in the east.

Patrick Gallivan had hoped his son would enter railroading, but Ezra Gallivan had other interests. For a while he did work in the Indiana Northern's Michigan City offices, where he was more impressed with working conditions than with the line's finances and expansion. Ezra developed a sympathy for the poor and a desire to improve their lot that appalled his father. The elder Gallivan vowed that any poor man with ambition could rise to the top through hard work, while Ezra argued that C.N.A. business had become oppressive and must be regulated. When Ezra joined the People's Party in 1878, Patrick disowned him. The elder Gallivan marked the occasion with a large donation to the Conservative Party, and the two never spoke to each other again.

Ezra Gallivan was a tough, shrewd leader. He had won his mayorality by moderating his language and making strong appeals to Conservatives and Liberals in Michigan City, generally ignoring his own P.C. backers. "Why preach to the converted?" he asked Kelsony. "You do not offer bait to a fish that's already hooked." Now he proposed to do the same on a national scale, and having achieved a position of prominence in the party, went to New York with that in mind.

Gallivan would not seek the nomination himself; in 1883 he was content to wait in the wings, build up the party, and then seize power. Instead, he backed Councilman Scott Ruggles of the Northern Confederation. Ruggles had a reputation as a moderate, and was known to have misgivings about some of what he privately called "the crackpots" in the party. He was respectable, hard working, and responsible, albeit a dull speaker and plodding thinker. Ruggles won the nomination with ease, and pledged himself "to the quest for social justice in our land." The Convention cheered, and there was the kind of wild celebration expected by the press and public. But behind the scenes, the messianic and radical People's Coalition of 1878 had been transformed into a pragmatic and reformist organization.

This was not realized by most voters in 1883, and in any case, McDowell was unbeatable. The Governor-General won a second term with ease. But Gallivan's victory was just as great, for the People's

Coalition surged ahead in most of the confederations, and now became the official opposition in the Grand Council, replacing the Conservatives.[11]

### Results of the C.N.A. Elections of 1883

| STATE | LIBERAL | CONSERVATIVE | PEOPLE'S COALITION |
|---|---|---|---|
| | PARTY AFFILIATION OF COUNCILMEN | | |
| Northern Confederation | 28 | 6 | 11 |
| Southern Confederation | 10 | 8 | 11 |
| Indiana | 15 | 4 | 10 |
| Northern Vandalia | 8 | 1 | 2 |
| Southern Vandalia | 6 | 2 | 2 |
| Manitoba | 11 | 0 | 2 |
| Quebec | 4 | 2 | 7 |
| | 82 | 23 | 45 |

Source: New York *Herald*, February 16, 1878.

The first year of McDowell's second administration was the most fruitful legislatively in the history of the C.N.A. Within days of the election McDowell called for a special session of the Grand Council to consider his proposals. He now led a majority in the Council; on the opposite side of the bench was Ruggles, the Minority Leader. Not knowing where to sit, the majority of the Conservatives took their place in the back row of the Liberals, while five members, all from Quebec and the Northern Confederation, went over to the Coalition.

McDowell asked for speedy passage of a series of bills, which he claimed would "enable us to enter the Age of Renewal." The most important of these were:[12]

—An act to guarantee employment to every person seeking a job. If none were available in private industry, then the government would have the obligation of giving him a position at a national installation.
—A guaranteed minimum wage of N.A. £1 a day.
—A reform of the school system, which would guarantee a secondary education "to all who can profit thereby."
—A transportation act, to create a national agency with power to order changes in railroad policies.

11. Fowler. *McDowell*, pp. 438–46; Frederick Powell. *Theodore Lindsay: The Black and the Blue* (New York, 1956); Harvey Connery. *The Early Life of Ezra Gallivan* (New York, 1909), pp. 79–96; Milton Hull. *The Politics of 1883: McDowell and His Campaign* (New York, 1970).

12. Worthington Fowler. *Reform at Flood Tide: McDowell's Year of Glory, 1883* (New York, 1908); Jay Phister. *The Age of Renewal: McDowell at His Prime* (New York, 1952); Maxwell Stuart. *The Trap Is Set: Gallivan in Opposition* (London, 1966), pp. 143–59.

—A "fair trade act," which would encourage exports by the granting of bounties.

—The establishment of a new central bank, along the model of the Bank of England and the Bank of Mexico.

—Expansion of the NFA, so as to enable the agency to grant more and larger loans to distressed corporations.

—Expansion of the RCA, so that farmers could receive loans of N.A.£ 1,000 at low interest rates.

—Expansion of the Confederation Bureau of Investigation, so that it would be enabled "to better root out subversives in our midst."

—An army appropriations bill, designed to increase the army from 80,000 in 1883 to 200,000 by 1886.

—A naval appropriations bill, which would "make our navy second to none."

All of these measures, most in their original form, passed the Council in 1883. McDowell was hailed by the Liberal press as the greatest reformer in C.N.A. history. "With these new laws, our nation has forged into the lead in the area of social benefits," wrote the Burgoyne *Times*. The Michigan City *Dispatch* went so far as to call McDowell "the greatest reformer the English-speaking world has known since Kensington," while the Boston *Word* considered the Governor-General "the leading light of the century." Lindsay, writing in the *Herald*, claimed "The Governor-General will destroy our moral fibre with his nostrums, and our exchequer with his taxes," but his warnings fell on deaf ears. The Coalition press was sharply critical of the legislation, arguing that "Mr. McDowell, while well meaning, is treating symptoms, but ignoring the illness. The nation needs surgery, not more pills."[13]

The situation was pretty much the same in the Grand Council. Conservatives argued against the costs of the measures and the freedom they would take from the average C.N.A. citizen, and they usually voted against the bills *en masse*. The People's Coalition's response, however, was more guarded. Ruggles seemed to echo the Conservatives on occasion, wondering how the funds for McDowell's programs could be raised. He also criticized the Governor-General for having "good intentions but poor advice." In particular, Ruggles thought the nation's school system could not support the new education program, and that the administrative structure was no place "to dump, unceremoniously, those whose skills are other than that of paper-pushing." Ruggles reserved his sharpest barbs for other aspects of the Age of Renewal, however, and in particular, those dealing with business and

---

13. Egbert Pierce. *John McDowell and the Press: A Study in Manipulation* (Burgoyne, 1947), pp. 196–207.

foreign relations. The North American Bank, he said, would be used to benefit large-scale enterprises at the expense of their smaller competitors.[14] The program to aid exports, which was carried out by the North American Export Council, would also be used to assist bigger units and not their smaller rivals. The expansion of the N.F.A. and R.C.A. would not assist distressed small businessmen and farmers, said Ruggles, but rather "aid the large contributors to Mr. McDowell's campaign chest. Why not increase the total amount of money available and ease the requirements for loans, instead of enlarging upon the maximum amount for each loan? The former policy would aid marginal producers, the latter the secret friends of the Governor-General."[15]

Meanwhile, Ezra Gallivan spoke out against McDowell from his office in Michigan City. Leaving the nuts-and-bolts work to Ruggles, he spoke in generalities, concentrating on McDowell's ideas on foreign affairs. He asked why the Governor-General insisted on a larger armed force, "since we are not being threatened by any outside foe." And why the need for an enlarged C.B.I., "when the dislocations of the early part of our decade have diminished, and our nation fortunately has been spared the pains of our neighbors across the Atlantic."[16] For the most part, however, Gallivan concentrated on city administration, leaving the reply to the McDowell programs to Ruggles.

The Age of Renewal programs were passed by large majorities, made possible by splits in the Coalition delegation to the Grand Council. Some Liberals saw in this the disintegration of their opposition, but McDowell thought otherwise. At a Cabinet meeting he said, "Mr. Gallivan hopes to give us sufficient rope to enable us to hang ourselves. We must be cautious in the future. A loud hyena is not as dangerous as a stealthy tiger."[17]

McDowell was correct. The Gallivan strategy, as discerned later on, was to permit the Governor-General to have whatever legislation he thought necessary to bring about what the Mayor called "the McDowell Golden Age."[18] Then, when the measures fell short of the mark, Gallivan would come forward to argue that having failed, McDowell should make way for a more intelligent and dedicated leader. In a letter to his mother, written in 1884, Gallivan outlined his thoughts on the matter succinctly.

14. Jay Phister. *Front Man for Reform: The Ruggles Opposition* (New York, 1949).
15. New York *Herald*, October 5, 1884; Burgoyne *Constitution*, November 16, 1884.

16. Michigan City *Ledger*, January 12, 1885.
17. Michigan City *Ledger*, February 19, 1885, December 12, 1885.
18. John McDowell, *Papers*, McDowell Library, North City.

The Governor-General is a good man, probably the best we can hope for in this kind of society. His ideas and programs, however, are doomed to failure, and that is why we can let him do what he wishes, in the full knowledge that just as he has accepted the power, so must he bear the consequences. If the Age of Renewal programs were not enacted, then McDowell could claim that he hadn't been given a proper chance. Now this door is closed for him. Every time McDowell succeeds, it is a sign to the people that change was indeed necessary. Every time he fails, the people learn again that half-way measures are not enough for this corrupt society. Thus, whatever happens, the Liberals are doomed to defeat.[19]

As might be expected, McDowell's thoughts on the matter were quite different. Writing of them fifteen years later, the Governor-General said:

We knew from the start that legislation could mildly coerce, but never convince. That can only be done through the passage of time. It was my hope in introducing, and then passing, the Age of Renewal programs to create the kind of atmosphere in which human nature itself might gradually be transformed. Claims to the contrary notwithstanding, we were successful enough, and were able to develop programs which benefitted all the citizenry, and which prevented the kind of violence that was seen in France during the Great Depression.[20]

By 1885, however, it seemed Gallivan's strategy had worked. Most of the Age of Renewal programs proved either unworkable or poorly managed. The school system could not expand rapidly enough to handle the increased numbers of individuals wanting education; the N.F.A. and R.C.A. did operate to the betterment of big business and tended to ignore smaller units; there was a public outcry against C.B.I. investigations in the Northern and Southern Confederations; and the North American Bank proved unable to handle the tasks assigned it. The nation was in the midst of a general inflationary wave while, at the same time, full recovery from the Great Depression had not yet been achieved. Taxes were at an all-time high. Small-scale insurrections continued, especially in Quebec and parts of the Northern Confederation and Indiana. These were crushed by the C.B.I. and the army, leading to talk of a possible military dictatorship. And in the midst of all this, the Governor-General appeared powerless. "Let Mr. McDowell ask us for what he will," said Ruggles. "He has a majority in the Grand Council, and can have anything he wants from it. Indeed, we would be willing to support his plans, for the People's Coalition wants peace and har-

---

19. Bernard Gallivan. *Letters from My Father* (New York, 1920), p. 339.

20. John McDowell. *The Age of Renewal:* (New York, 1892), p. 108.

mony as much as anyone else." The truth of the matter, said Ruggles, was "the Age of Renewal is, and always has been, a sham. The Liberals have had their chance, and have failed. Now it is time for true reform, and not just fancy maneuverings."[21]

McDowell's second administration, which had begun with high hopes, political success, and the passage of the Age of Renewal programs, ended on a note of despair. The Governor-General asked for more time "to correct the abuses of a century," but by 1888, the public clearly wanted a change. The only alternative at the time seemed the People's Coalition, headed by Ruggles and Gallivan.

21. New York *Herald*, April 3, 1887.

# 19

# THE CRISIS OF MEXICAN REPUBLICANISM

THE Great Depression and the violence that followed came at a time when the U.S.M. was already in the midst of an economic downturn, with a revolution in the making. Historians like to compare the impacts the Bloody Eighties had on France, the C.N.A., and the U.S.M. In France, the crisis ended centuries of feudalism and, in the end, left a nation in the midst of partisan fighting, with a shaky republican government. The C.N.A. survived the Eighties comparatively well; despite the flaws in the Age of Renewal, it did serve to satisfy the demands of all but the more radical members of the People's Coalition and the *Patriotes* of Quebec (who would not have been satisfied with anything that emanated from Burgoyne).

Mexico, on the other hand, was shattered by the crisis. Flaws already evident in society and political life now became jagged scars; economic injustices that had existed since the founding seemed intolerable. In retrospect, we can see that the U.S.M. had never been a true nation in the sense that France or the C.N.A. had become. Instead, it was artificially created by the superimposition of a dynamic elite upon a society ready for social revolution. According to Marx, "In the early nineteenth century the Hispanos of Mexico were on the point of being overthrown by the Mexicano masses. Then the Jeffersonians arrived, to support and eventually replace the Hispanos, and then form an alliance with the old ruling class." But the industrialization of the U.S.M. and the coalescence of the ruling class led to a growing awareness of this plight on the part of the Mexicanos, and in time increased their demands for what they believed to have been rightfully theirs. "In this way, the rulers have armed the ruled, and have prepared the way for their own destruction. Doubtless the revolution, when it arrives, will be led by Mexicano intellectuals, and the masses will raise some of them to the status of heroes. But the true father of such a rebellion will not be a Mexicano trained in Anglo schools, but men like Jackson and Huddleston, who through reforms, helped lay the foundation for their own destruction."[1]

The major impact of the Great Depression and news of the European revolutions arrived in Mexico at a time when Conceptión's guerrillas had begun regular attacks on Mexico City and the Gulf and Pacific ports. Moralistas seemed everywhere at the time, and the government itself in danger of collapse. Then, a year later, Kinkaid was assassinated, and the acting President seemed a man of straw, to be crushed at the first direct blow.

The aged George Vining proved tougher than any of his friends imagined possible. The first act of his administration was to receive Cabinet and Senate recognition of his powers; Vining was not to be an "acting President," but a true President in every respect. Then he deployed a major part of the army to the western Sierra Madre. "We shall uproot the Moralistas, and destroy them and any other group that threatens the republic," he told the Senate. "I shall not shrink from the use of any weapon at my disposal to keep order in the U.S.M." Toward this end, Vining created the Constabulary, an elite corps of police and soldiers, operating in civilian clothes, whose function was to discover the traitors in the cities, expose them, and then bring them to justice. The Constabulary was obviously copied from the C.N.A.'s Bureau of Investigation; indeed, Superintendent Geoffrey Prentice's text, *The Nature of Rebellion*, became required reading for Constabulary members, while Prentice sent Mark Forsyth to Mexico City in 1880 to help in establishing the new organization. In order to win support for the Constabulary, Vining searched for a leader who would be respected and trusted. He surprised many, however, by choosing a man with a name from the past: Benito Hermión, who was Pedro Hermión's second oldest son.

Benito Hermión was thirty-nine years old when he was named to the post of Commandant of the Constabulary. His career up till that time had not shown great promise. Benito had gone to the best schools in Mexico City, then on to Jefferson University, where he was better known for his escapades than his scholarly endeavors. After graduation, young Hermión studied law under Egbert Wilkes, whose firm, Bigham & Wilkes, was general consul for the Jefferson & California Railroad. In 1879 Benito became a director of the line, and

1. The quotation is from Karl Marx. *On the Coming Revolution in Mexico*, 2nd edition (London, 1869), p. 95. Also, see Carlos Ortez. *Mexico, France and North America: One Problem, Three Answers* (Mexico City, 1964); Barbara Brooks. *Historians and the Bloody Eighties: A Study in Interpretation* (New York, 1970).

at the time of his nomination for the Constabulary post, was president of the J & C.[2]

Those who knew him realized Benito was a sensualist, a man of limited intellectual accomplishments, and a person who traded on the reputation of his father for all of his positions. But in a time of distress, the name of Hermión became a major asset, and so Vining named Benito Commandant, hoping he would be able to spark the imagination of older Mexicans who remembered Pedro, and of younger ones to whom he was a legend.

Benito did a creditable job with the Constabulary, much to the surprise of his friends. He found that he had a talent for investigation, and enjoyed the plaudits of the crowd. Within months of being sworn in, Mexico City politicians were talking of his great political future, and Continentalists smacked their lips at the thought of his running for the presidency when "the Vining interlude" ended in 1881. Insiders in government knew, however, that Hermión would not make a move without the advice and permission of Egbert Wilkes. And behind Wilkes were the Kramer Associates and Petroleum of Mexico, as well as several other Anglo-Hispano firms.[3]

By the time of the 1881 conventions, the situation in Mexico was more peaceful than it had been a year before. The Constabulary and the army had limited the Moralistas to the Sierra Madre. Although Conceptión was still popular among many Mexicanos, others had left his cause, perhaps because victory had not come as soon as it had been promised. Still, the conventions were well guarded, as was all of Mexico City, for during the past year Mexico—in the large urban areas at least—had become a police state.

As expected, the Liberty Party nominated Thomas Rogers for the presidency. In his acceptance speech, Rogers lashed out at the Moralistas, calling Conceptión "a cancer that would destroy our society, and bring to an end this noble experiment in republicanism." On the other hand, the candidate conceded the need for reform. "The large corporations of California and Jefferson control not only those states, but the rest of the nation as well. Large problems require large solutions. If elected, I promise to curb the influence of those elements in our society that operate against the common good." Thus, Rogers threw down the gauntlet to Kramer and Benedict.[4]

The Continentalist caucus was a wild affair, full of surprises and drama. The party had expected Vining to step down in 1881; the President was sixty-nine years old, and could hardly expect to survive

2. Linda Carlista. *The Heir: The Life of Benito Hermión* (Mexico City, 1946).
3. Robert Kinsolving. *Feet of Wood: The Life of Benito Hermión* (New York, 1969), pp. 93-110.
4. *Mexico City Times*, July 5, 1881.

a full six-year term. But Vining had tasted power and would not relinquish it so easily. On the first day of the caucus, he spoke to friends of his desire to spend the rest of his life at his Jefferson City ranchero. But that night, Vining told the convention he was prepared "to assume the burdens of the presidency if the Almighty and this Convention so desires."

Only one other candidate was put before the caucus, and that was Benito Hermión. As might have been expected, Benito's nominators spent as much time talking of his father's glories as they did of the son's abilities. "Hermión was there when our party and nation needed him in 1843. Now, when we once again need a strong man, Hermión is here." In this way, Senator Patrick Mahoney of Jefferson presented the nominee to the delegates. Benito did not make an appearance, however. "It would be unseemly," he told a reporter. But the real reason for Benito's seclusion was that he was not the speaker his father had been, and he had orders from Kramer to refuse the nomination if tendered, and to do nothing to encourage his supporters. Kramer was well content with the way Vining had handled matters during the past year, and was willing to accept him as President for the time being.[5]

Although Conceptión had formally disbanded the Workers Coalition after the 1875 elections, the organization remained intact, and planned an open convention, "and not the secret affair of the Anglos," to take place in Palenque, a Mexicano stronghold. There were rumors Conceptión himself would appear at the convention, and days before, the area was infiltrated with Mexicano newcomers. There were also some Hispanos and Anglos, many of whom later on were identified as members of the Constabulary. To most Mexicans, the Palenque Convention seemed a dangerous affair. To those who knew of the arrival of Moralistas and Constabulary, it appeared fraught with dangers. But none—with the possible exception of Bernard Kramer, Benito Hermión, and Monte Benedict—realized at the time that the Palenque Convention might be a turning point in Mexican history.[6]

The Workers Coalition delegates gathered in Montezuma Hall on the morning of July 15, 1881, to hear a speech by José Godoy, the former mayor of Medira, the man expected to win the nomination, and a reputed lieutenant of Carlos Conceptión. As Godoy began to speak, Constabulary agents entered the hall, marched to the podium, and arrested him. A riot erupted on the floor, shots rang out, and a panic

5. Kramer did not control Vining, but thought the aged President could be counted on to maintain order in the U.S.M., especially since the Kramer Associates all but controlled the Constabulary. But Kramer made no secret of his willingness to get rid of anyone who might threaten his interests. Dow. *Giants of Mexico*, p. 475.
6. Orrin Macon. *The Palenque Convention in Mexican History* (Mexico City, 1960).

developed. Before it was over, twenty-three people, all of whom were members of the Workers Coalition, were dead on the floor, and one of them was José Godoy. Another seventy-five were badly injured, of which ten were Constabulary officials.[7]

Godoy's death and the "massacre of innocents" at Montezuma Hall, led to insurrections in the Chiapan countryside, which spread to Durango, and from there to parts of California, Arizona, and Mexico del Norte. Only Jefferson was safe from rebellion, the result of harsh oppression at the hands of the Jefferson Brigade, a para-military organization controlled by Petroleum of Mexico. There were rumors of a plot to kill all Mexicanos, and another to dynamite the capital. In late July, 1881, most of the U.S.M. seemed either to withdraw behind closed doors or enter the streets, prepared to kill.

Vining's response was immediate and forceful. The President called a special meeting of his Cabinet, to which he invited Thomas Rogers and Liberty Party leaders in the Senate. He told them of looting and destruction, and of anarchy throughout most of the nation. Both he and Rogers agreed the elections scheduled for August 14 would have to be postponed until conditions had returned to normal. The nation was placed under martial law; the Constabulary officers were given powers over the regular army, and Benito Hermión was to direct the effort at bringing internal peace to the U.S.M.

During the next month, the Constabulary rounded up thousands of Mexicanos and placed them in internment camps "for safekeeping." Its agents roamed the countryside, holding "courts," which arrested, tried, and executed suspected Moralistas, the same day in many cases. There were rumors of slave rebellions in Jefferson and Chiapas, and the Constabulary entered the slave areas, killing wantonly. In the end, over 4,000 slaves were dead and the rumor, later, proved false. Army guards were posted outside industrial plants and around agricultural locations in California; Petroleum of Mexico installations were safe, so employees came to the plants to live. The canal zone, reportedly the target of terrorists, was under careful patrol, and several innocents were shot to death when they wandered into the area. On August 1, the newspapers were closed down "in the interest of public safety." Internal passports were required by August 10, and curfews established in the ten leading cities on August 21. By month's end, the nation was under police control. Almost every semblance of republicanism had been destroyed by the Constabulary or the Moralistas, and Mexico was a battlefield between revolutionaries and reactionaries.[8]

President Vining excused these excesses in the name of the great

7. Palenque *Pueblo*, July 18, 19, 1881; Mexico City *Times*, July 19, 1881.
8. William Berry. *The Dead Are Un-* *buried in the Plaza: The Mexican Repression of 1881* (Mexico City, 1956).

emergency of the period. Both he and Rogers had always been passionate believers in republicanism, and now, ironically, they presided over its destruction. But Vining drew the line on two freedoms. The Congress would not be touched; free expression remained inviolate in the capital, while the President stubbornly insisted on holding the elections on September 21.

Mexico seemed in a state of nervous peace on September 12, 1881. Moralistas had made attacks on major cities in Durango and Chiapas, and on each occasion had been repulsed. Concepción himself led the raid on Mexico City, and had been badly wounded in the attempt. The Moralistas were dispirited, but all Mexico was a police state, with Hermión in charge of the repression. Thus, Vining seemed to have won his gamble; the fight against anarchy had ended in a success, but republican institutions had been severely damaged. On the morning of September 12, the President was visited by a delegation of Libertarians from the Senate, who protested the abuses of the Constitution. "Have no fear of the Constitution," said Vining. "I have it here in the Palace, and will release it once peace returns to our land." Clearly, Vining intended to restore all constitutional freedoms by the end of the month, no matter what happened in the election. But that afternoon, Arthur Vining, three days short of his seventieth birthday and nine days before a certain victory in the election, suffered a heart attack, and by nightfall was dead.[9]

The Senate was called into immediate session by Secretary of State Marcos Ruíz, so as to select a new President. The Libertarians supported Rogers, while the Continentalists thought Ruíz would be the best person to serve until after the election, which was only a few days away.[10] Senator Frank Hill of California suggested a compromise: there would be no president for the next week, in which time the Cabinet would rule the nation, acting as a corporate body. The period was one of great tension and fear; under ordinary circumstances, the Hill proposal would have been rejected. But at the time it seemed sensible, and so, on the evening of September 13, the nation was ruled by the eleven man Cabinet. On that day, Mexican republicanism died.[11]

---

9. Watson. *The Right Man*, p. 405.
10. Berry. *The Dead Are Unburied*, p. 354.
11. Senator Hill was a tool of the Kramer Associates, and had been in its pay since his election twelve years earlier. His suggestion originated in San Francisco, and was part of Kramer's plan to solidify his control in Mexico City. Apparently Kramer wanted Hermión to be elected President. He planned to have him nominated by the Continentalist caucus which would meet on August 15, and then elected through massive vote buying. Kramer was willing to corrupt the spirit of republicanism, but held the forms to be sacrosanct. See Dow. *Giants of Mexico*, p. 493.

The first Cabinet meeting was held on September 15, with Secretary Ruíz the presiding officer. Ruíz began the meeting by asking for a discussion of plans for the September 21 elections. Hermión then rose to oppose holding the elections on that date. "I have information that several important members of the Liberty Party are under the control of the French revolutionaries, who in turn have been financing the Moralistas. Should the people, ignorant of these fact, elect a Libertarian government, then Mexico will be doomed." Ruíz asked Hermión to present his information to the Cabinet, but the Commandant refused. "Even here, in the Cabinet, are two members who are in the pay of the French. I cannot divulge my information until a full investigation is made, and then only to the people, and not to traitors." The Cabinet was shocked, but supported the Hermión proposal for "an indefinite delay of the election" by a vote of seven to four.[12] Then came a second vote, one which created the post of "chief of state." This too passed, and then Hermión was slected for the position.

The next day, September 16, 1881, Hermión appeared before the Senate to ask confirmation for the Cabinet's decisions. Immediately a roar erupted from the Libertarians. Homer Sheridan of Arizona called the move "cynical and contrary to law," while Rogers branded Hermión "a man of great ambition but little character." Nothing was decided at the meetings, however, and the vote was postponed for the next day. That night the Constabulary seized and imprisoned five Libertarian senators, among them Fritz Carmody of Mexico del Norte, Rogers' chief lieutenant. Rogers himself was warned of the action and escaped from the capital, along with his family and those of Senators Schuyler Stanley of Durango and Winthrop Sharp of Arizona.[13] By morning, every major Libertarian politician was either in jail, a fugitive, or a defector to the Continentalists. In addition, three were mysteriously "dead by accidents."[14] That afternoon the Senate, with only fourteen of the twenty-four members present, confirmed the Cabinet decisions of the previous day unanimously. Thus, Benito Hermión became chief of state.

Those Libertarians who remained in Mexico City and supported the new regime, tried to explain their actions to their followers, usually behind closed doors and after a thorough search was made for Constabulary listening posts. After all, they rationalized, the country was

---

12. The strong anti-revolutionary sentiment in Mexico that followed the French revolution and the Conceptión defection made such charges not only believable, but politically potent. Felix Lombardi. *Francophobia in Mexico:* *The Summer of 1881* (Mexico City, 1952).

13. Bernard Mix. *The Night of the Caballeros: The Hermión Seizure* (London, 1964).

14. New York *Herald*, October 1, 1881.

in danger of anarchy, and a strong man needed at the helm; when the dangers had passed, full constitutional rights would be restored. Others who now opposed Hermión, had previously accepted Vining's actions, and so were hopelessly compromised when they attempted to protest the new regime.[15] The few who had been against Vining's strong-arm methods from the first, were afraid to talk in public; those who did, were jailed or interned, often to disappear forever. Even this was excused by some Libertarians; Hermión might be a fool and a knave, they explained, but he was only the front man for people of intelligence and force, the kind of men Mexico needed at a time of trouble. They were referring, of course, to Kramer and Benedict.

Kramer and Benedict, however, would not remain on the scene for long. They did indeed control Hermión in 1881 and 1882, but the Chief of State (or El Jefe as he came to be called) was gradually escaping from their influence even then. Kramer suffered a stroke in February, 1882, and died in April, at the age of seventy-one. Later that year Benedict, having reached his seventieth birthday, retired from active leadership at Petroleum of Mexico. Kramer was succeeded by Diego Cortez y Catalán, who appeared to lack Kramer's power and boldness, and was willing to concede Hermión political power in return for freedom in the economic sector. Monte Benedict's post at P.M. was taken by his nephew, Andrew Benedict, whose attitude was much the same as that of Cortez.

Thus, the conservative opposition to a Hermión dictatorship vanished, while El Jefe's brutal tactics drove the Moralistas still further into the Sierra Madre. By mid-1883, Benito Hermión was in complete power in Mexico City, and none there would challenge his rule. His lieutenants had taken control of Chiapas, Durango, and Mexico del Norte. California's leaders were under the control of the Kramer Associates, which was allied to El Jefe, while Arizona's politics were dictated from San Francisco. Jefferson remained a Petroleum of Mexico fief, ruled in harmony with the cotton barons who supported the Hermión dictatorship. Only the Sierra Madre, parts of Baja California, and the Yucatan were Moralista strongholds. The Indians of northern Arizona and Mexico del Norte also opposed the Mexico City government, but Hermión was wise enough not to send his troops into the

---

15. As Rogers put it, "We did much that was wrong and foolish, but at the time these actions seemed prudent and sensible. Our liberties were taken from us by stealth and over time, and not in a single day. And we helped those who had robbed us of our freedoms." Interview with Thomas Rogers, June 12, 1884, in Victoria, the Bahamas, as reported in the London *Times*, July 8, 1884.

area to fight the best warriors on the continent, and these areas became semi-autonomous in fact, if not in theory.[16]

The pacification of Mexico, begun by Vining and completed by Hermión, enabled that nation to recover economically from the Great Depression. By 1883, almost all sectors of the economy were operating at full capacity. The export trade was still in the doldrums, but this was due more to continuing overseas problems than to internal difficulties within Mexico. Vining had refused to recognize France's revolutionary government, and relations with Paris, once so strong, had deteriorated. Hermión was as anti-revolutionary abroad as he was at home, and he refused to meet with representatives of the French Republic and hinted at an alliance with the Germanic Confederation.

The unspoken issue in Mexican politics at this time was the debt owed France by the preceding governments, which by 1879 had amounted to 100 million dolares. An additional 160 million dolares had been invested by Frenchmen in Mexican enterprises, not only in Kramer Associates and P.M., but large and small businesses in all areas and in each state. In 1882, Hermión announced Mexico would repudiate the foreign debt owed France. "This money had been borrowed from the Kingdom of France, which unhappily no longer exists. It would be immoral to repay the funds to the men who so brutally butchered the royal family. France will have a legitimate government some day, and when it does, Mexico will be glad to repay the moneys. Until then, I say we shall not pay the assassin and reward him for his deeds."[17] Investments of those Frenchmen who swore loyalty to the Republic were also confiscated by Hermión, and soon found their way into the portfolios of his most trusted supporters.[18] By 1883, then, some eighty percent of Mexico's foreign debt had been repudiated, while half the foreign investment in Mexico had been nationalized or redistributed.[19]

When Hermión had seized power, his critics considered him a man of mediocre ability and intelligence, whose grasping nature would suck Mexico dry for his personal profit. While El Jefe never showed extraordinary abilities at management, lacked an innovative mind and his father's magnetic personality, he did have ambitions to be remem-

16. James Mudd. *The Hermión Regime: A Study in Corrupt Power* (London, 1954); Henry MacMurray. *Benito Hermión: The Peace Years* (New York, 1966).
17. Benito Hermión. *The Mexico of My Heart* (Mexico City, 1886).
18. Mudd. *The Hermión Regime*, pp. 254–67.

19. In 1889 Hermión agreed to repay part of the investment of private citizens. But the state debt was never repaid. Arnold Jackobson. "Benito Hermión as a Money Manager." *The London Journal of Economics*, XXXVI (December, 1954), pp. 560–87.

bered as a "good man." Thus, in 1883 he announced a massive social welfare program for the nation, calling it necessary to create a "Free Society."

The major elements of Hermión's Free Society were free education for all, with salaries paid those who entered professions deemed vital to the nation's security and welfare; free health insurance; a guaranteed annual wage of $1,000 for each household; free government-paid vacations; the establishment of a "Youth Patrol," in which every boy and girl would serve; government-sponsored housing, in which rents would be no more than ten percent of a person's salary; and special benefits for each child born into a family.[20]

To pay for the Free Society, Hermión announced new taxes on corporations, a sharply graduated income tax, a tax on foreign holdings, and an increase in import duties. Other funds came from sharply increased exports of petroleum as well as from confiscations. In addition, El Jefe was able to float a large loan in the Germanic Confederation after the signing of the Amisdad Treaty of 1886. Finally, he forced Kramer Associates and P.M. to sell the government half-ownership of the Kinkaid Canal at a very low price. As might have been expected, Cortez and Benedict protested this and other actions, but Hermión soothed their ruffled feelings by granting them new concessions, promising to crush their rivals, and writing provisions in the tax laws exempting the Associates and P.M. from the new levies.[21] Cortez and Benedict had little choice but to accept this deal. Without their companies, Hermión would have remained a railroad president for the rest of his life. Now he had power, and there was little his creators could do to stop him.

Hermión's Free Society programs were popular, although Mexico's debts were far greater in 1888 than they had been prior to the confiscations. On the other hand, production in most sectors had increased even more dramatically. In 1888, the U.S.M. produced more than three-fifths of the world's petroleum, a quarter of its cotton, and impressive amounts of metals, hemp, produce, and other products. "When at peace, Mexico may be the most prosperous nation in the world," wrote Sir Elbert Hayes. "All she lacks is coal, and that may be gained without too much difficulty."[22] This was, of course, an overstatement when written in 1887. But Hermión recognized Mexico's

---

20. Although the Free Society programs were proclaimed, none were carried through to completion with the exception of establishment of the youth patrols and the childbirth allowance. Hermión. *The Mexico of My Heart*, pp. 210–19; Mudd, *The Hermión Regime*, pp. 300–15.
21. Arnold Jackobson. *Big Business in the Free Society* (Melbourne, 1958).
22. Sir Elbert Hayes. *The Economies of the World* (London, 1887), p. 1065.

essential strengths, and proposed to enlarge upon them while the rest of the world was still recovering from the Great Depression. The first step in this direction came in 1886.

### Selected U.S.M. Statistics, 1878–1888
(IN MILLIONS OF DOLARES)

| YEAR | GROSS NATIONAL PRODUCT | FOREIGN DEBTS AND INVESTMENTS | IMPORTS | EXPORTS |
|------|------|------|------|------|
| 1878 | 1304 | 440 | 367 | 572 |
| 1879 | 1430 | 435 | 386 | 509 |
| 1880 | 1234 | 405 | 328 | 447 |
| 1881 | 1153 | 403 | 252 | 300 |
| 1882 | 1158 | 138 | 234 | 310 |
| 1883 | 1345 | 130 | 289 | 498 |
| 1884 | 1540 | 206 | 357 | 692 |
| 1885 | 1682 | 364 | 540 | 794 |
| 1886 | 1762 | 492 | 629 | 809 |
| 1887* | 1894 | 706 | 795 | 905 |
| 1888 | 1958 | 907 | 926 | 1086 |

* Includes Guatemala.
Source: U.S.M. *Statistical Abstract*, pp. 110, 540.

# 20

# THE MEXICAN EMPIRE

WHEN Benito Hermión achieved power in September of 1881, few Mexicans had a clear idea of what he would accomplish domestically. On the other hand, there was no doubt El Jefe would be interested in territorial expansion, for everything in his background indicated such would be the case. As a Continentalist, a long-time associate of the Kramer Associates and P.M., and finally, the son of Pedro Hermión, he was an imperialist by inclination, by training, and by birth.

El Jefe's first interest in foreign affairs was in his dealings with France and the Germanic Confederation, but his abruptness to the French and his sudden friendship and admiration for all things German were based more on emotional and financial than diplomatic considerations.

More significant, however, were his relations with the C.N.A. Governor-General McDowell had considered Mexico a menace to North American security when he came to office in 1878. He was particularly concerned with the growth of Mexican business interests in the Caribbean, for if that sea came under Mexico City's control, then Georgia might easily be threatened by hostile ships in case of war. McDowell had not been troubled by President Kinkaid, however, but by the Kramer Associates and P.M. When Kramer's power increased during the Vining interlude and, then, when Hermión seized power, McDowell feared a worsening of relations. Pedro Hermión's last words had been, "We shall never give up! Our cause is just!" Would not the son of such a father, backed by expansionist forces of the Continentalist Party, naturally attempt to revive the memories, and perhaps the actions, of the Rocky Mountain War?

Such was not to be. Instead, Hermión made every effort to assure the North Americans of his desire for good relations between the two nations. He encouraged exchanges of professors, students, artists, and the like, and named Simon Cardenes, Mexico's leading author and a particular favorite in the C.N.A., the new Ambassador to Burgoyne.

Cardenes proved an excellent choice, for he was able to negotiate several important agreements with Minister for Foreign Affairs Malcolm Kitteridge that bettered Mexican-North American relations. The most important of these, the Kitteridge-Cardenes Treaty of 1884, clearly established the boundary line between the two nations in the Indiana-Mexico del Norte area, provided for an "open Caribbean," and set down the principle that each nation would encourage trade with the other by lowering tariffs.

All of this puzzled McDowell, who had believed Hermión would prove difficult and aggressive. But his Commandant of the Confederation Bureau of Investigation, Mark Forsyth, who had spent a year in Mexico working with Hermión and knew him better than any North American, had expected such a policy. Forsyth, who had become a major power behind the scenes in Burgoyne, was the Governor-General's unofficial expert on Mexican affairs. In the summer of 1884, he told McDowell that North America need not fear aggression from Mexico "for the time being." According to Forsyth, "Benito has always preferred warmer climates than those we enjoy in the C.N.A., and he lacks both the desire and stamina for a struggle with a nation as powerful as ours. He is a bully and a coward, and will fight only those nations and peoples he can defeat with ease. If we remain strong, he will grovel before us, while stabbing his southern neighbors in the back." Forsyth predicted Hermión would expand to the south "as soon as his house is in order in Mexico City," and he advised McDowell "to assure our Caribbean friends of our best wishes, and desire for their continued independence, and to let Benito know our feelings in the matter."[1] This was done, and may have had an effect on Mexico's expansionism. Whatever the cause, Hermión remained a convinced believer that nothing should be undertaken to disturb C.N.A.-U.S.M. relations—at least not until other matters were disposed of.[2]

The first important indication of Hermión's ambitions—and the accuracy of Forsyth's predictions—came in 1886. Two weeks before the signing and ratification of the Amisdad Treaty with the Germanic Confederation, Hermión lashed out at the French, who by that time had become his favorite whipping boy. "Paris is not content to support the Moralistas and encourage the Indians to revolt against their own government, but is even now planning to attack us more directly. We must be watchful, for the French invasion will come, and when it does, we shall be ready for it."[3] Although such statements created a great

1. Mark Forsyth. *Under Three Governors: My Life in the C.B.I.* (New York, 1900).
2. James Boatwright. *The Birth of Mexican Imperialism* (Mexico City, 1957), p. 98.
3. *Ibid*, p. 114.

stir in Paris, they were also considered hyperbole, and not taken seriously. In reality, they were the first step in Hermión's expansionist policies.

On October 4, 1886, Hermión ordered Minister to Guatamala George Pierson to negotiate with President Vincenzo Martinez for a widening of the Kinkaid Canal Zone "to enable us to better protect that vital passage." Martinez was agreeable, but considered the price to be paid an insult. After two weeks of talks which led nowhere, El Jefe told the Senate, "The jackals of Guatamala City will not agree to the transfer because they are being encouraged by Paris. The bloody francs of Paris are more acceptable to Martinez than the honest dolares of Mexico." Martinez protested the insult to Minister Pierson, but the next day Hermión told the Senate, "I will delay no longer, for even now the French are preparing to attack from bases on Guatamalan soil. Unless Señor Martinez signs this treaty, so necessary to our safety, we shall take the land in self-defense." As Hermión spoke, elements of the Mexican navy steamed toward Guatamalan waters, and the Mexican Fourth Army, stationed on the Guatamala border, was ordered to combat readiness.

Martinez learned of this, and called Pierson to his offices. There, at 1:00 P.M. on October 18, he agreed to Hermión's terms for an enlarged canal zone. Pierson, who throughout acted in good faith, wired the news to Mexico City at 2:06 P.M. There is every reason to believe El Jefe received Pierson's wire soon after. Still, at 3:35 P.M., Hermión appeared before the Senate and asked for a declaration of war against Guatamala, "so as to strike a blow at Martinez and his French friends before they can attempt to destroy us." The Senate approved the declaration unanimously; Mexico and Guatamala were at war.[4]

The Isthmian War began on October 18 and was over by the morning of November 15, when Guatamala City fell to General Miguel Aguilar's forces. Hermión himself went to the capital a month later, celebrating Christmas at the San Sebastian Church. While there, he met with Guatamalans who were known opponents of the Martinez regime, and before he left for home El Jefe named one of them, García Ramírez, as Governor of the nation. Benito promised Ramírez that Aguilar's army would remain only so long "as to prevent a French seizure of the nation, assure domestic tranquility, and free elections in Guatamala." Aguilar's army would remain in Guatamala for fifteen years, during which time it crushed several nationalist movements and presided over a police state. The free elections never took place, al-

4. London *Times*, October 20, 1886.   *in Mexican History* (Melbourne, 1954). Edward McGraw. *The Isthmian War*

though the Mexicans did stage two travesties of elections in 1892 and 1895, in which no opposition to the favored politicians was permitted. Needless to say, the French menace was pure fabrication throughout.[5]

The seizure of Guatamala brought protests from Britain, the C.N.A., Spain, and New Granada. Hermión ignored the Spanish note; answered the British and North American messages politely, assuring London and Burgoyne that his move into Guatamala had been necessitated by self-defense; and turned his full wrath on New Granada.[6]

El Jefe claimed that documents had been found in Guatamala City linking Martinez and New Granadan Premier Adolfo Camacho to French interests determined to destroy the U.S.M. On March 17, 1887, Hermión called representatives of leading European, Mexican, and North American newspapers to his office to tell them of his findings, and display proof of a plot. Letters from Camacho to Martinez indicated the two men had been planning an alliance, and perhaps even a union of their nations. Camacho did write that Hermión was "not to be trusted in any case, since this lunatic believes he has a destiny to control the world." But there was no evidence of French help, or even that Camacho or Martinez had contact with French agents. When a London reporter asked about this, Hermión replied that "these papers are now being processed and analyzed, and will be released at the proper time." Indeed, two months later Hermión did allow reporters to see such documents and letters, and they did indicate a conspiracy had been organized to attack Mexico. Premier Pierre Fornay of France denied the purported conspiracy, however, charging Hermión with falsification. El Jefe said Fornay was "incapable of truth," and then alleged that members of the French community in Tampico knew of the plot, and were "agents in our midst, vipers in the bosoms of those who offered them protection and freedom."[7]

In September of 1887, the Mexican Congress passed a series of laws proscribing the freedom of "those aliens dangerous to the nation." Soon after, the French quarters of Tampico and other Gulf cities were entered and prominent leaders seized, to be sent to detention camps or prisons, and there held for trial. During the next two years, Hermión purged the nation of the last of his political foes, in the process nationalizing almost every French-connected firm in the nation. Over 120,000 French aliens and French-born Mexicans, some of whom had

5. *Ibid*, pp. 354, 367–69.
6. Edward McGraw. *The Mexican Empire and Its Cost* (Melbourne, 1957), pp. 226–39.
7. It has been proven that the documents released in May, purporting to be from Premier Fornay to Martinez and Camacho, were Hermión forgeries. See New York *Herald*, October 4–10, 1900; Lydia Sulloway. *El Jefe and the Lust for Empire* (New York, 1943), pp. 197–214.

arrived in Tampico from France only six or seven years before, were now obliged to flee once again, and many found their way to the Bahamas, the Southern Confederation, and New Granada. By 1889, Hermión's grip on the nation was complete with the exception of those few Moralistas who remained in the Sierra Madres, and these were too dispirited to be a threat to Mexico City. Conceptión himself died of natural causes in 1887, and his passing was barely noticed at the time.[8]

Throughout this period El Jefe continued his verbal assaults on "the devils of Bogotá," as he usually called Camacho and his cabinet. Then, on February 10, 1890, he told the Senate of his having learned of a plot "hatched in Bogotá to assassinate leading members of this body, the Cabinet, and the Chief of State." Four days later shots were fired through the windows of the homes of five senators, and bombs were found in the Presidential Palace. Hermión promptly ordered Aguilar's Fourth Army to a state of readiness, and alerted elements of the Gulf and Pacific fleets to prepare for action.[9]

Premier Camacho learned of El Jefe's actions the following day, and knew what they meant. Ever since the Isthmian War, he had been ready for such a moment. The New Granada army was at full readiness, and the small navy prepared to defend the key ports of La Guaira, Cartagena, and Santa Maria. Camacho called the ambassadors of Britain, the C.N.A., and Mexico to his offices the next morning and told them of what had transpired the previous day. "We will fight the Mexicans if it comes to that," he said, "but in our struggle we may need help. What will your countries do in this time of trouble?" Camacho warned C.N.A. Ambassador Wesley Eagen that "today Hermión threatens La Guaira, tomorrow he may attack Norfolk. You must realize that we will fight, and may be able to defeat this madman without your help. But if we fail, you will be next. Guatamala was the doorway to Bogotá, and Bogotá may prove the gateway to Burgoyne."[10]

Eagen returned to the embassy and wired the news to Gallivan. The Governor-General sympathized with the New Granadan cause, but was not then prepared to do more. He ordered the Foreign Ministry to inform Mexican Ambassador Edmundo Roa of his "grave concern," but Gallivan would do nothing else. Britain, which had been more willing to act, also withdrew after Gallivan's actions, as did

---

8. Carlista. *The Heir*, pp. 436–39.
9. There is good reason to believe the bombs were planted by Hermiónistas, and the shots may have come from the same source. Kinsolving. *Feet of Wood*, pp. 436–37.
10. Wesley Eagen. *In the Twilight* (New York, 1909), pp. 228–39.

Spain. Thus, by late February, 1890, New Granada was open to attack, and without allies.[11]

Realizing how desperate his situation was, Camacho decided to strike the first blow. The New Granada army, led by General Roberto Bermúdez, crossed into Guatamala on March 1, and was soon at the Kinkaid Canal. Meanwhile, Mexican Admiral Frank Butland's First Fleet landed at La Guaira on March 2, and took Caracas the following day. Admiral Howard Loyo's Third Fleet captured Santa Maria on March 4, and marines of the 34th Brigade under the command of Colonel David Brewster began the march to Bogotá. The New Granada armies put up a strong resistance, but the Mexicans overwhelmed them. Brewster was in Bogotá on June 8, while General Francisco Goodspeed's First Army secured the eastern part of the nation. Camacho, who had fled to the hills with his government, was captured on September 18. Three days later Bermúdez surrendered to Aguilar at Puebla. The conflict, which Hermión called the War for Salvation, but which is more commonly known as the New Granada Expedition, was over.[12]

New Granada was too large and important to treat as a mere dependency. The nation had a population of over 12 million in 1890, and had been independent for over seventy years. It was rich in raw materials, especially petroleum, which had just been discovered by a P.M. affiliate in the La Guaira region. In addition, New Granada was the world's leading coffee producer, had a rapidly-growing middle and professional class, and was considered the most powerful nation in South America at the time of the Expedition. Three years after the Mexican victory, large deposits of iron ore, as well as several major coal mines, were found in New Granada. While Hermión had not captured the nation because of its wealth alone, New Granada soon made its economic contribution felt, providing vital iron and coal lacking in the U.S.M., as well as enriching Kramer Associates and Petroleum of Mexico.

Such a prize was a jewel in Hermión's crown. El Jefe sent his older brother, Victoriano, to rule from Bogotá. Quiet and more moderate than Benito, Victoriano proved the right man for the job. Although unable to win the affection of the New Granadans, he did earn their respect, and toward the end of his life, came to consider himself more a New Granadan than a Mexican. For the time being, however,

11. John Pritchard. *The Formation of the Mexican Empire* (Mexico City, 1960), pp. 276–79.
12. John Earley. *A History of the New* *Granada Expedition* (New York, 1914); Miguel Olin. *El Jefe's War for Salvation* (New York, 1956).

Victoriano succeeded in incorporating New Granada into the Mexican economic matrix.[13]

The conquest evoked expressions of concern from Madrid, London, and Paris. In Burgoyne, Governor-General Gallivan "deplored the seizure of this land which had done no harm," and offered asylum to its refugees. He maintained cool relations with El Jefe, but it went no further than words; in fact, he refused to allow New Granadans to form a government-in-exile in Tampa in 1891, and took no steps to disturb trade with the U.S.M. He did, however, ask the Grand Council for a larger military and naval appropriation in 1892, and within two years the C.N.A. was prepared for war. "So long as El Jefe seeks his destiny to the south we shall do nothing," said Gallivan. "But if the tyrant looks to the north or to the east, he shall be dealt with severely."[14]

Hermión had always claimed the U.S.M. had no desire for additional territory, and had warred with Guatamala and New Granada in the interests of self-preservation. After the victory of 1890, Mexico could no longer claim to be threatened from the south. Guiana on the Atlantic coast was a British colony, while Quito and Rio Negro were poor countries, with little in the way of economic wealth or political power. "Mexico will never go to war again," proclaimed El Jefe in 1892. But he added ominously, "We stand guard against any who would threaten us. The nation that transgresses U.S.M. rights must be prepared to accept the consequences."[15]

Mexico was at peace from 1890 to 1897, but this did not mean an end to Hermión's expansionism. The leaders of Quito and Rio Negro conceded Mexico to be the most powerful nation in the continent, and became Mexican dependencies in fact, if not in law. The Empire of Brazil was more independent, but Dom Pedro V could be counted on not to take any important step without first consulting Mexico City. The same was true of the other South American nations, all of which in one degree or another became dependencies, allies, or cohorts of Benito Hermión. Mexico's influence even extended into the Pacific. In 1892, the Kramer Associates financed a revolution in Hawaii, putting its puppet on the throne, and the following year, the islands petitioned

13. Despite the claims of Humbert Eames, in *The Drive for Wealth* (New York, 1941), Hermión did not invade New Granada for economic reasons. Petroleum of Mexico and Kramer Associates both opposed the war, although afterwards they shared in the exploitation of New Granada. By 1890 El Jefe had come to believe his own stories of a French plot, and had developed signs of paranoia. Willkie Devlin. *Formation of the Mexican Empire* (Mexico City, 1967).

14. John Earley. *The Drums of War: Ezra Gallivan and Benito Hermión* (New York, 1966), p. 143.

15. Mexico City *Times*, June 3, 1892.

Hermión to be made a dependency of the U.S.M. Hermión accepted, and Hawaii was thus added to the nation.[16]

The Mexican economy, to which was now added those of Guatamala, New Granada, and Hawaii, expanded greatly, so that Hermión was able to boast that his was the most rapidly growing nation in the world. While still very poor by C.N.A. standards, Mexico was obviously thriving under the Hermión regime. Of course, much of this was due to the fact that the nation had only two major companies in the 1890's—the Kramer Associates and Petroleum of Mexico—and these worked in close cooperation with the government. Mexico had little wasteful duplication, no labor unions or powerful agrarian lobbies, or any other economic or political force that could hinder or complicate the coordination Hermión was trying to introduce in the economy.

### Comparative C.N.A. and U.S.M. Statistics, 1888–1896

| | CONFEDERATION OF NORTH AMERICA | | UNITED STATES OF MEXICO | |
| | | G.N.P. | | G.N.P. |
| | POPULATION | (MILLIONS OF | POPULATION** | (MILLIONS OF |
| YEAR | (MILLIONS) | N.A. POUNDS)* | (MILLIONS) | DOLARES) |
| --- | --- | --- | --- | --- |
| 1888 | 69.3 | 20657 | 50.2 | 1958 |
| 1889 | 70.4 | 21630 | 51.9 | 2289 |
| 1890 | 71.6 | 22335 | 52.8 | 2554 |
| 1891 | 73.2 | 24987 | 65.5 | 3178*** |
| 1892 | 74.7 | 27564 | 66.8 | 3543 |
| 1893 | 76.0 | 30046 | 68.2 | 3870 |
| 1894 | 77.1 | 33425 | 69.7 | 4298 |
| 1895 | 78.8 | 33285 | 71.0 | 4559 |
| 1896 | 80.0 | 35539 | 73.1 | 4893 |

\*   five North American pounds = four Mexican dolares
\*\*  excluding slaves
\*\*\* including New Granada and Hawaii

Sources: C.N.A. *Statistical Abstract*, pp. 382, 487; U.S.M. *Statistical Abstract*, pp. 843, 1056.

By 1895, the Kramer Associates was the third largest business organization in the world, engaged in many kinds of manufacturing, foreign trade, railroads, food production, etc., with interests on all continents. Petroleum of Mexico was the largest producer of refined products, and owned more than three-quarters of the world's known reserves. Other

---

16. Swithen Hudd. *We Took the Islands: My Role in the Annexation of Hawaii* (Mexico City, 1899); Nathan Durfree. *Hawaii: Its History* (London, 1969).

companies existed in the U.S.M., but only with Hermión's permission, which was granted after consultation with the Kramer Associates and P.M. Even those national leaders who deplored Hermión's methods were obliged to admit he achieved results, and his ideas and the performance of the Mexican economy were studied throughout the West.[17]

But to what use was all this? Had he so desired, Hermión might have concentrated all his efforts on domestic growth. Already he had eclipsed every other figure in U.S.M. history; given another decade of peace, he might have performed additional wonders, and be considered one of the greatest men of the century. Under such circumstances, the harshness of his rule and the nature of his conquests might have been overlooked by historians of today. Such was not to be. The conquests of Guatamala and New Granada had whetted his appetite for blood, and more would flow before he passed from the scene.

---

17. This is not to say Mexico was a garden as a result of the Hermión programs. There was still widespread suffering in Chiapas and Durango, as well as parts of Baja California. The Indians of Mexico del Norte and Arizona remained aloof from U.S.M. society, and did not benefit from any of the Hermión programs. Political repression remained the rule in Mexico, and those basic freedoms of speech, assembly, and the like enjoyed in the C.N.A. and in pre-Hermión Mexico were all gone. Furthermore, El Jefe viewed Guatamala and New Granada as conquered lands fit only for exploitation, and the peoples of these countries suffered while he ruled in Mexico City. Edgar Witherspoon. *A Critical Look at the Hermión Regime* (London, 1943); Stuart Blue. *Nine-Tenths of the Iceberg: The Hermión Years* (New York, 1967).

# 21

# EZRA GALLIVAN'S CREATIVE NATIONALISM

B Y 1888, John McDowell was tired, and bereft of new ideas for his Age of Renewal. The Governor-General had earned the respect and gratitude of all North Americans, regardless of party, for his many accomplishments. He had led the crusade for honesty in government, and had succeeded in creating a more equitable society in the C.N.A. North America had been spared the violence and turmoil of the Great Depression, and McDowell was credited, perhaps unduly, with this as well. Finally, the Governor-General had made the C.N.A. a major power within the Empire, and this was a remarkable tonic for national pride. "McDowell destroyed a major party and obliged his political rivals to become an echo of Liberalism. He found corruption and inequities and eliminated the former and corrected the latter. Because of him, the C.N.A. entered the twentieth century a generation before the rest of the world."[1]

Perhaps these words were overly effusive, but McDowell was indeed the most important figure in North American history since the Rocky Mountain War. "McDowell was invincible; no man or party could destroy or stop him. Gallivan realized this, and so devised a brilliant strategy. Only McDowell could destroy McDowell, and so he did. Gallivan allowed the Governor-General to pass every law he introduced, and he then capitalized on the failures. In the process, he became a national leader over the prostrate form of his political enemy."[2] Gallivan, who was a fair man, realized as much as anyone how important a leader McDowell had been. "Mexico was unfortunate enough to become a tyranny as a result of the Great Depression, while North America remained a republic. There are those who say this was due to the natures of the two countries. Perhaps this is so. But men, not

---

1. Paul George. *John McDowell: An Appreciation and Assessment* (Bur- goyne, 1930), p. 11.
2. *Ibid*, pp. 145–46.

impersonal forces, rule nations. Mexico had Hermión; North America had McDowell. That was the difference."[3]

Gallivan was not so kind during the 1888 political campaign, however, when McDowell received Liberal endorsement for an unprecedented third term. McDowell's slogan was simply, "Let us Continue," and the Governor-General pledged himself to the completion of the Age of Renewal. Gallivan was nominated over Ruggles to lead a united Coalition Party at the polls. He appeared at many large meetings at which he would praise McDowell for his many achievements, but subtly criticize him as, "a man worn out by the burdens he has carried for so long."

In 1888, Ezra Gallivan was thirty-eight years old, vigorous, charming, and handsome, while McDowell was sixty-two, and his difficult years as Governor-General had taken their toll of his health. In addition, the Liberals had ignored important organizational work, as though resting after their defeat of the Conservatives. Gallivan's agents organized well, and their programs were coordinated personally by Senator Peter Higbe of the Northern Confederation, Gallivan's shrewd manager. Under Higbe's guidance, the Coalition achieved an internal consistency and efficiency the Liberals would not have for another two elections.[4]

Finally, and most important, Gallivan's party had become a great deal more conventional since its inception in 1869. While McDowell's Liberals had gained strength among the Conservative voters who had deserted their sinking party, the People's Coalition under Gallivan and Ruggles had come, imperceptibly, to stand for vigorous, but orderly, reform.[5]

A week prior to the elections the New York *Herald* claimed, "Mr. McDowell will win a new mandate, and the Liberals will dominate the new Grand Council." The Burgoyne *Times* had a special issue on "The Next Five Years: Completing the Age of Renewal." Gamblers in Norfolk were accepting wagers at 11–3 that the Coalition would win, and offered 20–1 on the Conservatives, running a poor third under an able moderate, Abraham Reese. They were no longer taking wagers on the Liberals.[6] Thus, it was a shocked nation that awoke the morning of February 17 to learn that the Coalition had won an amazing victory, and that Ezra Gallivan might be the next Governor-General.

---

3. Ezra Gallivan's Eulogy at John McDowell's Funeral. New York *Herald*, October 4, 1892.

4. Howard Arthur. *The Impossible Victory: The Coalition in 1888* (New York, 1934), p. 335.

5. Ernest Foy. *The Anatomy of North American Politics: An Analysis* (New York, 1956), pp. 395–97.

6. Arthur. *Impossible Victory*, pp. 209, 215, 227.

### Results of the C.N.A. Elections of 1888

| STATE | LIBERAL | PARTY AFFILIATION OF COUNCILMEN PEOPLE'S COALITION | CONSERVATIVE |
|---|---|---|---|
| Northern Confederation | 19 | 24 | 2 |
| Southern Confederation | 9 | 19 | 1 |
| Indiana | 12 | 15 | 2 |
| Northern Vandalia | 8 | 3 | 0 |
| Southern Vandalia | 6 | 4 | 0 |
| Manitoba | 10 | 3 | 0 |
| Quebec | 2 | 5 | 4* |
| | 66 | 73 | 9 |

* Three councilmen in Quebec won as independents.
Source: New York *Herald*, February 18, 1888.

Had he so desired, McDowell could have contested the election in the Grand Council; since the Coalition lacked a clear majority, he might have been able to prevent Gallivan's election there. But McDowell refused to consider the possibility, and at a party caucus on February 19 asked the Indiana Liberals, twelve in number, to cast their ballots for Gallivan. "This is unprecedented," he told them, but "new forms may be better than indecision and uncertainty at this time."[7] Only eight agreed to the plan, but this was sufficient to make Gallivan the next Governor-General.

A flushed Gallivan told reporters of his pleasure at being elected, and of his intention "to lead the nation into new paths and continue the drive for national greatness." With tears of gratitude in his eyes, the usually emotionless Gallivan thanked his predecessor for "his graciousness, his selflessness, and his sacrifice." "It would be arrogant of me to express the gratitude of the nation to John McDowell for his many services to our people, for I cannot speak in its name. But the Governor-General knows well how we all feel about him. He has performed many tasks for our nation, and all of them with dignity and honesty. Now he has shown the measure of his devotion to republi-

---

7. There are those who believe the Indiana delegation was prepared to make the move in any case, and so McDowell was merely bowing to the inevitable when he asked the members to vote for Gallivan. To others, the McDowell move is explained by memories of his own difficulties in obtaining a majority in 1873, and fears Gallivan would not be able to stand up under pressure to make a deal with the French-Canadians. A third group believes McDowell cared more for his reputation than anything else, and thought such an action would enhance it in the eyes of his fellows. But most North Americans continue to hold that it was an act of unselfish patriotism on his part. Worthington Fowler. *McDowell in Retirement* (New York, 1901); Fenton. *McDowell*, pp. 467–69.

canism by his actions in the Liberal caucus. Mr. McDowell informs me that he will retire to his Manitoba home. Let us hope he will not become too involved with the beauties of his native confederation, and will be ready to return to Burgoyne if we need him again."[8]

The People's Coalition, which had started life as a radical S.C. movement in 1869, now had national power in Burgoyne. Prior to the appearance of Gallivan, the Coalition had been viewed by some Liberals and most Conservatives as a dangerous mob of Neiderhofferian radicals, intent on destroying the economic and social fabric of the nation. Gallivan (and to a lesser extent Ruggles) changed all this; they had made the party over into a middle-class movement of intellectuals and workers, and had done so because McDowell had been so successful in blunting the cutting edge of radicalism with his reforms. By 1888, the Norfolk Resolves of 1869 seemed antique and outdated, as irrelevant to the needs of the C.N.A. as the Declaration of Independence had been to Benito Hermión. Still, there were those in the Coalition who had fought for almost two decades for power, and now that they had it, they meant to transform the C.N.A. into some kind of Neiderhofferian society. They had viewed McDowell as a natural enemy, but reserved even more scorn for Gallivan, who having obtained power, refused to use it. During his early years in Burgoyne, Gallivan would continually fight the radical wing of his own party, usually with success, but often causing bitter divisions.

Gallivan's administration was pragmatic rather than doctrinaire, in this respect making the Governor-General more like McDowell than his own more rabid supporters. But the coming of a P.C. government did bring certain changes to Burgoyne. First of all, the personnel was different. McDowell had relied to a large extent on professional politicians, businessmen, and members of the Mechanics National Union. Most of them left when Gallivan took office, and their places were taken by technicians, representatives of small business, and professors from the nation's leading universities, particularly Georgia, Webster, and Northwest. The worker representatives of the M.N.U. were replaced by their counterparts in the more radical Consolidated Laborers Federation. These new men did not lack intelligence or dedication, but few had any important government experience, and efficiency suffered until they learned their new craft.

There was a change, also, in the drift of foreign policy. McDowell had been a strong believer in the Empire, and had not only tied the

---

8. *Ibid*, p. 470; Arthur. *Impossible Victory*, p. 506. McDowell died of a heart attack on October 1, 1892. At that time he was preparing to write his memoirs, but did not get past the first five chapters. The book, published as *The Age of Renewal*, contains an account of his boyhood in Manitoba as well as notes collected for the rest of the work.

C.N.A. closer to Britain than before, but hoped the nation would take the lead in what Prime Minister Cadogan was already referring to as the "United Britannic Commonwealth." The Coalition, in contrast, was cool toward the idea of collaboration with Britain, which during the Bloody Eighties had been considered a reactionary regime. Instead, the Coalition tended to favor the French, especially after the Revolution and the establishment of the Republic. French Premier Antoine Phillipe sent a message of congratulations to Gallivan after his election, in which he expressed "the hope that our two nations may march side by side toward the universal goal of mankind—peace and plenty." Gallivan thought Phillipe a fool, but nonetheless worked to better Franco-North American relations, while rejecting proposals for a Third Imperial Conference.

Gallivan, however, would not join with France in opposition to the Hermión regime. He felt strongly that too much time had been spent by Liberal and Conservative governors-general on foreign affairs; that a strong foreign policy was a conceit, not necessary for the C.N.A. At one Cabinet meeting in 1890 he told Minister of Finance Patrick O'Shea, "If I could have one wish, it would be that the C.N.A. could be severed from this earth and put into orbit, somewhere near the moon. There is nothing we need from other nations. We export grain, manufactured goods, and other items they need badly, and in return we import trouble. Let Hermión have the world, if only he allows us our own land."[9] Perhaps more because of his desire than his knowledge, Gallivan did lower the military budget in 1888 and 1889, cut back on the naval construction program, and used the funds saved to lower taxes on incomes.

In his inaugural address, Gallivan set five objectives for his new government, saying they would be accomplished within a year of that date. They were:

1. An end to ... this ruinous inflation. ...
2. ... full employment is necessary for our nation, and it will be the goal of this administration to see to it that every worker . . . has a meaningful job.
3. Although a police force is necessary, the CBI has become far too powerful for a free people to bear. I have arranged to meet with the necessary authorities and will . . . report later on. . . .
4. Quebec has real and long-standing grievances against the national administration . . . every attempt will be made to secure the full loyalty of every citizen of that important state.
5. The People's Coalition wants the people to have power over their

9. Michael O'Shea. *A Diplomat in the Family: The Life of Patrick O'Shea* (New York, 1922), p. 253.

lives, and not government control of every aspect . . . of activity.
. . . New means will be found for the people to . . . share more
fully in the profits their work made possible.[10]

The five points were all well-taken, and represented problems
McDowell had not handled well or which he had ignored. But they
were hardly radical, although some Liberals wondered anxiously what
Gallivan meant by finding new means for workers to share in the
wealth they produced. It was a good political speech, however, delivered well and dramatically. Gallivan even had a name for his new
program, calling it "Creative Nationalism." But like the Age of Renewal, Creative Nationalism was a rubric that contained everything
and anything the Governor-General wanted.

Soon after taking office, Gallivan visited Quebec. This in itself
required courage, since the *Patriotes* were still on the rampage and had
been heartened when one of their number won election to the Grand
Council. Despite assassination threats, Gallivan walked through the
crowds in Quebec City and delivered a speech to the assembled French-
speaking citizens, which ended with the words, "I have heard, and I
have understood." The population cheered, although more than one
onlooker admitted he didn't know why.

Whether or not Gallivan did understand the Quebec tangle, he
did offer a solution. On February 1, 1889, the Governor-General appeared before the Grand Council to deliver a message on Quebec. He
offered a plan "to determine the future of the Confederation of Quebec, its relations with the national government, and the will of its
people." "There is no room in our nation for individuals or confederations which would be happier without ties to Burgoyne. After all, we
are the *Confederation* of North America, and Burgoyne, Dickinson,
Galloway, and men of their time always believed in the power of
confederations within the union. Thus, I propose to give the people of
Quebec a choice as to their future." Gallivan then went on to propose
that a plebiscite take place in Quebec that summer, with three alternatives on the ballot. Quebec could remain within the Confederation as
presently constituted; it could become an "associated state," with a
great degree of local autonomy but without full membership in the
Confederation; or it could be granted independence, in which case
those residents who wished to leave would be assisted in so doing by
the central government.[11]

The speech was received in shocked silence by the majority of the
Council. When it ended, the entire Quebec delegation rose to cheer
the Governor-General. After some hesitation, there was polite ap-

10. Ezra Gallivan. *Under Fire and the Sword* (New York, 1898), p. 56.

11. Howard Arthur. *Creative Nationalism* (New York, 1939), pp. 99–100.

plause among the other members. The next day most C.N.A. newspapers supported the Gallivan proposal. It was ratified by the Grand Council on February 9, and the plebiscite set for July 6.

Almost immediately the confederation of Quebec divided into three parties. The largest was the Free Quebec Coalition, made up of those who desired independence and who hinted of a future alliance with France. In it were found the *Patriotes* and their supporters. The Loyalty Party, a small group of wealthy business and French-speaking immigrants, desired no change at all. In between was the Justice and Peace Party, which desired association, and which appealed to middle-class farmers and individuals with ties to Nova Scotia, which from the founding of the C.N.A. had enjoyed a great deal of local autonomy.

It was generally assumed the Free Quebec Coalition would win an overwhelming victory. There was violence in Quebec that spring, as Free Quebec forces destroyed opposition offices, threatened voters, and in general, indicated war would erupt unless their victory was assured.

### *The Quebec Plebiscite, July 6, 1889*

| ALTERNATIVE | VOTES |
| --- | --- |
| Association | 995,289 |
| Independence | 756,344 |
| Confederation Status | 92,456 |

Source: Burgoyne *Register*, July 10, 1889.

More than anything else, however, the Gallivan proposal had served to precipitate sentiments in the confederation, which for years had asked for such a vote. But now that the French-speaking citizens had the right to seek independence, they had second thoughts. The violence must have appeared a foretaste of what would follow a Free Quebec victory. Thus, the voters rejected demands for independence with a clear majority for association. Gallivan called for a special session of the Quebec legislature "to implement the will of the people." The plan was ratified within three months; Quebec now had control of all internal affairs while remaining associated with the C.N.A. "on issues of common interest." Thus ended a half-century of contention, for which Gallivan deservedly received the credit.[12]

The Quebec plebiscite was the most dramatic event of Gallivan's

---

12. Under the plan, Quebec lost its representation in the Grand Council, with the lost seats being redistributed after the 1890 census. Quebec was given the right to send three "observers" to the Council, just as Nova Scotia, and came to resemble that region in its relations with the C.N.A. Armond Fleur. *We Leave as Friends: The 1889 Plebiscite* (New York, 1945).

first year in office, but the Governor-General was also busy elsewhere. Mark Forsyth was retired as Commandant of the C.B.I., a move that delighted critics of the powerful security chief. But Gallivan named Vice-Commandant Norton Kamen his successor, the man Forsyth had been grooming to take his place. Kamen's selection assuaged the sentiments of the Forsyth supporters, while the Commandant's removal pleased those who considered the C.B.I. too powerful an institution in the life of the C.N.A.

Gallivan had more difficulty in ending the inflation and assuring full employment. The Grand Council voted special grants to the confederations for the purposes of public projects, and this did serve to increase the payrolls. But the money was raised through the flotation of bonds, which increased the money supply and so contributed to more inflation. Gallivan tried to balance this by cutting back on other expenditures, especially those for the army, navy and the C.B.I. By year's end, however, inflation had declined only slightly, while unemployment, though not as severe as in 1888, was still a problem. In spite of these setbacks, Gallivan was able to convince the public that progress was being made.

The Fifth Point of his program was by far the most contentious of the Gallivan plans. The Governor-General had promised that "new means will be found for the people [to] share more fully in the profits their work made possible." But what did this mean? To his enemies, it implied a heavy dose of Neiderhofferian economics, which would destroy the confidence of the business class and end its uneasy cooperation with Burgoyne. Gallivan knew this, and made it clear he never considered Neiderhofferism the answer to C.N.A. problems. Instead, he offered a program of his own, based on political and economic pressures, ideas of his resident intellectuals, and suggestions set forth by President Whitney Popper of the Consolidated Laborers Federation.

Under the proposals, the national government would act through the National Financial Administration to make loans to those individuals who wished to establish businesses. The N.F.A. would be granted the right to float bonds at preferred rates, and would use the money so obtained for the loans. The new entrepreneur would become a partner of the government in his operation, for depending upon circumstances, the government would receive from ten to forty-nine percent of the common stock of the new company in addition to the bonds for the loan. In this way, Gallivan hoped to encourage workers to become businessmen, while at the same time retain the confidence of an already powerful business community.[13]

---

13. Robert Sobel. *The Fifth Point: Ezra Gallivan and His Creative Nationalism* (New York, 1967).

Burgoyne politicians focused their attention on the Fifth Point, which became the symbol of the Gallivan administration. Liberals called the program socialistic, while Conservatives believed it "destructive of all that has made our nation great." Radical members of Gallivan's own party broke with him on the issue, demanding government seizure of established businesses rather than the new plan. But Gallivan was able to muster sufficient votes to pass the measure, which became law in 1891.[14]

The Fifth Point opened a new era in C.N.A. history; it had far more important implications than Gallivan himself had realized. The economic climate was improving in 1890, due more to natural causes than to anything the government had done. Increasing numbers of ambitious and often talented young men wanted to start their own businesses, and they applied to the N.F.A. rather than the commercial banks for loans, since the government agency had lower qualifications and would accept equity as well as bonds as collateral and payment. Given the beneficial economic climate of the 1890's, most were able to succeed at least modestly; the failure rate for the N.F.A. loans was only fifteen percent in 1890 and even lower for each of the next ten years. Some companies, most notably Associated Motors, Confederation Locomobile, Kenton, Ltd., and New York Airmobile were spectacular successes, so that the government's stock in them came to be worth a great deal. The Fifth Point "worked," but never lacked for critics.

During his first term in office the Governor-General proved a skillful, adept, and flexible politician. The five points of his Creative Nationalism program had been carefully drawn so as to be realizable within five years, and so they were. They were also calculated to please both Liberals and Coalitionists in different ways, sufficient to gain votes in 1893, but not so specific as to alienate potential supporters. Thus, Gallivan's expectations of a second term were not disappointed. He defeated Liberal candidate N.C. Councilman James Hare by a wide margin, leading some observers to note that the Liberals might follow the Conservatives to oblivion, ushering in a new Era of Harmonious Relations.[15]

---

14. Under the terms of most contracts, the N.F.A. had the option of selling its stock to the entrepreneur at current market value within ten years of its issuance, assuming the value was at least ten percent over its original price. The N.F.A. could also sell shares to outsiders, or on Broad Street. It should be stressed that had not the economy been so strong, the experiment might have failed. Julius Nelson, head of the N.F.A., proved a wise and sophisticated administrator. Later on, when lesser men succeeded him, the agency caused at least as much harm as good. Julius Nelson. *Financing a Nation: My Years at the N.F.A.* (New York, 1910).
15. Arthur. *Creative Nationalism*, pp. 443–45.

### Results of the C.N.A. Elections of 1893

| STATE | PARTY AFFILIATION OF COUNCILMEN | | |
| --- | --- | --- | --- |
| | PEOPLE'S COALITION | LIBERAL | CONSERVATIVE |
| Northern Confederation | 29 | 15 | 1 |
| Southern Confederation | 23 | 6 | 1 |
| Indiana | 22 | 7 | 1 |
| Manitoba | 6 | 9 | 1 |
| Northern Vandalia | 10 | 6 | 0 |
| Southern Vandalia | 8 | 5 | 0 |
| | 98 | 48 | 4 |

Source: New York *Herald*, February 17, 1893.

Such statements show a lack of understanding of Confederation politics. Although elected by a record margin, Gallivan was walking a political tightrope. His powerful machine had secured full control of the Coalition's central organization. Thus, he felt free to woo the Liberals, which he did with great effectiveness in his first administration. But this created resentment among many rank-and-file Coalitionists, as well as a vocal minority in the Grand Council. To them Gallivan had betrayed the spirit of the Norfolk Resolves, had gone over to the enemy, and was no longer a true political partisan. Such individuals had opposed the Quebec plebiscite, and considered the Fifth Point a sop to skilled workers that ignored other laborers. They also thought Gallivan's attempts to end inflation had been half-hearted, while he had done little to alleviate unemployment. They demanded an end to the C.B.I., and not just a change in its leadership.

Gallivan was usually able to outmaneuver his opponents within the People's Coalition, but he could not defeat them. Under the leadership of Thomas Kronmiller, a former official of the Consolidated Labrers Federation who had won election as Councilman from Indiana in 1893, the radical coalitionists organized their own caucus and prepared to pressure Gallivan for more radical legislation. "I can take care of my opponents on the other side of the aisle," said the Governor-General. "What I need now is some elixir to transform my supposed comrades into supporters."[16]

Both the dissident Coalitionists and the majority of Liberals were united in opposition to Gallivan's foreign policies. The Governor-General remained an isolationist, caring little for overseas expansion, a major role in the Empire, or the glories of war. In speaking before the North American Congress of Historians in 1894, he enlarged on these ideas.

---

16. Foy. *The Anatomy of North American Politics*, p. 406.

Look at the map and you will see why this nation has been so blessed as to be able to afford a neutral stance on the world scene. We are bounded by the Atlantic moat, the Arctic, the Gulf, and the Mexico frontier. Those who would attack us from Europe cannot do so, while on this continent the only threat could come from Mexico. Figures soon to be released will show that our economy is ten times as large as that of the U.S.M. Last year the *addition* to production *alone* was greater than that of the *total* Mexican output. Our population is some 7.5 million larger than that of Mexico. We are a united people; Mexico faces internal dislocations. We have the good will of the rest of the world; Mexico has only a shaky alliance with the Germans, which may mean little in time of trouble. Yet there are those who say Mr. Hermión is preparing to resume the Rocky Mountain War. He would not be so foolish, but even if troubles do develop, we can arm rapidly enough to meet any challenge that may come our way.[17]

Gallivan's critics replied that El Jefe had more than two million men under arms, and that his was a tough, experienced force. In contrast, the 500,000 man C.N.A. Army had not fought since the Rocky Mountain War, and lacked modern equipment. The Mexican Navy in the Gulf alone was larger than the combined C.N.A. Navy, and was better-trained. Finally, size alone did not assure safety. As Councilman Kronmiller in his reply to Gallivan pointed out:

In 1845, when the war with Mexico began, our population was fifty percent larger than theirs. The Mexican Army never had more than 650,000 men under arms, while we raised almost three times that amount. The difference between the economies was more startling then than it is today. Yet the Mexicans of a half-century ago were able to fight us to a standstill. What might they do today if we do not prepare for all eventualities?[18]

Kronmiller was even more specific and warlike in private. He would have the C.N.A. fight Mexico in a "great moral crusade," whose goals it would be to "liberate the enslaved peoples of Guatamala and New Granada, return Hawaii to its former free state, and most importantly, rid the world of its last vestige of slavery."[19] Unable to create enthusiasm for his own domestic programs, Kronmiller attempted to win support for his foreign policy. He knew, of course, that in such a struggle North America would have the support of France, which would attempt to regain its lost investments, and this suited the radical Coalitionists well, since they considered the European revolutionaries brothers-in-arms.

17. Burgoyne *Register*, December 28, 1894.
18. Borgoyne *Register*, December 30, 1894.

19. Henry Kurtz. *The Moral Imperative: Its Origins and Development* (New York, 1968).

The Liberal protest took a different form. They argued that Gallivan should not reject an imperial role. The Empire would form a natural trade area tied together by bonds of mutual interest, trust, and language. Then too, the Liberals were still emotionally bound up with the concept of remaining Englishmen. To them the Queen was their monarch, while Gallivan was only their political leader.

Even had these protests not existed, the peoples of the C.N.A. might still have desired a wider world role for their nation. This was the result of what came to called the Moral Imperative by its supporters and by journalists. It had its origins among Darwinian scientists, journalists, poets, and politicians, many of whom were in the British Tory Party, but whose counterparts could be found in every nation of Europe and the Americas. According to this view, it was the "Moral Imperative" of their nation to bring the blessings of civilization to less fortunate peoples. Gallivan eschewed the whole idea of a world role; his opponents embraced the idea, and had the support of important elements of the society.[20] Such people could understand Hermión's expeditions, or while criticizing them, could wish the C.N.A., and not Mexico, had become a great colonizing nation. The desire for the supposed glories of war and combat, held by a people who had lived at peace with their neighbors for half a century, was a force Gallivan had to face, and it would provide the major challenge of his second administration.

---

20. The term came from a novel by Burnet Mayfield, *The Moral Imperative* (London, 1893), in which the hero becomes a missionary to the Congo and leads the peoples of the region to Christianity and industrialization. Badly written though it was, *The Moral Imperative* found a wide readership in Britain, and an even more enthusiastic audience in the C.N.A. Despite Neiderhofferian claims, the Moral Imperative was never a mask for economic gain, since its most ardent supporters were the lower classes and professionals, while business generally fought the idea of mission, preferring instead trade and investment. In the C.N.A. its most famous advocate was Professor Henry Newton of Burgoyne University, while journalist William Hearst of the San Francisco *Examiner* was its leading supporter in the U.S.M. See Henry Newton. *The North American Mission* (New York, 1882); William Hearst. *The Blood in Our Veins* (Mexico City, 1897); Franklin Nunn. ed. *The Moral Imperative* (London, 1945). The best survey of the movement is William Paca. *When the World Went Mad: The Utopians of the 1890's* (New York, 1968). A more sympathetic view can be found in Russell St. John. *The Cutting Edge of Civilization: The Moral Imperative* (New York, 1967).

# 22

# THE GREAT NORTHERN WAR

"UNDER El Jefe, the United States of Mexico was the skin. The Kramer Associates was the skeleton, flesh, heart, and mind."[1] This is the judgement of a modern Mexican economic historian, who views the Hermión regime as the political manifestation of a company which, at its peak, controlled more assets than any other in the world. But such an evaluation is both unfair and an oversimplification. It is doubtless true that Benito Hermión could not have come to power without the aid of Bernard Kramer and his ally Monte Benedict, but once in control, Hermión struck out on his own. Kramer's death in 1882 and Benedict's subsequent retirement made his task in seizing complete power all the easier. Had he lived, Kramer would probably have challenged many of Hermión's programs and tactics; as it was, such a confrontation proved unnecessary. Hermión found Kramer's successor, Diego Cortez y Catalán, more than willing to forgo politics in return for a free hand in his sphere. Thus, the nation was actually divided into sectors, with Hermión controlling the army and political apparatus while Cortez had the economy under his direction. And since the interests of these two men were similar, few power conflicts arose between them at first.[2]

While Hermión solidified his grip on the nation and fought his wars, the Kramer Associates expanded from its California base to control almost seventy percent of Mexico's non-petroleum industry by 1890. In 1891 it began its international operations, financing railroads in Manchuria and the Argentine, a copper mine in the Congo, and the Burger Steel Company in Belgium. In 1892, Cortez and Andrew Benedict worked out an arrangement whereby Petroleum of Mexico was merged into the Kramer Associates through an exchange of securities. At the same time, Cortez' interests in Hawaii were threatened by the natives. He spoke to Hermión about it, and within four months the islands were annexed to Mexico. In 1894 Cortez joined with the

1. Walter Sepúlveda. *An Economic History of the Hermión Regime* (Mex-ico City, 1968), p. 2.
2. Mudd. *The Hermión Regime*, p. 89.

Krupps in a venture to take control of the Ottoman Empire. Although nothing came of it, the very fact that the company was able to think on such a scale indicates its world importance.[3]

### The Kramer Associates, 1888–1898

| STATE | ASSETS | SALES | PROFITS | SALARIED EMPLOYEES (MEXICO AND FOREIGN) |
|---|---|---|---|---|
| | (IN MILLIONS OF MEXICAN DOLARES) | | | |
| 1888 | 470 | 464 | 51 | 34,000* |
| 1889 | 569 | 509 | 57 | 38,000* |
| 1890 | 634 | 556 | 60 | 40,000* |
| 1891 | 700 | 697 | 71 | 46,000* |
| 1892** | 1576** | 1799 | 198 | 98,580 |
| 1893 | 1657 | 2006 | 230 | 120,045 |
| 1894 | 1893 | 2225 | 254 | 144,368 |
| 1895 | 2040 | 2469 | 276 | 170,098 |
| 1896 | 2249 | 2685 | 307 | 203,008 |
| 1897 | 2546 | 2965 | 330 | 237,364 |
| 1898 | 2768 | 3123 | 339 | 272,057 |

\* approximate
\*\* Inc. Petroleum of Mexico
Source: Tulin. *The Cortez Years*, p. 726.

Both Hermión and Cortez were seeking new worlds to conquer in 1894. El Jefe was interested in the Caribbean, where Cuba, Dominica, and Porto Rico seemed ready victims to his threats.[4] Cortez found little there to merit his attention; the world had no great need for the agricultural products of these islands in the mid-1890's. On the other hand, there was a world shortage of copper, the result of the rapid electrification of Europe and the C.N.A.[5] Cortez' experts had told him that copper in large quantities was to be found in the Yukon area of Alaska. Armed with this information, Cortez contacted Tzar Nicholas II's foreign minister, Prince Sviatopolk-Mirsky, and arranged for the Kramer Associates to receive concessions in the Yukon to search for copper "and whatever other minerals might be found." Under the terms of the agreement, the Kramer Associates would pay all costs, while sharing profits with the Imperial government on a fifty-fifty

3. Stanley Tulin. *The Kramer Associates: The Cortez Years* (London, 1970), pp. 3–19.
4. Hermión was not prepared for military action in the Caribbean, however, for he did not want to arouse the warhawks in the People's Coalition of the C.N.A., who might pressure Gallivan into taking strong action. O'Shea. *A Diplomat in the Family*, pp. 309–14.
5. Tulin. *The Cortez Years*, p. 243.

basis. All company employees would have to be acceptable to Russia, and the Russian agents in Alaska would retain complete political control of the mining towns if any were to be established.[6]

The first exploring parties entered the Yukon in the spring of 1895. They searched for a year, finding little of value. Then, in July of 1896, a party led by Winston Carew struck a vein of gold. Further exploration indicated it to be the most valuable find since the California gold rush. By the end of the year, the Carew party was able to report that "the nature and full extent of the fields cannot be determined. But there is no doubt that this is the most important gold discovery in the history of mankind."[7] Even allowing for exaggeration, the Yukon gold fields certainly appeared the most valuable property controlled by the Kramer Associates.

Word of the discovery soon reached St. Petersburg. At the time Russia was in the midst of a financial crisis, having made commitments for railroads without having the funds for their payment. Now these moneys seemed a trifle when compared with the promises of the Yukon. Tzar Nicholas wired his personal congratulations to Cortez and Carew, wishing them "continued good fortune in our joint enterprise."[8] Within a year, however, the Russian would change his tune. In a memorandum of October 21, 1897, Prince Sviatopolk-Mirsky claimed the agreement with Kramer Associates covered only copper discoveries. "Since little or no copper has been discovered in the Yukon region, the mines when opened, will be controlled by the Imperial Government." Then he went on to suggest the Kramer Associates might operate the mines "for which the company would, of course, be well-compensated."[9]

Diego Cortez had a reputation for coolness under fire, and a passion for anonymity. The Mirsky telegram, however, caused him to rush shouting from his office; never before had he been treated in such a way. As he saw it, the Russians had not only cheated him, but then had the gall to suggest he collaborate in selling the stolen goods! Cortez realized, however, that the handling of such matters must be conducted at the highest level. He telephoned Hermión immediately and asked for an appointment for October 25. The two men met in the Palace the morning of that day, and Cortez returned that evening for another conference.

The Hermión-Cortez talks were behind closed doors, and we may

6. Carl Needham. *The Great Northern War* (New York, 1963), p. 89.
7. Tulin. *The Cortez Years*, pp. 299–305.
8. Needham. *The Great Northern War*, p. 137.

9. Telegram from Prince Mirsky to Diego Cortez, dated October 21, 1897, as quoted in Knute Neuberger. *The Background of the Great Northern War* (London, 1965), p. 176.

never know exactly what happened. Apparently Cortez wanted Hermión to send a strongly-worded note to Mirsky, demanding Kramer Associates' rights in the Yukon be respected. If all else failed, Cortez wanted war with Russia. El Jefe knew, of course, what was transpiring in Alaska, but his attention was still riveted on the Caribbean, and he had no desire to become entangled in what he later called "the frozen wastes of the north." Thus, the meeting ended without a decision having been made. As of that evening, it would seem the Russians had been able to carry off their *coup*.[10]

Unable to win the support of the Mexico City government for his policies, Cortez returned to San Francisco in disgust. While on the train, however, he planned to obtain his "rights" on his own, without the aid of the national government, and to do so in such a way as to force Hermión to act in his behalf. Most of the California legislature had been purchased by the Kramer Associates, while Governor Alberto Puente, though nominally loyal to Hermión, was also on the Kramer payroll. Cortez sent his private secretary, Russell Smith, to see Puente on November 7, apparently to discuss how best to translate his ideas into actions.

The Cortez plan, as formulated the week of November 7–15, was both diabolical and almost certain of success. A ruse would be found to spark armed conflict at the California-Alaska border. The Russians would be allowed to "invade" California and be stopped before they reached San Francisco. Governor Puente would then ask Hermión for aid. The Chief of State would have no choice but to send national troops to California. In this way, the war would begin, and would end with Mexico occupying all of Alaska, and with the Kramer Associates given the right to develop the land.[11]

On February 27, 1898, Puente notified Hermión of "repeated violations of the border by Russian Imperial forces." El Jefe promptly sent an investigating team to the area, but realizing Cortez might be behind the message, called Kramer Associates and told Cortez that "under no conditions will you involve Mexico in a squabble with the Russians. If you start trouble with the Russians, you will have to end it, and not I."[12]

The investigating team reported its findings on March 15. The team noted that border violations had indeed taken place, and that the Russian officer in charge of the border, Captain Boris Tschakev, had

---

10. This episode alone should indicate that the Kramer Associates did not control Hermión on the eve of the war. Still, the belief persists. See Sepúlveda. *Economic History*, pp. 343–48.

11. Andrew Stirling. *The Secret His-* *tory of the Great Northern War* (London, 1923), pp. 111–18.
the summer, so as to avoid fighting in the harsh Alaska winter.

12. Apparently Cortez waited till February to put his plan into operation because he wanted the war to begin in

been "most uncooperative throughout."[13] As a matter of form more than anything else, Hermión sent a mild note of protest to St. Petersburg, believing the matter would end there. But it didn't. Instead of the expected assurances of investigation and friendship, Prince Mirsky sent an insulting note to El Jefe, warning him of the consequences "should California continue its attacks on Russian territory."[14] This initiated a series of communications, five on each side, with each round becoming harsher and more belligerent than the one before. Cortez' plan was working well; by early May he was ready to spring his trap.

On May 4, 1898, Hermión ordered extensive summer maneuvers, and told Admiral Ephraim Small to prepare the Pacific Fleet for a cruise to Hawaii. News of this led Prince Mirsky to command General Andrei Mishikov of the Alaska command to be on guard "against the possibility of sudden attack." There was a major incident at the California border on May 17, but both sides withdrew soon after. What happened next is still unclear, but on May 21 a Russian regiment entered California and headed in the direction of San Francisco.[15]

The California Guard had been well-prepared for this eventuality, but fell back, clearly on command from Kramer Associates' headquarters. The Guard stiffened twenty miles north of San Francisco, while Governor Puente called upon Hermión for "immediate and large-scale help." El Jefe had acted even before receiving the message. Admiral Small entered San Francisco harbor on May 30, and 20,000 crack Mexican marines disembarked and headed for the northern battleline. The marines easily repulsed the Russian attack, and then followed the fleeing enemy northward. The first Mexican force entered Alaska on June 11. There it was met by an additional 40,000 Mexican soldiers, under the command of General Richard Stockton. The Great Northern War had begun.[16]

The first phase of the war was over in four months. Admiral Small's Pacific Fleet landed at Nikolaevsk on July 5, and the Mexican marines began their march south, trapping the Russian army led by General Mischa Kornilov in a pincers movement. Kornilov surrendered to General Stockton in August, and with this the most important

13. Stirling. *Secret History*, p. 145.
14. There is reason to believe the telegram was badly translated by the language section of the State Department. It is interesting to note that Henry Wilson, the chief Russian translator, had worked for the Kramer Associates prior to accepting a government post. It is entirely possible he exaggerated the tone of the Mirsky telegram. See William Reilly. "Henry Wilson's Role in Initiating the Great Northern War." *The Journal of Russian Studies.* XXVII (June, 1934), pp. 105–56.
15. Most accounts indicate that the first attack came from the California side, but to this day it is impossible to be certain. Stirling. *Secret History*, p. 209.
16. Needham. *The Great Northern War*, p. 156.

fighting of the war ended. Stockton sent troops to the Yukon, while other contingents were landed along the Alaska coast by Small and elements of the Caribbean fleet under the command of Captain Nicholas Seger, which had come through the Kinkaid Canal in June. By early October of 1898 all of Alaska, with the exception of the Aleutians, was under the Mexican flag.[17]

Cortez was delighted with the campaign. Kramer Associates' engineering teams went along with Stockton's brigades and set up camps in the Yukon, preparatory for mining the following spring. The mines were every bit as rich as Carew had indicated, and production figures caused celebrations in San Francisco and Mexico City.[18] Cortez congratulated Hermión on "your great and complete victory." He and other company officials naturally assumed the war was over, with a minimum loss of life and property and maximum gains. All that remained, thought Cortez, was the signing of a peace treaty.

### Alaska Gold Production, 1897–1905

| YEAR | PRODUCTION (IN THOUSANDS OF OUNCES) |
|------|------------------------------------|
| 1897 | 449 |
| 1898 | 403 |
| 1899 | 1869 |
| 1900 | 2326 |
| 1901 | 2335 |
| 1902 | 2769 |
| 1903 | 3056 |
| 1904 | 3560 |
| 1905 | 4067 |

Source: U.S.M. *Statistical Abstract*, p. 371.

Without informing Hermión, Cortez contacted officials in Japan asking that nation to offer its good offices to end the war. The Japanese were more than willing to do so, since the Premier, Count Matsukata, was fearful of Mexican influence so close to Japan. On January 5, 1899, the Japanese Ambassador to the U.S.M., Ono Yamashira, met with Secretary of State Felicio Montoya and asked whether Hermión was prepared to set down his terms for peace, and at the same time, Ambassador to Russia, Baron Kiyouri spoke with Prince Mirsky regarding the possibility of Japanese mediation. The Russians were prepared to

---

17. Needham. *The Great Northern War*, pp. 345–49.   18. *Ibid*, p. 376.

discuss peace; Mirsky suggested that Tokyo might be a suitable site for the meetings. But Hermión was loath to end the war. Thus, Montoya told Yamashira that Mexico would discuss peace only if Russia admitted she had violated California territory, would cede Alaska to Mexico, and pay an indemnity of $2.5 million. Such terms were clearly out of the question, and so the war continued.[19] It was generally believed Hermión would order the capture of the Aleutian Islands that spring or summer, and force Russian vessels from the Bering Sea, making that area a Mexican lake.[20]

On May 28, a Mexican naval force began the occupation of the Aleutians as expected. Then, before the outer islands were secured, the Pacific Fleet left Hawaii and steamed in the direction of Siberia. Elements of the Fleet landed marines at Petropavlovsk on the Kamchatka Peninsula on June 28. A second landing took place at Okhotsk in Siberia on July 15, while the third and largest force seized Nikolaevsk on July 26. The first two landings came as surprises, and were unopposed. But the Russians had been prepared for the Nikolaevsk invasion, and engaged the Mexican fleet in combat the morning of July 23. The Battle of the Okhotsk Sea ended in a complete Mexican victory. Sixteen Russian ships, including two battleships, were sunk, with a total loss of 20,000 men. The Mexicans lost not a single ship, and casualties were nine dead and fourteen wounded, and all of these the result of a boiler explosion aboard the battleship *Andrew Jackson*.[21]

The three Mexican beachheads were joined by August 10, while at the same time Mexican soldiers marched inland and secured all territory within two hundred miles of the coast. By early October, all the major population centers in the north up to the Kolyma River were in Mexican hands, while in the south the Mexican marines ruled the region as far inland as Kharbarevsk. Admiral Small was named Administrator of Siberia, with headquarters at Udsk.[22] At this point winter approached, and all military activity ground to a halt.

Mexico's success in Alaska had interested other nations, but had not disturbed normal activities in the world capitals. The invasion of Siberia, the utter defeat suffered by the Russians, and lack of knowledge of Hermión's future plans, were other matters. "The Siberian campaign of 1899 was important enough in its own time, for it catapulted Mexico to a position of world power," wrote C. Hadley McCoy. "But its implications were not understood, or even barely glimpsed, by the participants. The Great Northern War had taken on a new meaning. It was no longer merely a power struggle between

19. Stirling. *Secret History*, pp. 406–7.
20. *Ibid*, pp. 405–17.
21. Felix Noland. *A Military History*

of the *Great Northern War* (London, 1925), pp. 243–46.
22. *Ibid*, p. 279.

Russia and the U.S.M. It now became one of those pivots upon which world history revolves."[23]

The most obvious result of the Siberian campaign was the Russian Revolution. Ever since the Bloody Eighties the ruling class in St. Petersburg had feared revolution. In order to maintain itself in power, the nobility came to rely upon the operations of the secret police, the army, and informers within the various revolutionary movements. During the late 1880's and early 1890's, 80,000 republicans, democrats, and socialists were denounced, captured, and sent to Siberia without trial, many to the Kamchatka Peninsula prison camps. The Mexicans freed these men when they captured the camps, and some 7,000 organized the Free Russian Brigade, which fought alongside the Mexicans and rendered invaluable assistance during the campaign. With Hermión's permission, Admiral Small permitted them to form a "Provisional Free Russian Government," which was recognized by Mexico City as the legitimate authority in Siberia on November 23, 1899. Its premier, George Tsukansky, was more than willing to allow the new Siberian state to become a puppet of the U.S.M. with the understanding that Mexican troops would protect Free Siberia from the Tzarist forces.[24]

Such guarantees were not necessary, for on February 2, 1900, revolution erupted in St. Petersburg and from there spread throughout all of European Russia. The inept handling of the Siberian campaign, the inability of the secret police to discover all radical organizations, an economic and financial crisis—all contributed to the uprising. There were several leaders, but the most important were Count Serge Witte, Paul Miliukov, and General Vladimir Malenkov.[25] In the Ukraine General Malko Hrishchiev formed his own provisional government, with true power in the hands of a group of young officers headed by Major Simon Petlura. Poland declared itself independent, as did the Baltic States. By early July, Russia was dismembered, with the new national armies and the revolutionaries uniting to defeat the Tzarist forces in every corner of the Empire. Tzar Nicholas was obliged to abdicate on July 17, naming his brother Michael his successor. Then most of the Imperial family fled the country, eventually taking up residence in Britain. After two months Michael too abandoned hope, and on the evening of September 5 left for exile in Sweden, taking

23. C. Hadley McCoy. *The Beginning of Modern Times* (London, 1965), p. 1.
24. Michael Suzanov. *Siberia Under Mexican Domination: the First Year* (London, 1910), pp. 8–29.
25. These three men could agree to overthrow the Tzar, but differed as to their plans for the future. Witte wanted Michael to replace Nicholas, Miliukov dreamed of a republic, while Malenkov hoped to become the El Jefe of Russia. See Zoë Montgomery. *The Russian Revolution* (New York, 1967), pp. 97–118.

with him those members of the Imperial family that had remained after Nicholas' abdication. On that day the Russian Empire died.[26]

The Revolution would continue for five years, and end only after the intervention of Britain, France, the Germanic Confederation, and Austria. As McCoy put it, "Russia died in 1900, ending almost three centuries of Romanov rule. The assassin was not the feared Germans, the Poles, or the Ukrainians, but Benito Hermión, the dictator of Mexico."[27]

The combination of the Mexican victory in Siberia and the Russian Revolution also led to changes in Japan. That nation had attempted for centuries to remain aloof from the rest of the world, and had succeeded in doing so to a great degree. But the presence of an aggressive U.S.M. in Hawaii, Alaska, and now Siberia, and the violence in European Russia that soon spread to the Asiatic part of the Empire, led Emperor Meiji to adopt a radically different policy. Count Matsukata was commissioned to approach the western nations to ask for increased trade and technological assistance. Britain, France, and the Germanic Confederation were all eager to invest in and trade with Japan, but only Britain had the necessary funds, abilities, and technology for the task. By 1900, Britain and Japan had become trading partners, and the following year saw the signing of the Yamagata-Macmillan Treaty, which provided for increased commercial contact and, most importantly, pledged each nation to support the other in case of war in the Pacific.[28]

The Siberian campaign also affected the U.S.M., and in a way Hermión would scarcely have expected. In 1897, he had no interest in northern wars; three years later he controlled Alaska and his puppet ruled Siberia. Together, these lands were twice as large as the Mexico he had led on assuming power in 1881. In 1901, Mexico (together with dependent nations) was the second largest power in the world in terms of land, being exceeded only by the weak and divided Chinese Empire. The U.S.M. was still third-rate economically, but in military terms, its army and navy were second to none. Little wonder, then, that Hermión began to have fantasies of world domination, and dreams of becoming "the second Alexander."[29] The world got an inkling of these dreams when, on April 2, 1901, El Jefe announced the end of the United States of Mexico, and its replacement by The Mexican Empire, with himself as its first Emperor.[30]

26. *Russia in Exile* (London, 1911), p. 17; Noland. *Military History*, p. 465.
27. McCoy. *Modern Times*, p. 89.
28. Isadore Klineburg. *Count Matsukata and the Emergence of Japan* (Melbourne, 1960).
29. Carlista. *The Heir*, pp. 387–89.
30. Bernardo Silvera. *The Private Thoughts of Benito Hermión* (New York, 1920), p. 113; Mexico City *Times*, April 3, 1901.

It was the peak of his career, and Hermión obviously hoped for still greater honors. He was sixty years old in 1901, apparently in good health, and full of vigor. His son, who was now Prince Frederick, was thirty-three years old, and considered even more ambitious than his father. Privately Hermión predicted his dynasty would one day "rule not only continents, but the great globe itself."[31]

News of such talk precipitated the opposition to El Jefe, which had always existed, but previously had been disorganized, cowed into silence, or willing to go along with the Mexico City regime. Its elements included students, exiles, some newspaper editors, old former Libertarian senators, and the remnants of the Moralistas. But the major figure in the movement was Diego Cortez.

At the time, Cortez' political role was little known. Not until the release of the first of his files in 1937 did the import of Cortez' actions become focused, and even now there are gaps in our knowledge of his thoughts and actions in this critical period.[32] We do know that Cortez had strongly opposed the Kuriles expedition in May of 1899, and was deeply distressed by the Siberian expedition. It was in this period he probably decided to dispose of El Jefe. "The man is mad," he wrote in his journal on July 17, 1899. "Benito will destroy the nation, Kramer Associates, and perhaps the world if he continues this way."[33]

In November Cortez met with Hermión in San Francisco, and warned him that "Siberia has nothing we need. Alaska was another matter entirely. Unless we can extract ourselves with honor and dignity, we will either be expelled by the European powers or sink into the icy morass of a useless land."[34] The Russian Revolution convinced Cortez that Hermión would have to be disposed of; a change in policy alone would not suffice. The Yamagata-Macmillan Treaty, which Kramer Associates considered dangerous to its interests in the Pacific, led Cortez to contact those dissident elements that might aid in Hermión's overthrow. The proclamation of the Empire led him to speed up the timetable considerably. Cortez never liked to act quickly; in 1901 he surprised even himself by his boldness.[35]

On the evening of August 1, 1901, Cortez met with a band of El

31. *Ibid*, pp. 200–10.
32. Most of what follows comes from the released papers of Diego Cortez, the first of which were opened to scholars in 1937, with subsequent files opened at ten year intervals thereafter. At the time of this writing (1972) some fifty percent of the papers have been released. Thus, our knowledge of Cortez' actions is necessarily incomplete. See Jack Nathanson. ed. *From the Cortez Files* (Mexico City, 1938); Jack Nathanson. ed. *More From the Cortez Files* (Mexico City, 1947); Frank Dana. ed. *Recent Discoveries in the Cortez Collection* (New York, 1958); Miguel Señada. ed. *Cortez and Hermión: Bitter Friendship* (Mexico City, 1968).
33. Dana. *Recent Discoveries*, p. 795.
34. Nathanson. *Cortez Files (1938)*. p. 354.
35. *Ibid*, pp. 134, 237, 556.

Jefe's opponents at a hacienda outside Sacramento, and there they planned Hermión's "removal." Pedro Sanchez, the exiled former editor of the Mexico City *Times*, who had been spirited into the city by Kramer Associates' police, suggested a surprise *coup*, followed by a public trial of Hermión and his closest supporters. Edward Van Gelder, formerly a Senator from Jefferson but forced from office by Hermión, thought El Jefe too popular to be tried successfully, and suggested assassination. Richard Polk, a Durango Senator who like Van Gelder had been expelled from office, wanted Hermión to be captured and exiled. Others spoke (there were fifteen at the meeting), while Cortez listened carefully. He showed emotion only once, when Moralista Carlos Lincoln said he would have nothing to do with the plot if Cortez meant to take Hermión's place as what he called "El Jefe Segundo." With this, Cortez offered his thoughts, which were taken down verbatim by his secretary.

> First of all, the Kramer Associates has no desire to play a political role. Neither I nor anyone else even remotely connected with the Associates will take a position in any new or provisional government established when Hermión departs. You have my word on this. Second, we have no fear of retribution at the hands of a new government, no matter what its complexion, for to be frank, gentlemen, Kramer Associates is strong enough to withstand any blow any of you might deliver. Third, we hope for a return to the Constitution, with free elections held as soon as possible. I note that Senator Van Gelder seems surprised. Let me remind him I have no reason to deceive any of you. If we wanted, we could get rid of El Jefe ourselves. You are here precisely because we are convinced that only through constitutionalism can Mexico return to any degree of sanity. Like Mr. Lincoln, I too have no desire to see a second El Jefe in power. Fourth, Benito must not be killed. Such an action made his father a martyr, and so paved the way for his son to gain power. Fifth, he must not go into involuntary exile, for such a man could easily return to cause all of us great embarrassment. Sixth, a trial is out of the question, for while it would be taking place, pro-Hermión forces might stage a revolution of their own. Finally, gentlemen, Kramer Associates has a plan, simple but precise, by which we can rid ourselves of this danger to us all. We intend to put it into operation in a matter of weeks. Although I appreciate your ideas, I'm afraid they do not take into account many facets of the problem which we have been considering for the past two years. We will rid Mexico of Benito. Then it will be up to you to remake our nation, and it is for that purpose you are here today.[36]

Cortez then went on to note that Hermión was, despite his braggadocio, a physical coward. "I know him better than any of you,

---

36. Señada. *Cortez and Hermión*, pp. 119-21.

and I swear it is a fact. If faced with danger to his person, he will panic, and then run. We must give him that opportunity. And when the Mexican people see him flee, they will know him for what he is, a craven coward, and his aura of power will vanish." Then let him leave Mexico, said Cortez; "Such a self-imposed exile would pose no problem to us, or to the nation."[37]

None would rise to refute this line of argument. Later on, Van Gelder wrote that, "to do so would have been useless in any event. Cortez had the soldiers. In any case, his was the best plan we had, the frankest statement, and the most convincing presentation. I believed him. So did we all."[38]

The plan went off with geometric precision and a swiftness that was dazzling; the London *Times*, writing of the *coup*, said "it was the most successful Kramer Associates' production since Alaska."

On October 15, Hermión was in the Palace entertaining the diplomatic corps at a dinner in honor of Germanic Confederation Ambassador Heinz von Kron. That evening some two thousand Kramer guards, disguised as laborers, slipped into the city and took posts in the vicinity of the palace. While El Jefe slept, forty-nine of them entered the compound, overcame the police, opened the gates to others, and then cut communications to the outside. When Hermión looked out the window the next morning he saw what had happened, and as expected, panicked. Martin Cole, head of the Kramer force, shouted that the compound was in his hands, hinting strongly that he was a Moralista. "We will harm no one who is innocent," he said. "All we want is El Jefe." Then Cole said, "Servants and others may leave in peace, and must do so within the next fifteen minutes."[39]

Hermión thought of how best to escape. Donning a butler's uniform and shaving his mustache and beard, he slipped out of the palace, joined the servants, and went through Kramer lines to freedom. This too had been foreseen by Cortez, and although Hermión did not realize it then (and never would) a path to Tampico was cleared for him even as he left the city. For the next two months El Jefe travelled at night, and slept days where he could, not knowing, of course, that his journey was being tracked by over three hundred Kramer agents. He arrived in Tampico the evening of September 27, and the next day, bribed the captain of the Argentinian oil tanker *Tierra del Fuego*, bound for Spain, to take him aboard as a passenger. (As might be expected, the captain was in the employ of Kramer Associates, and the ship under Kramer registry.)

37. *Ibid*, p. 122.
38. Edward Van Gelder. *The Victory of Republicanism* (Mexico City, 1912), p. 56.
39. *Ibid*, p. 116; Tulin. *The Cortez Years*, p. 509.

El Jefe arrived in Spain on October 20, 1901, where he went into exile. He did not live poorly, since he had deposits of well over $5 million in two Madrid banks. But his political career was over. When the Mexico City newspapers printed the external facts of his escape, he appeared cowardly to the public, and all but his most devoted admirers deserted the Hermión camp. The Mexican Empire was ended, after only four months of life.[40]

---

40. Hermión never left Spain, settling down in an armed villa on the outskirts of Barcelona. He died there on August 16, 1911. His family was permitted to join him later on. Although Frederick Hermión hoped for several years to return to Mexico in triumph, he never did. Instead, he settled down to a banker's existence in Spain, taking out citizenship in 1910. The Hermión clan still resides in Barcelona, amid a rather bizarre "court." It has contacts with the Russian royal family, and Joseph Hermión, the pretender "Emperor" son of Frederick, married "Princess" Alexandra Romanov in 1924. Joseph's son, Benito, was born in 1920. He is a professor of linguistics at Madrid University, and appears embarrassed by the shabby pomp affected by others of the family. His son Pedro—El Jefe's great-great-grandson—is a famous horseman, and in 1969 was permitted to return to Mexico City to purchase horses. When asked whether he harbored political ambitions, he cracked to a reporter, "What's the matter, didn't Mexico have enough of my family?"

# 23

# THE STARKIST TERROR

THE so-called "Mexican problem" dominated Ezra Gallivan's second term as Governor-General, as Burgoyne, in common with other major world capitals, kept a weather eye on El Jefe's activities in the late 1890's. When gold was discovered in the Yukon, Liberals criticized Gallivan for neglecting the mineral development of northern Manitoba. "While the Kramer Associates finds a fortune in Russian lands, Mr. Gallivan allows the Athabasca region to remain frozen and isolated. Perhaps the Governor-General should ask Diego Cortez for assistance, since he appears incapable of action on his own." Thus, Councilman Hare, leader of the opposition, took Gallivan to task. To this the Governor-General replied: "Mr. Hare should know, or should be informed, that private investigations of the Athabasca region have shown little or no gold in the district. Any North American who so desires can go to Athabasca and search to his heart's content, and what he finds, will be his alone. It is the role of the individual, and not the government in Burgoyne, to go on gold-seeking expeditions. Does Mr. Hare, who has opposed every measure this government has taken in the field of social welfare on the grounds that such actions limit freedom, now suggest the government expand its scope to include gold mining? I think not."[1]

Actually, Gallivan wanted North Americans to remain out of northwest Manitoba, for fear of complications with Mexico or Russia. In 1897, Gallivan knew of several border clashes, but kept the matter secret, realizing such violations would only spark war talk in Burgoyne. Instead, he notified Cortez of the incidents, and the Kramer Associates' President assured Gallivan they would not be repeated.[2]

Gallivan's life-long antipathy to foreign involvements was a major factor in determining his attitude toward the Yukon gold strike. An-

1. Arthur. *Creative Nationalism*, p. 500.
2. It is interesting to note that Gallivan contacted Cortez, and not Hermión, regarding the violations. Apparently this was done because the Governor-General did not want to discuss matters with El Jefe, whom he did not trust, but with a man whose ideas of proper behavior were not unlike his own. *Ibid*, pp. 530–34.

other was the election campaign of 1898. As late as August of 1897, he had planned to retire from the governorship-general after his term had ended, and take a seat in the back benches in the Grand Council. His Creative Nationalism program had run its course; "I have made my contribution," said Gallivan. "Let someone else taste of power now." But the burst of nationalist fervor, sparked by spokesmen for the Moral Imperative, to which was added increased talk of expansion toward Alaska, led Gallivan to reconsider his position.

There were several Liberal contenders in 1898 and all were committed to some kind of union with Britain and development of Athabasca. If Gallivan stepped down, there was a good chance Thomas Kronmiller would succeed him as People's Coalition leader, and Kronmiller spoke every day more stridently of "the North American mission." Gallivan had once said, "No man is indispensable, but by the time he reaches the age of forty, every man thinks he is." Now he, too, came to believe he was the indispensable man for 1898, and probably with more reason than most.[3] With this in mind, Gallivan told the Coalition central committee that he would run for a third term.

As expected, the Liberals selected an expansionist as their candidate. Governor Douglas Sizer of Manitoba, a protégé of McDowell's, won the nomination, and pledged himself to "the fulfilment of national destiny" in his acceptance speech. Gallivan won nomination by acclaim, despite grumbling from the Kronmiller forces. Kronmiller all but demanded Gallivan step down. "We have a Queen already; now Mr. Gallivan wants to be king," he told the convention. Soon afterwards he announced that he would "not be bound by this convention." Thus, a deep split widened in the Coalition. On the one side was Gallivan, the moderate isolationist, while on the other was the radical expansionism of Thomas Kronmiller.

Gallivan was easily the most popular man in the C.M.A., as well as its most adept politician. The People's Coalition machine did its job well in 1898; although the Liberals made slight gains, this was to be expected after the massive P.C. victory of 1893. What was unusual, however, was the P.C. caucus' vote for Governor-General. Kronmiller challenged Gallivan at the meeting, and received 20 votes to the Governor-General's 71. This was the first time in C.N.A. history that the Council caucus of a political party faced such a challenge, and it indicated a serious division within P.C. ranks that even Gallivan would not be able to heal.

An ominous note was added by the fact that the People's Coalition had suffered its worst setback in Southern Vandalia, where its delegation had been reduced from eight to four. The Negroes of that state

---

3. Henry Tracy. *Gallivan: The Third Stage* (Burgoyne, 1961), pp. 4–6.

resented what they called "the all white program of Massa Ezra." Unlike McDowell, Gallivan had included not a single Negro in his cabinet, and this was viewed as either racism on his part or insensitivity. Sizer instructed the Liberal Party in Southern Vandalia to ignore all other issues and concentrate on the question of race, and the strategy paid off at the polls. Furthermore, all four P.C. councilmen from Southern Vandalia voted for Kronmiller at the caucus.[4]

### Results of the C.N.A. Elections of 1898

| | PARTY AFFILIATION OF COUNCILMEN | | |
|---|---|---|---|
| STATE | PEOPLE'S COALITION | LIBERAL | CONSERVATIVE |
| Northern Confederation | 27 | 18 | 0 |
| Southern Confederation | 25 | 5 | 0 |
| Indiana | 19 | 9 | 2 |
| Manitoba | 7 | 8 | 1 |
| Northern Vandalia | 9 | 7 | 0 |
| Southern Vandalia | 4 | 9 | 0 |
| | 91 | 56 | 3 |

Source: New York *Herald*, February 16, 1898.

Whether or not Gallivan intended to mend fences with Kronmiller or the Southern Vandalia Coalitionists, he had little time or energy for such matters in 1898. With the coming of the Alaska phase of the Great Northern War, he had to face increased opposition in the Grand Council. The easy Mexican victory frightened many in the C.N.A., who now felt unprotected and exposed to any threat El Jefe might make. For the first time in its history, the Manitoba legislature passed a resolution asking for increased military spending; Northern Vandalia followed, fearful of incursions by the Mexicans. By autumn the movement had spread to the eastern states, as new organizations sprang up protesting Gallivan's isolationism. The Students Defense League, with headquarters at Georgia University, claimed over 100,000 members, all of whom were dedicated to "the defense of our land from its enemies, both internal and external." By this they meant Gallivan, who they charged "works either together with or for foreign powers who would destroy our nation." Frank Mitchell, the S.D.L. leader, called for Gallivan's removal "by whatever means necessary." Edward Byrnes, of the more militant but smaller, For North America Movement, hinted that assassination might be the best way to rid the nation of the Governor-General. Friends of Burgoyne, an organization con-

---

4. Horace Smyser. *Origins of Modern Negro Thought* (New York, 1966).

sisting of individuals who could trace their ancestry back to soldiers who had fought in the Rebellion, called for Gallivan's resignation "for the good of the nation." According to unofficial tallies, the mail of councilmen ran two to one against Gallivan, and was most critical of his defense stance. In an address of January 10, Sizer asked for Gallivan's resignation. "He should leave government," he concluded. "Mr. Gallivan has stayed too long." Meanwhile, Kronmiller organized the opposition within the Coalition, finding many willing to come out against the Governor-General.[5]

At first Gallivan said nothing, perhaps hoping the "belligerency craze" as he called it would pass. Then, when sentiment favoring expansionism and of some way of meeting the "Mexican menace" grew, the Governor-General spoke. In an address to the nation on May 17, 1899, he called for reason and "a proper perspective of our problems and their possible resolution."

> As we all know, Chief of State Hermión has led his country in a war with Russia. It would appear that war is about to draw to a close, and there are those among us who now fear he will turn his attention eastward, and attack North America. Such a possibility does exist; to deny it would be to hide from reality. And to dissuade any intentions Mr. Hermión may have, the C.N.A. army and navy are being fortified. Our armed strength will reach 700,000 by year's end; border patrols are being manned; the state governors have informed me that they are prepared to call up the guards, which will add an additional million men to our defense force. I know this. Mr. Hermión knows this. And so does Mr. Kronmiller and Mr. Sizer.
>
> I do not believe war will come to our land. I will do everything within my power to prevent conflict. But if such a tragedy does strike, we will be prepared. There is no cause for alarm. No nation or combination of nations can defeat the Confederation of North America. We are so strong we can afford to accept calmly events abroad that might frighten lesser nations. . . . And so I ask you, my fellow North Americans, to maintain your perspective in this troubled time. It will pass, and when it does, we should be proud of our actions and deeds.[6]

The Gallivan speech did have some calming effect, and for the next month, the situation appeared to have returned to normal. Then came news of the Mexican invasion of Siberia on June 28, and opposition to Gallivan reappeared overnight, stronger than before. New leaders also appeared, the most important of whom was Fritz Stark, a Liberal councilman from the Southern Confederation.

Stark was fifty-five years old in 1899, a three-term councilman and, before that, a prominent figure in Georgia politics. He was universally

5. Allen Watterson. *The Great Fear: Starkism in the C.N.A.* (London, 1956), 6. New York *Herald*, May 18, 1899, pp. 34–56, 118–20, 203–9.

respected, even loved, and considered a mild and cautious man. He had
not participated in the earlier attacks on Gallivan, although his expansionist views were well-known. It came as a surprise, then, when he
rose in the Council on July 10 to deliver a speech on "shocking information" he had discovered the previous day. "We all know what is
behind El Jefe's attack on Siberia," he began. "It is the Kramer Associates, which is another name for the United States of Mexico. Diego
Cortez controls Mexico, as he does many other nations throughout the
world. He is using the Mexican people and their blood to increase his
profits, and now he has added Russia to the list of victims." Then Stark
looked across the aisle to Majority Leader Winthrop Fields. "The
Governor-General has told us Mexico cannot conquer North America.
I believe him. No nation is strong enough to accomplish such a task.
Then he tells us that only North Americans can destroy their nation.
Once again, I believe him. And now I know what he meant. I have
information which, if correct, would seem to indicate that Ezra Gallivan is in the pay of the Kramer Associates, which has purchased our
foreign policy, lock, stock, and barrel."

Such a charge, coming from any councilman at that time of superheated passions, would have created a great stir. But since it was made
by the sober, respected Fritz Stark, it caused an even greater shock
than might otherwise have been the case. Without waiting and with
passion in his voice, Stark detailed the nature of his information. John
Montalban, a clerk in the Mexican embassy in Burgoyne, had visited
him the previous week to tell him of the plot. He brought documents
to prove the case, which indicated that since 1893, Cortez had paid
Gallivan N.A. £1.5 million a year to "protect our common interests."
"I have investigated Señor Montalban's charges carefully; I do not
speak rashly. I am satisfied they are true. The Governor-General cannot ignore these documents, as he has ignored public opinion since the
Great Northern War commenced."[7]

The public reaction to the Stark speech was electrifying. Pande-
monium erupted throughout the nation. Not a city was spared the
violence that followed. Coalition offices were entered, looted by people
searching for "evidence," and burned. Councilman Dudley Graves of
Indiana was assassinated; attempts were made on the lives of at least
fifteen councilmen who had supported Gallivan. In New York and
Philadelphia mobs entered immigrant quarters searching for "foreigners" who were sympathetic to "anti-North Americans." Gallivan
was obliged to remain sequestered in his mansion, surrounded by capital guards; it was said that not even the army would be permitted near

7. Watterson. *The Great Fear*, pp. 223-26.

him, since elements of the Burgoyne regiments were prepared to assassinate the Governor-General. Revolution was in the air.

The terror lasted two weeks. In all, 436 people were killed, another thirteen thousand were wounded, and countless others were forced to flee their homes. The total property damage was estimated at N.A. £980 million. What was worse, for the first time in its history, most North Americans appeared to have lost confidence in their leaders.[8]

Gallivan himself was shocked by the Stark speech. As soon as he recovered, he called the Councilman and asked for a meeting "to examine these grave and irresponsible charges you have made." Gallivan noted that Stark had used the phrases "if correct" and "seem to indicate" in his speech. "This would imply, Councilman, that you may have doubts; if so, you had no right to speak as you did. I would like to explore them with you at the earliest possible moment." Stark agreed to come to the Governor's Mansion, but only if accompanied by a delegation from the Council's Committee on Rules.

Gallivan accepted, and the meeting was held the evening of July 19. At that time, Stark gave Gallivan the documents he had received from Montalban. The Governor-General denied them all, stating they were forgeries. He then asked the councilmen present for "a full investigation of these slanders, at the earliest possible moment." The members agreed, and the following day established the Special Subcommittee f the Rules Committee to Investigate Charges of Treason. Its Chairman, Councilman Henderson Nelson of the Northern Confederation, was a Liberal. Although under normal circumstances the post would have been filled by a Coalitionist, Gallivan insisted a member of the opposition chair the Subcommittee "to remove any doubts as to its impartiality." He might have also added that all the Coalitionists on the Subcommittee were members of the rapidly-growing Kronmiller Cabal, dedicated to the overthrow of the Governor-General in the P.C. caucus.[9]

The Subcommittee did a most difficult job with care and dispatch. Nelson proved an admirable choice for the position; his fairness and willingness to hold open hearings were admitted by all. Despite frequent interruptions and threats, the Subcommittee was able to complete its investigations within two weeks, but even before the final session on August 4, important disclosures were made.[10]

The first was that of Gallivan's accounts. The Governor-General was worth N.A. £324,954, most of which was in government bonds.

---

8. *Ibid*, pp. 299–310.
9. *Ibid*, pp. 320–23.
10. Confederation of North America. Subcommittee of the Rules Committee. *Report of the Inquiry into Charges of Treason* (Burgoyne, 1900).

A meticulous search disclosed no other funds or secret accounts. Thus, the moneys supposedly paid by Cortez could not be found.

Then it was learned that John Montalban had a record of mental illness, which included delusions of grandeur and abnormal fear of death. Handwriting analysis indicated the documents he had given Stark had been carefully forged. Stark's "experts" were proven to be incompetent. In effect, the entire affair had been a hoax.[11]

Stark accepted these pieces of evidence with a growing horror of what he had brought about. As the Subcommittee met, violence continued in the nation, and the movement had acquired a name—"Starkism." Now Stark realized he had been deceived. In a public address on August 6, he admitted his errors. "I have wronged a good and honest man, irreparably. I ask Governor-General Gallivan's forgiveness and understanding. I acted out of love of country, but I have done more harm to it than any man since the Rebellion." Then Stark announced his resignation. The next day he was found dead in his Burgoyne home, apparently from a self-inflicted wound in the head. In his hand was a note, with the words, "It is ended."[12]

This recantation and death did not put an end to the terror. Gallivan's opponents now claimed he had coerced Stark into making his admission and then had him killed. Within a week it was as though the Subcommittee had not met, and Stark had not admitted his errors. Newspaper articles appeared, books were published, speeches delivered, all purporting to show how the Kramer Associates controlled every aspect of Mexican life, and was now doing the same in the C.N.A. A play opened in New York, entitled "The Merry Life of Patrick Henry," which was a barely disguised attack on Gallivan, implying he was guilty of the most heinous crimes imaginable. It received good notices, became an immediate hit, and the slander was spread to other cities soon after.[13]

At first Gallivan tried to ride out the storm. He had the support of moderates, the Indiana P.C., and majority elements in other P.C. organizations in Northern Vandalia and the N.C. But the coalition of nativists, radicals, believers in the Moral Imperative, expansionists, and students remained intact. Clearly the nation was dividing; revolution was still a threat. Gallivan had earlier warned of such a possibility; in 1901 it seemed the C.N.A. was indeed destroying itself.

Thus, on July 24, 1901, Gallivan called a special meeting of the Coalition caucus and announced his resignation as Governor-General. That evening he informed the nation of his decision. "For many years I have cherished the grace with which John McDowell left office, and

11. Watterson. *The Great Fear*, p. 505.
12. The best study of this phenomenon is Alice Welsch. *Who Killed Cock Robin? Starkism in Perspective* (New York, 1959).
13. *Ibid*, p. 204.

had hoped I could match it. This was not meant to be. Therefore, let me be blunt and direct. Events of the past two years have shown I have become an embarrassment to many in the nation, a source of serious contention. North America as a whole would be better served by my resignation than if I stayed in office."[14]

The Coalition caucus met the next day to select a new Governor-General. The meeting was unprecedented; not since William Johnson had resigned in 1856 had a Governor-General left office before the end of his term, and Johnson had done so voluntarily, while Gallivan was, in fact, deposed. As expected, Kronmiller made a strong bid for the position. But he had been too identified with Starkism in the past, was a contentious individual, and was much resented as a backwash of pro-Gallivan sentiment increased after the speech. Minister for Home Affairs Leonidas Rubey had support. A moderate, one who had remained in the background during the previous two years, he was considered a "unity candidate." But the party was not seeking a Governor-General alone, but also a candidate for the 1903 elections, and Rubey was not the stuff chief executives are made of. Rubey himself suggested Councilman Harry Burroughs of Manitoba, then sixty-nine years old and much beloved by the party. He thought Burroughs might serve as a *de facto* interim Governor-General, and then step down just prior to the elections, to be succeeded by the party's candidate. This might have won support were it not for objections that the Mexicans had done the same with George Vining, who had opened the door for El Jefe. In the end, the caucus settled on Northern Vandalian Councilman Clifton Burgen. "Burgen had everything in his favor," said Kronmiller afterwards. "No one knew who he was, and neither did he." Burgen was given to understand he was an interim appointee, and would be replaced at the 1903 caucus. He accepted this role, and on July 29, with Gallivan by his side, he took the oath.[15]

The Burgen administration was uneventful, though blessed by fortuitous happenings abroad. Three months after Burgen assumed office, Hermión was deposed, and the Starkist wave swiftly receded. Within a year there were second thoughts about the way Gallivan had been treated. Now the tables were turned on the Starkites, as they were purged from their positions on newspapers and in universities, voted out of office in the 1902 elections, and avoided at public meetings. "It was amazing," said Edward Byrnes. "Former comrades were embarrassed to be seen in public with me, and would not even talk to me on the telephone. We were right in 1899, and we are right today. Nothing has happened to change that. But even if we were wrong, so were the

14. Burgoyne *Record*, July 25, 1901.
15. Warren Wallgren. *The Burgen Ad-*   *ministration: A History* (New York, 1960).

turncoats. Today they deny it, but most of them were ready with the torch in 1899, while today they fall over each other awarding medals to Gallivan."[16]

There were some in the party who urged Gallivan to assume leadership of the party once again, and run for a fourth term in 1903. But Gallivan had had his fill of politics. In 1903, he would be fifty-four years old and, as he said, "too old and worn for such a task." He had had a minor heart attack two months after leaving office, and though recovered, could rightly claim to be in poor health. By 1903, however, his rehabilitation was complete. He received a tumultuous ovation at the People's Coalition Convention; Councilman Jonathan Caldwell, who only four years earlier had called for Gallivan's removal, now said that the difference between Mexico and North America is that "they had Henry, we had Dickinson; they had Jackson, we had Webster; they had Benito Hermión, and we had Ezra Gallivan."[17]

Although retired from office, Gallivan was not through with politics. He now moved to prevent Kronmiller's selection by the P.C. caucus, and so great was his influence, that he was able to succeed. Thus, the Coalition named another moderate, Christopher Hemingway, a Councilman from the Northern Confederation, as its candidate. Hemingway was committed to Creative Nationalism, was an isolationist, and believed Gallivan to have been the greatest Governor-General in C.N.A. history. He was handsome, well-spoken, and friendly, but had little else to recommend him to the public.

### Results of the C.N.A. Elections of 1903

| STATE | PARTY AFFILIATION OF COUNCILMEN | |
| --- | --- | --- |
| | PEOPLE'S COALITION | LIBERALS |
| Northern Confederation | 25 | 17 |
| Indiana | 21 | 13 |
| Southern Confederation | 22 | 6 |
| Manitoba | 6 | 12 |
| Northern Vandalia | 7 | 7 |
| Southern Vandalia | 2 | 12 |
| | 83 | 67 |

Source: New York *Herald*, February 17, 1903.

The Liberals turned to Clark Nelson, who had made his reputation on the Subcommittee that investigated the Stark charges. Nelson had a reputation for integrity, and like Hemingway, was a moderate. While

---

16. Edward Byrnes. *Rebel* (New York, 1920), p. 46.

17. Tracy. *The Third Stage*, p. 445; New York *Herald*, January 4, 1903.

more willing to join with Britain in common programs, he was no internationalist. Thus, the Liberals too rejected extremism, and nominated a man who could promise a calm administration. The Conservatives also met, but so few appeared, the meeting adjourned the first day. With this, the party disappeared into C.N.A. history.

Hemingway won election without too much difficulty. But the people did not vote for him; instead, as one reporter put it, "they expunged their guilt by voting Gallivan his fourth term."[18] Another put it more strikingly. "Gallivan and Hermión are both gone from the scene, and their like will not be seen again for many a year. We have left the Time of the Giants, and are about to enter the Years of the Pygmies."[19]

---

18. Burgoyne *Times*, February 20, 1903.    19. Boston *Register*, March 1, 1903.

# 24

# THE YEARS OF THE PYGMIES

THE Mexico City *coup* of October 15, 1901, was carried off with precision. Less than an hour after El Jefe had fled the Palace, Kramer Guard Commandant Martin Cole arrived to take his place. Surrounded by his men, Cole proclaimed a provisional government, which would rule until elections could be held. After he had spoken, onlookers raised their fists and shouted, "Viva Cole!" Within the past decade there had been six *coups* in South American countries; in each a military man had overthrown a civilian government, which then promised elections. In none of these cases were the elections held, and so the Mexicans had reason to believe Cole meant to become El Jefe II.

Those who had planned the *coup* knew this was not to be so, and more importantly, that Cole had no such ambitions. A trusted officer in Kramer Associates, he took orders from Cortez and from no one else. Cole would be provisional President for seven months, but all of his directives were written by Cortez personally, and emanated from Kramer headquarters in San Francisco.[1]

During October and early November, the Mexican army, the state constabularies and rangers, and the Kramer Guard established civil rule in those areas where it had broken down. Admiral Small was informed to retain the lands already held in Siberia, but not to advance any further. The Free Russian Government, headed by Boris Tschakev, would be permitted to establish its rule over Mexican-occupied lands, and Small was to prepare for an eventual withdrawal. The gold operations in Alaska proceeded well, as did manufacturing in California and Jefferson and agriculture elsewhere. The nation's economy had scarcely been disturbed by El Jefe's leaving, and Kramer Associates management of political life was as efficient as its work in the factories and mines.

On November 15, Cole announced full amnesty for all who had been exiled by Hermión, and in addition, promised the Moralistas "a

---

1. Raymond Vun Kannon. *The Phoenix: Mexico's Rebirth* (London, 1958).

role in the new Mexico if they want one." This meant little, since Hermión had all but destroyed the last vestiges of Moralista opposition by 1898. But as a sign of good faith, the Cole offer was a wise move. Political life resumed soon after, with exiles and those who remained establishing offices and preparing for the promised campaign. Even the Hermiónistas participated, for the amnesty covered them as well as the exiles. Cortez was determined there would be no bloodbath after El Jefe left, and with the exception of minor acts of retribution in Chiapas and Durango, there was none.[2]

At first, attempts were made to resurrect the Continentalist and Liberty parties, but these failed. The Continenalists were now considered Hermiónistas in disguise, while the Libertarians had for the most part cooperated with El Jefe in his early years. Few of those who had remained in Mexico ran for state office in 1902, fully expecting to meet disaster at the polls. Much to their surprise, the public returned many Hermiónistas to power, indicating perhaps that memories of El Jefe were not all bad. For the most part, however, the exiles were able to make stronger appeals, and so had control of the new state legislatures.

Cortez had decided, even before overthrowing Hermión, that he would restore the old Constitution. To do so would be an act of good faith on his part and would avoid the complexities and delays of a constitutional convention. He felt it important that Cole should never go back on his word. Cole had promised elections for June 14, and Cortez would brook no delays or debates on this subject.

No less than fourteen candidates stood for the presidency in 1902. The campaign was lively, and thanks to army control and Kramer Associates' supervision, probably the most honest in Mexican history.[3] Naturally, no candidate received a majority; Pedro Sanchez, the exiled former editor of the Mexico City *Times*, received the largest number of votes, and this was only twelve percent of the total. Cortez had

---

2. The *coup* created difficulties in New Granada, where Victoriano Hermión had ruled since 1890. Victoriano was able to survive the *coup*, however. When the Bogotá politicians considered the chaos of other Latin American nations and compared this with their own security, they asked Victoriano to remain in office. He died in 1906, after having secured New Granada as a dependency of the U.S.M. Willkie Devlin. *The Other Hermión: The New Granadan Experiment* (Mexico City, 1970).

3. Because of its great power, Kramer Associates has often been charged with controlling nations and men to its own ends. Such beliefs and accusations do not come to grips with the basic philosophy of men like Kramer and Cortez. They were willing to allow *any* government to rule in areas where they had interests, with the understanding (1) order would be maintained, and (2) Kramer properties would be protected. Cortez himself always preferred republican rule, for he felt that such governments were more stable than tyrannies or monarchies. And he insisted on free elections in 1902 because he felt that only by creating a trust in the new government, could stability be assured in post-Hermión Mexico.

expected this to happen, and speaking through Cole, ordered a runoff between Sanchez, Anthony Flores (a Continentalist Senator from Durango who had been exiled by Hermión) and George Craig (who had been Secretary for Postal Affairs in the Hermión Cabinet). Flores won, receiving slightly over forty-five percent of the vote, with Craig second and Sanchez third.

### The Mexican Presidential Run-off Election, 1902

| STATE | FLORES | CRAIG | SANCHEZ |
|---|---|---|---|
| California | 1,967,945 | 2,135,496 | 892,342 |
| Jefferson | 1,554,672 | 2,045,529 | 769,082 |
| Durango | 1,546,730 | 436,945 | 431,940 |
| Chiapas | 1,554,048 | 645,034 | 293,405 |
| Arizona | 761,087 | 843,455 | 340,136 |
| Mexico del Norte | 660,978 | 452,970 | 530,578 |
| | 8,045,460 | 6,559,429 | 3,257,483 |

Source: U.S.M. *Statistical Abstract*, p. 113.

There were several interesting aspects to the 1902 vote. In the first place, all candidates in the run-off could be considered "moderate" and "republican," and all were the kind of men Cortez could work with easily. Next, Kramer Associates had insisted on an honest election, and one was held. Speaking at a meeting later on, Cortez said, not in a bragging fashion, that "Kramer Associates will underwrite honesty in Mexican politics." Flores was a Hispano, but his mother was a Mexicano; for the first time in U.S.M. history a person with such a background had been elected to the presidency. The vote showed Flores most popular in Mexicano districts; he carried Chiapas and Durango easily, and did well in Mexicano enclaves elsewhere. Flores also was able to win significant pluralities in several key Anglo districts in Jefferson and California. This was made possible by the work of Kramer Associates executives, many of whom campaigned for Flores. As indicated before, the election was honest, the ballot secret. But Cortez let it be known he favored Flores, and this helped turn the tide in his favor.[4]

---

4. Cortez thought all three candidates were acceptable, but preferred Flores because of his mixed ancestry. Easily the most informed man in the U.S.M. if not the world, as well as being a person of great intellect, Cortez saw signs of trouble between the races long before anyone else. He believed Mexico might be spared turmoil if the Mexicanos were given important positions before they could gather to demand them. Thus, he backed Flores, who was really a Hispano in all but his mother's background. Tulin. *The Cortez Years*, p. 789.

The Flores presidency was uneventful politically. Under his leadership civil liberties were restored, public works projects were continued, and the nation prospered. The last Mexican marines evacuated Siberia in 1903, leaving Tschakev in charge of the area politically, while Kramer Associates' engineers remained to search for mineral wealth. Relations with New Granada and Guatamala were satisfactory; the rest of the world was assured that under Flores, the U.S.M. would engage in no wars or drives for territorial expansion. Running under the banner of the United Mexican Party, Flores won a smashing victory over his Liberty Party opponent, Frank Everhart, in the 1908 elections. His motto, "Security in Your Home and Prosperity in the Land," seemed fulfilled. And all of this was underwritten, as promised, by Pedro Cortez and Kramer Associates.[5]

Political life in the C.N.A. was equally languid. As expected, Governor-General Hemingway proved competent and popular. A follower of Gallivan all his previous political life, he remained so during his term. Hemingway maintained the C.N.A.'s isolationist stance, and successfully turned back Kronmiller's attempts to have the country annex Cuba and Porto Rico. Nor did North America join the United British Commonwealth of Nations, formed in 1906 by Britain, Australia, New Zealand, India, Victoria, and Egypt, although Hemingway accepted "associated" status. King Edward VII visited the C.N.A. in 1907, and his tour was a triumph, as North America renewed its ties with the mother country. But this allegiance was emotional, not political, and so it would remain.[6]

Hemingway himself toured Quebec and Nova Scotia in 1905, and was well-received, indicating that antagonisms between those provinces and Burgoyne were dying. That same year, the Governor-General spoke at all the confederation capitals, taking over four months to make the journey. Clearly Hemingway was popular; he enjoyed the title of "most beloved Governor-General in history." But he introduced no new measures, started no crusades, and did not call the people to new reforms. All was going well, and Hemingway saw no need to rock the boat.

Hemingway could have won re-election easily in 1908 had he wanted to stand, but he announced on September 6, 1907, that he would retire to the back benches "and the company of my friend and mentor, Ezra Gallivan," after his current term was over.[7] He and

5. The vote was 12,045,360 for Flores and 7,540,723 for Everhart. It was the greatest electoral triumph in Mexican history, and a sign to some that the nation would accept "half-breed" leadership. *Ibid*, 930.

6. Christopher Hemingway. *The Way of the World* (New York, 1911).

7. *Ibid*, p. 406. Gallivan had accepted a Council seat in 1904. He remained there until 1910, when he resigned to become Chancellor of Burgoyne University, a post he filled until his death in 1914, at the age of sixty-five.

Gallivan selected his successor, Councilman Albert Merriman of Indiana, who defeated Liberal Councilman Guy St. Just of the Northern Confederation with ease. Merriman appeared a carbon copy of Hemingway, having no desire to innovate and a great love of crowds and travel. On learning of Merriman's election, a bitter Thomas Kronmiller remarked, "In this way we enter the fifth term of King Ezra Gallivan."[8]

### Results of the C.N.A. Elections of 1908

| | PARTY AFFILIATION OF COUNCILMEN | |
|---|---|---|
| STATE | PEOPLE'S COALITION | LIBERALS |
| Northern Confederation | 22 | 20 |
| Indiana | 25 | 9 |
| Southern Confederation | 24 | 4 |
| Manitoba | 8 | 10 |
| Northern Vandalia | 8 | 6 |
| Southern Vandalia | 3 | 11 |
| | 90 | 60 |

Source: New York *Herald*, February 16, 1908.

From 1902 to 1913 the U.S.M. was led by Anthony Flores and the C.N.A. by Clifton Burgen, Christopher Hemingway, and Albert Merriman. All seemed cut from the same cloth. Each in his own way was a moderate, an isolationist, and a person unwilling to innovate or take risks. Most of this period has been labeled "Years of the Pygmies" by historians more attracted by the action, dangers, and rapid changes that had taken place in the Hermión and Gallivan periods.[9] But such an analysis misses an important point. After the empire-building of El Jefe and the reforms of Gallivan, followed by the bout with Starkism in the C.N.A., the peoples of both nations desired peace and tranquillity. When Anthony Flores said "The people know me. I am one of them," newspaper columnist Diego Santiago replied that "The President is the lowest common denominator, and what is more surprising, he appears proud of it."[10] Governors-General Burgen and Hemingway were always more at home at a church supper than at a university forum, while Albert Merriman spent two weeks each winter skiing in Northern Confederation resorts, and admitted that "books over two hundred pages in length usually bore me."[11]

8. New York *Herald*, February 17, 1908.
9. Arnold Marriot. *Years of the Pygmies* (New York, 1923); Leland French. *In the Shadow of the Giants: The Burgen-Hemingway-Merriman Years* (New York, 1969) are representative works of this genre.
10. Mexico City *Times*, June 5, 1909.
11. French. *Shadow of Giants*, p. 203.

Such men frustrated reformers and disturbed intellectuals, but all three were popular, well-liked, and probably reflected the mood of North America in their day as well as McDowell and Gallivan had in theirs.[12] It is worth noting that Ezra Gallivan, a hero to North American intellectuals, considered the three men that followed him to office worthy of the post, and looked forward to his annual "fishing fortnight" with Hemingway off the Georgia coast.[13]

### Selected C.N.A. Statistics, 1900–1910

| YEAR | POPULATION (MILLIONS) | G.N.P. (MILLIONS N.A.£) | ELECTRICITY (1,000 EDISONS) | LOCOMOBILES (1,000S) | RADIOS (1,000S) |
|---|---|---|---|---|---|
| 1900 | 87.1 | 42934 | 65670 | 18 | 29 |
| 1901 | 89.9 | 45986 | 86975 | 23 | 50 |
| 1902 | 91.8 | 48008 | 120324 | 37 | 98 |
| 1903 | 92.4 | 52030 | 150658 | 56 | 156 |
| 1904 | 95.0 | 56189 | 190434 | 97 | 298 |
| 1905 | 97.7 | 60243 | 230434 | 134 | 406 |
| 1906 | 99.8 | 63452 | 280767 | 198 | 689 |
| 1907 | 102.0 | 67874 | 350654 | 252 | 946 |
| 1908 | 104.5 | 71089 | 456453 | 324 | 1656 |
| 1909 | 107.1 | 74554 | 540543 | 443 | 2055 |
| 1910 | 109.8 | 77998 | 605602 | 769 | 3145 |

Source: C.N.A. *Statistical Abstract*, pp. 383, 487, 1104, 1434, 1499.

After a quarter of a century of turbulent and, at times, violent change, Mexico and North America enjoyed slightly more than a decade of political calm. Such was not the case in the economic sphere, however; in this period, the lives of the average Mexican and North America were transformed as much as they had been in the last fifty years of the nineteenth century. Even if one concedes that pygmies administered political affairs in Mexico City and Burgoyne, it can be said that giants dominated San Francisco, Tampico, and Jefferson, and they were matched by the titans of New York, Michigan City, and Norfolk.

The economic advances of the C.N.A. were less dramatic than many of those of Mexico, but more substantial. In every year from 1900 to 1914, gross national product increased a minimum of six percent. The production of electricity rose from 65.7 million edisons in

---

12. The best and most recent defense of Gallivan's three successors is Hubert Lodge. *Men for Their Age: The Hemingway and Merriman Administrations* (New York, 1971). Also see James Green. *Frustrated Prometheus: The Role of Intellectials in the C.N.A. in the Twentieth Century* (London, 1969). 13. Ezra Gallivan. *At the End of the Day* (New York, 1912), p. 143.

1900 to 605.6 million in 1910. In 1900 there were only 18,000 locomobiles registered in the C.N.A., and these were owned by either the very rich or experimenters. By 1910, over 769,000 locomobiles were registered in the C.N.A., and the cost of the lowest-priced model had fallen from N.A. £5,040 to N.A. £1,540.[14] Edison's first radio appeared in 1896, and at the time it was an oddity. In 1900 there were only five stations in the nation—three in New York, one in Burgoyne, and one in Michigan City. By 1910, one in every nine North American families had a radio, which in the past decade had declined in price from N.A. £200 to N.A. £10 for the least expensive model. Governor-General Burgen had delivered a message over radio in 1902, and it was heard in only six cities. On February 15–16, 1908, the entire nation stayed up to listen to the election returns, in the first Nova Scotia-to-Manitoba hookup.[15]

These were the most dramatic changes in the lives of North Americans in the first decade of the new century. But older technologies also kept pace, and made life easier for the average man. By 1910 one of every fifteen urban housing units had indoor plumbing, or five times as many as in 1900. By 1910, every population center of more than 10,000 inhabitants was within fifteen miles of a railroad, and sleeping cars were available for all who could afford them. The inexpensive generators, which Edison had marketed in the 1880's to power his lights, were replaced by central power stations in the 1890's, which were less expensive and more efficient. But the thousands of generators were not wasted; instead, they were sold to farm families, so that by 1910, only a scattering of farms in the more remote parts of the western states were without electrical power.[16]

To this should be added the new developments, some of which were known but considered exotic in 1910. Edison's airmobile, invented just before his death in 1903, was the first heavier-than-air craft to fly successfully. But it was not until National Union licensed the Edison patents to Whitney Forster in 1905 that aviation had its real beginnings. Forster, a former carriage maker who received his financing from the N.F.A., organized Forster Airmobile Ltd. in 1904, and armed with the Edison patents began to turn out small, sturdy, and at the time, safe airmobiles in 1906. Others followed soon after. Glenn Curtiss' Curtiss Aviation Ltd., Samuel Baker's North American Airmobile, and Arnold Franklin's Franklin Transportation, Ltd. all appeared in 1907–8, and each was organized with N.F.A. support. None

14. Wyatt Turner. *The Story of the North American Locomobile* (New York, 1969).
15. John Flaherty. *The Sound and the Fury: Radio in the C.N.A.* (London, 1965).
16. Dame Maria Carlyle. *Everyday Life in North America in the Early Twentieth Century* (London, 1967).

survived more than a few years, however. It was not until 1915, when the restructured Forster Aviation, Ltd. was formed and Forster produced the Falcon and at the same time managed to obtain a government mail contract, that the history of commercial aviation in North America would begin.[17]

The same initial failures greeted vitavision, although for different reasons. Edison's first vitavision demonstration took place in 1900, and two years later, National Union established the first vitavision transmitting unit in Toms River, New Jersey, N.C. But the expenses of the process, technological failures, and the success of radio, doomed the experiment to failure. Not until the early 1920's would vitavision reappear, but when it did, it caused a minor social revolution of its own.[18]

Motion pictures were another matter. Although the public would not pay N.A. £2,000 for a vitavision receiver that showed only one program a day, it would put down a shilling for a motion picture entertainment at one of the many theatres that appeared all over the country in the century's first decade. By 1910 there were some 98,000 such theatres, while weekly attendance was almost 50 million. Thus, on the average, the North American went to a motion picture show once every two weeks.[19]

Two distinct types of firms led the way to this new kind of society that was developing in the C.N.A. The first were the old-line, pre-N.F.A. companies. The North American United, the Grand National, and the Indiana Northern continued to dominate the railroad scene, as through amalgamations and mergers they came to control almost ninety percent of the nation's rail traffic. Dawes Marine was the leading force in ocean transport, Borden Provisions, Ltd. was the nation's leading canner, North American Steel was the world's leading producer of the metal, while Peabody Chemical Works and Holt Mills set the pace in chemicals and textiles. National Union and its several subsidiaries were the dominant force in electric motors and lighting equipment, and developed many of Edison's inventions. North American Communications, formed in 1890, controlled the nation's telephone lines, while Great North American Stores was a burgeoning food chain even in 1900.

More vigorous and innovative than any of these (with the exception of National Union) were those firms financed by the National Financial Administration. Originally begun by McDowell in 1884 to assist corporations in economic difficulty due to the depression, it had

17. Carlos Snyder. *The Eagle's Wings* (New York, 1955), pp. 58–108.
18. John Flaherty. *The Little Black Box: Vitavision's Early History* (London, 1969).

19. Isaac Stephenson. *Dreams for a Shilling: The Early History of the Motion Picture* (New York, 1955).

been remade by Gallivan into an agency committed to finance new business ventures, the famous Fifth Point of his 1888 inaugural address. Julius Nelson, named N.F.A. Administrator in 1889, served in that capacity for fifteen years. At the time of his retirement in 1904, Governor-General Hemingway called him "the greatest banker of his age." While this was doubtless true, Nelson was more than that; he was in large part responsible for the great economic growth of the C.N.A. during his lifetime and after, and in his own way, was a more powerful figure than even Diego Cortez.[20]

Nelson restructured the N.F.A., established state offices, and arranged for new financings during his first two years in office.[21] Few loans were granted in this period, since the nation was still recovering from its economic downswing, and in addition, not many of those who wanted loans understood the program. The first important financing began in 1891; among the new firms supported that year were Kenton Ltd. (dry goods), Indiana Milling, Ltd. (flour), and Parkins, Ltd. (construction). Others followed, and their requests were handled with a skill rare in government agencies. Major credit for this rested with Nelson. To be sure, he had failures, but at the time of his retirement in 1904, thirty-nine of the leading one hundred C.N.A. corporations had originated with National Financial Administration loans.

The N.F.A. also proved a financial boon to the government. Nelson's total capitalization in 1889 had been N.A. £50 million. At the time of his retirement, the Agency had N.A. £175.8 million in cash, N.A. £203.4 million in secured bonds, and common stock valued at N.A. £259.9 million, against N.A. £265.7 million in liabilities.[22]

Much of Nelson's success could be attributed to easy money policies and a rapidly rising securities market, which went from 93.4 on the SEB Index on March 5, 1889 to 325.6 on the day Nelson retired from office. The vigor and intelligence of the men he backed were certainly an important factor in the N.F.A.'s growth. Nelson himself attributed his record to "sound, conservative procedures in evaluating and making finance arrangements."[23] His critics, however, charged it was just this conservatism that enabled Nelson to maintain his record

20. Nelson. *Financing a Nation*; Rupert Price, *Julius Nelson of the N.F.A.* (New York, 1967); Case Springer. *The Remembered Man: Nelson in Action* (New York, 1965).
21. On assuming office, Nelson floated a N.A. £46 million bond issue, managed by Henry Clews in New York and J. P. Morgan in London. The flotation established Morgan as the leading banker in the English-speaking world, a position he held for almost a quarter of a century. Nelson. *Financing a Nation*, p. 144. National Financial Administration. *Annual Report, 1904* (New York, 1905), pp. 13–15.
22. National Financial Administration, *Annual Report*, 1905 (New York, 1906), pp. 15–16.
23. Nelson. *Financing a Nation*, p. vii.

## The National Financial Administration, 1889-1904

| YEAR | FINANCINGS | AVERAGE FINANCING | FAILURE RATE | CURRENT ASSETS* (IN MILLIONS | CURRENT LIABILITIES N.A. POUNDS) |
|------|-----------|-------------------|--------------|------------------------------|----------------------------------|
| 1889 | 21  | N.A. £1430 | 12.0% | 50.0  | 46.5  |
| 1890 | 34  | 1355 | 15.0 | 52.3  | 47.1  |
| 1891 | 97  | 1659 | 14.2 | 65.3  | 55.2  |
| 1892 | 155 | 2034 | 14.0 | 87.4  | 65.7  |
| 1893 | 176 | 2134 | 13.8 | 109.3 | 75.4  |
| 1894 | 201 | 2364 | 13.8 | 143.4 | 99.8  |
| 1895 | 222 | 2298 | 13.8 | 178.9 | 106.9 |
| 1896 | 256 | 2306 | 13.6 | 204.4 | 130.6 |
| 1897 | 280 | 2443 | 13.4 | 301.5 | 150.8 |
| 1898 | 305 | 2697 | 13.4 | 443.7 | 196.8 |
| 1899 | 314 | 2662 | 13.3 | 487.5 | 213.4 |
| 1900 | 330 | 2587 | 13.3 | 509.2 | 225.6 |
| 1901 | 341 | 2599 | 13.5 | 515.2 | 230.5 |
| 1902 | 340 | 2605 | 13.5 | 550.6 | 240.6 |
| 1903 | 337 | 2546 | 13.7 | 598.7 | 256.4 |
| 1904 | 355 | 2650 | 13.6 | 642.8 | 287.5 |

* Includes secured bonds and common stocks, valued at New York Stock and Exchange Board and Curb quotations of December 30 of year indicated.
Source: Nelson. *Financing a Nation*, p. 605.

while—in the words of one writer—"subverting the intent of the N.F.A."[24]

The N.F.A. had been established to enable ambitious, talented workers to become entrepreneurs. In Gallivan's words, ". . . New means will be found for the people [to] share more fully in the profits their work makes possible." While this statement was subjected to many interpretations, there was no doubt Gallivan meant the government would help workers help themselves. Under Nelson's direction, however, the N.F.A. had financed only those individuals who showed an excellent chance of success, ignoring the others. Andrew de Molay, head of the New York Bankers Association, charged Nelson with "stealing business from commercial banks, and not serving the purposes for which he has been named to office. Almost every N.F.A. financing could have been handled by a member bank of this Association, but the borrowers went to Nelson instead, since by law his rates can be lower than ours. This is not creating new business; it is taking money from one pocket and putting it in the other." Samuel Frier of

24. Marshall Perkins. *Behind the Mask: The Life and Works of Julius Nelson* (New York, 1920), p. 4.

the Textile Union argued that Nelson's own statistics indicated the extent of his failure. "The N.F.A. was not supposed to be a money-making operation, but a service to the people. A commercial bank might be pleased to show a failure rate of 13.3. To us it indicates that Mr. Nelson has not been taking the kind of risks he should. In 1899 the N.F.A. granted 314 loans and financings, nine more than the previous year. Mr. Nelson does not tell us that the N.F.A. processed 2,539 applications and culled the 314 from that amount. What of the other 2,225 men who failed Mr. Nelson's test? These are the people the Governor-General told us were to be helped, and these are the men the N.F.A. ignores." Columnist Milton Fields charged the "N.F.A. should be making 30,000 loans and financings a year, and not 300." And so it went.[25]

Nelson had sufficient stature and support to ignore such charges, but he was *sui generis*, and his successor would have greater difficulty with the critics on both sides of the argument. In order to ease the pressures, Hemingway ordered a re-study of the N.F.A., and under his direction, the charter was amended. Now there would be three administrators, each named for a six-year term, with one being up for reappointment every two years. The three men, who took office on August 6, 1904, were Hugh Neill, Edward White, and Maxwell Boatner. Neill and White were bankers, while Boatner was a former Governor of Indiana.[26] Together these men continued the work of Nelson, making only a few changes in the next ten years. Throughout this period they were subjected to great pressures, difficult to withstand, from banks, workers' organizations, and politicians. Despite this, the N.F.A. remained essentially conservative, and because of it, the Association became a political issue by the end of the 1920's.[27]

The economic progress of the C.N.A. was more than matched by the growth of the Mexican economy in this period. With the establishment of a popular and stable government, the end to costly wars, and a strong market for Mexican products, the U.S.M. prospered in the first decade of the century. The advance was sparked by petroleum exports (in 1910 the U.S.M. produced seventy-four percent of the world's petroleum), gold, cotton, and to a declining extent, food. But iron deposits in New Granada and Alaska, Alaskan coal, Mexico del Norte's copper, and other raw materials from other states and dependencies were developed rapidly and profitably. The gross national product almost doubled in this period, a feat unmatched by any other country

25. *Ibid*, pp. 143, 156, 189, 203.
26. John Friendly. *A History of the National Financial Administration* (New York, 1967), pp. 346–387.

27. James Harper. *The Mexican Miracle: The Economy Under Flores and Parsons* (Mexico City, 1955), pp. 109–23.

in the world. At the same time foreign trade boomed, due in large part to petroleum exports and the importation of machinery from the Germanic Confederation. President Flores could well boast that "ours is the most dynamic country in the history of mankind," and be forgiven the hyperbole.[28]

### Selected U.S.M. Statistics, 1900–1910

| YEAR | POPULATION** (MILLIONS) | GNP | EXPORTS (MILLIONS OF DOLARES) | IMPORTS | PETROLEUM (THOUSANDS OF BARRELS) |
|------|------|------|------|------|------|
| 1900* | 88.9 | 5834 | 1645 | 1598 | 280870 |
| 1901 | 92.4 | 5959 | 1876 | 1787 | 320432 |
| 1902 | 95.0 | 6498 | 2032 | 2197 | 354657 |
| 1903 | 97.1 | 7043 | 2244 | 2398 | 375690 |
| 1904 | 99.3 | 7478 | 2398 | 2543 | 394537 |
| 1905 | 101.3 | 8034 | 2654 | 2657 | 414476 |
| 1906 | 103.4 | 8723 | 3042 | 2954 | 444392 |
| 1907 | 105.9 | 9443 | 3397 | 3587 | 485506 |
| 1908 | 108.8 | 9799 | 3685 | 4065 | 520476 |
| 1909 | 111.0 | 10323 | 4035 | 4152 | 555879 |
| 1910 | 113.4 | 11899 | 4454 | 4356 | 578047 |

\* Includes Guatamala, Hawaii, New Granada, and Alaska
\*\* Excludes slaves
Source: U.S.M. *Statistical Abstract*, pp. 110, 540, 945, 1034, 1576.

Like the C.N.A., Mexican industrialization meant that a portion of the population entered a consumer economy in the first decade of the new century. There were motion picture theatres in Jefferson and Durango just as there were in Indiana and the Northern Confederation. Radios were in use in the U.S.M. by 1910, but at that time, only the wealthy could afford receivers. Similarly, the U.S.M. had locomobiles. The first were imported from North America, but by 1906 Jefferson Motors was producing its own models, with a radically different power system than that in use in the C.N.A.[29] Almost all of

---

28. Mexico City *Times*, November 16, 1909. What Flores did not say, however, was that this prosperity was unevenly divided. The average wage in California and Jefferson was still three times that in Chiapas, where people still starved to death in the streets as late as 1908. Oswald Marcusson. *The Shame of Mexico* (London, 1935).
29. The C.N.A. locomobiles were powered by a conventional steam engine.

Since Mexico was so rich in petroleum, the nation could afford a more sophisticated model that used a greater amount of the fuel. The vulcazine engine, which ignited a mixture of vulcazine and air internally, was introduced by Jefferson Motors in 1905, and was adopted throughout the U.S.M. President William James of Jefferson Motors predicted his car would soon overcome the "iron horses" of the C.N.A. in

Jefferson and California had electricity by 1906, but generating plants made their appearances later in the other states.[30] Given these and other comparatively minor differences, it was far easier for a middle-class citizen of Michigan City to adjust to life in Jefferson City in 1910 than it would have been only a generation earlier.

This development and great growth was spearheaded by the Kramer Associates. After having assured himself the nation was in safe hands, Cortez planned for his retirement, which was accomplished in 1904, when he reached the age of sixty-seven. His successor at Kramer Associates was Douglas Benedict, the grandson of Monte, who Cortez had been grooming for the position since 1899. Like the other Benedicts, Douglas was withdrawn, a good manager, and a person who avoided the limelight. In a rare interview on assuming the presidency, Benedict said simply, "I will do my best." Within a year he had decentralized operations, creating twenty operating units, each with its own vice-president who had a great deal of power in day-to-day transactions. Kramer Associates owned Jefferson Motors, the Carminales Lighting Company, and other new firms that sprang up in this period. Of the $20.4 billion of the Mexican G.N.P. in 1910, Kramer Associates accounted for $10.9 billion. In addition, the company controlled the economies of Free Russia and Cuba, and had important interests elsewhere in the world. There is no way of knowing exactly how powerful the company was at the time, or even its sales total (if all operations are included). The most learned estimate is that, in 1910, Kramer Associates' worldwide sales reached $16.1 billion, which, if true, would make it four times as large as the next biggest firm in the world.[29]

---

world sales. Through aggressive salesmanship, the Jeffersons did sell well on the world market, forcing improvements in the C.N.A. locomobiles, and the eventual formation of a single company, North American Motors, in 1921. James' prediction came true, but later than he thought. The vulcazine locomobiles would not pass the steam cars in world sales until 1929. Wyatt Turner. *The Rise of the Vulcazine Engine* (New York, 1966).

30. The tardy introduction of electricity in the U.S.M. was not due to backwardness, but rather the cheapness of domestically-produced natural gas. In 1895 Vincenzo Carminales invented the Carminales mantle lamp, which burned natural gas and gave off a better light than the Edison bulbs, and at less than half the cost. Not until 1946, did the number of Carminales

lamps fall below the electric lights in use in the U.S.M., and even today they are the rule in Chiapas and Durango. John Flaherty. *The Carminales' Legacy: Mexico's Edison* (London, 1971).

29. Stanley Tulin. *The Kramer Associates: The Benedict Years* (London, 1971), pp. 67–156. It is worthy of note that four of the new vice presidents were Mexicanos, a continuation of Cortez' plan to incorporate the Mexicanos into the economic life of the U.S.M. Between 1904 and 1909, Cortez donated $9 million for college scholarships for Mexicanos in Chiapas and Durango. The Cortez Fund, formed after his death in 1909, was capitalized at $200 million, all in Kramer Associates stock, and the dividends were used for these scholarships, and are being so used to this day.

Thus, the C.N.A. and the U.S.M. found different ways of exploiting the new technologies that appeared early in the twentieth century. Each had its advantages and disadvantages, but at the time it seemed that, as before, the U.S.M. was more efficient in its organization, while the C.N.A. offered more freedom to its citizens.[30]

---

30. Thomas Boyd, *The Difference Is Freedom: A Comparison of the C.N.A. and the U.S.M.* (London, 1954).

# 25

# THE MORAL IMPERATIVE

"THE Moral Imperative provided the rationale for modern imperialism, just as Protestantism offered heavenly justification for seventeenth century capitalism." In this way, Neiderhofferian historian Martin Van Beeck stated that the drive to open Asia and Africa to the West would have occurred even had not that great intellectual movement taken place. "There is something in Western man that requires him to have a mandate from God whenever he wants to enrich himself materially. If he wants it enough, the mandate will always come, in one way or another."[1]

Doubtless Van Beeck oversimplifies, and there are other historians who differ strongly on this point.[2] Be that as it may, there is no doubt that the Europeans who plundered Africa and Asia in this period spoke of the need to "enlighten" those whose lands they conquered, just as the *conquistadores* had claimed in their period. The U.S.M. viewed its conquests of Guatamala and New Granada in this light. "The people there have had their chances for greatness, and have failed due to a lack of the divine spark. Mexico possesses such inspiration, and therefore will carry Civilization southward." Thus wrote one of El Jefe's strongest supporters.[3] "They will give us sugar, and we will give them Civilization. It is a fair trade." In this way, Hermión justified the taking of Hawaii.[4] Later on, he would say of the Russian expedition, "Under the Siberians the land lay fallow. We will make it bloom. All will benefit thereby. It is God's will as well as our own."[5]

In so commenting, El Jefe echoed similar statements being made in other parts of the world by the rulers of France, the Germanic Confederation, Britain, the Netherlands, and Italy; each had his own version of the Moral Imperative, and each tried to turn a profit

1. Martin Van Beeck. *A World Gone Mad and Its Cure* (The Hague, 1945), p. 45.
2. For a summary of the argument, see Benjamin Neely. ed. *The Moral Imperative* (New York, 1970). Also, Nunn,

*The Moral Imperative*, pp. 2–15.
3. Harry Doxey in the *Jefferson Courier*, May 5, 1896.
4. Durfree. *Hawaii*, p. 332.
5. St. John. *The Cutting Edge of Civilization*, p. 111.

thereby. Only in the C.N.A. were the followers of the Moral Imperative frustrated, and this frustration provided the fuel for Starkism and the violence that it evoked.[6]

The Moral Imperative served to unite a formerly divided France. Paris was the scene of a *coup* in 1909—the fifth in twenty-five years—and after the dust settled, Marshal Henri Fanchon became the head of a provisional government. Fanchon was a devoted expansionist, a clever propagandist, and a man of considerable personal magnetism. Speaking of Joan of Arc, glory, and duty, Fanchon noted that much of Africa and Asia had been taken by the British and Germans. "France has a mission," he said. "We cannot fail our blood and our history."[7]

Under Fanchon's leadership France became a unified nation once more; for the first time since the Bloody Eighties, the nation had a strong government able to control all parts of the nation. Within two years the French economy had fully recovered. In 1911 Fanchon promulgated a new constitution, elections were held, and he was selected President of the Republic. France's republican forms satisfied the reformers; Fanchon himself appealed to the monarchists. "France is now at peace," said British Prime Minister Stanley Martin. "The republicans have their republic, and the royalists their king."[8] In 1912, however, Fanchon acted to destroy the balance of power that had existed in Europe since the Bloody Eighties, and Martin no longer made such glib statements about him or about France.

At the time the world's major powers were interconnected by alliances that were confusing, and often outdated. For example, Britain was leader of the United Commonwealth, had close relations with the C.N.A. (but no formal treaty), had signed a nonaggression pact with the Germanic Confederation in 1883 that was still in force and which was directed against revolutionary France, and one with Japan in 1901 to prevent further Mexican advances in Asia. The Germanic Confederation had treaties with the Ottoman Empire, Poland, and minor Baltic principalities, all directed against the Russian successor nations, a treaty with Mexico, and an "understanding" with Italy. France was allied with the Ukrainian Republic, Serbia, Greece, and the Argentine, in addition to cultivating China. The U.S.M. had treaties with Free Russia, the Brazilian Empire, and the Germanic Confederation. The C.N.A. was the only major power without such treaty commitments,

6. According to Van Beeck, "Gallivan was as much an imperialist as any European leader. But his was the imperialism of the market, rather than that of the sword. The North American flag did not fly over Africa, but North American merchants had their part in dismembering the continent economically." This view is partisan, however, and does not satisfactorily explain the Gallivan programs. Van Beeck. *A World Gone Mad*, p. 187.

7. Claude Elizy. *Fanchon and the Rebirth of France* (London, 1966), p. 98.

8. London *Times*, September 21, 1911.

but was considered "friendly" to Britain as well as being tied to the United Commonwealth by the Crown. Given these relationships and obligations, troubles might easily erupt. No nation was quite certain what the others would do if it acted in one way or another; no nation could tell whether one or another movement would, or would not, result in a war that could involve most of the world.[9]

Marshal Fanchon understood this, and was prepared to test the system at its weakest points. Fanchon judged rightly that the revolutionary spirit of the Bloody Eighties had not died, but rather had been frustrated and suppressed, and that, given the proper stimulation, might be restored—to France's benefit. Fanchon had a sophisticated understanding of the implications of the Moral Imperative, and meant to use ideology to advance his nation's destiny. He understood perfectly the spirit that had led to world disarmament in the early twentieth century—a sense of security engendered by the alliances; the hope that man was too intelligent to fight modern wars with their potential for destruction and revolution; the strong desire of people everywhere to benefit from the new peacetime technologies. Fanchon was convinced that a strong France, with a modern armed force, prepared to probe at will world trouble spots, might succeed in conquering the globe. Not since the days of El Jefe had the leader of a major power had such dreams, and given the history of France and Fanchon's almost mystical belief in her destiny, such fruits seemed obtainable.

Fanchon's first efforts were tentative and exploratory. He let it be known that he believed France to be the aggregate of all Frenchmen, united by bonds of history—and wherever a Frenchman resided, "there is a portion of our home." Thus, he sent fraternal greetings to the Quebec government, the Santos colony in Brazil, and the United Townships of Ghana, letting each in turn know "Your Mother remembers."[10]

His attempts in this direction produced mixed results. Fanchon was rebuffed by Quebec, now that that land had entered into a more satisfactory relationship to the C.N.A.; was invited to visit Santos (but did not go after the Emperor refused to admit him to the country); and was asked for economic assistance by the United Townships of Ghana. Fanchon's "grand survey of 1912" did serve to alert other nations to his plans, and as the Marshal had hoped, made France the center of world attention.[11]

Fanchon's objectives were laid bare the following year. He reopened discussions with Mexico regarding properties seized in the

---

9. Clifford Jones. *At the Watershed: The World in 1916* (London, 1966).
10. Jones. *At the Watershed*, p. 227.

11. Maxwell Horan. *The Paper Marshal: The Life of Henri Fanchon* (New York, 1944).

aftermath of the French Revolution. "Ever since taking power in 1909, Fanchon concentrated on fighting a war and obtaining the tools with which to win that war. By 1913 he had the weapons in hand. The New French Army was strong and well-equipped. The French Navy was on guard."[12]

Marshal Fanchon then laid the groundwork for his much-desired war. Should Mexico refuse to make restitution, Fanchon was prepared to call upon the Franco-Mexican residents of Tampico to remember their homeland, sponsor a Moralista revival, call for an end to slavery—in short, support all elements in Mexico that might help his cause, and there were some who appeared ready to listen in 1913.[13]

Fanchon believed the Mexican-German Treaty of 1886 to be a dead letter. Thus, he assumed Berlin would not assist Mexico if French ships seized Tampico. Fanchon also concluded the C.N.A. would either remain neutral or sympathize with France in such a conflict. "Burgoyne will be with us in spirit as we enter Mexico City," he said.[14]

In this way, Fanchon hoped to isolate Mexico, attack the nation while it was still in a state of relative disarmament, and win a great victory to hearten his people and raise France to the position of first-rate power. A war with the Germanic Confederation might end with France dominating Europe; conquest of the U.S.M. would make France the major reformist power in the world, and could conceivably result in a French "mission" in South America and, ultimately, a Pacific destiny.

Fanchon's plans were based on several colossal miscalculations. The United Empire and the C.N.A. would hardly stand by and allow France to so upset the world's balance of power. The Marshal hadn't taken into consideration the role to be played by Kramer Associates; Benedict would certainly throw his firm's considerable power behind Mexico City. Fanchon's information regarding the pro-French attitude of the Franco-Mexicans was inaccurate; they would not rise to his call. As for the Moralista support for a French invasion—he did not realize the Moralistas were no longer powerful in the Sierra Madres. "Fanchon was blinded by dreams and visions. A true romantic, he still thought France capable of conquering the world. Any competent economist or person conversant with power could have told him otherwise. But Fanchon surrounded himself with poets and pseudo-historians, who heightened his already lively imagination. This poor deluded wretch was doomed to failure from the start." The Marshal had

---

12. Jones. *At the Watershed*, p. 304.    14. *Ibid*, p. 220.
13. Elizy. *Fanchon and the Rebirth of France*, p. 212.

parlayed the jerry-built treaty system and his admittedly clear percep-
tion of its weaknesses into a world reputation, "but he lacked the
actual power to turn dream to reality."[15]

The two party system had reappeared in the U.S.M. by 1914.
Flores was the head of the United Mexican Party, which was based on
an alliance between businessmen in California and Jefferson, and peasants, most of whom were Chiapan and Durangan Mexicanos. The
U.M.P. had direct antecedents in the Continentalists. The major difference between the two was the mild isolationism of the United Mexicans, contrasted to the Continentalist expansionism, and its increased
interest in social welfare, especially in the south. Libertarian critics
often remarked that the U.M. leaders wanted to preserve their own
areas for the wealthy, while having the middle class pay the bill for the
rehabilitation of the poor. Whether for idealistic or political reasons,
the United Mexican Party tended to support state intervention in favor
of the poor, and encouraged the emergence of Mexicano leaders in the
states.[16]

The Liberty Party was more isolationist than the United Mexicans, claiming Kramer Associates was behind Flores, trading support
for contracts, and had backed Hermión in order to enrich itself. The
Libertarians included many small businessmen—individuals who lived
off the scraps left by Kramer Associates—as well as professionals, intellectuals, and independent farmers. The Party favored the abolition of
slavery, government encouragement of private enterprise, and a high
tariff to protect infant industries.[17] In 1914, the Libertarians charged
that Douglas Benedict was financing the United Mexicans; such was
not the case. Indeed, Kramer Associates money found its way into the
campaign chests of "friendly" politicians of both parties that year.[18]

The Libertarians had little hope of victory in 1914. Flores had
been a popular President, the nation was prosperous, and the party
lacked a magnetic candidate. The convention nominated Albert Ullman, a former history professor at Kinkaid University who had been
elected to the Senate in 1908. Ullman was young, able, and intelligent,
but no match for Victoriano Consalus, his United Mexican opponent.
Secretary of State in the Flores administration, Consalus was well-
known, flamboyant, and shrewd. Like Flores, he was half-Mexicano,
and also a man dedicated to raising the living standards of the southern
poor. Consalus won an easy victory, and the Libertarians returned to
the opposition side of the Senate. Ullman noted that "not since 1857—
over a half century ago—has a Libertarian occupied the Presidential

15. Flinders. *The Road to War*, p. 259.
16. Charles Adkins. *A History of the United Mexican Party* (Mexico City, 1959).
17. Charles Adkins. *Always the Brides-maid: The Liberty Party, 1851–1960* (Mexico City, 1961), pp. 337–39.
18. Tulin. *The Benedict Years*, p. 308.

Palace. Our last successful candidate, Hector Niles, was elected when the public turned against the Rocky Mountain War. Perhaps it will take a similar tragedy to get us back in office."[19] At the time, Ullman could scarcely have realized how accurate his musings would be.

### The Mexican Elections of 1914

| STATE | CONSALUS (UM) | ULLMAN (L) |
|---|---|---|
| California | 3,954,809 | 1,839,450 |
| Jefferson | 2,767,304 | 1,695,320 |
| Durango | 1,940,205 | 934,206 |
| Chiapas | 1,545,454 | 1,004,947 |
| Arizona | 804,394 | 1,104,302 |
| Mexico del Norte | 690,304 | 943,203 |
| | 11,702,470 | 7,521,428 |

Source: U.S.M. *Statistical Abstract*, p. 113.

Even before the election, Flores consulted with Consalus and Ullman as to possible responses to the French challenge. Both agreed that Fanchon was capable of launching an attack on Mexico, but neither thought a French attack, if it came, could be successful. Consalus thought the best response would be to order partial mobilization, station elements of the Pacific Fleet in the Caribbean and outside the Kinkaid Canal, and place guards in the large French quarter in Tampico. Ullman thought a conference with Fanchon might be fruitful, and considered some of the Marshal's criticisms of the U.S.M. partially justified. Flores said little, indicating the problem would belong to one or the other of the candidates in a few days, and that he would conduct a holding operation until his successor took office. Matters stood there, until Consalus was inaugurated on February 16.[20]

In his inaugural address the new President promised "a better life for all our people," and in general limited his short speech to generalities. The only firm note came when he talked of foreign policy. "Our land has had more than its share of war. Its history has been written in blood. From the days of the *Conquistadores*, to the North American Rebellion, through the Rocky Mountain War and the bloodshed of the

---

19. Mexico City *Times*, February 18, 1914.
20. Mexico City *Times*, February 9, 1914. Somehow the story of this meeting leaked to the newspapers. Ullman was made to appear weak in the report, and this may have added to the large majority by which Consalus won. Since Ullman made no attempt to deny the story, we may assume it was accurate.

Hermión dictatorship, we have suffered. We want no war, and so we prepare for combat sadly, hoping it will not fall to this generation to suffer the fate of its ancestors."[21]

Despite this, Consalus did not shrink from combat; indeed, within a few days he appeared to relish the idea.[22] He rejected all attempts at mediation from the other powers. When France held naval maneuvers in Argentine waters, he sent a note to President Lopez Vargas warning him of "dire consequences should the Argentine continue its warlike alliance with France." On April 1, Mexico broke diplomatic relations with the Argentine; three days later, France recalled its ambassador to Mexico. On May 16, French troops began arriving in the Argentine, "to assist that government in repressing guerrilla activities near the capital." Fanchon told reporters that "There is evidence that the Argentine guerrillas are being supplied from Mexico. If this is true, France may have to take actions stronger than words to aid its ally."[23] On June 2, a French brigade disembarked in Martinique. As the world watched, the two nations inched closer to war.

A major riot erupted in Tampico on June 12, 1914. Government troops entered the city to stop the fighting, which ended in four days. Fanchon sent the French fleet toward the port, "to assist our country-men in their fight against tyranny." The fleet arrived in the Caribbean on June 22, and anchored just beyond the fifteen kilometer limit, as though awaiting further developments. Then, on the night of June 27, the riots erupted once again. With this, the French navy steamed toward the harbor, obviously intent on landing. Mexican coast artillery fired on the ships, sinking four and crippling another two, but ten troopships made the beaches and the French marines entered Tampico. The conflict—known as the Hundred Day War—was on.[24]

During the first month of the war it appeared France might succeed in defeating Mexico. The French marines were able to consolidate their position in Tampico, while a second force landed at the Kinkaid Canal and secured the Caribbean end. A third force steamed in the direction of Vera Cruz, but this was turned back by elements of the Mexican Navy after the Battle of Campeche Bay. By the end of the

21. Mexico City *Times*, February 17, 1914.
22. "For all its peaceful words and deeds, Mexico remains warlike in its heart. Never in modern times has a people so gladly gone to war, so willingly sacrificed its young, so joyfully tasted blood." Barrington Gray. *Mexico: The Modern Sparta* (New York, 1955), p. 1.

23. New York *Herald*, May 17, 1914.
24. After the war it was discovered that the Tampico riots had been started by French agents, as were similar demonstrations in all cities with sizable Franco-Mexican populations, in addition to the bombings at the Kinkaid Canal. Edward McGraw. *The Hundred Day War: An Analysis and History* (Melbourne, 1950), pp. 446–49.

second week, however, the Mexican and Guatamalan units at the Canal had forced the French into the nearby mountains, leaving the Tampico salient the only successful French beachhead. Additional troops landed on July 15, and under the command of General Jacques Beauchamp, began to drive in the direction of Mexico City.

The Mexican army had been prepared for the advance, but fell back steadily in the face of determined French assaults. Aged General Vincent Collins, who had fought in the Great Northern War and was sixty-nine years old in 1914, was removed from command on August 13, and replaced by General Emiliano Calles, whose previous position had been commander of the Durango district. Calles was forty years old at the time, the youngest general in the army, and its only Mexicano of that rank. Consalus selected him as Collins' replacement primarily because he was available at the capital at the time, but the appeals the French were making to the Mexicanos doubtless had some influence on the decision. Calles marched fresh regiments to the front, and met the main body of the French Expeditionary Force on the outskirts of Chapultapec. There, on August 28, 1914, Calles engaged Beauchamp in the war's only important battle.

As Beauchamp sent his cavalry to reconnoiter the enemy's flanks, a squadron of Mexican airmobiles appeared overhead, and diving on the massed French artillery, began dropping charges in clusters. Simultaneously, Mexican soldiers attacked on two sides, blowing up French machine gun emplacements while a second wave followed, throwing down coils of barbed wire as it went. The Mexicans withdrew then through openings in the wire barriers, which were closed immediately by special squads. Within two hours the French were encircled by a band of barbed wire, through which they could not escape. Beauchamp led three charges against the barrier, and on each occasion the advancing troops were slaughtered by Mexican mortars and machine guns, while the airmobiles returned to use their guns on the hapless French force. Beauchamp himself died in the third charge, amid the bodies of over 2,000 dead members of the F.E.F. At dawn the next day General Pierre Bordagary surrendered unconditionally, thus ending the drive to Mexico City. "Within thirty-eight hours France lost the war, Calles made his reputation, and warfare was revolutionized."[25]

The French garrison in Tampico was now besieged, and although the defenders managed to hold on until September 29, they were doomed men and knew it, since the Mexican Navy had sealed the port from future landings. Finally, on October 3, Fanchon sued for peace.

---

25. Field Marshal Sir Wesley Gabor. *Emiliano Calles and the Art of War* (London, 1955); Emiliano Calles. *Wars to Come* (Mexico City, 1918).

An armistice was declared on October 10, 1914; the Hundred Day War was over.[26]

Had it ended there, the war would have been considered a brief episode of relatively little consequence, no more or less important than the three German interventions in the Argentine in the late nineteenth century, or the many small wars in Asia and Africa in this period. This was not to be, for the French brought revolution as well as soldiers on their ships.

Only Mexico, of all the western nations, maintained slavery in 1914.[27] Over the years, many slaves had escaped into Southern Vandalia, most of them crossing from Jefferson, while a few brave souls arrived by small boat from Durango and Chiapas. In addition, more than 50,000 former slaves took refuge in Cuba and the Antilles, where they usually found employment as fishermen. The Mexicans made little attempt to prevent them leaving, since slaves were considered "marginal economic goods" in the late nineteenth century. Only in Chiapas did slavery flourish, and even there, the institution was limited to coastal areas.

Despite this tacit encouragement of migration, there were some 100,000 Negro slaves in the U.S.M. in 1914. Over half were house servants, another quarter worked in factories, the oil fields, or the ports, while the rest were on plantations as field hands.[28] The last slave insurrection had taken place in Chiapas in 1885, and at the time of the Hundred Day War, it appeared they were content with their lot.

Such was not the case. Although treated well compared to their ancestors, many slaves resented their station. Their desire to be free was fueled by the example of Southern Vandalia, the reforms and promises that followed the Hermión era, the rising standard of living in the U.S.M., and the growth in literacy that accompanied industrialization. The spark came with the French invasion. Wherever the French soldiers went in Durango, they freed the slaves. According to contemporary observers, about half the freed slaves refused to leave their posts, but others did. Before the war was over, approximately 8,000 slaves were fighting side by side with the French.[29]

The French refused to take their Negro allies with them when the last ships left on September 17, leaving them to shift for themselves.

26. As a result of the Treaty of Caracas, the U.S.M. was granted an indemnity of $200 million, with an additional $200 million set aside to pay claims of Mexican nationals. In addition, France ceded Mexico the islands of Martinique and St. Thomas in the Caribbean. Phillip Daley. *The Hundred Day War* (New York, 1966), pp. 504–5.

27. Slavery persisted in Arabia, central Africa, and parts of east Africa in 1914, and an attempt was being made in Australia to impose a form of slavery on the natives there. Jenkins. *The Last to Go*, p. 400.

28. U.S.M. *Statistical Abstract*, p. 504.

29. Daley. *The Hundred Day War*, p. 353.

Consalus ordered them seized, put into jails, and held for treason trials. Ullman protested; their actions were understandable under the circumstances, he argued, and that this would be a good opportunity to free all slaves. He also observed that slaves could not be tried for treason, for only citizens could commit such an act, and slaves were not considered citizens under Mexican law. The question of the deserting slaves provided Mexico with its first important political issue since the Hermión era, and gave the Liberty Party a major political issue to take to the people in future elections.[30]

The forthcoming trials also had their impact abroad. Britain, the Germanic Confederation, and Italy protested the actions, and others followed. The Pope sent a special plea to Consalus asking for clemency. But the greatest reaction came in the C.N.A.[31]

In 1914, the Governor of Southern Vandalia was Howard Washburne, an able and intelligent Negro whom many thought would soon make an attempt for the governorship-general. Few gave him any chance of success in such a drive, but the fact that the ruling People's Coalition even considered him seriously, indicated both his attractiveness and the racial harmony prevailing in the C.N.A. in the early twentieth century. It would have been prudent for Washburne to have said nothing of the trials; to raise the issue would certainly harm him politically in the other confederations. But early in 1915 Washburne spoke out, demanding the captured slaves be released. Then he went further; on February 10, the Governor called for an end to slavery in the U.S.M. "Our brothers are in chains, and their cries never leave our ears. We can no longer tolerate it. Either Mexico will end slavery, or we will do it for her."[32]

Of course, Washburne's statements had no binding effect on the national administration, and four days later Governor-General Merriman apologized to Consalus. But the damage had been done. Southern Vandalia rallied behind Washburne, and he had sympathizers in other confederations as well, especially the N.C. and Manitoba. Within a week a national organization had been formed, Friends of Black Mexico, which at its height numbered almost a million members outside Southern Vandalia and at least three million in that Negro confederation. Thirty-four of the one hundred and fifty councilmen signed a petition supporting the Washburne statement; Washburne himself resigned as Governor to devote all his efforts to the F.B.M.[33]

30. Harold Walker. *The Boil: Free Slaves in the Hundred Day War* (New York, 1955), p. 116.
31. Clyde Herman. *The Gathering Storm: The End of U.S.M. Slavery* (New York, 1967), pp. 176–89.

32. Harold Walker. *Black Lloyd: The Life of Howard Washburne* (New York, 1970).
33. *Ibid*, p. 337.

As the Friends of Black Mexico held rallies, diplomats in Burgoyne and Mexico City worked hard to keep the peace between their two countries. Both Merriman and Consalus remained calm in the face of provocations. Merriman ignored Washburne and skillfully parried the thrusts of those Council Liberals who in 1914 had embraced the Washburne position, and who talked of nominating the former Governor as their candidate in 1918. By late 1915, the tumult had died down somewhat. The closed-door trials of the Mexican slaves were almost completed, and the judges in Chapultapec were prepared to hand down their verdicts on January 5, 1916. Washburne planned a day of mourning on that date, and demonstrations were planned in Paris, London, Berlin, and Rome. These would not take place. Instead, on January 5, the world seemed prepared for a new war, one that would result from what already was called "The Chapultapec Incident."

# 26

# A TIME OF DIFFUSION

THE Mexico Tribunal presided over the treason trials of the rebel slaves in late 1915, and on December 20, Judge Homer Mattfield announced a final verdict would be handed down on January 5, 1916.

Crowds began to gather in Chapultapec on December 30. Many were there for the New Year celebration, but many more came to hold a "silent vigil" in support of the prisoners. The two elements clashed, and the police called upon the capital to send reinforcements to defend the city. The extra troops were sent back to Mexico City on January 3, as all seemed quiet once again. But the Chapultapec police and a select unit of the Guard remained close to the Federal Prison, in case of future disturbances.

Just before dawn on January 4, fires broke out in the ghetto area of Chapultapec, and riots followed. Police rushed to the area to quell the disturbance, but no sooner had they arrived than a force of more than 2,000 young people rushed the Federal Prison, overpowered the exterior guard, and began to batter down the doors. The guard inside fired on the mob, but some got through. Once inside, they freed the prisoners, who then joined with the attackers in subduing the remaining guards. Some 4,000 individuals were wounded in the Chapultapec Incident; 188 guards were killed, as were 549 of the attackers and 429 slave prisoners.[1]

Army elements were rushed to the city, followed by an investigating team. On January 5, the investigators reported that some of the interior guards had cooperated with the attackers, and that at least two hundred of the dead "Mexican students" were citizens of the C.N.A.[2] The Mexican Army was ordered on the alert, the Navy was ordered out of ports, and Anglo and Hispano districts began to arm against a feared slave rebellion and possible attack from the C.N.A.

President Consalus and Governor-General Merriman were in al-

---

1. New York *Herald*, January 5, 1916; Herman. *The Gathering Storm*, pp. 214–35.

2. Harold Walker. *The Chapultapec Affair: Doorway to Today* (New York, 1958), p. 59.

most immediate contact as soon as the investigators' report was released. Both knew wars had started with less provocation; neither man
wanted a conflict. According to an agreement arrived at after a series
of telephone conversations on January 5–6, Merriman announced that
those C.N.A. citizens who had participated in the Chapultapec Affair
had done so "without the knowledge of this government and certainly
without its sanction. Measures will be taken at once to ensure that
further incidents involving C.N.A. citizens in Chapultapec and other
parts of the United States of Mexico will be prevented." The words
were carefully selected so as to be firm, yet vague. Within the next
two weeks, the passports of 10,970 North Americans then in Mexico
were revoked, and their holders told by Mexico City to leave the
country within three days. Eventually 232 of them were seized by the
C.B.I. and charged with "actions injurious to the nation." Of this number, 154 were directly or indirectly involved in the Chapultapec Incident, and sentenced to jail terms. Relations between Burgoyne and
Mexico City returned to normal; the feared war did not take place.[3]
But a residue remained that was even more corrosive than war. The
Chapultapec Incident had set off a chain reaction of protest in the
C.N.A., while in Mexico the freed slaves caused consternation in a land
still bedeviled with social and political problems.

The most obvious reactions came in North America, where Merriman's announcement, expected though it was, resulted in protest rallies throughout the nation, many organized and led by Friends of Black
Mexico. Washburne himself spoke at the Burgoyne rally, pledging
himself to the "unceasing effort to bring freedom to our brothers in
Mexico, to free not only the Negro, but the Mexicano and Indian as
well." Washburne announced a boycott of all Kramer Associates'
products then being sold in the C.N.A., and twenty-four-hour vigils
outside U.S.M. consulates. "We shall not rest until we reach the conscience of the Mexicans, and when we do, slavery and other evils of
that benighted land will come to an end."[4]

In themselves, the vigils and boycott accomplished little; Benedict
wasn't impressed by the slight falloff in sales, and was even amused that
the Kramer Associates, which had led the movement for equality in
the U.S.M., had been singled out for attack. The vigils were also harm-
less, and proved a tactical mistake, since they were not well-attended.
But there was violence in New York, Boston, Philadelphia, Newport,
and other cities along the eastern seaboard, as anti-F.B.M. forces
clashed with the demonstrators. Other fights erupted in Indiana, the

---

3. The swiftness of the action was a
further indication of the power of the
C.B.I., which by 1916 had dossiers on
more than 100,000 suspected C.N.A.
radicals. Will Scott. *The Power Behind
the Throne: A History of the C.B.I.*
(New York, 1960), pp. 443–56.
4. Burgoyne *Herald*, February 19, 1916.

Southern Confederation, and Northern Vandalia, which in themselves were minor, but indicated a serious fissure in C.N.A. society at the time.

For a half century the C.N.A. had prided itself on its race relations. Southern Vandalia, now almost completely Negro, was a prosperous part of the nation, its citizens free to travel in the other states, its agricultural and political leaders honored throughout the nation. Despite this, the C.N.A. was a nation divided against itself racially. When poor Negroes moved to Indiana and Northern Confederation cities in search of industrial jobs, they were shunted into ghettoes and discriminated against by businessmen and government alike. No Negro outside of Southern Vandalia held an important political post; there were no Negro directors of the hundred leading C.N.A. industrial and financial corporations; a survey of N.F.A. loans showed that few Negroes had been granted assistance by that powerful agency. As one writer put it, "North America resolved its racial problems by denying contact between the races. If the Wilkins area of Michigan City was the Negro section of that industrial complex, then Southern Vandalia was the Negro section of the nation."[5] Another wryly observed that "White North Americans care little how powerful Negroes become, so long as that power does not touch them."[6] "We do not have a raceless society," said another, "but two societies, each without knowledge of the other. White North Americans have less contact with Negro North Americans than they do with the Chinese."[7]

The 1916 demonstrations changed all this, and exposed the raw nerve of race in North America. So long as the F.B.M. was exclusively concerned with Mexican slavery, the movement was tolerated and even encouraged. In 1920 the movement changed gears, however, and at that point the public response changed.

The Friends of Black Mexico had been organized as a protest against slavery. When Mexico seemed on the verge of ending the institution in the spring of 1920, Washburne decided to retain its form, but change its appearance, program, and constituency. Now he would attempt to end racism in the C.N.A. itself, and speak out on a variety of other problems which troubled the nation. On April 14, 1920, the F.B.M. held a mass meeting to celebrate "the crossing of the River Jordan in Mexico." On this occasion, Washburne announced "the beginning of a new crusade, one to remake the face of our own land. Like the ending of slavery in Mexico, this too has been long overdue." That night Washburne declared "the F.B.M. is dead, felled by its own

5. Wilton Harmaker. *The Genesis of Twentieth Century North America* (Burgoyne, 1970), p. 4.
6. Montgomery Farmer. *Making A New World* (New York, 1966), p. 87.
7. James Chester. *Washburne of the C.N.A.* (London, 1928), pp. 110-11.

success. Now the fight for democracy will be spearheaded by a new organization, the League for Brotherhood, which will welcome support from all men of good will, whatever their race or stations in life." He concluded by saying the fight for manumission in Mexico had lasted four years. "This new struggle will take more than four times four years. We may not see its end, just as Moses did not enter the promised land. But the path is open. The way is clear. We shall prevail."[8]

At first the League for Brotherhood had the same constituency and leadership as the Friends of Black Mexico, although Washburne strove to broaden both. He dreamed of a nationwide organization that would, through capitalist and republican paths, obtain a greater share of jobs and power for Negroes than had previously been the case. He soon found the new organization attracted other reformers and radicals, who hoped to use it as a vehicle for their own programs. These were men and women who had rejected capitalism and republicanism, who found even the old radicals such as the Neiderhofferians irrelevant. To them Washburne himself was an antique, and they scoffed at his call for greater power for Negroes in institutions they considered evil. This new group of radicals and reformers rejected urbanization and industrialization, what they called "the suffocation of the cities and the horrors of the factory," and issued a call to return to "a more natural way of life." The movement—if we can call it that—had no leaders; to strive for leadership would be "to accept the rationale of the capitalists, who cannot thrive without regimentation. Each of us is a free man; he needs no dictator." But through sheer weight of numbers they were able to take control of the League for Brotherhood late in 1920. The League, which began with a membership of one million whites and two million Negroes in the spring of 1920, had seven million members by mid-1921. Most of them were dissatisfied middle-class whites and intellectuals, who, while sympathizing with the Washburne group, thought it unsuited by temperament and values for a leadership role.

Burgoyne's political leaders did not know what to make of this great reformist wave. Governor-General Merriman, who retired to the Grand Council in 1918 after what most commentators thought had been a successful ten year term, had hand-picked his successor, Councilman Calvin Wagner of Indiana, who had no trouble defeating Liberal Governor Chester Phipps of the Southern Confederation in the

---

8. Burgoyne *Times*, April 15, 1920; Farmer. *Making A New World*, p. 294; Chester. *Washburne of the C.N.A.*, pp. 465–69. Washburne left the movement in 1923, by which time he had been relegated to a minor post in the League. He died in 1929, an almost forgotten man. His last words were, "I have been trampled to death by history." Burgoyne *Herald*, August 29, 1929.

election. Like Merriman and Hemingway, Wagner was an amiable politician, friendly to all and one who liked the title of "judge," which referred to earlier duty on the Indiana courts.[9]

Wagner became leader of a nation that was prosperous, at peace with its neighbor and the rest of the world, with nothing but further advances in sight. In 1918 the population of the C.N.A. was 131.8 million, its gross national product N.A. £985 billion, and its industry and inventiveness the envy of the world. The great reform programs of the McDowell and Gallivan eras had borne rich fruits; the blueprint for future development appeared set. When Phipps argued that the election of a Coalition Council would mean "more of the same," Wagner agreed. "If by more of the same, Governor Phipps means still greater prosperity and continued peace and tranquillity, then I plead guilty to that desire."[10]

What neither Phipps nor Wagner realized was that prosperity, like depression, brings problems. Wagner once said, "This is a business century, and we are a business country." By this he meant that in an age of industrialization, North America would prosper mightily. What he did not understand was that many North Americans were coming to reject the values of that business civilization. The dilemma was ably summed up by historian Fritz Webern in 1933.

> North America was the first nation to understand the full implications of the modern industrial revolution, the most blessed by natural resources, population, and stable government so as to benefit from it, and the most brilliant example of the potential for prosperity that movement implied. Under the Age of Renewal, revolutionary forces were subdued with the creation of a strong government encouraging initiative and controlling the forces of big business that, if unchecked, could have made the C.N.A. a plutocracy. With Creative Nationalism the nation defused the radical People's Coalition, ended the troublesome Quebec issue, and went still further in opening economic opportunities to ambitious, capital-short men. From 1878 to 1901 the nation was led by two remarkable men—John McDowell and Ezra Gallivan—who overcame the problems of faction to unite the nation's middle class as never before. Their successors—Burgen, Hemingway, and Merriman —lived off the intellectual capital and reforms of the McDowell-Gallivan era. And so great was that heritage that on the surface, at least, the C.N.A. seemed happy and content.
>
> What none of these men realized was that, in reality, McDowell and Gallivan had re-written the constitution so as to enable the C.N.A. to undergo a great quantitative revolution. These two men were both

---

9. Milton Schuster. *The Quiet Election: The Wagner Victory of 1918* (New York, 1929), p. 88.          10. *Ibid*, p. 243.

middle-class in orientation, and saw their nation as a place in which the poor could not only aspire to middle-class status, but with the help of the government, attain it, given hard work and intelligence. . . .

Neither McDowell or Gallivan could have foreseen the problems that followed the Hundred Day War. Unwittingly, Fanchon set off a string of minor explosions that unmasked the next set of problems the nation would face. Many people in the C.N.A. had long felt that McDowell and Gallivan had succeeded in climbing the mountain, but that it was the wrong mountain. While conceding the remarkable economic gains of the past half century, they argued that they only affected the *quantity* of life in the C.N.A., and brought prosperity that in time destroyed the *quality* of existence in the nation. Merriman and Wagner saw great cities, highways, large universities, prosperous farms, and a happy middle class. Their critics saw slums, pollution, ghettos, the poor who for one reason or another could not avail themselves of opportunities, Negroes denied a true role in C.N.A. society, and a nation gone mad with an obsession with materialism. . . .

In essence, the great reform wave of this period was directed toward engaging the problems men like Wagner denied *were* problems, or if they did exist, were the proper concern of government. . . . The earlier reformers had shown they could accomplish anything that could be measured; their successors cursed them for their dreams, hated them for their successes, and determined to crush the inheritance so proudly given them by their fathers.[11]

None of those who joined the Friends of Black Mexico understood this. Even Washburne, considered the most brilliant leader of the movement, did not realize what would follow. As he saw it, the Negro had to be further incorporated into the warp and woof of C.N.A. society, to get a greater quantitative share of the wealth and power in those confederations where they were denied the chance to improve themselves. In 1919 Washburne said, "What the Negro wants is the same kind of home, job, and life that his white brothers enjoy east of the Mississippi."[12] Only two years later novelist Jeremy Slater would write, "For years we have been begging for a share of the poison. If we get it, we will die; if we don't, we will bloom. Washburne means well, but he will destroy us if he succeeds."[13]

This mass movement lacked a single name, never achieved a fully-developed rationale or "philosophy," had many leaders and programs, each of which seemed to contradict the others, and no clearly-defined goals. Its largest organization, the League for Brotherhood, had begun

---

11. Fritz Webern. *The Dilemma of Our Times* (New York, 1933), pp. 119–25.
12. New York *Herald*, November 11, 1919.

13. Jeremy Slater. *Essays of the Revolution* (New York, 1921), pp. 56–57.

as a Negro movement, expanded to include whites in 1920, and by 1921 had taken positions on the relationships between the confederations and Burgoyne, foreign policy, the use of natural resources, the role of the N.F.A., and other matters not directly concerned with the Negro as a Negro. Each time it broadened its platform new members would join, but at the same time the movement grew more diffuse, and this loss of focus hindered effective action. "The League resembles the fat woman at a circus," said one of its detractors. "It can't help eating more of each tempting dish placed before it, and each time it does, it becomes more slovenly and incapable of movement."[14]

Washburne himself retained his popularity; indeed, by 1921 the protest movement seemed to be whatever he said it was. But Washburne proved incapable of using his power effectively. Increasingly he spoke in biblical language, talked of a "moral regeneration" of the nation, and the need for brotherhood. His followers applauded his speeches enthusiastically; his critics noted that rarely did Washburne offer concrete proposals. Nor would he seek political power, although the Liberals had a large minority willing to support him in the 1923 elections. "Mr. Washburne is a saint," said Phipps. "But saints are notoriously poor politicians."[15]

Other leaders were better organized though less popular. Ivan Falls of the Agrarian Alliance demanded a limit to the size of cities and a return to the soil; Fred Harcourt of the Workers' Army wanted Neiderhofferian reforms; Arnold Gelb of the Universities for Justice called for an end to all forms of government; Bryan Coleman thought "the leaders of our dictatorship will not listen, so they must be done away with by any means we have." None of them, however, could command the respect and attention of Washburne and his co-leaders at the League for Brotherhood.[16] "The movement had popular leaders without programs, and programs without popular leaders. Let us hope that the right program does not find the right leader. If this happens, the nation is doomed."[17] So said a "conventional politician" in 1922.

Such a man did appear in 1922, but he was not at all what either the protestors or their governmental opponents would have expected. There were major riots and demonstrations that summer, the worst since the 1880's. Wagner attempted to rally the nation behind him, but only succeeded in antagonizing his enemies and making his supporters more militant. "The faint aroma of Starkism has made its appearance," said James Kilroy of the New York *Herald*, and both the opponents of

14. Winslow McGregor. *A Child Shall Lead Them: The Idiocy of Our Times* (New York, 1921), p. 165.
15. New York *Herald*, August 5, 1922.
16. Farley Shaw. *Voices of the Great Protest* (New York, 1930).
17. Benjamin Morrison, as quoted in New York *Herald*, October 15, 1922.

our civilization and its supporters seem pleased by the possibility of its return."[18] The economy continued to boom, as the nation's wealth and industrial plant were scarcely affected by the riots. But the feeling of moral decay that had made its appearance six years before was becoming dangerous. At this time, Owen Galloway appeared on the scene to attempt a reconciliation of the nation.

The Galloway name was one of the most honored in the C.N.A. Owen Galloway could trace his ancestry to Joseph Galloway, the hero of the North American Rebellion, whose ideas were instrumental in the formulation of the Britannic Design. For six generations, the Galloways had served in Confederation and local governments. Franklin Galloway was one of the C.N.A.'s leading authors; Joseph Galloway IV a major philosopher, and Theodore Galloway a close friend and organizer for Edison. Owen's father, Samuel Galloway, had been a pioneer in the locomobile industry, and Galloway Locomobile, Ltd. was the builder of the finest steam-driven locomobiles in the world.[19]

Owen Galloway had been raised in a typical, upper-class atmosphere in Galloway Point, on the outskirts of Michigan City. He had private tutors till the age of seventeen, at which time he went to Oxford, where he graduated in 1905. On his return to the C.N.A., he took a position at Galloway Locomobile and soon became vice president in charge of development. It was his idea to turn out low-priced locomobiles, a move his father opposed at first, but later supported. The Dickinson, a small, simple vehicle, made its appearance in 1915. Selling for N.A. £923 and containing the simplest mechanism of any locomobile on the road, it won quick acceptance by the public. In 1919 the C.N.A. turned out 1.7 million locomobiles, of which 486,000 were Galloways, and of that amount, 397,354 were the spartan Dickinsons.[20] In that year, too, Owen Galloway at the age of thirty-five, became president of Galloway Locomobile.

During the next two years Galloway moved swiftly and boldly. He bought out seven other locomobile manufacturers (many of whom were on the verge of bankruptcy due to the popularity of the Dickinson), and in 1921 formed North American Motors, the first North American locomobile company capable of competing with Jefferson Motors. That same year, Galloway's engineers developed an improved vulcazine engine, which appeared in the Dickinson in 1922; the new car became the most popular in the world within three years. Galloway also formed a petroleum affiliate, which at first attempted to find

18. New York *Herald*, June 23, 1922.
19. Maryann Milton. *A History of the Galloway Family* (New York, 1944); John Collins and Edwin Foster. *Galloway* (New York, 1967).

20. Edwin Foster. *The Business Career of Owen Galloway* (New York, 1961); Dwight Pendleton. *The Galloway Years* (New York, 1964), pp. 344–405.

new sources of the fuel in North America, but by 1922 was seeking it throughout the world. North American Fuel organized a series of service stations that spanned the nation; North American Inns became the nation's leading hotel keeper; North American Finance, the second largest company of its kind in the C.N.A., led in the financing of locomobiles. By the end of 1922, Owen Galloway had put together the largest company in the nation, and one that was second only to Kramer Associates on the world scene.[21]

The most popular radio program in the C.N.A. in 1922 was the Galloway Playhouse, which presented plays drawn from contemporary and classic novels. The playhouse went on vitavision that September, causing sales of receivers to zoom. By year's end, it was estimated that the two presentations—on radio and vitavision—drew some 40 million listeners and viewers.[22]

That Christmas Day, the Galloway Playhouse presented *The Christmas of the Magi* by Charles Dickens, a long-time seasonal favorite, which featured Rudolph Vincent as Charles Wilson and Dame Mary Willingston as Carole Doolittle. The program was two hours in length, presented at 5:00 P.M., and was heralded as the dramatic event of the year. An estimated 60 million people heard and watched the program, after which Owen Galloway was scheduled to deliver a "seasonal greeting."

The play was superb, but was overshadowed by Galloway's speech. The listeners and watchers expected the usual message of brotherhood so familiar during the Christmas season, and the first part of Galloway's speech was just that. Then he turned to "the problems that beset the nation this day of peace and brotherhood," and presented what came to be known as the Galloway Plan.

> There is little good will in our land this season of good will. We have succeeded in conquering nature, but many of our citizens tell us the price for this victory has been our souls. Our political leaders tell us the nation has never been more prosperous than at present, while from the universities and pulpits come messages of moral and spiritual decay. One person tells us we are the greatest nation since Rome, while another recites the sad tale of Rome's destruction. Intelligent and sincere spokesmen for all causes offer solutions, but each is rejected by the others. Indeed, we cannot find a solution until we isolate the problem. And that is why I speak of it to you this Christmas season.
>
> We have come a long way together as a nation, and longer still as a people. Always in our moments of greatness we have tried to preserve the rights of individuals and the continuation of civil order. As

21. Ezra Ripley. *A History of North American Motors: The Early Years* (New York, 1945).

22. Flaherty. *Little Black Box*, p. 400.

John McDowell put it, "Without freedom, there is no just state. Without a just state, there is no freedom. . . ."

At times part of the nation may find it intolerable to live in a society which it considers immoral, but which the majority views as just and honorable. At such times tempers rise and rhetoric is fiery. One side may call the other "anarchists," while it, in turn, is characterized as "tyrants." Then each may try to destroy the other, in which case no group can be victorious. Civil strife destroys all, the victor included. . . .

Such a moment was demonstrated in tonight's play, which deals with the voyage of the Pilgrims to a New World on a Christmas many years ago. Unable to live in Britain, these brave people struck out for North America. They helped make a continent bloom. But what of their impact on the land they left? Had they remained in Britain, civil war might have ensued. By leaving they benefited all. . . .

Another such moment occurred after the Rebellion, when some of our countrymen took the Wilderness Walk to Jefferson. Think what we may of their descendants, the Pilgrims of that day were honorable and brave men and women. By leaving, they not only prevented continued conflict in what would soon become the Confederation of North America, but they went on to found a new nation and so realize their dreams. We honor the Pilgrims who arrived at Plymouth. We should recognize the same qualities in Greene, Hamilton, and Monroe.

What does all this have to do with our current problems? In this season of love it would be gratifying to hope the factions of our divided land could come together in a spirit of brotherhood. But we know, realistically, this will not come to pass. Like the Pilgrims and the North American rebels, some dissenters have said, "It is time to leave." Perhaps they are right. After all, the present wave of reformism had its origins not in hate, but in the hope on the part of some that brotherhood of the races was possible in the nation. Apparently this is not the time for such a dream. Sad to say, many of our fellow-countrymen still judge the value of a man's skill and intelligence by the color of his skin. . . .

I am not suggesting the destruction of the nation. My family has done too much to hold it together for me to wish its dismemberment. But even this should be considered. When Ezra Gallivan gave Quebec its autonomous status, the people of that province were in arms against Burgoyne; today we live in peace with them. It appears Quebec is more a part of the C.N.A. as a province than it had been as a confederation. . . .

If all the dissenters were located in a single confederation or region, the Gallivan solution might be tried once again. Such is not the case today; many of our communities have those on the verge of rebellion, while every town and city appears to have a majority that supports the nation as presently constituted. We are a nation of two societies, each with different values, ideals, and goals. . . .

If this is true—and I believe it is—what can be done? If two peoples cannot live together, they may better live apart. Bryan Coleman tells us we are immoral; the Heirs of the Rebellion, speaking through its central office, replies by demanding Mr. Coleman and those who think like him leave the country, to which Mr. Coleman responds by saying that the C.N.A. will be changed, and that in the new nation he will create, the Heirs of the Rebellion will be crushed.

What neither group realizes is that *separation may be the answer.* Mr. Coleman must know he cannot obtain the kind of support he needs to change the C.N.A. The Heirs of the Rebellion must know that to destroy Mr. Coleman would be to destroy part of our freedom. Cannot Mr. Coleman and those who feel as he does consider our heritage? Others have left societies they considered oppressive for new worlds, and in so doing benefited both that land and the one they left. . . .

Such a parting should be undertaken in a spirit of love, however, and not that of hatred. In this season especially, we should recognize that honest differences are possible between honorable men, and that withdrawal is preferable to destructive conflict and chaos.

With this in mind, my brothers and sisters and I, with the blessing of my father, have decided to organize a national trust dedicated to the healing of our nation's ills through separation. The trust will be capitalized at N.A. £ 100 million, in the form of securities of North American Motors and other large corporations. The dividends and interest will be used for the purpose of helping those who desire to relocate, be it in other parts of our nation, the United Empire, or elsewhere. Transportation will be provided by ships owned by North American Motors. Each emigrant will be provided with sufficient captial to make a new start. And this will be done in the spirit of brotherhood and love. Further details will be released within the week, and I will speak to you of them at a press conference scheduled for January 5.

Let me close with the words of tonight's play. "We go to a better land, to a future gained and paid for by the sacrifice of our ancestors. In so doing we assure the continuance of our people, and not their destruction."[23]

The "Galloway Plan" was received with amazement at first, and then mingled scorn and hope. James Kilroy, a Galloway supporter, said, "It came like a spring rain on a muggy day," while Morton FitzPatrick, a critic, thought Galloway a fool. At a press conference, Washburne called the Galloway Plan "worthy of study, and the child of a man of unquestionable sincerity." But there were those who looked upon the Plan as a scheme to sell more Dickinsons, a ploy to enable Galloway to become the new Governor-General, the work of a religious fanatic, or a clever plot to take over the government, and

---

23. The full text may be found in *American Speeches* (New York, 1966), Maxwell Parkes. ed. *Great North* pp. 1105-24.

make "Galloway and North American Motors the C.N.A. equivalent of Kramer Associates."[24]

None of these reckless charges had substance. As promised, the Galloway Trust was established in February, 1923. Even before that time, thousands of would-be emigrants flocked to its temporary headquarters and their sub-stations in every large city in the nation, asking to be placed on the rolls. "We are in a time of diffusion," said Washburne in March, "but good will prevails among men of honor." Governor-General Wagner promised cooperation, but none was asked of the government. The entire operation, the bulk of which took seven years, was handled without partisan or political involvement.

The Galloway Plan destroyed much of the basis for the protest movements. Pro-government critics argued that the Galloway Plan would "shut up the anarchist units for good. Now these weepers will have to accept the Plan or show themselves the cowards they are," while the more radical reformists welcomed the opportunity to "denude the nation of its most precious possession, its people. Galloway has done more to destroy this corrupt society than any man in history."[25] Of course, both sides exaggerated, but neither could restrain their emotional outbursts. Within months, however, it was clear Galloway had no covert purpose in his Plan, and that he himself was, as promised, free of malice toward either side. Galloway's managers neither praised the emigrants nor condemned them, but for the most part treated all with dignity and respect.

### Resettlement Under the Galloway Plan, 1923–1930

| YEAR | OVERSEAS | EMIGRANTS INTERIOR | TOTAL |
|------|----------|--------------------|-------|
| 1923 | 154,978 | 223,545 | 378,523 |
| 1924 | 95,654 | 200,453 | 296,107 |
| 1925 | 65,998 | 219,986 | 285,985 |
| 1926 | 51,198 | 176,232 | 227,430 |
| 1927 | 30,978 | 155,877 | 186,855 |
| 1928 | 31,725 | 187,989 | 219,714 |
| 1929 | 22,243 | 126,923 | 149,166 |
| 1930 | 12,649 | 93,080 | 105,729 |

Source: New York *Herald*, January 21, 1931.

According to Galloway Trust records, 1,074,532 North Americans accepted assistance to leave the country from 1923 to 1970. Of

24. Lewis Sayers. *The Galloway Plan: The Modern Moses* (New York, 1966),  pp. 19, 24, 38, 118, 145.
25. Sayers. *Galloway Plan*, p. 335.

this number, 551,236 went to Australia, 101,326 to New Zealand, and 95,685 to Scandinavia. More important, 3,987,940 accepted aid in resettling to Manitoba, while an additional 1,047,632 went to sparsely settled areas of Northern Vandalia, Quebec, and Nova Scotia. Most went from 1923–1930, but a trickle of emigrants continues to this day.

Historians still debate the impact of the Galloway Plan on C.N.A. society, but the riots and demonstrations that so badly divided the nation in the early 1920's had disappeared by 1925. "We may differ as to the effectiveness of the Galloway Plan, the motives for its introduction, and its wisdom," said a noted historian at the 1970 meeting of the North American Historians Association, "but it was clearly the most important event in North American history since the Starkist terror, with Galloway himself the most interesting public figure of the century."[26] For this reason, the period from 1923 to 1934 was called "The Galloway Era."

---

26. Wilton Harmaer as quoted in the Burgoyne *Examiner*, December 28, 1970.

# 27

# THE DEWEY ERA

THE *malaise* of 1916–1924 has never been satisfactorily diagnosed, but if we may judge the sickness by the cure, it was caused by changes in society too rapid for the protestors to absorb, a rebellion against the idea of progress that dominated the western world, and a desire for "a more simple life" on the part of the rebels. The vast majority of the emigrants went to rural and semi-rural areas overseas, while the popularity of Manitoba for those who resettled within the C.N.A. gives further evidence to support this conclusion.

Doubtless such a move would have occurred without the Galloway Plan; as early as 1915, there was evidence of disenchantment with urban life in that the ten leading cities of the C.N.A. had not increased in population for the past five years. But Galloway gave impetus to the diffusion. The C.N.A.'s population in 1920 was 136.7 million; even with emigration, its 1930 population reached 156.3 million and the distribution of this population was radically different.

### C.N.A. Population Statistics, 1920–1930

| YEAR | N.C. | INDIANA | S.C. | MANITOBA | CONFEDERATION N. VANDALIA | S. VANDALIA | TOTAL |
|------|------|---------|------|----------|------------|-------------|-------|
|      |      |         |      | (MILLIONS) |          |             |       |
| 1920 | 35.1 | 28.8 | 21.8 | 19.0 | 16.8 | 15.2 | 136.7 |
| 1921 | 35.3 | 29.2 | 21.9 | 20.1 | 17.0 | 15.0 | 138.5 |
| 1922 | 35.5 | 29.4 | 22.1 | 21.0 | 17.4 | 15.1 | 140.5 |
| 1923 | 34.9 | 28.9 | 22.2 | 23.2 | 17.4 | 15.0 | 141.6 |
| 1924 | 34.7 | 28.9 | 22.1 | 24.5 | 17.6 | 15.1 | 142.9 |
| 1925 | 34.7 | 29.0 | 22.2 | 26.0 | 18.1 | 15.2 | 145.2 |
| 1926 | 34.8 | 29.2 | 22.2 | 27.3 | 18.3 | 15.3 | 147.1 |
| 1927 | 34.8 | 29.4 | 22.8 | 27.9 | 18.9 | 15.2 | 149.0 |
| 1928 | 35.0 | 29.5 | 22.9 | 30.4 | 19.1 | 15.3 | 152.2 |
| 1929 | 35.4 | 29.9 | 23.2 | 31.0 | 19.5 | 15.6 | 154.6 |
| 1930 | 35.6 | 30.2 | 23.4 | 31.5 | 19.7 | 15.9 | 156.3 |

Source: C.N.A. *Statistical Abstract*, p. 956.

In 1920 some 69 percent of the population lived in urban areas (populations more than 200,000); in 1930, the figure had declined to 65.4 percent. Manitoba had become the second largest state by 1930, as the populations of all the others stagnated at first, and then increased at a sluggish rate. Even those who remained in their home confederations tended to move to rural areas or suburbs. By 1928 it was estimated that the typical North American family moved once every five years.[1]

Southern Vandalia was the one major exception to this pattern. The confederation lacked large cities, being comprised for the most part of medium sized farms. For twenty years prior to the Galloway Plan, many young Negro men and women would leave their homes for opportunities in northern and southern cities. From 1922 that movement increased sharply, so that by 1930, one-quarter of the population of New York was Negro, while almost half that of Michigan City, Norfolk, and Boston were recently-arrived Southern Vandalians. As might be expected, many went to all-Negro sections, but a substantial number found their ways to the suburbs, where they lived side-by-side with their white counterparts.[2] This changed the nature of the Negro Rights Movement, and, as we shall see, channeled it into new directions.

The great migration had profound implications for the C.N.A. One of the most obvious of these was a decline in the economic growth rate, as Manitoba's newcomers, seeking a simpler life, foreswore many luxuries and tried to live a frontier-style existence. On the other hand, there was an increase in sales of vitavision receivers, attendance at motion pictures, and publishing, all the results of isolation in new surroundings. The expected drop in locomobile production did not take place; instead, sales rose, partly the result of the need for transportation in a nation on the go, the lack of rail transport in isolated regions, and the requirement for an auxiliary power source on the farms.[3] There was a religious revival among the uprooted, which may be explained in part by the need for stability in a time of change and the return to the soil.

Necessarily, there was a political change as well. Long neglected, Manitoba now became a major political force in the C.N.A., soon to surpass even the Northern Confederation. The Manitoban style, individualistic and anti-governmental, was strikingly different from that of

1. C.N.A. *Statistical Abstract*, pp. 106, 794, 1358.
2. Inter-racial mixing caused less friction than had been feared, since the individual families were usually of the same social status. "The North American does not hate so much on the basis of race and religion as he does on social and economic status," writes June Zaccone. *The Galloway Plan and the Races* (New York, 1930), p. 14.
3. Some claimed Galloway had put forth his plan to increase sales. Milton Hart. *Galloway: The Other Side* (Burgoyne, 1929).

the older confederations, where strong government was taken for granted and cooperation had become the norm. This conflict of styles and goals would determine the nature of C.N.A. politics during the late 1920's and 1930's, and traces may be seen to this day.[4]

What of those who left the country? Life was hard and bitter for many. Although the economic climate of Australia provided opportunities for ambitious individuals, most of those who went there lacked the skills needed in that country. Similarly, the emigrants to Scandinavia and New Zealand suffered. There is every reason to believe the emigrants were well-educated and intelligent, in addition to having a sincere belief in their causes. But most were educated in the classical liberal arts curriculums; there were many philosophers on the Galloway ships, but few engineers, doctors, or mechanics. Many sought teaching positions in their new homes, but when it appeared that the educational apparatus of Australia and New Zealand would come under expatriate control, those countries banned such employment to all those with less than ten years' residence. Because of this, many newcomers became economic drains on the nation, and were deeply resented by the natives. In addition, the countries to which they went had heard of the *malaise* in North America, and many of their new neighbors had little sympathy for the rebels, who were shunned and denied opportunities. Needless to say, N.A. Negroes found few countries willing to accept them, and this in turn led to a revival of Southern Vandalian regionalism. The emigrants, as a whole, may be called a lost generation.[5] Those who remained in the C.N.A. suffered; those who returned to the C.N.A. in the 1930's faced scorn from their opponents.[6] Their children did better, and in most cases appeared to adjust well to the new nations and become "natives." But many appear to have had clashes with their parents over the emigration question, and the generation break seems evident even a half-century after the Galloway Plan's announcement.[7]

If the plan did not unroll as its founder thought it would, it did serve to make Galloway the most popular person in North America. Galloway's weekly addresses on the Galloway Playhouse became a ritual with millions of citizens, just as attendance in church or at the motion pictures. At first these talks dealt with the Plan, but by February, 1923, Galloway was using his weekly speeches as a vehicle for the articulation of his philosophy.

Galloway believed strongly in the power of tradition; this was to

4. Edward Keith. *The Manitoban Century* (New York, 1966), pp. 106-45.
5. Phyllis Potter. *The Lost Generation: The North American Emigrants of the 1920's* (London, 1955).
6. Phyllis Potter, Carole Ching, and Melville Spencer. *The Returnees: The Bitter Pill* (London, 1961).
7. Potter. *Lost Generation*, p. 310-23.

be expected from a man obsessed with his own family's past. Change was necessary, he said, "for in a changing world, to stand still is to be a radical." But alterations in the social fabric must be made with care; "better to delay a reform than to bring about an undesirable alteration which may do more harm than the evil it seeks to correct." Galloway was a regular church-goer, but conceded "a man may be as religious at work or play, as in the house of God." Most of all, he believed in the inherent goodness of the individual when unhampered by institutions, "which often are the dead hand of the past on the actions of the present and the hope of the future." Thus, he applauded attempts at mutual aid, societies formed to correct problems which disbanded when the problems were no longer pressing, and people who made their way without asking aid of government. "One cannot endow the individual with dignity," he said in 1924. "Only man himself may earn self-respect. The giver of freedom is too often the bearer of invisible chains." On one occasion he suggested the regular "peaceful dissolution of our governments, churches, corporations, clubs—all organizations to which we belong—and a fresh start for each, in which needed changes may be made."[8]

Much of Galloway's thinking was muddy, contradictory, and banal. For the head of the nation's leading corporation to suggest an end to organizations appears bizarre today; for a man so interested in history to ask for continual "fresh starts," while at the same time preserving past values, is also confusing. North American intellectuals admired Galloway's good heart, but more often than not considered him hopelessly bourgeois and incapable of deep thought. "No one denies Mr. Galloway's beauty of spirit," wrote Professor Ernest Armstrong of Burgoyne University in 1925. "It would be pleasant, however, to find a brain to match the soul."[9]

The people who listened to Galloway's radio and vitavision addresses regularly had few such doubts of his intelligence. To them, he appeared the greatest North American of his time. Galloway was not a brilliant speaker; indeed, he tended to read his talks in a dull monotone. The words were simple, often confused, and rarely stirring in themselves. But Galloway had a *mystique* nonetheless, one that puzzled conventional public figures, worried politicians, and attracted a horde of imitators. Scarcely an important national politician of the 1920's and 1930's dared appear anything but shy, homespun, simple, and innocent.

Some believed Galloway had timed his Plan to coincide with the

8. Owen Galloway. ed. *Selected Addresses* (New York, 1935), p. 354 *passim.*

9. New York *Herald*, February 10, 1925.

elections of 1923. The conventions had been held by the time of the speech, but by mid-January a group of Indiana councilmen suggested the formation of the "Galloway Coalition," consisting of politicians who had pledged themselves to the selection of Galloway as governor-general in February. Galloway firmly rejected their overtures, insisting, "Even if selected for the post, I will not serve in it." This ended the movement, but not his influence. Governor-General Wagner endorsed the Galloway Plan, "and all it entails." His opponent, Councilman Henderson Dewey of Indiana went further, promising to bring Galloway into the government if elected. To this Wagner countered by coming out in support "of Mr. Galloway's future plans, of which I have been informed by none other than that gentleman himself." But Galloway denied talking to the Governor-General in anything but vague generalities.

Both candidates appeared on vitavision regularly; this was the first election in which the public could watch the leading candidates day-by-day. At first it appeared Wagner would win an easy victory—the People's Coalition was the nation's majority party, and Wagner was the incumbent, which gave him additional power. But Dewey ran a clever race. He spoke in generalities, consciously imitating Galloway's prose, his style, and even his appearance. Without saying so, Dewey implied he was closer to Galloway than was the Governor-General. The plan worked. Dewey won election by a wide margin, thus ending a thirty-five year control of the executive by the People's Coalition.[10]

### Results of the C.N.A. Elections of 1923

| | PARTY AFFILIATION OF COUNCILMEN | |
| STATE | LIBERALS | PEOPLE'S COALITION |
| --- | --- | --- |
| Northern Confederation | 17 | 19 |
| Indiana | 19 | 13 |
| Southern Confederation | 14 | 13 |
| Manitoba | 13 | 10 |
| Northern Vandalia | 10 | 6 |
| Southern Vandalia | 8 | 8 |
| | 81 | 69 |

Source: New York *Herald*, February 17, 1923.

Ever since the Gallivan era, the Liberals had protested against the growth of big government and ineptness in Burgoyne that was transmitted to the states. This stance was more the result of being out of

10. Franklin Drew. *The Guard Changeth: The Elections of 1923* (New York, 1931).

office than any significant ideological commitment, but in time, the goal of limited government came to be important to many leading Liberals. Dewey was not one of these, although he realized the mood of the country favored decentralization. "Governors-General Hemingway, Merriman, and Wagner were reformers who were content with the *status quo*, and so did nothing," he later wrote. "There was I, a moderate who opposed the drift of C.N.A. central politics, who was obliged to sponsor the most important legislative program in decades. It was highly paradoxical."[11]

Soon after his election, Dewey sent a series of bills to the Council for its consideration. Unlike Gallivan and McDowell before him, Dewey did not tag the proposals with a romantic name, such as the Age of Renewal or Creative Nationalism. Instead, they were introduced simply, with little prologue, by low-keyed councilmen. Thus did Dewey bow once more to the popular Galloway style as he began what he later called his "dismantling operation." Although Dewey sent over one hundred measures to the Council from 1923 to 1928, only four could be considered of major importance. These were:

1. The Spargo Bill to redistribute federal revenues to the states on a *per capita* basis.
2. The General Education Bill, which replaced older legislation. Education through professional schools was now guaranteed all intellectually qualified citizens, to be paid for by the states but reimbursed by the Confederation government.
3. The Simmons Toll Road Bill, which provided for the construction of confederation-sponsored toll roads, which would be self-liquidating financially in fifty years.
4. The Transportation Control Act, which created the Confederation Transportation Authority, with wide powers to control railroads, airmobile lines, and interstate truckers.

All four measures passed with little difficulty, after being praised as "liberating" by Dewey and his party. The Coalition leaders noted that the four bills were all popular with rural and underdeveloped areas, and with Manitobans in particular. Not until 1928 did they understand that Dewey's strategy was even more far-reaching than they had imagined. The Governor-General was attempting to remake not only the Liberal Party, but the structure of C.N.A. politics. Believing the central government would, in any case, lose power to the confederations, he buttressed confederation Liberal organizations through the judicious use of contracts, jobs, and other favors, while often ignoring

11. Henderson Dewey. *Commonwealth* (New York, 1930), p. 2. This posthumous book was edited by Edith Dewey, although she does not receive credit on the title page.

councilmen in Burgoyne. Dewey did not seem to believe the Liberals could retain power in Burgoyne beyond his administration, but he saw great possibilities for the Manitoba, Indiana, and Northern Vandalia Liberals.

Dewey also tried to use Galloway to advance his programs. He met with the industrialist eight times from 1923 to 1928, telling the press and vitavision reporters that he "wanted to draw upon the wisdom of this great man."[12] On at least four occasions, Dewey asked Galloway to serve as chairman of special commissions; each time he was politely refused. In 1927, Dewey offered to step down the following year and support Galloway's candidacy on the Liberal line, but this too was rejected.[13] Clearly, Galloway meant to hold to his earlier determination not to enter politics.

Dewey's first term must be considered a success. Under his leadership major steps were taken to decentralize the C.N.A. and cut the Burgoyne bureaucracy to the bone. Agencies established by McDowell and Gallivan, important at the time of inception, but now moribund, were swept away or combined into new, streamlined offices. Greater autonomy was given to field representatives, and care was taken that these men were ambitious and talented Liberals. Total Confederation government spending, which consumed 8.8 percent of the GNP in 1923, had fallen to 6.4 percent by 1928, while that of local governments rose dramatically.

Dewey also brought the spirit of the Galloway Plan into C.N.A. government. Although there was no direct connection between the Galloway Trust and the Confederation bureaucracy, government men cooperated whenever possible with the Trust, and did more to aid in relocations than was believed at the time. Minister of Home Affairs Douglas Watson noted that more individuals relocated within the C.N.A. *without* Trust assistance than did so with its aid, and that only 29.7 percent of those who emigrated received more than N.A. £40 from the Trust, while 31.8 percent asked for no such aid. "If the truth were to be told," he told the Liberal Party Convention of 1938, "the

---

12. Burgoyne *Examiner*, July 19, 1925.
13. Galloway's decision may not have been as simple as it appeared to contemporaries. Richard Maltz has concluded Galloway believed he could wield greater power as a private individual than as a partisan politician. Thus, he could and did judge every important act of government while lacking responsibilities for his criticisms. In 1917, long before the Gallo-

way Plan, he wrote, "Queen Victoria was far more intelligent than is generally believed. By refusing an active political role she was able to act as a stabilizing force, a symbol for *all* Britain, and a major check on those politicians she rightly despised." Richard Maltz. *Better Than Any of Us? The Ambitious Galloway* (New York, 1970), p. 440.

Dewey government was more instrumental in aiding emigration than the Trust."[14]

Wisely, Dewey did not publicize this fact. Instead, Home Office agents were ordered to assist the emigrants, and to be especially helpful to those who relocated within the nation. "Since most of the emigrants were intellectuals or thought themselves as such, and since the Coalition was the natural home of intellectuals, Dewey was in fact exporting his political opposition. Those who relocated within the C.N.A. were more often middle-class and professional in background, likely candidates for the Liberal parties in their new homes. Aid from the Home Office oftentimes made a vacillating Coalitionist into a staunch Liberal."[15]

The People's Coalition appeared inept in the face of this kind of program and approach. Dewey had managed to make it appear as though Galloway favored his administration, even though the industrialist remained scrupulously neutral politically. Diffusion of power was the order of the day in the nation, and the Coalition was known as the party of centralization. Dewey had brought many able and attractive young men to Burgoyne, and had done a remarkably good job in building up the Confederation organizations. Douglas Watson, Emery Collins, John Hopkins, and Dennis Mitchell of the Cabinet were articulate and popular men; Governors Foster McCabe of Manitoba, David Heald of Indiana, and Councilman John Jenckinson of the Northern Confederation were intelligent politicians. Like Dewey, they were able to present an appearance of modesty, understatement, and coolness— and all appeared to great advantage on vitavision.

The People's Coalition, by contrast, seemed a party of old men. Former Governor-General Wagner was, in the words of a Burgoyne journalist, "a decent and fairly intelligent man who unfortunately has the appearance of a contented hog; Governor Elbert Childs of the Northern Confederation has the faint aura of a circus-master, while N.C. Councilman Frank Evans, the party's most attractive candidate, manages to alienate potential supporters by his automatic opposition to every Dewey program."[16]

Because of this, the results of the 1928 elections were a foregone conclusion. The Liberals won a smashing victory in February over the inept Evans, gaining Council majorities in every Confederation but the N.C., and winning five of the six governorships and control of four legislatures. Dewey was now hailed as the most brilliant politician since

14. New York *Herald*, November 30, 1938.
15. Maltz. *Better Than Any of Us*, p. 500.
16. Franklin Drew. *The Guard Is Confirmed: The Elections of 1928* (New York, 1933).

## Results of the·C.N.A. Elections of 1928

| STATE | PARTY AFFILIATION OF COUNCILMEN | |
| --- | --- | --- |
| | LIBERALS | PEOPLE'S COALITION |
| Northern Confederation | 17 | 19 |
| Indiana | 20 | 12 |
| Southern Confederation | 17 | 10 |
| Manitoba | 19 | 4 |
| Northern Vandalia | 12 | 4 |
| Southern Vandalia | 9 | 7 |
| | 94 | 56 |

Source: New York *Herald*, February 16, 1928.

Gallivan. His enemies said "Mr. Dewey is certainly popular, but what is his record? He has done nothing of importance as Governor-General except to parrot Galloway." Such an analysis ignores the quiet work of five years of politicking and gauging the public pulse. More perceptive was Edward Brewster's post-election analysis.

The Liberals have won a major victory, one that was hardly unexpected. Mr. Dewey will be Governor-General for another five years. Of equal importance is the change in the political complexion of the nation. Five years ago this was considered a Coalition country; now a Liberal majority has appeared. This majority will not last for only a season or two, but perhaps for decades. Mr. Dewey has shown remarkable strength in those areas where the population is rising. He lost votes in the Northern Confederation, which has fewer people today than it did in 1920. The 1930 census may show Manitoba to be larger than Indiana and the Southern Confederation, and this confederation is the base of Dewey's power and of his new Liberalism. When the Council is restructured on the basis of the coming census, the Liberals will benefit still more. Indeed, had the election been held under redistricting, Dewey would have received not 94 votes, but a minimum of one hundred and two.[17]

Certainly Dewey was the equal of Gallivan in political astuteness, if not in brilliance and imagination. "He knew what the country wanted, and he delivered the goods. Governor-General Dewey understood the average North American. He was so average himself."[18] An unfriendly comment, perhaps, but with more than a grain of truth in it.

17. Edward Brewster in the New York *Times*, February 18, 1928.
18. Don Brokow. *Henderson Dewey:* *A Study in Mediocrity* (New York, 1945), p. vii.

Dewey's second administration began quietly, with no changes in the Cabinet or statements of new initiative. On December 1, 1928, Dewey announced a major study of the National Financial Administration "to see how this important agency may better serve the interests of the nation and its people."[19] At the time, it seemed the most important action Dewey had undertaken.[20]

The N.F.A. had barely been touched by the quiet reforms of the 1920's. The administrators—Carl Bixby, Norris Jones, and Philip Koch —had all served since the early part of the decade and seemed certain of continuing in office indefinitely. All three had been conservative New York bankers, although Bixby's home was in Michigan City and Koch's in Norfolk. They maintained good relations with the New York bankers, were well-thought of on Broad Street, and considered above politics. In 1923, the N.F.A. had authorized 958 financings with an average of N.A. £5,406 each. Its assets were N.A. £2,437 million, with liabilities of N.A. £1,996 million. Five years later, the N.F.A. authorized 1,009 financings averaging N.A. £5,334 each.[21]

The N.F.A. had never lacked for critics. Their most persistent argument was that the agency was too conservative, and had refused financings to thousands of ambitious people who needed help and merited consideration. By 1923 the N.F.A. was also a major force in the securities market, and in the atmosphere of anti-urbanism of the time, a prime target for reformers. But the agency could be criticized on less ancient or emotional grounds in 1928. Dewey noted that of the 4,698 loans granted the previous five years, half were to entrepreneurs in the Northern Confederation, while another fifth went to Indianans; either entrepreneurs in the other Confederations lacked the qualities of their eastern counterparts, or the N.F.A. was remiss in its duties.

Actually neither was completely true or false. In the past, most N.F.A. financings went to young companies with potential to succeed in an industrial economy, and since the N.C. and Indiana were the most industrialized areas of the nation, it was only natural they would dominate its market. But the N.F.A. had not taken cognizance of the period of diffusion. Nor would it consider favorably most financing requests from agriculture-based operations, and, in particular, seemed to discriminate against Southern Vandalian Negroes. In 1928, the regional offices of the N.F.A. had initiated only forty percent of all financings, and of this amount, only seven percent were approved for Manitobans. These statistics had not caused alarm in Burgoyne as long as the nation was stable, but now that the political and economic

19. New York *Herald*, December 2, 1928.
20. "Dewey's most important actions were so well executed that few knew of them before they were completed." Drew. *The Guard Is Confirmed*, p. 394.
21. Jules Whitney. *The N.F.A. Story* (New York, 1966), pp. 354, 368.

climate was changed, Dewey felt a readjustment in N.F.A. policies should follow. What he had in mind was a distribution of financings according to population. Thus, the N.F.A. would be obliged to finance a certain number of Manitobans, Southern Vandalians, etc. This would help make the economic map of the C.N.A. conform to its new demographic outlines, aid newcomers to Manitoba in their resettlement plans, and enable Negroes to better share in the nation's wealth.

The administrators protested the plan as "arbitrary" and "unjust." Bixby complained the N.F.A. was being asked to finance "unworthy enterprises" because of their geographical location. Jones said he would have resigned in protest, "had I not known that the Governor-General would name a diffusionist to take my place." Koch called upon the business community for support, and opined that "I see the fine hand of Mr. Galloway behind all this." Such charges and statements were counter-productive, and only served to make Dewey appear more a reformer than he actually was. In fact, the Governor-General realized, as did the administrators, that within the next four years he could replace two of them, and so have his way without controversial legislation. Still, the newspapers and vitavision commentators made it appear as though Dewey was locked in battle with the N.F.A.; the Governor-General emerged as the protector of individualism and diffusionism, while the administrators were castigated as "secret little men with untold power and no public mandate for its use."[22]

Dewey's study proceeded over the administrators' protests, and on May 5, 1929, the Governor-General went on vitavision to report to the nation on his program to "bring the N.F.A. to more people, to increase its usefulness, not detract from it."[23] The speech was well-received, and there is no doubt that this modest reform would have passed the Council with an overwhelming majority if offered for a vote the following day.

As was his wont, Dewey moved slowly. He met with his party leaders in the Council on May 8, and together they decided to schedule a vote for the following week, to avoid opposition claims that opinion had been stifled. This vote did not take place. On the morning of May 10, 1929, Dewey was found dead of a heart attack, which he apparently had suffered in his sleep. "In death as in life," wrote a friend, "Henderson moved quietly, so that it was all over before we realized it had begun."[24]

22. Jack Norris in Burgoyne *Inquirer*, April 1, 1928.
23. New York *Herald*, May 6, 1929.

24. Alton Gibbs. *A Friend in Burgoyne* (New York, 1931), p. 364.

# 28

# THE SLAVE DILEMMA

LIKE the C.N.A., Mexico faced serious racial problems in the aftermath of the Chapultapec Incident. For decades, Anglos and Hispanos had insisted the slaves were content, while the Mexicanos in
general opposed manumission, fearing competition from the freedmen.
Only in the universities and intellectual circles in the capital and
Tampico did free Mexicans talk seriously of an end to slavery. The
issue was not of paramount importance in national politics; prior to
1916, even the Kramer Associates did not consider manumission
necessary for a stable nation. Indeed, during the early part of the
century, Mexican reformers concentrated their attention on equal
rights for Mexicanos and women; the slaves were the forgotten people
of the land.[1]

After Chapultapec the Mexicans discussed little else. Every unfamiliar Negro was suspected of being a runaway; there was talk of
insurrection. Reluctantly, Consalus instituted a program of internal
passports, and curfews were enforced in Tampico, Vera Cruz, and the
capital. There were continuous demonstrations outside Mexican lega-
tions in Europe and the C.N.A.; several had to be closed. Those in
Paris, Birmingham, Michigan City, and Flange, Manitoba, were burned
to the ground. By mid-1916, any Mexican Negro found in Anglo or
Hispano neighborhoods ran a strong risk of being killed. The repression was severe. Libertarian politicians known to favor manumission
were hounded by opponents. In March Albert Ullman was shot at
while entering his home, and government guards were assigned to protect him.[2]

Clearly such a situation could not be allowed to continue. Presi-

---

1. Of course, the Indians were less in
evidence in all states than the Negroes,
with the exceptions of Mexico del
Norte and Arizona. Staying to themselves, they developed their own economic structure, largely divorced from
the rest of the nation. In 1971, only

4.6 percent of all Indians lived in urban
areas of states other than Mexico del
Norte and Arizona. Guy Fowler. *Indians: The Quiet Mexicans* (New York,
1971), pp. 233-36.
2. Walker. *The Chapultapec Affair*,
pp. 287-98.

dent Consalus recognized the dangers inherent in such a situation, but did not seem capable of finding a solution. He established a number of commissions to investigate slavery in the U.S.M., which issued a series of reports on the subject in 1916 and 1917. In time, the nation tired of Consalus' commissions, and demanded action. There were those in the United Mexican Party who wanted the slaves to be shipped to Africa, or indeed, any place outside of Mexico. A small group wanted the slaves to be given land of their own, separated from the rest of the nation, where they could work out their own destiny. Many of Mexico's leading writers and artists demanded immediate freedom, but their demonstrations only alienated many middle-class Hispanos and Anglos. The Catholic Church remained quiet on the issue, as did the leading Protestant ministers.

In early 1917 it seemed a majority of Mexicans wanted slavery to continue as it was, but a poll of January, 1917, showed that 60.5 percent of the free Mexican population was "dissatisfied" with the institution; 79.8 percent would be happy if the Negroes "vanished," while 61.2 percent wanted still more studies of the subject. No solution appeared in sight; yet the *status quo* had become intolerable. Neither Consalus nor Benedict could find the proper formula for dealing with slavery; Albert Ullman remarked, "We are harvesting the crop sown even before the Wilderness Walk. Do the people of Mexico actually believe they can avoid responsibility for their past?"[3]

The most perceptive student of the subject of Mexican slavery, Theodore Holmes, headed a sub-committee of the main committee to study slavery in 1917. Only twenty-seven years old at the time, but already recognized as a major scholar, Holmes wrote an essay on race relations in Mexico which was widely quoted, and became the basic document for future studies of the subject. In his conclusion, Holmes noted that the U.S.M. was "the most rainbow-like nation in the world today."

> First were the Mexicanos, who were here long before the first conquistador. Those whom we now call Indians were, in fact, a group of northern Mexicanos, but the two were different culturally and perhaps even ethnically in the fifteenth century, and so should be considered distinct and separate. The Hispanos came in the fifteenth century and, within a few years, mingled easily with the Mexicanos, creating a halfbreed group that grew larger each decade until the early nineteenth century. Then came the Anglos, and with them, the first important infusion of Negroes. The Anglos made common cause with the Hispanos, and by the mid-nineteenth century intermarriage was not at all

3. Mexico City *Times*, January 18, 1917.

uncommon. As religion became less a factor in Mexican life, this mingling came to be expected, especially in upper class circles.

Today this rainbow nation is dominated by a relatively small group of Anglos. The Hispanos are next in the pecking order, but the line between the two is vague and to all intents and purposes meaningless. Then came the Mexicanos, but centuries of intermarriage with the Hispanos had made that line, too, a matter of academic, not practical, importance. Few Anglos marry Mexicanos, but fewer still can claim that one or more cousins is not at least half-Mexicano. It seems clear that with three or four generations, these three peoples will be one, with education and wealth more important than race in determining status.

The Indians remain aloof. They have done so in the past, and will continue to do so in the future. At one time, Indians served in presidential cabinets and rose to high position in the army. Today there is no Indian in Mexico City's political elite, and only 439 Indians in the Mexican Army, none above the rank of captain, and all serving in Mexico del Norte and Arizona posts. Only 19.8 percent of qualified Indians voted in the 1914 elections, although encouraged to participate by the government. Clearly the Indians as a group have rejected Mexican society as a whole, and as long as this remains the case, frictions between them and the rest of the nation will be minimized.

But what of the Negro? He is different from the Indian in status, despised by the Mexicano, ignored by the Hispano, and considered animal-like by the Anglo. It is difficult to believe that, even given a century, he will merge into the mainstream of Mexican life. One may admire the brotherhood of those whose claim this will happen, but are they being realistic?

Fortunately, we have a model of the future. In North America, the Negro freedmen at first attempted to live side-by-side with their white countrymen, some of them former owners. This having failed, the Negroes moved to Southern Vandalia, where many prospered. Their great-grandchildren are now settling in the other states. For the most part these men and women are indistinguishable culturally from their white countrymen; only color provides a difference. There have been problems in some cities, however, and even now the races are just beginning to mingle.

Today, eight decades after manumission, that nation has not solved its racial dilemma.

Despite this, we should not despise the C.N.A. model. No man can foretell the future, but wise ones may formulate plans for the present. With this in mind, I propose consideration of the following:

1. Some way must be found to grant the Negro slaves their freedom. Internal peace will not be possible unless this is done.

2. There must be recognition that the races will not live at peace with one another in our lifetime. This is sad, but nonetheless true.

3. For the benefit of both races, they must be separated. This can

be done through sponsorship of an emigration policy, or resettlement in some part of the C.N.A. where the Negro may flourish. . . .[4]

The Holmes Report was widely read, discussed, and quoted. One major criticism was its obvious reliance upon the North American experience as a guide; in 1917, few Mexicans were prepared to say their nation resembled the C.N.A. Another was the relocation issue. Holmes had not said where this "Negroville" would be, and Anglos, Hispanos, and Mexicanos would be unwilling to relocate to provide such a spot. Nor did Consalus take seriously the plan to "export" Negroes. "One day they may return to haunt us," he said. Thus, the dilemma was crystalized, though unresolved, in 1918. "If I retain the institution I will be pilloried," said Consalus. "Should I ask for its end, I will be crushed."[5]

The resolution came not in the form of a program, but a man. Ever since his great victory at Chapultapec, General Emiliano Calles had been Mexico's hero. Calles found this role uncomfortable. A moody, withdrawn, and scholarly man, he was far more interested in military matters than in politics. Furthermore, he was grossly over-weight, a poor speaker, and tended to be obscure in his statements. Still, Calles was a popular hero, and had he so desired, could have had either party's nomination for the presidency in 1920.

The General rejected all such overtures after the war, going so far as to say "I would rather die than serve in that awful office." At first reporters believed this attitude the result of Calles' origins. After all, he was a full-blooded Mexicano, and no man of that background had ever been seriously considered for the presidency. But there was no indication that the Mexican people would not elect Calles despite this, and Calles himself was not overly sensitive on the issue, although it was well-known he had had difficulties with Anglo and Hispano officers prior to the Battle of Chapultapec.

In December of 1919, President Consalus called Calles into his office and asked him to consent to being nominated at the United Mexican convention of 1920. "There is no reason to hurry your reply, Emiliano," said the President. "But if you are interested, it would be best that some of us know now."[6] Calles reiterated firmly that he had no interest in politics. Later on it was learned that Consalus wanted very much to run himself in 1920, and had been none too eager to press Calles into this new career.[7]

The Libertarians made their play for a Calles candidacy in Feb-

4. Theodore Holmes. ed. *The Rainbow Nation and Other Papers* (Mexico City, 1925), pp. 9–43.
5. Jerome Krinz. *Victoriano Consalus* and the Politics of Race (New York, 1960), pp. 200–17.
6. Emiliano Calles. *The People and the Nation* (Mexico City, 1931), p. 58.
7. Krinz. *Victoriano Consalus*, p. 416.

ruary, 1920, a month before the convention. Ullman was the leading candidate for the nomination, and, at the time, seemed to have a majority of the delegates on his side. There was reason to believe the General was becoming interested in the office. He had made several short political speeches that summer, in which he showed he was aware of problems in Mexico, although he had offered no solutions to them. Ullman listened to these talks carefully; earlier he had openly opposed a Calles candidacy, and was making the race primarily because of his desire to head off a drive to draft the General. Ullman feared Calles might prove another Hermión, believed him unsympathetic to the plight of the slaves, and thought he would prove a willing tool of Benedict and the Kramer Associates once in office. Besides, Calles was a Mexicano, and the United Mexican Party, not the Libertarians, had made the great drive to register the Mexicanos.

On February 15, Ullman met Calles at a government dinner, and afterwards the two talked at great length. The meeting was planned, although Calles did not know it at the time. The discussion was not "leaked" and even now its specific content is unknown, but they did talk about slavery in Mexico and "related subjects." No pledges were made, and afterwards, when asked by reporters if he was interested in the Libertarian nomination, Calles said he "planned to remain in the army the rest of my life. In any case, Mr. Ullman will doubtless be that party's nominee."[8]

As expected, the United Mexican Party renominated Consalus at its Mexico City Convention. But the Libertarians, contrary to expectations, bypassed Ullman, and "drafted" Calles. The General accepted the designation, pledging himself in trivialities and meaningless generalizations. "It was the worst acceptance speech in the history of Mexican politics. Yet the crowd cheered as they did in the old days when El Jefe delivered his diatribes."[9]

Calles proved a poor campaigner, but so great was his reputation

8. Mexico City *Times*, February 24, 1920.
9. In 1929 Samuel Slate, a C.N.A. historian, claimed Ullman had engineered the draft. At the time, the story was discounted, but more evidence has been uncovered to indicate that is what happened. According to the plan, Ullman would allow his name to be presented first, and, at the proper moment, Senator Frank Armstrong of Jefferson would nominate Calles, after which a carefully-planned demonstration would take place. Calles was nominated on the first ballot, as Ullman knew he would be. Apparently Calles did not know of the details of the draft, but was told he might be nominated "by acclamation." The General made no promises to the party, which in effect was accepting him on character. Ullman was supposed to have told Armstrong, "I think I know what we are getting, but I'm not certain. We are throwing dice with destiny." Samuel Slate. *The Rise of Emiliano Calles* (New York, 1929); James Clark. *The Slate Thesis Vindicated: How Calles Became President* (Mexico City, 1966); Dwight Hermon. *Albert Ullman and the Calles Conspiracy* (Mexico City, 1969).

that this did not matter. Consalus correctly pointed out that Calles had no political experience; had gone back on his word that he would not run for office; and had no solutions to Mexico's problems. Ullman suggested Calles challenge Consalus to a debate, expecting the President to reject it. To his surprise, Consalus agreed, and the debate, which was vitavised, saw the President score point after point against Calles, who was visibly ill at ease. When asked what he would do about slavery, the General replied "He would study the matter." Apparently he didn't know the question had been under study for four years. "Consalus destroyed Calles as a matador finishes off a dull bull."[10]

Despite all his failures as a candidate, Calles was able to win election in April. Thus, he entered office, apparently without a plan or much in the way of knowledge as to his powers and responsibilities.

### The Mexican Elections of 1920

| STATE | CALLES (L) | CONSALUS (UM) |
|---|---|---|
| California | 2,007,895 | 4,108,079 |
| Jefferson | 2,587,697 | 2,869,706 |
| Durango | 2,593,495 | 1,000,596 |
| Chiapas | 1,945,697 | 940,956 |
| Arizona | 1,403,468 | 799,893 |
| Mexico del Norte | 1,304,398 | 495,605 |
| | 11,842,690 | 10,214,835 |

Source: U.S.M. *Statistical Abstract*, p. 113.

Calles, however, was no fool. He realized he was unprepared for the presidency, but quickly set about learning its functions and exploring the limits of his power. His mentor in this was Albert Ullman, who became Secretary of State, and was Calles' chief advisor in his first two years in office. Ullman understood the situation completely. Unlike most Libertarian politicians, he neither underrated Calles' intelligence nor considered the President a wonder-worker. Ullman believed Calles to be a man of good instincts who would learn quickly. "Some of my colleagues seemed to consider the President rather stupid and slothful. Had they forgotten the Battle of Chapultapec? They also considered him a poor politician. Did they realize what it takes to rise to field command in an army commanded by Anglos if you are a Mexicano? They were the fools, not Emiliano Calles."[11]

---

10. Fernando Mordes in Mexico City *Tribune*, March 30, 1920.
11. Albert Ullman's interview by Miguel Callendra. October 12, 1929, on *I Remember*, a vitavision show of the time.

The stolid former General and the imaginative former college professor worked well together. At first, most of Calles' ideas were borrowed from Ullman, and even some of his phrases sounded like those of his Secretary of State. Thus, many of the reforms of 1920–1921 may be credited to Ullman as much as to the President, a fact Calles did not bother to deny. By 1922, however, Calles was his own man, and Ullman gracefully withdrew into the background. Not once did the two men appear at odds with one another; their friendship was genuine, and based on mutual respect. Even so, some commentators thought Calles was under Ullman's power, while others considered him no more than a tool of the Mexico City Libertarians. Writing in this vein, Josephine Williams of the Jefferson *Times* fantasized: "Mr. Calles resembles nothing more than petrified wood, not only in appearance, but in chemistry. Wood when placed in mineral solution changes gradually, as the wood molecules are replaced by those of stone. Thus, the appearance is wood, but the reality is calcium. President Calles seems the Hero of Chapultapec, but in reality he is the miserable professor from Kinkaid."[12] To this, Ullman had his usual ready quip. "Miss Williams had better consult some good geology and chemistry texts before she pontificates so wisely!"[13]

On April 15, Calles announced he would present his legislative program to the Senate within a week. He appeared before that body on April 21 to read his requests, an act unprecedented since the restoration of the republic. The speech was far shorter than anyone had expected, lasting less than four minutes. It dealt exclusively with the slavery issue. In blunt, choppy sentences, Calles outlined the background of the situation, and then offered his solution. "Slavery must be abolished in Mexico. We shall try to do so by constitutional amendment, but if this is not possible, other ways will be found. We have talked long enough of this subject. In all the reports I have yet to find one reasonable argument in favor of keeping the Negro enslaved. The free population of Mexico numbers 132 million. There are some 103,000 Negro slaves in the country. Giving these poor wretches their liberty will not dilute our national bloodstream; nor will it poison our lives. It is a small price to pay for the benefits manumission will bring."[14]

Calles purposely did not spell out the details of the plan; he had wisely decided to allow public shock and discussion to run its course before detailing the mechanics of manumission, or the way the amendment would be handled. Ullman, who managed the program, and who had helped write the speech, later said that "We had no specific plan

12. Josephine Williams in Jefferson *Times*, February 12, 1921.
13. Albert Ullman, as quoted in Mexico City *Times*, March 1, 1921.
14. Mexico City *Herald*, April 16, 1920.

worked out in advance. All we knew was that freedom was the only answer. We were willing to allow the defenders of slavery to guide us in the way they would end the institution, and listened carefully in the next two weeks. Then we acted."[15]

Surprisingly, few major political figures of either party attempted to respond forcefully to Calles' speech. To challenge a recently-elected popular hero would have been foolhardy, while the plan itself was too nebulous to attack. No politician with hopes of a national career could expect immediate benefits, for no one knew whether or not Calles would succeed. Finally, word spread throughout the capital that Douglas Benedict supported manumission. With Kramer Associates' backing, Calles could scarcely fail in his drive for freeing the slaves.

Benedict's role in Mexican politics since the end of the Hundred Day War was one of watching and waiting. Kramer Associates had a better intelligence-gathering force than the government itself, and yet he could not fathom the slavery situation. To threaten the destruction of a mighty nation for the sake of a hundred thousand slaves, most of whom seemed contented enough, seemed bizarre to the cold, business-like Benedict. The Mexicanos were another matter entirely; for two decades Kramer Associates had been involved in programs to raise the standard of living of Mexicanos and involve them to a greater extent in Mexican political and economic life. But Benedict was unprepared for the manumission movement, and true to form, the aged businessman did nothing until the dust had settled.

Kramer Associates had been neutral in the 1920 elections; rumors to the contrary, Benedict had no contact with Calles, and, as usual, Kramer money found its way into both parties' campaign chests. It was no secret that Ullman was opposed to the giant corporation; six years earlier he had indicated that, if elected, he would sponsor legislation to curb its influence. Benedict did not take this talk seriously, since he controlled more than enough senators to prevent the passage of such bills. Calles was another matter. Benedict had more power at his disposal than the national government itself, but Calles was more popular than any Mexican since El Jefe. Thus, Benedict determined to support Calles' efforts so long as they did not touch upon the core of Kramer Associates' interests. When and if Calles turned his attention to reforms that might harm the company, Benedict would take action, but not before that time.[16]

On April 29, Senator Rodrigo de la Casa of Durango, a major pro-slavery leader, asked for a meeting with Ullman. The Secretary agreed, and the two met in his office at noon the following day. De la

---

15. Callendra Interview, October 12, 1929, on *I Remember*.  16. Tulin. *The Benedict Years*, p. 445.

Casa's anxiety concerned the President's speech; he argued that amendment of the Constitution was a dangerous practice, and that Calles should think twice before submitting such a fiery issue to the people. Ullman queried de la Casa how he thought Calles should proceed—given the fact that the President was determined to end slavery. The Senator had obviously prepared his reply; a simple bill, submitted to the Senate and Assembly and passed by a voice vote, would be far more appealing to the legislators. Ullman recognized that de la Casa thought the measure would surely pass, indicating the pro-slavery forces knew they lacked the votes to block manumission. He told de la Casa he would report the discussion favorably to Calles.[17]

Calles was not surprised to learn of the conversation. Several hours before, the President had granted an audience to Benedict. Their meeting had been friendly, though each man was wary of the other. Benedict expressed his hope that the question of manumission could be settled with as little disturbance as possible, and Calles had agreed. Then Benedict had said that he had long favored an end to slavery, "a barbaric practice that has no place in modern society." Calles told him he knew that Kramer Associates had refused to deal with firms that employed slave labor, and that company executives had been forbidden to use household slaves regardless of local custom. Benedict seemed pleased the President knew of this practice, and responded that he saw no reason why "the institution of slavery should receive official sanction for another season." Neither man mentioned Kramer Associates' power in Congress, but each realized what the other was saying. Calles implied the government considered Kramer Associates a progressive firm which would not be legislated against, while Benedict had indicated he would influence those congressmen under his control to vote for manumission.[18]

During the next two weeks, word went out to United Mexican senators who had received financial aid from Kramer Associates to support a manumission bill. Benedict's voice in the Senate was de la Casa, while Hernando Cromwell acted for Kramer Associates in the Assembly. Sufficient senators went along with the plan to make passage possible, but there was a party revolt in the Assembly, where Pedro Fuentes of Chiapas refused to follow orders from San Francisco. For the moment, it appeared that Fuentes had invited political destruction. Actually, his revolt enabled Fuentes to become the leader of a new, major mass movement in the nation.

The Manumission Act was introduced in the Assembly on May 13, 1920. That morning, the Mexico City newspapers predicted swift

17. Callendra Interview, October 12, 1929, on *I Remember*; Rodrigo de la Casa. *Life at Court: An Observer of the*   *Calles Regime* (Mexico City, 1934), pp. 115–19.
18. Tulin. *The Benedict Years*, p. 505.

passage even though, as one reporter put it, "the nation is still not satisfied that manumission is the answer." The measure provided for token payments to owners of slaves, a one year "grace period" during which slavery would be "phased out," and the establishment of the Manumission Bureau, which would assist freedmen to adjust to their new status. "The plan seems reasonable," wrote Vincent Pierson in the Mexico City *Journal*, "and judging from the temper of the Assembly, it will pass. But if the legislators accept the measure, Mr. Calles' problems will not be over. The courts may rule the law unconstitutional. Or the people, as is their way, may simply refuse to accept the bill. In such a case anything can happen, and President Calles may yet become General Calles once more."[19]

Fuentes spoke out against the measure, calling it "legal theft." He recited the history of slavery in the U.S.M., quoting liberally from Jackson and every other pro-slavery hero he could muster. Then he turned to Cromwell, and pointing his finger, shouted, "We know who is behind you in this. It is Kramer Associates, more particularly Douglas Benedict. Kramer gold put you where you are, and Kramer gold is buying manumission for the administration. You were elected on a pledge to retain slavery, and now you have conveniently changed your mind. I challenge you to tell us why you have so acted." The Assembly rose as a man, protesting Fuentes' lack of decorum. Cromwell simply smiled and shrugged his shoulders. But the damage was done. Fuentes correctly assessed the public mood as opposing manumission. Manumission passed by a voice vote, and the next day the Senate ratified the measure. Slavery was thus ended in Mexico; within a year the last Negro was free. By that time, however, the nation was in a revolutionary mood, with Fuentes on a collision course with Calles and Benedict.[20]

19. Mexico City *Journal*, May 13, 1920.
20. Dwight Hermon. *Starkism in Mex-* *ico: The Public Career of Pedro Fuentes* (New York, 1955).

# 29

# MANUMISSION
# AND EXPANSION

"UNDER most circumstances, republicanism is the most stable form of government. Should a nation have an incompetent as monarch or tyrant, it may easily be destroyed. But the government of a republic springs from the people themselves, and so long as it follows the will of its constituents, it will survive. Should a tyrant clash with his people, the people will be obliged to adjust; in a republic, the people will turn out their leaders, and replace them with men more in harmony with their desires."[1] In this way, John Quincy Adams, Secretary of State in the Jeffersonian government of the early nineteenth century, wrote of the importance of maintaining republicanism in his new nation. A hundred years after these words were written, the U.S.M. would learn what Adams meant, as Mexican republicanism would face its most severe test.

In many ways the crisis of 1920–1921 was more dangerous than that of 1881, when Benito Hermión seized power in Mexico City. Mexico was in little danger of anarchy in 1881; Hermión had insisted on retaining republican forms, even if he distorted their contents. Hermión truly recognized the value of maintaining a commonwealth, that is, a community of people living under law. Furthermore, Kramer Associates not only maintained its power, but actually expanded rapidly in the Hermión era, and the company added to Mexico's stability while functioning as a counterweight to Hermión's excesses. In this way, Cortez had organized the overthrow of El Jefe, not because Hermión threatened Kramer Associates, but because he endangered Mexican stability.

Pedro Fuentes, a self-educated U.M. Assemblyman from Chiapas, realized this better than did Calles and Benedict. A leading representative of Mexicano interests in the Congress, he knew the vast majority

---

1. J. Q. Adams. *Diary*, Vol. 4, pp. 335–36.

of his constituents opposed manumission. Like Benedict, Fuentes did not believe the slave issue a major problem prior to 1919. Indeed, in 1917 he called slavery "a pain, but not a cancer," and had even signed a petition against slavery to please a friend. As the issue became paramount in Mexican politics, however, Fuentes became the leader of the pro-slavery forces. In so doing he claimed to be representing the will of his people; Ullman later called it "demagoguery of the worst kind."[2] It would seem both men exaggerated somewhat, but each was doubtless correct as well.

Calles knew the Mexicano population was opposed to manumission, much as the nation hated slavery. He felt that his popularity would suffice to convince the public the institution must be ended. Doubtless his military background influenced his attitudes; Calles was used to having people take orders, and he believed the population would consider manumission an order from the capital, to be obeyed, not questioned.

Similarly, Douglas Benedict assumed Calles would be able to win manumission, given his help. Kramer Associates had no ax to grind in 1920, but was willing to help free the slaves to establish working relations with the new government. Thus, he commanded those legislators backed by Kramer funds to support the President. In the world of the corporation, as in the army, leaders are used to being obeyed.

Ullman led the battle for manumission, wrote its pamphlets, and rallied support for the movement. Prior to entering politics he had been a college professor, and, as such, considered truth his primary objective. Ullman had long before determined that slavery was wrong, and now, as Secretary of State, he joyfully presided over its extinction. He believed himself the possessor of the truth, and would pursue it no matter what others thought. Such an attitude may be commendable, but it hardly was in the spirit of what Adams would call republicanism.

Thus, the battle for manumission was led by three men—a former general, the head of the largest corporation in the world, and a man who had spent most of his life on the college campus. In their own areas, none were required to take "public opinion" into consideration. For different reasons, each was convinced slavery must be ended. Fuentes, who had more practical political experience than any of them, now took command of the pro-slavery forces. Paradoxically, this great democratic movement was headed by people whose training had led them to be authoritarian, while their opposition was led by one who understood the public better than most Mexicans. It puts one in mind

2. Callendra Interview, October 12, 1929, in *I Remember*.

of Hamilton's response to Adams when his Secretary of State spoke of his beliefs. "And what should be done if the people, as is often the case, are unjust? At such a moment wise men will yearn for a benevolent tyrant to bring about needed stability."[3]

Had manumission been placed before the Congress by a colorless figure who lacked Kramer Associates' support, it would have been defeated easily. Fully three-quarters of the Assembly had been elected in 1920 on platforms opposing manumission. Yet the Assembly, and then the Senate, passed the measure by voice votes. Calles signed the Manumission Act into law on May 21, 1920, while Ullman proclaimed it "the removal of a stain, long overdue." There were rumors of dissension in the nation, but Calles took little note of them; the measure had passed and now the people must accept it. The decision made, he turned to other matters, which he considered "even more pressing than the freeing of a small number of slaves."[4]

The issue would not die, however. Even without leadership, manumission would have created havoc in the nation, especially in Chiapas and Durango, the centers of the anti-manumission movement. Slaves were set upon by hooded bands, beaten up, and in 154 cases, killed, often in horrible ways. Pro-manumission legislators were also attacked; in 1920–1921 seventeen Assemblymen and two Senators were obliged to resign in the face of mounting pressure from constituents. Even Fuentes was shocked by this reaction, and although he had assumed leadership of the anti-manumission forces, was unable to prevent such violence, which continued for more than a year.

The issue was further complicated by the reaction of the slaves. Doubtless most wanted their freedom, but as terrorism increased, many feared for their lives. On January 6, 1921, Calles was presented with a petition signed by more than 10,000 slaves, who asked to retain their status. Some of the names were forged, while others signed under pressure. A majority, however, sincerely felt that under the circumstances, slavery was preferable to a questionable freedom.[5]

This is not to say that Calles lacked support. Kramer Associates used its power to compel acceptance in areas it controlled. The vast majority of slaves who received freedom under the Manumission Act were vocal in their appreciation. Members of the Exodus Society, formed by several gifted slaves led by Jackson Williams, vowed to lay down their lives if necessary to preserve their new status. The pro-manumission white forces were strongest in California and Arizona.

3. Adams. *Diary*, Vol. 4, pp. 465–69.
4. Mexico City *Herald*, February 19, 1921; Calles. *People and Nation*, p. 354.
5. See a series of polls of the period, collected in Howard Litwin. ed. *The People Speak: Voices of Mexico in the 1920's* (Mexico City, 1933), pp. 335–67.

Paradoxically, Jefferson was anti-slavery; the state that introduced the institution to Mexico was now controlled by men who were glad to see it ended. The Indians, usually silent on such matters, supported Calles, as did the university and college communities. Calles was hailed as a liberator overseas, and was singled out for praise particularly in the C.N.A. and Britain. Even the French, whom he had defeated in the Hundred Days War, were pleased by his actions, and in 1921, the Assembly in Paris voted him a member of the Legion of Distinction.[6]

The summer of 1920 has been called the "Bloody Season" in Mexican histories.[7] The riots and demonstrations were so severe that Calles was obliged to call out the troops to separate the pro- and anti-manumission forces. Mexico seemed on the verge of racial war, with Anglos and Hispanos battling Mexicanos over the Negroes, few of whom participated in the movements. There was even some talk of dissension in the army, and had it not been for Calles' great personal following there, many officers might have deserted to the anti-manumission side. By late August, the opposition had taken to burning down offices of the Manumission Bureau, and threatening its officials with death if they attempted to raise them again. By then, too, Fuentes had decided to cast his lot with the anti-manumission groups, despite their incendiary activities. Later on, he would claim to have done so to moderate the violence; "You cannot lead a people unless you accept the heart of their beliefs," he said. But at the same time it seemed he was preparing a *coup*, to overthrow Calles and make himself a new El Jefe.[8]

Calles said little throughout this period, although backing Ullman, who had become the chief administration spokesman. Ullman did his best to calm the anti-manumission forces. He pointed out that although the freedmen would no longer be bound to their masters, "most will doubtless prefer to remain where they are." Indications were that he was correct. Few household servants left their masters, going on wages rather than subsistence. There was a great exodus by the fieldhands and dockhands, the former to get better jobs, the latter due to pressures from Mexicanos on the docks. Only forty-two percent of the industrial workers remained at their posts, the rest leaving either through their own will or because of pressures exerted by Mexicano-led unions.[9] Kramer Associates let it be known that freedmen would be welcomed at its plants, but this policy was impossible to enforce on the individual manager's level. Instead, many freedmen made the trek to

6. Calles. *People and Nation*, p. 507.
7. Miguel San Martín. *The Bloody Season* (Mexico City, 1930).
8. Hermon. *Starkism in Mexico*, p. 276.
9. *Ibid*, p. 314–29.

Arizona and Mexico del Norte, where they found refuge and employment in Indian areas.[10]

The climax of the Bloody Season came in late September, when the Manumission Bureau in Mexico City itself was threatened with destruction. A group known as the Sons of the Wilderness Walk let it be known that if slaves were processed through the Bureau in the capital, it would be destroyed. The first slaves were due for processing on September 22, and Calles firmly announced that "Nothing will be allowed to interfere with the orderly processes of government."

That morning an anti-manumission crowd appeared outside the Agency, awaiting the appearance of the first freedman. Before he could emerge, however, a government locomobile appeared in the plaza, and Calles got out unaccompanied. The crowd jeered and swung clubs in his direction. Undaunted, the President went through the mob, looking straight ahead, his face stony, his jaw firm. He entered the Agency, and the mob buzzed with rumors. Some thought the President would close down the Bureau; others spoke of army interference. Neither happened. Instead, at 9:30, Calles emerged, arm-in-arm with John Walker, the first freedman to receive liberty in the capital, and walked with him to the center of the crowd. As the two made their brave walk, tension mounted, as the shouts of derision swelled to a roar. Calles and Walker stopped, and stood quietly, as though daring the anti-manumission group to do its worst. For fully three minutes—it seemed like an hour to those present—nothing happened. Then, slowly, the crowd began to disperse. By 10:00 the plaza was empty with the exception of Calles and Walker, and some twenty reporters. The Bloody Season came to a close soon after, although sporadic violence continued for another decade. Writing of the incident that evening, Miguel Casey noted:

> The President said nothing, but his eyes challenged those about him. Never before had I seen such an act of bravery. At that moment Calles was not a president, a general, or even the hero of Chapultapec. He was El Primero, the legendary matador, facing the bull. I do not know whether Calles thought of this before he entered the plaza; I doubt it very much. But, by this act, he won the day not only for manumission, but for his own reputation. Now he has done it all. No Mexican has ever so drained the cup, and so magnificently.[11]

10. Within two generations, intermarriage had become common between the Indians and Negroes, and the distinction between them became blurred. Today, only a quarter of Mexico's Negro population can claim to have "pure blood." Douglas Wayne. *The Black Indians of Arizona: An Anthropological Study* (New York, 1969).

11. Mexico City *Herald*, September 22, 1920.

Journalist Walter Anderson was more realistic about the meaning of the Bloody Season and Calles' political future.

> Our posterity will consider Calles a great man; the sons and grandsons of his opponents will praise him as a liberator. But their parents will not forgive him. The Mexicanos consider Calles a traitor to his people; the Anglos and Hispanos have not forgotten he is a Mexicano. The Indians will support him as will the freedmen, but they count for little in the way of numbers. Calles will be president for five more years, and in this time he will lack a constituency. It will be a difficult period for him, and a sorry one for Mexico.[12]

There is little reason to believe Calles considered the political implications of his actions. Ullman did, and urged the President to mend his fences, but this advice went unheeded. The two men remained friends, and Ullman would be the second-most influential man in Mexican politics for the rest of the Calles presidency, but after 1920, the President's ideas were his own.

In 1920–1921, Ullman tried to win a mass following for manumission, and failed miserably. By March, 1922, it was evident that Calles could hope for little in Mexicano areas in the future. Thus, Ullman urged the President to cultivate the Anglos and Hispanos and—much against his own inclinations—advised Calles to seek more support from Benedict. The President received such words politely, but he ignored them. Instead, he appeared before the Congress on March 22 to present his second "bombshell."

The President began by observing that manumission was "proceeding not as smoothly as we might prefer, but proceeding nonetheless." The nation would be free of slavery in a short time, he said, and that was "all to the good." Now he wanted to "further broaden the republican base of our nation."

> We are a nation in ideology, but an empire in form. Our constitution speaks of the six states, but we control five more, which we rarely discuss. I am referring to New Granada, Guatamala, Hawaii, Alaska, and the Siberian Republic. The Mexican flag does not fly over these lands; each is led by its own government, but otherwise, they are as Mexican as California or Chiapas. We control them, but they have no voice in what we do. I propose, therefore, that we permit them to make a choice. Plebiscites shall be scheduled in these nations; I have communicated with their leaders, and believe they will accept. If the peoples there want to join us, they shall be permitted to do so. If not, then we should remove ourselves from their midst.[13]

12. Mexico City *Times*, September 24, 1920.

13. Mexico City *Herald*, March 23, 1922.

This plebiscite speech came as a complete surprise to all but Ullman, who had been consulted a week before and who had advised against it. The Secretary noted that there was no great pro-Mexican party in any of the nations and dependencies involved, and no reason to create new difficulties when the old had not been conquered. "If the leaders of New Granada, Siberia, and Guatamala accept our proposal—and I doubt they will—and the people vote for incorporation into the U.S.M., then they will become a burden we can barely afford to carry. If they don't, it will be a slap in the face from which we may not recover for many years." As Ullman summed it up, "there is everything to lose and nothing to gain in such a proposal." He could have noted, too, that New Granada and Guatamala were dominated by peoples closer to the Mexicanos than to the Anglos and Hispanos, and would doubtless vote against Calles if allowed to do so in the 1926 elections. Still, Calles was determined to have his way, and delivered his speech as planned.[14]

When they recovered from their surprise, the legislators divided into several groups. Fuentes applauded the plan, saying "the President will not expunge all his mistakes with this act, but it is right nonetheless, and should be supported." Fuentes sincerely believed Calles was acting wisely, but doubtless also realized it was political dynamite, to be used against him in the future whatever happened. Franklin Adams, the California Assemblyman, thought the idea "harebrained." His opposition was significant, since Adams was known as "the legislator from Kramer," and could be counted upon to reflect San Francisco's views on all matters. Benedict, though ill, openly opposed the plebiscites. His subsidiaries controlled all the territories and nations involved, and he thought any change would be for the worse. By April, Kramer Associates' representatives were busily at work attempting to block Calles' plan.[15]

The proposal foundered badly. Premier Oleg Khmirinovsky of the Siberian Republic rejected it out of hand, as did President Carl Hermión of New Granada. The legislatures of Alaska, Hawaii, and Guatemala accepted, however, but the plebiscites, held in early 1923, showed no great enthusiasm for joining Mexico. Still, majorities were gained in Alaska and Hawaii, both of which received statehood in November of the year.

Calles had lost a great deal of political support through his manumission efforts, and more followers left his side as a result of the plebiscites. In both cases he refused to consider the political implica-

---

14. Callendra Interview, October 12, 1929, on *I Remember*.

15. Tulin. *The Benedict Years*, p. 896.

tions of his actions, doing "what was right," as he put it, rather than "what was correct."[16] But his actions did alienate his following in the Congress, and made it impossible for him to obtain other reforms during the remainder of his presidency. Calles hoped to provide a minimum wage for all Mexicans, introduced a measure to enlarge upon social welfare benefits, and sponsored proposals to fund a center for scientific research, to be located in the capital with branches in all the states. None of these measures passed. By 1925 it was clear that, although he remained personally popular, Calles could not hope for a second term in the presidency. The party was surprised, therefore, to learn that Calles planned to seek vindication at the polls the following year.

Despite minor opposition, the Libertarians renominated Calles in 1926. As expected, the United Mexicans turned to Fuentes, who had spent the previous two years organizing his campaign. In his acceptance speech, Fuentes promised to "explore every avenue, every facet of the Calles record, and expose this man for the fraud he is." The convention cheered. Interestingly enough, no major figure noted that Fuentes himself was a full-blooded Mexicano. Whether he would admit it or not, Fuentes could not have received the designation had not Calles broken the ice for him six years before. In 1914, neither party would have considered a Mexicano for the presidency; in 1926, both nominated Mexicano leaders.

The campaign began in fire and ended in ice. Calles called Fuentes a "would-be tyrant," while the United Mexican characterized the President as "a failure, simple and complete." The two met in a vitavision debate on January 5, at which time both were wary and spoke more guardedly. Then, on January 10, Fuentes told a Tampico audience that he considered both the slavery and annexation issues closed. From that point on, the campaign was dull, with neither candidate making a major speech.[17]

As expected, Fuentes won handily. He captured the new states with ease, while winning large majorities in Mexicano areas in the old ones. Calles did better than expected in California and Jefferson which, ironically, were the only two states that had gone against him in 1920. The President left office as quietly as he had arrived six years before. The Mexico City *Times*, in writing of his departure, noted that "General Calles was important in spite of himself, but he was no republican. Without realizing it, Calles was in the mold of El Jefe. Fortunately for

16. Calles. *People and Nation*, p. 444.
17. According to some, Calles ran for a second term only to protect the freedmen. Once Fuentes accepted manu-mission, Calles lost interest in the contest. Winston Clark. *The Calles-Fuentes Campaign of 1926* (Mexico City, 1945).

## The Mexican Elections of 1926

| STATE | FUENTES (UM) | CALLES (L) |
|---|---|---|
| California | 3,343,493 | 3,330,406 |
| Jefferson | 3,056,406 | 2,879,455 |
| Durango | 2,599,989 | 1,545,695 |
| Chiapas | 1,802,346 | 1,243,587 |
| Arizona | 1,006,598 | 1,546,807 |
| Mexico del Norte | 1,000,059 | 945,334 |
| Hawaii | 495,695 | 399,796 |
| Alaska | 456,354 | 385,697 |
| | 13,760,940 | 12,276,777 |

Source: U.S.M. *Statistical Abstract*, p. 114.

the nation, he lacked the sophistication to know this."[18] But in 1931, the same newspaper editorialized that "Emiliano Calles was doubtless the greatest president this nation ever had,"[19] while a public opinion poll of 1934 showed him to be the most popular President in Mexican history. This meant little to Calles. As Ullman put it, "Calles doesn't care what people think. He lives in his own skull. It isn't that he has contempt for the masses. Having known him all these years, I feel his republican instincts were always strong. It's just that he has always placed personal conviction above all else. Criticize him for this if you will, but without it, the slaves would still be with us and Hawaii and Alaska would not be states."[20]

18. Mexico City *Times*, April 2, 1926.   20. Callendra Interview, October 12,
19. Mexico City *Times*, December 3,   1929, in *I Remember*.
1931.

# 30

# THE FUENTES-JACKSON DUEL

I N Pedro Fuentes, the U.S.M. found a man whose personality and philosophy were antithetical to those of Emiliano Calles. Both were Mexicano, but there the similarity ended. While Calles considered his birth a matter of accident, Fuentes was always aware of his origins and determined to build his support on a Mexicano base. Calles supported democratic programs in a dictatorial fashion; Fuentes followed public opinion, and given the mood of the time, this often resulted in acceptance of anti-democratic ideas. Calles was a former general who hated war; Fuentes never served in the army and yearned for a foreign conflict. Calles brought Hawaii and Alaska into the nation because he thought it was "right," while Fuentes supported him in this because he wanted Mexico to grow. Fuentes joined the United Mexican Party because he admired its Continentalist forbears, and because it supported Mexicano aspirations. Calles became a Libertarian by accident, but he had been one all his life without knowing it, since even as a youth his ideas and those of Libertarian leaders tended to coincide. Even in appearance the two men differed. Calles was short and heavy, while Fuentes was tall and thin.[1]

After manumission, Mexico suffered the horrors of internal dissension, but by the time Fuentes took the oath the situation in the country had returned to normal. Manumission had not brought about the great social upheaval its opponents had feared. A visitor to the U.S.M. in 1928 noted that conditions had not changed much from the situation eight years earlier. "There are fewer Negroes to be seen in Tampico, Jefferson, Vera Cruz, and other cities in the south, while there may be more in San Francisco and Crooked Bow. Those I saw seemed courteous enough, while the servants at my host's mansion were as pleasant as ever.... I asked to visit Negro areas of Arizona and Mexico del Norte, but was told . . . this was out of the question."[2]

1. Harry McGraw. *Calles and Fuentes: The Yin and Yang* (Mexico City, 1950), pp. 10–15.

2. Dame Jane Forster. *My Mexico* (London, 1930), p. 194.

Prior to manumission, slaves could be divided into four economic classes and two social groups. There were the household servants, industrial workers, agricultural workers, and teamsters, while the social line was drawn between those who were literate (usually household workers) and the rest. After freedom, these lines tended to disappear, to be replaced by a new division between the majority, who remained at their old jobs, and the rest, who went to the Indian areas. The former group was by far the larger. Their situations did not change much with freedom, although within a generation most of them were literate, and by 1960, the Negroes who had remained were to be found in secondary management posts, teaching jobs, as foremen, and so forth. In other words, there is an indication today that these Negroes will, in time, become an integral part of a free Mexican society. Intermarriage, unusual prior to manumission and frowned upon by all segments of society, is now making its appearance, although most marriages of this kind are between Negroes and Mexicanos of low social and economic level.[3]

The situation was different in the Indian areas; there intermarriage began almost immediately, and today the race line is partly obliterated. The Negroes who went to Indian areas were among the most militant of their race. By 1960 they, too, had a literate and intelligent leadership cadre. James White Eagle, Jefferson Collins, James Dunn, and Robert Red Wing were political leaders of great intelligence, while Franklyn McCabe became the first Negro assemblyman in U.S.M. history in 1958. Alan Kilburn rose to leadership of the Homeland Society in 1945, and under his direction, over 20,000 Negroes returned to Africa. Philip Harrison, the founder of Black Justice, became the most noted dissident in the U.S.M. in the 1940's, demanding payment for "centuries of slavery" and "war against the rainbows" as well as a separate Negro state. Harrison was shot to death in a gun battle in 1948, but the movement has continued to this day, although it attracts a smaller number of Negroes each year.[4]

President Fuentes ignored the freedmen while in office. The Manumission Bureau continued its work, and Fuentes even increased its appropriation in 1928. But he had little interest in the matter, and turned his attention to other problems soon after taking office. The most important of these concerned Kramer Associates.

Never before in Mexican history had Kramer Associates been so

3. In 1949 Carlotta Hernandez, whose father was a leading businessman in Mexico City, married Arthur Fox, the son of a freedman. She was banned from society, and the couple obliged to relocate to Arizona. Mexico City *Times*, August 1, September 30, December 23, 1949.
4. William Argylle. ed. *Voices of Protest: Black Mexicans After Manumission* (Mexico City, 1970).

unpopular with the masses. Benedict had failed to understand the strength of the anti-manumission forces, and had underestimated the resentment of many Mexicans regarding the giant corporation. Reformers who applauded Benedict's attitude toward slavery were the same people who earlier had called for a breakup of the Associates; Mexicans who appreciated Benedict's program of hiring them and raising Mexicanos to administrative posts were angered by the Associates' manumission policy. Between them, these two groups could find reasons to want the organization under greater control than before, and together they constituted a large majority of the Mexican population.

Benedict was an old, sick man by 1925, but he held onto the reigns of power until after the 1926 elections. Then, when he saw how the political winds were blowing, he retired in June of that year in favor of John Jackson, his heir apparent for the past ten years.

Jackson was both a logical and intelligent choice. He had a fine grasp of international business, and was not associated with any political faction. Perhaps because he expected trouble, Benedict had named Jackson to head Kramer Associates Asian operations in 1923, and he had been out of the country since that time. Now he assumed command of the giant firm, which, in 1926, had assets estimated at $9,000 million, sales of approximately $11,000 million, and employed some million workers in various parts of the world. (The exact amounts must be estimated, for after 1915, Kramer Associates stopped publishing figures for its combined operations, perhaps in fear of hostile governmental interference.) By 1926 three-quarters of its sales originated outside of Mexico. France, the Netherlands, and the Germanies had passed legislation limiting its subsidiaries within territories under their jurisdiction. Japan refused to allow the corporation to operate in its lands, and placed import quotas on its products. Kramer Associates controlled the Philippine economy (under a contract signed with that nation's president), and all but controlled the Argentine and the Empire of Brazil. Although still Mexican insofar as its charter was concerned, it was a force in and of itself. "There are only three first-rate powers in the world today," said Bruno Kauffman in 1926, "and these are the United Empire, North America, and Kramer Associates."[5] This was the juggernaut Fuentes prepared to assault in 1928.

Fuentes sincerely felt Kramer Associates had become too powerful and influential in Mexican life. This had been true for the past six decades, but Benedict's support of manumission changed the situation drastically. The only previous action to which it could be compared was Cortez' activities in deposing El Jefe. In so acting, however, Cor-

---

5. New York *Herald*, March 23, 1926.

tez had mirrored the public will of the time, while Benedict had gone against public opinion.

Fuentes also believed Kramer Associates might use its enormous influence in areas where its interests clashed with those of the nation. Fuentes was particularly concerned with the Associates' activities in the Pacific, where Benedict and then Jackson were trying to woo the Japanese, while Mexico and Japan had differences of opinion regarding the future development of Asia.

Finally, Fuentes believed Kramer Associates meant to keep the Mexicanos subservient to the Anglo-Hispano coalition that still controlled the company from San Francisco. Of all his charges, this one was the most unrealistic. Cortez and Benedict had done more to raise the Mexicano standards of living and education than all the Mexico City political leaders combined. Had Fuentes known more of conditions in Jefferson and California he might not have felt this way; but as a Chiapan, he saw the misery of his people, and early in life blamed it on Kramer Associates. This thought never left him.[6]

At first Fuentes considered expropriation, but such a drastic action would raise more problems than it would solve. For example, the bill might not pass the legislature, where Kramer Associates still had much power. And if it did, who would manage the Kramer facilities if the company pulled its skilled personnel off their jobs?

Fuentes then considered using the taxation powers of his office to force Kramer Associates out of key power positions. Constitutionally, this would have been possible, but such taxes would also harm other Mexican businesses and banks, thus setting off a major panic and depression. Fuentes knew his enemy, but did not know how to defeat him.

In desperation, Fuentes began to study Dewey's attack on the N.F.A. in North America. Like Kramer Associates, though much smaller in size, the N.F.A. had come to dominate much of North American business. Unable or unwilling to make a frontal assault on the agency, Governor-General Dewey had named a commission to "study the matter." The commission helped turn public opinion in his favor, brought out several problems that excited the public and, in the end, proved a useful tool in the North American reform movement. Fuentes decided such a commission might perform the same function in Mexico. Thus, on June 17, 1929, he proclaimed the formation of the Zwicker Commission, headed by Secretary of the Exchequer Stanley Zwicker, which would "investigate large corporations in the United

---

6. Stanley Zwicker. *The Heart and   from Life* (Mexico City, 1935).
*Soul of Pedro Fuentes: A Portrait*

States of Mexico, and make suggestions for legislation." Kramer Associates was not mentioned, but everyone knew it was the first shot in the battle against the giant firm.[7]

Jackson was prepared for the challenge. He did not underestimate Fuentes, but at the same time, he believed the U.S.M. could do nothing to harm the corporation, while Kramer Associates could crush Mexico if it so desired. In the tradition of Benedict, however, Jackson wanted to avoid a direct confrontation. Thus, he put a plan into operation that presented the Zwicker Commission at first with a moving target, and then with no target at all.

On May 5—a month and a half before the formation of the Zwicker Commission—Jackson called a press conference, at which time he announced a major restructuring of Kramer Associates. "After three years in this chair I have learned that no one man can run this business or even understand it completely. For this reason the board and I have decided to deploy power much in the same way as a general deploys troops, or a bank its assets. There isn't much more I can tell you right now, gentlemen, but I can assure you that Kramer Associates will look quite different in the 1930's than it does today."[8]

During the next six months, Kramer Associates lawyers labored overtime to implement Jackson's ideas.[9] By the end of the year they came up with a new plan of organization so complicated that the registration materials alone numbered over 200,000 pages.[10] The essence of the plan was, as Jackson had promised, decentralization. In place of the monolithic giant, eleven large corporations appeared— Kramer of Mexico; Kramer of the Philippines; European Kramer; Kramer Finance, S.A.; World Petroleum, Ltd.; World Locomobile; World Transportation; Technology, Ltd.; United Dry Goods, Inc.; Benedict Machine Tools, S.A.; and Cortez Mines, Ltd. Each firm was incorporated in a different country, and each had its own board of directors and president, always a national of the country of incorporation. In turn, these eleven firms spun off a total of eighty-seven subsidiaries, which in turn had 165 sub-subsidiaries. The firms were interconnected at the second and third levels through gentlemen's agreements, individual contracts, and joint directorships. Stock in subsidiaries and sub-subsidiaries was sold, in the countries of origin whenever possible. Each financing differed from the rest; Technology, Ltd., for example, had three different classes of common stock and no bonds,

7. Mexico City *Times*, June 18, 1929.
8. Mexico City *Times*, May 6, 1929.
9. I am indebted to Prof. Stanley Tulin of Kinkaid University for material in preparing this section. Mr. Tulin, who has devoted his life to the study of Kramer Associates, is presently preparing a new book, *The Kramer Associates: The Jackson Years*, which will be published in 1974.
10. Kramer Associates. *Proposals for the Restructuring of Kramer Associates*, 94 volumes. (Mexico City, 1929–1931).

while World Locomotive had a single class of common, three preferreds, and floated twelve bond issues in different countries in its first year. Some analysts have called the structure a pyramid, since indirectly the entire conglomeration was controlled by Kramer Associates, S.A., headed by Jackson. But it was not really pyramidal in form, but rather resembled a tangled ball of twine, which defied separation.[11]

This restructuring operation took four years to complete, and served to thoroughly confuse the Zwicker Commission. Zwicker and his staff were confounded; Fuentes was enraged. He had hoped the matter would be completed within a few months; on the eve of the 1932 elections only the surface had been scratched, and that barely. Fuentes had been obliged to forego his other programs and his interest in foreign affairs in order to concentrate his attention on Kramer Associates. What was worse, news of the struggle dominated the newspapers and vitavision programs, and by 1932, Fuentes had been made to appear inept, while Jackson was hailed as a genius, even by his enemies. There were rumors of Jackson himself running for the presidency in 1932, or, at the very least, supporting a Libertarian against Fuentes. None of this was true. Jackson, in fact, wanted Fuentes to remain in office. "We are better off with Fuentes than with anyone else," he told a director in private in 1931. "The President is a dolt; his successor might have more intelligence, and cause us real trouble."[12]

Fuentes received the nomination of a sullen United Mexican convention in 1932, and pledged himself "to the completion of this great task before us." By then he was obsessed with destroying Kramer Associates; all other programs were forgotten as the President said: "If we end the influence of this behemoth over our lives and do nothing else in the next six years, posterity will consider our efforts well worth it." Many of the delegates disagreed, but Fuentes controlled the party, and they were obliged to remain silent.

The Libertarians entered their convention with high hopes. After hearing an address by former Secretary Ullman, who charged Fuentes with "monomania of the worst kind," they set about writing a platform that called for increased public works, encouragement of private initiative in the states, better relations with other nations, and increased social insurance. One section pledged "effective action to control big business," but this was vague, and Kramer Associates was not even mentioned. Thus, the Libertarians promised the electorate everything imaginable, criticized Fuentes for his failures, and then swore to do a better job with the Fuentes program! It was poor logic, but good politics.

---

11. Interview with Stanley Tulin, December 3, 1970.

12. Interview with Stanley Tulin, December 3, 1970, and the Tulin Files.

The Libertarians selected Councilman Alvin Silva as their candidate. Silva had entered the legislature in 1920 as a Senator from Durango, had supported the Calles programs faithfully, and in the Fuentes years had emerged as a leading critic of the attack on Kramer Associates. In 1931 he had written a book, *The Search for the Mexican Soul*, in which he called for an end to "old programs and ideas that were useful when conceived, but which mean nothing today." Silva was a strong believer in national unity, a defender of Negro rights, and had worked long in defense of the Mexicanos (he himself was a Hispano). "We must search out the national destiny," he wrote. "It is to be found within ourselves, but also outside the country. Mexico has a destiny in the world which it has long ignored. This can continue no longer."[13] Later on, during a vitavision interview, Silva spoke of Mexico's "Pacific Destiny." "While the President worries about Kramer Associates, the world is changing rapidly. A visit to Honolulu would do him a world of good, not only to refresh his sagging spirit, but to give him a better perspective on the world as it is, not as it was."[14] Such talk was effective, and Silva was wise enough not to say so much as to earn him enemies.

### The Mexican Elections of 1932

| STATE | SILVA (L) | FUENTES (UM) |
|---|---|---|
| California | 4,256,892 | 2,895,602 |
| Jefferson | 3,214,759 | 3,201,945 |
| Durango | 2,296,972 | 2,495,394 |
| Chiapas | 1,935,496 | 1,557,978 |
| Arizona | 1,909,935 | 1,100,065 |
| Hawaii | 496,965 | 416,596 |
| Alaska | 439,996 | 455,998 |
| | 14,531,015 | 12,123,578 |

Source: U.S.M. *Statistical Abstract*, p. 114.

The campaign was a spirited one, with Silva attacking Fuentes' ineptness, "even when he concentrates his attention on a single objective," while Fuentes replied by making reckless accusations against his opponent, calling him a tool of Kramer Associates and a pawn for Jackson. The public was tired of this single refrain. Fuentes, the master of the public mood, had at last miscalculated and he lost the election by a substantial margin.

13. Alvin Silva. *The Search for the Mexican Soul* (Mexico City, 1931), pp. 15, 145, 196.

14. Mexico City *Herald*, November 15, 1931.

Soon after, Silva took office and the Zwicker Commission was wound up. John Jackson had triumphed for Kramer Associates, but Silva would soon challenge the company on a front where it was more susceptible to attack. This struggle would not be against Kramer Associates as a firm, but against those foreign nations where it had substantial investments and markets.

Silva cared little about internal affairs. As he saw it, Mexico was as united as it ever would be through internal reforms. "No matter what the people receive, they will always want more, and will look to their neighbors for it."[15] True unity, he told his future Secretary of the Exchequer, Tito Señada, could come only through foreign adventures, and in particular, war. "Mexico fought as one people in the Rocky Mountain War; Mexicans rejoiced in the Great Northern War; with all its drawbacks and problems, the Hundred Day War was fought by a united people. I do not say we should seek war; rather, our goal should be national greatness. But if national greatness requires a clash with a foreign power, so be it."[16]

Silva, of course, spoke differently to the public. In his inaugural speech, Silva talked of foreigners "who would threaten our nation. Even now, Hawaii is in danger of attack."[17] "The voice was Silva's," wrote Charles Martin, "but the words sounded suspiciously like those of El Jefe."[18] It was an accurate judgement; whether he knew it or not, Silva had paraphrased a speech delivered by El Jefe just before the Great Northern War.

The nation had been at peace since 1914. Under Consalus, Calles, and Fuentes, the government had concentrated on internal problems and reforms. Now the pendulum swung again, as was the custom in Mexican history. The Silva regime would see further war and bloodshed. When asked later on whether he knew what the future held when he supported Silva in 1932, Ullman replied, simply, "We could not guess."[19]

15. Tito Señada. *Mexico's Destiny and My Role in It: A Concession* (Mexico City, 1939), p. 98.
16. Señada. *Mexico's Destiny*, p. 119.
17. London *Times*, April 24, 1932.
18. Charles Martin in Burgoyne *Herald*, July 17, 1936.
19. Mark Jernigan in Mexico City *Herald*, July 18, 1936.

# 31

# THE FIGHT FOR PEACE

GOVERNOR-GENERAL Henderson Dewey's sudden death threw official Burgoyne into turmoil. Half the members of the Liberal caucus, which would select his successor, were out of town, while many others had no candidate in mind. The country was leaderless, nonetheless, and in the afternoon of May 10, 1929, Majority Leader John Jenckinson told the press a caucus would convene the following morning at 9:00, and would not adjourn until a new governor-general was selected.[1]

A quorum was not achieved, however, until the following morning, and then it consisted of only 71 of the 94 councilmen. The rest—including ten Liberal councilmen from Manitoba—arrived in Burgoyne a day or more after the caucus had finished its work. The nation had a new Governor-General by then, and the method by which he had been chosen was roundly criticized.[2]

From the first, three candidates stood out from the rest. Minister of Home Affairs, Douglas Watson, had been Dewey's advisor on domestic matters. An early supporter of the Galloway Plan, he had still criticized it as usurping the power of the government. Watson also was more internationally minded than the other candidates, supporting an enlarged navy. His major opponent, Minister of Finance John Hopkins, agreed with Watson on domestic matters, but was an isolationist in foreign policy. Governor Foster McCabe of Manitoba, leader of the strongest confederation party in the nation, presented the caucus with a man personally popular, unsophisticated but knowing his limitations, and an unquestioning supporter of all the Dewey programs.

---

1. According to the Britannic Design, a new governor-general should have been selected immediately. Since this was not possible, Jenckinson actually served as governor-general in the interim.

2. In 1936, the nation approved an amendment providing for the office of Council President, to be selected by the Council itself, and who would preside over the Council and succeed the Governor-General in case of death or incapacitation. Most Council Presidents have been either old veterans honored for service, or defeated rivals selected in the name of unity. John Deak. *The Britannic Design in the Twentieth Century* (New York, 1959), pp. 156–69.

Had the caucus met a year and a half earlier, or three years later, McCabe would have been chosen easily. He would have been a perfect interim Governor-General, and could have held the party and nation together until the next election. But there would be no new election for another three and a half years. The nation could not afford a man of less than the highest abilities, and only McCabe's closest friends could claim he was in that category. Of the other two candidates Watson had the closest grip on the caucus, and had taken good care to mend his political fences. In spite of some apprehension concerning his ideas on foreign policy, he was selected as Dewey's successor.[3] That evening he appeared on vitavision to pledge himself to the fulfilment of Dewey's programs, "with priority given those . . . which will increase opportunity for young North Americans."[4]

Watson was a shrewd political leader, who understood the way the Council operated and the niceties of politics, better even than Dewey. In addition, he had his predecessor's ghost as an ally. Whenever Watson needed extra votes, he would evoke Dewey's magic name, and more often than not, it would provide him with his majority. If anything, Watson overdid it; in 1932, after being in office more than three years, he told reporters, "I am only serving in his place." "Mr. Watson protests too much," editorialized the Burgoyne *Times*. "We all know what Mr. Dewey did and did not do, and how Mr. Watson's plans differ from those of his predecessor. The Governor-General is a most adept and effective leader, and to continue to use the name of Henderson Dewey is not only unnecessary, it is unseemly."[5]

Watson's record, however, was indeed impressive. He retained all the Dewey appointees and in time won their loyalty; even his former opponent, Hopkins, remained in the Cabinet until 1932. Watson met with Galloway on several occasions in 1929 and 1930, and managed to create the impression that he, like Dewey, had the industrialist's support. Reviving a practice started by Hemingway, Watson made annual tours of the country, and did not limit his public contacts to vitavision as had Dewey. In this way, he not only retained the Dewey constituency; he enlarged upon it.

His first concrete political act in 1930 was to persuade the council to pass Dewey's plea to revamp the National Financial Administration. Under the new legislation, semi-autonomous branches were established in the capitals of all the states, as well as in Quebec and Nova Scotia. Each would be financed independently, and would serve the needs of the people of the individual confederation. Total financings would be determined by a formula which took into account population, re-

3. Jules Whitney. *The Accidental Executive: The Political Life of Douglas Watson* (New York, 1961), pp. 55–67.

4. Burgoyne *Herald*, May 12, 1929.
5. Burgoyne *Times*, October 15, 1932.

sources, interest rates, money supply, and other similar variables. Administrators Jones and Koch resigned in protest, but Bixby became administrator of the Northern Confederation N.F.A., where he served until 1932. Watson selected local bankers to head the other branches, in each case making certain the man was a loyal Liberal.[6]

### The National Financial Administration, 1929–1934

| YEAR | FINANCINGS | AVERAGE FINANCING | FAILURE RATE | CURRENT ASSETS (IN MILLIONS OF N.A.£) | CURRENT LIABILITIES |
|---|---|---|---|---|---|
| 1929 | 1,018 | N.A.£5,296 | 13.7% | 3,594.2 | 1,978.3 |
| 1930 | 1,102 | 5,045 | 13.7 | 3,687.4 | 2,065.4 |
| 1931 | 1,698 | 4,117 | 15.4 | 4,099.4 | 2,612.7 |
| 1932 | 2,090 | 3,495 | 16.0 | 4,550.1 | 3,229.0 |
| 1933 | 2,394 | 3,107 | 16.3 | 4,958.5 | 3,890.7 |
| 1934 | 2,444 | 2,895 | 16.9 | 5,394.3 | 4,529.9 |

Source: C.N.A. *Statistical Abstract*, pp. 1445–46.

The N.F.A. of 1931 was quite different from its predecessor. Financings increased immediately, especially in the western confederation, while at the same time, the amount of the average financing declined sharply and the failure rate rose steadily. Conservative bankers warned that a continuation of such practices might cause an economic collapse. They noted that the N.F.A. was going to the bond markets more often than before, and that the flotation of N.F.A. bonds was an upsetting influence on the general market. The N.F.A.'s balance sheet, always conservative prior to 1930, was now changing so as to resemble what one critic called "a Manitoban enterprise of dubious nature." The ratio of assets to liabilities fell steadily and, what was more dangerous, the assets of 1930 had been of a far higher quality than those of four years later.[7]

Defenders of the restructured N.F.A. called these critics "fossils of a bygone era," and thought the Administration was "at last serving the needs of the people." They claimed that "in an expanding economy, risks are really opportunities, and so are acceptable."[8] The economic statistics seemed to bear them out. From 1930 to 1934 the GNP increased from N.A. £97.8 billion to N.A. £120.6 billion, its most rapid increase since the early part of the century.[9] The C.N.A. was

6. Whitney. *The N.F.A. Story*, pp. 400–1.

7. Charles Gross. "The Coming Crisis in the N.F.A." in New York *Herald*, March 12, 1934.

8. See "Replies to Mr. Gross" in New York *Herald*, March 15, 18, 1934.

9. C.N.A. *Statistical Abstract*, pp. 487, 1184.

prosperous, but its financial underpinnings were dangerously weak, and the public seemed not to know or care.

Besides leading in the restructuring of the N.F.A., Watson increased expenditures for roads, provided subsidies for airlines, and established the National Health Administration, whose goal was to discover the causes of diseases and find their cures. Throughout this period Watson continued the isolationist foreign policies of his predecessors, although he noted, when signing the airline subsidy measure, that "The old isolation will not do. We are hours from the major cities of Europe and the Orient, and not days or weeks. We must rethink our positions constantly."[10]

Watson seemed unbeatable in 1933, and this presented the People's Coalition with a dilemma. Two men vied for the nomination that year. Councilman from the Southern Confederation Harley Shaw, the minority leader in the Council, had supported many of Watson's programs, but claimed they were being mishandled. Like the Governor-General, Shaw felt a stronger foreign policy would be needed, and he pledged himself "to seek a more reasonable relationship with the United Empire if elected." His opponent, Northern Vandalian Councilman Bruce Hogg, charged the N.F.A. with "irresponsibility," and the Governor-General with "pandering to the basest elements of our society." He called his tentative explorations overseas, "an invitation to disaster." The supporters of these two men engaged in a bitter struggle at the Michigan City convention, one that left the party divided and dispirited. In the end, Shaw won the nomination and Hogg conceded gracefully, pledging himself to work for a Coalition victory.

As expected, Watson won easily, surpassing even the Dewey landslide of five years before. The combination of prosperity, the memory of the idolized Dewey, and redistricting, led to the greatest sweep in C.N.A. history to that time. Afterwards, Shaw remarked that "In the beginning I thought we might take it all. Then I hoped we might squeak out a victory. Toward the end I became assured that we would lose by a fairly large margin. But I was not prepared for Armageddon."[11]

Flushed with victory, Watson pledged himself to a continuation of the policies "which have worked so well in the past, and will benefit us still more in the future." A month later, on March 12, he announced that he would embark on a European tour, "so as to better understand the peoples and leaders of these nations, which, in turn, will enable our country to more effectively play its proper role in international affairs."[12] The move was unprecedented; for the first time in North

10. Burgoyne *Times*, June 19, 1932.  
11. George Black. *Armageddon, Wat-* *son Style* (Burgoyne, 1934), pp. 78–116.  
12. New York *Herald*, March 13, 1933.

### Results of the C.N.A. Elections of 1933

| STATE | PARTY AFFILIATION OF COUNCILMEN | |
| --- | --- | --- |
| | LIBERALS | PEOPLE'S COALITION |
| Northern Confederation | 17 | 15 |
| Manitoba | 20 | 7 |
| Indiana | 21 | 9 |
| Southern Confederation | 20 | 7 |
| Northern Vandalia | 15 | 4 |
| Southern Vandalia | 11 | 4 |
| | 104 | 46 |

Source: New York *Herald*, February 17, 1934.

American history, a Governor-General would leave the national soil while still in office.[13]

The "grand tour" lasted a month, during which time Watson was in constant communication with Burgoyne, and Minister of Home Affairs Emery Collins presided over Cabinet meetings. Watson visited Berlin, Paris, Amsterdam, and ended his tour in London, where he had a private meeting with the King and addressed Parliament. Prime Minister George Bolingbroke called Watson "the leader of a great nation, a man of extraordinary vision, and a most welcome visitor to our shores." He recounted the excellent relations between Britain and North America, calling them "a model for all mankind." "We are brothers because men wiser than we saw the need for self-government in North America, and we shall stand united no matter what the foe, no matter what the problem." Watson responded by saying that "Our loyalty to the Crown remains undiminished, and our relations with the Empire continue to be that of brothers."[14] The tour was an unquestioned success; Watson charmed his hosts, and won new popularity in the C.N.A.

Watson reported on his tour to the Grand Council and nation in a vitavised session of the legislature on May 7, 1933. In his talk he stressed the bonds between Britain and North America, spending relatively little time on his activities in the Germanic Confederation, France, and the Netherlands. To those who listened, the tour seemed a great success, in which much good will had been created, but nothing concrete accomplished.

---

13. Watson had wanted to fly to Europe so as to dramatize the closeness of the two continents in terms of time. But he was talked out of his plan by the Cabinet, who feared the airmobiles were not yet safe enough for the voyage. He did, however, fly from capital to capital in Europe. Whitney. *Accidental Executive*, p. 404.

14. London *Times*, April 18, 1933.

The following day, during a special Cabinet meeting, Watson told of more important activities during the tour. For the past decade, the Germanic Confederation had been expanding into British spheres of influence in Asia and Africa. More important, German businessmen had received oil concessions from the Ottoman Empire, which would threaten the supplies of Britain, France, and the C.N.A. Should Germany displace Britain in that part of the world, North America would be obliged to rely upon Mexico for its oil, a condition five governors-general had worked to avoid.

The Germans were also enlarging their army, which in 1933 numbered 1.9 million men. The German air arm consisted of over 900 airmobiles, more than Britain and the C.N.A. combined, and most were of a more advanced design than those of the rest of the world. "Like it or not, we must enlarge our military and naval forces, and create an air arm second to none."

Some Cabinet members protested, implying that Watson had exaggerated the dangers from the Germanic Confederation. "After all, Mr. Governor, the Germans are thousands of miles away. I can understand French and Dutch fears of an armed Germany, but need we worry unduly?" Minister of Agriculture Henry Evans, who asked the question, went on to suggest that "it would even be cheaper to purchase Mexican oil than to defend the Turks. We should give this matter a great deal of thought."

Watson rose dramatically, went to the door, and opened it to admit Ambassador to the U.S.M., Marshall Gipson. He asked him to take a seat by his side and then called on Gipson to "tell us what you told me last night." Gipson then related rumors in Mexican diplomatic circles of a forthcoming German-Mexican alliance. Evans protested that such an alliance would make no sense. Germany and Mexico were clashing for markets in South America and Africa, while Kramer Associates faced strong German competition on the world petroleum markets. "Nonetheless, I believe the rumors have substance," answered Gipson. "Germany and Mexico have always been allied in one way or another, and so the news should come as no surprise."

Minister for Foreign Affairs Courtney Judd then rolled down a large map, and pointing to various spots as he spoke, outlined the problem as he saw it. "The United Empire spans the globe, but it is not as strong as it appears. Australia and India indicate they will not permit themselves to be drawn into a war which does not affect their vital interests. Britain has a strong alliance with Japan, while Mexico has Siberia as a client state and has recently fortified Hawaii. Japan already has clashed with Germany and Mexico in China, and Japanese suzerainty over Taiwan and Indo-China has been challenged. War may erupt next year here (pointing to China) and here (pointing to the

Ottoman Empire). If it does, Britain will surely be defeated." Watson then added, "Do not think of Kramer Associates as a Mexican firm. It is autonomous and answers only to John Jackson. And we don't know what Jackson will do in case of war." Then Watson rose slowly, and said, simply but dramatically, "In the face of this, we must draw closer to the Empire and rearm. There is no alternative. If Britain falls, North America will be next."[15]

Despite Evans' protests, the Cabinet voted to support the Governor-General. Three weeks later negotiations were begun in London for a "treaty of alliance," and on August 1, 1933, Watson asked for an increase in military and naval spending.

This new interest in foreign affairs stirred a great debate in the nation. Councilman Hogg, who led the Coalition forces, charged Watson with "taking us to the edge of the chasm. Whether he will be able to bring us back, remains to be seen." Evans left the Cabinet in September, announcing he would "work for peace," and if that meant leaving the Liberals, "so be it." Twenty-nine Liberal Councilmen sent Watson a petition asking him to "reconsider the appropriations bill," but the Governor-General stood firm. "If you are correct, we shall have spent several tens of millions of pounds unnecessarily; if war comes, then the replenished armed force will save the nation. An army is like an insurance policy. You hope you will not need it, but if you do, then its value is difficult to measure."[16]

Watson appeared on vitavision regularly in the autumn and winter of 1933–1934, and by March it appeared he had won his battle for the appropriations bill. Then, on July 1, Owen Galloway spoke out on the issue, changing the situation overnight. Never before had he taken a political stance, but "conditions are such that silence might be taken as assent, and this must not be." Galloway strongly opposed the armaments program, calling it "unwise, unnecessary, and more likely to bring us to war than prevent a conflict." He urged councilmen of both parties to reject the Watson proposals, and devote their times to the "more pressing internal problems that face us today."[17]

Public opinion turned against Watson overnight. There were demands for Watson's impeachment; a citizens' committee was formed to support Galloway for governor-general; there was a march on Bur-

15. This section is drawn from Jeffrey Martin. *The Secret History of the Watson Administration* (New York, 1944). While undoubtedly exaggerated (the speeches, for example, were probably fabrications) it appears accurate in its basic outline. Martin himself was active in the peace movement in 1934, however, and this casts even greater suspicion as to his accuracy.
16. Benjamin Williamson. *Watson Against the World: The Crisis of 1934* (New York, 1955), pp. 155–59.
17. Galloway. *Selected Addresses*, p. 665.

goyne a week later joined by over two million North Americans who came to protest the arms program. On July 24 Council Majority Leader Herbert Lee, who had supported the arms program, was deposed by the caucus and replaced by Charles Dorsey, an opponent of armament. A week later, three members of the Cabinet resigned in protest against the Watson programs. On January 10, 1935, Hogg introduced an impeachment proposal in the Council.[18]

Watson remained surprisingly cool in the face of this assault. He continued to spend the moneys voted him earlier for national defense, and diverted other funds in discretionary accounts to the new air arm. He was now convinced that without a strong C.N.A., war in Europe and Asia would be inevitable. "It is strange," he told his son. "If I am right and our arms program prevents war, no one will know it, and I will be destroyed. Should I be wrong, and war does not come, then I will be destroyed anyway. It seems my destiny is already determined, but we shall never know why or how."[19]

Mexican President Alvin Silva watched happenings in North America with keen interest, as did German Chancellor Karl Bruning. A Mexican-German accord had been signed in 1934, and both nations were indeed enlarging their armed forces in preparation for war. At the same time, Britain and France joined together in an alliance and they, too, increased military spending. The Japanese Navy was ordered on alert in March of 1935, and during the rest of the year tensions in Europe and Asia increased. The C.N.A. was the key to the situation. Should that nation join with Britain, France, and Japan, then the Mexicans and Germans would be outnumbered. Without North America, however, the alliances would be evenly balanced, and Silva and Bruning could hope for victory.[20] The world was at a stalemate in 1935, to be resolved by events in Burgoyne.

Watson managed to ride out the impeachment proceedings, as his defenders, stressing the world arms race, convinced sufficient councilmen that "Douglas Watson's insurance policy is worth having." By March, 1936, even Hogg was talking about the possibility of war in the Balkans and the Near East, but he still believed the C.N.A. should stay neutral should it come. The Council continued to reject arms appropriations measures, but Watson was able to find funds elsewhere for the military and air arms.[21] By the end of the year, the C.N.A. army numbered 2 million; the navy, 590,000; and the air arm had 600 airmo-

18. Williamson. *Watson Against the World*, p. 298.

19. Douglas Watson, Jr. *The Last Hope for Peace* (New York, 1940), p. 197.

20. Manfred Ohrens. *Origins of the Global War*, 2 vols. (New York, 1941), Vol. 1, p. 354.

21. Watson. *Last Hope for Peace*, p. 233.

biles of the latest design. "Our forces may not be sufficient to win a war," he told Minister of Finance Ezra Clarkson, "but they should do to prevent one."[22]

By February of 1936 it appeared Watson had won his gamble. After three years of tension, war had not come. The world's major powers were still at combat readiness, but most leaders expected peace to continue. On February 22, Watson went to Georgia to take his first vacation in two years. Silva was in Acapulco at the time, also resting from struggles in the capital. Bruning was cruising in the Mediterranean, on a private yacht so as to allay suspicions. Prime Minister Bolingbroke was at his daughter's wedding in East Anglia. There seemed no reason to expect a new crisis that week, but after months of fear and excitement, the crisis came.

On the afternoon of February 24, 1936, John Jackson announced that Kramer Associates would move its headquarters to Luzon in the Philippines "to be closer to our Asian interests." Soon after, it was learned that Kramer Associates had been selling securities in the world stock exchanges for weeks, converting its funds to gold. The gold price, which had been £7.23 on February 18, had risen to £7.65 by February 23 and closed at £7.99 the following day. The next morning gold opened in London at £8.89, rose to £9.56 by noon, at which time trading was halted. There was panic on all the world's securities markets that day, and one by one they closed their doors, in fear of helping create a liquidity crisis.

The New York Stock and Exchange Board was hard hit, as prices tumbled fifteen percent in a single day, February 25. Watson rushed back to Burgoyne to take charge of affairs, and Minister of Finance Clarkson flew to New York, where he pledged Treasury support to the banks. Within days, a measure of confidence had been restored. The London Exchange reopened on February 28, and the other world markets followed soon after. Jackson issued a statement to the effect that Kramer Associates had "complete confidence in the world's economies," and noted that the move to the Philippines had "been planned several months ago, and should be no surprise to the international community." The New York market opened on March 1, and recorded its heaviest volume in history when prices rose more than sixteen percent in five hours. The crisis was over, so it seemed.[23]

Informed businessmen and statesmen knew differently. The world had enjoyed an economic boom during the past decade, in which capital commanded premium prices. On top of this came the arms pro-

22. Ezra Clarkson. *The Financial Crisis of 1936: Prelude to Tragedy* (New York, 1940), p. 66.
23. The best study of this period is

Jack Buchanan. *The Financial Crisis of 1936 and Its Causes* (London, 1966). Also see New York *Herald* for excellent contemporary views of the panic.

grams of the major powers, which increased taxes and spending, created inflation, and caused interest rates to soar even higher. "The rubber band of world finance was stretched thin. In 1936 it snapped and then broke."[24] While uninformed speculators and investors hastened to buy securities in early March, those who realized the danger of the situation sold out, and converted their funds to gold.[25] Later on, it was learned that Kramer Associates had never stopped buying gold, so that by March 5 it had almost ten percent of the world's coin and bullion supply.[26]

The financial tensions hit the weakest firms first, and there were reports of failures and bankruptcies in all the major nations in early March. This, too, was not taken as seriously as might be expected, for the large companies all seemed in good shape. Then, on March 15, the C.N.A. and then the world was struck by a financial bombshell from North City.

The N.F.A. branches had continued their expansionist programs throughout 1935, processing 2,687 separate financings that year, with a record failure rate of 17.1 percent. All the branches were short of capital, but the Manitoba office was in particularly bad shape. Administrator Wilson McGregor probably deserved much of the blame for this situation, although it should be said that he was no more derelict in his duties than administrators in other states. Indeed, had he tried to hold back on financings, he probably would have been removed from office. Burgoyne knew of the situation, but did nothing. Clarkson told Watson of the problem, but the Governor-General was so deeply concerned with foreign affairs and the isolationism debates that he allowed the matter to slide. Thus, he was distressed, but not surprised, when word reached him on March 14, 1936, that McGregor would not be able to meet interest payments on Manitoba N.F.A. bonds that were due that day. Treasury funds were rushed to North City to meet the crisis, and the bondholders were satisfied, but news reached the media, and, by nightfall, all North America knew of the problems in North City.[27]

The next morning, March 15, the New York Stock and Exchange Board was struck by a new panic, one that was worse than that of February 25. The N.F.A. was unable to sell its bonds, and the prices of outstanding issues plummeted. Not even government assurances of solvency were taken seriously any more. That evening, the Manitoba N.F.A. closed its doors. By 10:00 the next day, the branches in all other capitals except New York followed, and the New York branch

24. Buchanan. *Financial Crisis of 1936*, p. 997.
25. Clarkson. *Financial Crisis of 1936*, p. 443.
26. Interview with Stanley Tulin, December 3, 1970.
27. Buchanan. *Financial Crisis of 1936*, p. 476.

had to close on March 17. The N.F.A., the largest purely financial corporation in the world and the backbone of C.N.A. commerce and industry, was, in fact, bankrupt.[28]

The panic of 1936 severely crippled the C.N.A., and is even now considered the single most important event in the modern history of the nation, eclipsing even the crises of the 1920's. The nation's business was paralyzed for weeks, and its financial institutions would not recover from the shock for years. For the moment, however, its immediate effect was to turn the Watson Administration from foreign affairs to domestic considerations once again. Clearly, the nation could not participate in war after such a damaging blow. This was the reading in London, Berlin, Mexico City, and Tokyo, as the North American financial disaster altered the course of world events and brought the major powers to a new conflict.

---

28. Buchanan. *Financial Crisis of 1936*, p. 495.

# 32

# THE GLOBAL WAR

THE C.N.A. financial panic of March, 1936, had spread to western Europe by early autumn, and to Japan by November. The world financial outlook that Christmas season was bleak, as in every country, capital went into hiding. Interest rates continued to rise, but investors refused to purchase new bonds. Industrial concerns cut back on expansion plans; consumers put off new purchases. Even Kramer Associates felt the pinch, as its profits were halved in 1936, and halved again in 1937.[1] The armaments industries were the only ones not to suffer; in the midst of the worst world depression in history, the major powers continued to prepare for war.

The war might easily have come in 1937 were it not for three factors. The first of these was the depression itself. The powers had to set their internal affairs in order before embarking on military adventures and recovery was slower than expected. Toward the end of 1937, it appeared the world's economies had leveled off, but would not rise without some major impetus. Many economists in Britain and France argued that war would provide such a push; Geoffrey De Bow expounded that the increased government spending that would come with war would lead to new prosperity and Bernard Morris agreed. "The key is to be found in consumption. If people will not purchase goods, factories will remain closed. Thus the government must step in and become a major buyer of the nation's commodities. And the most logical place to spend such funds, given the nature of the world today, is on the military."

Lawrence French of Burgoyne University disagreed. If a war did come, he wrote, "the world's economies would be totally destroyed, as would republicanism wherever it may be found. Munitions makers will insist on payment for their goods. To meet such payments, governments will print inflationary paper money. When the manufacturers demand gold instead, the gold supply will be exhausted within months,

---

1. Interview with Stanley Tulin, January 6, 1971.

if not weeks. At this point, the governments will be forced to take over the factories. When this happens, every nation in the world will become a dictatorship."[2] Such debates continued throughout the year, but no formula was found to bring about recovery, and without it, war seemed improbable.

The second factor was an unusual "peace offensive," which began spontaneously and which, by mid-1937, had led to a great international effort. There were demonstrations in Berlin, Mexico City, and London that summer. The Army barracks in Michigan City was overrun with protestors, and the city was in a state of anarchy for three days. Intellectuals and opposition leaders in all major nations spoke out against the arms race, and dire predictions as to what would happen if war broke out were published, translated, and spread all over the world. Owen Galloway, who led the C.N.A. peace movement, organized a "world conference for peace," which took place in Madrid on September 8, and which attracted delegates from almost every nation in the world. The turnout was large, but the meeting was a failure, as squabbles between rival peace groups led to a riot in the city on September 11, after which Premier Aldo Figuroa ordered the delegates out of Spain. Still, in terms of numbers alone, the peace movement was impressive, and gave the political leaders of the major powers reason to pause. Galloway predicted that "any nation that goes to war will find itself engaged in two conflicts—one with the foreign enemy, the other with its own people."[3]

A final and most important factor in delaying war decisions was the elections pending in the Germanic Confederation and Britain in November of 1937 and in early 1938, in the C.N.A. and the U.S.M. No statesman in any of these countries wanted to take his nation to war without first receiving a mandate; "war waited on the people."[4]

The German elections of November 5 resulted in a victory for Karl Bruning's Deutschland Party, which captured control of the legislatures of Baden-Baden and Bavaria as well as increasing its majority in the all-important Prussian Diet. Bruning's opponent, Gustaf von Holtz of the Democratic Party, was a leading peace advocate, and Bruning's

---

2. Howard Buley. *Economists and the Global War* (London, 1966), pp. 105–9, 145–56, 223–29.
3. Thomas Kelley. *The Peace Crusade of 1937: A Study in Group Behavior* (New York, 1949).
4. After the war, revisionist historians would claim that the people throughout the world did not want to fight. Their opponents would, on such occasions, bring out the votes in the four coun-

tries to prove the opposite. My own view is that the war was popular in its first few months, but then public opinion turned against it in all countries. In the words of Charles Plimpton, "the only unjust and immoral war is the one you lose." See Walter Verity. "Historians and the Global War" in the *Australian Historical Review* XXXVII (January, 1955), pp. 454–99.

victory was seen as a mandate for war. Similarly, the Tories won in Britain, and Prime Minister Bolingbroke was returned to office. Although less belligerent than Bruning, Bolingbroke was known as a "Great Englander," as opposed to his Whig opponent, Malcolm Hart, who favored accommodation with Germany. In this way, Europe's two leading powers cast the ballot for war.

The North American election campaign was one of the most hardfought in years. Watson had won a decisive victory in 1933, but the depression, his support of the unpopular arms policy, the defection of Owen Galloway, and the growth of urban violence, had led his majority to melt away. "By late 1937, Watson's reservoir of good will had been drained. In 1933 he had looked like Samson; by 1937 his locks had been shorn."[5] Still, Watson was able to win his party's nomination, and vowed to make the C.N.A. election a plebiscite on war or peace. "Only a strong nation can be free and peaceful. If you vote for me, you are voting for the arms program. A vote for my opponent is a mandate for weakness, which would invite aggression and perhaps destroy not only Europe and us with it, but the world."[6]

The Coalition candidate was Councilman Bruce Hogg, who had opposed the arms program from the first. In addition, he was able to make capital of the government's failure to bring about economic recovery and Watson's seeming ineptness in his last two years in office. "We have sufficient problems at home not to have to worry about the rest of the world," said Hogg in his acceptance address. "This February, the people will choose between the bankrupt candidate of a bankrupt party who would engage us in a war which we neither want nor need, from which we gain nothing; and the party of peace and recovery, one that is concerned with the Confederation of North America, and not the globe."[7] Of equal interest was the Coalition choice for Council President. If elected, Hogg pledged himself to support Councilman James Billington of the Northern Confederation for the post. Billington was one of only ten Negroes in the Council, and if the Coalition won, would assume the highest post in the national government ever held by one of his race.[8]

The election was close, with the Liberals doing well in urban areas while the Coalition swept the farms and suburbs. Most analysts credit Billington's selection with swinging Southern Vandalia into the Coalition ranks, and as it turned out, this was sufficient for a Hogg victory.[9]

---

5. Charles Gross in New York *Herald*, December 5, 1937.
6. New York *Herald*, January 10, 1938.
7. Burgoyne *Times*, January 18, 1938.
8. Arthur Heide. *The Emergence of*

*James Billington* (New York, 1960), pp. 23–39.
9. Jeffrey Martin in New York *Herald*, February 20, 1938.

The Hogg victory, razor-thin though it was, enabled him to take command in Burgoyne on February 20, at which time he said, "One thing can be promised without a shadow of doubt. Unless attacked, this country will not fight in a foreign war while I am in office."[10]

### Results of the C.N.A. Elections of 1938

| STATE | PARTY AFFILIATION OF COUNCILMEN PEOPLE'S COALITION | LIBERALS |
|---|---|---|
| Northern Confederation | 20 | 15 |
| Manitoba | 17 | 15 |
| Indiana | 10 | 15 |
| Southern Confederation | 7 | 17 |
| Northern Vandalia | 11 | 8 |
| Southern Vandalia | 11 | 4 |
| | 76 | 74 |

Source: New York *Herald*, February 17, 1938.

The Mexican elections followed those of the C.N.A. by little more than a month. President Silva's administration was considered a moderate success by Mexico's political analysts. The nation had suffered less than most as a result of the financial depression, and the loss of Kramer Associates had not caused as severe a dislocation as had been expected. Although the firm's headquarters were now in Luzon, much of its business remained in Mexico. Kramer Associates had survived the depression better than any other major firm in the world; its Mexican operations were not unduly harmed. From the time of its formation in 1865, the company had set the tone for the Mexican economy. In 1938, Kramer Associates was in sound condition, and so, too, was Mexican industry and agriculture. "All around us there is poverty, yet we are rich; all around there is weakness, yet we are strong." In order to retain this strength, said Silva, his re-election would be necessary.[11]

The United Mexicans had two potential candidates in 1938. Former President Fuentes was most eager to make the race, as was Governor Richard Brace of Jefferson. Both men were considered peace candidates, and each had substantial backing. Brace won the designation

10. Burgoyne *Times*, February 21, 1938. The closeness of the election resulted in the passage of a new constitutional amendment in 1939, under which the votes of the Senate would be combined with those of the Council in case of a tie vote for governor-general.
11. Mexico City *Journal*, April 2, 1938.

on the fifth ballot, after which Fuentes pledged his support "in the fight to maintain peace and honor in Mexico."[12]

Of all the nations involved in the arms race, Mexico was perhaps the most belligerent. No nation had fought in as many wars as she in the past century; no people so honored military men and prized militarism as the Hispanos and Mexicanos. The population, stirred by talk of a conflict, gave Silva a substantial victory in 1938, one that was clearly a mandate for war. "The vote would have been different had Watson won his race in February," editorialized the Mexico City *Diario*. "Now that North America has opted for neutralism, war seems inevitable, and Silva is the man for such a task."[13]

### The Mexican Elections of 1938

| STATE | SILVA (L) | BRACE (UM) |
|-------|-----------|------------|
| California | 4,545,620 | 3,056,945 |
| Jefferson | 3,422,934 | 3,495,694 |
| Durango | 2,587,945 | 2,446,587 |
| Chiapas | 2,223,437 | 1,767,598 |
| Arizona | 1,900,956 | 1,465,687 |
| Hawaii | 489,576 | 520,920 |
| Alaska | 506,930 | 479,934 |
|  | 15,677,398 | 13,233,365 |

Source: U.S.M. *Statistical Abstract*, p. 114.

The world political situation was far clearer in mid-April of 1938 than it had been six months earlier. If war came, the Mexican-German alliance would face Britain, France, and Japan. Other nations would surely enter once the war began, but North America could be counted out. Hogg had pledged himself to peace, and statesmen in all the world capitals believed he would keep his nation out of war. Ironically, by so doing, his position guaranteed such a war would come.

The arms race continued throughout 1938 and 1939, while at the same time, international tensions grew and the expectation of war in-

---

12. Had it not been for Fuentes' long history of opposition to Kramer Associates, he might have won the nomination and presented Silva with a more difficult opponent. There is evidence that Jackson subsidized the United Mexican campaign of 1938, hoping for a Silva defeat. Recent studies indicate that Kramer Associates gave large quantities of money to the peace movements, and in every way possible tried to prevent the war. According to Tulin, "From 1936 to 1939, Jackson spent more time searching for a way to peace than in running his companies." Interview with Stanley Tulin, January 10, 1971.

13. Mexico City *Diario*, April 14, 1938.

creased. "Today it seems bizarre. But in 1939 it appears all the major nations *knew* war would come, though not how or when. And throughout all this, no major world leader lifted a finger to prevent the bloodshed."[14] "Nothing is inevitable in history, but given the nature of political leadership in the world in 1939, no one but a fool would have predicted peace."[15]

The immediate cause of the Global War came in August of 1939, when the Ottoman Empire was struck by revolution. At the time, Britain controlled most of the Empire's petroleum production, but the Germans had made inroads in the country ever since receiving their first concession in 1933. The Shah was playing one side against the other, with great success, and seemed capable of doing so indefinitely. At the same time, he ignored internal problems in the Empire, especially those regarding his large Arab minority. On August 5, Abdul el Sallah, a Bedouin leader, raised the standard of revolt in Damascus, and within a week, had won the Arabs to his side. In order to obtain arms, he had made similar promises to both the British and Germans regarding petroleum rights. Neither side knew what el Sallah had told the other, and each assumed he was "their man."

The Shah's forces rallied, and in the battle of el Khibir on September 10, defeated the Arabs, causing them to flee to the coastal areas and mountains. Now el Sallah called upon the Germans for help, warning that unless it were given, he would be vanquished, and Germany's hope of obtaining new concessions would be gone. On September 16, Bruning called a council meeting where it was decided to send elements of the air arm to the Middle East to "buttress the Arab position." The first German aircraft landed at the only Arab airstrip on September 19, discharging 2,000 elite troops. Within the next two days others followed, bringing the total contingent to 6,000.

On learning of the German decision, the Shah contacted Prime Minister Bolingbroke, warning that he could not withstand a combined Arab-German assault, and asking for the aid of British marines stationed at the Victoria Canal. Determined to protect British oil and strategic interests and angered at el Sallah's duplicity, Bolingbroke met with his cabinet on the morning of September 20 to ask support for the dispatch of 10,000 marines from Victoria to Constantinople. This was given, and that afternoon Bolingbroke notified Commons of his decision. "This may mean war," he said. "If so, then so be it. We cannot allow Mr. Bruning to destroy a century and more of progress in that part of the world." That evening 3,500 marines were airlifted to Arabia, while another 20,000 were sent to Constantinople by ship.

---

14. Miguel Alavarces. *The Global War: A Diplomatic History* (Mexico City, 1960), p. 66.

15. James Ross. *Inevitability in History: A Dialogue* (London, 1949), p. 198.

The first clash between German and British troops took place on September 30, near Damascus. The next day, Bruning declared war on Britain. The British declaration followed on October 2, and France joined on October 3. By the end of the week, all western Europe except Italy and Scandinavia was involved. The Global War had begun.[16]

Germany won a series of dazzling victories in the first six months of the war. Two armies swung into France and crushed the inferior and poorly-equipped defenders, taking Paris on November 17 and forcing the government to capitulate ten days later. Meanwhile Spain left the Anglo-French alliance and proclaimed its neutrality, while Italy, seeing what had happened to France, joined the Germans in a military pact. Several of the Russian states and the Ukraine joined in the anti-German Coalition, but most remained neutral, at least until the "Time of Troubles" in 1947. The Germans also had successes in the Middle East. The British and Arabs were defeated in a series of battles in present-day Arabia in late November, and on Christmas Day, 1939, the Germans took both Alexandria and the Victoria Canal.

Late in 1940 three German armies marched eastward from the Ottoman Empire, while a large German task force steamed into the Indian Ocean to assist them. The goal was India, which fell by the end of 1941. The only German failure throughout this period was in the English Channel, where an invasion attempt on December 1, 1940, failed due to poor weather conditions and insufficient naval support.[17]

Coming where it did, the war was a mild surprise and a disappointment to the Mexico City government. Silva's attention had been riveted on China and Japan, which he prized for Mexico. He had hoped to involve Germany in a Pacific War, but the war had begun in the Middle East. Thus, Silva spent the first years of the fighting honing his armed forces to a fine edge, enlarging the Hawaii arsenals, and waiting for the proper moment to strike. At first he cheered his German ally on, though ignoring requests for assistance in the Ottoman campaign. Then, as he watched with amazement the power and precision of the German war machine, Silva began to have doubts about his alliance with Germany, perhaps fearing Bruning would conquer other areas Mexico coveted. Clearly, the strength of Britain and France had

16. The bibliography on the Global War is extensive, but much of the material found in this chapter has been derived from Alavarces. *The Global War;* Field Marshall Sir Alexander Hunter. *A Military History of the World Conflict* (London, 1957); and Hans Schuster. *The War of the World* (New York, 1958).

17. "Had Bruning turned to Britain after defeating France he could have conquered the nation with ease. Instead, he was seduced into his Indian expedition. The naval force that might have captured Dover was used instead at Bombay. This was his greatest error of the war." Hunter. *Military History*, p. 365.

been overestimated by general and political analysts; their armies and navies were no match for the smaller but better equipped and better led German forces. Only the British Royal Air Arm managed to hold its own against its German counterpart, and then it did so with great difficulty.

Silva determined to enter the war sometime late in 1941. There appear to have been three reasons for his decision. He had long chafed at Mexico's inaction as Europe and the Middle East were at war. Then, Silva had information that Japan was preparing to strike a new blow at China, and if successful, would become the leading Pacific power. Finally and most importantly, Silva had come to fear Germany's might. Although allied with Berlin, Mexico now caught a glimpse of the future—a world dominated by a Germany which would control all of Asia, Europe, and Africa. If Bruning was able to crack through the last British defenses in South-East Asia and go on to Australia and China, he would be the most powerful man in the history of the world. And in such a world, Mexico would count for little.

In early December, just before the fall of Pondicherry, Silva signed a secret treaty with Siberia, under the terms of which Mexican troops were transferred from Alaska to Siberia. On New Year's Day, 1942, a combined Mexican and Siberian air strike was launched against Nagasaki, while a second wave hit Tokyo from Mexican aircraft carriers based in Hawaii. Declarations of war followed on January 2, opening a new stage in the Global War.

Throughout the rest of 1942 and all of 1943, the Germans and Mexicans continued their conquests, though with more difficulty than before. The Germans were able to conquer Indo-China, but bogged down in the East Indies, where native troops, fighting on their own terrain, did what the French could not—they stopped the Germans and actually forced them to withdraw from Borneo in late 1942. Mexico and Siberia were able to conquer Manchuria and occupy much of northern China, but failed in their attempts to invade the Japanese islands and Taiwan, while Kramer Associates' private army put the Philippines off limits. Australia also defied two Mexican attacks and one from the German base on New Guinea. But the Germans did conquer the eastern rim of Africa, thus turning the Indian Ocean into a German lake, while the Mexicans took Midway, Guam, the Marshalls, the Marianas, and other island groups in the Pacific.

The turning point in the war came in mid-1944, and was signaled by the failure of the fourth German assault on the British Isles and the disaster of the Mexican airmobile invasion of Honshu, which ended with the slaughter of 26,000 Mexican and Siberian troops. In November there was an uprising in Paris which caused Bruning to withdraw troops from Africa to keep order in Europe. Other riots followed in Warsaw, Amsterdam, and Brussels in 1944; by the end of the year, the Germans found themselves re-fighting the European campaign, but this time the foe was civilian and anonymous. German installations were dynamited, troops trains derailed, and in September, the Berlin Opera House was bombed only minutes before Bruning arrived to deliver a speech. Bruning, who only a month before had been named Chancellor of the German Empire, was enraged. He ordered hostages taken in every city that rioted, and began a terrorist campaign directed against Europe's civilian population. During the next year, over one million civilians were killed in continental Europe, but the Germans also paid a heavy price. Bruning's armies were obliged to withdraw to positions in India, abandoning all of Indo-China and the Pacific.

The Mexicans had problems of their own in China, where resistance not only continued, but intensified. The battle line stabilized in central China in mid-1944, and from that point on the Chinese armies began to retake land. The Japanese recovered from earlier blows, and retook the Marshalls and Iwo Jima from combined Mexican-Siberian occupiers. In December, 1944, a Japanese airmobile carrier task force bombed Honolulu, and in March, 1945, San Francisco was bombed from the air for the first time.

The British, Europe's civilians, and the New Guineans had forced Germany to a stalemate early in 1945. They could not defeat Bruning's legions, but the Germans were no longer believed invincible; the insurrections in Europe continued, while the British Isles no longer feared invasion. Similarly, the Japanese, Australians, and Chinese had forced the Mexicans and Siberians to a deadlock. By 1945 it was clear China would not fall, and Australia and Japan were no longer under constant attack. Instead, Silva was obliged to reinforce Hawaii against the possibility of a Japanese invasion that summer. The Mexican elections of 1944 had been suspended due to the war, and in 1945 guerrilla bands, opposing governmental policies for a variety of reasons, were active in all the states, especially Jefferson, Durango, and California.[18]

The Germans and Mexicans had not been surprised by local opposition to their rule; nor did they expect their enemies to continue to lose battle after battle as they had in the early stages of the war. But neither Silva nor Bruning had foreseen the ability of their enemies to obtain arms after their economic bases had been crushed by bombings and invasions. The two world leaders still distrusted each other, but by 1943 each realized he had a common enemy, which was not to be

---

18. All of the above material may be found in any standard history of the Global Conflict, but see Hunter, *Military History*, in particular.

found in London, Tokyo, or Peking. "The road to Australia passes through Luzon," said Bruning in 1945, while in the same year Silva said, "We fight in the Pacific, but the real enemy is in the Atlantic."[19] Thus, they recognized that their foes were not in uniform or civilians in occupied regions, but rather two powers supposedly neutral in the Global War—Kramer Associates and the C.N.A.

---

19. Alavarces. *The Global War*, pp. 809, 815.

# 33

# THE ASHES OF WAR

GOVERNOR-GENERAL Hogg devoted the major part of his energies in 1938 and the first half of 1939 to combatting the depression. He proposed and got Council approval for food distribution programs for the poor; assistance to municipalities and townships in the form of outright grants (the moneys to be used for public works which would provide employment); and the establishment of an insurance affiliate of the N.F.A., which, in effect, insured all financings up to N.A. £1,000. At the same time, Hogg slashed the budget and raised taxes. "The world will not respect us if we are weak; a strong economy is the best defense against potential aggressors," he said. Following the suggestion of his economics advisor, Lawrence French, Hogg strove mightily to "put our finances in order" by running the budget at a surplus. To do this he attempted to cut back on arms programs, as well as eliminating some of the older social services such as emigrant aid. The road building program was curtailed, as was the subsidy to the merchant marine.[1]

After a year and a half of the program, the economy was still moribund, with no major recovery in sight. Hogg blamed the Liberals in the Council, who had defeated his programs for arms cuts and forced the government to end the 1938–1939 fiscal year with a deficit. Council Minority Leader, Hugh Devenny of the Northern Confederation, retorted that "Mr. Hogg has gone back on every one of his campaign promises, has shown amazing ineptness in handling even the simplest problem, and has managed the extraordinary feat of keeping us in a state of near-bankruptcy while the rest of the world is recovering. And now he blames the Opposition for the failure of Majority programs!"[2]

In the autumn of 1939, when Hogg realized that Arabia might provide the tinder for a major war, he was still certain that North

---

1. Lawrence French. *Economic Responsibility: The Early Years of the* Hogg Administration (New York, 1948).

2. New York *Herald*, May 4, 1939.

America could avoid involvement, and did nothing to prepare for conflict. When war finally came in October, Hogg ordered the merchant marine to remain in coastal waters, placed the coast artillery on alert, and then proclaimed North American neutrality. "We are the enemy of war itself, not of any nation. We shall defend ourselves against attack, but shall take no action either side could consider belligerent. North America is at peace. North America will remain at peace. I give you my word on this."[3]

Both Germany and Britain attempted to win North American support. Germany offered North America "a share in a new world order, a partnership of equals after the aggressors are destroyed."[4] Prime Minister Bolingbroke was less direct, instructing Ambassador to Burgoyne Quentin Ritchie "to stress the implications of a German victory in the Atlantic . . . have Mr. Hogg consider the nature of the German-Mexican pact . . . a strong neighbor to the west is hardly in North America's interests. . . ."[5]

Hogg was unmoved by these appeals. At a Cabinet meeting on November 10, he predicted: "The war is going badly for Britain and France, but this is temporary. Soon we may expect a stalemate in Europe, as both sides will have exhausted themselves in a futile exercise in destruction. At that time, North America will act in the interests of peace." The following day Hogg spoke with Galloway, and the industrialist agreed to act as an official government representative "when and if North America's good offices are needed to effect a peace."[6]

The fall of France, and Germany's almost-successful invasion of Britain came as a surprise in Burgoyne as elsewhere. In December of 1939—sometime between the attempted Channel crossing and the German conquest of the Victoria Canal—North American attitudes toward the war changed, as did Hogg's policies. Public opinion polls of August showed that 78.9 percent of North Americans wanted to remain out of the war if and when it came. In November, 80.2 percent indicated they supported Hogg's neutrality policies, but significantly, 65.8 percent believed North America would be drawn into the fighting nonetheless. A poll of January 8–15, 1940, showed that 79.9 percent "would feel safer if Britain defeated Germany," while only 10.1 percent "would feel safer if Germany defeated Britain." In early December, 14.7 percent agreed that "North America should aid Britain, but should not send troops to Europe." By mid-January, 1940, 55.8 percent would "give Britain the aid it may need but not send troops there,"

3. Burgoyne *Times*, October 4, 1939.
4. James Radamaker. *Secret Files of the Global War: Correspondences With North America, 1939–1941* (Melbourne, 1959), pp. 395, 446.
5. Radamaker. *Secret Files*, p. 946.
6. James Radamaker. *Bruce Hogg: Armed Neutral* (Melbourne, 1951).

while 21.4 percent favored "aid to Britain, even should it mean war." In early February, 33.1 percent favored "a North American declaration of war against Germany if Britain is defeated," and the figure rose to 39.9 percent in late March. Significantly, 47.4 percent believed "Mexico is allied with Germany, and poses a threat to North America."[7]

Policy in Burgoyne followed the polls. In January, Hogg and Premier Olaf Henderson of Iceland announced the signing of a mutual defense pact. North American troops arrived in Iceland in early February, with, as one reporter noted, "far more ordnance and airmobiles than they could possibly use."[8] In late February, a British flotilla docked in Kopavogur harbor, and within minutes, hundreds of what seemed to be Icelandic fishermen arrived to load armored terramobiles and aquamobiles, guns, and fifteen airmobiles on the ships, which were then taken to Britain.[9] More such "thefts" took place during the next nine months, as North American arms became instrumental in saving Britain from defeat and providing material for continental guerrilla forces. Bruning protested the actions to Hogg, who replied that "there have been serious thefts at North American installations in Iceland, and we are taking all precautions to assure the safety of our base."[10] But the supplies continued, and for diplomatic and military, as well as legal reasons, the Germans were forced to ignore it.

By late 1943, British pilots were ferrying North American-built warmobiles to the home islands. North America remained neutral in theory, but no leader in Burgoyne attempted to hide what was really happening. The Hogg policies were successful, not only in stemming the German advance, but in helping bring North America out of the depression. A war-based industry, not balanced budgets, restored full employment and prosperity to the industrial cities and the farmlands.[11]

In July of 1940, Hogg met with Hugh Devenny, Douglas Watson, and other Liberals to tell them of his plans to aid Britain and to ask their support. The meeting went well, and as Devenny told reporters afterwards, "there will be a political moratorium until the 1943 elections."[12] Watson became Minister of Foreign Affairs, while other Liberals entered the Cabinet in lesser posts. Hogg proclaimed a "unity

7. Janette Michaelson. ed. *North America and the War: A Public Opinion Analysis* (New York, 1953), pp. 89, 194, 223, 265, 305, 319.
8. Quebec *Liberator*, February 15, 1940.
9. The Icelandic fishermen were, of course, North American soldiers. In 1947 Hogg said that "I got the idea from my readings in North American history. The rebels, as you may know,

dumped tea in Boston harbor during the Tea War, dressed in Indian costume." Hugh Devenny. *War and Men: Politics in North America, 1943–1952* (New York, 1955), p. 117.
10. Radamaker. *Secret Files*, p. 405.
11. Schuster. *War of the World*, pp. 335–49.
12. New York *Herald*, July 10, 1940.

government" on July 27, one that would remain in power "for the duration of the war, or until the voters decide otherwise."[13]

The coalition government was a success, so much so that neither party thought it wise to introduce politics into the situation in 1943. On the other hand, neither Hogg nor the Liberals considered not holding elections. In the Cabinet meeting of November 18, 1942, both sides agreed that neither party would hold a national convention that year, but instead, candidates for the Council would run unpledged, and the next governor-general would be selected by the party that won a majority. Furthermore, if the Coalition received a majority and Hogg remained in office, he would retain all Liberals who were then in the Cabinet. Should the Liberals win (and either Devenny or Watson be selected governor-general) Hogg would become Minister for Foreign Affairs and other Coalitionists then in the Cabinet would remain at their posts. This agreement was released to the press in early December, and was stressed by most candidates in the elections.[14]

### Results of the C.N.A. Elections of 1943

| STATE | PARTY AFFILIATION OF COUNCILMEN | |
| --- | --- | --- |
| | PEOPLE'S COALITION | LIBERALS |
| Northern Confederation | 22 | 13 |
| Indiana | 19 | 10 |
| Manitoba | 12 | 19 |
| Southern Confederation | 11 | 10 |
| Northern Vandalia | 10 | 9 |
| Southern Vandalia | 10 | 5 |
| | 84 | 66 |

Source: New York *Herald*, February 16, 1943.

Hogg and the Coalition won a clear majority in February, and the Cabinet remained intact, while Billington remained at his post as Council President. "North American republicanism was strengthened by the Global War, which showed, among other things, that a republic need not forget its heritage while under attack. Hogg never forgot this; Silva did. It is the difference between a nation that honors John Dickinson and one that honors Andrew Jackson."[15]

Kramer Associates filled North America's role in the Pacific war, but in a quieter and even more effective manner. In the process, it

---

13. New York *Herald*, July 28, 1940.
14. Charles Simonson. *The Year Without Politics: The C.N.A. in 1942* (New York, 1950).

15. Karen Markey in Burgoyne *Tribune*, September 12, 1949; Heide. *James Billington*, p. 187.

emerged not only as a powerful company, but a political force in its own right, one might even say a nation.[16]

In 1939 and 1940 Kramer executives in Melbourne and Tokyo met secretly with government leaders to warn them of Mexico's Pacific plans. The Australians and Japanese knew them in outline, but were gratified to learn the details provided by the company. John Jackson was not content merely with providing intelligence, however. He proposed in 1940 to form an alliance of Australia, Japan, and the Kramer Associates "to guarantee peace in the Pacific, and, more particularly, defend the area against a potential Mexican challenge."[17] Such an informal alliance was agreed upon, so that when the Mexican attack on Nagasaki and Tokyo took place in 1942, Japan and Australia were ready for war.

Far less is known today about the history of the Pacific war than of its European and Middle Eastern counterparts. Until and unless the Kramer Associates files are opened, we must guess as to what happened behind the scenes. If we may extrapolate information from reports of Kramer member firms, however, it would seem that the firm spent over N.A. £20 billion to subsidize the anti-Mexican efforts in China alone, and an equivalent amount in the rest of the Pacific region.[18] "When the war began Jackson listened to the Japanese and Australians as a lawyer listens to a client. By 1943, they functioned as equals. A year later, Jackson was recognized as leader of the alliance."[19]

Alvin Silva knew this, as did the rest of the world. Accordingly, on March 22, 1944, he announced that all Kramer properties in the U.S.M. would be seized and nationalized. Kramer executives put up no resistance, but many key workers left their jobs and went into hiding. Expropriations thus resulted in a crippling of the Mexican war effort. Furthermore, after the war it was learned that due to the complexities of the Kramer structure, only one-fifth of the firm's properties had been nationalized, while the rest continued to operate independently. This was not due to largess on Silva's part. Rather, it was because by

16. "Ever since the Cortez era Kramer Associates was a nation, and not merely a company. It had an army, a population, a budget, laws, etc.—indeed, everything a nation possesses except territory. This last point has always confused scholars and statesmen, and worked to the benefit of the Associates. After all, you can declare war on a nation, but how do you combat a company, especially one that knows laws and how to use them as well as did the Kramer people? I still believe Kramer Associates to have been the world's most powerful nation since the 1880's, and consider victory in the war impossible without its aid and leadership." Letter from Stanley Tulin to the author, dated December 1, 1970, and reprinted with Mr. Tulin's permission.

17. Interview with Stanley Tulin on November 11, 1970. All material regarding Kramer Associates in this chapter is derived from this and subsequent interviews.

18. Mr. Tulin's estimate.

19. Letter from Tulin to the author, December 1, 1970.

1943, no one knew exactly what the company owned and what was independent of its control.[20]

German war activities slowed down considerably in 1946, as the Empire seemed to have reached both the limits of its power and a realization of its situation. Continued guerrilla activity in Europe enraged Bruning, but he could do nothing to stop it. Germany's population was tired of war, and could see no further gains from continuing the fighting. Opposition to the Bruning policies increased in Berlin, so that he lost his majority in the summer of the year. In desperation, Bruning tried to suspend the Diet, but on the evening of August 18, he was arrested by contingents of the Berlin guard and placed under "safekeeping." The next day Heinrich von Richter of the Democratic Party attempted to form a government, but failed. A parliamentary crisis ensued, which was ended when von Richter agreed to accept Deutschlanders into his Cabinet as the price of becoming Chancellor.[21]

Although a leader in the anti-Bruning camp, von Richter had no intention of signing a humiliating peace. Instead, he withdrew all but token forces from India and the now-defunct Ottoman Empire, strengthened his garrisons along the Russian front, and concentrated his attentions on Europe. So as to end the inconclusive guerrilla war, he permitted elections in conquered countries, with the proviso that these nations "must remain allied to the German Empire, and permit German troops to defend them against British aggression." Many guerrilla groups refused the offer, especially those in the Netherlands, but sufficient nationals cooperated with the programs to enable the elections to take place. By the end of 1948, the new governments were established, most of the guerrilla fighting was over, and a measure of peace returned to Europe. But the war against Britain continued, in theory if not in fact. The Germans would never again attempt an invasion of the islands, while Britain could hardly expect to fight the German army. Thus, in 1948 the European war came to an effective if not a legal end.[22]

A similar situation developed in the Pacific. The Chinese and Japanese forced the Mexicans and Siberians out of China by the beginning of 1947, and then two Japanese armies conquered Siberia and stood poised for an invasion of Alaska. Australian contingents mopped up the Pacific islands, destroying Mexican bases and forcing the defenders either to surrender or to withdraw to Hawaii. Japanese task forces assaulted Hawaii and the Aleutians in December, 1948, but were turned

20. Mr. Tulin believed the figure closer to ten percent, but notes that he has been denied access to the files and can only estimate.

21. Schuster. *War of the World*, pp. 594-98.
22. Hunter. *Military History*, p. 894.

back after suffering heavy losses. These were to be the last battles of the Pacific War, and with them, the Global War came to an effective end. Still, Mexico would not sign a peace treaty with its foes, and legally at least, the war continued.[23] After 1948, the world was in a situation of "War Without War," and to this day, we cannot really say who won the war. But it was over, and for the moment at least, there were celebrations throughout the world.[24]

The world looked very different in 1948 than it had a decade earlier. Britain and France, formerly considered important powers, were now subordinates of North America and Germany respectively, although having achieved that status in strikingly different ways. Japan now controlled Siberia, and was judged a major power, but, in fact, was dependent on Kramer Associates and would be for many years. The United Empire was crushed; Australia went its own way after 1944. Nationalist revolts in Africa caused the weakened and war-weary Europeans to leave that continent, although Germans remained on the eastern coast of the Indian Ocean until 1951. China and Indo-China became battlegrounds for rival war lords, who even now cause new uprisings to break out every year or so. In Africa and Asia, then, the war that began in 1939 continues to this day, but for the rest of the world, peace prevailed, although it was a dangerous and unstable peace. "We are living in a time of truce," said Hans Schuster, "and we all know a truce can be broken at any moment."[25]

The cost of the war cannot easily be measured; statistics tell only a small part of the story, and even then, they are incomplete. The Russian upheavals of 1947–1955, for example, are not usually considered in Global Conflict statistics, but the wars between the Free Russian Republic, the Ukrainian Empire, and the Russian Confederation were actually started during, and as a direct result of, the global conflict. Nor do they include the continuing unrest in the Ottoman successor states, or in Africa and Asia. Remembering this, one should view official statistics with a degree of caution, and yet, even so, they strike a note of horror.

In addition to the 25.4 million battle deaths, well over 35 million civilians were killed (excluding Africa) and an additional 30 million were wounded, while 50 million servicemen suffered war wounds. The influenza epidemic of 1946–47, which crippled the war effort and had been caused in part by the conditions of war, claimed 25 million deaths world wide. Thus, well over 165 million people either died or were wounded as a result of the war. Since many civilians died from lack of

---

23. Hunter. *Military History*, pp. 903-9.  25. Schuster. *War of the World*, p. vii.
24. Schuster. *War of the World*, p. 783.

medical attention because of the war, starvation, and the like, it would not be exaggerated to say that the war claimed at least 200 million casualties. Various census figures indicate the world's population in 1940 was approximately 2 billion. Thus, the Global War claimed or partially destroyed the lives of one of every ten people on the planet. It was the worst tragedy in the history of the world.[26]

### Global Battle Deaths, By Countries, 1939–1948

| COUNTRY | TOTAL ARMED FORCES | TOTAL COMBAT DEATHS |
|---|---|---|
| German Empire | 12,500,000 | 3,800,000 |
| China | 13,000,000 | 4,100,000 |
| Japan | 6,000,000 | 1,300,000 |
| U.S.M. | 12,000,000 | 3,900,000 |
| Britain (inc. Empire) | 12,500,000 | 2,700,000 |
| All Others | 19,000,000 | 9,600,000 |
| | 74,000,000 | 25,400,000 |

Source: C.N.A. *Historical Statistics*, p. 1168.

It would appear that Germany had emerged from the war its leading victor, as well as the most powerful nation on the globe. She controlled all of western continental Europe except Scandinavia and Switzerland, but Germany was in shambles after the war, and would not recover for another decade and more.

Kramer Associates was one of the two winners, if such a term may be used. The firm was now truly a world power, with interests in every corner of the planet. Jackson had taken Taiwan in 1948, and that island as well as the Philippines became the base for his huge business empire. Kramer Associates had no army, but needed none, since it controlled almost everything else. In 1950, its constituent firms employed over 2 million people; with families included, it had a "population" of over 5 million. Since the company had always provided well for its employees, and in the wake of disillusionment after the war, Kramer workers tended to think of themselves more as company people than as nationals of countries.

The C.N.A. was the other great power. The nation had not entered the war; there were only 34,658 North American combat deaths, and these were either military personnel on detached duty or civilians. The nation's industrial machine, already the greatest in the world, was not only intact, but was modern and well-prepared. The C.N.A. popu-

26. Dominick Fea. *The Cost* (New York, 1959), pp. 255–57.

lation was healthy and well-fed, while most of the rest of the world was in ruins and starving. The 1938 depression was only a memory; it had ended in 1940, to be replaced by war prosperity. North America was an island of plenty in a world of desolation and disease. This provoked feelings of guilt on the part of many, but the great majority of North Americans in 1948 were thankful to have been spared the burdens of war.

# 34

# THE GUILT QUESTION

AS North Americans went to the polls in February of 1948, war still raged on three continents, with no end in sight. Following the procedures of five years before, the Liberals and the Coalition nominated candidates for the Council without indicating choices for the governorship-general. Once again the Coalition received a majority, 77–73; Hogg thus became the first three term governor-general since Ezra Gallivan, and the second in C.N.A. history. The Liberals retained their seats in the Cabinet, but Hugh Devenny, now the recognized party leader, took over as Minister for Foreign Affairs from the aged and tired Douglas Watson. As before, James Billington was selected Council President.[1]

Within a half year of the elections, the change in the nature of the war had become noticeable. Burgoyne intelligence sources informed Hogg that all the warring nations were on the point of exhaustion, and that none could afford another year of fighting. Thus, the C.N.A. was prepared for the *de facto* peace that followed the Hawaii and Alaska assaults of December. Under the direction of Minister of Home Affairs William Williams, war-based industries were converted to civilian production, while the wartime farm subsidy program was gradually phased out.

As peace returned to Europe, Africa, and Asia, the C.N.A. found itself in the midst of a great debate which divided the nation, and revolved around the Hogg Administration's actions prior to and during the war. Liberals in the Council, led by Southern Confederationist Chester Lang, argued that Hogg had been as responsible for the war as anyone else. As he saw it, the Watson programs of the late 1930's had put the nations of the world on notice of C.N.A. intervention in case of war. This caused Mexico and Germany to move cautiously, fearful of a C.N.A.-British-Japanese alliance that could overwhelm them.

---

1. Charles Simonson. *The Oak Has Fallen: Hogg's Last Stand* (New York, 1952); Heide. *James Billington*, p. 243.

# The Guilt Question

Hogg's insistence on neutralism had encouraged the war parties in Mexico City and Berlin, who had then initiated the war. "Bruce Hogg kept his promise. The C.N.A. did not go to war. But because of it, over 100 million innocents are dead, and their blood is on our hands. Our selfishness will never be forgotten, nor should it be. For the next century and more, North Americans will be cursed by other peoples. This is Mr. Hogg's legacy to the nation."[2]

Hogg's defenders—who included Devenny and other Liberals in the Cabinet—replied that the war would have come, even had North America indicated its willingness to join in efforts at prevention. "The peace crusade was North American in inspiration. Owen Galloway's efforts in the cause of peace, supported at all times by Governor-General Hogg, were only a token of his massive efforts to keep the peace. When the whole story is known, Mr. Hogg will be recognized as the peacemaker he was and is today." Thus, Billington defended the Governor-General, and others joined in similar statements.[3]

We can never know which school of thought is correct; history cannot be rerun like a vitavision program. But what is clear is that many North Americans had a sense of guilt at having been spared the horrors of war, and this feeling grew markedly in 1948–1949, as information on casualties was released, and North Americans saw films of the desolation in Europe and Asia on their vitavision sets. The "guilt question" would haunt North American life for the rest of the generation, and provide the *leit-motif* for political, economic, and artistic decisions to this day.[4]

The first and perhaps most important manifestation of this guilt feeling was the "Mason Doctrine," enunciated by Councilman Richard Mason, a Liberal, in March of 1949. Mason proposed a massive program of foreign aid, to run "for as long as is necessary" and which would help "stricken people to reconstruct their lives, which have been so brutally shattered by war." Mason would make no distinction as to nationality: "German and Briton, Japanese and Siberian, need help, and we must extend our hand to them in their time of need." He concluded by calling upon other nations "unblemished by war" to join in the program. Later on, he indicated that "Mexico, which has been a major cause of world suffering and which herself has hardly felt the sting of the bomb, should devote a portion of her wealth to this cause. It is the least the Silva regime can do under the circumstances."[5]

The Mason Doctrine won instant approval in the nation and the

2. New York *Herald*, March 2, 1949.
3. Heide. *James Billington*, p. 256.
4. Leon Bloch. *The Question That Will Not Die: War Guilt in the C.N.A.* (New York, 1967).
5. Jerome Lass. *Richard Mason: The Nation's Conscience* (New York, 1955); Herbert Losee. *The Magnificent Anachronism: Mason of the Southern Confederation* (New York, 1969).

*For Want of a Nail*

Council, although there were several major debates as to its implementation and avowed purposes. Generally speaking, the Liberals wanted to make outright gifts to individuals and governments in such a way as to make them appear an admission of C.N.A. guilt in the war. The Coalition, while willing to approve a major budget for reconstruction abroad, would have tighter controls over who would be given the funds and in what way they would be spent, and would not accept the "guilt clause." Hogg was able to keep the Coalition councilmen in line and won a quarter of the Liberals to his side, so that the Coalition proposal was accepted. Nonetheless, the program, which lasted from 1950 to 1963 and cost N.A. £25 billion, was still called the Mason Doctrine, and catapulted the Councilman into a major leadership position in the party.[6]

When, in November of 1949, the Liberals left the Cabinet and partisan politics resumed in the C.N.A., it was Mason, and not Devenny, that took command of the party in the Council as well as in the national committee. Soon after, Mason announced that "the election campaign of 1953 had begun," and almost three years before the conventions, began organizing his campaign staff.

Governor-General Hogg took little note of Mason's activities. The reconstruction of the N.F.A. and its activities in the conversion effort occupied a good deal of his time, as well as that of his Cabinet. Hogg was also concerned with revolutions in South America, Mexico's maintenance of her armed forces even though the war had ended, and negotiations with Kramer Associates regarding international investment procedures. "The world is too complex to worry about Mr. Mason," he told Minister of Home Affairs Perry Jay in early July, 1950. "Besides, I have a hunch things will work out far differently than Mr. Mason expects."[7] Jay, who had become the strong man in the Cabinet after the Liberals had left, believed "Hogg had something up his sleeve."

Twelve years as Governor-General had transformed Hogg from an often intemperate and brash rebel to a shrewd politician. It had also taken a toll of his health. Hogg appeared tired in 1950—he was sixty-two years old at the time, and never physically strong. Later on, Jay would write:

> I suspected Hogg was tired of the job, tired of Burgoyne—tired of the world, in fact. After the Cabinet meeting of September 15, he told me to "get ready for something big." Two days later we had a long talk on a range of subjects; it was as though Hogg was preparing to turn over the reins of government to me, although he said nothing of it at the

6. Lass. *Richard Mason*, p. 306.
7. Perry Jay. *The Way It Happened:*   *The Transition of Power in 1950* (New York, 1958), p. 96.

time. As I left he said, "So long Perry, and keep slugging." That was the last time I saw him before the tragedy.[8]

After dinner on September 16, Hogg suffered a severe stroke that paralyzed the left side of his body as well as his vocal cords. His wife notified the Palace doctors, and then called Jay. Within an hour the Cabinet was gathered in the Square Room, along with Devenny, Mason, and Council President Billington, who now became Acting Governor-General. The doctors reported Hogg hadn't long to live. Billington, Jay, and Devenny tried to communicate with the stricken Governor-General through his personal physician, General John Russell. None could make out what he said, although Russell claimed he looked at Billington and said "you" on two occasions. He died moments afterwards. Thus, Billington became the new Governor-General.[9]

Billington described the scene later. "Frankly, I was shocked. I hadn't expected this to happen. Mr. Hogg and I were on the best of terms, but we all knew he had been grooming Jay as his successor, and we accepted the designation. Perry Jay was, and is, an intelligent and able man; no matter what our differences, we were friends then." Thus, Billington reminisced about his reaction to Hogg's death and his relations with Jay a decade after the event.[10]

James Billington was sixty years old in 1950, and had served as Council President since 1938. Now he was Governor-General, the first Negro to serve in that post in C.N.A. history, and given the nature of the world in 1950, one of the two most powerful men in the world.

Billington was a fascinating and complex individual. His paternal grandfather had been the first Negro councilman ever elected from the Northern Confederation, while his maternal grandfather had been Minister of Finance in the Southern Vandalian state government. Ferdinand Billington, James' father, had been a lawyer, who for the last ten years of his life had worked for North American Motors, and was a personal friend of Owen Galloway. When Galloway died in 1948, James Billington delivered the eulogy, and he had expected to become general counsel for the Galloway interests when he left office as Council President in 1953.

James Billington had never been concerned with the various movements for Negro rights. As a young man, he had considered Friends of Black Mexico an interesting organization, but had not joined. Ferdinand Billington had thought Howard Washburne had

8. Jay. *The Way It Happened*, p. 178.
9. John Russell. *Beck and Call: My Life as Palace Physician* (Burgoyne, 1959), p. 265.

10. James Billington, *Memoirs: Vol. I. At the Helm* (New York, 1960), p. 336. Also, see Jay. *The Way It Happened*, pp. 245-56; Devenny. *War and Men*, pp. 498-99.

been a "dangerous crank," and his son seemed to share the feeling. As far as the League for Brotherhood was concerned, James Billington had said openly, in 1921, that "They are misguided, and led by Pied Pipers who cannot even find the river."[11] At that time, he was the youngest member of the Northern Confederation state assembly, and was almost immediately put forward by anti-League Coalitionists as their answer to radicals who hoped to create a racial confrontation in the C.NA. Billington was elected to the Council in 1933, where he was considered a competent but not necessarily outstanding legislator. On the other hand, he quickly made a host of friends in Burgoyne. "James Billington was an unusual man," wrote Jasper Alcott, Councilman from Indiana in 1939. A noted opponent of racial mixing, Alcott's opinions had been altered by his association with Billington.

> At first, I thought of him as a fine Negro, and then, after I got to know him better, as one of the best people I had ever known. Jim and I never talked race; to this day I have no idea of his feelings on the subject. But I gladly concede that he convinced me in those days that race is the least important factor among civilized men.[12]

Alcott's views were shared by almost all the members of the Burgoyne political community. "More than any other person, Billington prepared the way for color-blindness in the C.N.A.," was the judgement of capital correspondent Jerome O'Brian.[13] His selection as Council President was recognition of his reputation among his fellows in the legislature. At the time, Margaret Salmon thought "Billington would have been selected no matter what his race, but the fact of his blackness certainly boosted the Hogg candidacy."[14]

As Council President, Billington sat in on Cabinet meetings, toured the country, and, in 1939, was named to head the Governor-General's Commission on the Defense Effort. By the time he succeeded Hogg, he was well-known, generally respected, and considered an asset to the Administration. Some had already thought that, were he younger, he might aspire to the governorship-general itself, so that there was less fear of his abilities on assuming office than might otherwise have been the case.[15]

Billington's first weeks in office were difficult, but most of his problems had little or nothing to do with race. The nation had been used to Hogg for so long that a new face—perhaps especially one that was black—seemed strange. But Billington, though almost as old as Hogg,

---

11. New York *Times*, March 30, 1921.
12. Jasper Alcott. *Autobiography* (New York, 1939), p. 505.
13. Jerome O'Brian in Burgoyne *Herald*, November 10, 1948.

14. Margaret Salmon in New York *Herald*, January 2, 1938.
15. Jerome O'Brian in Burgoyne *Herald*, April 23, 1950.

had a far more vital presence, was a better speaker, and possessed of a delicate sense of humor that came over well on vitavision. He pledged himself to continue Hogg's work, including "the search for peace" and "the reconstruction of a shattered world"; spoke of the need for "a carefully organized program for the agricultural sector"; and concluded with an analysis of economic affairs in general. Billington was privately nervous, as might be expected, but the speech came off well, as did others that followed. The nation as a whole accepted Billington; the feared racial difficulties did not develop among the C.N.A.'s white population.[16]

Nor did Billington have serious problems with the Cabinet. As expected, Jay was disappointed at not having succeeded Hogg, as he might well have done had the dead man lived another month or so. Under ordinary circumstances, he might have mounted a political challenge to Billington's party leadership, if not to his official powers, but Jay had always been a strong supporter of Negro rights organizations, and to do so seemed to him a betrayal of his principles. For the time being at least, Jay cooperated with Billington, and helped make the transition smoother than might otherwise have been the case.

Billington's major difficulties were with C.N.A. radicals, especially the remnants of the League for Brotherhood, who considered him "a racial traitor." He was outspoken in defending Hogg's policies, and denied C.N.A. guilt in the war, thus earning the opposition of intellectuals in New York, Norfolk, and Michigan City, especially those affiliated with or members of the newly-formed Reconciliation Committee of One Hundred Million. Unlike Hogg, he believed in a strong military machine in time of peace, and this, too, won him the opposition of anti-war factions. By 1953 Billington had his share of strong supporters, but many in the Confederation opposed his programs and approaches.

There are those today who believe Billington's subsequent political problems were based on race, but with the exception of a small group of Negro militants, all his other opponents would have attacked any leader who stood for the programs Billington wanted. "Billington had many detractors in 1953," wrote one contemporary, "but the nation could be proud of the way he was attacked. These people hated his programs, not his skin. Even in defeat, Billington was able to prove a point. In its public life at least, the C.N.A. had become color-blind."[17]

Toward the end of 1952, Jay resigned from the Cabinet and announced he would challenge Billington at the convention. He opposed

16. New York *Herald*, September 19, 1950; New York *Times*, September 25, 1950.

17. James Lawrey. *From the Fifth: Inside the Council* (New York, 1959), p. 387.

the development of the Governor-General's arms program; labeled as premature his ending of the agricultural subsidies; and thought more funds should be granted the Mason Doctrine programs. The convention fight was bitter, but Billington obtained the nomination, although the party remained divided in the election.

As expected, the Liberals nominated Mason on the first ballot, and the candidate pledged himself to make "just retribution for errors of judgement committed by previous administrations." He ran a forceful campaign, as did Billington, and the temper of the nation was such that he won an easy victory.[18]

### Results of the C.N.A. Elections of 1953

| | PARTY AFFILIATION OF COUNCILMEN | |
|---|---|---|
| STATE | LIBERALS | PEOPLE'S COALITION |
| Northern Confederation | 15 | 20 |
| Indiana | 22 | 9 |
| Manitoba | 15 | 14 |
| Southern Confederation | 11 | 9 |
| Northern Vandalia | 10 | 10 |
| Southern Vandalia | 9 | 6 |
| | — | — |
| | 82 | 68 |

Source: New York *Herald*, February 15, 1953.

The election of 1953 was the first completely partisan political struggle since 1938, and the positions of the candidates indicated the great changes that had taken place in party positions during the war. The Liberals were now strong believers in international cooperation and aid to the stricken nations, while, at the same time, opposing arms programs. On the national level, the Liberals tended to favor strong central government and direction of the economy. Thus, the party of Dewey and Watson had changed strikingly since 1939.

By contrast, the People's Coalition, isolationist under Wagner and Hogg, opposed to arms programs, and favoring a strong central government, was now led by Perry Jay, an internationalist who criticized the general management of the Mason Doctrine programs and the

---

18. A careful analysis of the vote indicates that the race issue played but a small role in the election, and then only in parts of Indiana, the Northern Confederation, and Southern Vandalia. "The major issue of 1953 was war guilt, not race. Billington lost because he seemed insensitive on the issue. Mason won because he had become identified with the acceptance of guilt." Frank Rusk. *A Statistical Analysis of the 1953 C.N.A. Councilmen's Elections* (New York, 1958), p. 315.

power centered in Burgoyne. This ability of the major parties to switch roles on key issues provided one more illustration of the pragmatic and flexible nature of C.N.A. politics.

War guilt, not race or the power of government, was the key to the 1953 elections. Mason hammered away at Billington throughout the campaign, but there was never a particle of evidence that he used or intended to use racial prejudice as a political tool. Nor did Billington believe his opponent had so acted.[19] After the election Billington gracefully bowed out of politics, and soon after, was named president of North American Motors. But the Coalition remained divided between the Billington and Jay factions, and while this continued, Mason was able to exercise great political power in Burgoyne. This added to the new Governor-General's zeal. It was to be the beginning of a strange period in C.N.A. history, led by one of the most unusual governors-general the nation had ever had.

---

19. Billington. *Memoirs*, pp. 586–89.

# 35

# THE MERCATOR REFORMS

O F all the major belligerents, Mexico suffered the least. With the exception of three bombing attacks on San Francisco and isolated ones on other California ports, an abortive attempt to seize the Kinkaid Canal, and raiding parties that did little damage in Alaska, the mainland was untouched by foreign assaults. Hawaii was under siege for several months and suffered from regular air raids for a while, but the islands were fairly quiet after 1945 and prior to the last invasion attempt in December, 1948.

On the other hand, some 3.9 million Mexican troops had died in combat, most of them in China, while another 4 million were wounded. When one considers that, in 1939, Mexico had a population of 154 million, the impact of the dead and wounded becomes better focused; scarcely a family from Alaska to Chiapas hadn't lost a member to war or seen one crippled.

At the same time, the nation was plagued by guerrilla bands, which caused President Silva to withdraw troops from Asia to keep the peace at home. Philip Harrison, leader of the Black Justice Party, took advantage of the war to demand reparations from Mexico for centuries of slavery. A former slave himself, Harrison had relocated to Arizona after manumission where he married an Osage Indian and organized the freedmen for what he called "justice day." On March 12, 1944, he declared a "war against the Rainbows" and from that time until his death four years later in a gun battle in Armadillo, he headed a movement that consisted of at least 5,000 Negro guerrillas, who terrorized the Anglo, Hispano, and Mexicano populations of Arizona, Mexico del Norte, California, and Jefferson. His counterpart in the south, Miguel Calhoun, joined in the Rainbow War, and after Harrison's death took command of a movement that in 1949 took the lives of some 3,000 of his opponents. Armondo Santa Cruz, a Mexicano politician in Durango, led some 20,000 of his people in "Causa de Justicia," in which he demanded land for poor peasants. Santa Cruz punctuated his fiery speeches with bombing attacks on Anglo and Hispano areas. He was also strongly anti-Negro, and on several occasions, the Santa Cruz and Calhoun forces clashed in bloody battles. In the judgement of a sympathetic historian, "Santa Cruz and Calhoun together might have toppled the Silva government, taken Mexico out of the war, and instituted a new era of social justice in the U.S.M. But each man hated the other more than they did the Anglos and Hispanos, and so the viper of racial bigotry destroyed Mexico's best chance for a true revolution."[1] Other groups, many of them simply outlaws seeking loot, were formed in each of the states, and although none was as important as Black Justice or Causa de Justicia, they added considerably to the nation's internal dislocation.

Silva was able to prosecute the war with a substantial majority of the population supporting him. He constantly repeated his claim that Japan had instigated the war, and that the Nagasaki and Tokyo attacks only beat the Japanese to the draw. He also charged Kramer Associates with collusion with Mexico's enemies after the first Mexican setbacks, so that by 1944 John Jackson was considered a war criminal of the first magnitude in Mexico City. Silva told the nation that Black Mexico and Causa de Justicia were being financed by Kramer money, and he added that Kramer agents were advising Harrison and Calhoun as to where and when to attack. Since Silva had seized control of all Mexican newspapers, radio and vitavision stations in 1944, and mounted a skillful propaganda campaign, he was able to convince the nation not only of the justice of his position, but of the need to continue the war. In 1949, when the other belligerents longed for peace, only Mexico seemed eager to press the assault. Had it not been for the sorry state of the Mexican economy, Silva might well have ordered his troops to stand fast in China and fight to the end.[2] As it was, news of the withdrawal came as a shock to the Mexican people, who had been led to believe they were winning the war.

Silva promised an invasion of China for 1948, but none came. Some in Mexico welcomed the hiatus, but others, a war group in Silva's own Liberty Party, cried for "complete victory against the aggressors." The President was able to control the opposing factions, but found it increasingly difficult to rule without grass roots support. Thus, in July of 1949, he announced that national elections—the first in twelve years—would be held in January of 1950.

Silva had no problem winning the Libertarian nomination. The

---

1. Mitchell Armitage. *Justice Now!: A History of Domestic Opposition to the Silva Regime in the Global War* (Mexico City, 1969), p. 570.

2. Walter Davis. *At Home: Life in the U.S.M. During the Global War* (Mexico City, 1965), pp. 249-55.

*For Want of a Nail*

United Mexican Party, which had opposed entry into the war, and then given it only lukewarm support, had more difficulty. None of its leading figures could hope to win against Silva, since the President had successfully branded them little better than traitors. In desperation, the United Mexicans turned to Admiral Paul Suarez, who had been Commander of the Pacific Fleet from 1939 to 1944, and had resigned as a protest against Silva's leadership. Suarez was no peace advocate, but he saw little to be gained from the China expedition. Instead, he favored a blockade of Japan and a naval war against the Philippines, Taiwan, and Australia, which he judged would cost fewer lives and bring the U.S.M. greater gains.

### The Mexican Elections of 1950

| STATE | SUAREZ (UM) | SILVA (L) |
|---|---|---|
| California | 4,376,894 | 4,335,454 |
| Jefferson | 3,820,076 | 3,668,790 |
| Durango | 2,796,059 | 2,465,968 |
| Chiapas | 2,395,496 | 1,895,695 |
| Arizona | 1,550,695 | 2,054,687 |
| Alaska | 657,698 | 557,832 |
| Hawaii | 480,879 | 534,659 |
| | 16,077,797 | 15,513,085 |

Source: U.S.M. *Statistical Abstract*, p. 114.

Suarez accepted the nomination, and despite protests to the contrary, became the "peace candidate"; he attracted the minority who wanted the war to end with the *status quo ante bellum*, as well as those Mexicans who supported his strategic concepts. Internal opponents of the Silva regime voted for Suarez, as did those who resented the suspension of the 1944 elections. Taken together, they were sufficient to enable the Admiral to win a close victory over Silva in the January elections.

The campaign was marked by violence; each party accused the other of terrorizing opposition voters, and afterwards both charges were substantiated. Suarez criticized Silva for not making provisions for servicemen's ballots; "The President fears the voice of those whom he would send to useless slaughter in China," he said. Silva replied by charging Suarez with "demagoguery of the meanest kind, and serving the interests of the warlords of Japan and Taiwan."[3] After the Suarez

---

3. Armitage. *Justice Now!*, pp. 510–17.

victory, Silva claimed irregularities in the California and Jefferson balloting, to which Suarez countered by noting that "government agents
counted the ballots, and all these are Silva appointees."[4]

The violence escalated as January 19, the date set for Suarez'
inauguration, came near. There was a mass protest in Mexico City the
evening of January 15, in which fifteen were killed. Similar demonstrations took place the following day, as the nation neared a state of
anarchy. In the name of order and to "defend the constitution," Colonel Vincent Mercator, leader of the Guadalajara garrison, took it upon
himself to proclaim martial law in his district, and others followed.
Mercator arrived in the capital at dawn on January 18 and went into a
secret meeting with ten other garrison commanders. When they
emerged, Mercator proclaimed that it would be impossible for Suarez
to take office the following day, since such an action would provoke
civil war. He went on to proclaim a "provisional government not of
politicians, but of those whom the politicians have betrayed." Within
an hour Suarez had been taken into "protective custody," while Silva
was arrested for "crimes against the republic." That evening Mercator
proclaimed the formation of his provisional government, to be led by
Field Marshal Felix Garcia, in which he would serve as Secretary of
War.[5]

Garcia was never more than a front man for Mercator, who in
1950 became the *de facto* dictator of Mexico. Not until 1954 would
Garcia retire, at which time Mercator assumed the post of President,
although no election had confirmed him in office. Mercator was forty-
four years old in 1950, a reserve colonel who before the war had been a
lawyer in Jefferson with a modest practice and little hope of advance-
ment. Like many of his profession, he viewed the war as an opportunity to gain public acclaim, but had a certain contempt for professional
soldiers. By 1950, however, Mercator had become convinced that only
the army could save the nation; though lacking in intelligence, the
senior officers were at least honest and prepared to make the sacrifices
necessary for victory. He considered Silva little more than a weakling
for the China withdrawal, while he characterized Suarez as "a turncoat
at best, and perhaps a traitor." In 1950, Mexico had voted for a candidate whose actions as president would have served to lighten the burdens of war. Instead, by late January, they were led by a colonel's
clique and an aged field marshal, both determined to re-escalate the
war.

4. Kenneth Zarb. *Guns and Wood: The Life of Paul Suarez* (New York, 1969), p. 447.

5. Kenneth Zarb. *Garcia!* (New York, 1965), p. 287.

Working through Garcia, Mercator enlarged the constabulary and set about crushing the Negro and Mexicano rebels. At the same time, he proclaimed a nationalization policy for industry, in which all designated firms were obliged to sell their operations to the government. The prices were based on a formula involving earnings, assets, and patents, and were paid in the form of fifty-year bonds that paid no interest for the first five years, and which were not transferable for the first ten. "I have cast a wide net," said Mercator. "Who can say what I will catch in it."[6] Both programs were executed with the precision that was the hallmark of the Mercator regime. By 1952 the guerrillas were crushed and forced to retire to the mountains, while some seventy percent of all U.S.M. industrial plants hiring over one hundred employees was under government control.[7]

Mercator also embarked on a wide-ranging social welfare program. Government health clinics were established in all the large cities by 1957, while mobile ones were dispatched to the villages. Land confiscated from the large companies was distributed to peons; by the end of the decade, the class of wealthy citizens was almost obliterated. The Mexican road system, always one of the finest in the world, was now extended to formerly isolated areas, and at the same time, railroad charges were lowered on a sliding scale, so that by 1968 such transportation was free. All of this was paid for, of course, from the profits of confiscated companies. After ten years of Garcia and Mercator rule, Mexico had few wealthy citizens, but much of the nation's poverty, especially in rural areas, was ended.

The nation paid a price for all this. Some half million middle-class Mexicans fled the country from 1950 to 1960, many going to the Caribbean island states, while one-fifth took up residence in the C.N.A., especially the Southern Confederation. Their loss was a blow to the Mercator social programs, but the Colonel was able to weather it by encouraging immigration from less fortunate lands, especially South American nations, and by expanding upon and radically accelerating the university structure and system. Medical and technological schools now became trade colleges, where students would learn nothing but those skills needed for the job. "A doctor is little different from a plumber," said Dr. William Chron, Mercator's Secretary of Education, and he went on to claim that he could transform a secondary school graduate of slightly better than average intelligence into a doctor in three years. Through the use of a radical curriculum and intensive

6. Arnold Saypoe. *A Life of Vincent Mercator* (London, 1961), p. 387.

7. John Silver. *Vincent Mercator and His Mexico* (Mexico City, 1968), p. 338.

study, Chron was able to fulfill his pledge to have the lowest ratio of population to doctors in the world, but even now the quality of Mexican medicine leaves much to be desired. Still, it was far better than what had existed prior to 1950, and for this the poor Mexicans were grateful.[8]

To assess Mercator's programs, one must weigh the value of freedom against that of security and even prosperity. Prior to the Global War, Mexico could be considered a parliamentary republic. After the Hermión era, freedom flourished in Mexico, to be capped by the manumission effort of the Calles presidency. Nowhere in the world outside of the C.N.A., Britain, and Australia was there so free a press, or were the rights of individuals so well-protected. On the other hand, Mexico's peons had not shared in these freedoms, and were in a miserable state. In 1940, the life expectancy of an Anglo male at birth was 70.4 years, while that of a Chiapan Mexicano was only 49.8 years. Today, the Anglo expectancy is 72.4 years, while that of the Mexicano is 58.9.

While Mexico has yet to achieve Mercator's goal of equality, it is closer to it today than while under a parliamentary regime. Prior to Mercator, starvation was not unknown in Chiapas and Durango; today it is only a bad memory. Youngsters in Chiapas have heard of the "starving times" only from books; their parents lived through it, and many of their ancestors died of the hunger.[9]

On the other hand, Mercator was ruthless in crushing dissent and in expropriating from the rich. In 1958, he promulgated a law limiting individual incomes to $4,600 a year. The figure was raised somewhat in future years, so that by 1968 it stood at $6,000. The Estate Law of 1960 ordered the nationalization of all individual wealth on the death of its owner, the only exception being houses of less than six rooms. At the same time, Mercator instituted a major housing program which was geared to replace slums with decent dwellings for all Mexicans. This program was judged a failure by most historians; even today, a quarter of all Mexicans lack decent plumbing, and outhouses are common sights, even in the capital. Furthermore, the Estate Law proved impossible to implement, as Mexico's wealthy leaders managed to find ways around it. Finally, Mercator saddled Mexico with a huge bureaucracy, which took an increasing share of the GNP each year. "Mexico is a utopia," wrote a German visitor in 1965. "But like all utopias, it is a vision with only the bones of reality."[10] By then many of the free-

---

8. David McAnson. *The Proud Humanitarian: Vincent Mercator of Mexico* (Mexico City, 1968), pp. 167-98.

9. Silver. *Mercator*, p. 405.

10. Heinz Kerl. *Mexico Under the Banner* (London, 1966), p. 447.

doms taken away in 1950 had been restored, but the Mexican press never fully recovered its earlier independence.[11]

This far-reaching social welfare program was carried out at the same time that Mercator busied himself with rebuilding the armed forces. "The war is not over," he said in 1954. "We will never rest until *all* our enemies are destroyed, and the revolution is completed."[12] Most laymen assumed this meant a Mexican assault on Japan, Australia, and China, and indeed the Hawaiian bases were enlarged in preparation for an attack. But the old war was not resumed. Instead, Mercator singled out other, more subtle enemies, for destruction. By 1954 he considered Kramer Associates not only the source of most of the nation's troubles, but part of a conspiracy whose goal was to return his enemies to power. As Kramer Associates did not have the armed might necessary to mount such an attack, Mercator reasoned the company had allied itself against him with the C.N.A.

John Jackson died on Taiwan on September 15, 1949, having seen his company move half a world from its original home, and increase its properties and assets while the world was engaged in a destructive war. Several years earlier Jackson had singled out Carl Salazar as his heir apparent, and Salazar was thus able to take over the administration of Kramer Associates within hours of Jackson's death.[18]

Salazar was quite different from his predecessors. Kramer had been a rough, self-educated German who embraced Mexican citizenship gladly, and was patriotically inclined throughout his life. Douglas Benedict was a well-educated Anglo, a quiet man who considered himself Mexican only because Jefferson was part of that nation. Cortez knew more of international finance and world affairs than either Kramer or Benedict, but left his San Francisco base only reluctantly. Jackson, born in Mexico but a resident of the Far East for many years prior to becoming leader of Kramer Associates, struggled against many rivals before winning designation for the post, and he too considered Mexico his true home. Salazar, on the other hand, had no particular feelings for Mexico. His grandfather and father before him had been Kramer employees. John Salazar had worked in the Jefferson oil fields

11. Freedom of speech and of the press was restored gradually, with no fanfare, since Mercator always denied he had ever attempted to silence opponents. Some anti-Mercator books and magazines were published prior to 1960 as a token of this deception. When full freedom was granted, John Massey of the Mexico City *Times* wrote, "The great power of Mercator was seen not only in his airmobiles and landmobiles, his warships and army, but in his willingness to allow the opposition freedom. So decimated and cowed are his enemies that he knows they can cause him no harm." Mexico City *Times*, November 4, 1964. On the other hand, Margaret Hale of the Jefferson *Herald*, a major Mercator critic, disappeared from her home on June 15, 1966, and has never been heard of since.

12. Silver. *Mercator*, p. 555.

13. Interview with Stanley Tulin, November 11, 1970.

as a foreman, while Edward Salazar had been a financial vice president based in San Francisco, a personal friend of Cortez. Carl had been born in San Francisco, gone to school in Jefferson and then on to London for graduate work in finance, before joining Kramer Associates. He had then spent two years at Kramer University (a special school open only to company employees) in Honolulu, after which he was placed in the legal department in San Francisco. He had been one of the experts Jackson had used in restructuring the firm, and knew more about it than anyone, Jackson included.[14] He preceded Jackson to Luzon by a year, and prepared the way for the transfer, after which he was elevated to the senior vice-presidency. According to Stanley Tulin, Salazar had no special loyalty to the U.S.M., and did not consider San Francisco his home at the time of his accession. "Carl Salazar was a legal citizen of Taiwan, but in truth, he was a citizen of Kramer Associates. Salazar was the ruler of a nation of over five million, stretched across the globe. He might be called a "Kramerite" for want of a better term. Most of the Kramer executives his age felt as he did. As I indicated in a previous letter, K. A. is a nation, and if you want to understand it, deal with it as such."[15]

Salazar expected Mercator to nationalize industrial properties in Mexico; soon after the *coup* he had informants in several key positions in Mexico City, and Kramer Associates often knew more of government affairs than did the Cabinet. Although some twenty percent of Kramer assets were still in Mexico, Salazar did nothing to prevent nationalization, and offered no protest. He merely accepted Mercator's questionable bonds, and withdrew as many men as he could from the nation, some in secret by submarine. "Nationalization was only a pinprick to Kramer Associates. Mercator could not realize it, but at the time, Salazar was more concerned with getting some 500 of his key men out of the country than with all the oil in Jefferson and California."[16]

Salazar ordered the industrialization of Taiwan and the abandonment of Luzon soon after assuming control of the company. Taiwan had a more skilled population and a better climate than Luzon, and in addition, was more stable politically. According to published statistics, Taiwan's growth rate in the late 1950's had reached the twelve percent *per annum* level. At that time it was the richest nation in Asia, and was slowly but persistently turning Japan and Australia into economic colonies. The Taiwanese government was separate from Kramer Associates; but the company had very much the same kind of relationship with the government that Kramer had developed with the U.S.M. in

14. Letter from Stanley Tulin to author, September 15, 1970.
15. Letter from Stanley Tulin to author, September 15, 1970.
16. Tulin letter, December 29, 1970.

the mid-nineteenth century. Kramer money and manpower—and most importantly, brainpower—were placed at the disposal of the Taiwanese government, and used most effectively. Premier Chiang Ching-kuo and Salazar became fast friends and golfing companions; each man respected the provinces of the other, and never spoke of K.A.'s "special situation" in the nation.[17]

This is not to say Salazar forgot the Mexican expropriation, but rather that he dealt with it in a manner far more subtle than bluster or war. In late 1953, Kramer affiliates ceased doing business with Mexican firms. Mexican petroleum became a glut on the market; Mexican foodstuffs, so badly needed abroad, could not be easily sold, while Mexican industries found difficulty in purchasing raw materials. This caused a depression in the U.S.M, which was a major cause for Garcia being deposed and Mercator taking his place. It is difficult to say exactly what Salazar hoped to gain from this action; Tulin believes he was "gratifying a strong desire. Powerful men often do these things." Whatever the reason, it angered the Mexican President, who increased his arms budget, indicating his intention to return to the Pacific, and then deal directly with his opponent on Taiwan. On January 4, 1955, Mercator proclaimed that "Mexico's enemies must not go unpunished. We will push in Mr. Salazar's ugly snout, and make him wish he hadn't thought of his slimy plan to destroy us." The Mercator speech is usually considered the first blow in the second stage of the War Without War era.[18]

---

17. Interview with Stanley Tulin, January 6, 1971.

18. Mexico City *Times*, January 5, 1955.

# 36

# THE NEW DAY

IN order to understand C.N.A. history in the 1950's, one must appreciate the magnitude of the Global War's impact on that society. It was the first major world conflict since the Thirty Years War of three centuries before; the wars of Louis XVI, the Anglo-French wars of the eighteenth century, the local wars of the nineteenth—all were military parades when compared with the campaigns of the Global War. The C.N.A., moreover, had not been involved even in local wars since the end of the Rocky Mountain War in 1855, and thus was psychologically even less prepared for the appalling aftermath of the world conflict.

When the Global War ended in 1948, C.N.A. citizens saw, in their newspapers and on vitavision, the utter desolation of Europe, the Middle East, and Asia. The well-fed, well-housed North Americans who had actually prospered selling war material to Britain and her allies, felt an increasing sense of guilt and horror. There was a growing conviction, moreover, that had the Watson program been followed, the war might never have taken place. By 1950, many North Americans said openly that their nation should have prevented the war by following Watson in 1938; but, in their hearts, they were thankful for the Hogg victory which had kept them at peace while the rest of the world was destroyed.[1] These factors—shock, the role of vitavision, and feelings of guilt—combined to make possible the political revolution of the 1950's. To this should be added the residue of enthusiasm for the Galloway Plan and the escapism of the pre-war period. On the one hand, the impact of the war convinced many North Americans that escape to

---

1. Jeffrey Martin, who had taken an extensive tour of the country in 1937–1938 to determine voter attitudes, revisited 476 of the people he had interviewed on a second tour in 1949. "It is interesting to note that of the 295 individuals who told me they planned to vote for Coalition councilmen and so elect Hogg, 203 claimed to have voted Liberal and had supported Watson. They apparently had convinced themselves that they had guilt for the war, and tried to expunge this sentiment with a retroactive PC vote." New York *Herald*, January 5, 1950.

the wilderness of Manitoba and Northern Vandalia was the only way one could avoid contamination by society; while on the other, there was the nagging feeling that the desire for such an escape had been the very thing that encouraged the warmakers to strike.[2] Clearly, the country was ready for something like the Mason Doctrine after the war, and Mason's election in 1953 was the natural result of the national mood.[3]

The Mason Doctrine has been called "the most unselfish proposal in the history of civilized man" by a supporter; and "a program that is well-meaning, but considering the realities of the world, mistaken in design" by a critic. One might easily conclude that both judgements were valid. There is no doubt that North American foodstuffs prevented the deaths of millions of people throughout the world, while without North American machinery, technological aid, and subsidies, the European and Asian nations could not have recovered as rapidly as they did from the war's destruction. When Mason became Governor-General in 1950 he doubled previous aid programs, and late in the year, went on a world tour to inspect conditions abroad and report back to the North American people. In a vitavised address of November 30, 1950, Mason spoke movingly of what he had seen, the desolation abroad, and the many lives North American aid had rescued. Indeed, he was unable to finish the speech, breaking down in tears toward the end. The speech touched the conscience of the nation, which already had been battered by years of self-doubt and self-hate. Mason sobbed, "We *must* lead the world to a new day" just before the end of his speech. Thus was born the name not only for his program, but the national mood of the 1950's.[4]

In recent years, the New Day movement has been compared with the diffusion movement of the 1920's. Both were rejections of urbanism, there were elements of anarchism to be found in each, and those who participated tended to be young, intellectual, and idealistic.[5] The differences between them, however, are even more striking. The diffusion movement, as symbolized by the Galloway Plan, was rational, well-considered, and on the whole, led by people with an ability to isolate a problem, find an answer, and organize to achieve results. The New

---

2. More than one analyst believes the willingness to accept Billington, and the amazing lack of racial bigotry during his administration, was due more to guilt feelings than anything else. "To hate anyone in the C.N.A., for any reason, was considered the worst crime of all in the immediate post-war era." Lass. *Richard Mason*, p. 32.
3. "In 1950 the nation wanted a Jesus, not a St. Paul. Sad to say, they got one. Nothing would have pleased Mason more than to be crucified." Jeffrey Martin in New York *Herald*, June 10, 1950.
4. Richard Mason. ed. *The New Day* (Burgoyne, 1957).
5. Carl Krauss. *The Messianic Trend in Twentieth Century C.N.A.* (New York, 1969).

Day movement, in contrast, was highly emotional, erratic and illogical (some would say anti-logical), and led by poets and artists, not politicians and businessmen. One may compare the speeches of Owen Galloway with those of Richard Mason to best understand this point. Galloway was almost always cool and collected, organized and disciplined; after the success of his New Day speech, Mason became even more emotional and erratic, at one point going so far as to deliver a vitavision speech with a chorale setting, in which he sang the last paragraphs of his report.[6] Another time, he urged his listeners to "seek the simpler life, avoid the fleshpots, eschew materialism, and find your souls," while in the same speech he called for increases in food and machinery production "to aid our brothers in other lands." "The Governor-General has not yet told us how rustic souls can increase wheat production ten percent and provide the amount of earthmovers for China that are needed. Perhaps on his next trip up the mountain he can ask his Friend for the answers, and then communicate them to the poor mortals below."[7] Jeffrey Martin thus criticized Mason for his simplistic solutions to all problems.

Martin and other, similar critics found it difficult to understand the national mood of the New Day period. They called Mason irrational, more a religious leader than a government head, and Mason's supporters agreed with them, replying that was why they loved him so. It was as though Martin and his circle were the only sober people at a drunken orgy, trying to discuss serious matters with individuals in a state of advanced inebriation. The two would simply talk past each other, with neither person understanding the other. "There is a split in North American society that is simply fascinating," wrote a German visitor in 1956. "One walks down the streets and sees two kinds of people. One is dressed in sombre garb, the other in the most colorful garments imaginable. The former, of course, is a critic of the Administration, the latter a Mason disciple. One need not speak with them to discover this."[8] Another wrote, "In North America the anti-Mason people work hard to produce the goods the New Day people give away to foreigners. It is a division of labor that works well, yet each group hates the other."[9]

The reaction in those nations receiving Mason Doctrine aid was also mixed. At first the peoples of the world applauded North America's gifts, but by 1956 other voices were heard. Mason had spoken so often of his country's guilt that foreigners came to believe him, and they looked upon Mason Doctrine aid not as a gift freely given, but reparations owed them. North Americans visiting Europe at that time

6. Burgoyne *Times*, April 27, 1956.
7. New York *Herald*, April 30, 1957.
8. Percival Prime. *Letters from North America* (London, 1957), p. 87.
9. Prime. *Letters*, p. 117.

were jeered at, spat upon, and in some cases, beaten. Yet few protested; seemingly they viewed this contempt as only their due. "Do you want to receive more Mason Plan aid?" asked the London *Times*. "Then just kill a few North American tourists and aid officials, and call Mason a criminal. Should you do this, your North American listener will nod his agreement, and give you all he has."[10] Thus, gratitude was transformed into contempt, and yet the Mason Doctrine programs continued.

Official government reaction was mixed. The Germans resented aid given the British, and *vice-versa*. Japan felt too much aid was earmarked for Australia, while in Melbourne, fears of a too-rapid Japanese revival led to criticisms of the Mason policies. By 1956, Germany was using some of the funds given by the C.N.A. for war material, a fact not learned until six years later. Soon other countries, many of which had achieved full economic recovery by 1957, were demanding military aid outright, and when Mason rejected their demands, anti-North American sentiment grew and multiplied. Mason's critics called the foreigners "ingrates," and demanded an end to aid programs when they were no longer needed; New Day advocates asked for understanding of such abuse, noting the ravages of war, and considered increases in aid budgets.

Mason had little time for, interest in, or inclination to understand domestic economic and political problems, and came to rely increasingly upon his Cabinet for such work. Minister for Home Affairs Grover Speigal became the Administrative strong man in day-to-day affairs, running the government as though Mason's prime minister. Under his direction, the N.F.A. was recentralized, though financing continued to be pro-rated among the confederations. He directed Mason Doctrine programs from Burgoyne, and insisted they be coordinated through his offices. Speigal called it "decentralization through centralization," but in reality, he managed to assume many powers which the confederations had obtained in the 1920's and 1930's. Doubtless this was necessary due to the needs of an increasingly complex economy, but Speigal was resented by confederation rights advocates, who more often than not also opposed New Day programs as well. Thus, the national divisions were intensified.

The Liberals renominated Mason in 1958, and the Governor-General accepted "the party's will and mandate." It was a most emotional convention, as might have been expected, but not nearly so interesting as the Coalition meeting in Norfolk. The party had three hopefuls that year. Councilman Roswell James of the Southern Con-

---

10. London *Times*, August 24, 1957.

federation controlled the party machinery in the S.C., Northern Vandalia, and Indiana, and believed this would suffice to win him the nomination. Perry Jay, the most famous Coalitionist, had become Mason's most trenchant critic in the Council debates, and had wide support in the legislature. The third candidate was Jeffrey Martin, who in 1958 was editor of the New York *Herald,* had a weekly vitavision news program, and was easily the most admired person among the rank-and-file. Martin had never served in a government post, and had no direct political experience. His support came from party members, not organizations or councilmen. Yet he was able to win nomination on the seventh ballot, accepting the frenzied cheers of the Convention with a dynamic speech attacking every aspect of the New Day. Paradoxically, Martin was the major political beneficiary of the emotionalism of the day, while at the same time its greatest critic.

The campaign of 1958 was marked by parades, vitavision political shows, and much ballyhoo. It also sharpened the distinction between those who favored New Day and its opponents.

### Results of the C.N.A. Elections of 1958

| STATE | PARTY AFFILIATION OF COUNCILMEN | |
| --- | --- | --- |
| | LIBERALS | PEOPLE'S COALITION |
| Northern Confederation | 18 | 17 |
| Indiana | 18 | 13 |
| Manitoba | 14 | 15 |
| Southern Confederation | 11 | 9 |
| Northern Vandalia | 9 | 11 |
| Southern Vandalia | 7 | 8 |
| | 77 | 73 |

Source: New York *Herald,* February 18, 1958.

Mason eked out a victory the meaning of which eluded analysts. Some thought it a vindication of his policies, while most saw in the close vote a sign the nation was weary of the emotional crusade. The most interesting facet of the election for many was the lack of sectionalism. Apparently voters in all parts of the country were divided not by regional interests, but by class, education, and occupation. Generally speaking, Mason appealed to professionals, those educated in the humanistic studies, and white-collar workers, while Martin was strongest among secondary-school graduates, businessmen, blue-collar workers, and those educated in the sciences. The Negro vote divided along the same lines as the white, a further sign of the growing color-blindness in the nation, and of the impact of the Billington administration.[11]

Mason viewed his re-election as a mandate for the continuation of New Day programs, especially foreign aid. But many North Americans had come to consider the programs as redundant, especially when Germany, Britain, and Australia were fully recovered from the war, and actually re-arming at a rapid rate. Then, too, there was the threat from the U.S.M. Ever since 1955, Mercator had spoken of the C.N.A.-Kramer "axis" as "a dagger at our hearts." By 1958, Mexico was stronger than before the war, and seemingly prepared to resume the fighting in the Pacific. Yet Mason had kept military spending to a bare minimum, using the funds instead to finance his aid programs and for Speigal's domestic enterprises. He sought a meeting with Mercator in 1958 to assure the Mexican that he had nothing to fear from the C.N.A., but the offer was rejected. Despite this, and in the face of mounting criticism by his opponents, Mason refused to increase C.N.A. arms. "Nothing has ever been solved by war," he told a vita-vision audience in early 1959. "If we have learned one thing from the horrors of the Global War, it is that arms solve no problems, but only bring disaster.[12]

Mercator's charges of C.N.A.-Kramer collusion had no basis in fact. That Mason would secretly prepare for war was transparently absurd, but Mercator apparently believed it to be true, and acted accordingly. By mid 1959, Mexican warships were regularly patrolling the west Pacific, not far from the Philippines, and at one time coming within range of shore batteries on Formosa. At the same time, Mercator acted to make the Caribbean a "Mexican lake," by fortifying Martinique, signing an agreement of friendship with Cuba under which Mexican troops were stationed at Guantanamo, and occupying St. Martaan's, which was transformed into a major naval and air base by the end of 1959.

These last actions caused alarm in North America, and, for the first time, even New Day advocates called for an arms program. By early 1960, the Mason coalition in the Council was breaking up, and the Governor-General could no longer ignore politics. Speigal pleaded with Mason to make concessions to dissidents in the Council to preserve the slim governmental majority. A sign of military readiness, a strong protest against the Cuban and other actions in the Caribbean, would serve the purpose, said the Minister, but Mason was adamant in his refusal to so act. "The world needs plows, not machine guns," he said on March 14, 1961, "and North America will produce the plows, thus treading the

11. Frank Rusk. *Statistical Analysis of the 1958 C.N.A. Elections* (New York, 1962), pp. 224–37, 376–98.
12. Burgoyne *Times*, February 5, 1959.

road to peace."[13] Martin led the critics of what he called "Mason's Disease." "Mexico had threatened; none can doubt it," he said. "Preparedness may prevent war, not cause it. That is why we must re-arm as soon as is humanly possible."[14] He also wrote, "Mr. Mason has lost his grip on reality. Now he thinks himself a re-incarnation of the Prince of Peace. He is presently measuring himself for the cross. Do we want to be crucified along with this megalomaniac?"[15]

Carl Salazar of Kramer also considered Mason deranged, but unlike the C.N.A. Coalitionists, he was able to do something about it. He had learned from contacts with the Governor-General in 1958 that an *entente* with North America, directed at preserving world peace, could not be expected while Mason occupied the Governor's Palace. Thus, Mercator had been wrong in his conclusions, but correct in his analysis of Salazar's plans; Kramer Associates, indeed, desired an alliance with North America to keep world peace.[16]

Having failed in this, Salazar turned to what he called "Project Taichung," named after the Kramer facilities located in that city. Manned by over five hundred scientists, many of whom had escaped Mexico after Mercator's expropriation, and guarded by Kramer police, Taichung was one of the most modern cities in the world, and also one of the most secret. No one but Salazar and five members of his board knew exactly what was happening there; other board members had been told, simply, that "our security rests in Taichung."

On June 30, 1962, the world learned what had been taking place there. That day, Kramer Associates exploded an atomic bomb in an isolated spot in the north Pacific, having first taken precautions against fallout and death. Salazar ordered the entire operation filmed, and on July 10, prints were delivered to the leaders of Germany, the U.S.M., the C.N.A., and Britain. Ten days later, Salazar called his first and only press conference in Taiwan. "We shall never use this device in the cause of aggrandizement," he said. "But we will not hesitate to destroy any nation that has the foolishness to re-open the Global War." The Kramer Bomb, as it was called, was "not a weapon of war, but one of peace." Still, the rest of the world was shocked by the explosion, and Kramer Associates became the most feared power on earth, and Salazar its most powerful man.[17] Thus began the third phase of the War without War.

13. New York *Herald*, March 15, 1961.
14. New York *Herald*, March 28, 1961.
15. New York *Herald*, April 4, 1961.
16. Interview with Stanley Tulin, November 11, 1970.
17. Letter from Stanley Tulin to author, September 15, 1970; New York *Herald*, July 1–29, 1962.

# 37

## THE WAR WITHOUT WAR

THE disclosure of the Kramer bomb led to a radical re-orientation of military thinking throughout the world. Leaders in the belligerent nations realized that had they had the bomb in 1948, they could have won the war with ease. As might be expected, each launched a crash program to find its secrets. Military spending, already at 1938 levels in 1962, soared even higher, and the chances for peace seemed slimmer in the early 1960's than at any time in the post-war period.

Salazar had expected this to happen. While he agreed with Watson that a pacifist nation invites attack from belligerent neighbors, he saw the validity in Hogg's belief that arms races lead to confrontations and wars. On the other hand, he had contempt for both Mercator and Mason; Mercator he considered a barbarian and a fool, while to him Mason appeared a man with no grasp of international politics and the use of power. If war was to come, Salazar wanted Kramer Associates powerful enough to defend its own interests. The Kramer bomb ensured that no nation would consider going to war until it had its own bomb, and that the possessor of the weapon would then think carefully before striking the first blow, knowing it would bring instant retaliation from Taiwan. Salazar believed he was buying at least a decade of peace, and perhaps more.[1]

Salazar's analysis proved accurate. Fear of conventional war lessened after the explosion of the Kramer atomic bomb, and the race for parity with K.A. was on. Britain was the first nation to crack the "atomic curtain." Its bomb was ready for detonation in late 1964, and was exploded in the Australian desert on February 14, 1965. Now the 1939 alliances were revived, as Japan and the United Empire closed ranks, apparently preparing to re-open the war against Germany. British bases in Scotland were placed on full alert in November of 1965, while a supposedly secret squadron of atomic armed airmobiles was

---

1. This is Stanley Tulin's analysis, which he states is based not on facts, but on his opinions after a lifetime of studying the Kramer archives. Letter from Stanley Tulin to author, September 15, 1970.

established in northern Australia, apparently to prevent a Kramer retaliation should Britain bomb Germany.

The bombing did not come. On November 16, 1965, Germany announced it had the bomb, and four days later signed a treaty of friendship with the newly-formed Associated Russian Republics. At first the claims were rejected, but on March 19, 1966, Germany detonated its bomb in eastern Russia. Within a year, German squadrons in France and the Netherlands had atomic-armed devices, thus leading to a stalemate with Britain in Europe.

The reaction to the Kramer bomb was more violent in the C.N.A. and the U.S.M., causing not only a change in governmental policies, but in the governments themselves.

Mason's slim Council majority had been eroded by Mexico's warlike moves in the Caribbean and elsewhere. The nation was also wearying of his passionate speeches and the long "rendezvous with guilt" that, by 1962, had lasted for over a decade. A new generation was growing up, one that barely remembered the war and certainly had no role in the Watson-Hogg debates of 1938. To many of them, the infatuation with the guilt issue seemed irrelevant, even boring. So did the Mason Doctrine and the aid programs, which had appeared so necessary in 1948, but which fourteen years later were outdated.

Mercator's warlike speeches did not result in an increase in Coalition strength, however, for Martin's insistence on arms programs also appeared old-fashioned. Many young people believed that war would not come because "it made no sense"; a naive sentiment, but held by a large number of individuals nevertheless. Thus, there had been a rejection of both the Mason and Martin positions in 1961–62, which caused grave consternation among the politicians, busily preparing for the 1963 elections.

The bomb changed all this. Mason appeared before the Council on July 11, 1962, to deliver a report on the Kramer films. He surprised the legislators by his cheery attitude and analysis of the situation. As he saw it, the Kramer bomb assured "world peace in our lifetime." Before it had been detonated, the nations of the world had the notion they could renew the Global War. "Now they realize war will be an impossibility. I see the flowering of this mushroom cloud as a harbinger of a generation and more of peace in the world, and in time, goodwill toward all men."[2]

The speech astounded not only the opposition Coalitionists, but Mason's own Liberal supporters. He seemed the only man in the chamber oblivious to the meaning of the bomb and the Salazar press conference. Didn't Mason realize that a new arms race had already

2. New York *Herald*, July 12, 1962.

begun, with each nation working to develop an atomic bomb before the others? Hadn't he a plan for a C.N.A. bomb? The answers to both questions were, obviously, in the negative. When Mason finished speaking, he seemed puzzled by the lack of applause. Instead, there was a buzzing among the councilmen, and hurried meetings in the back of the Chamber.

Were it not for the fact Mason's term had less than a year to run, the Governor-General might have faced a non-confidence vote, in which his own party would have participated. There was even talk of Mason's having lost his mind, although clearly such talk was exaggerated.

That evening the Governor-General met with Councilman Jay, who urged him to proclaim a "scientific emergency," and a crash program to develop a C.N.A. bomb. If he would do this, Jay would accept that year's budget for the Mason Doctrine programs, and so insure its passage without debate. Mason rejected the proposal, saying the two problems were not related. "We shall aid the starving," he said, "and remain a peaceful nation."[3]

Upon leaving the Palace, Jay went to Speigal's home and talked with the Minister through the night. Speigal was also disturbed by the speech, but was convinced Mason was rational. There is reason to believe Jay spoke to Speigal of the possibility of a no-confidence vote that week, perhaps to enlist his aid. Speigal rejected such a role, and may have convinced Jay to drop any idea he might have had of ousting the Governor-General.[4] When asked to comment on the rumors later on, Speigal and Jay both denied them, although Jay did say, "It would have set a bad precedent." Thus, Mason remained in office, and C.N.A. work on an atomic bomb was delayed almost a year as a result.

Perry Jay won the Coalition nomination in 1963, after defeating a hard-pressed challenge by Martin. Mason arrived at the Liberal convention convinced the nomination was his for the asking. Instead, a party struggle ensued. In the end, Mason prevailed over several rivals, including Speigal. That evening Mason called a press conference, at which he denounced his Minister for Home Affairs as a "turncoat and warmonger," dismissed him from the Cabinet, and announced he would support "independents who will stand for office in all the confederations, for each Council seat, and who will be pledged to peace."[5] Calling his new "coalition" the Justice Brigades, Mason predicted he would win a massive victory at the polls. Thus Mason ran as both a Liberal and a Justice Brigades candidate, a situation that divided the Liberals.

---

3. Jackson Randolph. *The Inner History of the War Without War* (New York, 1968), p. 168.

4. Randolph. *Inner History*, p. 199.
5. New York *Herald*, January 6, 1963.

To this day the party has not recovered. At the time, however, Mason expected victory.

Such was not to be. Jay won the elections by a comfortable margin, while not a single Justice Brigades' candidate was elected to the Council. Blaming his defeat on lack of time to mount a nationwide crusade, Mason pledged himself to continue "the fight for peace" as a private citizen.[6]

## *Results of the C.N.A. Elections of 1963*

| STATE | PARTY AFFILIATION OF COUNCILMEN | |
| | PEOPLE'S COALITION | LIBERALS |
| --- | --- | --- |
| Northern Confederation | 22 | 13 |
| Indiana | 15 | 18 |
| Manitoba | 16 | 11 |
| Northern Vandalia | 13 | 9 |
| Southern Confederation | 9 | 9 |
| Southern Vandalia | 5 | 10 |
| | 80 | 70 |

Source: New York *Herald*, February 17, 1963.

Jay's programs were strikingly different from those of his predecessor, but the new Governor-General avoided comparisons. He made no vitavision speeches and scheduled no press conference during his first three months in office, limiting contacts with the public to news releases. Almost deliberately, Jay hoped to present a contrast to the flamboyant Mason. "Mason was a showman, while Jay is an accountant. Perhaps it's all to the good," editorialized the Burgoyne *Times*. "We need a sober man today."[7]

The Jay administration concentrated on four problems in its first two years. Mason Doctrine programs were cut back sharply, so that by the end of 1966, only African and Latin American nations were receiving aid, and that at a lower level than in 1962. The day he entered office, Jay ordered work to begin on an atomic bomb, and assigned a special assistant attached to his office to report directly on progress. While awaiting the bomb, Jay cemented relations with the United Empire, signing a non-aggression pact with Prime Minister Harold Fuller in April of 1964. Thus, the C.N.A. was under British atomic protection until it developed its own bomb. The third program dealt with the National Financial Administration. After a long and drawn-

---

6. New York *Herald*, February 19, 1963.    7. Burgoyne *Times*, February 27, 1963.

out fight, the Council voted to decentralize the agency for a second time, and place limits on financing. Jay announced his intention to do away with the N.F.A. "by the end of the decade. . . ." The agency had been of great use while the nation was expanding rapidly. "But today, when we have entered an age of large corporations and complex relations, the N.F.A is no longer as necessary. The government will continue to aid new enterprises, but through a new, far more limited agency."[8] Jay's fourth program, an attempt to substitute direct voting for governors-general for the conciliar method of election, failed to pass, and represented his major defeat.

The North American atomic bomb was detonated in northern Manitoba on September 1, 1966, which was also Jay's sixty-fifth birthday. "It's the best present I could have had," said a happy Governor-General to the nation that evening. Then, at the end of his speech, Jay turned to another topic—the pace of change in the world. He noted that when he was born in 1901, Ezra Gallivan had just left the Palace; airmobiles and locomobiles were in their infancy; "and it seemed to us, growing up in what was still a quiet and peaceful world, that progress was inevitable. Later on, we learned that it wasn't progress that came with each new year, but change. And there's quite a difference between them." Then Jay threw his political bombshell. "I came to office convinced that certain changes had to be made, and that this nation had to abandon its honeymoon with romanticism and face the facts of the atomic era. This has been done; my work is finished. It is for this reason that I will call a meeting of the caucus tomorrow, to present my resignation and help pave the way for my successor." Jay then said goodnight, and prepared for the caucus. He had told no one of his plan, and that night Burgoyne buzzed with rumors of the succession. The choice would be most important, for whoever would become governor-general would also lead the party in the 1968 elections little more than a year away, and given the popularity of the Jay administration, was almost certain of election.

The caucus met at 9:00 on the morning of September 2, and did not leave the room until 3:30, at which time the new Governor-General was announced. The man selected by the caucus was Carter Monaghan, Minister of Finance in the Jay Cabinet, the former Governor of Southern Vandalia, and the second Negro to serve as Governor-General. That evening Jay held his last press conference. When asked whether Monaghan was his selection, he smiled and said, "Before the first vote I wrote a name on a piece of paper and handed it to Philbrick here (turning to his secretary) because I knew one of you would ask that question. Jake, give the envelope to Mr. Brook (Mr. Philbrick

---

8. New York *Herald*, January 30, 1966.

handed an envelope to Michigan City *Star* reporter Clem Brook). Now open it and tell us what you see. (Mr. Brook opens envelope) Mr. Brook: It says Carter Monaghan. . . ."[9] Later on Jay denied having indicated his choice at the caucus, and to this day it is not known whether he wanted Monaghan as his successor or merely had predicted his election. Whatever the case, Monaghan took the oath the following morning. Then he and Jay went into the governor-general's office together to take care of last partings. According to Jay, he said, "I've left you one problem, and that can be summed up in a single word. It's Mercator."[10]

News of the Kramer bomb caused more fear in the U.S.M. than in any nation on earth. Ever since expropriation, Mercator had feared an attack from Kramer Associates, and he viewed the bomb as the vehicle for Salazar's revenge. On July 8, two days before the films reached Mexico City, Mercator placed the nation under martial law, and that same day he ordered Secretary of War Diego Calvares to begin the search for a Mexican bomb. When it became obvious that Mexico would not be bombed, Mercator lifted the martial law and the nation returned to normal. But the crash program for the bomb continued, and until it would be exploded, Mercator intended to give no nation an excuse to attack Mexico.

On November 20, 1962, the President proclaimed "the Offensive of the Dove." At that time, he called upon all nations of the world to sign a non-aggression pact, which would also guarantee the neutrality of those countries which were not involved in the Global War. Furthermore, he asked for a world conference of the belligerents, to meet in Geneva the following summer to sign treaties ending the war. Finally, Mercator pledged Mexico to the cause of world peace, promising never to "start a war, and to destroy all offensive weapons after the treaties are signed."[11]

The non-aggression pact, which contained no enforcement provisions and was therefore meaningless, was signed by 113 nations in 1963–1964. Germany and Britain refused to attend the Geneva conference, because no agenda had been agreed upon. "This is a propaganda play and nothing more," said Chancellor Adolph Markstein, while Prime Minister Philip Halliwell observed that "The President would not be so anxious to have us in Geneva had he a bomb in Mexico City."[12] Needless to say, Mexico destroyed no arms, since the treaties

---

9. C.N.A. *Collected Papers of Perry Jay, Eighteenth Governor-General* (Burgoyne, 1969), Vol. XXXV, pp. 415–16.
10. Interview on vitavision of Governor Perry Jay by Arnold Bittle, Max-

well Jenkins, and Arthur Flick, June 4, 1969.
11. Kerl. *Mexico Under the Banner*, p. 694.
12. London *Times*, January 30, 1963.

were not concluded. Little came of the Offensive of the Dove. World public opinion turned in favor of Mexico for a year, and Mercator would spend the rest of his life complaining of how Germany and Britain sabotaged his peace offensive. At the same time, however, he urged his scientists on, pleading with them for an atomic weapon so that Mexico need not fear its enemies.

In 1965, Mercator announced elections for November, and to allay suspicions of personal ambition, swore he would not be a candidate. Neither the Liberty nor United Mexican parties were permitted to nominate candidates, since Mercator had declared both to be enemies of the people. Instead, his own party, formed in 1965 and called the Progressives, nominated Raphael Dominguez, a Mexico City attorney who had also served on the faculty of the University. The Progressives named a full slate for the Senate and Assembly, in some cases two candidates for an office so it would appear the voters had a choice. As might be expected, Dominguez won, but he received only 14.7 million votes of a total of 31 million. Since, under normal conditions, the elections would have seen approximately 37 million votes cast, clearly many Mexicans boycotted the ballot. Scattered votes were cast for hundreds of candidates, whose names were written in after that of Dominguez was crossed out. Finally, some 9 million Mexicans wrote in the name of Paul Suarez, whose victory in the 1950 election had sparked the Mercator revolution, and who had died in jail in 1955.[13]

Mercator was infuriated by the results, which he had not expected and for which he had not prepared. He ordered changes in the election law to ensure against future happenings of this kind, and on November 22, swore in Dominguez as president. He then joined the Cabinet as Secretary of War, and in fact continued to rule Mexico through his puppet.

On March 14, 1967 there was a commotion in the capital and a flurry of telephone calls to and from Point Harrington, Alaska. The matter was kept secret, but rumors had it that the scheduled Mexican atomic device test had ended in failure. Similar occurrences took place in 1968, twice in 1969, and three times in 1970. Whether or not the bomb was involved cannot be known for certain, but as of November 1, 1971, the U.S.M. remains the only major power without it.

Dominguez has blamed Mexico's failure to develop a bomb on sabotage, but there is a more likely explanation for the absence of a Mexican atomic device. When Mercator seized Kramer properties in 1951, most of Mexico's leading scientists fled the country. The Kramer bomb had been developed by a team headed by Carlos Sparling, a sixty-

---

13. Kenneth Zarb. *Inside the U.S.M.: Mercator's Folly* (New York, 1971), pp. 333–39.

year-old Mexican who fled to Taiwan by submarine. Mexicans also worked on the German, British, and North American bombs, which could not have been produced as rapidly as they were without them. "Mexicans developed the atomic bomb," wrote one author, "and Mexico is the only big power that lacks one!"[14]

Nor was Mexico able to reconstruct its scientific force in the 1960's. After the scientists fled in 1950, the middle class followed, especially technological students, and they are scattered around the world, although the best are to be found in Taiwan and in North American universities. Mercator had brought reforms to Mexico, "but he had only served to give the poor a bigger slice of an already shrinking pie. The people who had the knack of making the pie expand are now elsewhere."[15]

The Mexican higher education program, headed until 1966 by Dr. William Chron, was geared to produce far more specialists than ever before in Mexican history, but a price was paid for this, and it was quality. Mexico has more doctors, lawyers, teachers, engineers, and scientists today than it had prior to 1950, but their general level is far lower now than it was even a century ago. Chron had warned Mercator this would happen, but the President had been willing to support him anyway. By 1966, however, when Dominguez and Mercator found the atomic secrets could not be unlocked by their scientists, they discharged Chron and replaced him with Professor Albert Peck of the Mexico City Polytechnic Institute, who established new university centers in each state, where the cream of Mexico's students will be trained. But such programs take many years to mature, and one cannot expect much from Mexican science for decades.

Determined to have the bomb at any cost, Mercator has engaged in espionage work, and his agents attempted to bribe foreign scientists and technicians to defect to Mexico. Several such attempts were uncovered in Germany and Britain in 1966 and 1967, and in 1969 a major Mexican espionage ring was uncovered in Michigan City, causing the U.S.M. and C.N.A. to break relations. At the time Dominguez said, "We are surrounded by enemies, and a cornered nation, like a cornered man, often must strike out in self-defense. This is not a threat, merely an observation. I hope our enemies understand the meaning of my words and will act accordingly."[16]

14. Zarb. *Inside the U.S.M.*, p. 444.   16. Mexico City *Times*, February 1.
15. *Ibid*, p. 450.   1969.

# 38

# SCORPIONS IN A BOTTLE

CARTER MONAGHAN'S first year in office was devoted to continuing the Jay policies, tightening his grip on the party machinery, and establishing good relations with Britain and the rest of the United Empire. He also kept a close watch on Mexico, as fears of an attack from the west began, despite the fact that the C.N.A. had the atomic bomb.

In 1967 the nation's best selling book was James Volk's *The Bomb Myth*, in which the author, a political scientist at Burgoyne University and sometime advisor to governors-general, argued that the bomb hadn't really changed the power equation as much as had been believed. "The bomb is only effective as a deterrent," wrote Volk. "If a nation has atomic bombs and is prepared to use them, it may feel safe from attack. But should that nation consider employing them in a surprise raid on a putative enemy, it would soon realize that bombs from other nations could rain down on its cities. Former Governor-General Mason, whom many believe a crank, may be correct in his conclusions if not in his reasoning. War may be a thing of the past, and the chances for war may lessen, not increase, if the U.S.M. gets its bomb."[1]

Volk's arguments had wide appeal, not only in the C.N.A., but throughout the world. It was translated into every major language, and was known to have been carefully read by the leaders of Kramer Associates, Germany, Britain, and Mexico. There was talk of Volk standing for the governorship-general against Monaghan in 1968, of simply "giving" the bomb to Mercator, and establishing a world organization dedicated to peace, which would have bombs at its disposal, to be used whenever necessary. Nothing came of all this, but such ideas were in the air in 1967, and depending upon one's views, either gave Mexico more time to develop its bomb or demonstrated that peace would last indefinitely.

---

1. James Volk. *The Bomb Myth* (New York, 1967), p. 354.

*The Bomb Myth* re-opened the great debate on the arms policy that had been believed ended when Kramer Associates detonated its bomb. Monaghan rejected Volk's thesis, arguing that "It may be true that no sane and reasonable man will use the bomb. But who is to say sane and reasonable men do today, or will in the future, control the destinies of countries? We must have every safeguard at our command, and one is a strong deterrent force."[2] To this Mason replied, "Mr. Volk has showed conclusively that war is now an impossibility. And yet we maintain this frightening arms escalation. The Governor-General has said that we must beware of insanity in high places. I would reply that any man who would continue producing bombs must be insane."[3]

The Coalition nominated Monaghan for a term in his own right in 1968. The Liberal convention was divided down the middle. On one side was Mason, too old to stand himself in 1968, but now returned to the party to support either Volk or Councilman from Southern Vandalia, Fred Tryon, for the nomination. Both men favored retaining the bomb, but would end production of additional arms and concentrate attention on defense systems. Grover Speigal, who favored administration policy toward the bomb and believed Mexico a major threat to C.N.A. well-being, opposed both Volk and Tryon. He limited his objections to Monaghan on the Governor-General's domestic policies, especially his willingness to see the N.F.A. disbanded in 1970. "Should this happen the nation will be the province of giant firms, and the freedom of enterprise will be gone, with the others to follow soon after."[4] The convention deadlocked, with neither Volk or Tryon willing to bow to the other, while Speigal had all the anti-Mason votes. After four days of balloting and several major brawls on the convention floor, the party turned to a fourth man, Governor Jason Winters of Manitoba, who had not taken a stand on foreign policy "since it is not in the province of my office to have a foreign policy, except toward Burgoyne," and who supported retention of state N.F.A.'s, but would disband the national organization. The pro-Speigal delegates accepted Winters, but approximately half the Mason people walked out of the hall, pledging themselves to put forth a peace candidate on a peace platform.[5]

Since the Justice Brigades had done so badly in 1963, Mason decided not to resurrect it. Instead, he and Tryon organized the Peace and Justice Party, and within days were able to place members on the

2. New York *Journal*, July 18, 1967.
3. New York *Herald*, August 22, 1967.
4. New York *Herald*, January 7, 1968.
5. For a sympathetic analysis of the Peace and Justice Party of 1968, see

Robert Mead. *Peace and Justice, Sanity and Reason* (New York, 1970). A critical view may be found in Jay Knowles. *In the Day of the Cuckoo* (New York, 1970).

ballots in all the councilmanic races. The party also decided to nominate Volk for the governorship-general, since there was little time to build up a candidate, and Volk already had national exposure[6]

### Results of the C.N.A. Elections of 1968

| | PARTY AFFILIATION OF COUNCILMEN | | |
| STATE | PEOPLE'S COALITION | LIBERALS | PEACE AND JUSTICE |
|---|---|---|---|
| Northern Confederation | 16 | 10 | 9 |
| Indiana | 14 | 17 | 2 |
| Manitoba | 18 | 6 | 3 |
| Northern Vandalia | 14 | 7 | 1 |
| Southern Confederation | 10 | 7 | 1 |
| Southern Vandalia | 8 | 6 | 1 |
| | 80 | 53 | 17 |

Source: New York *Herald*, February 17, 1968.

The campaign was exciting and spirited, with all three candidates using vitavision exclusively, and not making speeches in the confederations as had previously been the norm. The highlight was the debate of February 7, in which the candidates appeared on vitavision to discuss the issues. The next day most reporters seemed to think Volk was the most attractive speaker, Monaghan's arguments the most convincing, and Winters the most confusing. Monaghan won the election by a substantial margin, while Volk did far better than had been expected.

An analysis of the 1968 vote confirms trends already visible in 1958 and 1963. Once again, class, occupational, and educational backgrounds outweighed sectional, religious and racial factors in the balloting. Monaghan did best with blue-collar, business and scientific voters, while Volk's backers were primarily among the humanistically-educated, in the college towns, and among intellectuals in the major cities. Winters captured the farms and small-city-minded, and "middle-of-the-road-compromiser" votes. Had the Jay Amendment been passed, and the vote been given the candidates directly instead of to councilmanic candidates, Monaghan would have received 52.8 percent of the votes, with Winters getting 25.0 percent and Volk, 22.2 percent.

It is believed the Coalition and Liberal voters are not as different in ideology and desires as had previously been the case, while the Peace and Justice voters differ from them at every turn. This may mean that the Liberals will disappear as a major force in C.N.A. politics, and the

6. Mead. *Peace and Justice*, pp. 97–110.

Peace and Justice Party replace it as the nation's second party. On the other hand, Volk was an extremely well-known and attractive candidate, and without him heading the slate, the party might not have done as well as it had. Then too, the issue of the bomb may not be as important in 1973 as it is today. If this is the case, the party may die.[7]

The Peace and Justice Party welcomed the results as a vindication of Mason's positions, even though garnering less than one in four votes. The party mounted a major demonstration program in 1969, which was crippled by disclosures of the Mexican spy ring in Michigan City. Most North Americans viewed the existence of such a network as proof of the need for a strong armed force. The Peace and Justice leaders rejected the charges as fabrications of the C.B.I., and warned of the dawn of a new era of Starkism in the C.N.A. The nation remained divided, with a clear majority in favor of arms, while a militant and increasingly radical Peace and Justice Party now (1971) calls for a disarmament of the nation and internationalization of the bomb.[8]

The world situation in mid-1971 is complex, fluid, and most difficult to analyze. It is commonplace to note that there are five major powers in the world today—the C.N.A., the U.S.M., Kramer Associates, Germany, and Britain, but it may be that two of these are not as strong as is commonly believed.

Britain has never fully recovered its pre-war vitality, and derives much of its strength from the United Empire, especially Australia, and its alliance with Japan. Australia and Japan are natural enemies in the Pacific, and Britain may be obliged to choose between them in the near future. If and when this happens, Britain may be relegated to the rank of a second-class power, and will then rely more upon its ever-closer ties with the C.N.A. than has previously been the case. Some go so far as to see an eventual union of the C.N.A. and the United Empire, with the C.N.A. assuming leadership of the Empire, or Britain and Australia joining the C.N.A. as new confederations. Such a happening is unlikely, but we live in an unlikely period, and union may indeed come in time.

Similarly, Germany's strength lies as much in her domination of Europe and the Middle East as in her own internal resources. In recent years, however, France, the Associated Russian Republics, and the Arabs have been showing signs of chafing at German rule. Anti-German riots erupted in Paris, Moscow, and Jerusalem in 1969, and more capitals were hit by demonstrations in 1970. It may well be that

---

7. Frank Rusk. *A Statistical Analysis of the 1968 C.N.A. Elections* (New York, 1971), pp. 111–18, 204–9. Interestingly enough, Rusk hardly mentions the fact that Monaghan is a Negro in his book.

8. Max Josephson. *The End of the Western Era* (New York, 1971).

the revival of European nationalisms and the re-birth of pan-Arabism may cause the breakup of the *de facto* German empire. Should this happen, Germany would no longer be a major power, and would probably seek safety in some ˇkind of confederation with her former client states, if indeed such is possible. Unlike Britain, Germany has no strong C.N.A. to lean upon. Thus, central Europe may become a source of international dislocation in the 1970's.

Kramer Associates may be the strongest power in the world today. There is no way of knowing exactly how powerful this company is, or even what its plans for the future may be. Its employees are in every nation in the world; it controls—indirectly—almost a sixth of the world's resources. Its leadership is unmatched in intelligence and knowledge by any other power. On the other hand, Salazar has always shown himself to be reasonable and peaceful. So long as Kramer's vital interests are not damaged or threatened, he will remain the balance wheel of international relations. Kramer bombs, now equipped with missile delivery systems, are poised to strike at all the major powers. Each knows that it will be crushed should it start a war against the others, or attempt in some other way to change the balance of power drastically. On the other hand, no nation knows for certain exactly *what* Kramer Associates owns or controls. Thus, an action against a firm or individual that might appear minor in Mexico City, Burgoyne, London, or Berlin, might be viewed in an entirely different light in Taipei. Such an eventuality is highly unlikely, but under certain circumstances, Kramer Associates could become a warlike power, and attempt to take control of the world.

The C.N.A. is the most powerful conventional nation in the world. Its GNP is now equal to that of the German and British nations and allies combined. As a result of the arms program initiated by Jay in 1963, its strong technological base, and its vital population, it is a powerful agent for world peace. But the nation remains divided between the supporters of the government, and the Peace and Justice followers. One cannot say which is correct in its assessment of the world scene and the C.N.A.'s role in it, but internal dislocations of a political nation cause grave fears in other nations, and are of especial interest in Taipei and Mexico City.

The U.S.M. is considered the world's trouble spot in 1971. Statesmen and political analysts cannot decide whether the world would be safer or more endangered should Mexico develop a bomb. After the uncovering of the Michigan City spy ring, the border between Mexico and North America was closed, and guerrilla activity has begun along the Jefferson-Southern Vandalia line. While not yet serious enough to warrant an international conference, it may easily escalate into a major confrontation. If this should occur, the other nations and Kramer Associates would surely be drawn into a new Global War.

The conflict between the C.N.A. and the U.S.M., then, is the key to the world's future. On the one hand we find a powerful industrial state with the most sophisticated population in the world, divided internally but retaining its republican heritage. On the other is Mexico, an even larger nation, growing more powerful each year under the leadership of what might best be described as a benign dictatorship masked as a republic. In 1970, Mexico's GNP passed that of the Germans, and next year it should surpass that of Britain, thus going to second place among the conventional nations, and to third if Kramer Associates is included.

Both the C.N.A. and the U.S.M. will remain united; neither will face the dislocations of Britain and Germany. In all probability tensions between them will continue, for there is no sign of a change on the horizon. For almost two centuries these two nations have faced each other. In a way, they have been at war since 1775, when the Rebellion erupted at Lexington and Concord. Today Mexicanos and Hispanos dominate Mexican politics, but the Anglos, though a small minority, are still the most powerful group in the nation, dominating Mexican business and providing the power needed by the government to do its work. Businessmen in San Francisco and Jefferson City can trace their lineage back to the North American colonial era, and when they do, they find they are distant cousins of their counterparts in New York and Burgoyne. Ironically, there is reason to believe that an ancestor of Frederick Buchanan, president of California Petroleum Corporation, once owned a slave who was the ancestor of Carter Monaghan, Governor-General of the C.N.A.

In 1843, Pedro Hermión delivered a speech in Henrytown that changed the course of C.N.A. and U.S.M. history. In it, he spoke of relations between the countries as being similar to those of scorpions in a bottle. "Slowly the scorpions circle each other, until one lashes out at the other, and strikes him dead." Hermión was referring to the North American continent when he spoke then, but his words might be remembered today and considered to our profit. To some observers it seems the U.S.M. and the C.N.A. are circling each other again, as they have so often in the past. Should one strike, the other will retaliate. Hermión was inaccurate then and now; he might have told his audience that when the game is played, more often than not, both insects die. The game seems to be on in 1971, and if one or the other lashes out, not only will the scorpions die, but the world may be destroyed.

# CRITIQUE

[ED. NOTE. *It was recommended at the decennial meeting of the Mexican Historical Association and the North American Historical Association in 1965 that critiques be appended to any work written by a scholar of one nation about the other. In this way, biases could be recognized and a healthy dialogue fostered between historians of the two nations. While such critiques were not mandated, they were strongly recommended, and some 65 percent of all such works published since 1966 have included them. Although this book is not of that variety, Professor Sobel has suggested a critique be amended. He agreed to the selection of Professor Frank Dana of the University of Mexico City as its writer, with the understanding that he would have no control over its editing and content. He has further agreed that the critique will replace the usual conclusion one might expect to find in a work such as this.*]

ROBERT SOBEL has in the past concentrated his attention on the business histories of the United States of Mexico and the Confederation of North America. His first book, *Men of Great Wealth*, was published fifteen years ago. It concerned the origins of Kramer Associates, was drawn largely from secondary sources, and although it added little to our knowledge of the company, did serve to create new interest in it. He then published a statistical survey of North American business, drawn largely from the census returns, in which he tended to glorify the North American businessman as second only to the K.A. men in skill, ingenuity, and intelligence. Then followed general studies of North American business from 1855 to 1910 and a biography of Ezra Gallivan. Although the former told us nothing new of the subject, the Gallivan book did reveal a side of that Governor-General which had not been stressed in earlier works, particularly his economic ideas. Clearly Mr. Sobel has matured over the years, and may now be prepared to undertake serious, scholarly work in the field. Sad to say, this present volume is not of that category.

*For Want of a Nail . . .* is the fourth major dual history of the C.N.A. and the U.S.M. to be published in the past decade. Of them, Lawrence Gilman's *Duel for a Continent* (Mexico City, 1959) and Henry Tracey's *The United States of Mexico and the Confederation of North America* (New York, 1969) were written from the points of view of Mexico City and Burgoyne respectively. Each tried to be fair, but in different ways, both were partisan. Although Mr. Sobel does not indicate as much in his bibliography, he appears to have drawn much of the material in his book from these earlier efforts. Indeed, one can think of several other works, all of which have left their marks on Mr. Sobel's thoughts, which he does not credit as such.

It is a work marred by minor errors and questionable conclusions. For example, Sobel's account of the Rocky Mountain War plays down the fact that most historians today consider the aggression to have begun by the C.N.A. attack at three points along the Vandalian border. While stressing the admittedly serious violations of the constitution by Mexican presidents in the past century, he hardly credits them with broadening the base of our representative structure. In writing of Benito Hermión he indicates the Emperor was a coward; no major Mexican historian would accept this assessment. But the most serious problem is his presentation of the North American Rebellion, in which the loyalists could do no wrong, while the rebels are presented as fools, clowns, traitors, and knaves. This section of the book appears to have been drawn largely from North American sources and written from Burgoyne's point of view. The author clearly admires the C.N.A., considers Burgoyne a hero and Sam Adams a villain, and believes the Britannic Design the most perfect document written by man. Fortunately, his biases are so clear that they will be obvious to the reader. As a corrective, I would suggest Oscar Jamison's *The Struggle for Liberty: Henry, Adams, and the American Rebellion* (Melbourne, 1969). Curiously, this work does not appear in the bibliography.

Like Jamison, Sobel is an Australian who has written of both the C.N.A. and the U.S.M., and taught in universities in both nations. Jamison is now in Melbourne. After completing his research for this volume, Sobel journeyed to Taiwan, where he now resides, teaches, and writes. He is sponsored there by Stanley Tulin, probably the most anti-Mexican historian in the world.

Sobel's present position explains a good deal of what may be found in the last part of his book. I am referring to those sections dealing with the growth of Kramer Associates. This monolith had dominated Mexican life for much of its existence, and was finally expelled from the nation after a long and bitter struggle. Many of Mexico's problems may be traced to the work of Kramer Associates. Like many of my colleagues, I believe our nation might have been spared most of its present difficulties had earlier presidents taken the strong actions of the Mercator regime.

Mexico's major enemy today is Kramer Associates. Indeed, no nation is safe from its influence, the more frightening since Kramer has power without responsibility. In recent years the company has allied itself with the C.N.A., and together these two have placed Mexico in a pincers and are prepared to squeeze at any moment. Robert Sobel, writing from Taiwan, late of Burgoyne University, and Stanley Tulin's heir apparent, is hardly the man capable of rendering a fair judgement on recent events in Mexico.

Sobel's biases are evident in two sections of this book. The first deals with the rise of K.A. At every turn Kramer executives are portrayed as wise and efficient, while Mexican leaders are either blunderers or tyrants. So we find Benito Hermión as a sensual dictator, saved from his own recklessness by Diego Cortez. According to Sobel, Cortez led his *coup* against El Jefe when the tyrant set out on an expansionist course that would have upset the world's power balance. In fact, Hermión not only rose to power through Kramer assistance, but most of his actions were directed from San Francisco. It was only when he tried to break this bond that Cortez deposed him.

*All* the Kramer Presidents, from Kramer himself to Carl Salazar, are described in glowing terms; not so Mexico's presidents. If Mexico gains power or a Mexican leader shows brilliance, Sobel gives the credit to a Kramer man operating from behind the scenes. Should Sobel believe Mexico's policy unwise, however, he blames it on Mexico City. The author must realize he cannot have it both ways; not only is it unfair to praise only the good in K.A. and the bad in Mexico, it is unscholarly.

The author's bias is also evident in those sections dealing with Mexican slavery. Except for a few radicals in Chiapas and Durango, no Mexican leader seriously considers the re-instatement of that institution. A recent poll of Mexican historians has shown they consider Calles second only to Jackson as the nation's greatest leader, and this largely because of his leadership in the manumission effort. During his administration Calles had wide support from many parts of the nation, from almost all groups in Mexico. Yet Sobel infers that Calles, together with K.A. President Benedict and Albert Ullman, defied the nation to end slavery. This is a gross oversimplification, as may be discovered by a reading of Jaime Milton. *The Manumission Years: Emiliano Calles and the People* (Mexico City, 1966). This work, along with many other pro-Mexican books, is not in the Sobel bibliography.

Having said this, it remains to analyze *For Want of a Nail* . . . itself. Sobel states in his preface that this is a "double history" of the C.N.A. and the U.S.M. Actually, as I have indicated, it is a triple history, for Kramer Associates must also be considered. The author implies that since their early histories, Mexico and the C.N.A. have been at each other's throats, like the scorpions in Pedro Hermión's famous speech. But the text does not support this contention. Rather, from the end of the Rocky Mountain War to the Global War, the two nations have developed to a large extent independent of each other. This generation is used to thinking of the C.N.A. and the U.S.M. as natural enemies, but such was not the view of men in both countries two generations ago. Thus, the merchandise is not exactly what we are led to believe it is.

This is not to say the book lacks a thesis, one that dominates the work, and the exposition of which makes this book an important one, though flawed. The key to understanding this work is not Kramer Associates, slavery, Galloway, etc., but rather John Burgoyne and the Rebellion. The histories of Mexico and North America are so crowded and eventful that by the time the reader finished the last page of this book, he may have forgotten the first three chapters. I would suggest that such a reader, on completion of this *critique*, re-read these chapters, for they contain the key to Sobel's thinking and the germs of his thesis.

It is the author's contention that the peoples of British North America were fairly united prior to 1763. Although he does not say as much and in so many words, he implies that the North Americans of that day had two political traditions. The first of these came from Britain, and consisted of an evolutionary road to a more perfect commonwealth. The second, a child of the Enlightenment, was a utopian view of man and nature, to be found, in differing ways, in such thinkers as Voltaire, Rousseau, Montesquieu, and others of that period. Following the Seven Year's War, some Americans—among them Galloway and Dickinson—held that the nation's future lay with the Empire, with Europe, with tradition, and with the evolutionary development of institutions. A second group, including the Adamses and Jefferson, were utopians, who believed in free will, held that man could be the master of his fate, rule himself, and wash away the abuses of centuries in a generation. These two groups and ideologies clashed in the Rebellion, which saw the victory of the "evolutionists," if we may call them that. The hero of this book is John Burgoyne, first Duke of Albany, who wins the Rebellion and then sets the new C.N.A. along the evolutionary path.

Meanwhile, some of the rebels flee North America for Jefferson, where they attempt to put their ideas into practice. From this point on, Sobel contrasts the national developments of the two peoples. As he sees it, the North American way was by far the more successful. Ezra Gallivan frees the peoples of Quebec; El Jefe conquers New Granada.

The C.N.A. has little difficulty freeing the slaves; the Mexicans cling
to the institution long after it had been abandoned by the rest of the
civilized world. The C.N.A. develops a diversified economy; Mexico is
dominated by the Kramer Associates. Both nations have difficulties in
retaining their freedoms, but the C.N.A. overcomes the obstacles,
while Mexico does not. As Sobel views the two histories, the C.N.A.
evolves from its British base to a new kind of pluralistic civilization, a
model for the world. In contrast, the original utopianism of the first
Jeffersonians is so diluted by the Mexican admixture as to be unrecog-
nizable a few generations after the Mexican War. Sobel has written
elsewhere that "The C.N.A. was the realization not only of Dickinson's dreams, but also those of Sam Adams."[1] It is clear from this and
other, similar statements where his biases lie.

Doubtless the reader will consider these criticisms harsh. If so,
they have succeeded. I have grave reservations about certain sections
of this book and disagreements with Professor Sobel's interpretations
of many issues. The author would probably respond that I have my
biases just as he has his, and he would be correct. There is nothing
wrong with this. The historian must strive for objectivity, knowing he
can never succeed. Professor Sobel, in other writings, has indicated his
understanding of this problem. I commend him for his willingness to
accept this *critique* under the terms outlined in his preface. If Mexican
historians on the one side and C.N.A.-K.A. historians on the other are
ever to transcend narrow nationalism, such trust must become the
norm, and not the exception.

*July 17, 1972*                          FRANK DANA
                                         *James Marshall Professor*
                                         *University of Mexico City*

---

1. New York *Herald*, June 15, 1969.

# APPENDIX I

*Governors-General of the Confederation of North America*

| | Governor-General | Political Party | Administration |
|---|---|---|---|
| 1. | Winfield Scott | UNIFIED LIBERAL | 1843–1849 |
| 2. | Henry Gilpin | UNIFIED LIBERAL | 1849–1853 |
| 3. | William Johnson | NATIONAL CONSERVATIVE | 1853–1856 |
| 4. | Whitney Hawkins | CONSERVATIVE | 1856–1858 |
| 5. | Kenneth Parkes | LIBERAL | 1858–1868 |
| 6. | Herbert Clemens | CONSERVATIVE | 1868–1878 |
| 7. | John McDowell | LIBERAL | 1878–1888 |
| 8. | Ezra Gallivan | PEOPLE'S COALITION | 1888–1901 |
| 9. | Clifton Burgen | PEOPLE'S COALITION | 1901–1903 |
| 10. | Christopher Hemingway | PEOPLE'S COALITION | 1903–1908 |
| 11. | Albert Merriman | PEOPLE'S COALITION | 1908–1918 |
| 12. | Calvin Wagner | PEOPLE'S COALITION | 1918–1923 |
| 13. | Henderson Dewey | LIBERAL | 1923–1929 |
| 14. | Douglas Watson | LIBERAL | 1929–1938 |
| 15. | Bruce Hogg | PEOPLE'S COALITION | 1938–1950 |
| 16. | James Billington | PEOPLE'S COALITION | 1950–1953 |
| 17. | Richard Mason | LIBERAL | 1953–1963 |
| 18. | Perry Jay | PEOPLE'S COALITION | 1963–1966 |
| 19. | Carter Monaghan | PEOPLE'S COALITION | 1966– |

# APPENDIX II

## Leaders of the United States of Mexico

### The Republic

| | Presidents | Party | Administration |
|---|---|---|---|
| 1. | *Andrew Jackson* | CONTINENTALIST | 1821–1839 |
| 2. | *Miguel Huddleston* | LIBERTY | 1839–1845 |
| 3. | *Pedro Hermión* | CONTINENTALIST | 1845–1849 |
| 4. | *Raphael Blaine* | CONTINENTALIST | 1849–1851 |
| 5. | *Hector Niles* | LIBERTY | 1851–1857 |
| 6. | *Arthur Conroy* | CONTINENTALIST | 1857–1869 |
| 7. | *Omar Kinkaid* | CONTINENTALIST | 1869–1879 |
| 8. | *George Vining* | CONTINENTALIST | 1879–1881 |

### The Hermión Period

| | | | |
|---|---|---|---|
| | *Benito Hermión* | CHIEF OF STATE | 1881–1901 |
| | | EMPEROR | 1901 |

### The Restored Republic

| | | | |
|---|---|---|---|
| 9. | *Martin Cole* | . . . . . . . . . . . | 1901–1902 |
| 10. | *Anthony Flores* | UNITED MEXICAN | 1902–1914 |
| 11. | *Victoriano Consalus* | UNITED MEXICAN | 1914–1920 |
| 12. | *Emiliano Calles* | LIBERTY | 1920–1926 |
| 13. | *Pedro Fuentes* | UNITED MEXICAN | 1926–1932 |
| 14. | *Alvin Silva* | LIBERTY | 1932–1950 |

### The Mercator Period

| | | | |
|---|---|---|---|
| | *Felix Garcia* | . . . . . . . . . . . | 1950–1954 |
| | *Vincent Mercator* | . . . . . . . . . . . | 1954–1965 |
| 15. | *Raphael Dominguez* | PROGRESSIVE | 1965– |

# APPENDIX III

*Presidents of the Kramer Associates*

| | |
|---|---|
| *Bernard Kramer* | 1865–1882 |
| *Diego Cortez y Catalán* | 1882–1904 |
| *Douglas Benedict* | 1904–1926 |
| *John Jackson* | 1926–1949 |
| *Carl Salazar* | 1949– |

# SELECTED BIBLIOGRAPHY

ADAMS, JOHN. *Collected Works.* 20 vols. Mexico City, 1912.

ADAMS, JOHN QUINCY. *The Diary of John Quincy Adams.* 3 vols. Mexico City, 1856.

ADAMS, SAM. *Letters of a Rebel.* 14 ed. Mexico City, 1965.

ADKINS, CHARLES. *Always a Bridesmaid: The Liberty Party, 1851–1960.* Mexico City, 1961.

———. *A History of the United Mexican Party.* Mexico City, 1959.

AGISSIZ, CHARLES. *The King on a String: The Last Years of Louis XVII.* London, 1956.

ALAVARCES, MIGUEL. *The Global War: A Diplomatic History.* Mexico City, 1960.

ALCOTT, JASPER. *Autobiography.* New York, 1939.

ALMOND, EDGAR. *Michael Doheny: The War Years.* Mexico City, 1969.

ALMOND, JAMES. *The Man of the People: Emiliano Calles.* Mexico City, 1952.

ANDERSON, ADOLPH. *The Rise of C.N.A. Nationalism.* London, 1967.

ANDREWS, GEORGE. *Business Cycles in Nineteenth Century Britain.* London, 1959.

ARGYLLE, WILLIAM. *Voices of Protest: Black Mexicans After Manumission.* Mexico City, 1970.

ARMITAGE, MITCHELL. *Justice Now! A History of Domestic Opposition to the Silva Regime in the Global War.* Mexico City, 1969.

ARNOLD, BENEDICT. *Toward a New Jerusalem.* Jefferson City, 1800.

ARTHUR, HOWARD. *The Impossible Victory: The Coalition in 1888.* New York, 1934.

BAKER, ALGIE. *Understanding the Constitution.* Mexico City, 1967.

BANCROFT, GEORGE. *Hamilton and Madison: The Grand Collaboration.* Mexico City, 1886.

BARKINS, MORTON. *Long-Term Dislocations in the C.N.A. Economy in the Great Depression.* London, 1970.

BARRETT, JAMES. *Counting the Cost: The Legacy of Tecumseh.* Mexico City, 1960.

BARTLEY, SIR EVELYN. *The Treason Trials of 1778–1779: Transcripts and Records.* 31 vols. London, 1800.

BAYARD, ETIENNE. *The Sputtering Fuse: The French Question in Quebec in the Nineteenth Century.* Quebec, 1967.

BEDOYA, MARCOS. *El Jefe Superiór: La Vida de Hermión.* Mexico City, 1882.

BENEDICT, MARYANN. *Secret Correspondences of the Rebellion.* Mexico City, 1956.

BENNETT, RICHARD. *The First Group: Pioneers in the Wilderness.* Mexico City, 1933.

———. *Nathanael Greene: Portrait of a Founder.* Mexico City, 1929.

BERRY, WILLIAM. *The Dead are Unburied in the Plaza: The Mexican Repression of 1881.* Mexico City, 1956.

BILLINGTON, JAMES. *Memoirs: Vol. I. At the Helm.* New York, 1960.

BJORNSON, ERIC. *The Failure of the Middle: The Triumph of Radicalism in America in 1774.* London, 1965.

———. *The Radical Mind: Studies in Power.* London, 1967.

BLOCH, LEON. *The Question that Will Not Die: War Guilt in the C.N.A.* New York, 1967.

BOATWRIGHT, JAMES. *Pedro Hermión: A Hero in His Own Land.* Mexico City, 1954.

BOSTWICK, SIDNEY. *Every Man Has His Own Price: The Election of 1858.* Burgoyne, 1958.

BOYD, THOMAS. *The Difference is Freedom: A Comparison of the C.N.A. and the U.S.M.* London, 1954.

BRAYBACK, MALCOLM. *Conversations with President Jackson: Being a Record of My Friendship with the Founder of Our Country.* Mexico City, 1855.

BRINKERHOFF, HERBERT. *The Price of a Man: Oil and Produce in Mexican Politics.* Mexico City, 1970.

BROKOW, DON. *Henderson Dewey: A Study in Mediocrity.* New York, 1945.

BROOKS, BARBARA. *Historians and the Bloody Eighties: A Study in Interpretation.* New York, 1970.

———. *Historians and the Britannic Design: A Study in Interpretation.* New York, 1965.

BROOKS, PAUL. *Jacob Little and the Panic of 1836.* New York, 1967.

BROWN, MICHAEL. *Burgoyne in the Seven Years' War: The Development of the Military Ideas of John Burgoyne, First Duke of Albany.* London, 1809.

BROWN, RODNEY. *Parliament and the Cabinet in the Age of North.* London, 1911.

BUCHANAN, JAMES. *The Paris Mission and Other Episodes in a Busy Life.* New York, 1868.

BUTLER, MARSHALL. *The Paradox of the Black Vote.* Burgoyne, 1955.

BYRNES, EDWARD. *Rebel.* New York, 1920.

CALHOUN, JOHN. *Defense of the Realm and Other Essays.* Norfolk, 1845.

CALLES, EMILIANO. *The People and the Nation.* Mexico City, 1931.

CARLISLE, SIR DOUGLAS. *The Four Viceroys: Burgoyne, Carleton, Howe, and Clinton.* New York, 1967.

CARLISTA, LINDA. *The Heir: The Life of Benito Hermión.* Mexico City, 1946.

CARMICHAEL, ZELDA. *The Flames of February: Europe in the Winter of 1880.* London, 1967.

———. *In the Wake of the Red Witch: Reform in Europe in the 1880s.* London, 1970.

CHESTER, JAMES. *Washburne of the C.N.A.* London, 1928.

CHRISTMAN, DAVID. *The Founding of Jefferson City: The First Three Decades.* Mexico City, 1967.

———. *The Origins of Political Parties in Jefferson.* Mexico City, 1960.

CLARK, HERBERT. *The True Story of the Kinkaid Canal.* Mexico City, 1889.

CLARK, WINSTON. *The Calles-Fuentes Campaign of 1926.* Mexico City, 1945.

CLINTON, JOSEPH. *The Life of George Clinton and the Clinton Family of the Northern Confederation.* New York, 1882.

COCKE, WILLIAM. *Caesar in Broadcloth.* New York, 1910.

———. *John Dix: The Great Healer.* New York, 1905.

———. *Sir Alexander Haven: Proconsul in the Wilderness.* New York, 1910.

COCKRILL, FRANK. *What Happened in Michigan City?* London, 1968.

COLBY, SIR EDWIN. *The Parliamentary Experience of John Burgoyne.* New York, 1855.

COLLIER, BALDWIN. *The Lost Opportunity: Slavery in Jefferson City, 1782–1795.* New York, 1948.

COLLINS, HENRY. *Lord North and the Rise of Parliament.* New York, 1956.

COLLINS, JOHN and FOSTER, EDWIN. *Galloway.* New York, 1967.

COLLUM, SAMUEL. *The Home Front: A History of the C.N.A. in the Rocky Mountain War.* New York, 1967.

COMMONS, LELAND. *Jackson and the Mexican Campaign.* Mexico City, 1951.

CONFEDERATION OF NORTH AMERICA. *The Rocky Mountain War.* 37 vols. Burgoyne, 1888–99.

———. Bureau of Statistics. *Historical Atlas and Statistical Abstract.* Burgoyne, 1971.

———. Department of Statistics. *The Census of 1870.* Burgoyne, 1872.

———. Department of Statistics. *The Census of 1880.* Burgoyne, 1881.

———. Department of Statistics. *The Census of 1890.* Burgoyne, 1891.

———. Department of Statistics. *The Census of 1900.* Burgoyne, 1901.

———. Subcommittee of the Rules Committee. Grand Council. *Report of the Inquiry in the Charges of Treason.* Burgoyne, 1900.

CONROY, HOMER. *The Collected Papers of Nathanael Greene.* 28 vols. Mexico City, 1910.

CONTENT, HARRY. *Never Give Up: Rebels after the Rebellion.* New York, 1950.

COPELAND, REYNOLDS. *The Legacy of Failure: Europe and the Rebel Defeat in British America.* London, 1929.

CORAZÓN, HECTOR. *La Vida y Obras de Benito Calzón de Durango.* Mexico City, 1962.

CORDOVAN, PEDRO. *Jackson at the Convention: The Strokes of Genius.* Mexico City, 1962.

CORNELL, LLOYD. *The Quiet Reformers: Jefferson and Slavery.* Mexico City, 1970.

CORNWALL, SIR BARTLEY. *Hamilton and Continental Destiny: The Lost Struggle.* New York, 1961.

CROWN, ELLSWORTH. ed. *A Bibliography of the Rocky Mountain War.* New York, 1966.

DALEY, PHILLIP. *The Hundred Day War.* New York, 1966.

DANA, FRANK. *The Cotton Culture of Jefferson: White Gold in the Sun.* Mexico City, 1967.

———. ed. *Recent Discoveries in the Cortez Collection.* New York, 1958.

DAVIS, ALAN. *Patriotism Knows No Boundaries.* Mexico City, 1954.

DAVIS, PHILIP. *Second But To God: The Works of Thomas Edison of Indiana.* New York, 1911.

DEAK, JOHN. *The Britannic Design in the Twentieth Century.* New York, 1959.

DE LA CASA, RODRIGO. *Life at Court: An Observer of the Calles Regime.* Mexico City, 1934.

DENNY, MARTIN. *The Northern Confederation in the Era of Harmonious Relations.* New York, 1967.

DEVENNY, HUGH. *War and Men: Politics in North America, 1943–1948.* New York, 1955.

DEVLIN, WILLKIE. *Formation of the Mexican Empire.* Mexico City, 1967.

———. *The Other Hermión: The New Granadan Experiment.* Mexico City, 1970.

DEWEY, HENDERSON. *Commonwealth.* New York, 1930.

DICKINSON, SIR JOHN. *The Late Rebellion.* 3 vols. Philadelphia, 1784.

———. *My Life and Work.* Philadelphia, 1804.

DILL, SIR HARRY. *The Battle of Saratoga.* London, 1888.

DOW, MORTIMER. *The Growth of Mexico: The Political Maneuverings of Kramer and Benedict in the Industrial Era.* Mexico City, 1950.

DREW, FRANKLIN. *The Guard Changeth: The Elections of 1923.* New York, 1931.

———. *The Guard is Confirmed: The Elections of 1928.* New York, 1933.

DUFFY, ROBERT. *George Clinton: The New York Magician.* New York, 1968.

DURFREE, NATHAN. *Hawaii: Its History.* London, 1969.

EAGEN, WESLEY. *In the Twilight.* New York, 1909.

EARLEY, JOHN. *A History of the New Granada Expedition.* New York, 1914.

———. *The Drums of War: Ezra Gallivan and Benito Hermión.* New York, 1916.

ELIZY, CLAUDE. *Fanchon and the Rebirth of France.* London, 1966.

ELSON, JAMES. *Dickinson and Galloway in the Crisis Years.* New York, 1901.

ENGLISH, WILLIAM. *New Friends in an Old Bed: The Immigrant-Conservative Alliance of 1878.* New York, 1969.

FARMER, MONTGOMERY. *Making a New World.* New York, 1966.

FAULKNER, CLARK. *Burgoyne in Parliament: Preparation for Greatness.* University of North America, 1970.

FAY, SIR HUMPHREY. *The Canada Campaign of 1775.* Montreal, 1887.

FEA, DOMINICK. *The Cost.* New York, 1959.

FENTON, REUBEN. *And Close the Door: The Decline of C.N.A. Conservatism.* New York, 1955.

————. *McDowell: Appearance and Reality.* New York, 1957.

FIGUEROA, SIMON. *La Vida de Liberdad.* 13th ed. London, 1955.

FINNIGAN, MAX. *Organizing the Elite: A History of the M.N.U.* New York, 1968.

FLAHERTY, JOHN. *Builders of North America.* London, 1967.

————. *The Carminales Legacy: Mexico's Edison.* London, 1971.

————. *The Little Black Box: Vitavision's Early History.* London, 1969.

————. *The Sound and the Fury: Radio in the C.N.A.* London, 1965.

FLEUR, ARMOND. *We Leave as Friends: The Plebiscite of 1889.* New York, 1945.

FLINDERS, ALEXANDER. *The Road to War: The Fanchon Proposals.* London, 1934.

FOLLOWS, THEODORE. *Reason and Race in Jefferson.* New York, 1952.

FORBES, HARRY. *In Peace Friends: Jefferson and the Politics of Expediency.* New York, 1933.

————. *The Franco-American Alliance: Its Origins and Consequences.* Burgoyne University, 1962.

FORREST, HARVEY. ed. *Philosophers of Crisis.* London, 1958.

FORSYTH, MARK. *Under Three Governors: My Life in the C.B.I.* New York, 1900.

FORTEZ, MIGUEL. *The Rocky Mountain War in Mexican History.* Mexico City, 1956.

FOSTER, EDWIN. *The Business Career of Owen Galloway.* New York, 1961.

FOWLER, SIR EDWIN. *That Chameleon Franklin! The Life and Times of Benjamin Franklin of America and England.* London, 1800.

FOWLER, HARTLEY. *Burgoyne as a Playwright: The Last of the Restoration Writers.* Philadelphia, 1954.

FOWLER, WORTHINGTON. *John McDowell and the Fruits of Reform.* New York, 1899.

————. *McDowell in Retirement.* New York, 1901.

————. *Reform at Flood Tide: McDowell's Year of Glory, 1883.* New York, 1908.

FRENCH, LAWRENCE. *Economic Responsibility: The Early Years of the Hogg Administration.* New York, 1948.

FRENCH, LELAND. *In the Shadow of the Giants: The Burgen-Hemingway-Merriman Years.* New York, 1969.

FREUND, FRANZ. *The Work of Three Decades.* 2 vols. New York, 1869.

FRIENDLY, JOHN. *A History of the National Financial Administration.* New York, 1967.

FULLER, MARTIN. *Rose Fuller and the Attempts to Prevent the Rebellion, including a Biography of Important Members of the House on the Eve of the Conflict.* London, 1799.

GABOR, FIELD MARSHALL SIR WESLEY. *Emiliano Calles and the Art of War.* London, 1955.

GALLIVAN, BERNARD. *Letters from My Father.* New York, 1920.

GALLIVAN, EZRA. *At the End of the Day.* New York, 1912.

————. *Under Fire and Sword.* New York, 1898.

GALLOWAY, OWEN. ed. *Selected Addresses.* New York, 1935.

GARNER, BURGOYNE. *Origins of the Conservative Party in the Northern Confederation.* New York, 1929.

GARNETT, HIRAM. *Fruitful Years and Good Friends.* Mexico City, 1907.

GEORGE, PAUL. *John McDowell: An Appreciation and Assessment.* Burgoyne, 1930.

GIBBS, ALTON. *A Friend in Burgoyne.* New York, 1931.

GIBBS, HENRY. *The Gilpin Legacy.* New York, 1889.

GILMAN, LAWRENCE. *Sam Adams and the Rebellion: A Study in Revolutionary Leadership.* Mexico City, 1954.

GILPIN, HENRY. *No Apologies are in Order: My Term as Governor.* New York, 1860.

GIPSON, WALLACE. *The Wilderness Walk: Greene in the Desert.* London, 1959.

GOULD, DAVID. *Gold and Railroads, Profits and Losses.* Mexico City, 1948.

GRADY, ROBERT. *The Age of Neiderhoffer.* New York, 1965.

———. *The London Conspirators.* Mexico City, 1966.

GRAY, BARRINGTON. *Mexico: The Modern Sparta.* New York, 1955.

GREEN, DAVIS. *A President Dies: The Assassination of Omar Kinkaid.* New York, 1960.

GREEN, JAMES. *Frustrated Prometheus: The Role of Intellectuals in the C.N.A. in the Twentieth Century.* London, 1969.

GREENE, MARTIN. *The Britannic Design: Symbol for an Age.* Canberra, 1965.

———. *The Britannic Design and the Lafayette Constitution of 1793: Comparisons and Contrasts.* New York, 1968.

HALL, SIMON. *How Much?* New York, 1890.

HAMILTON, ALEXANDER. *Farewell to Change: Thoughts on Leaving the C.N.A.* New York, 1785.

———. *Government and the Nature of Man.* Jefferson City, 1793.

———. *Memoirs.* 3 vols. Jefferson City, 1814.

———. *The War With Mexico.* Jefferson City, 1818.

———, MADISON, JAMES, DUER, WILLIAMS, and JAY, JOHN. *Federal Governance.* Jefferson City, 1800.

HARCOURT, PERCY. *The Vipers in their Bosoms: Clinton and Bland in 1788.* London, 1956.

HARGRAVE, PERCY. *Dickinson of North America.* 6 vols. London, 1960–66.

HARGROVE, LADY JANE. *The Flaw in the Design: Suffering during the Crisis Years.* London, 1899.

HARMAKER, WILTON. *The Genesis of Twentieth Century North America.* Burgoyne, 1970.

HARNETT, JOHN. *A History of Slavery in the Southern Confederation.* London, 1930.

HARPER, ALEXANDER. *Banking Policies in the United States of Mexico During the Arkins Years.* Mexico City, 1950.

HARRIS, WILLIAM. *The Bloody Ballot: The C.N.A. Election of 1878.* New York, 1943.

HARRISON, WILLIAM HENRY. *The Autobiography of William Henry Harrison.* Burgoyne, 1840.

HART, MILTON. *Galloway: The Other Side.* Burgoyne, 1929.

HARTWICK, H. C. *Black Skin and Red Ink: Profits in the Slave Trade, 1820–1840.* New York, 1967.

HAWES, ALBERT. *Jackson and the Mexican Indians: Partners in Opportunity.* Mexico City, 1958.

——. *Jackson the Man.* Mexico City, 1952.

——. *Jackson of Mexico: A Hero's Story.* Mexico City, 1956.

HAWKES, LORD HENRY. *Peace and Victory: The Last Stage of the American Rebellion.* London, 1884.

HEARST, WILLIAM. *The Blood in Our Veins.* Mexico City, 1897.

HEIDE, ARTHUR. *The Emergence of James Billington.* New York, 1956.

HEMINGWAY, CHRISTOPHER. *The Way of the World.* New York, 1911.

HENDLEY, SIR JOSHUA. *Travels Through the Southern Confederation in the Winter of 1833.* London, 1935.

HENRY, LAWRENCE. *Washington: Reluctant Rebel.* New York, 1925.

HERMON, DWIGHT. *Albert Ullman and the Calles Conspiracy.* Mexico City, 1969.

——. *Starkism in Mexico: The Public Career of Pedro Fuentes.* New York, 1955.

HERMIÓN, BENITO. *The Mexico of My Heart.* Mexico City, 1886.

HETHERINGTON, EDWARD. *Urban Riot: The Northern Confederation Cities in the 1870's.* London, 1956.

HIMMELSTEIN, HEINRICH. *The War of the World.* London, 1907.

HINTON, GEORGE. *Rebel Rapacity: Land Speculation and Smuggling in North America in the Late Eighteenth Century.* London, 1943.

HOLLENBERG, JACK. *It Began in Triumph.* London, 1962.

——. *It Ended in Tragedy: Huddleston in 1845.* London, 1966.

HOLMES, THEODORE. ed. *The Rainbow Nation and Other Papers.* Mexico City, 1925.

——. *Slave Rebellions of the 1820's.* New York, 1945.

HOLT, JANET. *Demagogue and Dictator: The Life of Pedro Hermión.* New York, 1954.

HOOVER, BARBARA. *The Role of Mineral Investigations in Mexico del Norte, Arizona, and Jefferson During the 1840's and 1850's.* Jackson University, 1962.

HOPKINS, BEAUREGARD. *The Pearl of the Southern Confederation: Life in Early Georgia.* Atlanta, 1906.

HOPKINS, GILBERT. *Burgoyne: The Early Years.* London, 1899.

HORAN, MAXWELL. *The Paper Marshal: The Life of Henri Fanchon.* New York, 1944.

HOSKINS, SIR ROBERT. *Opinion on the Rebellion in the Colonies in 1775–1778.* London, 1832.

HOSKINSON, STEWART. *The Loyal Americans: The Negroes of Southern Vandalia.* New York, 1962.

HOWARD, FRANK. *The Strange Death of President Kinkaid.* New York, 1899.

HOWE, GEN. SIR WILLIAM. *Memoirs of the Late Rebellion, including a diary of events and recollections of a busy life.* London, 1865.

HUDD, SWITHEN. *We Took the Islands: My Role in the Annexation of Hawaii.* Mexico City, 1899.

HUDDLESTON, MIGUEL. *Portrait of the Founder: Arthur Younger of Mexico del Norte.* Mexico City, 1875.

HULL, MILTON. *The Politics of 1883: McDowell and his Campaign.* New York, 1970.

HUNTER, FIELD MARSHAL SIR ALEXANDER. *A Military History of the World Conflict.* London, 1957.

IRWIN, THOMAS and MCLEAN, DONALD. *Manitoba: Athens of the North.* New York, 1966.

JACKOBSON, ARNOLD. *Big Business in the Free Society.* Melbourne, 1958.

JACKSON, ANDREW. *Our People: Views and Observations on the Population of the United States of Mexico.* Mexico City, 1841.

JACKSON, GEORGE. *The New Day: The First Years of the C.N.A.* New York, 1967.

JAMES, FRANCIS. *Decision at Brant.* Mexico City, 1967.

JAY, JOHN. *Notes on the Perfidy of Our Former Friends.* Jefferson City, 1800.

JAY, PERRY. *The Way It Happened: The Transition of Power in 1950.* New York, 1958.

JENKINS, ARCHIE. *And So We Began: The First Days of the United States of Mexico.* London, 1951.

———. *The Last to Go: U.S.M. Slavery.* London, 1949.

JENNINGS, WALTER, GROSS, EDWARD, and FIELDS, EDWARD. *New England and the African Slave Trade.* Oxford, 1823.

JONES, CLIFFORD. *At the Watershed: The World in 1916.* London, 1966.

JONES, WARNER. *Lord North: The British Richelieu.* Mexico City, 1958.

———. ed. *Lord North's Master Plan: Genius or Ignorance?* Mexico City, 1960.

JOSEPHSON, MAX. *The End of the Western Era.* New York, 1971.

KAHN, JOAN. *Secret History of the Kinkaid Assassination.* New York, 1970.

———. *The Unknown History of the Hermión Assassination: The Gilpin Connection.* New York, 1968.

KEITH, EDWARD. *The Manitoban Century.* New York, 1966.

KELLEY, THOMAS. *The Peace Crusade of 1937: A Study in Group Behavior.* New York, 1949.

KELLY, ARTEMAS. *Origins of the Trans-Oceanic War.* Mexico City, 1967.

KENNEDY, HARMON. *The North American Rebellion: The Crisis in Leadership.* Mexico City, 1965.

KERR, ROBERT. *Carlos Concepción and the Birth of the New Radicalism.* New York, 1960.

———. *The Life and Times of George Vining.* New York, 1955.

KINSOLVING, ROBERT. *Feet of Wood: The Life of Benito Hermión.* New York, 1969.

KIRK, ROSWELL. *Edmund Burke: The Great Dissenter.* London, 1898.

KLEBERG, MARTIN. *The Politics of Vandalian Separation.* New York, 1957.

———. *The Pugh Thesis Revisited.* New York, 1961.

KLINEBURG, ISADORE. *Count Matsukata and the Emergence of Japan.* Melbourne, 1960.

KLUCHANSKY, FEODOR. *Russia in Exile.* London, 1911.

KNOWLES, JAY. *In the Day of the Cuckoo.* New York, 1970.

KRAMER ASSOCIATES. *Proposals for the Restructuring of Kramer Associates.* 94 vols. Mexico City, 1929–1931.

KRONOVET, ESTHER, *New York in the Crisis Years: 1836–1837.* New York, 1960.

KURTZ, HENRY. *The Moral Imperative: Its Origins and Development.* New York, 1968.

LA LUMIA, VICTOR. ed. *One Hundred Years Under the Britannic Design.* New York, 1882.

LAMB, MARTHA. *The Resolution of Conflict: Constitutional Case Studies.* Canberra, 1956.

LANGELL, ELIZABETH. *Thomas Edison: America's Genius.* Burgoyne, 1955.

LEA, DAVID. *The Birth of Vandalia.* Galloway, 1951.

———. *Vandalia in the C.N.A.: A History.* Galloway, 1946.

LEFEVRE, DESMOND. *Lord Dorchester and the Britannic Design.* New York, 1945.

LETTS, DICKINSON. *Origins of the Two Party System.* New York, 1923.

LEVER, FANNY. *The Second Britannic Design.* New York, 1850.

LEVINSON, BLANCHE. *The Lost Colony of Louisiana.* New York, 1967.

LICHTENSTEIN, HYMAN. *On the Seventh Day He Rested: Jackson in Retirement.* Mexico City, 1969.

LODGE, HUBERT. *Men for their Age: The Hemingway and Merriman Administrations.* New York, 1971.

LOMBARDI, FELIX. *Francophobia in Mexico: The Summer of 1881.* Mexico City, 1952.

———. *The Three-Cornered Hat: Kinkaid, Rogers, and the Election of 1875.* Mexico City, 1955.

LORING, GEORGE. *Origins of the Rocky Mountain War.* London, 1969.

———. *The Right Man: Gilpin in Command.* London, 1956.

MACKREITH, ROBERT. *Lord Howe and the Rebellion.* New York, 1965.

MACON, ORRIN. *The Palenque Convention in Mexican History.* Mexico City, 1960.

MADISON, JAMES. *The Course of Human Events.* Jefferson City, 1819.

———. *Government and the Proper Concern.* Jefferson City, 1793.

MALONE, DAVIS. *The History of Quebec.* Dorchester, 1967.

MALTZ, RICHARD. *Better than Any of Us: The Ambitious Galloway.* New York, 1970.

MARCOS, FERDINAND. *Henry Colbert: Militant Libertarian.* New York, 1956.

MARKS, DAVIS. *Hector Niles: The Mexican Augustus.* Mexico City, 1949.

MARCUSSON, OSWALD. *The Shame of Mexico.* London, 1935.

MARRIOT, ARNOLD. *Years of the Pygmies.* New York, 1923.

MARTIN, CARTER. *Visits to Strange Lands: My Struggle for Peace and Justice.* New York, 1865.

MARTIN, JEFFREY. *The Secret History of the Watson Administration.* New York, 1944.

MARX, KARL. *On the Coming Revolution in Mexico.* 2nd ed. London, 1869.

MASON, RICHARD. ed. *The Better Day.* Burgoyne, 1957.

MASON, THOMAS. *The Jefferson-California Axis of 1866–1876.* London, 1968.

MATES, GEN. SIR HENRY. *George Washington: The War Years.* 4 vols. New York, 1932.

MATTHIAS, WILLIAM. *Like an Old Shoe: The Decline of Slavery in Jefferson.* Mexico City, 1961.

MAXWELL, RICHARD. *The Prostitutes of Burgoyne: Conservative and Liberal in the Glory Years.* Mexico City, 1967.

MAYFORD, BURNET. *The Moral Imperative.* London, 1893.

McANSON, DAVID. *The Proud Humanitarian: Vincent Mercator of Mexico.* Mexico City, 1968.

McCAULEY, SIR BARTON. *Origins of the Franco-Mexican Alliance.* London, 1954.

McCOY, C. HADLEY. *The Beginning of Modern Times.* London, 1965.

McDOUGALL, GEN. WESLEY. *The Lessons of the Rocky Mountain War.* London, 1914.

———. *The Relative Strengths of the C.N.A. and the U.S.M. during the Rocky Mountain War.* London, 1911.

McDOWELL, JOHN. *The Age of Reform.* New York, 1893.

McGOVERN, FRANCES. *They Stuck in their Thumbs! The Selection of Vining.* London, 1967.

McGRAW, EDWARD. *The Hundred Day War: An Analysis and History.* Melbourne, 1950.

———. *The Isthmian War in Mexican History.* Melbourne, 1954.

———. *The Mexican Empire and its Costs.* Melbourne, 1957.

McGREGOR, WINSLOW. *A Child Shall Lead Them: The Idiocy of Our Times.* New York, 1921.

McGUIRE, MARGARET. *The Hermión Craze: Mass Delusion in Mexico.* London, 1910.

McKINLEY, FRANK. *Winfield Scott and the Sin of Pride.* Mexico City, 1957.

McMULLAN, WILLIAM. *A Half Century of Life and Labor.* Mexico City, 1869.

McNEE, SIR HARTLEY. *Adams and the French Conspiracy.* London, 1888.

MEAD, ROBERT. *Peace and Justice, Sanity and Reason.* New York, 1970.

MENZER, SAMUEL. *The Huddleston Conspiracy: The Brown Menace of 1851.* London, 1970.

———. *Who Killed Kinkaid?* London, 1967.

MICHAELSON, JANETTE. ed. *North America and the War: A Public Opinion Analysis.* New York, 1953.

MILTON, MARYANN. *A History of the Galloway Family.* New York, 1944.

MITCHELL, PAUL. *The Jenkinson Cabinet and the Five Years' War.* London, 1958.

MIX, BERNARD. *The Night of the Caballeros: The Hermión Seizure.* London, 1964.

MONTEZ, BARBARA. *A History of the People's Coalition.* London, 1960.

MONTGOMERY, ZOE. *The Russian Revolution.* New York, 1967.

MONTOYA, HERNANDO. *Strange Places and Strong Men.* Mexico City, 1857.

Morales, Jose. *My Cause is Mexico*. 4th ed. New York, 1902.

Mudd, James. *The Hermión Regime: A Study in Corrupt Power*. London, 1954.

Muller, Herman. *Hermión of Jefferson: Patriot or Traitor?* Mexico City, 1969.

Muncrief, Harold. *Nova Scotia Forever!* London, 1959.

Murphy, Paul. *Ants in the Sugar: The Problems of Honesty in the Huddleston Administration*. Mexico City, 1960.

———. *New York of the South: The Rise of Henrytown in the 1840's and 1850's*. Mexico City, 1967.

———. *The First Years of the Huddleston Administration*. Mexico City, 1962.

Murray, Henry. ed. *Gilpin and the Historians*. New York, 1970.

Nathanson, Jack. ed. *From the Cortez Files*. Mexico City, 1938.

———. *More From the Cortez Files*. Mexico City, 1947.

Needham, Carl. *The Great Northern War*. New York, 1963.

Neiderhoffer, Erich. *My People, My Life*. London, 1890.

Nelson, Julius. *Financing a Nation: My Years at the N.F.A.* New York, 1910.

Newton, Henry. *The North American Mission*. New York, 1882.

Nightingale, Charles. *An American Journey: Views of Mexico and North America in 1877*. London, 1880.

Nunn, Franklin. ed. *The Moral Imperative*. London, 1945.

O'Brian, William. *Hermión, Scott, and the Rocky Mountain War*. New York, 1955.

Ocon, Ralph. *The People We Left Behind: The Remnant in the C.N.A.* Mexico City, 1959.

O'Connor, Max. *The Men of Lafayette*. New York, 1960.

Ohrens, Manfred. *Origins of the Global War*. 2 vols. New York, 1941.

Olin, Miguel. *El Jefe's War for Salvation*. New York, 1956.

Ortega, Ferdinand. *The First World War: 1795–1799*. Mexico City, 1937.

Ortez, Carlos. *America and the Struggle for the World*. Mexico City, 1970.

———. *The Mexican Civil War*. Mexico City, 1960.

———. *Mexico, France, and North America: One Problem, Three Answers*. Mexico City, 1964.

O'Shea, Michael. *A Diplomat in the Family: The Life of Patrick O'Shea*. New York, 1922.

Paca, William. *When the World Went Mad: The Utopians of the 1890's*. New York, 1968.

Papineau, Francois. *My Father: His Cause was Just*. Mexico City, 1854.

Parkes, Bamford. *Benedict Arnold: The Rebel Genius*. New York, 1965.

Parkes, Maxwell. ed. *Great North American Speeches*. New York, 1966.

Passman, Ernest. *Lloyd of Carolina: A Political Biography*. New York, 1965.

Paulding, James. *The Indian Question in Indianan Foreign Policy*. New York, 1959.

———. *One State, Two Nations: Indiana and the Indians*. New York, 1967.

PAVELLE, HECTOR. *Paris During the Insurrection.* London, 1956.

PENDLETON, DWIGHT. *The Galloway Years.* New York, 1964.

PERKINS, MARSHALL. *Behind the Mask: The Life and Works of Julius Nelson.* New York, 1920.

PETERSON, HENDRICK. *The Philosophy and Works of Karl Marx: His Epistemology, Ontology, and Gestalt.* London, 1943.

PHISTER, JAY. *The Age of Renewal: McDowell at his Prime.* New York, 1952.

——. *Front Man For Reform: The Ruggles Opposition.* New York, 1949.

PITCHON, DANIEL. *Vermont and Western Virginia in the Decades Following the Britannic Design.* Mexico City, 1965.

POPPER, VINCENT. *A Demographic Study of the C.N.A., 1783–1825.* London, 1954.

POWELL, FREDERICK. *Theodore Lindsay: The Black and the Blue.* New York, 1956.

PRENTISS, ALEX. *A More Perfect Union: The Concordia Accords.* New York, 1967.

PRESS, STANLEY. *The Doctrine of Continental Destiny.* Mexico City, 1965.

PRICE, RUPERT. *Julius Nelson of the N.F.A.* New York, 1967.

PRITCHARD, JOHN. *He was First! The Governorship-General of General Winfield Scott.* New York, 1960.

——. *The First Shot: Origins of the Rocky Mountain War.* Mexico City, 1958.

——. *William Lloyd: The Southern Emancipator.* New York, 1956.

PUGH, HOWARD. *The Era of Harmonious Relations.* New York, 1890.

——. *Potter's Vandalia.* New York, 1888.

QUEEN, JAMES. *North America's Age of Genius: 1855–1880.* London, 1959.

QUESNAY, FLORIDE. *Travels Through the C.N.A.* London, 1854.

RABBINO, SIMON. *Except in His Native Land: The Irony of the Niles Presidency.* London, 1970.

——. *The Invasion of the Pound: British Investments in the C.N.A. from 1840 to 1880.* London, 1965.

——. *The Impact of the Rocky Mountain War on the North American Economy.* London, 1967.

RADAMAKER, JAMES. *Bruce Hogg: Armed Neutral.* Melbourne, 1951.

——. *Secret Files of the Global War: Correspondences with North America, 1939–1941.* Melbourne, 1959.

RAMSPECK, WALTER. *The California Gold Rush of '39.* New York, 1956.

RANDOLPH, JACKSON. *The Inner History of the War Without War.* New York, 1968.

RAYMOND, JOSEPH. *Portrait in Oil: The Making of Consolidated Petroleum.* New York, 1968.

REICHART, HARPER. *The Election of 1845: The Mandate for War.* Mexico City, 1956.

——. *The Quiet Messiah: Arthur Conroy of Arizona.* Mexico City, 1952.

REINS, LEWIS. *John Gaillard: Nobility in Chains.* Mexico City, 1943.

REVELL, WINSTON. *Wymess, Kramer, and the Big Ditch.* New York, 1968.

REYNOLDS, JOHN. *Background for Rebellion: Quebec, 1800–1838.* New York, 1956.

———. *The Shame of Western Civilization.* New York, 1960.

RIBOT, PIERRE. *My Life and Works.* London, 1829.

RIPLEY, EZRA. *A History of North American Motors: The Early Years.* New York, 1945.

RIPLEY, JAMES. *The Webster Legacy: The Creation of an Industrial Commonwealth.* New York, 1967.

RITTER, HARVEY. *Allen's Irregulars: The History of a Brave People.* London, 1967.

RIVERS, THOMAS. *Daniel Webster and His Confederation.* New York, 1970.

ROBINSON, JOHN. *The Kinkaid Presidency and the Men Behind It.* London, 1950.

RODRIGUEZ, RICARDO. *Slavery as an Issue in the Southern Confederation.* Mexico City, 1970.

ROSENBAUM, HERBERT. *The Hoskins Thesis and its Critics.* Melbourne, 1969.

ROSS, JAMES. *Inevitability in History: A Dialogue.* London, 1949.

RUSK, FRANK. *A Statistical Analysis of the 1953 Councilmanic Elections.* New York, 1958.

———. *A Statistical Analysis of the 1958 Councilmanic Elections.* New York, 1962.

———. *A Statistical Analysis of the 1968 C.N.A. Election.* New York, 1971.

RUSSELL, JOHN. *Beck and Call: My Life as Palace Physician.* Burgoyne, 1959.

ST. JOHN, RUSSELL. *The Cutting Edge of Civilization: The Moral Imperative.* New York, 1967.

SAN MARTIN, MIGUEL. *The Bloody Season.* Mexico City, 1930.

SAYERS, LEWIS. *The Galloway Plan: The Modern Moses.* New York, 1966.

SCHULTZ, GEORGE. *The Great Migration: The Dispersion of the 1880's.* London, 1963.

SCOTT, HUGH. *Giant In Chains: Van Buren and the Conservatives.* Mexico City, 1960.

SCOTT, ROBERT. *John Hancock: The Profiteer and the Patriots.* New York, 1959.

SCOTT, WILL. *The Power Behind the Throne: A History of the C.B.I.* New York, 1960.

SEABURY, ROBERT. *Historians and the Trans-Oceanic War.* London, 1967.

SEÑADA, TITO. *Mexico's Destiny and My Role In It: A Confession.* Mexico City, 1939.

SENNETT, BERNARD. *The Growth of the North American Steel Industry.* New York, 1970.

SEPÚLVEDA, WALTER. *An Economic History of the Hermión Regime.* Mexico City, 1968.

SHEPARD, ANDREW. *The Northern Confederation in the Violent Years, 1835–1839.* New York, 1945.

SIDNEY, ROBERT. *Horatio Gates: The Man Who Lost the Rebellion.* New York, 1970.

SILVA, ALVIN. *The Search for the Mexican Soul.* Mexico City, 1931.

SILVERA, BERNARDO. *The Private Thoughts of Benito Hermión.* New York, 1920.

SIMONSON, CHARLES. *The Oak Has Fallen: Hogg's Last Stand.* New York, 1952.

———. *The Year Without Politics: The C.N.A. in 1932.* New York, 1950.

SIMPSON, JULIA. *Historians and the Demography of the Rebellion: A Case Study.* Queens University, 1962.

SLATE, SAMUEL. *The Rise of Emiliano Calles.* New York, 1929.

SMALL, ROBERT. *The Role of the Railroad in the History of the Northern Confederation.* Mexico City, 1960.

SMITH, SIR MALCOLM. *An Address to the People of the Southern Confederation.* Norfolk, 1834.

SMYSER, HORACE. *Origins of Modern Negro Thought.* New York, 1966.

SNOW, RUSSELL. *Decision in London: Forging the Britannic Design.* New York, 1953.

———. and BARCK, HARMON. *A Constitutional History of the Confederation of North America.* New York, 1959.

SOBEL, ROBERT. *The Fifth Point: Ezra Gallivan and His Creative Nationalism.* New York, 1967.

———. *Men of Great Wealth: Operations of the Kramer-Benedict Combine.* Melbourne, 1956.

———. ed. *A Statistical Survey of North American Business, 1855–1910.* New York, 1957.

———. *The Epic Age of North American Industry.* Melbourne, 1960.

SPINNER, SYLVIA and SMALL, ANDREA. *Views of Tampico: Being an Investigation of the Growth of Our City.* Tampico, 1940.

STEPHENSON, DAVID. *The Townshend Alternative.* London, 1955.

STEWART, HORTENSE. *The Lost Colony and the Shawnee: The Emergence of a New Civilization.* San Francisco, 1971.

STRAWBRIDGE, JAMES. *Butcher Jackson.* New York, 1961.

STREET, CORBY. *Compromise and Conciliation as Factors in the Jeffersonian Constitution of 1793.* Mexico City, 1936.

SULLOWAY, LYDIA. *El Jefe and the Lust for Empire.* New York, 1943.

TAFT, FRANK. *The End of the War: The Hague in 1853–1855.* Melbourne, 1967.

TAFT, RALPH. *The Keystone: Petroleum of Mexico.* Mexico City, 1954.

TELFORD, BERNARD. *Georgia and the Rise of the S.C.* Mexico City, 1965.

THOMPSON, WINSTON. *The Flawed Design: Problems at Lafayette.* London, 1967.

TINKER, GEORGE. *The Monroe-Jackson-Carter Administrations.* New York, 1967.

TRACY, HENRY. *Gallivan: The Third Stage.* Burgoyne, 1961.

TUCKER, MARTIN. *The Rise of the New Southern Confederation.* New York, 1960.

TULIN, STANLEY. *He Straddled the Continents: The Life of Bernard Kramer.* London, 1960.

———. *The Kramer Associates: Its Origins.* London, 1965.

———. *The Kramer Associates: The Cortez Years.* London, 1970.

———. *The Kramer Associates: The Benedict Years.* London, 1971.

TURNER, LELAND. *The Tin Cup Governor-General: The Parkes Estate.* New York, 1967.

———. *Three Bags Full: The King Conspiracy.* New York, 1970.

TURNER, WALDO. *Utopia Across the River.* New Jerusalem, 1903.

TURNER, WYATT. *The Rise of the Vulcazine Engine.* New York, 1966.

———. *The Story of the North American Locomobile.* New York, 1969.

UNITED STATES OF MEXICO. *Statistical Abstract and Guide.* Mexico City, 1970.

———. Congress. *Commission to Inquire into the Assassination of President Pedro Hermión: Final Report.* Mexico City, 1852.

———. Congress. *Report on the Death of President Omar Kinkaid.* Mexico City, 1880.

———. Department of War. *The History of the Rocky Mountain War.* 29 vols. Mexico City, 1910–1925.

VALDEZ, RICARDO. *Mexico: The Spanish Era.* Mexico City, 1960.

VAN BEECK, MARTIN. *A World Gone Mad and its Cure.* The Hague, 1945.

VAN GILDER, EDWARD. *The Victory of Republicanism.* Mexico City, 1912.

VAN LUVENDER, WESLEY, ed. *Burgoyne on War.* New York, 1950.

———. *The Life and Times of John Burgoyne.* New York, 1949.

———. *The Military Thought and Actions of John Burgoyne.* New York, 1944.

VENDERGRIFT, ARTHUR. *The Faith of Historians.* London, 1959.

VENZICCHIO, JACK. *The Life of Emiliano Calles.* New York, 1933.

VUN KANNON, RAYMOND. *The Phoenix: Mexico's Rebirth.* London, 1958.

WADSWORTH, WINTHROP. *King George III and Lord North: The Struggle for the American Soul.* London, 1971.

WAINWRIGHT, EDGAR. *Bloody Patrick Henry: The Cromwell Who Failed.* New York, 1917.

WALKER, HAROLD. *The Boil: Free Slaves in the Hundred Day War.* New York, 1955.

———. *The Chapultapec Affair: Doorway to Today.* New York, 1958.

WALLGREN, WARREN. *The Burgen Administration: A History.* New York, 1960.

WATKINS, ARTHUR. *The Baring Crisis of 1835.* London, 1910.

———. *The Great Depression of 1880–1883.* London, 1915.

———. *Mexico on the Eve: Society in the U.S.M. in the 1870's.* London, 1920.

WATSON, EARL. *The Right Man: The Vining Administration.* Mexico City, 1943.

WAYNE, DOUGLAS. *The Black Indians of Arizona: An Anthropological Study.* New York, 1969.

WEBERN, FRITZ. *The Dilemma of Our Times.* New York, 1933.

WEBSTER, DANIEL. *The Program for Progress.* New York, 1838.

WECHLER, HERBERT. *George III and His Circle.* New York, 1939.

———. *Sam Adams' Plans: Blood and Boston.* New York, 1944.

WELLES, SIR JOHN. *A Love That Never Died: The Letters of Queen Victoria and Prince Albert.* London, 1935.

# 426 *For Want of a Nail*

———. *Queen Victoria's Table Talk.* London, 1929.

WELSCH, ALICE. *Who Killed Cock Robin? Starkism in Perspective.* New York, 1959.

WHITNEY, JULES. *The Accidental Executive: The Political Life of Douglas Watson.* New York, 1961.

WILCOX, SIR JAMES. *Isaac Barré and the Conspiracy.* London, 1965.

———. *Royal Leadership: George III and the Crisis.* London, 1970.

———. *The Triangle of Treason.* London, 1962.

WILKERSON, FRANK. *Reaping the Whirlwind: The Crisis Philosophers of the Late Nineteenth Century.* London, 1970.

WILLKIE, BURGOYNE. *Good Friends and Fair People.* Fort Lodge, 1895.

WILMINGTON, MARTIN. *Charles IV and Spain's Lost Opportunities in Mexico.* New York, 1959.

WINSLOW, CHARLES. *Peasants in Brocade: The Oil Millionaires of Chiapas and Durango.* New York, 1962.

WITHERSPOON, EDGAR. *A Critical Look at the Hermión Regime.* London, 1943.

WRIGHT, PHILIP. *The Marroista Interlude: The Decline of Liberty in Mexico.* Mexico City, 1952.

WYMESS, COURTNEY. *Remaking a Continent: My Life and Work.* Mexico City, 1892.

YORK, MARTIN. *Huddleston, Scott, and the Rapprochement of 1844.* Mexico City, 1929.

———. *The Election of 1841.* Mexico City, 1970.

YOUNG, GAMALIEL. *Carnegie and Scott: Rivals on the Rails.* London, 1969.

ZACCONE, JUNE. *The Galloway Plan and the Races.* New York, 1930.

ZARB, KENNETH. *Gems and Wood: The Life of Paul Suarez.* New York, 1969.

———. *Garcia!* New York, 1965.

———. *Inside the U.S.M.: Mercator's Folly.* New York, 1971.

ZWICKER, STANLEY. *The Heart and Soul of Pedro Fuentes: A Portrait from Life.* Mexico City, 1935.

# INDEX